Lecture Notes in Computer Science   10766

Commenced Publication in 1973
Founding and Former Series Editors:
Gerhard Goos, Juris Hartmanis, and Jan van Leeuwen

More information about this series at http://www.springer.com/series/7409

Gobinda Chowdhury · Julie McLeod
Val Gillet · Peter Willett (Eds.)

Transforming Digital Worlds

13th International Conference, iConference 2018
Sheffield, UK, March 25–28, 2018
Proceedings

Editors
Gobinda Chowdhury 🆔
Northumbria University
Newcastle upon Tyne
UK

Julie McLeod 🆔
Northumbria University
Newcastle upon Tyne
UK

Val Gillet 🆔
University of Sheffield
Sheffield
UK

Peter Willett 🆔
University of Sheffield
Sheffield
UK

ISSN 0302-9743   ISSN 1611-3349   (electronic)
Lecture Notes in Computer Science
ISBN 978-3-319-78104-4   ISBN 978-3-319-78105-1   (eBook)
https://doi.org/10.1007/978-3-319-78105-1

Library of Congress Control Number: 2018937366

LNCS Sublibrary: SL3 – Information Systems and Applications, incl. Internet/Web, and HCI

Printed on acid-free paper

This Springer imprint is published by the registered company Springer International Publishing AG
part of Springer Nature
The registered company address is: Gewerbestrasse 11, 6330 Cham, Switzerland

Preface

Established in 2005, the iConference is an annual gathering of a broad spectrum of scholars, researchers, and practitioners from around the world who share a common concern about critical information issues in contemporary society. The iConference pushes the boundaries of information studies, explores core concepts and ideas, and creates new technological and conceptual configurations—all situated in interdisciplinary discourses. iConference 2018, the 13th annual iConference, co-hosted by the Information Schools at the University of Sheffield and Northumbria University in Newcastle, took place in Sheffield during March 25–28, 2018. The theme of this first-ever UK-based iConference was "Transforming Digital Worlds," and the aim was to bring together thinkers and leaders from academia, industry and not-for-profit organizations to discuss emerging challenges and potential solutions for information and data management in today's rapidly changing world. Given the theme and the mission of the iSchools, which is to connect people with information using technologies, the conference keynotes addressed three areas, viz, information, people, and technologies. The keynote speakers were three world-renowned researchers – Dr. Lynn Silipigni Connaway from OCLC Research, Dr. Susan Dumais from the Microsoft Research Lab, and Professor Luciano Floridi from the Oxford Internet Institute.

iConference 2018 attracted a total of 139 completed papers, 80 preliminary papers, and 91 posters. Two track chairs were chosen for each area of submission, i.e., completed papers, preliminary papers, and posters. A total of 391 recognized experts from around the world took part in the review process. Each paper was reviewed by three reviewers and each poster by two reviewers, both through a double-blind review process. Finally, 42 completed papers, 40 preliminary papers, and 69 posters were selected for the conference. The quality of the accepted papers was ensured by the high level of competition and rigorous review process resulting in acceptance rates of 30% for completed papers and 50% for preliminary papers. Our grateful thanks to our reviewers and, in particular, to Noa Aharony, Kendra Albright, and Mei Mei Wu, who oversaw the reviewing of all the completed and preliminary papers.

This is the first time in the history of the iConference that the proceedings are being published by Springer in their *Lecture Notes in Computer Science* (LNCS) series. These proceedings comprise abstracts of the keynotes and the full version of the completed and preliminary papers presented at the conference. These papers have been grouped under eight broad themes: social media, communication studies and online communities, mobile information and cloud computing, data science/mining and data analytics, information retrieval, information behavior and digital literacy, digital curation, and information education and libraries. Although these categories or themes are not strictly mutually exclusive, we believe they will give the readers an idea of the different research areas and topics covered in the iConference series. Posters are not included in the proceedings, but they are available through the IDEALS open access repository (https://www.ideals.illinois.edu/handle/2142/14872).

We hope that together the three keynote addresses and 82 papers presented in the proceedings will stimulate interesting discussions and debates surrounding the issues of information and data in today's digital worlds.

March 2018

Gobinda Chowdhury
Julie McLeod
Val Gillet
Peter Willett

Organization

Organizers

iSchool, University of Sheffield, UK
iSchool, Northumbria University, UK

Conference Chairs

Val Gillet	iSchool, University of Sheffield, UK
Gobinda Chowdhury	iSchool, Northumbria University, UK

Program Chairs

Julie McLeod	iSchool, Northumbria University, UK
Peter Willett	iSchool, University of Sheffield, UK

Paper Chairs

Kendra Albright	Kent State University, USA
Noa Aharony	Bar-Ilan University, Israel
Mei Mei Wu	National Taiwan Normal University, Taiwan

Poster Chairs

Hideo Joho	University of Tsukuba, Japan
Frank Hopfgartner	University of Glasgow, UK

SIE Chairs

Jenna Hartel	University of Toronto, Canada
Theresa Anderson	University of Technology Sydney, Australia

Doctoral Colloquium Chairs

Kevin Crowston	Syracuse University, USA
Elizabeth Shepherd	University College London, UK

Early Career Colloquium Chairs

Kalpana Shankar	University College Dublin, Ireland
Carsten Oesterlund	Syracuse University, USA

Doctoral Dissertation Chairs

Joseph Tennis   University of Washington, USA
Vivien Petras   Humboldt-Universität zu Berlin, Germany

iSchool Best Practices Chairs

Ann-Sofie Axelsson   University of Boras, Sweden
António Lucas Soares   University of Porto, Portugal

iSchools and Industry Partnership Chairs

Yvon Kermarrec   IMT Atlantique, France
Sean T. McGann   University of Washington, USA

Technical Chair

Andy Stones   University of Sheffield, UK

Sponsorship Chair

Stephen Pinfield   University of Sheffield, UK

Conference Coordinator

Clark Heideger   iSchools

Program Committee

Pamela Abbott   The University of Sheffield, UK
Alison Adam   Sheffield Hallam University, UK
Waseem Afzal   Charles Sturt University, Australia
Shameem Ahmed   Western Washington University, USA
Kendra S. Albright   Kent State University, USA
Hamed Alhoori   Northern Illinois University, USA
Suzanne Lorraine Allard University of Tennessee, USA
Robert B. Allen   Yonsei University, South Korea
Lu An   Wuhan University, China
Muhammad Naveed Anwar   Northumbria University, UK
Clément Arsenault   Université de Montréal, Canada
Paavo Arvola   University of Tampere, Finland
Diane Bailey   UT Austin, USA
Alex Ball   University of Bath, UK
Peter Bath   University of Sheffield, UK
David Bawden   City University of London, UK
Antonis Bikakis   University College London, UK

Bradley Wade Bishop	University of Tennessee, USA
Phuritsabam Bobby	Manipur University, India
Toine Bogers	Aalborg University Copenhagen, Denmark
Leanne Bowler	University of Pittsburgh, USA
Jenny Bronstein	Bar-Ilan University, Israel
Vanda Broughton	University College London, UK
Caroline Brown	University of Dundee, UK
Steven Buchanan	University of Strathclyde, UK
John M. Budd	University of Missouri, USA
Jennifer Jane Bunn	University College London, UK
Gary Burnett	Florida State University, USA
Christopher Sean Burns	University of Kentucky, USA
Biddy Casselden	Northumbria University, UK
Tiffany Chao	University of Illinois, USA
Tamy A. Chambers	Indiana University, USA
Hsin-liang Chen	University of Massachusetts Boston, USA
Jiangping Chen	University of North Texas, USA
Steven Siu Fung Chong	University of Arizona, USA
Heting Chu	Long Island University, USA
Adrian Clear	Northumbria University, UK
Paul D. Clough	University of Sheffield, UK
Josep Cobarsi-Morales	Universitat Oberta de Catalunya, Spain
Gilbert Cockton	Northumbria University, UK
Andrew Martin Cox	University of Sheffield, UK
Shannon A. Crawford Barniskis	University of Wisconsin-Milwaukee, USA
Kevin Crowston	Syracuse University, USA
Hong Cui	University of Arizona, USA
Mats Dahlström	University of Borås, Sweden
Gabriel David	University of Porto, Portugal
Sharmistha Dey	Queensland University of Technology, Australia
Philip Doty	University of Texas at Austin, USA
J. Stephen Downie	University of Ilinois, USA
Heidi Enwald	University of Oulu, Finland
Donald Everhart	University of California, San Diego, USA
Lesley Suzanne Johnson Farmer	CSULB
Melanie Feinberg	University of North Carolina at Chapel Hill, USA
Antonia Ferrer Sapena	Universitat Politècnica de València, Spain
Bruce Ferwerda	Jönköping University, Sweden
Eugenia Gabrielova	University of California, Irvine, USA
Tali Gazit	Bar-Ilan University, Israel
Val Gillet	University of Sheffield, UK
Paula Goodale	University of Sheffield, UK
Tim Gorichanaz	Drexel University, USA
Michael Gowanlock	Northern Arizona University, USA

Ola Pilerot	University of Borås, Sweden
Angela Pollak	University of Alberta, Canada
Nathan Richard Prestopnik	Ithaca College, USA
Susan Rathbun-Grubb	University of South Carolina, USA
Ehsan Sabaghian	Syracuse University, USA
Laura Saunders	Simmons College, USA
Laura Sbaffi	University of Sheffield, UK
Kirsten Schlebbe	Humboldt-Universität zu Berlin, Germany
Mette Skov	Aalborg University, Denmark
Richard Slaughter	University of California, Irvine, USA
Emma Spiro	University of Washington, USA
Hrvoje Stancic	University of Zagreb
Caroline Stratton	The University of Texas at Austin, USA
Shigeo Sugimoto	University of Tsukuba, Japan
Qiong Tang	Sun Yat-sen University, China
Carol Tenopir	University of Tennessee, USA
Tien-I Tsai	National Taiwan University, Taiwan
Andrew Tsou	Indiana University, USA
Pertti Vakkari	University of Tampere, Finland
Julie Sara Walters	Northumbria University, UK
Lin Wang	Tianjin Normal University, China
Peiling Wang	University of Tennessee, USA
Xiaoguang Wang	Wuhan University, China
Ian Watson	Northumbria University, UK
Michael Majewski Widdersheim	Emporia State University
Lorna Wildgaard	Royal School of Library and Information Science/Copenhagen University, Denmark
R. Jason Winning	UC San Diego, USA
Jian Xu	Sun Yat-sen University, China
Lifang Xu	Wuhan University, China
Lijun Yang	Sun Yat-sen University, China
Siluo Yang	Wuhan University, China
Ying (Fred Ying) Ye	Nanjing University, China
Geoffrey Yeo	UCL, UK
Liangzhi Yu	Nankai University, China
Bin Zhang	Wuhan University, China
Mei Zhang	University of Wisconsin-Madison, USA
Lihong Zhou	Wuhan University, China
Dhary Abuhimed	McGill University and PwC Advisory, USA
Noa Aharony	Bar-Ilan University, Israel
Dharma Akmon	University of Michigan ICPSR, USA
Michael Albers	East Carolina University, USA
Nicole D. Alemanne	Valdosta State University, USA
Daniel Gelaw Alemneh	University of North Texas, USA
Judit Bar-Ilan	Bar-Ilan University, Israel

Leah A. Lievrouw	University of California, Los Angeles, USA
Zack Lischer-Katz	University of Oklahoma, USA
Elizabeth Jane Lomas	UCL (University College London), UK
Irene Lopatovska	Pratt Institute, USA
Kun Lù	University of Oklahoma, USA
Quan Lu	Wuhan University, China
Anna Hampson Lundh	Curtin University, Australia
Jessie Lymn	Charles Sturt University, Australia
Lai Ma	University College Dublin, Ireland
Sirkku Maennikkoe Barbutiu	Stockholm University, Sweden
Jens-Erik Mai	University of Copenhagen, Denmark
Agnes Mainka	Heinrich Heine University, Germany
Rita Marcella	Robert Gordon University, UK
Andrea Marshall	Drexel University, USA
Crystle Martin	University of California, Irvine, USA
Jorge Martins	The University of Sheffield, UK
Eleanor Mattern	University of Pittsburgh, USA
Matthew S. Mayernik	National Center for Atmospheric Research (NCAR)
Athanasios Mazarakis	Kiel University, Germany
Claire McGuinness	University College Dublin, Ireland
Elspeth McKay	RMIT University, Australia
Pamela Ann McKinney	University of Sheffield, UK
Julie McLeod	Northumbria University, UK
Shawne D. Miksa	University of North Texas, USA
A. J. Million	Drury University, USA
Matthew Ryan Mitsui	Rutgers University, USA
Lorri Mon	Florida State University, USA
Robert D. Montoya	Indiana University, Bloomington, USA
Camilla Moring	University of Copenhagen, Denmark
Michael Moss	Northumbria University, UK
Hui Nie	Sun Yat-sen University, China
Karine Nahon	Interdisciplinary Center (IDC) Herzliya, University of Washington, USA
Gustaf Nelhans	University of Borås, Sweden
Bryce Clayton Newell	University of Kentucky, USA
Chaoqun Ni	University of Iowa, USA
David M. Nichols	University of Waikato, New Zealand
Jan Nolin	University of Borås, Sweden
Rebecca Noone	University of Toronto, Canada
Ragnar Nordlie	Oslo and Akershus University College, Norway
Karen Nowé Hedvall	Swedish School of Library and Information Science, Sweden
Nasrine Olson	University of Borås, Sweden
Felipe Ortega	University Rey Juan Carlos, Spain
Virginia Ortiz-Repiso	University Carlos III of Madrid, Spain

Keynotes

People's Modes of Online Engagement: The Many Faces of Digital Visitors and Residents

Lynn Silipigni Connaway

OCLC Research, 6565 Kilgour Place, Dublin, OH 43017-3395, USA
lynn_connaway@oclc.org

Abstract. This keynote will discuss the findings of research on how individuals engage with technology and get their information. The research has been published in an OCLC report, The Many Faces of Digital Visitors & Residents: Facets of Online Engagement, and was conducted in Hong Kong, Italy, Spain, the UK, and the US. The results of the research provide insights for teaching and learning as well as the development of programs, services, and events in libraries and information centers.

Large-Scale Behavioral Analysis:
Potential and Pitfalls

Susan T. Dumais

Microsoft Research Lab, One Microsoft Way, Redmond, WA 98052-6399, USA
sdumais@microsoft.com

Abstract. Over the last decade, the rise of web services has made it possible to observe human behavior in situ at a scale and fidelity previously unimaginable. These large-scale behavioral traces enable researchers to understand how information diffuses through social networks, examine individual learning strategies influence to educational outcome, identify possible adverse drug reactions and interactions, etc. Using examples from web search, I will highlight how observational logs provide a rich new lens onto the diversity of searchers, tasks, and interactivity that characterize today's information systems, and how experimental logs have revolutionized the way in which web-based systems are designed and evaluated. Although logs provide a great deal of information about what people are doing, they provide little insight about why they are doing so or whether they are satisfied. Complementary methods from field observations, laboratory studies, and panels are necessary to provide a more complete understanding of search behavior and to enable the development of new search capabilities.

What Human Project Should Be Pursued by a Mature Information Society?

Luciano Floridi[1,2]

[1] Oxford Internet Institute, University of Oxford,
1 St Giles, Oxford, OX1 3JS, UK
[2] The Alan Turing Institute, 96 Euston Road, London, NW1 2DB, UK
luciano.floridi@oii.ox.ac.uk

Abstract. Today, in many advanced information societies, asking whether one is online or offline has become meaningless. Imagine being asked whether you are online by someone who is talking to you through your smart phone, which is linked up to your car sound system through Bluetooth, while you are driving following the instructions of a GPS, which is also downloading information about traffic in real-time. The truth is that we are neither online nor offline but onlife, that is, we increasingly live in that special space that is both analog and digital, both online and offline. An analogy may help. Imagine someone asking whether the water is sweet or salty in the estuary where the river meets the sea. That someone has not understood the special nature of the place. Our information society is that place. And our technologies are perfectly evolved to take advantage of it, like mangroves growing in brackish water. In the mangrove society, all relevant (and sometimes the only) data available are machine-readable, and decisions as well as actions may be taken automatically, through sensors, actuators, and applications that can execute commands and output the corresponding procedures, from alerting or scanning a patient, to buying or selling some bonds. The consequences of such radical transformation are many, but one is particularly significant and rich in consequences: what is the human project we should pursue in designing the mangrove society? This is the question I shall discuss in the talk, in view of exploring a possible answer.

What Human Project Should Be Pursued by a Mature Information Society

Luciano Floridi

Oxford Internet Institute, University of Oxford,
1 St Giles, Oxford OX1 3JS, UK
The Alan Turing Institute, 96 Euston Road, London NW1 2DB, UK

Contents

Communication Studies and Online Communities

Mobile Information and Cloud Computing

Information Retrieval

Information Behaviour and Digital Literacy

Digital Curation

Information Education and Libraries

XXXII   Contents

Social Media

Social Content Management: A Study on Issues and Challenges

Wan Azlin Zurita Wan Ahmad$^{(\boxtimes)}$, Muriati Mukhtar,
and Yazrina Yahya

National University of Malaysia, 43600 Bangi, Malaysia
azlinzurita@gmail.com, {muriati,yazrina}@ukm.edu.my

Abstract. Organisations are facing challenges in managing the diverse social content resulting from the active interactions between them and their customers on social media platforms. The increasing opportunities from social content have led to the concept of social content management (SCM). However, research in SCM is yet to receive more attention, especially in the context of its issues and challenges. Therefore, this paper has evaluated the issues and challenges in SCM research from the academic and practical viewpoint. Since the number of academic research in SCM is limited, this paper offers a point of departure for future studies in the SCM field. In the context of practical contribution, this study aimed to offer better understanding of the issues and challenges in managing social content.

Keywords: Social content · Social content management

1 Introduction

The enterprise content management (ECM) has overarched the term for the technical and managerial capabilities in content management [1]. In an organisation, ECM is often used to manage all types of content in the content lifecycle [2, 3]. The unstructured contents, such as presentations, word files, emails as well as social content were managed by the ECM [4]. Social content has its own potential, for example, in innovating the services offered by the organisation [5]. Such innovation is obtained through the interaction process between an organisation and its customers as well as information that were gathered for enhancing the organisation's outreach [6]. Social content, as a result of the interaction process, is used to assist organisations in their decision-making process towards providing innovative services to their customers.

However, the growing usage of social media has increased the volume of social content, which was not being properly managed [7]. Due to the compliance and quality issues, ECM was facing challenges in managing social content. Therefore, the SCM was introduced, specifically to manage the social content. The SCM has shown its importance to an organisation in the context of managing its social content, which could become an asset to the organisation. Despite the importance of SCM to the organisation, the number of research that identify the issues and challenges in SCM has been limited. To highlight the study gap, this study has aimed to examine the issues and

© Springer International Publishing AG, part of Springer Nature 2018
G. Chowdhury et al. (Eds.): iConference 2018, LNCS 10766, pp. 3–9, 2018.
https://doi.org/10.1007/978-3-319-78105-1_1

challenges in the field of SCM by conducting a literature review and obtaining the viewpoints of experts who are experienced in managing social content.

2 Method

A qualitative method was adopted, which consisted of three phases as follows.

2.1 Phase 1: Selection of Document and Document Analysis

The first phase was conducted to identify the relevant research papers and to explore issues and challenges in SCM. The processes applied in this phase included in Table 1.

Table 1. Characteristics of the document analysis proses

Criteria	Details
Search	• Research databases, such as ISI, Scopus, IEEE, and science direct • Open search engines, such as Google, Google scholar, and research gates • Reliable websites, such as the AIIM website and consulting firm's website
Keyword	• "Issues", "challenges", and "gap" in SCM and ECM
Inclusion	• Journals, conference proceedings, books, theses, working papers • Due to the limited research on SCM, ECM research that include social content as part of the content management were selected in this study • Articles written in English
Exclusion	Articles written in other languages

2.2 Phase 2: Experts Review

A series of semi-structured interviews were conducted with experts from government agency to identify the issues and challenges faced in managing social content from a practical viewpoint. Details of the selected experts are listed in Table 2.

Table 2. Panel of experts

Expert ID and position	Agency	Category and experience	Length of interview session
Expert 1 Head of ICT consultant (Strategic)	Agency A	Top management-36 years, with 10 years of experience in ECM and SCM	50 min
Expert 2 ICT expert - Information Management (IM)	Agency B	Middle management-26 years, with 6 years of experience in ECM and SCM	55 min
Expert 3 ICT expert - IM	Agency B	Operation-11 years, with 5 years of experience in ECM and SCM	1 h
Expert 4 Public relation officer	Agency C	Operation-11 years, with 8 years of experience in SCM	1 h

The processes applied in this phase were:

a. Preparing the interview sessions that included the schedule and interview guide that based on leading question. The topics in the interview guide covers: the scenario in managing social content in an organisation, and the issues and challenges in SCM.
b. Conducting the interview with the experts. The experts were interviewed face-to-face and follow-up sessions were conducted via email and other communication tools. Each session was manually recorded and taped.

2.3   Phase 3: Analysis and Conclusion

Results from the document analysis and experts review were grouped and discussed.

3   Results and Discussion

Issues and challenges in SCM are concluded in Table 3.

Table 3. Issues and challenges in SCM

Issues and challenges in SCM	Authors	Interview session
Lack of academic references	[8]	
Lack of research on business model	[8]	√
Challenges in the SCM system	[4, 7, 9–12]	√
Lack of governance	[13–15]	√
Lack of privacy and security control	[13, 14]	√
Lack of commitment from management and team		√

Explanations on the issues and challenges are as follows:

3.1   Lack of Academic References

Although SCM has its own potentials, specific academic studies related to this field are still lacking [8]. Previous studies have shown, only nine studies were conducted specifically for the SCM [7, 8, 13, 14, 16–20]. A study by [16] on the platform for SCM has been adopted by American to discuss on health care policies. Studies by [13] and [14] had focused on the evolution of the ECM system into the SCM system and the importance of managing social content to maximise value and reduce risks. [7] conducted a study on managers' perceptions on the potentials and challenges of SCM systems for internal organisations. Meanwhile, studies conducted by [19, 20] were focused on the elements and factors that could be affecting SCM based on findings in the ECM. Nonetheless, these studies have not thoroughly analysed how social content is being managed. Several studies have been conducted on the models of SCM. A study by [8] was on a process-oriented model that could assist organisations in managing social media content and improve their business performance. Meanwhile, studies conducted by [17, 18] were focused on SCM models based on the service science perspective, namely, from the theory of service dominant logic and the DART model. Both studies had focused on managing content in the content lifecycle.

3.2 Lack of Research on Business Model

Previous studies have reported that there is a lack of research related to business models to guide and improve SCM efforts in businesses [8]. As previously mentioned, only three studies have been conducted on the models of SCM. The experts had agreed with the importance of business model. Expert 1 from Agency A stated, *"We don't adopt any business model and only follow the best practices. We do face challenges because without a proper business model, we missed out on some important elements that could foster the management of social content."*

3.3 Challenges in the SCM System

There were also challenges within the SCM system. A study conducted by [7] revealed the challenges faced by internal organisations while using the SCM system. These challenges include; (1) users are reluctant to contribute, in the context of willingness to use the system, (2) limited time and effort to use the system, (3) the user feels that the system is a barrier, (4) the fear of losing power if the user shares information, and (5) the transferring of knowledge in an accessible and applicable format. Apart from these challenges, there are also other issues related to the system itself. [13] revealed that there is a concern in integrating the social system into the enterprise system. A study by [14] highlighted issues related to the ability of the system, such as its search ability and the retrieval of the content. Studies conducted by [4, 10] were focused on the quality of the system. A study by [11] had shown concern over the strategic decision-making capabilities in such system.

From the perspective of practical usage, there is an issue in using the system. Expert 3 from Agency B stated, *"The use of the system is an issue. The organisation feels that the system is a burden and therefore, the reluctance to use is there."* Minor use of the system has also become a challenge in resolving SCM operational issues in organisations. Social content involves a huge volume of data that need to be managed using a specific system. Dialogue management is also a concern as not all social contents could be adopted in a decision-making process. Hence, intelligent analysis through the system could assist organisations to analyse suitable contents and weigh them against the value of the content provided by the customers. Expert 4 from Agency C stated, *"We manually analyse the social content. With the huge volume of data, it becomes a problem and there is a need for a system. The system should have suitable capabilities, especially while analysing the content, specifically to manage the enthusiastic comments, thoughtful dialogues, and openly hostile threats."*

3.4 Lack of Governance

Social content requires a policy to rapid the management of social content [13, 14]. There is also a need to control the content, which includes the effectiveness and efficiency of all kinds of processes, depending on the availability and quality of the underlying data [15]. This includes a clear content ownership, an established routing for evaluating the content, and services related to content management inside the portfolio or the organisation. Based on previous studies, there is also a concern in maintaining the governance over the defined content lifecycle [14].

From the perspective of practical usage, there is a lack of control in governing SCM. SCM needs a proper body of control. This is because the management of social content involves various human resources and content assets. In addition, apart from developing new policies, the SCM also needs to comply with the existing policies to ensure that it supports the organisation's goals and objectives. Expert 2 from Agency B stated, *"We discussed the issues from social content in the management meeting. Only critical issues were discussed and not all results are revealed to the customers. This is the time to have a firm structure to complement the need from customers who use the social media platform as a formal channel to communicate with us. Besides having a new policy, there is also a need to comply with existing ones."*

3.5   Lack of Privacy and Security Control

Social media embarks in openness, therefore, privacy and security are of concern [21]. According to [13], there is a need to balance between collaboration and agility with security and privacy considerations. There is also a concern in maintaining the security over the content lifecycle [14]. The experts have also agreed with the findings from the literature review. Expert 4 from Agency C stated, *"Social content triggers the issue of privacy and security. Hence, there is a need to give attention to legal perspective, which controls the privacy and information technology perspective, which controls the security".*

3.6   Lack of Commitment from Management and Team

The interviews with experts have revealed that there is a lack of commitment from managements and teams in SCM. Social content is a new and unstructured content that must be managed by the organisation. Therefore, commitment from management and the various teams are important to ensure the overall success. Expert 1 from Agency A stated, *"Commitment from both parties is a critical issue, to ensure that new business processes and new types of content are incorporated into the practice to benefit the entire organisation."* Expert 2 from Agency B also stated, *"It is important to obtain corporation-wide commitment in the SCM to support the decision-making process. Therefore, change management programs are essential to gain the support by justifying the investment, as well as for addressing user hurdles".*

4   Conclusion

This paper contributes to the mitigating efforts against the issues and challenges in the SCM field. Document analysis and expert review have revealed six issues in the SCM field, namely; (1) lack of academic references, (2) lack of research in business model,

(3) challenges in the SCM system, (4) lack of governance, (5) lack of privacy and security control, and (6) lack of commitment from managements and teams. Due to the limited number of academic research in the SCM field, this paper is expected to be the starting point for future researchers to conduct new studies in this field. Meanwhile, for practical purposes, this study is expected to assist organisations in understanding the issues and challenges in sustaining SCM.

Acknowledgement. The study is financially supported by Public Service Department of Malaysia.

References

1. Herbst, A., Simons, A., vom Brocke, J., Müller, O., Debortoli, S., Vakulenko, S.: Identifying and characterizing topics in enterprise content management: a latent semantic analysis of vendor case studies. In: 22nd European Conference on Information Systems, pp. 1–15. AISel, Tel Aviv (2014)
2. Tyrväinen, P., Päivärinta, T., Salminen, A., Iivari, J.: Characterizing the evolving research on enterprise content management. Eur. J. Inf. Syst. **15**, 627–634 (2006)
3. Smith, H.A., McKeen, J.D.: Developments in practice VIII: enterprise content management. Commun. Assoc. Inf. Syst. **11**, 647–659 (2003)
4. Hopkins, P.J.: Engaging with web 2.0 technologies: implementing enterprise content management at Bond University. In: EDUCAUSE, pp. 1–13. Bond University, Gold Coast (2009)
5. Criado, J.I., Sandoval-Almazan, R., Ramon Gil-Garcia, J.: Government innovation through social media. Gov. Inf. Q. **30**, 319–326 (2013)
6. Zheng, L., Zheng, T.: Innovation through social media in the public sector: information and interactions. Gov. Inf. Q. **31**, 106–108 (2014)
7. Herbst, A., vom Brocke, J.: Social content management systems: challenges and potential for organisations. In: Piazolo, F., Felderer, M. (eds.) Innovation and Future of Enterprise Information Systems. LNISO, vol. 4, pp. 19–28. Springer, Heidelberg (2013). https://doi.org/10.1007/978-3-642-37021-2_4
8. Aladwani, A.M.: The 6As model of social content management. Int. J. Inf. Manag. **34**, 133–138 (2014)
9. Itahriouan, Z., Abtoy, A., El Kadiri, K.E., Aknin, N.: Validated CMS: towards new generation of web content management systems on web 2.0. Int. J. Inf. Technol. Comput. Sci. **4**(12), 40–49 (2012)
10. Perez-Montoro, M.: Theoretical perspectives of content management. In: Ferrer, N., Alfonso, J. (eds.) Content Management for E-Learning, LLC, pp. 1–24. Springer, Heidelberg (2011). https://doi.org/10.1007/978-1-4419-6959-0_1
11. Alalwan, J.A., Thomas, M.A., Weistroffer, H.R.: Decision support capabilities of enterprise content management systems: an empirical investigation. Decis. Support Syst. **68**, 39–48 (2014)
12. Escalona, M.J., Domínguez-Mayo, F.J., García-García, J.A., Sánchez, N., Ponce, J.: Evaluating enterprise content management tools in a real context. J. Softw. Eng. Appl. **8**(8), 431–453 (2015)
13. Moore, G.: Systems of Engagement and The Future of Enterprise IT. White paper, AIIM (2011)

14. Miles, D.: Managing Social Content - To Maximize Value and Minimize Risk. White paper, AIIM (2011)
15. vom Brocke, J.: On the Role of Enterprise Content in Business Process Management. BPTrends Coloum (2013)
16. Davies, T., Mintz, M.D., Tobin, J., Ben-Avi, N.: Document-Centered Discussion and Decision Making in the Deme Platform 1 (2009)
17. Wan Azlin Zurita, W.A., Muriati, M.: A social content management model based on S-D logic. In: 5th Asian Conference on Information System, pp. 274–281. ACIS, Krabi (2016)
18. Wan Azlin Zurita, W.A., Muriati, M.: A social content management model based on the DART model. Am. J. Appl. Sci. **14**(1), 25–33 (2017)
19. Wan Azlin Zurita, W.A., Muriati, M.: Elements affecting social content management. In: SOFTAM Postgraduate Symposium, pp. 102–108. UKM, Bangi (2016)
20. Wan Ahmad, W.A.Z., Mukhtar, M., Yahya, Y.: Exploring elements and factors in social content management for ICT service innovation. In: Saeed, F., Gazem, N., Patnaik, S., Saed Balaid, A.S., Mohammed, F. (eds.) IRICT 2017. LNDECT, vol. 5, pp. 851–859. Springer, Cham (2018). https://doi.org/10.1007/978-3-319-59427-9_88
21. Kilgour, M., Sasser, S.L., Larke, R.: The social media transformation process: curating content into strategy. Corp. Commun. An Int. J. **20**(3), 326–343 (2015)

Measuring the Effect of Public Health Campaigns on Twitter: The Case of World Autism Awareness Day

Wasim Ahmed[1](✉), Peter A. Bath[1] ⓘ, Laura Sbaffi[1],
and Gianluca Demartini[2]

[1] Information School, University of Sheffield, Sheffield, UK
wahmed1@sheffield.ac.uk
[2] School of Information Technology and Electrical Engineering,
University of Queensland, Brisbane, Australia

Abstract. Mass media campaigns are traditional methods of raising public awareness in order to reinforce positive behaviors and beliefs. However, social media platforms such as Twitter have the potential to offer an additional route into raising awareness of general and specific health conditions. The aim of this study was to investigate the extent to which a public health campaign, World Autism Awareness Day (WAAD), could increase Twitter activity and influence the average sentiment on Twitter, and to discover the types of information that was shared on the platform during a targeted awareness campaign. This study gathered over 2,315,283 tweets in a two-month period. Evidence suggests that the autism campaign, WAAD, was successful in raising awareness on Twitter, as an increase in both the volume of tweets and level of positive sentiment were observed during this time. In addition, a framework for assessing the success of health campaigns was developed. Further work is required on this topic to determine whether health campaigns have any long lasting impact on Twitter users.

Keywords: Social media · Health campaigns · Twitter

1 Introduction

Millions of pounds are spent each year in order to encourage behavior change among the public, e.g., campaigns that encourage the public to eat healthily, undertake exercise, or cease smoking [1]. The purpose of mass media campaigns is to promote healthy behavior changes and to discourage unhealthy behaviors by raising awareness [1]. However, there has been limited empirical research to measure the extent to which health campaigns have the potential to raise awareness on social media (e.g., Twitter). Although there have been evaluations of traditional public health campaigns [2], the effectiveness of social media health campaign is an important issue that is currently under-researched. Understanding the effectiveness of public health campaigns on social media, such as Twitter, would enable policy makers and public health experts to develop more focused campaigns that could target specific messages and improve understanding of health issues. World Autism Awareness Day (WAAD) is an

© Springer International Publishing AG, part of Springer Nature 2018
G. Chowdhury et al. (Eds.): iConference 2018, LNCS 10766, pp. 10–16, 2018.
https://doi.org/10.1007/978-3-319-78105-1_2

internationally recognised day taking place on April 2nd each year and encourages Member States of the United Nations to raise awareness for people with autism around the world [3]. The campaign aims to bring together different autism organizations as well as information around diagnoses, treatments, and to generally raise awareness of the disease [3]. The main aim of this study was to assess the extent to which the public health campaign, WAAD influenced standard sentiment on Twitter, in order to determine whether the campaign was successful. In particular, the research objectives were:

- To investigate the extent to which WAAD raised awareness on Twitter by investigating the volume of tweets that were sent and received using specific keywords, and to investigate the effect on positive or negative sentiment during WAAD.
- To better understand the different classes of WAAD tweets during April 2nd 2015 by training a machine learning classifier to categorize tweets on this day.
- To analyse the structure of the conversation during WAAD, by creating a network graph of tweets related to WAAD.

A successful health campaign defined for the purposes of this study are those which:

- Raises awareness of a health disease and or condition, so that it makes members of the public conscious about the impact of a disease. In relation to Twitter we developed a framework for assessing the successfulness of a campaign.
- The volume of tweets should increase during the day of the campaign.
- The positive sentiment of tweets should increase during the campaign.
- When examining the structure of the network an isolates group should be identifiable which is important because it indicates a number of unique and unconnected users will be tweeting.
- When examining the content shared on the platform the majority of tweets should relate to the campaign.

2 Methodology

This study employed a case study research design, which seeks to concentrate on one aspect in detail [4]. This study follows a pragmatic approach, and the research methodology consists of a mixed methods approach utilizing machine learning, network analysis, and time series analysis. Twenty-four hashtags and keywords were used to monitor discussions on Twitter which related to various aspects of Autism which were most popular at the time, and included the following: #measles, Measles, #measlesoutbreak, MeaslesOutbreak, #MMR, Vaccination, Vaccinate, Vaccines, #Vaccines, MMR Vaccine, Vaccination AND MeaslesOutbreak, Vaccinate AND Measles, #Vaccinedebate, #Vaccineswork, #cdcwhistleblower, #Vaccinateyourkids, #Vaccineinjury, #VaccinesSaveLives, #adhd, #aspergers, #autism, adhd, aspergers, and autism. Data were collected between March 19th 2015 and the 9th May 2015, which included the 2015 WAAD day (April 2nd); a total of 2,315,283 tweets were gathered.

Once duplicates and non-English tweets were removed, 1,710,121 tweets remained. This final dataset contained data that was collected over 1,234 h and which contained 637,969 unique Twitter users. The data collection on WAAD day started Thu Apr 02 00:00:00 +0000, 2015 and ended Thu Apr 02 23:59:59 +0000, 2015. DiscoverText [5], a cloud-based text analytics software was used to classify tweets by machine learning. The time series analysis program Mozdeh [6], which uses Twitter's Search API, was used to gather Twitter data. Mozdeh uses the SentiStrength algorithm. SentiStrengh, when tested on Myspace comments, was able to predict positive emotion with 60.6% accuracy [7].

2.1   User Demographics

Twitter provides geolocation data with each tweet; this is known as 'gold standard' geolocation data, as location information from users Twitter biography may not be accurate. However, not all users enable this feature, thus not all tweets will contain geolocation data. In total 15,601(0.91%) out of the 1,710,121 tweets contained valid latitude and longitude data. The majority of tweeters were based in the USA and the UK (see Fig. 1).

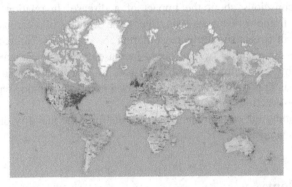

Fig. 1. World map to show the geographic spread of tweets that contained geolocation information for the tweets collected in this dataset.

3   Results

This section provides the results of the study. Figure 1 displays a time series graph of all tweets that were sent during the period, and Fig. 2 shows the volume of tweets related to WAAD over time alongside the average positive and negative sentiment. It is important to note that, for the time series graph, some of the fluctuations are caused by the time of day, with peaks during the daylight hours and troughs during the night. This is because up to 60% of all tweets have English language settings, and this may indicate sleeping time for the majority of English speaking users [8]. Note that for this

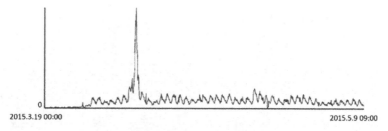

Fig. 2. Time series for all tweets from 2015.3.19.00.00 to 2015.5.9.09.0.

graph and others there is poor coverage during the initial phase of data collection due to Twitter's rate limiting. Rate limiting occurs when the number of requests to Twitter exceeds their maximum number of requests, and can also occur when there is unusually high traffic on the platform requests for data may be limited.

As can be seen from Fig. 2, the largest peak corresponded to World Autism Awareness day, when a total of up to 245,463 tweets (in all languages) were sent and received during April 2nd 2015. This accounted for 14.4% of the total sample of tweets collected. Figure 3 shows the frequency of the sentiment expressed by WAAD related tweets over time: positive sentiment is represented by a red line, and negative sentiment is represented by a black line. The tweets were consistently more positive than negative as positive sentiment lines (red) are higher than the negative sentiment lines (black). There is also an increase in the frequency of subjective posts. When examining exact duplicates it is possible to investigate the most frequently occurring tweets in this dataset. We found that that 8 out of the 10 most popular retweets were related to WAAD, therefore there was an observed increased interest in this during this time period. The manually-coded set of tweets was used to train a machine learning classifier using a Naïve Bayes algorithm. The entire dataset of tweets was then classified: 68,547 (81%) of tweets were classified as related to WAAD and 16,455 (19%) of tweets were not related to WAAD. In order to undertake additional analyses, a network graph was developed using NodeXL [9]. The resulting graph is shown in Fig. 4.

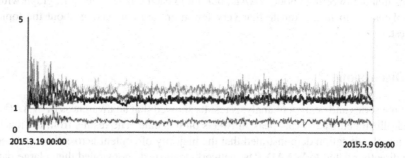

Fig. 3. The average positive and negative sentiment strength for tweets containing all of the hashtags used to gather the data. Average tweet sentiment (1 to 5) +ve = red, −ve = black (0 = no posts), Grey/Pink: subjective posts only; Green = proportion of subjective tweets (Color figure online)

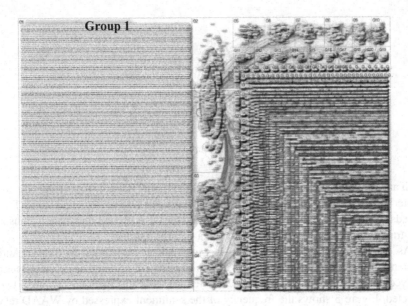

Fig. 4. Network analysis for tweets send and received on April 2nd, 2015 related to the keywords used to retrieve data

The network graph shows how different structures were formed during WAAD on April 2nd 2015. The network graph demonstrates (in group 1) that more than half of the tweets do not contain an '@' sign in their tweet, that is to say users do not mention other Twitter users. This can be inferred from G1 (group 1), which lists users by themselves, i.e., tweeting using one of the keywords without mentioning other users. It can also be inferred from the network graph that there are many disconnected participants, and these isolated cases are on the left hand side of the network graph within G1 (group 1). Therefore, the majority of tweets on Twitter over this time period corresponded to the occurrence of WAAD, and there are large fragmented Twitter populations that are tweeting about WAAD, but not to each other. A network graph without an isolates group may indicate that very few users are conversing about the topic of interest.

4 Discussion

The time series and sentiment analysis results showed that an awareness of WAAD was raised, illustrated by the vast peak in tweets on this date. The results from the machine learning classification demonstrated that the majority of content across this time period were directly related to WAAD. The network analysis demonstrated that a large part of the conversation was driven by WAAD tweets due to the large isolated group. Thus, by taking into account the four separate analyses above, the categories for a successful health campaign outlined earlier in the study were fulfilled, as shown in Table 1 below:

Table 1. Criteria for a successful campaigns in relation to WAAD

Criteria	World Autism Awareness Day
C.1 Volume of tweets should increase during the day of the campaign	Volume of tweets increased as demonstrated by the results of the time series graph (Fig. 2)
C.2 Positive sentiment of tweets should increase during the campaign	Positive sentiment of tweets increased during the campaign as demonstrated by the sentiment analysis graph (Fig. 3)
C.3 An isolates group should be identifiable in the network graph	An isolates group was formed during the campaign (Fig. 4)
C.4 When examining the content shared on the platform the majority of tweets should relate to the campaign	The majority of tweets (57%) related to WAAD

The implications of these results are that campaign managers could seek to promote the creation of news stories which are shareable. Moreover, for post-campaign monitoring examining the number of unique users in the form of isolates would provide an indication of the number of unique users engaging with a health campaign. Therefore, this study provides evidence to suggest that the WAAD campaign successfully raised awareness on Twitter. It is possible that all campaigns may look like this, therefore future research could seek to compare the success of different campaigns. Moreover, future research could seek to examine other aspects which correlate with awareness, such as donation amounts, which could form a further measure of success. Moreover, additional data sources such as Google Trends could be utilised in order to strengthen future work. A more in-depth study could use the Firehose API (all available tweets); however, it may be that the tweets gathered for this study are upwards of 70% [8]. Future research could compare traditional media and marketing campaigns with social media with regard to raising awareness about autism. It would also be useful to examine whether awareness on Twitter increases awareness in the offline environment.

5 Conclusion

This initial study found some evidence to suggest that the autism campaign, WAAD, was successful in raising awareness on Twitter, in that, across this time period, there was an increase in both the volume of tweets, and their positive sentiment. However, we do not make any conclusions on whether the increased awareness on Twitter had an impact on individuals. Instead, we provide evidence that the WAAD campaign did appear to increase awareness on Twitter. Further work is required which examines the longevity and also compares a number of health campaigns in order to reach such a conclusion. Further work will seek to build a custom sentiment algorithm to classify tweets, and to utilise multiple coders to train the classifier. Moreover with the increase in text-characters in English language tweets this may present greater further opportunities in this area [10].

References

1. Randolph, W., Viswanath, K.: Lessons learned from public health mass media campaigns: marketing health in a crowded media world. Ann. Rev. Public Health **25**, 419–437 (2004). https://doi.org/10.1146/annurev.publhealth.25.101802.123046
2. Hornik, R.: Public Health Communication Evidence for Behavior Change. Lawrence Erlbaum Associates, Mahwah (2002)
3. General Assembly Resolution 62/139. Resolution adopted by the General Assembly on 18 December 2007. http://www.un.org/ga/search/view_doc.asp?symbol=A/RES/62/139
4. Bryman, A.: Social Research Methods, 2nd edn. Oxford University Press, Oxford (2004)
5. DiscoverText: DiscoverText. https://www.discovertext.com/. Accessed 12 Feb 2015
6. Mozdeh: Mozdeh Twitter Time Series Analysis. http://mozdeh.wlv.ac.uk/. Accessed 19 May 2015
7. Thelwall, M., Buckley, K., Paltoglou, G., Cai, D., Kappas, A.: Sentiment strength detection in short informal text. J. Assoc. Inf. Sci. Technol. **61**(12), 2544–2558 (2010)
8. Gerlitz, C., Rieder, B.: Mining one percent of Twitter: collections, baselines, sampling. M/C J. **16**(2) (2013)
9. Social Media Research Foundation: NodeXL. http://www.smrfoundation.org/nodexl/. Accessed 28 May 2015
10. Ahmed, W.: More room for greater depth and detail: implications for academic research of Twitter's expanded character limit. LSE Impact Blog (2018). http://blogs.lse.ac.uk/impactofsocialsciences/2018/02/09/more-room-for-greater-depth-and-detail-implications-for-academic-research-of-twitters-expanded-character-limit

Automated Diffusion? Bots and Their Influence During the 2016 U.S. Presidential Election

Olga Boichak, Sam Jackson, Jeff Hemsley(✉) ,
and Sikana Tanupabrungsun

Syracuse University, Syracuse, NY 13210, USA
{oboichak,sjackson,jjhemsle,stanupab}@syr.edu

Abstract. In the 2016 U.S. Presidential election, some candidates used to automated accounts, or bots, to boost their social media presence and follow-ership. Categorizing all automated accounts as "bots" obfuscates the role different types of bots play in the spread of political information in election campaigns. Exploring strategies for automated information diffusion helps scholars understand and model online political behavior. This paper presents an initial effort aimed at understanding the disparate roles of bots in diffusion of political messages on Twitter. Having collected over 300 million tweets from candidates and the public from the U.S. presidential election, we use three OLS regression models to explore the strategic advantages of different types of automated accounts. We approach this by analyzing retweet events, testing a series of hypotheses regarding bots' influence on the size of retweet events, and the change in candidates' followers. Next, we develop an estimator to analyze the spread of information across the networks, demonstrating that, while 'benevolent bots' serve as overt information aggregators and have an effect on information diffusion, "nefarious bots" act as false amplifiers, covertly mimicking the spread of online information with no effect on diffusion. Making this important distinction allows us to disambiguate the concept of "bots" and reach a more nuanced and detailed understanding of the role of automated accounts in information diffusion in political campaigning online.

Keywords: Bots · Political elections · Viral events · Twitter · Social media

1 Introduction

In the aftermath of the 2016 U.S. Presidential election, studies found evidence of automated intervention on Twitter. Kollanyi et al. [10] showed up to 30% of pro-Trump and up to 20% of pro-Clinton Twitter traffic were driven by automated accounts, Woolley and Guilbeault [16] provided evidence of bots having had structural influence on online political behavior around major candidates, and Bessi and Ferrara [1] estimated that roughly 20% of political discussion on Twitter came from automated accounts. In light of their potential implications on public opinion and electoral outcomes, bots merit a critical inquiry. In this study, we aim to foreground the distinct roles of automated Twitter accounts in the 2016 U.S. Presidential election by analyzing their impact on diffusion of political information online.

© Springer International Publishing AG, part of Springer Nature 2018
G. Chowdhury et al. (Eds.): iConference 2018, LNCS 10766, pp. 17–26, 2018.
https://doi.org/10.1007/978-3-319-78105-1_3

We develop an estimator to analyze spread of information in a sample of 100 retweet events (RTEs). An RTE is comprised of an original tweet by one of the four general election candidates (Donald Trump, Hillary Clinton, Jill Stein, and Gary Johnson), and all instances when their message has been retweeted by the public. Using Botometer, a publicly-available classification model [15], and tracking a number of parameters related to information diffusion for each RTE, we outline two possible scenarios of bot involvement in political discussions. This allows us to distinguish between different types of automated accounts based on a 2×2 typology that intersects the number of followers with the tweet rate of the accounts, disambiguating the concept of "bots", and reaching a more nuanced and detailed understanding of their role in online political campaigns. We use this distinction to argue that categorizing automated accounts as bots obfuscates the role different types of bots play in the spread of political information in election campaigns. While benevolent bots serve as overt information aggregators [6] and have an effect on information diffusion, nefarious bots act as false amplifiers, covertly mimicking the spread of online information with no effect on diffusion.

2 Background

Twitter is a strategic component of political campaigning, used by candidates to broadcast messages directly to the public [3]. The public may share these messages into their own networks, expanding candidates' audiences as new followers tend to accumulate through retweets [9]. In this context, exploring strategies for information diffusion helps scholars understand and model online political behavior. Over the past few years, automated Twitter accounts, or bots, were shown to have a range of implications for electoral outcomes, from "manufacturing consensus" [16], to introducing noisy data for election forecasting [2].

Message diffusion (i.e., the spread of messages) through retweets is one way individuals can grow their audience on Twitter [9]. Research suggests numerous factors affect retweet diffusion, including who sent the tweet [11], followership [17], and hashtags, URLs and @mentions [14]. There is also evidence that emotional political tweets are more likely to be retweeted [13]. Candidates want to see their messages diffuse to reach more people. Journalists covering elections may also care about diffusion, using it as a measure of how popular a candidate is.

In political campaigns, useful (or benevolent) bots can be used to monitor user's activity (e.g. response time, or search categories), while harmful (or nefarious) bots may produce spam with the goal of persuading, smearing, or deceiving people [6]. Bot armies have been deployed to counteract criticism in Mexico during elections [12] and have been used by oppositional parties in Venezuela to attack the regime and spread misinformation [7]. In the 2016 U.S. Presidential election, bots had a disruptive influence on the information arena [10]. The prevalence of bots were estimated to have affected public discussion in negative ways, with a fifth of all political discussion in the U.S. elections being driven by bots [1].

Our paper contributes to this literature by examining the roles of bots in information diffusion in the 2016 U.S. Presidential election. Specifically, we ask: What was the role of benevolent vs. nefarious bots in diffusing political information on Twitter throughout the 2016 U.S. Presidential Election (RQ1)? Moreover, did automated accounts have an effect on candidates' followership on Twitter (RQ2)? Finally, can our estimate of the rate of diffusion in an RTE (as measured by the RTE signature which is the rate of retweets over time) be used to detect automated influence in RTEs (RQ3)?

3 Analysis

Our data come from the Illuminating 2016 repository [8], a collection of over 300 million Twitter messages from the 2016 U.S. Presidential candidates and the public (among them are approximately 80,000 original tweets from the candidates). Following Hemsley [9], our unit of analysis is a retweet event (RTE), which consists of an original tweet by a candidate and all the instances of the message being retweeted by users. Focusing on RTEs allows to us examine the effects of bots in terms of their ultimate reach in networks, how they might change those networks, and their future impact on information flows in those networks. For the purpose of this study, we generated a sample of 100 RTEs, stratified by the number of tweets in an RTE (in other words, the RTE size). Due to the fact that the size of RTEs are power-law distributed, we defined 4 categories based on the RTE's position in the distribution: Low (up to 80th percentile), Medium (80–90th percentile), Medium/High (90–99th percentile), and High (99–100th, or the top 1 percentile). Then, we took a random 10% from each category for each of the four U.S. Presidential candidates: Donald Trump, Hillary Clinton, Jill Stein, and Gary Johnson.

Next, we ran the 196,375 unique users in our dataset that participated in one of these 100 RTEs through Botometer, a feature-based classification algorithm that assigns scores to individual accounts on Twitter, indicating the probability that an account is a bot [15]. The distribution of bot scores is consistent with the findings of Bessi and Ferrara [1] that about 25% of all user accounts were identified as suspicious, i.e. have a high statistical probability of being automated. However, retrieving bot scores led us to discover three distinct groups of suspicious accounts, two of which have been traditionally excluded from analysis in other literature on automated accounts [16] (Fig. 1). The first group of accounts (shown in red) is comprised of user accounts with a bot score of over 50%; this type of account is commonly included in analyses of bots [16]. The second group of accounts (in yellow) are the 22,281 users who retweeted the candidates but have since deleted their accounts. Finally, the third group of accounts (in dark blue) are the 18,393 users who retweeted candidates' messages but have since switched their account to "protected" status, making their tweets accessible only to their followers. While one might speculate regarding the algorithmic nature of the last two groups of accounts (deleted and protected), they cannot be excluded from the analysis as they comprise almost 20% of our sample. There were also two much smaller categories of suspicious accounts: those who retweeted the same candidate's message more than once, and users who deleted all of their tweets after having participated in an RTE. As we demonstrate in our analysis below, some of these groups of accounts played distinct roles in diffusion of political information in the U.S. elections.

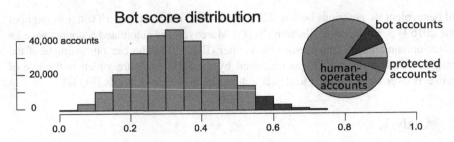

Fig. 1. Bot score distribution (Color figure online)

As a next step, after obtaining Botometer scores for each of the accounts in our dataset, we created a multi-dimensional plot to see whether these accounts cluster according to common bot indicators. Literature on bot detection [6] suggests that bot accounts exhibit patterns of high-volume activity that exceeds that of humans. For this reason, for each account in our dataset we computed a tweet rate, which would measure the number of tweets per day. We plotted the accounts' tweet rate by the number of followers, knowing from the literature that bot accounts usually (but not in all cases) have low followership counts. Finally, we overplotted each account with the color for each category of account: alleged human accounts (light blue), accounts with bot score >.5 (red), deleted accounts (yellow), and protected accounts (blue) (see Fig. 2). The distribution of human accounts (light blue) and deleted accounts (yellow) approximates normal, while the protected accounts (blue) and "bot accounts" are highly skewed to the left and to the right respectively.

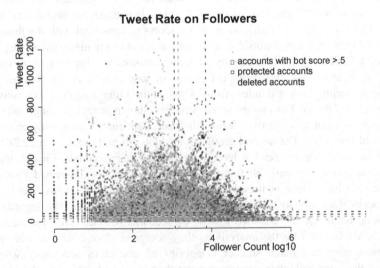

Fig. 2. Tweet rate by log 10 transformed follower count. Dashed lines show the mean values for each group. Human accounts (light blue) and deleted accounts (yellow) approximate normal distributions around their mean follower counts, while protected accounts (blue) and "bot accounts" (red) are skewed to the left and to the right, respectively. (Color figure online)

Contrary to the expectations, the alleged "bot accounts" tend to have comparatively high followership while their tweet rate is roughly average. This finding falls out of the line from the bot behavior described in the literature above. Upon closer examination, we see that those accounts with high followership, while possibly automated, perform a useful societal function by acting as information aggregators (examples include media organizations, high-profile journalists, and activist accounts). As we further explore in our regression models, these accounts actively participate in information diffusion despite the fact that they are automated. The second category of accounts – whose distribution is skewed up and left in Fig. 2 – are the protected accounts. Despite a higher-than-average tweet rate, many of them have relatively few followers. A closer investigation into a sample of these accounts reveals that they have other features associated with "bots," such as non-customized profiles, seemingly random usernames, and absence of geographical metadata [6].

We hypothesize that there are two distinct types of bots that can be distinguished by their goals: "information aggregators", or accounts with high tweet rate and high followership that play a useful role in the diffusion of political information; and "false amplifiers," or accounts with high tweet rate and low followership, which mimic the social spread of online political information without drawing attention to the fact that they are automated (and may hide with a protected status).

In this paper, we hypothesize on the ways in which automated accounts affect the spread of information: information aggregators increase the size of RTEs and diffuse messages, while false amplifiers increase the size of RTEs without increasing diffusion. To test these hypotheses, we examine the RTE signature, which is the plot of the number of retweets per minute (Fig. 3). Hemsley [9] shows that shape of the decay in the number of views per minute of a retweet event is related to how many new followers are gained during the course of a RTE. When the falloff from the peak number of retweets is more gradual, the person who posted the original tweet tends to gain more followers than when the signature is sharp. Hemsley argues that this reflects the length of the sharing path (from user A to B to C) and that longer paths bring content to new audiences, where new followers might be found. On the other hand, steep decays indicate that the message flowed in a linear pattern: out through the user's own followers, but not through the followers' followers (from A to B and A to C). For our purposes then, we expect that information aggregators will be associated with more relaxed decay phases in signatures, while for false amplifiers, the decay phase will be sharp. The rate of decay in retweets can be measured and compared by fitting a power law to the decay phase and estimating the shape parameter (alpha) [4].

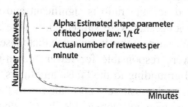

Fig. 3. A RTE signature model showing

We report on three regression models below. The dependent variables for these models are the size of the RTE (i.e., the number of retweets), the change in the number of followers for the candidate over the course of the RTE, and the parameter of the estimated power-law distribution shape for each signature (alpha). We ran a variance inflation factor to check for multicollinearity and use plots for regression diagnostics, all of which are available upon request [5].

Model 1 tests the impact of different factors on RTE size, to examine whether automated accounts had an influence on information diffusion (RQ1). For each RTE, we compute a mean bot score (an average of Botometer scores for all accounts that participated in an RTE), and calculate ratios of protected accounts and deleted accounts (% of all accounts that participated in an RTE). We include alpha as an independent variable in this model, to control for the relationship between the shape of the RTE signature and RTE size [9]. In each model, we also control for the number of users who deleted their tweets and the number of users who retweeted the same message more than once (Table 1).

Model 1: RTE size = mean bot score + protected account ratio + deleted account ratio + alpha + users with deleted tweets + duplicate users

Table 1. Model 1 regression results

	Estimate		Std. Err
intercept	−1936.460		1579.646
mean_bot_score	3181.095		3582.844
protected_account_ratio	34389.776	***	7211.896
dne_account_ratio	−18105.742	*	7157.455
alpha	1351.655	**	423.788
users_with_no_tweets	181.130	***	13.734
num_duplicate_users	74.899	***	5.495
Signif. codes: 0 '***' 0.001 '**' 0.01 '*' 0.05 '.' 0.1 ' ' 1			
Residual standard error: 953 on 93 degrees of freedom			
Multiple R-squared: 0.9714, adjusted R-squared: 0.9696			
F-statistic: 527.2 on 6 and 93 DF, p-value: 0.00			

The results above show a strong, statistically significant relationship between the ratio of protected accounts that participated in an RTE and its size. The shape of the RTE signature is also strongly associated with RTE size, as was expected [9]. We note that the variable for deleted account ratio is significant and negative, indicating that RTEs involving more accounts that were subsequently deleted tended to be smaller, holding all else constant. We suspect this is evidence that these accounts tended to have fewer followers and so were responsible for fewer "down-stream" retweets. These findings provide empirical grounding to the "false amplifiers" claim, showing that the number of protected accounts is positively correlated with the size of retweet events, but the relationship between mean bot score and RTE size is not statistically significant.

Model 2 tests the impact of bot involvement on the candidates' followership, to answer the RQ2. Results demonstrate that automated account involvement is not a significant factor in the increase of followers. In fact, little else mattered other than which candidate started the RTE: Donald Trump was much more likely to gain new followers than his fellow presidential candidates (Table 2).

Model 2: Change in followers = mean bot score + protected account ratio + deleted account ratio + alpha + users with deleted tweets + duplicate users + candidate effects

Table 2. Model 2 regression results

	Estimate		Std. Err
intercept	9359343	***	1335578
mean_bot_score	−3826193		0.2215
protected_account_ratio	8302106	.	0.0801
dne_account_ratio	−8238104		0.1318
alpha	−2063		0.9942
users_with_no_tweets	−6493		0.5708
num_duplicate_users	7589		0.1595
Gary Johnson	−7875482	***	0.0000
Hillary Clinton	−5808312	***	0.0000
Jill Stein	−7618885	***	0.0000

Signif. codes: 0 '***' 0.001 '**' 0.01 '*' 0.05 '.' 0.1 ' ' 1

Residual standard error: 598100 on 90 degrees of freedom

Multiple R-squared: 0.9669, adjusted R-squared: 0.9636

F-statistic: 292.4 on 9 and 90 DF, p-value: 0.00

Model 3 answers the question regarding the possibility of using an RTE estimator to detect automated diffusion (RQ3). These results show that both groups of automated accounts, the information aggregators as well as false amplifiers, have an impact on alpha (the RTE estimator). Information aggregators are strongly associated with an increased alpha, while false amplifiers on average are associated with a smaller alpha. This helps ground the claim about two distinct categories of automated accounts, which work in different ways and have divergent effects on the shape and size of the RTE (Table 3).

Model 3: alpha = mean bot score + protected account ratio + deleted account ratio + users with deleted tweets + number of duplicate users + RTE size + candidate

Table 3. Model 3 regression results

	Estimate		Std. Err
intercept	−0.206		0.6701
mean_bot_score	2.373	*	0.0325
protected_account_ratio	−5.238	**	0.0044
dne_account_ratio	5.204	**	0.0095
alpha	−0.009		0.1332
users_with_no_tweets	−0.006	*	0.0114
num_duplicate_users	0.00006	**	0.0082
Gary Johnson	0.217		0.1725
Hillary Clinton	−0.039		0.7338
Jill Stein	−0.071		0.5502

Signif. codes: 0 '***' 0.001 '**' 0.01 '*' 0.05 '.' 0.1 ' ' 1

Residual standard error: 0.2143 on 90 degrees of freedom

Multiple R-squared: 0.3573, adjusted R-squared: 0.293

F-statistic: 5.558 on 9 and 90 DF, p-value: 0.00

4 Discussion

Our work suggests that there are two distinct categories of automated accounts. These accounts work in different ways and their activities have different effects. False amplifiers increase higher RTE sizes, but do not engage new followers. False amplifiers are also associated with lower alphas, meaning a more relaxed decay phase for the RTE signature. This suggests that they tend to get more down-stream retweets compared to aggregators and other actors. In other words, their involvement in a RTE may result in longer sharing chains. But, since we don't see new followers associated with these accounts, "down-stream" in this case doesn't appear to mean they are reaching new audiences where new followers are typically found. Instead, this might be evidence of bot nets – networks of bots who all retweet each other. This points to further analysis we can do in the next iteration of this work. For example, if this is true, we might see a relationship between higher numbers of false amplifiers and the number of duplicate users in RTEs.

We also found that the number of information aggregators involved in an RTE seems to have no relationship with the size of the RTE. Nor is there a relationship with the change in the number of followers. Compared to false amplifiers, they tend to suppress down-stream retweets. That is, the more of this type of account are involved in a RTE, the higher the estimate of alpha is for the RTE signature, and, consequently, the less likely there will be followers of followers retweeting. This is surprising since aggregators tend to have a higher number of followers, on average, than false amplifiers (see Fig. 2). This may point to how people use aggregators or other factors, worth investigating in the next iteration of this work. Overall, this work suggests that while aggregators could be useful for some actors, they are not necessarily helpful to candidates in terms of getting the message out or gaining new followers.

We also note that compared to Trump, all of the other candidates tended to gain fewer followers, but alpha values for the candidates tended to be similar, indicating that there was no noticeable difference in the reach to new audiences for the candidates when controlling for other factors. We suspect that this reflects the fact that Trump received so much attention in the media about his tweets that he gained followers regardless of his Twitter behavior. Our data is limited in that we do not know which accounts followed which candidates; with different data, we could find out of any of the candidates had more of one type of bot following them than another.

In this work, we used RTE signatures to both measure and examine the effects of different types of bots on candidates' reach and change in followers during a RTE. Our work suggests that when coupled with changes in the number of followers, signatures might provide a signal for the presence of false amplifiers. In his paper on signatures, Hemsley [9] suggests that other measures (e.g. time to peak or number or retweets during the peak minute) might also be useful signals in identifying RTEs with a large percentage of bots.

5 Conclusion

In this work, we identify two different types of automated accounts (bots) that were active in retweeting the presidential candidates during the 2016 U.S. Presidential election. We find that neither information aggregators nor false amplifiers tended to bring candidates a significant boost in followers. Our work does find that when false amplifiers retweeted candidates, they did tend to produce more down-stream retweeting, but this could have reflected activity in bot nets.

This work begins broader comparative work on bot interference in election campaigns, and additional cases will be added as future elections take place. Future research will provide insight on the range of effects and roles played by bots in different political contexts - directly on the spread of information online [3, 9] and indirectly on public opinion and electoral outcomes. Most importantly, finding similar patterns across the U.S. presidential election and other elections would help ground claims about external actors interfering in the diffusion of political information online, and may provide evidence implicating the same actors at work across multiple elections.

One limitation of our analysis is that we treat false amplifiers as synonymous with protected accounts, but we can't know anything about these accounts with certainty. Also, we intend to refine the category of information aggregators by looking at whether accounts with high bot scores are "verified": organization accounts (i.e., those most likely to act as information aggregators) are likely to be verified.

References

1. Bessi, A., Ferrara, E.: Social bots distort the 2016 U.S. Presidential election online discussion. First Monday **21**(11) (2016)
2. Breur, T.: US elections: how could predictions be so wrong? J. Mark. Anal. **4**(4), 125–134 (2016)
3. Bruns, A., Highfield, T.: Political networks on Twitter. Inf. Commun. Soc. **16**(5), 667–691 (2013)
4. Clauset, A., et al.: Power-law distributions in empirical data. SIAM Rev. **51**(4), 661–703 (2009)
5. Faraway, J.J.: Linear Models with R. Chapman and Hall/CRC, London (2004)
6. Ferrara, E., et al.: The rise of social bots. Commun. ACM. **59**(7), 96–104 (2016)
7. Forelle, M.C., et al.: Political Bots and the Manipulation of Public Opinion in Venezuela (2015)
8. Hemsley, J., et al.: Collection and classification of illuminating 2016 social media data. In: Illuminating 2016 (2016)
9. Hemsley, J.: Studying the viral growth of a connective action network using information event signatures. First Monday **21**(8) (2016)
10. Kollanyi, B., et al.: Bots and Automation over Twitter during the First U.S. Presidential Debate (2016)
11. Kwak, H., et al.: What is Twitter, a Social Network or a News Media? p. 591 (2010)
12. Salge, C., Karahanna, E.: Protesting corruption on twitter: is it a bot or is it a person? Acad. Manag. Discov. (2016)
13. Stieglitz, S., Dang-Xuan, L.: Political communication and influence through microblogging–an empirical analysis of sentiment in Twitter messages and retweet behavior. In: 2012 45th Hawaii International Conference on System Science (HICSS), pp. 3500–3509, January 2012
14. Suh, B., et al.: Want to be retweeted? Large scale analytics on factors impacting retweet in Twitter network. In: 2010 IEEE Second International Conference on Social Computing (SocialCom), pp. 177–184 (2010)
15. Varol, O., et al.: Online human-bot interactions: detection, estimation, and characterization. In: Eleventh International AAAI Conference on Web and Social Media, May 2017
16. Woolley, S.C., Guilbeault, D.R.: Computational propaganda in the United States of America: manufacturing consensus online. Technical report #2017.5. Oxford Internet Institute, University of Oxford (2017)
17. Zaman, T.R., et al.: Predicting Information Spreading in Twitter, pp. 17599–17601 (2010)

Dribbble: Exploring the Concept of Viral Events on an Art World Social Network Site

Jeff Hemsley[(⊠)] and Sikana Tanupabrungsun

Syracuse University, Syracuse, NY 13210, USA
{jjhemsle, stanupab}@syr.edu

Abstract. While virality is a much-studied topic on popular social media sites, it has been rarely explored on sites like Dribbble, a social networking site for artists and designers. Using a mixed-method approach, we explore virality from a user-centric perspective. Interviews with informants confirm that viral-like events do exist on Dribbble, though what spreads are stylistic choices. While what spreads is different than on other platforms, our work suggests that the mechanics that drive these events are similar, suggesting an underlying social phenomenon that is reflected in different ways on different platforms. Our results are supported by regression modeling using variables identified by our informants. Our work contributes to social media studies since smaller sites like Dribbble are rarely studied, particularly using mixed methods approaches, as well as to the body of research around information diffusion and viral events.

Keywords: Dribbble · Social media · Virality · Art worlds · Mixed-methods

1 Introduction

This paper explores the concept of virality on Dribbble.com, a social network site created in 2009 for designers and artists to share and get feedback on their work. Virality is generally characterized as an emergent process where by many individuals simultaneously diffuse information, or content, into their own social networks [9]. The results can be that trending topics emerge or that otherwise localized information can spread to distant parts of the larger network. Virality is a much studied topic on sites like Twitter and Facebook, both of which provide functionality that directly supports resharing content. Dribbble, however, does not provide features for resharing the art of others, and yet design and art do evolve over time as designers and artists influence other artists [1]. In an effort to understand these processes, Becker [1] has called for diffusion studies in specific art worlds, networks of actors whose cooperative work produces art. Becker also notes that to truly understand social phenomena, such as virality, requires that we study more than the few central actors in a network, for example, sites like Twitter and Facebook. Thus, by studying a niche site like Dribbble, this work contributes to our understanding of virality on social media in general by allowing us to compare the similarities and differences of virality on a small and larger sites whose affordances differ.

In this work, we use a mixed method approach to understand if something like virality takes place on Dribbble and if so, what are the nature and driving factors of

© Springer International Publishing AG, part of Springer Nature 2018
G. Chowdhury et al. (Eds.): iConference 2018, LNCS 10766, pp. 27–36, 2018.
https://doi.org/10.1007/978-3-319-78105-1_4

these events. We use interview data from 14 participants to understand how Dribbble users use the site, and how they think about virality on the site and the factors that might influence it. We find that while works of art are not reshared, our interview informants do tend to map the concept of virality onto art that that becomes very popular, particularly when this happens suddenly. This is similar to how other studies have measured virality on sites like YouTube by using the number of views a video receives [2, 10]. Our informants also suggest a number of factors that drive these viral-like events, such as the number of followers one has. Using regression modeling on data collected from Dribbble's public Application Programming Interface (API), we confirm that some of the factors identified by our informants are related to the number of views an artwork receives, which allows us to discuss how these factors are similar and different to factors that drive viral events on sites like Twitter. Data from our informants also suggest that what spreads on Dribbble aren't specific works of art or design, but rather, that users 'borrow' elements from other's works, such as color palettes, design solutions and other stylistic choices, which they employ in their own works. These design flows can turn into 'trends' on the site and trends on the site can also be driven by larger design industry trends.

Our work makes a contribution to the study of viral events identifying common patterns on large and small sites that provides some insight into how emergent human behavior is played out through different affordances on different kinds of social media sites. We plan to conduct and analyze more interviews to verify we have reached saturation, and to build regression models that test additional variables. For example, initial results from work not reported here suggests that we can use Google Cloud Vision, an image content analysis service, to computationally label individual design and art posts that may shed light on the relationship between the number of views art receives and the types of content and elements of style, such as line work or color palettes. Our hope is that this work informs work on other niche social media platforms, such as on academic social network sites and music sites, which we believe will broaden our understanding of the social behaviors that underlie viral events.

2   Literature

We adopt Becker's [1] concept of an art world to understand and explore Dribbble. Art worlds are made up of a network of actors whose cooperative and collective activities result in the creation of works of art. In other words, an art world is where the mundane work of creating art is done. Conventions arise out of the interactions and activities of the actors that inform artistic production, mediate cooperation and define what qualifies as *good art* within the art world. Becker notes that art worlds have no boundaries, rather they are overlapping networks where artists are embedded with other actors who support the work of creating art. For example, the technical support agent at Adobe who answers an artist's question about Adobe Illustrator is part of the art world, as are those who view, give feedback and appreciate the art.

Dribbble, whose terminology is based on basketball terms, functions as the online part of an art world by enabling *players* (users), to form networks through follower and following relationships. Players can collectively signal what constitutes good art by liking and commenting on other player's shots (art or design work). Players also signal enthusiasm for other's shots by posting rebounds (i.e. response art – art that they make in response to other people's art that will generally be a variation of an original art). When a shot receives more than one rebound, it is referred to as a *playoff*, and is featured on the Playoffs page. Dribbble also has dedicated pages for shots that 'popular', 'recent', and 'debuts' which are for the first shot posted by those become a player after receiving an invite. The concept of 'good art', as defined by those in the art world, is an important one since it might be related to or overlap with viral-like phenomena. Also, Nahon and Hemsley [9] have theorized that social norms are reinstantiated and transformed through the process of diffusion. Thus, one explanation for the evolution of art on a site like Dribbble is that as artistic innovations diffuse through art worlds, they may change the conventions (roughly equivalent to social norms) that inform artistic production, mediate cooperation and define what qualifies as good art [1]. By focusing on Dribbble, we are examining a subset of an art world, one where viral-like events might happen. Note that while Dribbble is primarily thought of as a site for designers, we will generally use the term "art" since we are borrowing from Becker's conception of an art world.

There are not many studies that look at art related social media sites, much less with a specific focus on viral events. A different study looking at Dribbble used a database of U.S. baby names [18] and found that male designers tended to have more success at getting views and likes and that while women had fewer ties in the site's social network, they had more cohesive social networks than men [15]. Similarly, a quantitative study of Behance, another online social network site for designers, found that males tended to have more followers and that grayscale images tended to receive less attention [6]. Salah et al. [12] looked at the relationship between network clusters and artistic subcategories on DeviantArt, a site for a broad range of artists, and found that clusters of users on the site tended to form around production techniques, not types of art. None of the above sites focuses on viral, or viral-like events on an art site. However, Salah and Salah [11] explored the diffusion of art innovations on DeviantArt. They started by selecting artwork that was posted as a 'resource', or a downloadable stock image, which are intended to be mashed up or embedded in other artists work. When other artists use these stock images in their own work, Salah and Salah consider this a kind of diffusion of technique. We note that this work starts with content intended by the artists to be used by other artists, and so what Salah and Salah are looking at is not the emergent crowd driven event we typically associate with a viral event. Also, all of the work above only uses quantitative analysis, and so misses the experience and views of the site's users. We address this by taking a mixed methods approach, and specifically, we use interviews to get the player's perspective to answer our first research question: *RQ1: Does something like virality exist on the niche social media site Dribbble?*

Dribbble does not have a share or retweet button, so players cannot share the work of others directly into their own networks. Conceptually, Dribbble is more like YouTube in that messages themselves do not spread. On YouTube, the concept of virality is that users share links to a video, which is embedded on the poster's channel page [2]. So what is being shared is actually a Universal Record Locator (URL), and studies [10] typically use the number of views a video gets as a measure of virality. As mentioned above, there is some evidence that users on DeviantArt do adopt the style and technique of other users into their own work [11]. It is then reasonable to assume that the diffusion of aesthetic techniques might exist on Dribbble too. Thus, our next research question is: *RQ2: If viral-like events do happen on Dribbble, what is it that is diffusing in the Dribbble art world?*

Nahon and Hemsley [9] theorize that virality is a negotiated process between the crowd and more influential actors who exert disproportionate influence over the viral process. They refer to these influential actors as network gatekeepers, and their power is a byproduct of their position in networks. That is, they generally have between a few and many orders of magnitude more followers than the typical user, which gives them access to more information resources and gives them the "ability to link networks together, allowing information to travel far and fast and to connect people to information and ideas" [9:48]. Of course, virality does not happen without the crowd to propagate content, ideas or behaviors - we will use the cover term messages to mean all of the kinds of things that could go viral. In their view, network gatekeepers are needed to promote content and link together networks, but the crowd must also view, like, and share the message into their own networks for the message to be considered viral. Thus, gatekeepers may promote messages that do not go viral if the crowd opts not to adopt or share them into their own networks. Likewise, members of the crowd may find their messages stay stubbornly obscure because they lack the connections for the messages to spread much farther than their own followers.

Of course factors like timeliness, context, attributes of the sender, and the content of the message are also important factors in what spreads [9]. For example, on Twitter the number of followers and friends [14, 17], the account age and other profile information [8], and network relationships [7, 16], can all affect the diffusion of a message. Other large scale work has shown that the user's account age, number of tweets they have posted, and the number of their tweets that have been favorited are also related to how often they are retweeted [14]. Tweets with hashtags, URLs and @mentions all tend to be retweeted more than those without those textual features [13]. Given all this we should expect that if viral-like events happen on Dribbble we ought to find that similar factors are at work. Thus, our final research question is: *RQ3: What are the measures and factors of viral-like events on Dribbble?*

3   Methods

In this study, we adopt a sequential exploratory mixed-method approach [3]. We start with qualitative data collection and analysis to explore a phenomenon through semi-structured interviews with Dribbble's members. We use data from our informants to answer our first and second research question and to inform the variable selection for a regression model, which we use to answer the third research question. Data for the regression model was drawn from Dribbble's API, as described in the sections below. Where appropriate we include control variables suggested in literature for other sites, such as the number of hashtags [13, 14].

Recruitment of interviewees was conducted by email. Dribbble does not have an internal messaging system, though some players post their email addresses on their profile page. Using Dribbble's API we have collected over 400,000 user profiles and metadata for more than 700,000 shots. To select participants, we note that less than 5% of users include email addresses, and of those, we focus on players who list english as their language. From the remaining, we randomly selected batches of users to email to ask to participate. We offered a $20 Amazon Gift Card for an hour interview about their experience with the platform. Audio-only interviews took place on Adobe Connect, a web conferencing tool, and were recorded for later transcription.

We develop a linear regression model using number of views of a shot as the dependent variable. Our independent variables include metadata about the shot or the player who posted it. These include the number of followers of the player, the number of hashtags listed in the shot's description text, the age of the shot, the number of buckets a shot is in, where a bucket is a grouping mechanism for players to group their own or other shots into collections. The shots are drawn from 100 randomly selected players, stratified by their number of shots. The numbers of shots per user ranges from 29 to 688 with an average of 82.47. In total, we have 8,318 shots.

To satisfy the assumptions of linear regression (dependent and independent variables are linearly related, and errors are normally distributed with constant variance), we transformed our dependent variable with logarithm function. We also removed 6 outliers, each of which will be discussed separately. The variance inflation factor scores of the independent variables range from 1.0 to 1.2, indicating that our model does not suffer from multicollinearity. As is typical [4], we use plots for regression diagnostics, all of which are available upon request.

4 Results

In total, we conducted 14 interviews (11 males and 3 female) with ages between 18 and 34 (mean = 26.8). Most of our participants have been using the platform for more than 3 years. Our respondents describe themselves as UI/UX or product designers, graphic designers or illustrators, or motion graphic designers. Players posted shots to gain exposure for their work, get feedback, receive validation and to challenge themselves (participate in challenges or rebounds). All of them indicated that they used the platform for artistic and creative inspiration, while subsets indicated that they use the platform to get feedback on their work, promote themselves, maintain a public presence and portfolio, find jobs or other designers to work with, or to keep up with design industry trends. When asked about other platforms they posted art (designs) on, our participants listed, in order of frequency, Behance, Instagram, Facebook, Twitter, DeviantArt, Pinterest and Vimeo.

Dribbble allows users to view, like, comment on, rebound and save into buckets the shot of others. Several informants indicated that they would like, comment on or save into buckets shots that they thought were "good". When probed about what constituted good design (roughly, Becker's concept of good art), our respondents indicated work that solved design problems in a novel way, evoked emotion, conveyed meaning, or were visually appealing constituted good art. Some respondents said that they may also like or comment on other's work as a sign of support and that comments were also used to ask questions or provide feedback. In our conversations with them, we learned that many saw a hierarchy in the meaning of these features where rebounds to one's shots might be thought of as the highest compliment, followed by comments and finally likes. For example, informant 8 noted of rebounds that, "I think it's a way of complimenting the original artist." Thus, we find that Dribbble provides a number of indicators of good art, which is key element of an art world.

In discussing virality with our informants they frequently mentioned the idea of design trends on Dribbble, where many people posted shots with a similar look and everyone is responding to, or influenced by, others. One informant referred to this as a design "echo chamber". Our informants indicated that trends could originate outside of Dribbble. For example when Apple released its Touch Bar, designers across Dribbble quickly posted their own versions of Touch Bar icons. Informant 2 told us that their lead designer "designed a Touch Bar for Dribble right away and then we posted it on Dribble and then we got lot of likes because at that time everybody was interested in that and everybody was looking for it, so we got lot of likes and exposure." But design trends can also be local to Dribbble, such as when Dribbble noted on their blog that a wave of purple shots had washed over their Popular Shots page [19]. Thus, part of the answer to the first research question is that yes, something like virality exists on Dribbble, and one way it manifests is in the form of design trends.

One of the most important uses of Dribbble by our informants was to seek out inspiration and keep up with the trends e.g. "It usually happens early in the morning when I come to the office and see quickly okay what's happening in the design community, what's new" - Informant 6. While players indicate they do not copy the shots of others, the majority of our informants indicated that their own work was influenced by other players e.g. "I always end up with my own personally unique idea that got inspired by some users" - Informant 4. They describe adopting into their own work design elements like color palettes, line styles, textures, fonts and so on. Places they find such stylistic inspiration on Dribbble include their own landing page, which aggregates recent shots from those they follow, the Popular Shots page, which appears to order shots by a proprietary algorithm, or by using the site's search tools. The search tools allow players to find shots by keywords or colors. Thus, players may have a design problem in mind, or a set of requirements from a client, and after browsing Dribbble, they would borrow, for example, a color pallet or a line style that inspired them and incorporate it into their own work. Thus, in answer to research question 2, what seems to spread on Dribbble are stylistic elements of users.

All participants explained the concept of virality as shots that become very popular as measured by number of views. Informant 5 said, "The thing that is the top or get the most likes and views … I'd call it a viral". Several of our informants also noted that having their shot featured on the Popular Shots page was also a sign of virality since that seemed to results in shots getting even more views. Thus, part of the answer for research question 3 is that views can used to measure a viral-like event.

Some seemed to think that shots going viral was driven by luck, but most felt that those with more followers would get more views just because their shows would show up in more people's feeds. Specifically, one of our informants explained, "in order for your work to get viral, you need to have a lot of followers and you need to have a lot of exposure" (Informant 14). A few informants mentioned that Dribbble's algorithms seemed to prioritize some shots over others in the order of appearance on the Popular

Shots page. A couple of informants also clued us in about how to game the system by posting links to their shots on other sites to bump up the number of views their shots got. The idea being that this behavior might result in their shot getting featured on the Popular Shots page. Informants also linked the idea of virality to exposure, indicating that having your shot go viral could bring you a lot of attention in terms of likes, comments and new followers. So in terms of factors that could be drivers of viral-like events on Dribbble (research question 3), the number of followers seems to be the main factor that informants could identify.

Our regression model to confirms that followers are related to views, but as noted above, we included other variables as well. The results are presented in Table 1. Since we transformed the dependent variable, we report inverse log of the estimated coefficients, standard error, and confidence interval for easy interpretation. The R-Squared of 0.63 indicates that our predictors explain the variation in the outcome sufficiently well. All predictors are statistically significant. The estimated coefficient of the number of followers of 1.002 suggests that one more follower increases the number of views by 0.2%, while holding other variables constant. The hashtags' estimated coefficients of 1.07 suggests that adding one more hashtag increases the number of views by 7%, and the estimated coefficient of 1.06 for buckets suggests that being in one more bucket increases the number of views by 6%. Surprisingly, the estimated coefficient of shot age is 0.99, suggesting shots a day older decreases the number of views by 0.01%, suggesting the number of views shots receive has a short life span. It may also signal the upward spike characteristic of virality on other platforms [5].

Table 1. Regression results.

Variable	10^Est_Coef	10^Std. Error	LWR - UPR	t-val (p-val)
Intercept	204.55	1.02	196.2124 - 213.2510	250.47 (0.00)
Followers	1.002	1.00	1.0002 - 1.0002	58.09 (0.00)
Hashtags	1.07	1.00	1.0657 - 1.0737	39.33 (0.00)
Buckets	1.06	1.00	1.0589 - 1.0637	50.92 (0.00)
Shot age	0.99	1.00	0.9997 - 0.9998	−15.57 (0.00)
Signif. codes: 0 '***' 0.001 '**' 0.01 '*' 0.05 '.' 0.1 ' ' 1				
Residual standard error: 0.6943 on 8307 degrees of freedom				
Multiple R-squared: 0.6259, adjusted R-squared: 0.6258				
F-statistic: 3475 on 4 and 8307 DF, p-value < 0.00				

A closer look the 6 outliers removed from the model shows that they are among the top 6% of shots with most views and were created by 2 users, namely, A and B. These 2 users have relatively high number of followers (A: 5,825 and B: 6,198), but a relatively small number of shots (A: 68 and B: 129). The average number of followers and shots of the other top users is 2,648.35 and 151.25, respectively. We wonder if a high ratio of shots to followers signals exceptional artists and will pursue this in future work.

5 Discussion

For Becker [1], an art world is a place where the mundane work of making art gets done. Our informants suggest that one of the most important uses of Dribbble is as a source of inspiration. That is, when players have design problems, need to get ideas for a project, or are just looking for a challenge, they browse through the shots of other players. And, while players are quick to say they do not steal the work of others, they describe adopting elements of style, like color palettes or line work, from the shots of others and using them in their own work as an important use of Dribbble. Some even create buckets of themed shots for inspiration and others describe mixing elements of a set of shots together into a new shot. Thus, part of what happens on Dribbble is that users construct their artworks by leaning on the work of others. This is akin to how Becker describes artwork emerging out of the collective activates of the actors in an art world. That is, shots become useful resources for others.

We also see this as what is diffusing on Dribbble: elements of design. Like on other platforms, most things do not diffuse far from the source [9], and we suspect that few shots actually go viral (reaching many actors) even when they do influence the artwork of a few players. And yet, our informants do note that design trends do sweep through Dribbble: many players simultaneously posting shots with strikingly similar design elements in a phenomenon that seems reminiscent to the way Nahon and Hemsley describe viral trends on sites like Twitter [9].

Likewise, some of the mechanics that drive viral-like events on Dribbble are similar to factors that drive viral events on other sites. For example, we have shown that the number of views a shot gets is significantly related to the number of followers of the player who posted it. This is similar to studies showing a relationship between the of followers someone has and the number of retweets they get [13, 14]. Respondents also tell us that shots that reach the popular page get more views and that Dribbble's algorithms probably play a role in the number of views a shot gets. We can view both the popular page and the site's algorithms as performing the role of *network gatekeepers* in Nahon and Hemsley's view of viral events [9]. That is, some actors (technological ones in Dribbble's case) can select and promote messages such that they reach a much larger audience than they would otherwise. Without these network gatekeepers, users may find their messages staying stubbornly obscure because they lack the connections for the messages to spread much farther than their own followers.

Nahon and Hemsley claim that "viral events are not new" [9:1]. They note that on December 1st, 1955, Rosa Parks was arrested in Montgomery, Alabama, for not giving up her seat to a white person on a segregated bus, and that the news spread via phones, hand-bills and word of mouth, such that within 3 days, over 40,000 blacks had joined a boycott of the bus system. They say that what is new is that with social media "a viral video, a news story, or a photo can reach 40,000 people in hours, or even minutes, instead of days" [9:1]. We suggest that what we see as viral-like events on Dribbble reflects a basic human phenomenon that has always existed and is manifest in different ways depending on the context and the mechanisms available to people. Before the internet, phones, hand-bills and word of mouth spread news through crowds; on Twitter 140 characters can be retweeted by thousands; on Dribbble many people viewing the same artwork(s) may adopt elements of it into their own work, such that echo-chambers, or design trends emerge. In future work we intend to do more detailed comparisons to tease out the similarities and differences across platforms in an effort to isolate what is platform specific and what are the fundamental human behaviors that drive viral events.

6 Conclusion

This initial work examines the concept of virality in the Dribbble art world using a mixed-method approach. We began with the semi-structured interviews with the plat-form's users in order to understand the larger context of Dribbble's Art world, giving us a user's perspective of the site and of how viral-like events work there. With the interviews, we identified a construct for measuring virality as well as some influential predictors. We then used a linear regression model to confirm the relationships amongst variables. We discuss the form that virality appears to take on Dribbble, and note the possibility of using computational methods to identify and track the diffusion of design elements. This work serves as a bridge connecting an extensive body of literature concerning virality in social networks to a significantly smaller body of work looking at niche art sites, like Dribbble. Our work confirms that the mechanics that drive viral-like events on Dribbble are similar to factors found elsewhere such as number of followers and the practices of network gatekeeping.

It is important to note that we have conducted only 14 interviews although the coding of interviews suggested that we already reached data saturation. In future work we intend to use a computational method to detect the diffusion of design elements and improve our regression model by controlling for other factors such as artist's gender, age of account and other factors suggested by the larger body of viral events.

References

1. Becker, H.S.: Art Worlds. University of California Press, Berkeley; London (2008)
2. Burgess, J., Green, J.: YouTube: Online Video and Participatory Culture. Polity, Cambridge (2009)
3. Creswell, J.W.: Research Design: Qualitative, Quantitative, and Mixed Methods Approaches. Sage Publications, Thousand Oaks (2013)
4. Faraway, J.J.: Linear Models with R. Chapman and Hall/CRC, London (2004)
5. Hemsley, J.: Studying the viral growth of a connective action network using information event signatures. First Monday **21**(8) (2016). http://dx.doi.org/10.5210/fm.v21i8
6. Kim, N.W.: Creative Community Demystified: A Statistical Overview of Behance. arXiv preprint arXiv:1703.00800 (2017)
7. Kwak, H., Lee, C., Park, H., Moon, S.: What is Twitter, a social network or a news media? p. 591 (2010). https://doi.org/10.1145/1772690.1772751
8. Lee, J., Ahn, J.-W., Oh, J.S., Ryu, H.: Mysterious influential users in political communication on Twitter: users' occupation information and its impact on retweetability. In: iConference 2015 Proceedings (2015). https://www.ideals.illinois.edu/handle/2142/73456. Accessed 29 Sept 2015

9. Nahon, K., Hemsley, J.: Going Viral. Polity Press Cambridge, Cambridge (2013)
10. Nahon, K., Hemsley, J., Walker, S., Hussain, M.: Fifteen minutes of fame: the power of blogs in the lifecycle of viral political information. Policy Internet **3**(1), 6–33 (2011). https://doi.org/10.2202/1944-2866.1108
11. Salah, A.A., Salah, A.A.: Flow of innovation in deviantArt: following artists on an online social network site. Mind Soc. **12**(1), 137–149 (2013). https://doi.org/10.1007/s11299-013-0113-9
12. Salah, A.A., Salah, A.A., Buter, B., Dijkshoorn, N., Modolo, D., Nguyen, Q., van Noort, S., van de Poel, B.: DeviantArt in spotlight: a network of artists. Leonardo **45**(5), 486–487 (2012). https://doi.org/10.1162/LEON_a_00454
13. Suh, B., Hong, L., Pirolli, P., Chi, E.H.: Want to be retweeted? Large scale analytics on factors impacting retweet in Twitter network. In: 2010 IEEE Second International Conference on Social Computing (SocialCom), pp. 177–184 (2010)
14. Uysal, I., Croft, W.B.: User oriented tweet ranking: a filtering approach to microblogs. In: Proceedings of the 20th ACM International Conference on Information and Knowledge Management, pp. 2261–2264 (2011)
15. Wachs, J., Hannák, A., Vörös, A., Daróczy, B.: Why do men get more attention? Exploring factors behind success in an online design community. arXiv preprint arXiv:1705.02972 (2017)
16. Yang, Z., Guo, J., Cai, K., Tang, J., Li, J., Zhang, L., Su, Z.: Understanding retweeting behaviors in social networks, p. 1633 (2010). https://doi.org/10.1145/1871437.1871691
17. Zaman, T.R., Herbrich, R., Van Gael, J., Stern, D.: Predicting information spreading in Twitter, pp. 17599–17601 (2010)
18. Baby Names from Social Security Card Applications-National Level Data (2016). data.gov. https://catalog.data.gov/dataset/baby-names-from-social-security-card-applications-national-level-dat
19. Dribbble - Show and Tell for Designers. https://dribbble.com/stories/2017/08/24/shot-block-purple-reign. Accessed 11 Sept 2017

Understanding Interactions Between Municipal Police Departments and the Public on Twitter

Yun Huang$^{(\boxtimes)}$ and Qunfang Wu

School of Information Studies, Syracuse University, Syracuse, USA
yhuang@syr.edu

Abstract. Law enforcement agencies have started using social media for building community policing, i.e., establishing collaborations between the people in a community and local police departments. Both researchers and practitioners need to understand how the two parties interact on social media on a daily basis, such that effective strategies or tools can be developed for the agencies to better leverage the platforms to fulfill their missions. In this paper, we collected 9,837 tweets from 16 municipal police department official Twitter accounts within 6 months in 2015 and annotated them into different strategies and topics. We further examined the association between tweet features (e.g., hashtags, mentions, content) and user interactions (favorites and retweets) by using regression models. The models reveal surprising findings, e.g., that the number of mentions has a negative correlation with favorites. Our findings provide insights into how to improve interactions between the two parties.

1 Introduction

Social media (e.g., Facebook, Twitter, etc.) in government is a trending topic in both research and real practice [6]. Law enforcement agencies have realized that social media can be used to fulfill their organizational missions [26]. According to a survey by the International Association of Chiefs of Police (IACP), social media was used by more than 95% of 600 law enforcement agencies surveyed in 2014 [1]. Social media platforms allow people to share information instantly and facilitate mutual interactions, which enable police agencies to handle crimes more effectively and to promote the reciprocal relationship between police and the community [8,25]. Thus, an increasing number of municipal police departments intentionally try to employ social media for building community policing [2,14]. The idea of community policing is to develop collaborations between the people in a community and local police departments, resulting in solving issues and improving public safety together [5].

In order to effectively involve the community in regular daily operations [22], it is necessary to understand the day-to-day social media practices of law enforcement agencies [5]. Interview-based studies provide a great deal of information

© Springer International Publishing AG, part of Springer Nature 2018
G. Chowdhury et al. (Eds.): iConference 2018, LNCS 10766, pp. 37–46, 2018.
https://doi.org/10.1007/978-3-319-78105-1_5

that enables us to learn about how social media is used by law enforcement agencies, where different combinations of strategies are employed by law enforcement agencies to represent, engage, and network [22,23]. While valuable, these studies lack profound insights into what topics law enforcement agencies really tweet about on social media everyday and what topics users interact with the most. Models and tools are suggested to be built for better understanding of social media interactions [3]. On Twitter, such interactions can be measured in the form of favorites and retweets [16].

In this paper, we address the above research needs by examining the tweets of 16 municipal police departments in the U.S. We unpack police agencies' tweeting behavior and public interactions. Reflecting on our findings, we provided practical suggestions on how the agencies could improve interactions with their communities on social media.

2 Related Work

Law enforcement agencies have started using social media applications to broadcast information such as events, crime, traffic and safety, and to disseminate information to a large audience in a timely and accurately manner [11]. They also use social media to respond to the public's inquiries about incidents [4,7]. To describe how agencies interact with the public, researchers developed a framework consisting of three social media strategies, i.e., *Push*, *Pull* and *Networking* [22,23]. They found that agencies intended to use different combinations of these strategies. More specifically, when a *Push* strategy is applied, social media sites are used as an additional communication channel "to get the message out." Compared with *Push* (an one-way strategy to provide transparency), *Pull* is a two-way strategy with the goal of engaging the public by soliciting information or requesting certain actions. The *Networking* strategy, emphasizing the collaboration between the government agencies and the public, is also to promote a two-way interaction.

Researchers have studied how a variety of factors (e.g., length, hashtag, URL, topic, etc.) could impact user interactions [15,24,27,31,32]. For example, Suh et al. [31] tried to identify factors that influenced the retweetability of a user's tweet so that a prediction of the retweetability could be made; they found that URLs and hashtags as content features, numbers of followers and followees and age of accounts as contextual features are considered to have a strong correlation with the retweetability of a tweet. Vargo [32] also presented similar findings that the presence of hashtags boosted the retweet and favorite counts, while Petrovic et al. [27] proved that the number of followers and followees of the sender had correlation with retweetability. Naveed et al. [24] considered that the tweet topics affected the retweetability; they identified 100 topics in tweets and found that tweets with general topics or interests, such as social media, economy, Christmas and public events, were more likely to be retweeted, while tweets in specific or individual topics were less likely to be retweeted.

In our work, we apply the framework of three social media strategies, i.e., *Push*, *Pull* and *Networking* [22,23] to annotate agency tweets. In addition, to understand how the agencies used different strategies and the effectiveness of the strategies, we further examined agency tweets into several topics and received interactions from public users. Our work enriches the framework by materializing these three social strategies with different tweet topics.

3   Data Collection and Method

In this section, we present how we collected, prepared, and annotated the Twitter data for the following analysis.

We searched municipal police departments' Twitter accounts in the cities that either ranked in the top 50 most populated cities of the U.S. or ranked top 10 for high crime rates as these police departments are more likely to tweet safety-related events or topics in their community. Since not all of the departments have verified Twitter accounts, we found 52 official accounts and randomly selected 16 of them for analysis. We used Facepager [20] to collect tweets and Twitter REST API to collect interactions (i.e., favorite, retweet) these tweets received. Finally, 9,837 tweets in total sent by these 16 police departments with interactions between February 17 and August 13, 2015 were collected. Table 1 shows the account names, time of account creation, the number of followers (observed by August 13, 2015), the number of tweets that were sent by each account, the number of favorites and retweets received by these tweets.

Table 1. Basic information of the police departments' (PDs) Twitter accounts, their tweets and received interactions.

Twitter accounts	Account created time	Followers	Tweets collected	Received favourites	Received retweets
Los Angeles PD	2-Sep-07	11,500	320	373	338
Portland PD	30-Apr-08	52,800	1,492	7,698	9,996
Scottsdale PD	15-Aug-08	15,400	145	924	1,981
Boulder PD	14-Oct-08	7,608	317	182	330
New York City PD	14-Nov-08	167,000	1,469	45,062	54,792
Stockton PD	17-Jan-09	13,700	1,126	2,274	2,959
Baltimore PD	27-Feb-09	134,000	2,375	64,732	124,621
San Francisco PD	28-Apr-09	46,600	291	1,811	6,084
Virginia Beach PD	2-Jun-09	5,473	140	301	811
Burlington PD	9-Oct-09	3,594	113	74	83
St. Louis PD	4-Feb-10	30,000	492	3,384	4,570
Detroit PD	24-Mar-10	9,513	262	886	823
Oakland PD	6-Apr-10	20,100	198	882	1,608
St. Paul PD	14-Aug-10	12,900	516	1,064	3,358
Spokane PD	29-Aug-11	7,672	336	690	1,863
Cleveland PD	13-Mar-12	16,700	245	2,755	3,785

In order to understand the departments' tweets, we manually annotated all the tweets based on a two-tier code scheme in our previous work [18]. The first tier codes are three strategies which police departments utilized on social media, i.e., *Push*, *Pull* or *Networking* [22,23]. The second tier codes are 8 specific topics. The definition of topics are described briefly as below.

- Within the **Push** category, *Crime* defines tweets that convey information about a crime incident. The crime incident can be related to shootings, homicides, arrests, victims, guns, drugs, etc. *Traffic* defines tweets that are related to road conditions, such as real-time traffic, road construction alerts, and expected traffic delay alerts. *Announcement* defines tweets that communicate non-crime and non-traffic information.
- Within the **Networking** category, *Tip* defines tweets that communicate suggestions to improve public safety and to avoid potential dangers. *Personnel* defines tweets that address individual names of police department personnel. *Appreciation* defines tweets that express gratitude and appreciation. *Information* includes all other non-tip, non-personnel, and non-appreciation tweets. Unlike *Announcement* of the *Push* category about public safety alerts, *Information* of the *Networking* category is used to reach out to the public for building a long-term trust or relationship, e.g., for announcing a workshop for a safety-related topic.
- Within the **Pull** category, *Request* defines tweets that ask the public to provide information about critical issues, such as identifying a crime incident or finding a missing person.

We hired three coders and trained them to understand the coding rules and concepts. Two coders independently annotated the tweets into the first coding level. For each code in the first level, Cohen's Kappa [33] showed almost perfect agreement (0.81–0.99). We then asked the third coder to annotate the tweets independently where the first two coders had disagreed and to resolve the disagreement using the "majority rule" approach. Three coders then labeled the tweets into the second coding level using the same methodology. For *Traffic*, *Appreciate*, *Crime*, and *Request* in the second level, Cohen's Kappa also showed perfect agreement (0.81–0.99); for other codes in the second coding level, Cohen's Kappa showed substantial agreement (0.61–0.80).

4   Findings

In this section, we applied a variety of statistical methods to unfold the 16 police departments' tweeting behavior (e.g., tweeting volumes, strategies and topics), public interaction behavior (favorites and retweets), and their relationships.

4.1   Police Departments' Tweets and Interactions

We summarized the number of tweets and the number of favorites and retweets received for different tweet topics in Table 2. The descriptive statistics indicate that certain tweets received more interactions, e.g., *Personnel* received the largest favorites.

To examine the differences, we performed Multivariate Analysis of Variance (MANOVA) tests. Due to unequal sample sizes and unequal variances for different topics, we conducted Games-Howell tests [21] for post-hoc pair-wise comparisons. In terms of **favorites**, *Networking* ($M = 16.3$, $SD = 64.30$) received significantly more interaction than *Push* ($M = 13.4$, $SD = 43.21$, $df = 7,548$, $p < .01$) and *Pull* ($M = 5.1$, $SD = 43.21$, $df = 4,747$, $p < .001$); *Push* ($M = 13.4$, $SD = 43.21$) received significantly more interaction than *Pull* ($M = 5.1$, $SD = 43.21$, $df = 5,019$, $p < .001$). In terms of **retweets**, there was no significant difference between *Push* ($M = 28$, $SD = 102.33$) and *Pull* ($M = 24$, $SD = 53.12$, $df = 4,470$, $p = .11$); *Networking* received significantly less interaction than *Push* ($M = 28$, $SD = 102.33$, $df = 6,948$, $p < .001$) and *Pull* ($M = 24$, $SD = 53.12$, $df = 2,673$, $p < .001$).

Table 2. Descriptive statistics of received favorites and retweets for different categories and topics of police departments' tweets

Category	Topic	Total tweets	Favorites		Retweets	
			Mean	SD	Mean	SD
Push	Crime	1,793	10.96	27.19	19.53	60.32
	Traffic	584	7.57	15.74	11.27	38.03
	Announcement	1,804	17.60	58.97	39.85	141.23
	Information	3,519	13.42	48.38	12.58	38.56
Networking	Appreciation	308	24.82	89.24	21.12	88.52
	Tip	195	7.89	10.84	11.27	13.53
	Personnel	280	50.22	154.93	56.61	181.11
Pull	Request	1,354	5.12	8.50	23.72	53.12

Prior research found that emotion was critical to information seeking and sharing across social media [17]. When people feel emotionally connected to the social media messages, they are more likely to actively share these messages, accelerating the information dissemination process. *Networking* tweets, e.g. *Appreciation* and *Personnel*, showed that the police departments cared about their community or their police officers, which could trigger emotional connections, and therefore received more interactions.

We also performed clustering algorithms to partition the 16 police departments into clusters where police departments of each cluster share some common features. Each police department was represented as a three-dimensional vector, consisting of tweeting frequency for each category (*Push*, *Pull*, and *Networking*). For example, the frequency of *Push* is the count of *Push* tweets divided by the number of days. We applied the complete-linkage hierarchical clustering algorithm [19] and found that the optimum number of clusters was three by performing the canonical correlation analysis [9]. The first canonical dimension is strongly influenced by *Pull* (0.99) and *Networking* (0.80); the second canonical dimension is strongly influenced by *Push* (0.80). The results showed that cluster 1 included Baltimore PD and Portland PD where more *Push* tweets were sent; cluster 2 included NYPD and Stockton PD where more *Networking* tweets were sent; and the rest were grouped in cluster 3 where *Push* and *Networking* tweets were well balanced. All three clusters rarely used *Pull* strategies.

To examine if certain clusters received significantly more interactions than others, we conducted two univariate Analysis of Variance (ANOVAs) in terms of favorites and retweets. Due to unequal sample sizes and unequal variances, we performed the multiple pairwise comparisons by using the Games-Howell test [21] for the posthoc tests. To account for police departments' varying numbers of followers, we divided the number of interactions for a tweet by the total number of followers of the police department. In terms of **favorites**, cluster 3 ($M = 0.026$, $SD = 6.4E - 3$) received significantly more favorites than cluster 2 ($M = 0.019$, $SD = 2.3E - 3, df = 5,640, p < .001$); and cluster 2 ($M = 0.019, SD = 2.3E - 3$) received significantly more than cluster 1 ($M = 0.011, SD = 1.3E - 3, df = 3,809$, $p < .001$). In terms of **retweets**, cluster 3 ($M = 0.050, SD = 3.6E - 2$) received significantly more retweets than cluster 2 ($M = 0.024, SD = 3.6E - 3, df = 4,220$, $p < .001$); cluster 2 ($M = 0.024, SD = 3.5E - 3$) received significantly more than cluster 1 ($M = 0.014, SD = 1.5E - 3, df = 4,033, p < .001$). The results suggested that those police departments in cluster 3 that balanced their use of the *Push* strategy and *Networking* strategies received more interactions from the public.

4.2   Influential Factors for Interactions

In this section, by building regression models, we present several significant factors we identified in police departments' tweets, which influenced public interactions (favorites and retweets).

Factors' Selection and Regression Models. According to the reviewed literature, we initially selected a set of factors, e.g. hashtags, URLs, the length of tweets, the number of followers, tweet category, etc., and added mentions as a new factor. Then for each factor with the outcome variables (*Favorites* and *Retweets*), we ran a non-parametric Spearman's Rank Correlation Coefficient Test [28]. The test results showed that there were significant correlations between five factors (i.e., *Hashtags, Mentions, Followers, Days* and *Category*) and the outcome variables (*Favorites* and *Retweets*) ($p < .01$).

More specifically, the first four factors are numeric: *Hashtags* represents the number of hashtags (#) in the tweet; *Mentions* represents the number of mentions (@) in the tweet; *Followers* is the total number of followers of the police department when the police department sends the tweet; and *Days* represents the number of days between the account created date and the tweet created date. *Category* is a categorical variable, which represents the content feature of the tweet, i.e., *Push, Pull, Networking*.

We first performed a Grubbs' test to examine whether there were any outlier tweets in terms of favorites and retweets that may skew our models [13,29]. We removed 530 favorite outliers and 557 retweet outliers that accounted for about

5% of our data set. Then, we used the Negative Binomial Regression models [12] to investigate the associations between these influential factors and interactions. To build regression models, we took *Category* as a dummy variable [10] as there are three options, i.e. *Push, Pull, Networking*. For instance, for the *Push* category, D1 = 1 and D2 = 0; for the *Pull* category, D1 = 0 and D2 = 1; for the *Networking* category, D1 = 0 and D2 = 0. The two-way interactions between independent variables (e.g., *Hashtags * Mentions*, etc.) were also taken into consideration but no significant associations were found. As shown in Table 3, we separated three conditions of the *Category* variable into different models, i.e., FH (favorite-push), FL (favorite-pull), FN (favorite-networking), RH (retweet-push), RL (retweet-pull), RN (retweet-networking), and presented all the significant factors which impacted *Favorite* and *Retweets* ($p < .001$).

Table 3. The coefficients of significant factors for user interactions: H - Hashtags, M - Mentions, F - Followers, D - Days, FH - the model for Favorites and Push category, etc. The selected terms' coefficients in the above models all have $p < .001$.

Model	Favorites			Retweets		
	FH	FL	FN	RH	RL	UN
Intercept	1.9535	2.5219	2.1054	3.3864	4.2863	2.3940
H	0.1582	−0.0929	0.1648			
M	−0.5223	−0.1250	−0.3566			
F	0.1890	0.1947	0.3347	0.1696	0.1965	0.1272
D	−0.2510	−0.4493	−0.1732	−0.4508	−0.5535	−0.2037

Understanding the Factors. Table 3 revealed interesting observations. First, for *Favorites*, the coefficients of *Hashtags* varied from positive to negative for different categories of tweets; *Mentions* consistently had negative coefficients, and had strong coefficients under the *Push* and *Networking* models. Secondly, *Hashtags* and *Mentions* were not significantly related to *Retweets*. Below, we present further data analyses for *Hashtags* and *Mentions* that help explain the observations.

Hashtags. Prior work reported that the presence of *Hashtags* was associated with more *Retweets* [32], and it was also pointed out that not all *Hashtags* could improve the tweets popularity [31]. In *Favorites*, *Hashtags'* coefficients were positive for the *Push* and *Networking* categories, but negative for the *Pull* category. It indicated that certain *Hashtags* in *Push* and *Networking* tweets could be popular ones. Having examined the tweets, we identified that Baltimore PD's #communitypolicing and #BPDNeverForget, and NYPD's #happeningnow and #happeningsoon received the largest number of favorites. It was interesting that *Pull* tweets were negatively correlated with *Hashtags*. Having examined the data, we found that the tweets that received the largest number of favorites did not have *Hashtags*. However, many of them had the following words: REWARD, WANTED, MISSING PERSON, which usually were capitalized and appeared at the beginning of the tweets. This suggested that if the police departments used these capitalized terms in *Hashtags*, then potentially the relationships between *Hashtags* and *Favorites* might be consistent across all categories, because *Hashtags* increased message exposure by specifying content in metadata [30].

Mentions. That *Mentions* has consistent negative coefficients for *Favorites* is a surprising result. Intuitively, tweets with *Mentions* may draw more attention and subsequently receive more interactions. When we compared different topics, *Personnel* tweets received the most interactions. We suspected that those tweets would have many *Mentions*. However, when we reviewed the statistics of *Personnel* tweets, we found these tweets had significantly less number of *Mentions* ($M = 0.38$, $SD = 0.63$) than *Information* tweets ($M = 0.80$, $SD = 1.01$, $df = 390$, $p < .001$) whereas there were significantly more *Information* tweets than *Personnel* tweets ($X^2 = 3,420$, $df = 1$, $p < .001$). This may help us understand why *Mentions* had negative coefficients.

5   Discussion and Future Work

There have been extensive studies on how different factors are associated with interactions on Twitter. Our findings suggested actionable items that the police departments could consider to take so as to improve user interactions on Twitter. For example, our annotation results and clustering analyses showed that certain tweet topics (e.g., *Networking* tweets addressing *Personnel* or expressing *Appreciation*) were received more favorites; and balancing different types of tweets such as sending a similar number of *Push* and *Networking* tweets could improve user interactions than only pushing information on Twitter. Our findings revealed that hashtags and mentions could be used more effectively when combined with social media categories/topics. The use of the hashtag #communitypolicing receiving more interactions also indicated that police departments could leverage social media to implement community policing.

In this study, we started with 16 municipal police Twitter accounts from highly populated cities or high crime rated ones in the U.S. that may have more safety related issues, thus the findings may not be applied to those small cities that have significantly less safety issues. In our future work, we plan to evaluate our findings in more diverse contexts, e.g., across different countries or at different times (crisis and normal times).

Acknowledgement. This material is based upon work supported by the National Science Foundation under Grant No. 1464312. Any opinions, findings, and conclusions or recommendations expressed in this material are those of the author(s) and do not necessarily reflect the views of the National Science Foundation.

References

1. Survey on law enforcement's use of social media (2014). http://www. iacpsocialmedia.org/Resources/Publications/2014SurveyResults.aspx. Accessed 22 Sept 2015
2. Abramson, J.: 10 cities making real progress since the launch of the 21st century policing task force (2015)
3. Asur, S., Huberman, B.A.: Predicting the future with social media. In: 2010 IEEE/WIC/ACM International Conference on Web Intelligence and Intelligent Agent Technology (WI-IAT), vol. 1, pp. 492–499. IEEE (2010)
4. Brainard, L., Edlins, M.: Top 10 US municipal police departments and their social media usage. Am. Rev. Public Adm. **45**(6), 728–745 (2015)
5. Community Policing Consortium, Publicity Manager, United States of America: Understanding community policing: a framework for action. BJA Monographs, 79 (1994)
6. Criado, J.I., Sandoval-Almazan, R., Gil-Garcia, J.R.: Government innovation through social media. Gov. Inf. Q. **30**(4), 319–326 (2013)
7. Crump, J.: What are the police doing on Twitter? Social media, the police and the public. Policy Internet **3**(4), 1–27 (2011)
8. Denef, S., Bayerl, P.S., Kaptein, N.A.: Social media and the police: tweeting practices of British police forces during the august 2011 riots. In: Proceedings of the SIGCHI Conference on Human Factors in Computing Systems, pp. 3471–3480. ACM (2013)
9. Fern, X.Z., Brodley, C.E., Friedl, M.A.: Correlation clustering for learning mixtures of canonical correlation models. In: SDM, pp. 439–448. SIAM (2005)
10. Fox, J.: Applied Regression Analysis, Linear Models, and Related Methods. Sage Publications, Inc., Thousand Oaks (1997)
11. Frohlich, K., Hess, E.M.: The most dangerous cities in America (2014). http:// www.msn.com/en-us/health/wellness/the-10-most-dangerous-cities-in-america/ ss-AAfDo9R. Accessed 19 Nov 2015
12. Gardner, W., Mulvey, E.P., Shaw, E.C.: Regression analyses of counts and rates: poisson, overdispersed poisson, and negative binomial models. Psychol. Bull. **118**(3), 392 (1995)
13. Grubbs, F.E.: Sample criteria for testing outlying observations. Ann. Math. Stat. **21**, 27–58 (1950)
14. Hoffman, T.: NYPD turns to social media to strengthen community relations (2015). http://www.1to1media.com/view.aspx?docid=35385. Accessed 22 June 2015
15. Hong, L., Dan, O., Davison, B.D.: Predicting popular messages in Twitter. In: Proceedings of the 20th International Conference Companion on World Wide Web, pp. 57–58. ACM (2011)
16. Hu, Y., Farnham, S., Talamadupula, K.: Predicting user engagement on Twitter with real-world events. In: Ninth International AAAI Conference on Web and Social Media (2015)
17. Huang, Y.L., Starbird, K., Orand, M., Stanek, S.A., Pedersen, H.T.: Connected through crisis: emotional proximity and the spread of misinformation online. In: Proceedings of the 18th ACM Conference on Computer Supported Cooperative Work and Social Computing, pp. 969–980. ACM (2015)

18. Huang, Y., Wu, Q., Hou, Y.: Examining Twitter mentions between police agencies and public users through the Lens of Stakeholder theory. In: Proceedings of the 18th Annual International Conference on Digital Government Research, dg.o 2017, pp. 30–38. ACM, New York (2017). http://doi.acm.org/10.1145/3085228.3085316

19. Jain, A.K., Murty, M.N., Flynn, P.J.: Data clustering: a review. ACM Comput. Surv. (CSUR) **31**(3), 264–323 (1999)

20. Keyling, T., Jünger, J.: Facepager (version, fe 3.3). An application for generic data retrieval through APIs (2013)

21. Leichtle, A.: The Games-Howell Test in R (2012). http://www.gcf.dkf.unibe.ch/BCB/files/BCB_10Jan12_Alexander.pdf. Assessed 1 Oct 2012

22. Meijer, A., Thaens, M.: Social media strategies: understanding the differences between North American police departments. Gov. Inf. Q. **30**(4), 343–350 (2013)

23. Mergel, I.: A framework for interpreting social media interactions in the public sector. Gov. Inf. Q. **30**(4), 327–334 (2013)

24. Naveed, N., Gottron, T., Kunegis, J., Alhadi, A.C.: Bad news travel fast: a content-based analysis of interestingness on Twitter. In: Proceedings of the 3rd International Web Science Conference, p. 8. ACM (2011)

25. Newcombe, T.: Social media: big lessons from the Boston Marathon bombing (2014). http://www.govtech.com/public-safety/Social-Media-Big-Lessons-from-the-Boston-Marathon-Bombing.html. Accessed 24 Sept 2014

26. Nexis: Survey of law enforcement personnel and their use of social media (2014). http://www.lexisnexis.com/risk/downloads/whitepaper/2014-social-media-use-in-law-enforcement.pdf. Accessed 1 Nov 2014

27. Petrovic, S., Osborne, M., Lavrenko, V.: RT to win! predicting message propagation in Twitter. In: ICWSM (2011)

28. Pirie, W.: Spearman rank correlation coefficient. In: Encyclopedia of Statistical Sciences (1988)

29. Satapathy, S.C., Avadhani, P., Udgata, S.K., Lakshminarayana, S.: ICT and critical infrastructure. In: Proceedings of the 48th Annual Convention of Computer Society of India, vol. 1, pp. 773–780. Springer (2013)

30. Spiro, E., Irvine, C., DuBois, C., Butts, C.: Waiting for a retweet: modeling waiting times in information propagation. In: 2012 NIPS Workshop of Social Networks and Social Media Conference, vol. 12 (2012). http://snap.stanford.edu/social2012/papers/spiro-dubois-butts.pdf

31. Suh, B., Hong, L., Pirolli, P., Chi, E.H.: Want to be retweeted? Large scale analytics on factors impacting retweet in Twitter network. In: 2010 IEEE Second International Conference on Social Computing (SocialCom), pp. 177–184. IEEE (2010)

32. Vargo, C.J.: Brand messages on Twitter: predicting diffusion with textual characteristics. The University of North Carolina at Chapel Hill (2014)

33. Viera, A.J., Garrett, J.M.: Understanding interobserver agreement: the Kappa statistic. Fam. Med. **37**(5), 360–363 (2005)

#Depression: Findings from a Literature Review of 10 Years of Social Media and Depression Research

Julissa Murrieta[1]([⊠]), Christopher C. Frye[2], Linda Sun[2], Linh G. Ly[3], Courtney S. Cochancela[4], and Elizabeth V. Eikey[5]

[1] Prince George's Community College, Largo, MD 20774, USA
jmurrie61946@students.pgcc.edu
[2] University of Pittsburgh, Pittsburgh, PA 15260, USA
{ccfl5,lis69}@pitt.edu
[3] University of Washington, Seattle, WA 98195, USA
linhl2@uw.edu
[4] College of Westchester, White Plains, NY 10606, USA
ccochancela@cruiser.cw.edu
[5] University of California, Irvine, Irvine, CA 92697, USA
eikeye@uci.edu

Abstract. The purpose of our literature review was to understand the state of research related to social media and depression within the past 10 years. We were particularly interested in understanding what has been studied in relation to immigrant college students, as they are especially at risk for depression. Searching three databases, ACM Digital Library, PubMed, and IDEALS, we found 881 research articles. Based on our criteria, 78 research papers were included in our analysis. Although social media use is common among college students and depression is an issue for many immigrants and college students, we found few studies that focused specifically on college students, and we identified no studies on immigrant college students or college-aged immigrants. The research articles focused primarily on Twitter and general social media usage (rather than specific social media platforms) and commonly employed qualitative methods. We identify four gaps in the existing literature, why they matter, and how future research (our own included) can begin to address them.

Keywords: Social media · Depression · Mental health · Literature review
College student · Immigrant · Underrepresented populations

1 Introduction

Depression is the leading cause of disability across the world [1]. More than 300 million people suffer from depression worldwide [1]. According to the National Institute of Mental Health [2], approximately 16.1 million people in 2015, ages 18 and above, experienced at least one of the major depressive symptoms within the past year. Especially for college students in the United States, depression is a prevalent issue [3]. Within the college population, immigrant college students may be more susceptible to

© Springer International Publishing AG, part of Springer Nature 2018
G. Chowdhury et al. (Eds.): iConference 2018, LNCS 10766, pp. 47–56, 2018.
https://doi.org/10.1007/978-3-319-78105-1_6

depression [4]. In particular, they face more challenges as an immigrant that affect their academic success in college [4].

While the exact cause of depression is unknown [5], it can impact one's life dramatically. For example, depression is related to poor work performance, missing work, and increased suicide risk [5]. Additionally, it is the second leading cause of death for 15 to 29 year olds [2]. College students who experience depressive symptoms are often reluctant to seek treatment [6, 7]. This is especially problematic among immigrants [8]. Part of this can be attributed to the stigma of mental illnesses [6, 7]. Research has shown that perceived public stigma and personal stigma are barriers to individuals seeking treatment and help [6]. The stigma surrounding mental illnesses may partly explain why people are turning to technology to acquire and share information about health conditions, like depression. As of 2008, 72% of young adults looked up health information online, and 21% of adults used the internet to learn more about depression, anxiety, stress, or mental health issues [9]. As our society slowly evolves around technology, more people are using social media in relation to mental health conditions, such as depression [10, 11]. This is no surprise given the popularity and availability of social media in the United States. According to the Pew Research Center [12], approximately 79% of Americans have a Facebook account, 24% have Twitter, 32% have Instagram, 31% have Pinterest, and 29% have LinkedIn as of 2016. People are now using these types of general-purpose technologies to learn about different health-related topics and share health-related information that may be uncomfortable to discuss in person.

Therefore, understanding how social media is used in relation to depression is becoming increasingly important, especially among groups that depression significantly impacts, such as college and immigrant college students. What do we know about social media use and depression among immigrant college students? In order to begin to answer this question, we first sought to understand what has already been studied about the use of social media for depression with a particular focus on populations related to college or college-aged people and immigrants. Given the increase in social media use and the prevalence of depression, we believe this is the ideal time to look at the state of research about social media and depression. Therefore, in this paper, we report findings from our literature review, which aims to better understand how social media has been studied in relation to depression over the last 10 years in Human-Computer Interaction (HCI) and Health Informatics. This paper represents the first phase of our research and provides the basis for the second phase, which is described in the Future Research section. This literature review provides insights about research that has already been done in relation to social media and depression, emphasizing a lack of research on immigrant college students. Thus, our goal for this paper is to highlight these gaps and identify future research directions.

2 Methods

2.1 Research Questions

Our primary objective was to better understand what has been studied in relation to social media and depression in HCI and Health Informatics. While we were particularly interested in immigrant college populations, our goal was broader: we wanted to identify the types of methods, populations, and platforms studied. For this paper, we focus mostly on the quantitative analysis of the literature. Therefore, we identified three broad research questions:

RQ1: What methods are used in studies of social media and depression?

RQ2: What populations are specifically identified in studies of social media and depression?

   RQ2a: Are college students explicitly discussed in these studies?

   RQ2b: Are immigrants explicitly discussed in these studies?

   RQ2c: Are immigrant college students explicitly discussed in these studies?

RQ3: What social media platforms are studied in research on social media and depression?

2.2 Search Strategy

We sought to identify studies that were related to social media and depression in order to better understand what has been studied about social media use and depression among immigrant college students. We performed literature searches through three databases: (1) ACM Digital Library, (2) PubMed, and (3) IDEALS (iConference). These were chosen because they included many journals and conferences related to HCI and Health Informatics. The third author was assigned to search the ACM Digital Library, the first and fourth author were assigned to search PubMed, and the second and fifth author were assigned to search IDEALS.

In order to collect relevant studies, we conducted 18 keyword searches in each database with combinations of the following keywords: social media, depression, mental health, college student, university student, immigrant, first generation immigrant, and second generation immigrant. Broad and general searches (e.g., social media and depression) were used to obtain as many articles as possible in relation to social media and depression to help answer RQ1, RQ2, and RQ3. Additionally, specific searches (e.g., college and social media and depression) were used to identify articles specific to our population of interest and to explore RQ2 in more detail (particularly RQ2a, RQ2b, and RQ2c). Although our focus was depression, we searched for broader terms (e.g., mental health) in order to acquire more articles that may relate to depression. We applied filters to the searches: we restricted the keyword searches to abstracts only, focused on articles in the English language, included only scholarly and peer-reviewed articles, and limited the publication timeframe to 2007 to 2017. The timeframe was chosen to be within the last 10 years because social media usage in the United States hit a high point in 2007 and has been increasing [13].

2.3 Study Selection

Figure 1 shows an overview of the process to identify the relevant articles for analysis. The database searches resulted in 881 articles. Then, the articles were screened in relation to social media and depression. During this screening phase, only the abstracts were reviewed. If articles passed the screening, their citations were saved in Mendeley,

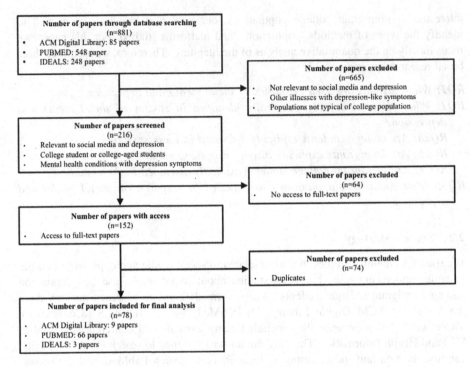

Fig. 1. Flowchart showing our process of identifying papers for our final analysis.

a reference manager. Articles were included if they discussed social media generally or named specific platforms. They were also included if they focused on a population that may have overlapped with college-aged students. This is because we found many studies were not explicit in identifying the population studied. In the United States, the enrollment rates for colleges comprised mostly of the 18 to 24 year old population (approximately 11.8 million students in 2015) [14]. Therefore, articles that used the term "adolescents" were included if they specifically focused on individuals who were 18 years old or older, and articles that used the term "adults" were included if their age ranges overlapped a typical college population. Additionally, articles about the general population were included because 90% of social media users are among the ages of 18 to 29 [15]. We included articles about mental health conditions generally if they mentioned depression-like symptoms.

Through the screening, a total of 665 articles were excluded. Studies were excluded if there was no relevant information about social media, depression, or if they focused on a population that typically would not overlap with college students. The excluded articles consisted of only mentioning one or two of our keywords (e.g., depression only but no mention of social media), focusing on a specific type of depression (e.g., postnatal depression), mentioning depression-like symptoms as a result of another illness or disease, and focusing on an older population (e.g., 65 year olds) or a younger population (e.g., 12 year olds), which would not be typical of a college population.

Next, the 216 articles that passed the screening were examined to see if the full-text was available. Two of the databases, ACM Digital library and PubMed, had restrictions with some of the articles. Only IDEALS provided access to all of the full-text articles. If we could access the full-text, we downloaded the PDF of each article into Mendeley. A total of 64 articles were excluded because we could not access the full-text.

Finally, the remaining 152 articles were examined for duplicates. As a result, 74 articles were excluded. A final total of 78 articles[1] were included in our analysis. The first author reviewed the final articles, and then an excel spreadsheet was compiled with the title, authors, year of publication, abstracts, methods, populations, technologies, and social media platforms of the final articles. We used this spreadsheet to track and organize the articles for our analysis.

3 Findings

As illustrated in Table 1, the articles were analyzed according to the types of methods (RQ1) and populations (RQ2) used in research studies. Qualitative (n = 30) followed by quantitative (n = 17) were the most popular types of methods used to study the relationship between social media and depression. There were only a few research studies that used both qualitative and quantitative methods (mixed methods) (n = 8). In addition, most of the research studies focused primarily on the general population (n = 40). Of those studies that explicitly named their target population, adults and adolescents were commonly discussed. While many studies specifically examined adults (n = 18) and adolescents (n = 15), the college student population (n = 5) was not thoroughly represented in these articles, and no identified studies focused on immigrants or immigrant college students.

Table 1. Method and Population types

Method type	# of Studies	Population type	# of Studies
Qualitative	30	Adults[a]	18
Quantitative	17	Adolescents[b]	15
Mixed (qualitative & quantitative)	8	College students	5
Literature review	9	General population	40
Other	14	Immigrants	0
Total	78		78

[a]Among the 18 articles, adults' ages ranged from 18 to 64 years old.
[b]Among the 15 articles, adolescents' ages ranged from 11 to 21 years old.

As Table 2 highlights, the articles were also analyzed according to the types of social media platforms (RQ3). For specific social media platforms, Twitter (n = 27),

---

[1] Due to Springer's page limitations, the final articles could not be included in this paper. A list of the articles can be obtained by contacting the first author.

followed by Facebook (n = 18) and then Reddit (n = 10) were the most frequently cited. However, it was commonly found that articles did not discuss specific platforms but rather discussed social media more generally in the research studies (n = 23). Articles that focused on adolescents and mentioned specific social media platform examined Twitter (n = 4), Facebook (n = 3), a health forum known as Horyzons (n = 1), and an online counseling service known as Kooth (n = 1). On another note, the articles that focused on adult populations mainly discussed unspecified social media platforms (n = 14), Facebook (n = 3), and Twitter (n = 2). The articles specifically identifying college students that also named a specific social media platform focused on Facebook (n = 2), Reddit (n = 1), and Yik Yak (n = 1). Only one article about college students did not specify any social media platforms (n = 1).

Table 2. Social media types

Social media type	# of Studies
Facebook	18
Google+	3
Instagram	5
Reddit	10
Twitter	27
YouTube, Forums	8
LinkedIn, Pinterest, Wikipedia	2
Myspace, Tumblr	4
Flickr, Livejournal, Orkut, Photobucket, Snapchat, Vine, WordPress, YikYak, Camoni, Douban, Horyzons, Kooth, Miki, PatientsLikeMe	1
No specific social media named	23

Articles about multiple social media platforms were counted individually for our analysis.

Social media has been studied in terms of social identity, social support, technology use, online community, and cyber victimization. The majority of the literature in the context of social media and depression has discussed mental health more generally (e.g., well-being, anxiety, self-harm). Social media was discussed in terms of general social media and mobile usage, specific social media sites (e.g., Twitter, Reddit, YouTube, etc.), and management and intervention for mental health (e.g., suicide prevention, reducing depressive symptoms, and increasing online peer-to-peer groups).

4   Discussion

From our literature review of 10 years of research, we found that studies of social media (most commonly about Twitter) focused on the general population (rather than explicitly naming a population), and the majority of research methods to collect and analyze data were qualitative. In this section, we discuss the gaps in the literature, why these gaps matter, and how our future research aims to address them.

4.1   Gaps in Literature

One of our primary contributions of this work is highlighting future areas of research based on our literature search. We identified four main gaps in terms of methods, populations, and social media platforms: (1) More researchers need to take a mixed method approach to understand depression and social media; (2) College students in general are not studied as the focal population group; (3) Immigrant college students specifically are understudied and; (4) There is a lack of diversity of social media platforms which are studied.

Based on our analysis, a majority of the studies involved the use of only qualitative or quantitative methods. Out of the 78 research articles, only 8 articles involved the use of mixed methods. However, mixed methods need to be utilized in more research studies as they benefit from the strengths of both qualitative and quantitative methods, which also means they compensate for the shortcomings of each of these methods alone [14]. Mixed methods strengthens the data collection and analysis [14] because it allows for more comprehensive information to be gathered on the research topic, and additional questions can be addressed.

As most of the literature focused on general social media users, there remains a gap in the literature examining the relationship between social media and depression among specific subgroups of social media users. Although we specifically looked for articles about college students, we only found 5 relevant articles. They are an important yet understudied population. In fact, it is reported that approximately 3 in 10 students have reported feeling so depressed that they found it difficult to function [15]. However, almost 75% of college students reported that they do not reach out for clinical services [16]. The articles that have researched college students and social media have focused on how social media sites, specifically Facebook and Reddit, are used in relation to mental health wellbeing. Because depression has become a very common health problem among college students in the United States [3], it is crucial we learn more about how they are using social media to manage depression and how social media may impact depression.

Although we also attempted to identify articles specifically about immigrant college students, they remain understudied. Immigrant college students are also an important population to research as they represent a large percentage of the college student population [17]. In fact, 24% of undergraduate college students were identified as first and second generation immigrant students in 2011 and 2012 [17]. They are also at an increased risk for depression [18]. First generation immigrants often carry the burdens of being an immigrant and a first-generation college student, which creates additional challenges in transitioning to college, achieving personal dreams, and abiding to familial expectations [18]. Additionally, these challenges have been associated with immigrant college students feeling more stressed and depressed compared to their non-immigrant college peers [4]. By understanding immigrant college students' challenges and mental health struggles, mental health can be better assessed and intervened.

Finally, we found the majority of studies focused on Twitter, followed by general social media, and Facebook. While Facebook and Twitter are common among 18 to 29 year olds, other social media platforms, such as Instagram, Pinterest, and messaging applications (e.g., Snapchat) are also popular among this group [12]. Additionally, college students have taken an interest in social media platforms that focus on pictures or videos (e.g., Instagram) [19]. However, we identified only 5 studies on Instagram, only 2 on Pinterest, and only 1 on Snapchat. Therefore, more research is needed on these types and other types of social media platforms. Additionally, more studies need to explicitly name the social media platforms on which they focus. This is important because social media platforms differ in their design, users, interaction, effects, etc. Without knowing the types of social media studied, it is difficult to translate and build upon these research findings.

4.2   Limitations

With our literature search, we aimed to be as exhaustive as we could in identifying articles related to HCI and Health Informatics. It is possible, though, that we may have missed some studies due to our keyword choices as well as the databases we searched. It is important to note that keywords were chosen in regard of our population of interest. Although our goals were broad, our intention was to identify literature around college students with a particular focus and interest in immigrant populations. Due to many articles not explicitly naming their population, we included general social media users, adults, and adolescents if they overlapped with college-aged individuals. Thus, we acknowledge that the populations discussed in these articles may not all be college students. Our paper highlights not only the lack of studies explicitly focusing on this group, but also the issues with generalizing findings when populations are not made explicit.

Furthermore, we only searched through three databases with a focus on HCI and Health Informatics as our goal was to draw attention to the gaps in these two fields, which have expertise and interest in social media and increasingly in mental health. Additionally, certain articles retrieved from ACM Digital Library and PubMed were not full-text and thus excluded from our literature review. Relevant studies involving social media and depression could have been omitted as a result. Finally, we acknowledge that there may have been selection bias during the screening process. While we met weekly as a team to discuss any questions about our search process, it is possible we may have missed studies due to each individual's interpretation of the articles.

4.3   Future Research

As mentioned beforehand, this literature review is phase one of a proposed research project. In order to begin to address the above mentioned gaps in phase two of our project, we are planning to conduct a study on how first and second generation immigrant college students with depression use social media. We will use a quantitative questionnaire on depression symptoms, social media usage, demographics, and culture and conduct qualitative semi-structured interviews with immigrant college students with depression. The goal is to better understand the use and impact of social media on immigrant college students with depression. We are also interested in how they navigate their social stratosphere through social media to manage their depression symptoms. We will group specific social media platforms together as part of our analysis in order to understand the benefits and drawbacks of particular platforms. Our research findings aim to create more inclusive social media platforms and services. We hope to gain insight on how immigrant college students use specific social media platforms as an alternative to clinical mental health services, which could lead to improvements in therapy and design recommendations for social media and other types of technology.

5 Conclusion

Because social media is so popular today, this is a perfect time to understand social media in relation to depression. In particular, we were interested on who is the focus of these studies. Our literature search reveals a lack of research on immigrant college students despite the prevalence of depression among this group. Searching through three databases related to HCI and Health Informatics, we found 78 articles related to social media use and depression. The majority of articles used qualitative methods, focused on a general population of social media users, and focused on Twitter or discussed social media generally. We found few articles specifically about college students and no articles about immigrant college students. This is problematic considering the prevalence of depression among college students and immigrants [3, 4] as well as the popularity of social media among college-aged people [19]. Therefore, we identify four gaps in terms of methods, population, and social media, which need further attention. We hope that through this paper, we can spark interest in addressing these gaps and emphasize the importance of studying social media use in relation to depression not only among college students, but also immigrant college students and other populations.

References

1. WHO - World Health Organization: Depression Fact Sheet (2017)
2. NIMH: NIMH » Major Depression Among Adults (2015)
3. Ibrahim, A.K., Kelly, S.J., Adams, C.E., Glazebrook, C.: A systematic review of studies of depression prevalence in university students. J. Psychiatr. Res. **47**, 391–400 (2013)
4. Soria, K., Stebleton, M.: Immigrant college students' academic obstacles (2013)
5. CDC Centers for Disease Control and Prevention: Depression - Mental Illness - Mental Health Basics - Mental Health - CDC (2016)
6. Eisenberg, D., Downs, M.F., Golberstein, E., Zivin, K.: Stigma and help seeking college students. Med. Care Res. Rev. **66**, 522–541 (2009)
7. Vidourek, R.A., King, K.A., Nabors, L.A., Merianos, A.L.: Students' benefits and barriers to mental health help-seeking. Heal. Psychol. Behav. Med. **2**, 1009–1022 (2014)
8. Derr, A.S.: Mental health service use among immigrants in the united states: a systematic review. Psychiatr. Serv. **67**, 265–274 (2016)
9. Lenhart, A., Purcell, K., Smith, A., Zickuhr, K.: Social Media & Mobile Internet Use among Teens and Young Adults. Pew Internet & American Life Project, pp. 1–16 (2010)
10. Andalibi, N., Ozturk, P., Forte, A.: Sensitive self-disclosures, responses, and social support on instagram: the case of #depression, pp. 1485–1500 (2017)

11. Andalibi, N., Ozturk, P., Forte, A.: Depression-related imagery on instagram. In: Proceedings of 18th ACM Conference on Companion Computer Supported Cooperative Work Social Computing, CSCW 2015 Companion, pp. 231–234 (2015)
12. Greenwood, S., Perrin, A., Duggan, M.: Social Media Update 2016. Pew Research Center (2016)
13. Perrin, A.: Social Media Usage: 2005–2015 | Pew Research Center. http://www.pewinternet.org/2015/10/08/social-networking-usage-2005-2015/
14. Ivankova, N.V., Creswell, J.W., Stick, S.L.: Using mixed-methods sequential explanatory design: from theory to practice. Field Methods **18**, 3–20 (2006)
15. American College Health Association: American College Health Association-National College Health Assessment II: Reference Group Executive Summary, Fall (2009)
16. Hunt, J., Eisenberg, D.: Mental health problems and help-seeking behavior among college students. J. Adolesc. Heal. **46**, 3–10 (2010)
17. Arbeit, C.A., Staklis, S., Horn, L., Simone, S.A.: New American Undergraduates—Enrollment Trends and Age at Arrival of Immigrant and Second-Generation Students (2016)
18. Deenanath, V.: First-Generation Immigrant College Students: An Exploration of Family Support and Career Aspirations. https://conservancy.umn.edu/bitstream/handle/11299/165446/Deenanath_umn_0130M_15232.pdf?sequence=1 (2014)
19. Knight-McCord, J., Cleary, D., Grant, N., Herron, A., Jumbo, S., Lacey, T., Livingston, T., Robinson, S., Smith, R., Emanuel, R.: What social media sites do college students use most? J. Undergrad. Ethn. Minority Psychol. – 2016 **2**, 21 (2016)

Analysing the Pattern of Twitter Activities Among Academics in a UK Higher Education Institution

Nordiana Ahmad Kharman Shah[1](✉) and Andrew Martin Cox[2]

[1] Department of Library and Information Science, University of Malaya,
50603 Kuala Lumpur, Malaysia
dina@um.edu.my
[2] Information School, The University of Sheffield, Regent Court,
Sheffield S1 4DP, UK
a.m.cox@sheffield.ac.uk

Abstract. This study explores the temporal patterns of Twitter use in academia, through quantitative and qualitative methods, answering the following questions: When do academics tweet? Where do academics tweet? and How often do academics receive feedback from their followers on Twitter? UK academics who are active users of Twitter in a specific institution were recruited for the study. Both the temporal patterns (daily and weekly) in the use of Twitter and the uses themselves suggest that the practice is seen primarily as a professional matter, and secondarily as personal. A significant pattern of 'microbreaks' is identified. The data indicates that where Twitter use becomes habitual, it is experienced as a positive addition to available communication tools.

Keywords: Social media · Twitter · Digital scholar · Higher Education

1 Introduction

Social media are communication platforms built upon Web 2.0 [1] principles [10] and are of importance because of their potential to change how people communicate, search for and exchange information online [6]. Through supporting User-Generated Content (UGC), they enable users to enter a more social and participatory phase of the web and to be dynamic contributors creating, managing, annotating, curating, reviewing and sharing information/data in online communities [10]. Higher Education (HE) has been one of the most active fields where attempts have been made to use such technologies to aid in learning, facilitate information sharing and foster collaboration among teachers and students, researchers and administrators. With the on-going development of social media applications, enthusiastic academics have been practical innovators taking steps to actively explore such tools in their pedagogic practice. A number of researchers have concluded that the use of social media in HE for the advancement of teaching and learning in education has been successful [20, 21, 25]. In addition to its use in support of teaching, academics have begun to expand their use for a wide variety of other purposes including for scientific and professional reasons [14]. Some authors have even

G. Chowdhury et al. (Eds.): iConference 2018, LNCS 10766, pp. 57–66, 2018.
https://doi.org/10.1007/978-3-319-78105-1_7

argued that social media use may transform the very nature of academic communication, writing, scholarship, research patterns, relationships and identity [12, 16, 23, 24, 26]. Microblogging via Twitter is one of the most common examples of social media being used in academia [13, 18]. Twitter is popular for its immediacy and efficiency. Although limited to messages of 140 characters yet it can include links to photos, videos or other online content [5, 7]. Despite the short length of messages, it can offer continuous public discourse in an open environment. This feature differentiates it from Facebook, which is more popularly used for establishing personal social networks rather than public discourse [5]. Twitter has been found to support communication activities and promote collaboration, through discussion, giving updates, questioning and answering and providing suggestions that facilitate an increase in awareness between scholars [8, 9].

While it has been seen that social media, and Twitter in particular, have been widely used in academic contexts, most previous research focuses on simply identifying the different ways Twitter is used. In contrast, this study emphasises the temporal patterns of Twitter use, through in-depth quantitative and qualitative analyses of Twitter activity by academics from the University of Sheffield. The paper seeks to answer the following questions: (1) When do academics tweet? (2) Where do academics tweet? and (3) How often do academics receive feedback from their followers on Twitter? While some researchers have established that Twitter has been widely used in the education sector [4, 15, 18, 23], the patterns of daily usage, posting, and replying are yet to be understood.

2   Methodology

This paper reports quantitative analysis conducted through a time-use analysis, specifically episode sampling, of the use of Twitter by 28 academics from the University of Sheffield, UK. Participants were selected based on the following criteria: having a Twitter account that was being used for professional purposes; that their account had been registered for at least a year; and that they were posting regularly – at least one tweet per week. The data was compared with qualitative responses gathered from the academics through interviews [22].

Participants were diverse in terms of disciplines, gender, age and levels of seniority. Tables 1 and 2 give an overview of the demographics of participants.

Table 1. Academic status of participants.

	Frequency	Percent
Professor	9	32.1
Senior lecturer	5	17.9
Lecturer	8	28.6
Research fellow	3	10.7
University teacher	3	10.7
Total	28	100.0

Table 2. Age groups of participants.

	Frequency	Percent
20–29	3	10.7
30–39	8	28.6
40–49	10	35.7
50+	7	25.0
Total	*28*	*100.0*

The sample made up a significant proportion of the early adopters of Twitter in the institution concerned. The tables above reveal that most participants were professors and lecturers and in the age group 40 to 49. The early adopters in this study show that Twitter was adopted among people of differing academic seniority levels and age groups in the university. This situation poses a challenge to the idea that digital tools are mostly relevant for 'young' people or the 'digital native'. The profile of the respondents in this research is like that in the studies by Carpenter and Krutka [2, 3] where they argued that most educators who use Twitter in the United States are in their 30s and 40s and suggests that the digital native stereotype is slowly changing despite the claims of Prensky [17] and Risser [19]. Despite the small sample size, because of the purposive sampling approach and the combination of quantitative data with insights from the qualitative stage of the research the insights generated in this paper gives an in-depth sense of the pattern of Twitter engagement, albeit not generalizable across the whole academic population.

3   Results

3.1   Hourly Distribution

As seen in Fig. 1, academics send most of their tweets during working hours. However, the peak period of tweeting is 7–9 am. This suggests that tweets are regularly posted as

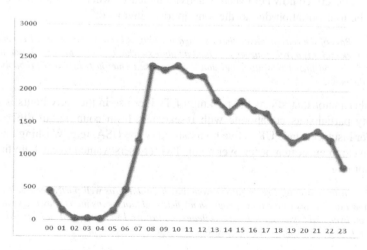

Fig. 1. Hourly distribution of tweets within a day

the academic search for news items while they are on their way to work or immediately upon arriving in the office.

3.2 Early Morning Twitter Activities

Participants mentioned that it had become automatic for them to browse the network even in the early morning. Twitter becomes a means for them to receive the first news of the day.

> "I tell you what I do, when I get up in the morning I will always, before I leave the house, I always look at Twitter, I always look at my timeline… You know what happens in the world and who is saying what. From the Twitter feed I follow BBC breaking news. If I want to get more information about that story I can follow them throughout the day; if I get time."

> "I look at it first the soonest I get out of bed on my phone but generally don't respond to anything then, I just look at it. Just see what is there."

Participants indicated that the habit of opening Twitter serves as their first source of information before performing other daily routines. The accessibility of social media applications through mobile devices seems to play a key role in determining this pattern. Twitter can be quickly and conveniently accessed because it is used on a mobile device that is always at hand.

One academic described how she deliberately engages on Twitter early in the morning, particularly when most of her colleagues are online.

> "Normally, if I'm going to do it, very often before work. I think that the time when a lot of people that I know are online is. You know you can get a report that tells you when your followers are online. I did that for the department feed and I did it for mine at the same time and my impression was that most of the people, you know… It's like between eight and nine in the morning when most people are at work, but not working."

The trend showing that the engagement of academics gradually increases from 5 to 7 in the morning can be attributed to Twitter's accessibility and mobility. As a consequence, academics have developed a habit of tweeting during their commute. One interviewee described how her tweeting activity increased when she started to commute with public transportation due to the long journey involved:

> "Part of the reason maybe that I started tweeting is because I commute, I commute 5 days a week and it is a train journey for about an hour so what tends to happen is I read all my twitter feeds and then I read the news and the response to me on twitter and probably post about the news."

Another factor that affects the peaking of Twitter use in the early hours is the fact that many participants collaborate with researchers from countries in different time zones. For instance, since UK is five hours ahead of the USA, (e.g. Washington DC) so major developments often occur over night. Twitter users wanted to catch up first thing in the morning.

> "In the morning, I see what everyone has been doing as well partly because as I say you know I am friends with a lot of people in my field and that means there is always something going on over night, you know I have colleagues who are I am interested in their work and tweet in Canada and the States, so Australia."

3.3 Microbreaks

As seen from Fig. 1, most tweeting activities occur during work hours. From the interviews, academics suggested that their Tweeting activity mostly occurs during work.

> *"When I have a kind of admin-type day, if I'm doing lots of bits, small things like emails, then I might well tweet in between, comment on things, retweet and so forth and when I see interesting tweets I just retweet them... it's sort of when it fits into what I'm doing other things. Sometimes if I'm at the computer doing bits and pieces, like emailing or writing short messages or something that perhaps doesn't require lots and lots of focus and concentration on doing one thing then I probably kind of tweet in between that."*

Academics seem to use Twitter while engaged in other work routines. This implies a significant relationship between work patterns and Twitter use. In the interviews academics mentioned that they use Twitter to *'kill dead time'*. This phenomenon could be referred to as a 'micro-break', a short period of social network engagement while at the workplace, with the aim to reenergize the self before returning to work routines. It is a practice where a person initiates a distraction, a 'self-interruption' to focus on lower level activities as a relief from the pressure of work. Micro-breaks can happen at any time within the day, and it is at these points scholars are mostly active on Twitter.

In microbreaking academics multitask to achieve something beneficial in terms of personal and academic endeavor, such as browsing for information to enlarge academic knowledge; sharing research interests and outputs to create future collaborations; and boosting visibility through communicating expertise in an academic discussion. Academics are typically multi-tasking: most of them have their Twitter account open along-side emails and other research work on different windows of a single browser.

Participants talked about setting their own rules or philosophy regarding tweeting. One professor strongly emphasized that he used Twitter only for purposes associated with his professional responsibilities, stating that:

> *"So, I do Tweet in the office, I mean on my iPhone, my iPad, or whatever but you know I, it's something that is definitely work associated [...] It's something I do when I'm working ... Twitter stays in the work compartment of my life."*

Another commented:

> *"It's like an accompaniment to my everyday work and because I think of Twitter more as a work thing in a way, that I connect it with my academic, kind of online identity and things like that [...] I think because most of the people I follow are academic-related in some way that I associate it with work space and work time."*

Thus, Twitter is seen mainly as a way to enrich professional working relationships. The user builds a profile in a convenient way interaction and the visibility of tweets. This shows how academics incorporate Twitter in their work routine, despite their tight work schedule.

3.4 Follower Feedback Frequency

Interactive communication is an important aspect of how academics use Twitter. As is evident in Fig. 2, the number of tweets made by academics is more than the replies received. However, there is strong correlation between when tweets are sent out and replies received as seen from the similarities in both curves of the graph. This suggests that Twitter is interactive, with a strong culture of replies being sent to those who Tweet.

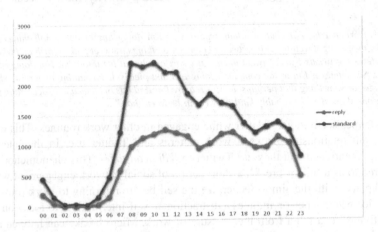

Fig. 2. Hourly distribution of tweets sent and replies received by academics within 24 h.

Most academics described how a significant use of Twitter was to connect with small or large groups of people who share common interests and goals. These networks included other academics, professionals, students, ex-students and people outside academia.

> *"I had very supportive, interesting interactions with all of these nice people who kind of then introduced me to other people and it made it feel like an actual community of people rather than just a receptive, you know, somewhere where people broadcast."*

For this user, the supportive environment of the community served as an inspiration for her to join Twitter. This meant that she was comfortable in actively communicating and sharing updates and information while expanding her network.

> *"Well I think it's very useful for keeping in touch with your colleagues and with people in your field and I think it helps you to feel like you're a part of the community of practice... it's very useful because you get to understand what people are talking about, what people are thinking is important, what the debates are, what the problems are, so I think it's very useful as a professional tool for feeling like you're a part of a community of researchers."*

Another academic believed that tweeting about her research collaborations with colleagues made her become more engaged with her work as well as with the community of people that participated in the project. This relates to the earlier findings that Twitter use peaks at different times of the day when collaborators are able to communicate across time zones, across temporal and geographical boundaries, as also shown earlier in the paper. The use of Twitter becomes interactive with tweets and replies.

> *"Twitter helps me connect with everybody in the project really fast and it helps me connect and helps me think about the project. I think the project has a Twitter excitement about it."*

4 Discussion

The active users recruited for this study were well distributed across ages and levels of seniority, rather than being clustered into younger age groups. This suggests that it should not be assumed that early adopters in this context are necessarily young or junior staff. Both the temporal patterns (hourly, daily and weekly) in the use of Twitter are suggestive that the practice is seen primarily as a professional matter. Although academics Tweet a lot in the two hours before the working day starts, they did not do so much in the evening or at the weekend. Indeed, most tweets are sent in working hours. Tweeting activity is spread across the whole day and week. Twitter offers a micro-break a "productive interruption" to routine work tasks, that when spread through the day can reenergize the scholar.

The data shows that academics use Twitter throughout the day but particularly in the morning and activity declines gradually later in the day. This finding is consistent with the findings of Carpenter and Krutka [3] that 84% of educators use Twitter daily or multiple times a day for their professional, as well as for personal purposes. In terms of communicative use, the content of the conversations generally included discussions of academic research and information; asking for help from other colleagues in regards to research ideas or teaching; providing assistance/feedback to those from a similar research background, which involves an informal collaborative purpose; teaching or research activity; participating in social conversation with the audience; occasionally voicing suggestions or concerns; and using the technology as another informal channel to receive teaching feedback directly from students. Participants reported that having a dialogue on Twitter is a supplement to existing communication mechanisms. This is in line with the findings of Carpenter and Krutka [2] where they observed that certain purposes have corresponding time signatures in terms of frequency and duration. In particular, they observed that academics mostly spend a longer time on Twitter when doing back channeling (77.39). However, they also frequently use the platform to participate in Twitter chats (36.49) and in networking (33.99), which is related to what was observed in this study.

Although scholars send more tweets than they receive replies, the rate and patterning of replying, is suggestive of a culture of supportive interaction through Twitter. Again, this is consistent with the interview data, which showed that academics felt a strong sense of participating in a wide and supportive community of interest through Twitter. Further, the data is suggestive that where Twitter use becomes habitual it is experienced as a positive addition to available communication tools. Although there is some blurring of boundaries between personal and public activities, as indicated by a significant use out of working hours, for these academics use of Twitter is experienced as beneficial. The finding, in relation to Twitter's role as a feedback channel through replies and retweets, supports Carpenter and Krutka's (2015) [3] conclusion that Twitter becomes "a space of enthusiasm, invigoration, empowerment and connection" (p. 722). Lalonde (p. 119) [20] notes similarly that 'the open nature of Twitter means these learning networks are now no longer confined to closed and private spaces, but are able to be open and public, which increases the opportunities for collaboration, connections and learning opportunities'. Harvey argues that low variation in the temporal location often indicates that actors have little freedom in exercising a given activity. But in this case academics' hourly, daily and weekly engagement in Twitter did vary. This reflects the fact that they engage freely with it, as part of their everyday academic and non-academic activities.

5 Limitations of the Study

The research only gathered one-off data from the academics from the University of Sheffield who are enthusiasts of Twitter, other research could be done by considering alternative data collection periods and sampling methods. A longer timeframe and wider geographic coverage could be carried out in future research. In undertaking such future research, it is suggested that diary writing would be a good method of data collection to supplement twitter data and interviews, because this would generate deeper insights based on the experiences, practice and time use of the academics. Further, analysis could also be done based on demographics to verify the difference of use among younger and less experienced teachers and their old-timer counterparts. Students' experiences and time-use might also be explored in future studies.

6 Implications for Policy and Practice

While it has been emphasized that this research could not generate a generalizable picture for the majority of academics who use Twitter, the authors still believe that the findings have significant implications for HE policy makers and faculty members. For example, institutional policy makers can find encouragement in the findings to acknowledge the potential of social media in the learning and teaching process, as well as in professional development of teachers. The temporal pattern of use, in short breaks spread through the day, is suggestive of alternative models for continuing professional development.

References

1. Aharony, N.: Web 2.0 use by librarians. Libr. Inf. Sci. Res. **31**(1), 29–37 (2009). https://doi.org/10.1016/j.lisr.2008.06.004
2. Carpenter, J.P., Krutka, D.G.: How and why educators use Twitter: a survey of the field. J. Res. Technol. Educ. **46**(4), 414–434 (2014)
3. Carpenter, J.P., Krutka, D.G.: Engagement through microblogging: educator professional development via Twitter. Prof. Dev. Educ. **41**(4), 707–728 (2015). https://doi.org/10.1080/19415257.2014.939294
4. Dunn, J.: 100 ways to use Twitter in education, by degree of difficulty (2012). http://edudemic.com/2012/04/100-ways-to-use-twitter-in-education-by-degree-of-difficulty/
5. Ebner, M., Lienhardt, C., Rohs, M., Meyer, I.: Microblogs in higher education - a chance to facilitate informal and process-oriented learning? Comput. Educ. **55**(1), 92–100 (2010). https://doi.org/10.1016/j.compedu.2009.12.006/

6. Grosseck, G.: To use or not to use web 2.0 in higher education? Procedia - Soc. Behav. Sci. **1**(1), 478–482 (2009). https://doi.org/10.1016/j.sbspro.2009.01.087
7. Harvey, A.S.: Guidelines for time use data collection and analysis. In: Pentland, W.E., Harvey, A.S., Lawton, M.P., McColl, M.A. (eds.) Time Use Research in the Social Sciences, pp. 19–45. Kluwer Academic/Plenum Publishers, New York (1999)
8. Holotescu, C., Grosseck, G.: Using microblogging in education. Case study: Cirip. ro. Procedia - Soc. Behav. Sci. **1**(1), 495–501 (2008). https://doi.org/10.1016/j.sbspro.2009.01.090
9. Honeycutt, C., Herring, S.C.: Beyond microblogging: conversation and collaboration via Twitter. In: Proceedings of the 42nd Annual Hawaii International Conference on System Sciences, (HICSS), Hawaii, USA (2009). https://doi.org/10.1109/hicss.2009.602
10. Junco, R., Heiberger, G., Loken, E.: The effect of Twitter on college student engagement and grades. J. Comput. Assist. Learn. **27**(2), 119–132 (2011). https://doi.org/10.1111/j.1365-2729.2010.00387.x
11. Kaplan, A.M., Haenlein, M.: Users of the world, unite! The challenges and opportunities of social media. Bus. Horiz. **53**(1), 59–68 (2010). https://doi.org/10.1016/j.bushor.2009.09.003/
12. Kirkup, G.: Academic blogging: academic practice and academic identity. Lond. Rev. Educ. **8**(1), 75–84 (2010). https://doi.org/10.1080/14748460903557803
13. Lalonde, C.: The Twitter experience: the role of Twitter in the formation and maintenance of personal learning networks. Unpublished MA thesis, Royal Roads University (2011). http://hdl.handle.net/10170/451
14. Lupton, D.: 'Feeling better connected': academics' use of social media. News & Media Research Center, University of Canberra, Canberra (2014)
15. Mulatiningsih, B., Partridge, H., Davis, K.: Exploring the role of Twitter in the professional practice of LIS professionals: a pilot study. Aust. Libr. J. **62**(3), 204–217 (2013). https://doi.org/10.1080/00049670.2013.806998
16. Nicholas, D., Rowlands, I.: Social media use in the research workflow. Inf. Serv. Use **31**(1–2), 61–83 (2011). https://doi.org/10.3233/ISU-2011-0623
17. Prensky, M.: Digital natives, digital immigrants. On Horiz. **9**(5), 1–6 (2001)
18. Reinhardt, W., Ebner, M., Beham, G., Costa, C.: How people are using Twitter during conferences. In: Hornung-Prähauser, V., Luckmann, M. (eds.) Creativity and Innovation Competencies on the Web, Proceeding of 5. EduMedia conference, pp. 145–156, Salzburg (2009). http://lamp.tu-graz.ac.at/~i203/ebner/publication/09_edumedia.pdf
19. Rhode, J.: Using Twitter for teaching, learning, and professional development. Northern Illinois University, Social Media Series (2012). http://www.slideshare.net/jrhode/using-twitter-for-teaching-learning-and-professional-development
20. Risser, H.S.: Virtual induction: a novice teacher's use of Twitter to form an informal mentoring network. Teach. Teach. Educ. **35**, 25–33 (2013)
21. Seal, K.C., Przasnyski, Z.H.: Using the World Wide Web for teaching improvement. Comput. Educ. **36**(1), 33–40 (2001). https://doi.org/10.1016/s0360-1315(00)00049-x
22. Selwyn, N.: Social media in higher education. In: Gladman, A. (ed.) The Europa World of Learning, pp. 1–9. Routledge, London (2012)
23. Shah, N.A.K.: Factors influencing academics' use of microblogging in higher education. Unpublished doctoral dissertation, University of Sheffield, United Kingdom (2015)
24. Veletsianos, G.: Open practices and identity: evidence from researchers and educators' social media participation. Br. J. Educ. Technol. **44**(4), 639–651 (2013). https://doi.org/10.1111/bjet.12052

25. Veletsianos, G., Kimmons, R., French, K.D.: Instructor experiences with a social networking site in a higher education setting: expectations, frustrations, appropriation, and compartmentalization. Educ. Technol. Res. Dev. **61**(2), 255–278 (2013). https://doi.org/10.1007/s11423-012-9284-z

26. Wankel, L.A., Wankel, C.: Connecting on campus with new media: introduction to higher education administration with social media. In: Wankel, L.A., Wankel, C. (eds.) Cutting-Edge Technologies in Higher Education, vol. 2, pp. xi–xviii. Emerald (2011). http://doi.org/10.1108/S2044-9968(2011)0000002003

27. Weller, M.: The digital scholar: how technology is transforming scholarly practice. Bloomsbury, London (2011)

Towards Understanding Cross-Cultural Crowd Sentiment Using Social Media

Yuanyuan Wang[1][(✉)], Panote Siriaraya[2], Muhammad Syafiq Mohd Pozi[3], Yukiko Kawai[2], and Adam Jatowt[4]

[1] Yamaguchi University, 2-16-1 Tokiwadai, Ube, Yamaguchi 755-8611, Japan
y.wang@yamaguchi-u.ac.jp
[2] Kyoto Sangyo University, Motoyama, Kamigamo, Kita-ku, Kyoto 603-8555, Japan
spanote@gmail.com, kawai@cc.kyoto-su.ac.jp
[3] Universiti Tenaga Nasional, Jalan Ikram-Uniten, 43000 Kajang, Selangor, Malaysia
syafiq.pozi@uniten.edu.my
[4] Kyoto University, Yoshida-homachi, Sakyo-ku, Kyoto 606-8501, Japan
adam@dl.kuis.kyoto-u.ac.jp

Abstract. Social media such as Twitter has been frequently used for expressing personal opinions and sentiments at different places. In this paper, we propose a novel crowd sentiment analysis for fostering cross-cultural studies. In particular, we aim to find similar meanings but different sentiments between tweets collected over geographical areas. For this, we detect sentiments and topics of each tweet by applying neural network based approaches, and we assign sentiments to each topic based on the sentiments of the corresponding tweets. This permits finding cross-cultural patterns by computing topic and sentiment correspondence. The proposed methods enable to analyze tweets from diverse geographical areas sentimentally in order to explore cross-cultural differences.

Keywords: Crowd sentiment analysis
Similar but sentimentally different · Cross-cultural studies

1 Introduction

Social media offers many possibilities for analyzing cross-cultural differences. For example, Silva et al. [8] compared cultural boundaries and similarities across populations in food and drink consumption based on Foursquare data. Park et al. [6] attempted to demonstrate cultural differences in the use of emoticons on Twitter. Other researches focused on cultural differences related to user multilingualism in Twitter [4,5]. In this context, sentiment analysis has become a popular tool for data analysts, especially those who deal with social media data. It has been recently quite common to analyze public opinions and reviews of events, products and so on social media using computational approaches. However, most of the existing sentiment analysis methods were designed based on a single language, like English, without the focus on particular geographic

© Springer International Publishing AG, part of Springer Nature 2018
G. Chowdhury et al. (Eds.): iConference 2018, LNCS 10766, pp. 67–73, 2018.
https://doi.org/10.1007/978-3-319-78105-1_8

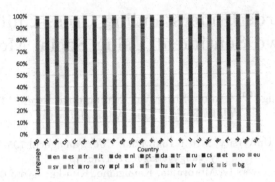

Fig. 1. European language distribution across different European countries in Twitter.

areas and on inter-regional comparisons. It is however necessary to develop new technology to be able to adapt sentiment analysis to a wide number of other cultures and areas [7] and to be able to compare the results. Most current methods cannot explore sentiment differences between diverse geographical areas to provide customized location-based approaches.

To foster cross-cultural studies between different spatial areas, we propose a novel crowd sentiment analysis to find similar semantics which are characterized by different sentiments based on social media data. We use data derived from different geographic places such as different prefectures, municipalities, or countries. In particular as an underlying dataset in our study, we utilize Twitter data gathered using Twitter Streaming API over Western and Central part of Europe issued during approximately 8 months in 2016. The data consists of 16.5 million tweets accumulating to 5 GB memory size. Fig. 1 shows the distribution of languages in our dataset (we show only European languages) accumulated from all users from each analyzed country. We can observe that English is a commonly used language across European countries in Twitter. Therefore, in this paper, for simplicity, we focus on English tweets. We then explore cross-cultural differences based on similar semantics but different sentiments in different geographical areas. Our method delivers two kinds of output based on the proposed crowd sentiment analysis: similar-but-sentimentally-different topics and terms.

For start, users need to select two locations. The method then returns the ranked list of similar-but-sentimentally-different topics (terms) in the form of term clouds, as well as the list of representative tweets for the extracted topics in both the locations. User can also select a time period (e.g., one of seasons) and, by this, the ranked topic (term) list, the term clouds, and the tweet list can be updated. When a user clicks a given term, the method presents the list of its most related tweets. We believe that such data could provide complementary knowledge to many social media studies interested in location-based sentiment analysis of user activities or in sentiment-based recommendation. The ranked term list could also help to improve methods that rely on sentiment analysis by adjusting and correcting sentiment lexicons. Note that although we focus on Twitter, our cross-cultural sentiment analysis can accept any datasets, e.g., services, products, or facilities, for discovering sentiments of topics over tweets. This should be useful for better recommending particular activities, products, services, events, or places to visit for a given segment of users.

2   Crowd Sentiment Analysis

The processing flow of our crowd sentiment analysis is shown in Fig. 2 on Twitter datasets for two geographical areas (e.g., France and Italy). Our approach consists of 3 stages: (1) *Sentiment Modeling* for categorizing tweets into positive and negative by applying neural networks, (2) *Topic Modeling (1, 2)* for detecting tweet topics through utilizing LDA model, and (3) *Topic-Topic Similarity Estimation* for finding similar topics based on output from *Topic Modeling 2*.

In order to identify each tweet's sentiment, we developed a sentiment classification model based on existing labeled tweet dataset used in [2]. The dataset consists of 1,600k tweets used as the training set and 498 tweets for the testing set. Re-tweets and tweets that contain URL have been removed from the dataset. We then use the deep learning approach to implement the classification model. There are three necessary steps in this stage: *preprocessing, transformation*, and *learning*. In the preprocessing step, every tweet is cleaned from non-word symbols and converted into a list of terms. Then, these lists are transformed into a vector representation before being fed into the learning algorithm.

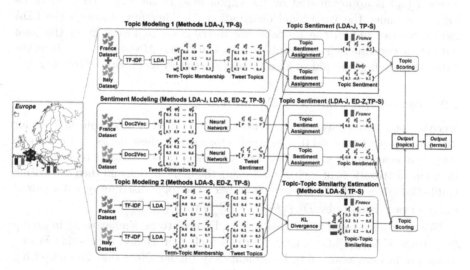

Fig. 2. Cross-cultural crowd sentiment analysis (e.g., France vs. Italy). For topic output, we propose two methods as listed in Sect. 3.2: LDA-J which is based on *Topic Modeling 1, Sentiment Modeling*, and *Topic Sentiment*; and LDA-S based on *Sentiment Modeling, Topic Modeling 2, Topic Sentiment*, and *Topic-Topic Similarity Estimation*. For term output, we propose ED-Z based on *Sentiment Modeling, Topic Modeling 2*, and *Topic Sentiment*; and TP-S based on LDA-S.

Next, every tweet is transformed into a feature vector using Doc2Vec algorithm. It can identify tweets that have similar meaning, which could not be well represented by other feature representation such as bag of words (BoW). Unlike Doc2Vec, BoW, or *TF-IDF* have tendency to produce sparse data. However, the set of human vocabulary consists of almost unlimited number of elements. Hence, representing a single instance over a set of universal vocabulary will always result in sparse vector. Doc2Vec allows large number of features (typically thousands of terms) to be represented in a lower dimensional space. We limit the feature number to 300 features. Each tweet will then have its own vector representation. These representations will be fed into a fully connected neural network for supervised learning.

2.1 Topic Modeling

We perform a topic modeling by using LDA model with *TF-IDF* scored terms of either the joint dataset of different geographical areas (*Topic Modeling 1*) or on separate datasets, each for a given geographical area (*Topic Modeling 2*).

LDA is a generative model in which the topic distribution is assumed to have a Dirichlet prior. After learning is completed, the probability of a term w to belong to a topic z_g ($g \in [1, G]$), $P(w|z_g)$, is known, where G denotes the topic number (G is set to 300 in the experiments). Then, the probability of z_g given a term w can be easily inferred by applying Bayes' rule, $P(z_g|w) \propto P(w|z_g)P(z_g)$, where $P(z_g)$ is approximated by the exponential of the expected value of its logarithm under the variational distribution [1]. Therefore, through the LDA model, we can obtain the probabilistic distribution of topics given the joint dataset of two different geographical areas in *Topic Modeling 1*, or given the datasets of each geographical area treated separately as in *Topic Modeling 2*.

2.2 Topic-Topic Similarity Estimation

Since we have two separate tweet datasets in two different geographical areas for *Topic Modeling 2*, we need to synchronize topics from these datasets. In the next stage, we measure the similarities between topics in two datasets by computing the topic distributions of each dataset using the LDA model, and then computing Kullback-Leibler (KL) divergence [3] between the topic distributions of a pair of topics in two datasets by $D_{KL}(P||Q) = \sum_w P(w) \cdot \log \frac{P(w)}{Q(w)}$.

We consider a topic z_i^x in area x (e.g., France) to be similar to z_j^y in area y (e.g., Italy) if $D_{KL}(P||Q) \leq 0.0002$ for this topic pair. Hence, tweets that belong to such topics are assumed to be semantically similar. Note that for computing KL divergence we always use joint vocabulary from the two datasets.

Finally, we assign sentiment to each topic based on the number of positive and negative tweets covered by the topic by computing the weighted average sentiment score over topics. Based on the computed sentiment scores of topics and the similarities of topics, we can then find semantically similar topics that have different sentiments. The topic pairs in two datasets of two geographical areas x and y are ranked by the Euclidean distance as follows:

$$dist(z_i^x, z_j^y) = \sqrt{(\#pos(z_i^x) - \#pos(z_j^y))^2 + (\#neg(z_i^x) - \#neg(z_j^y))^2} \quad (1)$$

Here, $\#pos(z_i^x)$ ($\#pos(z_j^y)$) returns the number of positive tweets about a topic z_i^x (z_j^y) in the dataset of geographical area x (y), and $\#neg(z_i^x)$ ($\#neg(z_j^y)$) returns the number of negative tweets about z_i^x (z_j^y).

3 Experiments

3.1 Dataset

We collected 8.81×10^6 English tweets produced by 7.41×10^5 unique Twitter's users in South-West Europe during 2016/4/30–12/21. Currently, we test the datasets of two countries: France and Italy. Table 1 shows the dataset statistics.

Table 1. Dataset statistics.

	France	Italy	Total
#Tweets	484,450	470,916	955,366
#Total unique terms	44,970	39,762	84,732
#Ave. unique terms per tweet	9.78	9.58	–
#Positive tweets: #Negative tweets	54k:27k	29k:12k	–

3.2 Metrics and Tested Methods

We use normalized Discounted Cumulated Gain (nDCG) at the following ranks: @5, @10, @20 and @30. Each result is judged using the 1-to-5 Likert scale, where 5 means the highest quality result and 1 indicates the lowest quality. We also compare all the methods using Mean Reciprocal Rank (MRR). The reciprocal rank of scored topics or terms is the multiplicative inverse of the rank of the first correct answer being the highest ranked result whose score is equal or above 4.

Topic Output Evaluation. For cultural studies of different geographical areas to show semantically similar but sentimentally different topics in those areas, we test two methods based on *Topic Modeling (1, 2)*:

1. **LDA without topic-topic similarity (LDA-J).** This method ranks topics on the joint dataset of different geographical areas by *Topic Modeling 1* using LDA based on their sentiment scores.
2. **LDA with topic-topic similarity (LDA-S).** This method ranks topic pairs on two datasets of different geographical areas by *Topic Modeling 2* using LDA based on their sentiment scores and topic-topic similarity.

Term Output Evaluation. We also return terms that have different sentiment values, while having the same semantics and syntactic forms. Such terms can be used for improving sentiment lexicons by geo-based customization. In this context, we set up one baseline and we propose two methods:

1. **Euclidean distance using tweet sentiments (ED-T).** This baseline ranks terms to find semantically similar but sentimentally different terms by the Euclidean distance scores using Eq. (1) where *#pos* (*#neg*) are simply the numbers of positive/negative tweets from the two datasets of different geographical areas, respectively. Here, we remove stopwords and low frequency terms if the frequency is less than 50 times in both datasets.
2. **Euclidean distance using topic sentiments (ED-Z).** This method ranks semantically similar but sentimentally different terms by the Euclidean distance scores in Eq. (1) where *#pos* (*#neg*) means the number of positive/negative topics on two datasets of different geographical areas. Here, we consider a term to belong to a given topic if $P(w|z) > 0.001$.
3. **Term probabilities with topic-topic similarity (TP-S).** We match topics in two datasets of different geographical areas by their similarity and then obtain top-ranked n ($n = 30$ by default) topic pairs (same as in **LDA-S**). Finally, this method ranks terms of the top-ranked topic pairs by computing the sum of their probabilities in the two datasets as given by LDA output within the top-ranked n topic pairs. The score of each term is the sum of its probabilities: $\sum_w P(w|z_i^x) \cdot P(w|z_j^y)$. Here, we remove stopwords and low frequency terms if the frequency is less than 50 times in both datasets.

3.3   Experimental Results

Results of Topic Output Evaluation. The main observation is that our proposed method **LDA-S** based on *Topic Modeling 2* outperforms **LDA-J** based on *Topic Modeling 1* and that **LDA-S** performs best according to nDCG@10, @20, @30, and MRR (see Table 2). Note that **LDA-J** does not perform topic-topic similarity but instead it is using the joint dataset of different geographical areas. Although **LDA-J** performs better than **LDA-S** according to nDCG@5, less important common topics in the joint dataset. Future work will improve **LDA-J** by using a new topic modeling based on Wikipedia corpus.

Results of Term Output Evaluation. The main observation is that our proposed methods **ED-Z** and **TP-S** outperform the baseline **ED-T** and that **ED-Z** performs best according to nDCG@5, @10, @20, and @30 (see Table 2). **ED-T** baseline does not perform any topic modeling. Instead it is just considering

Table 2. Results of topic (term) output evaluation in nDCG@5, 10, 20, 30, and MRR.

Output	Method	@5	@10	@20	@30	MRR
Topic	LDA-J	**0.898**	0.768	0.792	0.816	0.1
	LDA-S	0.861	**0.874**	**0.883**	**0.831**	**0.188**
Term	ED-T	0.826	0.763	0.762	0.784	0.077
	ED-Z	**0.887**	**0.893**	**0.835**	**0.836**	0.063
	TP-S	0.827	0.774	0.796	0.774	**0.1**

the difference of sentiments of the tweets containing a target term in the two datasets. This has the drawback of considering tweets where the terms do not have important role. It is necessary to detect topics and their key representative terms by using a topic modeling as our proposed methods. Comparing the results of the proposed methods **ED-Z** and **TP-S**, we found that **ED-Z** is better than **TP-S** according to nDCG@5, @10, @20, @30. Future work will combine **ED-Z** and **TP-S** to rank terms of top-ranked topic pairs based on **LDA-S** and compute the score of each term by the Euclidean distance scores of the number of positive/negative topics in the top-ranked topic pairs.

4   Conclusion

In this research, we have proposed a cross-cultural crowd sentiment analysis for finding similar topics or identical terms that are however subject to different sentiments as a part of wider cross-cultural study. In future, we will experiment using social media data in other geographical areas (e.g., Asia and America). We will also try to analyze cross-cultural crowd sentiment on each location based on the multilingual analysis of Twitter data similar to [5]. Furthermore, we plan to expand the current analysis method to recommend particular activities, products, services, events, or places to visit for a given segment of users.

Acknowledgments. This work was partially supported by MIC SCOPE (#171507010), and JSPS KAKENHI Grant Numbers 16H01722, 17K12686, 17H01822.

References

1. Blei, D.M., Ng, A.Y., Jordan, M.I.: Latent dirichlet allocation. J. Mach. Learn. Res. **3**(Jan), 993–1022 (2003)
2. Go, A., Bhayani, R., Huang, L.: Twitter sentiment classification using distant supervision. CS224N Project Report, Stanford 1, 12 (2009)
3. Kullback, S., Leibler, R.A.: On information and sufficiency. Ann. Math. Stat. **22**(1), 79–86 (1951)
4. McCollister, C.: Predicting author traits through topic modeling of multilingual social media text. Ph.D. thesis, University of Kansas (2016)
5. Mohd Pozi, M.S., Kawai, Y., Jatowt, A., Akiyama, T.: Sketching linguistic borders: mobility analysis on multilingual microbloggers. In: WWW 2017, pp. 825–826 (2017)
6. Park, J., Baek, Y.M., Cha, M.: Cross-cultural comparison of nonverbal cues in emoticons on twitter: evidence from big data analysis. J. Commun. **64**(2), 333–354 (2014)
7. Rudra, K., Rijhwani, S., Begum, R., Bali, K., Choudhury, M.: Understanding language preference for expression of opinion and sentiment: what do Hindi-English speakers do on twitter? In: EMNLP 2016, pp. 1131–1141 (2016)
8. Silva, T.H., de Melo, P.O.S.V., Almeida, J., Musolesi, M., Loureiro, A.: You are what you eat (and drink): identifying cultural boundaries by analyzing food and drink habits in foursquare. In: ICWSM 2014, (2014)

A Comparison of the Historical Entries in Wikipedia and Baidu Baike

Wenyi Shang[✉] [iD]

Department of Information Management, Peking University,
No. 5 Yiheyuan Road, Haidian District, Beijing, China
shang-wen-yi@pku.edu.cn

Abstract. This research chose two representative online encyclopedias, Wikipedia (English) and Baidu Baike, to compare their performance on historical entries. This research purposefully chose 6 entries and developed a framework to evaluate their performance in accuracy, breadth, depth, informativeness, conciseness and objectiveness. The result shows that: Wikipedia is superior in most cases while Baidu Baike is a little better in the entries on Chinese history. The operating mechanism is the main reason for it. The result implies that in the field of history, well-established online encyclopedias can be reliable for common users although improvement such as developing operating mechanisms is still needed.

Keywords: Wikipedia · Baidu Baike · Historical entries · Entry quality

1 Introduction

As a new way of creating and spreading knowledge, online encyclopedias are on the way of breaking the monopolization of the traditional academic world in knowledge dissemination. However, since they are edited by common users rather than scholars, their reliability is questioned. Among them Wikipedia receives the most attention, while Baidu Baike, a Chinese online encyclopedia is doubted by Chinese scholars.

Among the areas involved in online encyclopedias, humanity subjects, especially history, are attracting more and more attention since online resources are commonly used in popularization process of them. We thus focused on historical entries, evaluating the performance of Wikipedia and Baidu Baike. We try to develop a framework in order to evaluate their performance through multiple dimensions, therefore the research question is purposed as follows: how do Wikipedia and Baidu Baike perform in accuracy, breadth, depth, informativeness, conciseness and objectiveness?

2 Related Work

Rector (2008) did a research about the accuracy, breadth and depth of the historical article, directing at the reliability of historical entries in Wikipedia. The research provided a method of judging the quality of entries in online encyclopedias. The three factors were also emphasized by Spinellis and Louridas (2008).

© Springer International Publishing AG, part of Springer Nature 2018
G. Chowdhury et al. (Eds.): iConference 2018, LNCS 10766, pp. 74–80, 2018.
https://doi.org/10.1007/978-3-319-78105-1_9

More mature methods have been applied by researchers in order to judge the quality. Hu et al. (2007) have designed models based on author authority, review behavior and partial reviewership of contributors. Wöhner and Peters (2009) offered new metrics based on the lifecycle of articles, referring to the changes of contributions. Blumenstock (2008) proposed a simple metric, word count, to measure article quality.

Chinese scholars have noticed the difference of Wikipedia and Baidu Baike and tried to explain it. Liao (2014) used cultural factors to expound the difference. And in the following year, he focused on the mechanism of collaborative filtering and compared network gatekeeping of the encyclopedias (Liao 2015).

3   Methods

We used purposeful sampling method to choose 6 sample entries. We generated a list of randomly selected entries by continuously clicking the link of "random article", which is a function of Wikipedia that provides a link to another entry randomly. From the list, we chose first 6 historical entries based on the following criteria:

- They should also be contained in Baidu Baike.
- They should be attributed to the three categories, historic place, historical event and historical figure, with each category contains two entries.
- They should be attributed to three eras, ancient (before 476 A.D.), medieval (476 A.D.–1648 A.D.) and pre-modern (1648 A.D.–1914 A.D.). Each era should contain two entries. (Modern history is ignored since it may be effected by political reasons.)
- They should be attributed to four domains of World history, European, Asian (not including Chinese history), African, and American. Each domain contains one entry.
- Two entries on Chinese history are separately chosen.

The first 6 qualified entries selected from the list include *Fushimi* Castle, *Ciudad Bolivar*, Battle of *Torgau*, Battle of *Tangdao*, *Ezana* of *Axum* and *Fu Jian*.

In order to compare the above 6 entries in Wikipedia (English) and Baidu Baike, we divided the articles in both encyclopedias into many information items. Each piece of words that conveys a certain fact or judgement independently is considered as an "information item". Each item is given a binary value, where 1 means correct and 0 means incorrect, by referring to the authoritative historical works, traditional encyclopedias like Encyclopedia Britannica and news from official website. After judging all items, we got the precision rate of each encyclopedia.

Moreover, we also took breadth and depth into consideration. We picked out the information which appears in one encyclopedia but not in the other, and invited five graduates majored in history to give grades. Each information item received two grades: relevancy between the item and the article, and the depth of the item. The regulation of grading is based on a rubric of 0–5, where 0 means it is totally irrelative to the article or it is of no value at all, and 5 means it mightily matches the article or it is highly valuable in depth. After data collection, we summed up the grades to get the final grade of breadth of each entry. The formula is as follows (n is the number of information, and $G_j\,r_i$ stands for the grade of relevancy of information i by graduate j):

$$\sum_{j=1}^{5} \frac{\sum_{i=1}^{n} G_j r_i}{5} \tag{1}$$

And the grade of depth of each entry by each person is measured by the average score of every information. The formula is as follows (n is the number of information, and $G_j d_i$ stands for the grade of depth of information i by graduate j):

$$\sum_{j=1}^{5} \frac{\sum_{i=1}^{n} G_j d_i}{5n} \tag{2}$$

Both grades are measured with Pearson correlation coefficient in order to judge the inter-coder trustworthiness. Besides, because the grades given by graduates may be biased to some extent, the results were verified by referring to authoritative works.

The difference in languages was also considered in order to compare the informativeness. We fitted a function with a scaling factor of 1.9003 based on 5 paragraphs chosen from 5 entries in Encyclopedia Britannica and its Chinese translation. Based on researches such as Yu (1989), who calculated a factor of 1.735 and Wang (2004), who calculated a factor of 1.76, we affirmed our scale is reasonable since there is no obvious difference. Thus, the length is measured after dividing the Chinese words by the scale.

The framework of evaluation is shown in Fig. 1.

Fig. 1. Framework of evaluation

4 Findings

Wikipedia is superior in accuracy, breadth, depth and informativeness over Baidu Baike (except for the entry on Chinese history), and is more concise and objective Wikipedia has a higher precision rate in 5 out of 6 entries, and is 95.57% vs 88.03% in average. The difference between the encyclopedias in World history is clearer. Besides, the superiority in accuracy of Wikipedia appears in the usage of multimedia.

In the 4 entries on World history, Wikipedia has a higher grade in breadth. Moreover, in 4 entries out of 6, Wikipedia has a higher score of depth. The correlation is significant between most of the graders at the 0.05 level (except for grader D and E in relevancy, and grade A, C and B, E in depth), therefore, although still need further evaluation, results can be preliminarily explained as inter-coder reliable.

Table 1. Precision rate and average grades of breadth and depth (W stands for Wikipedia and B stands for Baidu Baike)

Entry	Precision rate of article		Precision rate of picture		Grade of breadth		Grade of depth	
	W	B	W	B	W	B	W	B
Fushimi Castle	95.65%	85.00%	100%	100%	41.4	23.8	3.44	3.44
Ciudad Bolivar	96.92%	94.12%	100%	N/A	79	12.2	3.93	3.13
Battle of Tangdao	92.00%	90.24%	100%	100%	23.4	40.2	3.50	3.04
Battle of Torgau	97.87%	85.71%	100%	0%	46.2	12.2	3.46	3.73
Ezana of Axum	95.45%	76.92%	100%	N/A	40	16.4	3.84	3.50
Fu Jian	95.52%	96.20%	N/A	50%	23.6	68	3.80	3.74
Average	95.57%	88.03%	100%	62.5%	42.3	28.8	3.66	3.43

Table 2. Information contained and normalized words per information items

Entry	Words contained		Number of information items		Number of pictures		Normalized words per information items	
	W	B (normalized)	W	B	W	B	W	B
Fushimi Castle	467	296	23	20	3	9	38.57	28.10
Ciudad Bolivar	1305	207	65	17	15	0	38.15	23.18
Battle of Tangdao	479	1361	25	41	1	2	36.40	63.10
Battle of Torgau	1049	631	47	28	3	1	42.40	42.86
Ezana of Axum	459	484	22	13	1	0	39.64	70.69
Fu Jian	1650	1849	67	79	0	2	67	44.48
Average	901.5	804.7	41.5	33	3.8	2.3	43.70	45.49

Wikipedia contains more words (normalized) in 3 out of 6 entries, however, since more words may result from redundancy, we calculated the number of information items in both encyclopedias to compare informativeness more accurately. Under this method, Wikipedia contains more information in all 4 entries on world history. Moreover, the number of pictures appearing in the 6 entries adds up to 23 in Wikipedia, while only 14 appear in Baidu Baike. Therefore, Wikipedia is more informative in general.

In order to compare the conciseness, we divided the number of normalized words by the number of information items in each entry, and found that the result is 45.40 in Baidu Baike and 40.32 in Wikipedia in average, implying Wikipedia is more concise.

We also judged their performance on objectiveness. In Wikipedia, there is no obvious subjective description in any of the entries, however, Baidu Baike showed non-neutrality especially in entries on Chinese history. For instance, in the entry Fu Jian, when Baidu Baike described the event of his coronation, it used the description "he arrogated the title of 'heavenly prince'", showing a strong emotional tendency.

Baidu Baike performs a little better in the entries on Chinese history

Above data shows that although Wikipedia is better under most circumstances, Baidu Baike is somewhat better in entries on Chinese history. Table 1 shows that the precision rate is relatively close in the entries on Chinese history, and that Baidu Baike performs better in breadth on those entries. Table 2 suggests that it contains more information.

5   Discussion

Referring to previous researches and studying the mechanisms of the encyclopedias, we try to briefly explain the findings in chapter 4.

The difference of accuracy may result from the fact that unlike Wikipedia, Baidu Baike lacks a mature consultation system to alleviate the problem caused by the editors' casualness. Because participation behavior of editors is mainly driven by interest, they lack enough motivation for precise verification. However, Wikipedia provides a way for consulting, the talk page. It is an auxiliary tool for the editors to discuss the content and correct the error, according to Wang (2004), which results in its high accuracy.

The difference of breadth results from the better organizing system and taxonomy of Wikipedia. Jia and Li (2013) found that Wikipedia has various taxonomies while Baidu Baike has only one, therefore entries in Wikipedia interact with each other more intimately. So more related entries will be considered when the editor is editing an entry. The result of depth is highly influenced by the talk page of Wikipedia, which provides editors a means to share information, making the editors with better academic attainment to participate more easily. Besides, the weakness in the academic field of World History in China also results in relative less valuable source for the editors.

The interest motivation influenced the result on informativeness. Editors tend not to include information beyond their interest, while Wikipedia editors can add information more easily with the help of talk page. The difference in conciseness can be attributed to the consultation system of Wikipedia, and that in objectiveness is a result of the neutrality principle. The first basic principle of Wikipedia is "articles should present an unbiased or neutral description of the entry," in contrast, there is no such restraint for editors of Baidu Baike. Personal emotional tendency has an impact on the words used in the entries. For instance, traditional view on legitimacy resulted in biased attitude.

Finally, resulted from a lack of the ancient books, study in the field of Chinese history in western world is relatively insufficient. In Baidu Baike, entry *Fu Jian* is completely based on *Jin Shu*, however, citations of ancient books in entries on Chinese history in Wikipedia are relatively insufficient. The lack of usage of ancient books resulted from language gap seriously influences Wikipedia's performance on Chinese history.

6   Conclusion

The result shows that Wikipedia is superior in general, while Baidu Baike is a little better in entries on Chinese history. Unlike previous studies that paid attention mainly on one encyclopedia, the research focused on the difference between historical entries of Wikipedia and Baidu Baike, which has never been studied previously.

Improvement is needed since the research is still preliminary. As a small-scale study, the size of sample needs increment, and the inter-coder trustworthiness need further analysis. Besides, more factors can be included in, such as relationship between entries and qualities of links provided. Future study may extend the research field to other subjects. Although difference between subjects results in different methods for collecting and analyzing data, the framework for evaluation is repeatable. It can be adopted in other studies on online encyclopedias, as well as specific methods such as dividing the article into information items and normalizing the words in different languages.

Based on findings of the study, we come to the conclusion that well-established online encyclopedias like Wikipedia can be reliable for common users in the field of history, proper evaluation on the online encyclopedias should not be totally negative. However, limitations still exist. Improving the reliability of online encyclopedias is not only of necessity, but is of great importance since they deeply influence the process of knowledge dissemination as well.

Online encyclopedias may improve their qualities by developing their operating mechanism. Building a better-organized knowledge community can be a good idea, which means constructing a communication platform for professionals to share ideas.

Moreover, since the development of Digital Humanities acts as an avoidable tendency, online encyclopedias should pay more attention to the quality of the historical entries and other entries on humanity subjects, trying to involve themselves in the tendency. In this way, they can fully exploit their advantages in the digitalization era and play a more important role in dissemination and development of humanity knowledge.

References

Blumenstock, J.E.: Size matters: word count as a measure of quality on Wikipedia. In: International Conference on World Wide Web, Peking, China (2008)

Hu, M., Lim, E.P., Sun, A., Lauw, H.W., Vuong, B.Q.: Conference on Information and Knowledge Management, Lisbon, Portugal (2007)

Jia, J., Li, Y.: Comparative analysis of the category organization systems of the Chinese Wikipedia and Baidu Baike. Inf. Stud.: Theory Appl. (6), 114–118 (2013). (Chinese)

Liao, H.: The cultural politics of user-generated encyclopedias: comparing Chinese Wikipedia and Baidu Baike. Unpublished doctor's thesis. University of Oxford, Oxford, UK (2014)

Liao, H.: Harnessing the power of collaborative filtering. Comparing the network gatekeeping of Baidu Baike and Chinese Wikipedia. China Perspectives, (4) (2015). http://chinaperspectives.revues.org/6854

Rector, L.H.: Comparison of Wikipedia and other encyclopedias for accuracy, breadth, and depth in historical articles. Ref. Serv. Rev. **36**(1), 7–22 (2008)

Spinellis, D., Louridas, P.: The collaborative organization of knowledge. Commun. ACM **51**(8), 68–73 (2008)

Wang, F.: Enlightenments of synergic edition system on the networking of traditional encyclopedias. Sci. Technol. Publ. (11), 76–80 (2014). (Chinese)

Wang, K.: The Development and Application of Bilingual Corpus. Foreign Language Teaching and Research Press, Beijing (2004). (Chinese)

Wöhner, T., Peters, R.: Assessing the quality of Wikipedia articles with lifecycle based metrics. In: International Symposium on Wikis, Orlando, Florida, USA (2009)

Yu, Y.: The Selected Readings and Translation of English and American Masterpieces. Xi'an Jiaotong University Press, Xi'an (1989). (Chinese)

Sentiments in Wikipedia Articles for Deletion Discussions

Lu Xiao[(⊠)] [iD] and Niraj Sitaula[(⊠)]

Syracuse University, Syracuse, NY 13244, USA
{lxiao04,nsitaula}@syr.edu

Abstract. Wikipedia provides a discussion forum, namely, Article for Deletion forum, for people to deliberate about whether or not an article should be deleted from the site. In this paper, we present interesting correlation between outcomes of the discussion and number of sentiments in the comments with different intensity. We performed sentiment analysis on 37,761 AfD discussions with 156,415 top-level comments and explored relationship between outcomes of the discussion and sentiments in the comments. Our preliminary work suggests: discussion that have keep or other outcomes have more than expected positive sentiment, whereas discussions that have delete outcomes have more than expected negative and neutral sentiment. This result shows that there tends to be positive sentiment in the comment when Wikipedia users suggest not to delete the article. This observation of differences in sentiments also encourages to further study influence of sentiments in decision making or outcome of the discussions. Our future analysis will include threaded comments, and examine the relationship between a discussion's sentiment and its other properties such as topic of the article and the characteristics of the participating users.

Keywords: Wikipedia · Sentiment analysis · Online discussion

1 Introduction

As a decentralized peer production system, Wikipedia uses various strategies to monitor and control the quality of the articles. One of which is its mechanisms for deleting articles from Wikipedia. According to the Deletion Discussion mechanism, an article proposed to be deleted may undergo the community discussion before a decision is made (e.g., to delete the article or to keep it). The article tagged for Deletion Discussion is called "Article for Deletion" (hereafter: AfD). The user who nominates an article for Deletion Discussion needs to provide a rationale to justify his nomination (i.e., the statement in the figure "Appears to not meet WP:GNG for reliable secondary sources to confirm notability"). In an AfD discussion, participants offer their opinions on what to do with this article as top-level comments. They may also respond to someone else' opinions by embedding their comments below the corresponding top-level comments. At the end of the discussion (e.g., after a week or two), a user who did not participate in this AfD discussion will review the discussion content and make the final decision. Wikipedia policy requires that the AfD decision should be based on the rationales provided by the participants.

© Springer International Publishing AG, part of Springer Nature 2018
G. Chowdhury et al. (Eds.): iConference 2018, LNCS 10766, pp. 81–86, 2018.
https://doi.org/10.1007/978-3-319-78105-1_10

While researchers have explored the sentiment aspect of Wikipedia talk pages' discussions (e.g., [2, 6, 10]), the sentiments in Wikipedia AfD discussions have not been looked at, not to say the role of sentiments in the decision-making process about the article.

Our work makes initial step to fill this gap and understand the sentiment aspect of AfD discussions along with its role in the discussion process and outcomes. We report here our current status of the research activities. Specifically, we examined the sentiment of the top-level comments in about 37,761 AfD discussions and their percentages in the AfD discussions of different outcomes.

2 Related Work

"On Wikipedia, notability is a test used by editors to decide whether a given topic warrants its own article" (https://en.wikipedia.org/wiki/Wikipedia:Notability). Lam and Riedl [4] found that the most common reason for deleting an article is its lack of notability. A later content analysis study (N = 229 AfD discussions) also found that notability is the most commonly used rationale for keeping or deleting an article [11]. These studies suggest that the discussions are logical and follow Wikipedia's policies in general.

On the other hand, it has been shown that besides notability of the article an AfD decision can be affected by various factors. For example, opinions offered at the early stage of an AfD discussion influence the later opinions [9]. Groups formed naturally and groups with a moderate diversity of newcomer and expert participants make better decision [5]. Additionally, Xiao and Askin [11] found an AfD discussion that has votes other than keep or delete (e.g., merge) is more likely to be suggested for actions other than delete. The authors also found that certain categories of an article correlates with the likelihood of the article to be deleted. For example, articles about people, for-profit organizations, or definitions are slightly more likely to be deleted than expected, while articles about locations or events are more likely to be kept than expected, and articles about nonprofit organizations and media are more likely to be suggested for other options (e.g., merge, redirect, etc.) than expected.

However, the sentiment in AfD discussions, and whether and how it affects the final decision has not been explored. Nonetheless, while all the AfD discussion data are available online, these earlier studies only had small samples, which made it challenging to generalize their findings to the AfD discussion study. Hence, our work explored larger number of AfD discussion and presents results from analyzing sentiments in the comments in the discussions.

3 Our AfD Corpus for Sentiment Analysis

Wikipedia manages the AfDs based on the date they are proposed for Deletion Discussion. The content of each proposed date is publicly accessible through URLs. An AfD discussion consists of several parts: article title, nomination reason, participants' votes, and outcome. A nomination reason explains why the article is proposed for deletion. A typical participant's vote includes the participant's opinion on the outcome of the article such as keep or delete, and the rationale to justify his/her vote. An outcome includes the final decision regarding the article and the rationale of this decision. Each of these three parts ends with a user signature. A user's signature consists of a username, and a timestamp (date and time).

Our PHP script visited the web sites through the URLs of the proposed dates from May 15, 2013, to May 15, 2015 (i.e., 720 dates) and stored the HTML content. These HTML pages become our raw data. We then applied regular expressions and filtered the noise from the data, e.g., the missing HTML tags, the mis-formatted user signature, etc. There are three possible views of an AfD vote or its outcome according to our database design: keep, delete, and other (Table 1).

Table 1. The mapping between a comment's view in AfD to the database

Participant's vote in following choices	Vote stored a
Strong delete, speedy delete, delete, weak delete	Delete
Weak keep, keep	Keep
Note, comment, question, speedy close, closing administrator, relisted, text, reviews, speedy decline, withdraw, userfy, move and dab, move, oppose, merge, redirect, redirect and merge	Other

Of the 183,007 top-level comments in the corpus, we observed that there comments which were not associated with any particular vote. In other words, they were not the justifications of participants' opinions. Examples of such comments are "Please add new comments below this notice. Thanks", "Please add new comments below this notice. Thanks, Mz7 (talk) 19:27, 15 May 2014 (UTC)", "Note: This debate has been included in the list of Football-related deletion discussions. Ascii002Talk Contribs GuestBook 12:24, 23 August 2014 (UTC)", and "Note: This debate has been included in the list of......", in comments text. There were also comments with only text "–" followed by username, for e.g. "Delete–Rpclod (talk) 02:42, 16 July 2014 (UTC)".

After removing these comments, we had 156,415 comments and we noticed that the median of the comments was found to be 2 and average number of sentences in each comment was found to be close to 2.62. In addition, distribution of outcomes in 37,761 AfD discussions consisted 21,589 as Delete, 8,196 as Other, and 7,976 as Keep.

4 Sentiment Analysis of Our AfD Corpus

Given the large number of sentences in this corpus, it is difficult and time consuming to manually annotate all the sentences for their sentiments. Therefore, we used available classifier to classify the polarity and intensity of a comment's sentiment.

4.1 Sentiment Classification

We preprocessed the data using nltk [1] as follows:

- Unwanted hyperlinks and html tags embedded in the comments were cleaned.
- Unwanted characters were also removed for e.g. \r\n, -, *comma (,), 's*, and others.
- Capitalization and punctuations were retained as it is.

To classify the sentiment of a sentence, we used VADER which stands for Valence Aware Dictionary for sentiment Reasoning [3]. Built with corpus like movie reviews, technical product reviews, opinion news article, VADER has been shown to perform better than many other methods in predicting sentiments in Social Media Text and accounts for different intensity of a sentiment [3].

4.2   Sentiment Analysis Results

We used the VADER library from nltk [1] library for the sentiment classifications. First we used VADER to find the sentiment of a comment, and then based on the sentiments of all the top-level comments of a discussion, we calculate the sentiment of the discussion by majority of the sentiments present in the discussion. When two or more sentiments with majority were found in discussion, to break the ties 100 random selection among the sentiments were taken and the one that occurred maximum number of times was picked as the sentiment of the discussion.

The result of sentiment labeling is shown in Table 2 along with the result from the classification. As shown in the table, majority of the discussions were neutral with respect to the sentiment of their content. This result is consistent with prior studies that AfD discussions are in general rational [11].

Table 2. Sentiment label distribution

Label	Comments count	% of comments	Discussion count	% of discussion
Positive	29886	19.11%	5697	15.09%
Neutral	111754	71.45%	30041	79.55%
Negative	14775	9.45%	2023	5.36%

For each discussion labeled with majority of sentiment, we observe the count of different votes i.e. Delete, Keep, and Other. This data is summarized in Table 3. Note that neutral means the emotional tone is neutral, not that the opinion on whether not to delete the article is neutral. We conducted a chi-square test based on this result and obtained a p-value < 0.001.

Table 3. Sentiment labels on discussion outcomes

Label	Delete discussion count	Other discussion count	Keep discussion count
Negative	1488	309	226
Neutral	17641	6389	6011
Positive	2460	1498	1739

The test shows the following results. Discussions that had delete outcome are more than expected to have negative and neutral sentiment and less than expected to have positive sentiment. Discussions that had keep or other outcome are more than expected to have positive sentiment and less than expected to have negative and neutral sentiment.

5 Discussion and Conclusion

When the inclusion of an article in Wikipedia article is questioned, Wikipedia may start an open discussion that encourages Wikipedia users to offer their opinions along with their reasoning. Such a discussion is called an Article for Deletion (AfD) discussion. While researchers have explored various aspects of AfD discussions (e.g., [5, 11]), the sentiments in these discussions have not been explored.

Addressing this gap, we seek to understand the sentiment aspect of AfD discussions and its role in the discussion process and outcome. Our analysis of 156,415 top-level comments in 37,761 discussions suggest that there is a correlation between an AfD discussion's sentiment and its outcome. The results showed that discussions with outcomes of keep or other have more than expected positive sentiment, whereas more than expected negative and neutral sentiment were found in discussions with delete as outcomes. While the correlation of positive and negative sentiment with the keep and delete discussion outcome is expected, we find it particularly interesting the correlation of neutral sentiment with the discussion outcome. The fact that delete discussions had more than expected neutral discussions indicates that even when participants argue for deleting the articles their comments were not that emotional hence more than expected neutral discussions were observed. The fact that keep or other discussions that had less than expected neutral discussions indicates that when users suggest not to delete the article there tends to be a positive sentiment than just a neutral statement. Prior studies have shown that in AfD discussions Wikipedia users tend to offer advice on how to improve the articles and be inclusive on controversial articles, as opposed to just arguing to delete or keep the article [11]. Our analysis result is consistent with this previous finding, as it indicates a constructive and inclusive discussion context.

In addition, our current analysis has only considered top-level comments. We next will include the threaded comments in our analysis, and examine the relationship between a discussion's sentiment and its other properties such as the topic of the article and the characteristics of the participating users. Another limitation of our study is the lack of performance measure for VADER for AfD discussion data. According to [3], VADER has F-1 measure of .63 for classifying the sentiment of an Amazon product review (performance of a human annotator is .85). While AfD comments are somewhat comparable with a product review, it would have been better if the performance of VADER was evaluated with a small sample of AfD discussion data before applying it to all the discussion comments. On the other hand, VADER is reported to be among the best sentiment prediction tool available for classifying social media texts and online review comments [7].

Earlier work in policy making has shown that the community sentiments have great influence in decision making processes of law makers [8]. It has also been shown that sentiment as a feature in a machine learning model has improved the prediction of decision making in process of loan granting [12]. As we have observed relationships between discussion's sentiment and its decision outcome, it will be interesting to explore the predictive power of an AfD discussion's sentiment on the outcome of the discussion.

References

1. Bird, S., Klein, E., Loper, E.: Natural Language Processing with Python: Analyzing Text with the Natural Language Toolkit. OReilly Media Inc., Sebastopol (2009)
2. Danescu-Niculescu-Mizil, C., Sudhof, M., Jurafsky, D., Leskovec, J., Potts, C.: A computational approach to politeness with application to social factors. arXiv preprint arXiv:1306.6078 (2013)
3. Hutto, C.J., Gilbert, E.E.: VADER: a parsimonious rule-based model for sentiment analysis of social media text. In: Eighth International Conference on Weblogs and Social Media (ICWSM-2014), Ann Arbor, MI, June 2014
4. Lam, S.T.K., Riedl, J.: Is Wikipedia growing a longer tail? In: Proceedings of the ACM 2009 International Conference on Supporting Group Work, pp. 105–114 (2009)
5. Lam, S.K., Karim, J., Riedl, J.: The effects of group composition on decision quality in a social production community. In: Proceedings of the 16th ACM International Conference on Supporting Group Work, pp. 55–64 (2010)
6. Laniado, D., Kaltenbrunner, A., Castillo, C., Morell, M.F.: Emotions and dialogue in a peer-production community: the case of Wikipedia. In: Proceedings of the Eighth Annual International Symposium on Wikis and Open Collaboration, p. 9. ACM (2012)
7. Ribeiro, F.N., Araújo, M., Gonçalves, P., Gonçalves, M.A., Benevenuto, F.: SentiBench-a benchmark comparison of state-of-the-practice sentiment analysis methods. EPJ Data Sci. 5 (1), 1–29 (2016)
8. Sigillo, A.E., Sicafuse, L.L.: The influence of media and community sentiment on policy decision-making. In: Miller, M., Blumenthal, J., Chamberlain, J. (eds.) Handbook of Community Sentiment, pp. 29–42. Springer, New York (2015). https://doi.org/10.1007/978-1-4939-1899-7_2
9. Taraborelli, D., Ciampaglia, G.L.: Beyond notability. Collective deliberation on content inclusion in Wikipedia. In: Proceedings of the 4th IEEE International Conference on Self-Adaptive and Self-Organizing Systems (SASO), pp. 122–125 (2010)
10. Wang, L., Cardie, C.: A piece of my mind: a sentiment analysis approach for online dispute detection. arXiv preprint arXiv:1606.05704 (2016)
11. Xiao, L., Askin, N.: What influences online deliberation? A Wikipedia study. J. Am. Soc. Inf. Sci. Technol. 65(5), 898–910 (2014)
12. Zhang, D., Xu, W., Zhu, Y., Zhang, X.: Can sentiment analysis help mimic decision-making process of loan granting? A novel credit risk evaluation approach using GMKL model. In: 2015 48th Hawaii International Conference on System Sciences (HICSS), pp. 949–958. IEEE, January 2015

Auto-Tracking Controversial Topics in Social-Media-Based Customer Dialog: A Case Study on Starbucks

Bei Yu[(⊠)] and Yihan Yu

Syracuse University, Syracuse, NY 13244, USA
{byu, yyu41}@syr.edu

Abstract. This study proposed and validated a topic modeling-based approach for auto-tracking customer dialog on social media, using Starbucks as a case study because of its pioneering social media practice in service industry. A topic model was fit based on nearly 150,000 customer comments posted to Starbucks' Facebook page in 2013. This model was able to identify not only business-related topics, such as customer responses to marketing campaigns, but also controversial topics regarding community involvement and corporate social responsibility, such as gay, gun, and government. Guided by this topic model, each topic's evolving dynamics and patterns of user participation were further revealed, providing a bird's-eye view of the topics and their evolution. The case study has demonstrated that the proposed approach can effectively track the main themes in the customer dialog on social media, zoom in on the controversial topics, measure their time spans, and locate the participants and the vocal activists. Such information would be valuable input for companies to design their intervention strategies and evaluate the outcomes in social media discussions.

Keywords: Topic modeling · Text mining · Customer dialog
Social media

1 Introduction

Nowadays, companies often use social media to engage customers and promote their products, services, brands, and reputation (Hays et al. 2013). Conversely, customers also take their opinions to social media with the belief that they can influence business practices by voicing opinions online. Gallaugher and Ransbotham (2010) conceptualized the social-media based customer dialog as a framework with three components (3M model): Megaphone, Magnet, and Monitor. Companies can use social media as a Megaphone to share messages with the world. They can also establish their social media presence as a Magnet to attract feedback from customers. Because customers may talk to each other on companies' social media platform, companies can even Monitor the inter-customer dialog, which they might not be able to directly observe through traditional media.

On the other hand, the openness of social media creates a number of challenges for managing the customer dialog, such as criticism, offensive comments, and rumors

© Springer International Publishing AG, part of Springer Nature 2018
G. Chowdhury et al. (Eds.): iConference 2018, LNCS 10766, pp. 87–96, 2018.
https://doi.org/10.1007/978-3-319-78105-1_11

(Gallaugher and Ransbotham 2010). For example, after Starbucks posted a promotion message on its gift card, some comments were responding to the promotion, e.g. "*I will buy few for gifts:))))*", some went off to other business practice topics, such as "*I was disappointed with their decision to stop the free coffee drink when purchasing a pound of coffee.*", and some would talk about the company's involvement in social issues, e.g. "*Starbucks has good coffee but supports gay rights.*" The last type of comments has ventured away from the company's business practice and into the field of community involvement and corporate social responsibilities (CSR) (Holcomb et al. 2007; Men and Tsai 2012). When customers engage in debate on controversial topics, companies will have to respond with an appropriate public relation management strategy (Coombs 2007) to avoid reputation damage.

Therefore, actively monitoring customer comments is critical for swift and effective response. The more traffic a company's social media platform attracts, the more challenging it becomes to track and address these controversial topics in customer dialog. Furthermore, since this type of comments is scattered around under all company posts, traditional methods of random sampling or keyword search fall short when the total number of comments is huge. For instance, our data collection shows that Starbucks received $\sim 150,000$ comments in 2013 and $\sim 180,000$ in 2014. The average number of comments on one post was 681 in 2013 and rose to 1079 in 2014.

In this study, we propose a topic modeling based method to automatically track the controversial topics in customer dialog on social media, monitor their evolving dynamics over time, and assess the level of user participation in these discussions. Using the 2013 Facebook comments on the Starbucks' wall as a case study, we seek to validate this approach and answer the research question whether this approach is effective in auto-tracking controversial topics in social-media based customer dialog.

2 Related Work

2.1 Content Analysis of Social Media in the Service Industry

To date, many studies have examined the company-initiated messages on social media. For example, Waters et al. (2009) conducted traditional content analysis to examine 275 Facebook profiles of nonprofit organizations. Some studies examined the relationship between the content of company posts and the customer feedback. For example, Kwok and Yu (2013) developed a two-tier taxonomy of Facebook messages from hospitality companies and found that conversational messages received more feedback than sales/marketing messages. Some studies focused on correlational analysis between customer feedback and other service quality measures. For example, Timian et al. (2013) found the number of likes that a hospital received on Facebook correlates with traditional measure of patient recommendation rate.

However, the main focus in these studies was on companies' messages and their receptions in quantitative measures such as the number of likes. These analyses addressed the Megaphone and Magnet components in the 3M model (Gallaugher and Ransbotham 2010), but left out the Monitor of customer dialog. Social media enables conversation between companies and customers; however, it also enables conversations that are not led by companies: directly talk between customers. This kind of interaction challenges traditional marketing communications (Mangold and Faulds 2009) because people are influenced more by communication between each other than from information broadcast by media (Lazarsfeld et al. 1968). Brown et al. (2007) argue that the action between customers online mainly consists of Word of Mouth (WOM) communication. This kind of communication is crucial for companies to use social media in a more productive way. Thus, analyzing user comments on social networks such as Facebook has become an increasingly important research topic. Unfortunately, the content of consumer comments was rarely systematically analyzed, probably due to the large amount qualitative data, which requires text mining techniques for analysis (He et al. 2013).

2.2   Topic Modeling

Topic modeling is a computational method that facilitates exploratory analysis of a large text collection. Assuming a text collection is generated based on a distribution of K topics, and each text document consists of these topics with various proportions, a topic modeling algorithm can fit a topic model that summarizes the main topics of a text collection and the topic distribution in each document.

LDA (Blei et al. 2003) has been used frequently as a technique for topic modeling of large text documents. For example, Maskeri et al. (2008) used LDA to explore business domain topics from source code Linked LDA, an extension of LDA, is used to filter spam information on web (Bíró et al. 2009). The Mallet topic modeling package (McCallum, 2002) contains an extremely fast algorithm, and has been used in many applications such as exploring the fashion trends in Vogue magazine in the last 100 years (Leonard 2014), the library engagement strategies on Twitter (Zou et al. 2015), and trends in the historical newspapers (Yang et al. 2011).

2.3   Studies on Starbucks' Social Media Strategy

Starbucks has been considered a role model in industry for its use of social media (West 2012). Prior research has often used Starbucks as an exemplar case (Gallaugher and Ransbotham 2010). While talking with customers about its products, store locations, and cultures on social media, Starbucks also maintains its customers' acceptance and support of its innovations (Chua and Banerjee 2013). Starbucks has also used more crisis communication practices than other organizations (Kim 2013). In 2010, Starbucks' then VP for brand and online content claimed that social media was an effective tool to stop rumors and misinformation. This distinction is the main reason why we chose Starbucks as the sample case in our study.

3   Method

Our research method consisted of multiple steps. First, we chose Starbucks as the study case and downloaded Facebook customer comments from 2013. We then used Mallet to summarize the main topics that consumers focused on, and thus identified controversial topics. After that, we visualized the dynamics of each controversial topic during 2013, and associated the key speakers on these topics.

3.1 Data Preparation

This study focuses on how customer comments on Starbucks' posts. Posts and comments in 2013 were downloaded from Starbucks' official Facebook page using the software package Facepager (Keyling and Jünger 2013). In 2013, Starbucks posted both photo messages (with accompanying text) and pure text status messages. According to Kwok et al. (2015), photo posts have replaced text updates as the main media type on Facebook. Therefore, we removed the text status updates and focused on photo posts only. Overall, we collected 218 photo posts and 148,562 comments.

3.2 Modeling Topics in Customer Comments

To explore the main topics in Starbucks' user comments, we chose to use the topic modeling algorithm implemented in the software package Mallet-2.0.7. Given a collection of text documents as input and a pre-selected value K, the algorithm assumes each document is more or less relevant to K number of topics. It then fits K topic clusters from the data, each topic being represented by a list of significant keywords (see a topic model in Table 1). For each document, the topic model assigns a distribution of probabilities to indicate the document's relevance to all topics (topic composition, see example in Table 2). For our data, all comments to one post are aggregated into one document, and thus 218 large documents in total were sent to Mallet for topic modeling. Such transformation would allow us to track the topic distribution in all comments to each Starbucks post.

A major challenge to accurate topic modeling is choosing the appropriate topic number K. Choosing a small K would result in a few big clusters that cover multiple topics, while choosing a large K would split similar topics to multiple clusters. Some studies have explored approaches to tune K, but insofar the problem is not fully solved (Chang et al. 2009; Greene et al. 2014).

In this study, we used two approaches to find the best K. The first approach was a qualitative, manual process. We manually read a sample of comments until we identified five topics. We manually labeled them as Tastes, Government, Gift Card, Deal, and Coffee. We then ran LDA from $K = 5$ and increased K by one every time. For each run, we checked whether the manually identified topics were split to multiple topic clusters. We found that the split occurred when $K > 15$. Therefore, we chose 15 as the best choice for K.

For a robustness check, we used the second approach which was a mathematical measure named "term-centric stability" (Greene et al. 2014) to test the topic model's stability. Given a range of K, this measure calculates a stability score for each K, and the K value with highest stability is considered the best choice. We chose the range of K from 5 to 50. We have explained our manual approach for determining the lower bound 5, and we chose 50 as the upper bound because it is a very large number for K based on prior literature. Figure 1. plots the stability test result, which shows that

Table 1. Topic clusters.

Topic	Keywords
Non-English	Starbucks; coffee; lol; de; love; dog; en; rico; drink; el; mi; la; es; hand; yo; se; nice; good; uno
Location	Portland; seattle; place; love; Oregon; pike; river; Willamette; market; miss; birthday; ve; city; Chicago; lake; dr; store; visit; home
Troops	Starbucks; coffee; support; don; troops; people; company; military; good; money; don't; post; send; doesn; work; sucks; http; true; give
Taste	Good; yummy; yum; love; drink; delicious; caramel; make; mocha; favorite; sounds; milk; starbucks; hazelnut; taste; sugar; iced; vanilla; omg
Free drink	Starbucks; lol; free; tomorrow; today; drink; work; buy; ll; holiday; didn; drinks; yay; lets; date; thought; told; stores; mine
Happy hour	Happy; starbucks; hour; love; green; mocha; frap; wait; today; Frappuccino; tea; lol; day; time; frapp; half; coconut; back; caramel
Praise	Starbucks; love; nice; awesome; cool; wow; lol; check; store; great; make; picture; don; idea; stores; pretty; life; amazing; beautiful
Flavor	Tea; orange; good; drink; Valencia; love; refresher; starbucks; iced; ice; berry; tastes; taste; tang; lime; lemonade; back; passion; peach
Gay	Marriage; espresso; gay; business; people; ceo; traditional; god; shot; don; thought; company; lol; face; man; brain; Christians; bad; make
Coffee	Coffee; love; starbucks; cup; roast; favorite; great; blonde; place; tea; miss; morning; café; ve; blend; black; beans; good; day
Promotion	Free; day; drink; starbucks; don; people; great; pay; give; store; make; time; morning; good; buy; deal; back; cup; money
Season	Pumpkin; spice; latte; love; fall; psl; favorite; back; year; caramel; mocha; peppermint; starbucks; gingerbread; wait; red; time; yay; season
Christmas	Love; Christmas; starbucks; cup; cups; blend; mug; coffee; year; gift; buy; tumbler; good; merry; bought; great; nice; mugs; holiday
Gift card	Card; starbucks; gold; gift; gaga; cards; free; lady; love; registered; rewards; troops; program; didn; drink; members; ve; support; seahawks
Gun&gov	Gun; people; guns; government; carry; amendment; pay; rights; stop; make; care; law; Obama; open; don; country; time; congress; petition

Table 2. Topic distribution.

Post message	"Cardamom, the recognizable spice of Chai makes its debut in our new Vanilla Spice Latte."			
Non-English	Location	**Troops**	Taste	Free drink
0.0191	0.0072	**0.0125**	0.5857	0.0179
Happy hour	Praise	Flavor	**Gay**	Coffee
0.01	0.0331	0.026	**0.0047**	0.0461
Promotion	Season	Christmas	Gift card	**Gun&Gov**
0.1213	0.0936	0.0125	0.0039	**0.0064**

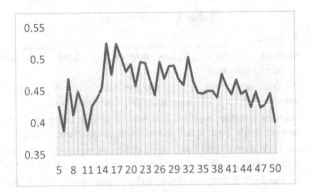

Fig. 1. Stability distribution

when $K = 15$, the topic model reaches the highest stability 0.5247. This result is consistent with our manual tuning result. We thus confirmed $K = 15$ as the best choice.

4 Result

4.1 Basic Data Summary

We have collected 148,562 comments made by 112,495 consumers. Among them, 92,890 people (82.6%) commented only once in 2013. The most vocal user gave 204 comments. This phenomenon is similar to other observations of long tails in social media participation (e.g. Mustafaraj et al. 2011).

4.2 Topic Clusters

Table 1 shows the top keywords for each of the 15 topics in the topic model. We manually labeled each topic based on the top keywords. Among the 15 topics 3 were controversial social topics: Troops, Gay, and Gun&gov. All other topics were about Starbucks products or services. The topic discoveries match with the major news events on Starbucks in 2013. Below is brief description of the social topics' context:

- Troops – a rumor said Starbucks does not support US troops. Although Starbucks has rebutted multiple times, the rumor enjoyed longevity.
- Gay – the Starbucks CEO re-stated support for gay marriage on March 21st, 2013. In 2012, Starbucks had announced support to legalize gay marriage (CNN 2013).
- Gun&gov – On September 17th, 2013, the Starbucks' CEO issued an open letter to ask customers to keep guns out of the Starbucks coffee shops. On October 10th, the CEO urged customers to sign the petition for government reopen. Note that it would be better if the topic modeling algorithm could divide this cluster to a gun cluster and a government shutdown topic. But probably because the two topics share some keywords, they were grouped together.

Table 2 shows the distribution of topic probabilities for one document containing comments on a specific post *"Cardamom, the recognizable spice of Chai makes its debut in our new Vanilla Spice Latte."* In this table, the biggest probability is Taste with a probability of 0.5857, meaning it accounts for 58.57% of the comments. The three social topics account for 2.36% of the comments under this post.

4.3 Topic Dynamics

Given each document's time stamp and topic composition, we then visualize the trend of customers' attention to social topics over time. For the Gun&gov topic depicted in Fig. 2, the topic trend shows the discussion had been heating up since July, peaked around September (when the open letter was issued), was followed by a Starbucks petition for the government to reopen after the 2013 federal shutdown, and resonated until the topic lost attention in November. In Fig. 3, the consumer attention to the Gay topic peaked around the March 21 and had a short attention span. In Fig. 4, the attention to the rumor that Starbucks does not support US troops seemed to linger throughout the year, with more attention received in the first half of the year.

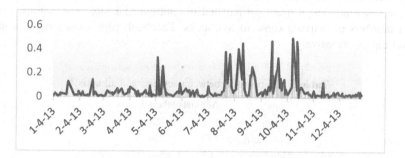

Fig. 2. Timeline for Gun&gov cluster in 2013

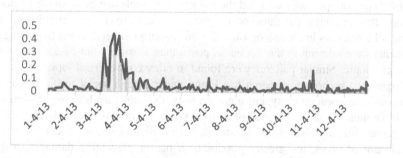

Fig. 3. Timeline for Gay cluster in 2013

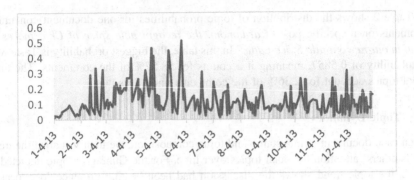

Fig. 4. Timeline for Troops cluster in 2013

4.4 Participants and Activists in Controversial Topics

We define "participants" in controversial topics as those who had commented under these topics, but not exclusively. We also define "activists" as those who posted exclusively on controversial topics and posted more than once. Table 3 shows that the while a large number of users participated in controversial topic discussions, only a small numbers of activists came to Starbucks' Facebook page to talk about controversial topics exclusively.

Table 3. Comparison between activists and all users

Topic	Activists	Participants
Troops	115	8809
Gay marriage	134	7264
Gun&gov	62	6541

The topic modeling result can further help tracking the behavioral patterns of those activists. For example, we examined the top seven gun-relevant posts in the Gun&gov cluster, after removing the three posts relevant to the government shutdown. After sorting all comments in chronological order, the pattern emerged: at the beginning, the comments were relevant to the Starbucks posts, then at some point an activist jumped to the gun topic. Similar patterns were found in other controversial topics.

Cognitive psychology research has found that although social media discussions often consist of vocal minority and silent majority, the public tends to over-estimate the size of the minority group because of its loud voice (Lewandowsky et al. 2012). Crisis management literature has also suggested that the earlier a company becomes aware of an indicator of crisis, the greater possibility it has of preventing damages, and the reason for an intensified crisis over time is an ignored crisis indicator (Veil 2007). Therefore, identifying the controversial topics and the vocal minority is also important for sending early warnings for crisis management. The topic model was able to lead the analysis to where the heated discussions happen, at what time, and by whom. Such information would also be valuable for companies to evaluate the outcome of its intervention strategies. For example, Starbucks posted several times in the Troops cluster to debunk the rumor; however, the time span in Fig. 4 shows that the topic lingered throughout 2013, which contradicts Starbucks' own claim that social media was an effective tool to stop rumors and misinformation.

5 Conclusion

In this study we proposed a topic modeling-based approach for auto-tracking controversial topics in social-media based customer dialog. The approach was validated through a case study by fitting a topic model based on nearly 150,000 Starbucks user comments in 2013. Out of 15 main topics, 3 were identified as controversial topics. The topics' time spans and the patterns of user participation were then further identified with the guidance of the topic model. The case study has demonstrated that the proposed approach can effectively distinguish discussions on controversial social topics from those on regular business practices, measure those topics' evolving dynamics over time, and locate where the discussions are happening and who are the participants and activists. Such information would be valuable for companies to design intervention strategies and evaluate their outcomes in social media discussions.

References

Bíró, I., Siklósi, D., Szabó, J., Benczúr, A.A.: Linked latent dirichlet allocation in web spam filtering. In: Proceedings of the 5th International Workshop on Adversarial Information Retrieval on the Web, pp. 37–40. ACM, New York (2009)

Blei, D.M., Ng, A.Y., Jordan, M.I.: Latent dirichlet allocation. J. Mach. Learn. Res. **3**, 993–1022 (2003)

Brown, J., Broderick, A.J., Lee, N.: Word of mouth communication within online communities: Conceptualizing the online social network. J. Interact. Mark. **21**(3), 2–20 (2007)

Chang, J., Gerrish, S., Wang, C., Boyd-Graber, J.L., Blei, D.M.: Reading tea leaves: how humans interpret topic models. In: Advances in neural information processing systems, pp. 288–296 (2009)

Chua, A.Y.K., Banerjee, S.: Customer knowledge management via social media: the case of Starbucks. Journal of Knowledge Management **17**(2), 237–249 (2013)

CNN: Starbucks CEO holds his ground on gay marriage (2013). http://money.cnn.com/2013/03/26/news/companies/starbucks-gay-marriage/. Accessed 26 Mar 2013

Coombs, W.T.: Protecting organization reputations during a crisis: the development and application of situational crisis communication theory. Corp. Reput. Rev. **10**(3), 163–176 (2007)

Gallaugher, J., Ransbotham, S.: Social media and customer dialog management at Starbucks. MIS Q. Exec. **9**(4), 197–212 (2010)

Greene, D., O'Callaghan, D., Cunningham, P.: How many topics? stability analysis for topic models. In: Calders, T., Esposito, F., Hüllermeier, E., Meo, R. (eds.) ECML PKDD 2014. LNCS (LNAI), vol. 8724, pp. 498–513. Springer, Heidelberg (2014). https://doi.org/10.1007/978-3-662-44848-9_32

Hays, S., Page, S.J., Buhalis, D.: Social media as a destination marketing tool: its use by national tourism organisations. Curr. Issues Tour. **16**(3), 211–239 (2013)

He, W., Zha, S., Li, L.: Social media competitive analysis and text mining: a case study in the pizza industry. Int. J. Inf. Manage. **33**(3), 464–472 (2013)

Holcomb, J., Upchurch, R., Okumus, F.: Corporate social responsibility: what are top hotel companies reporting? Int. J. Contemp. Hosp. Manag. **19**(6), 461–475 (2007)

Keyling, T., Jünger, J.: Facepager (version, f.e. 3.3). An application for generic data retrieval through APIs (2013). https://github.com/strohne/Facepager

Kim, E.: The role of social media in crisis communication - a case study of Starbucks (thesis) (2013). https://digital.library.txstate.edu/handle/10877/4619

Kwok, L., Yu, B.: Spreading social media messages on Facebook: an analysis of restaurant business-to-consumer communications. Cornell Hosp. Q. **54**(1), 84–94 (2013)

Kwok, L., Zhang, F., Huang, Y., Yu, B., Maharabhushanam, P., Rangan, K.: Documenting business-to-consumer (B2C) communications on Facebook: what have changed among restaurants and consumers? Worldwide Hosp. Tour. Themes **7**(3), 283–294 (2015). https://doi.org/10.1108/WHATT-03-2015-0018

Lazarsfeld, P.F., Berelson, B., Gaudet, H.: The People's Choice; How the Voter Makes Up His Mind in a Presidential Campaign, 3rd edn. Columbia University Press, New York (1968)

Leonard, P.: Mining large datasets for the humanities (2014). http://library.ifla.org/930

Mangold, W.G., Faulds, D.J.: Social media: the new hybrid element of the promotion mix. Bus. Horiz. **52**(4), 357–365 (2009)

Maskeri, G., Sarkar, S., Heafield, K.: Mining business topics in source code using latent dirichlet allocation. In: Proceedings of the 1st India Software Engineering Conference, pp. 113–120. ACM, New York (2008)

McCallum, A.: MALLET: A Machine Learning for Language Toolkit (2002). http://mallet.cs.umass.edu

Men, L.R., Tsai, W.H.S.: How companies cultivate relationships with publics on social network sites: evidence from China and the United States. Public Relat. Rev. **38**(5), 723–730 (2012)

Mustafaraj, E., Finn, S., Whitlock, C., Metaxas, P.T.: Vocal minority versus silent majority: discovering the opinions of the long tail. In: 2011 IEEE Third International Conference on Privacy, Security, Risk and Trust (PASSAT) and 2011 IEEE Third International Conference on Social Computing (SocialCom), pp. 103–10. IEEE (2011)

Timian, A., Rupcic, S., Kachnowski, S., Luisi, P.: Do patients "like" good care? measuring hospital quality via Facebook. Am. J. Med. Qual. **28**(5), 374–382 (2013)

Veil, S.R.: Crisis communication and agrosecurity: organizational learning in a high-risk environment. Ph.D. thesis (2007). http://search.proquest.com/docview/304844486/abstract?

Waters, R.D., Burnett, E., Lamm, A., Lucas, J.: Engaging stakeholders through social networking: how nonprofit organizations are using Facebook. Public Relat. Rev. **35**(2), 102–106 (2009)

West, T.: Starbucks tops social engagement study: what can your biz learn? - vote for the best company in Albuquerque's business competition. http://www.bizjournals.com/albuquerque/blog/socialmadness/2012/04/starbucks-tops-social-engagement.html. Accessed 27 May 2015

Yang, T.-I., Andrew, J.T., Mihalcea, R.: Topic modeling on historical newspapers. In: Proceedings of the 5th ACL-HLT Workshop on Language Technology for Cultural Heritage, Social Sciences, and Humanities, pp. 96–104 (2011)

Zou, H., Chen, H.M., Dey, S.: Understanding library user engagement strategies through large-scale Twitter analysis. In: 2015 IEEE First International Conference on Big Data Computing Service and Applications (BigDataService), pp. 361–370 (2015)

Lewandowsky, S., Ecker, U.K.H., Seifert, C.M., Schwarz, N., Cook, J.: Misinformation and its correction: continued influence and successful debiasing. Psychol. Sci. Public Interest **13**(3), 106–131 (2012)

Communication Studies and Online Communities

The Behavior and Network Position
of Peer Production Founders

Jeremy Foote(✉) and Noshir Contractor

Northwestern University, Evanston, IL, USA
jdfoote@u.northwestern.edu

Abstract. Online peer production projects, such as Wikipedia and open-source software, have become important producers of cultural and technological goods. While much research has been done on the way that large existing projects work, little is known about how projects get started or who starts them. Nor is it clear how much influence founders have on the future trajectory of a community. We measure the behavior and social networks of 60,959 users on Wikia.com over a two month period. We compare the activity, local network positions, and global network positions of future founders and non-founders. We then explore the relationship between these measures and the relative growth of a founder's wikis. We suggest hypotheses for future research based on this exploratory analysis.

1   Introduction

The surprising success of online peer production (OPP) projects like Wikipedia and open source software has shown that groups of motivated volunteers can successfully create high-quality goods without formal hierarchy. Scholars across a number of disciplines have studied why these projects work, sparking new research on the role of firms, intellectual property rights, and individual motivations in producing shared goods [1–4]. In this project, we focus on one aspect of OPP projects that has escaped much scholarly attention: its founding.

Founders have been shown to be influential in the similar context of entrepreneurship. Researchers have found both that people differ in their propensity to become an entrepreneur [5–9] and that the attributes and experiences of founders relate to a firm's success [10–14]. There are a number of reasons to think that OPP founders differ from entrepreneurs, such as the lower costs, risks, and benefits of founding. Learning about OPP founders can help us to understand why projects grow (or don't) in this increasingly important context.

We use measures of editing behavior and measures of social capital and social integration from over 60,000 contributors to Wikia.com to explore how founders differ from non-founders as well as how founders of high-growth projects differ from founders of low-growth projects. Our exploratory results suggest that compared to non-founders, founders are typically novelty-seeking and have low social capital. However, founders who are successful at creating larger communities have a different set of attributes: they have less diverse experience but are

© Springer International Publishing AG, part of Springer Nature 2018
G. Chowdhury et al. (Eds.): iConference 2018, LNCS 10766, pp. 99–106, 2018.
https://doi.org/10.1007/978-3-319-78105-1_12

actually more integrated in social networks, suggesting that they may use their social capital to recruit others.

2   Related Work

2.1   Entrepreneurship

Researchers have studied both who decides to become an entrepreneur and what attributes and experiences of entrepreneurs correlate with firm success. They have found that people with diverse experience and skills are more likely to become entrepreneurs [5,7,15], as are those who have worked with other entrepreneurs [8]. Given that someone has chosen to start a new firm, founders with more experience [10–12] have more successful firms, as do those with larger and more diverse social networks [14].

2.2   Peer Production

At first blush, online peer production projects seem very dissimilar to firms. They are composed of volunteers, without formal hierarchies and without paychecks. Indeed, much research on OPP focuses on how these organizations can work using structures and incentives so different from firms ([16] provides a survey). Surprisingly, much of this research has found that these supposedly decentralized, leaderless organizations are actually quite structured. For example, researchers have found that people select into different social and behavioral "roles" (like jobs) that are persistent over time [17], including leadership roles [18]. In other words, OPP looks more like firms than we would expect.

We argue that at its core the decision to start a new OPP project is very similar to the decision to start a new business. There are different costs to creating each type of organization, different tools for recruiting and encouraging contributors, and different benefits that accrue to founders. However, both founders and entrepreneurs organize the efforts of a group of people to create shared outputs. Indeed, the outputs of OPP projects and firms often directly compete.

Despite the similarity in context, very little research on peer production founders exists. Survey-based research suggests that OPP founders have diverse expectations and modest goals [19]. In the related context of online communities, researchers found that active and well-connected founders started longer-lived groups [20]. This paper extends these earlier works by comparing founders and non-founders and by exploring the relationship between founder attributes and the growth of a community rather than its survival.

Based on the entrepreneurship research, we focus on two questions:

RQ1: How do founders differ from non-founders?
RQ2: How do founders of large and small communities differ?

3 Methodological Approach

Our data comes from a dump of all edits to all wikis on Wikia.com as of April 2010. While wikis are used for different purposes, many of the wikis on Wikia are used for knowledge aggregation. The most popular wikis aggregate information about popular media, such as Disney movies or the Harry Potter books. These wiki projects represent an important strand of OPP but differ markedly from other OPP projects like open source software development.

We collected data at three different points in time (Fig. 1). We gathered behavior and network measures from the 60,959 users who made at least one edit from March to April 2009. We then identified the founders of the 16,904 wikis created in May and June 2009, and measured the number

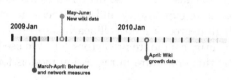

Fig. 1. Timeline of data collection

of unique contributors to each of these wikis as of April 2010. We used these data snapshots to compare the activity and network positions of those who became founders in May or June and those who did not, and to predict the relative growth of a founder's wikis between founding and April 2010.

Specifically, we measured behavior and attributes which have been found to relate to founding propensity or organization success in entrepreneurship. We created a number of *experience* and *activity* measures, such as tenure on Wikia, lifetime edits, recent edits, days since editing, and number of days with at least one edit. For *diversity of experience*, we measured the number of wikis that a user had contributed to and the Gini coefficient of edits per wiki. Finally, we measured the user's *founding expertise* and experience by measuring how many wikis users had started in the past, how often they started new pages, how often they participated in administering wikis, and the earliest point at which they contributed to a wiki (e.g., a value of 3 means they were the third editor on a wiki).

In order to measure a user's *social capital*, we created two different types of social networks based on two kinds of activities that occur on Wikia. We used article pages to create undirected collaboration networks, where edges are formed between an editor and the previous five editors of that page[1]. Communication networks are similar but are directed: users are assumed to be talking *to* the previous five editors on a talk page or *to* the owner of a user talk page. We created unweighted networks for each wiki and created each unweighted global network by combining the wiki networks. For each of the two network types, we measured the degree centrality, betweenness centrality, and PageRank of each user. There is, of course, no direct way to measure social capital, but these are somewhat overlapping measures of how prestigious and involved a user is in the network [22]. We also calculated "coreness", which is a measure of how integrated

---

[1] Similar analyses, (e.g., [21]) connect all editors, but a cutoff more closely approximates the social interactions we are interested in.

a user is [23]. We measured these values for each user in the global networks as well as in the wiki-level network for the wiki they were most active in.

We defined founders as the first three editors to a given project, since many founders start new wikis as groups [19]. We measured growth as the number of unique contributors to the wiki from the time of its founding until April 2010. Because a given user might start multiple wikis during our data collection, we used the median community size for all foundings that a user was a part of. We also included a control for when the median wiki was started.

Because there is so little research specifically on peer production founders we took an exploratory and hypothesis-generating approach. Our predictors had a high degree of multicollinearity, so we used elastic net regularized regression to identify candidate predictors [24]. We used the smaller set of predictors produced by this procedure in regression models for each of our research questions.

4   Results

There is one interesting result which doesn't require any modeling. We learned that founding is a rare activity for established users. Of the 60,959 users who were active in March and April 2009, only 822 founded a new wiki in May or June. That is not to say that founding is rare overall. There were 8,487 founders in May and June, meaning that nearly 90% of wikis were founded by new users.

For the rest of the analyses, we remove users with 'bot' in their username (N = 104) and low-activity users who don't appear in both the communication and collaboration networks (N = 45,775). There were also Wikia employees who we could not identify automatically, so we remove all users with edits to more than 100 different wikis (N = 24). This leaves us with a sample of 15,184 users and 470 founders.

For our first research question, we try to predict which users would become founders. Figure 2 shows the results of a logistic regression with the predictors identified by the elastic net procedure. Given our earlier finding that founders are likely to be new users, it is not surprising to see that tenure has a negative relationship with founding. However, both activity (edits) and diversity of activity (wikis edited, Gini of edits per wiki) predict becoming a founder, as was found to be the case in the entrepreneurship literature. This suggests that founders are *either* new users *or* active users. Founding experience is mixed, with creating pages and founding other wikis as positive predictors but being an early participant as a negative predictor. Social capital is also mixed, with communication network indegree as a positive predictor while PageRank and integration (coreness) are negative predictors. Overall, the difference between founders and non-founders is quite pronounced along many dimensions. On the right side of Fig. 2 we show a few density plots comparing the number of edits and the number of wikis edited, respectively. In both cases, there are clear differences between founders and non-founders.

In Fig. 3 we show the results of a negative binomial regression predicting the median number of contributors that a founder's wikis received as of April

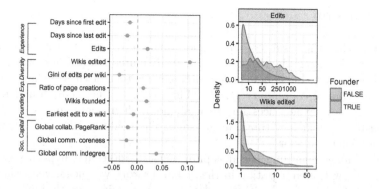

Fig. 2. Left: Scaled coefficient estimates with 95% confidence intervals for predicting of whether a user becomes a founder ($N = 15,184$). Right: Density plots of the number of edits and the number of wikis edited in March and April 2009 by those who become founders in May and June 2009 (blue) and those who do not (red). (Color figure online)

2010. This relationship is much noisier and much more difficult to model. The scatterplots on the right show two of the strongest predictors of growth and even these are incredibly noisy. This suggests that founder behavior and attributes do not have a strong effect on community growth. That being said, the analysis does offer a few insights. First, there is a benefit to experience, both tenure and editing activity, while experience as an admin has a negative relationship to community growth. Social capital is mixed, although most predictors show a positive relationship with growth. The median edit size of a founder's edits positively predicts growth. Finally, it is worth noting that the regularization step eliminated diversity measures from this model, suggesting that there is no significant relationship between diversity of experience and community growth in this dataset.

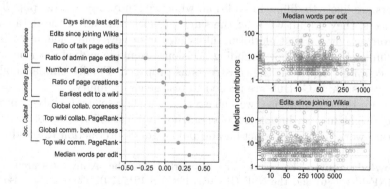

Fig. 3. Left: Scaled coefficient estimates with 95% confidence intervals, predicting the number of contributors to a community ($N = 470$). Right: Scatterplots of the median words per edit and total edits on the x axes and median community size on the y axes.

5   Discussion

We believe that the results of this exploratory study provide a foundation for future work. For example, founders in our study edited many different wikis and were more likely to start new pages. However, neither of these behaviors were good predictors of community growth. This suggests that many founders seek novelty and new experiences but then abandon their communities quickly to move on to the next new thing. Future research should look more explicitly at novelty-seeking behavior.

Our findings regarding social capital suggest additional hypotheses to be tested. We saw that integration in the global network was negatively related to becoming a founder but positively related to community growth. One explanation is that those who are on the periphery are discontent and thus more likely to start new communities but are ironically less able to grow their communities since growth requires spending social capital which they do not have.

Finally, we saw that a founder's typical edit size was the strongest predictor of growth. The reason for this relationship is not obvious, but one explanation is that people who make large edits typically add lots of information to a page and that wikis with more information are able to attract new contributors. Future work could test this hypothesis through experiments or causal inference.

6   Conclusion

There are important limitations to this work. Most obviously, we only look at founders who have previous activity on the site. Nearly 90% of the founders in our dataset were new to the site. This is consistent with research which shows that new communities can be founded as a way of learning about a site [19], but this also means that our approach cannot tell us anything about the majority of founders. Our results regarding the propensity to found and community growth only apply to existing members and the attributes and impact of new member founders are likely to differ. In addition, while we study a very large population of projects, they are all wikis on the same platform and all of the data comes only from activity on that platform. Interviews or surveys could help us to gain a richer understanding of how founding decisions are made and whether our measures accurately represent the constructs as proposed. Finally, similar analyses in contexts such as GitHub are needed to test generalizability.

Despite these limitations, we believe that this dataset and analysis provide unique insight into an important phenomenon and establish a set of intuitions for future work on peer production and public goods production to build upon.

Acknowledgments. This work was supported by the Army Research Office (W911NF-14-10686) and the NSF (IIS-1617468, IIS-1617129). The authors also wish to thank the iConference reviewers for their very helpful comments.

References

1. Benkler, Y.: The Wealth of Networks: How Social Production Transforms Markets and Freedom. Yale University Press, New Haven (2006)
2. Levine, S.S., Prietula, M.J.: Open collaboration for innovation: principles and performance. Organ. Sci. **25**(5), 1414–1433 (2013)
3. Raymond, E.S.: The Cathedral & the Bazaar: Musings on Linux and Open Source by an Accidental Revolutionary. O'Reilly Media Inc., Sebastopol (2001)
4. von Krogh, G., von Hippel, E.: The promise of research on open source software. Manag. Sci. **52**(7), 975–983 (2006)
5. Backes-Gellner, U., Moog, P.: The disposition to become an entrepreneur and the jacks-of-all-trades in social and human capital. J. Socio-Econ. **47**, 55–72 (2013)
6. Dobrev, S.D., Barnett, W.P.: Organizational roles and transition to entrepreneurship. Acad. Manag. J. **48**(3), 433–449 (2005)
7. Lazear, E.P.: Balanced skills and entrepreneurship. Am. Econ. Rev. **94**(2), 208–211 (2004)
8. Nanda, R., Sørensen, J.B.: Workplace peers and entrepreneurship. Manag. Sci. **56**(7), 1116–1126 (2010)
9. Zhao, H., Seibert, S.E., Lumpkin, G.: The relationship of personality to entrepreneurial intentions and performance: a meta-analytic review. J. Manag. **36**(2), 381–404 (2010)
10. Cassar, G.: Industry and startup experience on entrepreneur forecast performance in new firms. J. Bus. Ventur. **29**(1), 137–151 (2014)
11. Eisenhardt, K.M., Schoonhoven, C.B.: Organizational growth: linking founding team, strategy, environment, and growth among U.S. semiconductor ventures, 1978–1988. Adm. Sci. Q. **35**(3), 504–529 (1990)
12. Jo, H., Lee, J.: The relationship between an entrepreneur's background and performance in a new venture. Technovation **16**(4), 161–211 (1996)
13. Ostgaard, T.A., Birley, S.: New venture growth and personal networks. J. Bus. Res. **36**(1), 37–50 (1996)
14. Stam, W., Arzlanian, S., Elfring, T.: Social capital of entrepreneurs and small firm performance: a meta-analysis of contextual and methodological moderators. J. Bus. Ventur. **29**(1), 152–173 (2014)
15. Wagner, J.: Testing Lazear's jack-of-all-trades view of entrepreneurship with German micro data. Appl. Econ. Lett. **10**(11), 687–689 (2003)
16. Benkler, Y.: Peer production and cooperation. In: Bauer, J.M., Latzer, M. (eds.) Handbook on the Economics of the Internet. Edward Elgar, Cheltenham (2016)
17. Welser, H.T., Cosley, D., Kossinets, G., Lin, A., Dokshin, F., Gay, G., Smith, M.: Finding social roles in Wikipedia. In: Proceedings of the 2011 iConference, iConference 2011, pp. 122–129. ACM, New York (2011)
18. Zhu, H., Kraut, R., Kittur, A.: Effectiveness of shared leadership in online communities. In: Proceedings of the ACM 2012 Conference on Computer Supported Cooperative Work, CSCW 2012, pp. 407–416. ACM, New York (2012)
19. Foote, J., Gergle, D., Shaw, A.: Starting online communities: motivations and goals of wiki founders. In: Proceedings of the 2017 CHI Conference on Human Factors in Computing Systems (CHI 2017), pp. 6376–6380. ACM, New York (2017)
20. Kraut, R.E., Fiore, A.T.: The role of founders in building online groups. In: Proceedings of the 17th ACM Conference on Computer Supported Cooperative Work & Social Computing, CSCW 2014, Baltimore, Maryland, USA, pp. 722–732. ACM (2014)

21. Zhang, X., Wang, C.: Network positions and contributions to online public goods: the case of Chinese wikipedia. J. Manag. Inf. Syst. **29**(2), 11–40 (2012)
22. Wasserman, S., Faust, K.: Social Network Analysis: Methods and Applications. Cambridge University Press, Cambridge (1994)
23. Barberá, P., Wang, N., Bonneau, R., Jost, J.T., Nagler, J., Tucker, J., González-Bailón, S.: The critical periphery in the growth of social protests. Plos One **10**(11), e0143611 (2015)
24. Zou, H., Hastie, T.: Regularization and variable selection via the elastic net. J. Roy. Stat. Soc.: Ser. B (Stat. Methodol.) **67**(2), 301–320 (2005)

Data Journalism in 2017: A Summary of Results from the Global Data Journalism Survey

Bahareh R. Heravi(✉) (iD)

School of Information and Communication Studies, University College Dublin,
Dublin, Ireland
Bahareh.Heravi@ucd.ie

Abstract. Data journalism is an emerging discipline, which as a practice it is
rapidly becoming an integral part of many newsrooms. Despite this growth,
there is a lack of systematic research in this area to reveal the best practices,
knowledge sets, and skills required to develop the discipline. To address this
gap, this paper presents a brief overview of the results of the first Global Data
Journalism Survey, which includes the participation of journalists from 43
countries. Presented results shed light on a variety of aspects of data journalism
practice across the globe, including demographics, skills, education, and formation of data teams, as well as the opportunities and values associated with
data journalism.

Keywords: Data journalism · Data-driven journalism · Journalism
Computer assisted reporting · Precision journalism
Global Data Journalism Survey

1 Introduction

Data journalism is an emerging discipline, which – amongst other definitions [1, 2] – is
defined as 'finding stories in data – stories that are of interest to the public – and
presenting these stories in the most appropriate manner for public use and reuse' [3, 4].
Similar to other journalistic practices, data journalism puts the tenets of journalism first:
the investigation, the story, and communication of that story to the public. In data
journalism, data is the source, and computational methods and applications are the tools
to aid journalists in their work [3, 4].

Data journalism practice has been growing in the past 10 years. Despite this
growth, there is a lack of systematic research in this domain, and a divide between
academic and industry practices. Ausserhofer et al.'s [5] analysis of Data Journalism
literature suggests an increase of research publications on data journalism and related
fields since 2010. They note that although CAR (Computer Assisted Reporting) has
been practiced since the 1960s, the scientific investigation of it, also, has started only
recently.

© Springer International Publishing AG, part of Springer Nature 2018
G. Chowdhury et al. (Eds.): iConference 2018, LNCS 10766, pp. 107–113, 2018.
https://doi.org/10.1007/978-3-319-78105-1_13

To address this gap, the paper in hand presents a summary of the results of the first Global Data Journalism Survey[1], which studies the current state of data journalism in newsrooms across the globe, with a focus on knowledge, education and journalistic values when it comes to the practice of data journalism.

2   Method

This study was conducted through a survey, titled the Global Data Journalism Survey. The survey questions were designed in a collaboration between academic and industry partners, namely by the author and Mirko Lorenz, who is the Founder of Datawrapper and Innovation Manager at Deutsche Welle Innovation, following a set of interviews with industry experts. The survey consisted of 48 questions in 7 sections.

The survey was launched on the 3rd December 2016 and closed on the 10th May 2017. It was open to all data journalists and journalists globally. The survey was limited to those who identify as having worked as a journalist or a data journalist in the past year. It was carried out using the online Google Forms and was circulated and promoted as broadly as possible through various platforms and channels. A link to the survey was distributed widely through social media channels and relevant listservs, two Slack groups - News Nerdy and DJA 2017 - and a number of articles about the survey featured in the media [3, 6, 7]. This survey was conducted following an ethical approval from the University College Dublin's Research Ethics Committee.

3   Findings

Two hundred and six participants from 43 countries participated in this survey, with 181 respondents filling it out to completion. Given that the survey was circulated and promoted online, a definitive understanding of the total population size in not possible. However, as an indication of the size of the data journalism community, a data collection from LinkedIn on the terms "data journalist", "data journalism" and "'computer assisted reporting" OR "CAR"' on 'current jobs', at the time of the closing of the survey, returned a total of 463 journalists listed in these positions. This figure provides us with a crude estimate of the population size of the data journalism community. Considering the small community of data journalists, the data collected in this survey is considered to be a representative sample.

For the purpose of analysing the results, only responses completed to the end were considered and the rest were discarded.

3.1   Demographics and Newsroom Practices

The majority of participants were from the young, but not so young, generation of journalists with almost 75% being between 25 and 44 years old. Sixty-four per cent (64%) of participating journalists were in full time employment, while 18% were

---

[1] This survey was ran by Bahareh Heravi and Mirko Lorenz.

freelancers, 12% in part time employment as journalists, and 4% were casual/retainer. Thirty-two per cent (32%) of participants worked in large organisations of 500+ employees, 22% in organisations of size 10–49, 17% in organisations with 100–499 employees, 15% in small organisations of 2–9 employees and only 8% in mid-sized organisations of 50–99 employees. Forty-two per cent (42%) of participants worked in national organisations, 20% in local, 18% in international and the rest in a combination of these types, or other types of organisations. In terms of gender, 57.5% of our participants identified as male and 42.5% as female.

Tapping into experience, a majority of respondents (78%) were individuals with 1–10 years experience as a journalist with breakdown of 2% having less than a year experience, 41% having 1–4 years experience and 26% 5–9 years. Nineteen per cent (19%) of participants had 10–19 years experience and only 11% had over 20 years experience as a journalist.

In terms of content production, 43% of participating journalists produced content for online platforms of broadcast or print media outlets and 34% produced content for online-only publications. This makes a total 77% of all participants producing content for online publications. This figure is followed by print newspaper (8%), radio (4%), TV (4%), print magazines (3%), personal blog (2%) and producing content for news agencies made only 1% of the total.

We asked our participants about the status of data journalism in their organisations. Forty-six per cent (46%) claimed that they have a dedicated data desk/team/unit/blog/section. This figure was followed by 29% who expressed that they do not have a dedicated data desk/team/unit/blog/section, but publish data driven projects on a regular basis. Seven per cent (7%) of participants noted that they plan to work with data in the next six months and another 7% expressed that they have no immediate plan to start working with data. Of those who indicated they have a dedicated data desk/team/unit/blog/section in their organisations, 40% had a data team consisting of 3–5 people and 30% had a team of 1–2 people. This means a vast majority (70%) of organisations with data teams operate with small teams of 1–5. On the other side of the spectrum 22% of participating organisations had data teams of 6–10 people, 3% had a team of 11–15 people, and 5% had large data teams of more than 15 people.

When we asked journalists about the main hurdles in implementing data journalism in their organisations (they could choose more than one), 52% identified 'lack of resources' as the main hurdle, followed by 44% indicating that 'lack of adequate knowledge' was the main hurdle. Furthermore 40% believed that lack of time contributes to not being able to implement data journalism in their organisation.

3.2   Knowledge and Education

With an interest in education in this emerging area, we peeked into *knowledge* – which was rated as the second biggest hurdle in implementing data journalism – and *education*. Results show that while 86% of participants considered themselves as data journalists, in terms of data journalism proficiency only 18% rated themselves as experts in data journalism. Another 44% identified as having a better than average knowledge in data journalism and 26% identified as having average knowledge in the field. Nearly 13% of participants identified as novice or below average level of expertise in the field.

In terms of formal training, half of our participants (50%) had formal training in data journalism and the other half did not. With regard to a wider understanding of formal training in knowledge areas used in data journalism practices, most participants demonstrated a high degree of formal training in journalism, with less formal training in the more data oriented and technical aspects such as data analysis, statistics, coding, data science, machine learning and data visualisation. Figure 1 presents the breakdown of formal training in related fields.

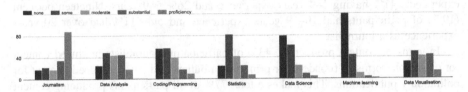

Fig. 1. Level of formal training in related knowledge fields, *N = 181*

In terms of education level, 97% of respondents had a university degree, with a breakdown of 40% university graduate (bachelor) level, 54% postgraduate level and 3% with a doctorate or above degrees. Looking into the degrees obtained by these participants, a 62% majority were formally educated in Journalism at the university level. This is followed by a combination of other degrees: Politics (15%), Computer/Information/Data Science/Engineering (12%) and Communication and Language/Literature each 10.5%, with 26% listing a combination of other degrees.

3.3   What Data Skills Are Journalists Interested to Learn?

To address the knowledge gap highlighted in the responses from participating journalists, we studied education needs in this sector. A remarkably high portion of participants in the survey (98%), expressed that they were interested in acquiring further skills to practice data journalism, with 81% being *very* interested. While nearly all participating journalists were interested in acquiring further skills, merely 42% expressed that they are interested in more formal higher education degrees in this area. However, if the training offered is shorter-term or more flexible, a striking 74% of participating journalists express interest in formal training in higher education, e.g. a postgraduate certificate or higher education diplomas.

In terms of specific data skills journalists are interested to acquire (Fig. 2), data analysis presented itself as the top skill, with 64% of individuals expressing interest in learning about it. This was marginally followed by learning "how to programme/code" at 63% and visualising data at 51%. These top three data skills were followed by another three skills: "how to clean data", "how to develop data-driven applications" and to learn "how to check if data is reliable", with over 48% of journalists expressing interest in each.

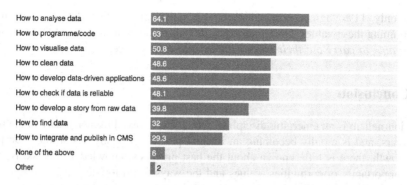

Fig. 2. Interest in acquiring skills listed skills (%), *N = 181*

3.4   Values Associated with Journalism and Newsroom Production

The topic of using data as a source, and means, of reporting has struck various debates around journalistic practices and associated values, e.g. [2, 8–10]. To study how journalists think about the values associated with journalism, and the inevitable requirements of viable story production in newsrooms, we asked our participants a series of questions covering a number of aspects associated, including topics of quantity and quality of data journalism storied published.

Sixty-five per cent (65%) of the respondents 'somehow agreed' or 'strongly agreed' that *data journalism allows them or their organisation to produce more stories*. On the end of the spectrum 13% 'somewhat disagreed' (10%) or 'strongly disagreed' (3%) with this statement.

Moving from quantity to quality, 90% of respondents 'agreed somewhat' (21%) or 'strongly agreed' (69%) that *data driven journalism adds rigour to journalism*, with only 5% expressing the opposite. Similarly 91% 'agreed' or 'strongly agreed' that *data journalism improves the quality of journalistic work* in their organisation, with only 4% believing the opposite (Fig. 3).

	Allows us to produce more stories	Improves quality of journalism	Adds rigour to stories	Opens up new fields of coverage	Undermines traditional journalistic values
Strongly agree	35	67	69	64	6
Agree somewhat	30	24	21	30	7
Neutral	21	6	5	3	6
Disagree somewhat	10	1	2	1	17
Strongly disagree	3	3	3	2	65

Fig. 3. Data Journalism, quantity, quality, rigour, opportunities and values (%), *N = 181*

Tapping into traditional journalistic values, while leaving the definition of these values to the participants, 83% of participating journalists 'disagreed somewhat' or 'strongly disagreed' that *data journalism undermines traditional journalistic values*, while only 11% 'agreed somewhat' or 'strongly agreed' that data journalism is undermining these values. On a final note, 70% of participants expressed that *they will not be able to carry out their work without data as a source.*

4   Conclusion

Data journalism is an emerging discipline, which has evolved tremendously in the past few years, and is rapidly becoming an integral practice in many newsrooms. Despite this growth, there is little known about the best practices, knowledge sets, skills, and more importantly opportunities, values and the ways to go forward in this discipline. To address this gap, this paper presented a brief overview of the results of the first Global Data Journalism Survey.

The results show that the data journalism community is a highly educated community, and it has its roots mostly in journalism and communication degrees, and less so in data/information and computer related disciplines. Additionally journalists engaged in data journalism form a younger cohort of journalists, with fewer than 10 years experience as a journalist. While technical, data analytics and statistical skills do not appears to be the strength of participating journalists put next to their journalism background, it appears that many newsrooms already have dedicated data team and/or produce data driven stories on a regular basis. This study further reveals that despite debates in the use of data for producing journalistic work, both in terms of quantity and quality, a vast majority of journalists believe that data journalism allows them to create more stories in terms of quantity, which are also more rigorous and of higher quality.

This paper presented a brief overview of the data collected in the Global Data Journalism Survey. A further, more detailed, analysis of the results will take place in the future.

References

1. Berret, C., Phillips, C.: Teaching Data and Computational Journalism. Knight Foundation, New York (2016)
2. Howard, A.: The Art and Science of Data-Driven Journalism. Knight Foundation, New York (2014)
3. SiliconRepublic: How is Data Journalism Changing the Newsroom? Q&A with Bahareh Heravi (2016)
4. Heravi, B.: Teaching data journalism. In: Mair, J., Keeble, R., Lucero, M., Moore, M. (eds.) Data Journalism: Past Present and Future. Abramis Academic Publishing, Bury St Edmunds (2017)
5. Ausserhofer, J., Gutounig, R., Oppermann, M., Matiasek, S., Goldgruber, E.: The datafication of data journalism scholarship: focal points, methods, and research propositions for the investigation of data-intensive. Journalism (2017)
6. Lorenz, M.: What is the current status of data journalism? Participate in our global survey to find out (2016)
7. Plaum, A.: Call for participation: global data journalism survey 2017 (2016). http://blogs.dw.com/innovation/call-for-participation-global-data-journalism-survey-2017

8. Diakopoulos, N.: Algorithmic accountability. Digit. J. **3**, 398–415 (2015)
9. Satell, G.: This is why data journalism is failing (2014). https://www.forbes.com/sites/gregsatell/2014/06/01/this-is-why-data-journalism-is-failing/
10. Houston, B.: Digging for truth with data: computer-assisted reporting. https://gijn.org/2015/03/05/digging-for-truth-with-data-computer-assisted-reporting/

iTransformation of a Digital Village:
A Community Development Initiative
Through ICTs

Safirotu Khoir[1](✉) ⓘ and Robert M. Davison[2] ⓘ

[1] Universitas Gadjah Mada, Yogyakarta 55281, Indonesia
safirotu@ugm.ac.id
[2] City University of Hong Kong, Tat Chee Avenue, Kowloon Tong, Hong Kong
isrobert@cityu.edu.hk

Abstract. The rapid diffusion of ICTs enables people to learn further and develop personal skills. Technology-based communication facilitates people to interact internally and externally, thus creating the opportunity for impacts on their lives in multiple respects. In the traditional life of a small village, the impact of ICTs may be even greater in terms of social life and the domestic economy. In this paper, we discuss how a village in Yogyakarta, Indonesia, embarked on a digital transformation initiative, transforming itself into a cyber-village to support its own community development. We draw on interviews with the local villagers and a village leader who was one of the key persons responsible for initiating the community development project. Our preliminary results show that the initiative successfully supported an increase in quality of life from economic and social perspectives.

Keywords: Digital village · iTransformation · ICT4D
Community development · Community participation · Cyber village
Community informatics

1 Introduction

When information is ubiquitous, we tend to ignore it yet the power of information is remarkable, even if it is invisible. When information is combined with Information Communication and Technologies (ICTs), it has the potential to provide effective support for individuals as they expand their knowledge. This is particularly noticeable in community development, where members of the community have a role to play as a key agent of change. Such participation has been found to constitute a strong component of the grassroots development approach [3] and to play a key role in supporting social harmony, i.e. "the peaceful interaction of people in a social group" (p.1) [2].

In information research, the linkage between ICTs and individual contributions and performance has attracted considerable attention [6]. In this paper, we explore how Kampoeng Cyber (Kampoeng means a small urban or rural neigbourhood or village in the Indonesian language) in the heart of Yogyakarta, Central Java, Indonesia, has transformed itself through the power of information to connect both internally (within

© Springer International Publishing AG, part of Springer Nature 2018
G. Chowdhury et al. (Eds.): iConference 2018, LNCS 10766, pp. 114–119, 2018.
https://doi.org/10.1007/978-3-319-78105-1_14

the village) and externally (to entities nearby and far away). Kampoeng Cyber, thereby, reinvents itself as a place in touch with its heritage yet also able to participate in contemporary society and avoid the ignominious fate of its residents seeping away, its identity disappearing. Recognising that more research is needed to explore the potential of Internet use to promote local participation and support community building [10], we address the following research question: how is Kampoeng Cyber transforming itself so that it can support its village members through ICTs? In this exploratory study, we aim to demonstrate how individual villagers in Kampoeng Cyber are involved in a learning process focused on how to use ICTs to increase their living standards with respect to their local business operations. We expect that the results can inform policy makers in the domains of social, technology and economic services, as to how they can provide better support for village iTransformation and community develpoment.

2 Kampoeng Cyber: Study Context

In this project, we investigate the role of information and ICTs in Kampoeng Cyber, a small village located in the centre of Yogyakarta, Indonesia's former capital. Kampoeng Cyber is located very close to Tamansari, one of the most famous tourist destinations in Yogyakarta. Inside the village, the streets are too narrow for cars, so people can only walk or ride (motor) bikes. The village decorates its walls with murals showing how ICTs can improve the village in terms of communication and increasing living standards. The population of the village comprises 143 people in 43 households. The vision of the village is to build an independent community that is well-informed with respect to technology and that will achieve improvements in the areas of social life, education, economy, art and culture. The village has the mission of bringing ICTs into the community with equitable access in order to improve communication and to provide wider knowledge and insight.

When Kampoeng Cyber was first established, the village leader and committee encouraged individual villagers to participate in a project that would support the whole community development through ICTs, including Internet access. This participative process triggered the villagers to form closer and more harmonious relationships with each other [7]. Mas Koko, the current village leader, stated that the village members not only became more aware of the role of the Internet after the establishment of Kampoeng Cyber, but they also showed their individual and community support emotionally. This was shown when they helped each other in terms of technology use (e.g. smartphones and the Internet use).

When we visited Kampoeng Cyber in May 2017, we noted that a spirit of harmony pervaded the village and the residents had a strong intention to improve their ICT skills. Davison [2] remarks how social harmony can be facilitated with ICTs. This is very apparent in Kampoeng Cyber, which the villagers report is a harmonious place to live in. As the village website makes clear "This is a village that always wants to develop, which it will do primarily through IT" [8].

3 Literature Review

Community development is "premised on the principles of local people themselves collectively identifying and prioritising their needs, goals and their own assets and taking charge of these" (p. 112) [9]. Related to community development, the World Bank provides a framework of poor relocation and encourages poor people to do better through participation in economic and social activities [1]. Participation is defined as bringing people into certain processes and institutional development through the project, planning and advisory board.

Several previous studies have discussed community development with respect to such issues as technology, community participation and the role of external parties. Recent research [9] discussed community development in Indonesia using two Non Government Organisations (NGOs) as case studies: Lumpuuk Resource Centre and Forum Bangun Aceh. The research described the power of NGOs in helping community development after the 2006 tsunami. Evidence showed that local participation was essential to support recovery from a devastating situation. Using a loan from outside/ international networks, the community developed infrastructure and started up a business to help it return to the normal previous life. In a different study, Ognyanove et al. [11] investigated community-oriented Internet participation in the relationship with civic activities and integration into a local communication media in Alhambra, California, USA. Using data from a phone survey and taking a communication infrastructure approach, the authors suggested that online platforms and activities constitute a mode of participation complementing more traditional indicators of civic engagement and inter-group communication.

A key theory describing how technology supports people through particular activities is Task-Technology Fit (TTF). TTF can be defined as the degree to which a technology assists an individual in performing particular tasks with respect to several related aspects such as task requirements, individual abilities, and the supporting tools [6]. Certain kinds of tasks (for example, setting up an online business requiring information from many sources including training and improving products) require certain kinds of technological functionality (for example, social media and other online tools for business). Maruping and Agarwal [12] explored how interpersonal interactions can be managed more effectively through ICTs. Using the TTF paradigm and media synchronicity theory, they argued that there were three key interpersonal processes: conflict management, motivation and confidence building, and affect management. The study proposed a theoretical model incorporating aspects (such as the richness of the medium and the synchronicity of communication) to examine how the communication needs as well as the need for ICT functionality, varies depending on the development stages of particular virtual team.

Particular tasks require particular types of technological support. In the case of Kampoeng Cyber, the main tasks include:

- Empowering villagers in their business and business processes (for example, introducing the Internet to expand their selling channels)
- Increasing villagers' technology literacy skills (for example: how to create, communicate by and maintain emails, social media accounts, blogs and websites)
- Maintaining communication internally and externally

In this paper, we frame our research from a TTF perspective with a focus on individual participation that supports iTransformation and community development through the use of ICTs. Focusing specifically on interpersonal interactions, the TTF paradigm helps us identify how such individuals can make use of the technological functionality as they work towards their goals [12].

4   Research Methods and Preliminary Analysis

In exploring the village, we draw on interviews with 5 villagers and a village leader. Data sources that we rely on include social media postings, the village website and our own observations made when we visited in May 2017. In this preliminary paper, we present the key themes by using content analysis [10]. We discuss the initial establishment, the early learning and adaptation process and what villagers have done so far with the help of technology. To enrich our perspective, we also participated in a regular monthly meeting in July 2017 in order to experience the inter-villager communication process. Mas Koko, the current village leader, enabled us to gain access to village residents. Our interview questions were based on the TTF framework: we focused on exploring how the villagers use ICTs to perform certain tasks related to expanding their business and improving their standards of living.

Recognising the power of the Internet, Mas Heri (the former village leader) intended not only to bring free Internet to each house in the village, but also to ensure that the villagers learned how to leverage the Internet effectively, through educational programmes. In 2008, the project kicked off with just five villagers, bringing the cable connection through an Internet provider company. These founding members used their own savings to purchase the computing resources, sharing this with their neighbours who gradually developed their own interest in the project. One university in Yogyakarta (Atmajaya University) supported the village and provided two services: the university technical support team came to provide computer training and the village members traveled to the university and used the computer lab to learn basic computer skills. The university provided computer literacy training, including how to create, manage and maintain a social media account, how to do basic communication with other people, how to create personal and business websites, how to post pictures and how to manage online shops. At the present time, the village has one IT consultant who voluntarily helps manage technology issues.

In the early years, growth was slow but in 2015 a private company provided funding which has permitted faster connections. At the time of writing, many of the villagers are informally employed or self-employed, seeking to sell their various products, e.g. batik, fishing equipment, T-shirt painting, snacks and traditional crafts, via the Internet. Consequently, living standards in the village have risen. Wifi hotspots have been installed, for access by the public as well as residents. Facebook is used as a village communication channel for sharing ideas, invitations and meeting minutes. Indeed, Mark Zuckerberg visited the village in 2014. Currently, we see a contagion effect with village members who have not previously had ideas of improving their living standards becoming inspired by those who are already online and using the Internet to promote their products. Most villagers operate offline shops while some operate both offline and online shops. For their online gallery, they use the free Wordpress blog. They also make extensive use of Facebook, with a few also creating their own websites. Sri Marpinjun, one of our informants, stated that more people from overseas came to the village and wider networks were easily created since people used ICT to sell their products.

While the villagers are now familiar with the affordances [4] offered by the Internet to communicate among each other, face-to-face meetings are still considered important and conducted regularly once a month. This meeting was used to gather more ideas, share information and discuss any issues and find possible solutions. Several improvement ideas emerged, such as villagers creating several programs such as how to make Batik and how to be a tour guide, and promoted them online. They also have an educational tour package for school children introducing ICTs and how to deal with the Internet using Kampoeng Cyber as a real example. This iTransformation promotes their businesses as individuals as well as for the whole community. The villagers who run the business have their own profit and they also voluntarily share their profit to support the community.

Overall, our preliminary study of Kampoeng Cyber lies within the TTF framework which provides a more general "fit" theory of tasks, systems, individual characteristics, and performance [5]. The use of ICTs for certain tasks was found to encourage the villagers to develop their potential skills using ICTs which then led to increases in their living standards. The village would like to promote itself nationally and internationally through ICTs with their products related to culture and arts which will benefit the village as a whole and each villager individually. The future plan of Kampoeng Cyber is to create a single e-trading platform that can bring together all village members with their own personal products that will be easier to manage.

5   Conclusion

This exploratory study of the way ICTs contribute to the iTransformation of Kampoeng Cyber demonstrates the willingness of the community to develop itself. While community development is sometimes a top down scheme, this iTransformation, in fact, is a bottom up initiative that later became of interest to the local and national government. While the community works together through ICTs, it has not eliminated the essence of face–to–face communication yet it has increased standards of living. This kind of initiative illustrates the potential for a village to develop through ICTs and thereby provide significant benefits for society. Community empowerment through a cyber-village is a success story that can inspire other villages in Indonesia and other (developing) countries. This early work should support a better understanding of ICT adoption in supporting villagers and therefore enable better preparation for more successful future projects. Future research should discuss further the social harmony that can be obtained through digital enablement as a by-product of village improvement and long-term sustainability.

Acknowledgement. The authors would like to thank Mas Heri, Mas Koko, Lek Iwon, Mbak Sri Marpinjun and other members of the Kampoeng Cyber village for their ideas, stories and sharing during the data collection process.

References

1. Cernea, M.M.: Using knowledge from social science in development projects. Proj. Apprais. **9**(2), 83–94 (1994)
2. Davison, R.M.: Facilitating social harmony through ICTs. In: Choudrie, J., Islam, M.S., Wahid, F., Bass, J.M., Priyatma, J.E. (eds.) ICT4D 2017. IAICT, vol. 504, pp. 3–9. Springer, Cham (2017). https://doi.org/10.1007/978-3-319-59111-7_1
3. Eversole, R.: Remaking participation: challenges for community development practice. Community Dev. J. **47**(1), 29–41 (2012)
4. Gibson, J.J.: The theory of affordances. In: Shaw, R., Bransford, J. (eds.) Perceiving, acting, and knowing: toward an ecological psychology, pp. 67–82. Lawrence Erlbaum Associates, Inc., Hillsdale (1979)
5. Goodhue, D.L.: IS attitudes: toward theoretical and definition clarity. DataBase **19**(3/4), 6–15 (1988)
6. Goodhue, D.L., Thompson, R.L.: Task-technology fit and individual performance. MIS Q. **19**(2), 213–236 (1995)
7. Jones, N.: The birth of Indonesia's cyber village. http://www.sapiens.org/technology/indonesia-cyber-village/. Accessed 3 Dec 2017
8. Kampoeng cyber (n.d). http://www.rt36kampoengcyber.com. Accessed 7 Dec 2017
9. Kenny, S., Hasan, A., Fanany, I.: Community development in Indonesia. Community Dev. J. **52**(1), 107–124 (2017)
10. Krippendorff, K.: Content Analysis: An Introduction to Its Methodology. Sage Publication, Thousand Oaks (2012)
11. Ognyanova, K., Chen, N.N., Ball-Rokeach, S.J., An, Z., Son, M., Parks, M., Gerson, D.: Online participation in a community context: civic engagement and connections to local communication resources. Int. J. Commun. **7**, 2433–2456 (2013)
12. Maruping, L.M., Agarwal, R.: Managing team interpersonal processes through technology: a task-technology fit perspective. J. Appl. Psychol. **89**(6), 975–990 (2004)

Enhancing Critical Infrastructure Resilience Through Information-Sharing: Recommendations for European Critical Infrastructure Operators

Paul Reilly[1,2] , Elisa Serafinelli[1,2] , Rebecca Stevenson[1(✉)] ,
Laura Petersen[2] , and Laure Fallou[2]

[1] Information School, University of Sheffield, Sheffield, UK
r.stevenson@sheffield.ac.uk
[2] European-Mediterranean Seismological Centre (EMSC),
Bruyères le Châtel, France

Abstract. This paper explores how critical infrastructure (CI) resilience can be improved through effective crisis communication between CI operators and members of the public. Drawing on academic and practice-based research into crisis and risk communication, as well as the results of 31 interviews conducted with key stakeholders from across Europe, the AESOP guidelines are proposed for enhancing the communication and information-sharing strategies of CI operators. These emphasise the importance of integrating both traditional and digital media into a multi-channel communication strategy that facilitates dialogue between CI operators and key stakeholders including emergency management organisations and representatives of local communities. The information-seeking behaviours of citizens should be evaluated by these organisations in order to ensure that this messaging reaches key demographics in disaster-vulnerable areas. This paper concludes by examining how post-disaster learning should be incorporated into a flexible framework for crisis and risk communication that manages public expectations about the time needed to restore services in the aftermath of large-scale incidents.

Keywords: Social media · Information sharing
Critical infrastructure resilience

1 Introduction

Much of the research in the fields of disaster management and crisis communication has focused upon the practices of key emergency management organisations, such as police, fire and rescue services (see Coombs 2010 for example). In contrast, there has been very little empirical investigation of the communication and information-sharing practices adopted by critical infrastructure (CI) operators during each stage of an incident (mitigation, preparedness, response, recovery).

© Springer International Publishing AG, part of Springer Nature 2018
G. Chowdhury et al. (Eds.): iConference 2018, LNCS 10766, pp. 120–125, 2018.
https://doi.org/10.1007/978-3-319-78105-1_15

This paper sets out to address this gap by exploring how CI resilience can be enhanced through the information-sharing practices of its operators. Building on the model of crisis communication proposed by Coombs (2015), it explores the ways in which CI operators might avail of the affordances of both traditional and social media in order to manage the expectations of disaster-affected populations about the timescale for the full restoration of services in the aftermath of a disaster. This paper concludes by proposing the AESOP guidelines for effective communication and information-sharing by CI operators during such incidents.

2 Crisis Communication and Disaster Resilience

2.1 Defining Crisis Communication

The importance of effective crisis communication has been acknowledged in key Disaster Risk Reduction (DRR) initiatives over the past two decades, including the United Nations International Strategy for Disaster Reduction (UNISDR) and The Sendai Framework for Disaster Reduction. Effective crisis communication is not just about what information is being shared; rather it is about using communication channels to enable dialogue with the public. Coombs (2015) argues that organisations responsible for crisis communication should *manage information* through the collection and dissemination of crisis-related information, while also *managing its meaning* through initiatives to influence how people perceive the crisis and related organisations.

2.2 Crisis and Emergency Risk Communication Model

The CERC model combines elements of crisis and risk communication in a framework that applies to each of the four phases of the disaster cycle. The model allows communicators to effectively "inform and persuade the public in the hope that they will plan for and respond appropriately to risks and threats." (Centers for Disease Control and Prevention 2014: 7). The model proposes that both local and national stakeholders should engage the public in information collection and dissemination, rather than relying on a small number of 'experts'. This move from 'top-down' to a 'shared responsibility' model of crisis communication was related to the increased volume of user-generated content (UGC) available on social media sites such as Facebook and Twitter. This UGC was said to provide emergency managers with unprecedented 'real-time' access to witnesses' information (Cassa et al. 2013). Furthermore, the ability to both push and pull information via social media was widely held to be increasing the reach of messaging designed to mitigate the impact of these incidents (Laituri and Kodrich 2008).

However, although the CERC model held out the possibility of a truly 'collaborative' crisis communication strategy, there remains little empirical evidence to show its influence on crisis communication practices outside the United States (MacDonagh et al. 2016). Furthermore, it could be argued that disasters such as Hurricane Katrina in the US in 2005 illustrated the need to extend the collaborative aspects of the model, especially in relation to the trust (or lack thereof) between minority communities and government during such incidents (Quinn 2008). There also remains a dearth of research exploring how CERC might be implemented by CI operators in order to increase critical infrastructure resilience by managing the expectations of citizens about the level of service that will be available during disasters.

3 Methods

3.1 Interviews and Focus Groups

This study set out to add to the limited empirical data on how operators can build more resilient critical infrastructures through crisis communication and information sharing during crisis situations. Interviews, focus groups and consultations were conducted with 31 relevant stakeholders between November 2016 and January 2017, including CI operators, professional journalists and other emergency management personnel. These participants were based in several EU countries including France, Portugal, Norway and Sweden. The participants were recruited via call for participation notices issued to relevant professional networks via email. These countries were selected on the basis that they hosted the living labs used in the IMPROVER project. Two different interview schedules were developed and used to explore the perspectives of CI and emergency management professionals, and journalists in relation to how crisis information is currently communicated and how this might develop in the future. CI and emergency management professionals were asked about current communication strategies; whether digital media had been incorporated, how traditional and digital media were used together, what feedback is collected, and what audiences they hope to reach using different platforms. Interviews with journalists focussed on their experiences of social media in detecting and verifying incidents, and whether they had come across any ethical and legal challenges of using social media in relation to emergencies. Ethics approval was sought and obtained from the host institution prior to data being collected and it was agreed with all participants would be anonymised in subsequent publications. Themes that emerged from the data were identified and explored using the six phases of critical thematic analysis proposed by Braun and Clarke (2006). Two coders read each transcript and compared notes in order to identify the communication practices that these interviewees believed would help build critical infrastructure resilience.

There were two limitations that should be acknowledged. First, a complete overview of every national resilience and crisis communication framework was not feasible. Rather, the aim of this study was to identify broad themes and patterns in crisis and risk communication and to reflect upon their respective strengths and weaknesses. Second, the data presented below is based upon a self-selected sample and could not be considered representative of these professional groups in these countries. Therefore, it was decided to focus instead on the identification of broad guidelines and tactics for effective communication that could be adopted by CI operators and applied to the context in which such incidents occurred.

4 AESOP Guidelines for Effective Communication Between CI Operators and Members of the Public During Crises

4.1 Analyse the Information-Seeking Behaviours of Local Populations Before Deciding Which Media Channels to Use During Disasters

As discussed earlier, understanding information-seeking behaviour is a pre-requisite for creating effective crisis communication strategies. A dearth of information during and after a disaster can create a vacuum in which rumours and disinformation emerge that have the potential to inflame tensions within affected communities. Our study suggested that some CI operators were still likely to prioritise action over communication with the public, the latter usually being facilitated via the traditional media. Therefore, we propose that operators should analyse the target-population's information-seeking behaviour prior to deciding which channels are used to share crisis information; incorporating traditional and digital media within their communication strategies in order to maximise the reach of these messages.

4.2 Engage Key Stakeholders in Order to Ensure Message Consistency Across Traditional and Social Media Platforms

The use of social media to share UGC during disasters can create challenges as rumours and misinformation spread on sites such as Facebook and Twitter can contribute to the strain placed on critical infrastructures during disasters while simultaneously creating unrealistic expectations about the amount of time required for full restoration of these services. Collaboration between CI operators, emergency management organisations, and news media organisations is essential in order to ensure that a consistent message is delivered to citizens from the sources they trust the most (Sutton et al. 2014). However, our interviewees identified the need to adhere to internal control structures and the absence of pre-existing relationships with such stakeholders as obstacles towards this level of cooperation. In order to rectify this, CI operators should cultivate positive working relationships with their counterparts in the news media, other emergency management organisations and other CI organisations. They should also ensure that consistent messages are shared via their own traditional and digital media channels (Stephens et al. 2013).

4.3 Social Media Should be Used to Provide Real-Time Updates to Citizens About Ongoing Efforts to Restore Services

CI operators should be aware that the exponential growth in social media use worldwide has increased public expectation about the availability of real-time crisis information. Social media use can also increase community resilience by encouraging engagement and a sense of community on a local and national level (Cheng et al. 2013). Our study suggested that although some operators used these sites on a regular basis, many did not appear to have a social media strategy to be deployed during crises. Several interviewees noted that their organisations lacked expertise in this area and failed to provide sufficient support to those in the communication team responsible for updating their social media accounts. Therefore, it is not only essential that CI operators use these sites to provide real-time updates to citizens about efforts to restore key services, but also that they integrate social media into their crisis communication strategies.

4.4 Observe and Adhere to Context-Specific Regulatory Frameworks for Emergency Management and Resilience

Efforts to increase CI resilience through information-sharing should always be complaint with their respective national and international regulatory frameworks (Melkunaite et al. 2016). For example, UK CI operators should adhere to the principles of JESIP (Joint Emergency Services Interoperability Practices), which aims to improve crisis response by encouraging communication, collaboration and interoperability between relevant stakeholders.

Whilst encouraging collaboration in crisis response, the European Programme for Critical Infrastructure protection[1] (EPCIP) notes organisations are only legally permitted to share information with personnel of an appropriate level of security who have been vetted by their respective EU state. Such frameworks should always underpin the communication and information-sharing practices of operators before, during and after disasters.

4.5 Post-disaster Learning Should be Employed in Order to Enhance and Develop Future Communication Strategies

Communication strategies need to be constantly reviewed and updated in light of the changing media landscape and the evolving consumption patterns of citizens. Hence, post-disaster learning is essential for CI operators to innovate and adapt their current practices to the changing requirements of their target audiences. Our analysis showed that many organisations already have regular reviews in place. Most organisations sought feedback on their practices, even though in some cases it tended to consist of complaints rather than actionable requests. Such initiatives are essential in order to create communication strategies that manage the expectations of citizens in relation to the services provided by CI operators.

5   Conclusion

The AESOP guidelines presented in this paper should inform the communication practices of CI operators at each stage of a crisis (mitigation, preparedness, response, recovery). The proposed tactics build on existing best practices in the field of crisis communication, aiming to establish the most effective channel(s) to be deployed during such incidents. With particular focus on how both traditional media and social media

[1] This project has received funding from the European Union's Horizon 2020 research and innovation programme under grant agreement no. 653390.

can help build resilience, this paper has explained how the frequency, clarity and consistency of crisis communication messaging can help build more resilient critical infrastructures. CI operators should work with other key stakeholders to ensure that the information shared with members of the public is both accurate and consistent. Finally, this study suggested that it was imperative for operators to constantly review and update their communication strategies in order to adapt to the changing media environment and the evolving information-seeking behaviours of their target audience.

References

Braun, V., Clarke, V.: Using thematic analysis in psychology. Qual. Res. Psychol. **3**(2), 77–101 (2006)

Cassa, C.A., Chunara, R., Mandl, K., Brownstein, J.S.: Twitter as a sentinel in emergency situations: lessons from the Boston marathon explosions. PLoS Curr. **5**, 1–12 (2013)

Centers for Disease Control and Prevention: Crisis and Emergency Risk Communication (2014). https://emergency.cdc.gov/cerc/resources/pdf/cerc_2014edition.pdf. Accessed 14 Sept 2017

Cheng, J.W., Mitomo, H., Otsuka, T., Jeon, S.Y.: The effects of ICT and mass media in post-disaster recovery - a two model case study of the Great East Japan earthquake. Telecommun. Policy **39**(6), 515–532 (2013)

Coombs, W.T.: Parameters of crisis communication. In: Coombs, W.T., Holladay, S.J. (eds.) The Handbook of Crisis Communication, pp. 17–53. Blackwell Publishing Ltd., Malden (2010)

Coombs, W.T.: The value of communication during a crisis: insights from strategic communication research. Bus. Horiz. **58**, 141–148 (2015)

Laituri, M., Kodrich, K.: On line disaster response community: People as sensors of high magnitude disasters using internet GIS. Sensors **8**(5), 3037–3055 (2008)

MacDonagh, P., Comer, M., Mackin, M., O'Byrnes, R., Dobrokhotova, E., Wendt, W., Kloyber, C., Elliot, A., McCarthy, S.: Best Practice in Communication for Civil Resilience. DRIVER D35.1 (2016)

Melkunaite, L. et al.: International Survey. IMPROVER Project, Deliverable 1.1 (2016)

Quin, S.C.: Crisis and emergency risk communication in a pandemic: a model for building capacity and resilience of minority communities. Health Promot. Pract. **9**(4), 18–25 (2008)

Stephens, K.K., Barrett, A., Mahometa, M.L.: Organizational communication in emergencies: using multiple channels and sources to combat noise and capture attention. Hum. Commun. Res. **39**, 230–251 (2013)

Sutton, J., Skiba, U.M., van Grinsven, H.J.M., Oenema, O., Watson, C.J., Williams, J., Hellums, D.T., Maas, R., Gydenkaerne, S., Pathak, H., Winiwater, W.: Green economy thinking and the control of nitrous oxide emissions. Environ. Dev. **9**, 76–85 (2014)

The Role of Stories in Three Non-12 Step Alcohol Online Support Groups

Sally Sanger(✉)⊙, Peter A. Bath⊙, and Jo Bates⊙

University of Sheffield, Sheffield, UK
Ssanger1@sheffield.ac.uk

Abstract. Health-related mutual aid groups provide an important source of information and support for people with a variety of illnesses and health problems. Research has demonstrated the important role of story-telling for people in Alcoholics Anonymous (AA) face-to-face meetings, for example, in informing new members about the organization's beliefs about alcoholism. There has been limited research examining the role that story plays in online AA, and even less research on story in non-AA/non-12 step groups. This paper explores the role of stories in three alcohol online support groups (AOSGs) that do not follow the 12-step philosophy, but offer very different beliefs about problem drinking and approaches to managing it. The paper reports on thematic analysis of the three groups' discussion forum messages, from which the role that story plays in the groups is identified. It is part of a wider study of the role discussion forums of AOSGs can play in informing users' 'representations' or beliefs about alcoholism/problem drinking.

Keywords: Online support groups · Alcohol · Story · Narrative
Mutual aid

1 Introduction

Lay beliefs about an illness or problem have now been shown to have important impacts on the clinical and social outcomes of treatment [7, 11, 14]. For example, the interpretation a person places on their 'symptoms' will influence what they decide to do about it, which in turn will impact on whether, and how, the issue is handled, and what the outcomes are from it. In terms of problem drinking, if an individual does not believe that they can stay sober, or does not believe that their drinking is a problem, they may not attempt to deal with it. The condition may escalate and lead to many of the social, personal, health and economic problems that can be caused by excessive drinking to an individual or society.

These influential lay beliefs can be formed in various ways over the course of an individual's lifetime, as a result of exposure to many different information sources. One possible influence in terms of alcohol is the information provided by support groups available to problem drinkers. (For the purpose of this paper no distinction is made between alcoholism and problem drinking, which are seen as points on a continuum of Alcohol Use Disorder in accordance with the Diagnostic and Statistical Manual 5 [1] definition.). Support groups are available in face-to-face and online formats, the latter

© Springer International Publishing AG, part of Springer Nature 2018
G. Chowdhury et al. (Eds.): iConference 2018, LNCS 10766, pp. 126–131, 2018.
https://doi.org/10.1007/978-3-319-78105-1_16

usually including discussion forums. Within these, people can seek information, ask questions and exchange knowledge, including that gleaned from personal experience.

The most influential and widespread alcohol online support group (AOSG) is Alcoholics Anonymous (AA), an international mutual aid group that espouses a definition of alcoholism as a disease, remedied by a 12-step programme. AA has influenced many state and private treatment programmes in the Western world. There has been much research into face-to-face AA and its effects, including into the central importance of members' use of story to convey the organisation's messages. There has also been some research into AA online in this regard. The aim of this paper is to explore whether similar processes are at work when stories are told in non-12 step AOSGs.

It is important to know more about this as problem drinking remains a significant problem in western society, and treatment figures are low. As more individuals turn to the Internet for help with health issues, improving understanding of, and access to the help available in online environments is vital. Given the centrality of 'story' to AA (as will be shown below), it is important to examine if this is used in the same way in other AOSGs. This study will briefly identify four types of story found in three AOSGs with contrasting beliefs, and will discuss the role of stories generally in the groups.

1.1 Definition of Story

Agreed by many to be a universal human activity [17], story-telling can be defined as follows:

> "A teller. . . takes a listener into a past time or 'world' and recapitulates what happened then to make a point, often a moral one" (Riessman [15] p. 3)

> "[Story-tellers] recount the events of their lives and narrate them into temporal order and meaning" (Sandelowski [16] p. 161)

For this study, narrative and story were deemed interchangeable, and the definitions above were adopted. Both indicate three elements: events or actions, a temporal element or sequence to these, and meaning, or how the person makes sense of what happened, what the point of the action is and therefore why the story has been told.

2 Literature Review

Cain [3, 4] showed how face-to-face AA teaches newcomers its culture, beliefs and practices, largely through stories. Newcomers learn to reinterpret their past and reconstruct their identities, moving from being drinking non-alcoholics to non-drinking alcoholics. They do this through listening to the drinking and recovery stories of others and identifying with them, interpreting their own story in the same way and telling it in their turn to help others. Newcomers also learn from others' reactions to their stories, and by observing how other members react to these, specifically which parts of the newcomers' narratives they endorse (identify with), and which they correct.

'Correction' happens when a speaker tells similar stories from their own life with alternate, AA-compatible interpretations and explanations. The original speaker is not overtly corrected: it is done implicitly, with "advice disguised as self-disclosure" to adopt Lewis's term [10] p. 10.

Storytelling in online support groups has received some research attention [e.g., 9]. However, there is little research on AOSGs [13] and storytelling. Coulson [5, 6] found that storytelling was used in a similar way to face-to-face AA in two online support groups which clearly followed an AA/12-step philosophy. Lyytikainen [12], using Howard et al.'s three-phase model of therapeutic change, also showed how storytelling is used to teach in the Russian version of AA online. Story there is central to the 'remoralisation' phase where an individual's ideas about a problem are re-worked and hope for change instilled. In 1999, Hanninen and Koski-Jannes [8] suggested that the stories of alcoholics online outside AA/12-step fellowships had received little in-depth analysis, and this situation remains the same today. There have been no in-depth studies of story in non-AA AOSGs: a gap which this paper begins to address.

3   Methods

A qualitative methodology was adopted for this study. Following ethical approval from The University of Sheffield, consent to analyse postings was obtained from the moderators of three AOSGs which do not follow the 12-step philosophy. These were groups with publicly available discussion forums on their sites, two of which also offered other facilities (e.g., information pages, blogs). They were aimed at adults with alcohol problems, written in English and differing in size, location and social norms. The three were purposively selected from a list as holding contrasting beliefs about alcoholism and its treatment (Cognitive Behavioural Therapy, medication, and harm reduction are the three different approaches to treatment). Five hundred messages per group were analysed from threads posted to between August and October 2015. This period was chosen to avoid current postings: in one case the group notified members that the study was taking place (and offered them the option of withdrawing their posts from the study which was not taken up). Whilst the researcher did not post on any of the forums, awareness of their presence analysing current posts could have been off-putting to the members of that group.

The samples of posts were downloaded and anonymised, then coded using NVivo 11 and analysed thematically using Braun and Clarke's method of thematic analysis [2]. The steps involved were:

- Familiarisation with the data
- Coding using a scheme partly derived from the literature review and partly arising inductively from the sampled material
- Grouping codes into themes relevant to the topic
- Reviewing and defining the themes.

Additionally the sites' information pages about problem drinking examined to establish the beliefs about alcoholism views promoted in them.

4   Findings

4.1   Types of Stories Identified

A key theme emerging from the analyses centred on the importance of stories and anecdotes. At least 98 were identified in the sampled material. Several common types of stories were found and their typical structure analysed, specifically:

- Drinking life-stories – accounts of an individual's drinking and recovery
- Moderate drinkers' tales – accounts of attempts at moderate drinking that escalate over time, leading back to problem drinking
- Experimenters' tales – stories of experimentation with alcohol or with medication to treat problem drinking
- Treatment tales – accounts focusing on treatment, which may or may not involve the medical profession.

Stories varied in length from one or two sentences to one or more lengthy posts, sometimes occurring over different threads.

4.2   The Role of Stories

Advice and Information Giving

The key use of story in AA was described above as giving "advice disguised as self-disclosure" (Lewis [10] p. 10). Story is also used to convey advice in the non-AA online groups:

> "I was trying to get through to [Alan] with my story...I wanted to turn him away from alcoholism, not to boast about my drinking" (John, B1, 11) (All quotations from the forums have been carefully re-worded to protect members' privacy, whilst retaining the original meaning).

Here a drinking life-story describing a sudden descent into alcoholism was used as a teaching mechanism, and its power was assumed to derive from the possibility that the reader would identify with it and listen to the writer as they were similar. However, there is a marked difference from AA in that in the actual telling of the story the writer was explicit about the meaning, and about applying this to the original poster [OP].

> "You meant to be funny, but it's not sensible to think like that. I had an ongoing joke that I wasn't an alcoholic, just working on becoming one. I didn't think I could just suddenly get addicted" (John, B1, 11)

The point of using a personal story was to reach someone through inviting iden-tification, and to exemplify or reinforce the simply stated message. In all three groups attempts to correct someone were overt: disagreement, feedback and correction were 'allowed' by the groups and therefore explicit: subtle correction through story was not necessary.

Through story, members can also provide information, experiential knowledge and a 'path' for others, showing them what may lie ahead:

"Your story has given me great information as to what emotions and thoughts to possibly expect" (Olivia, A1, 5)

Empowerment

Individual posters wrote about the effect and value of stories to them. Three common roles that they played for members which were explicitly stated by them include firstly, providing inspiration, motivation and encouragement. This was found in all three groups and the following is a typical example:

> "I like hearing stories of people succeeding...some posts and stories I've followed...have been so inspiring." (Deborah, A1, 4)

Secondly, hearing others' stories could reduce members' sense of being alone with the problem, or of feeling unique in being alcoholic, and this, along with inspiration, gave a sense of strength and self-efficacy:

> "The more stories we hear from others, the less alone we feel and we draw strength from others. That's what this group does" (Nancy A1, 9)

Thirdly, and as in this example, stories gave hope that a member could achieve what others have achieved. This was particularly prevalent in Group C where users of the method advocated to control drinking (The Sinclair Method or TSM) often felt frustrated at the slow progress they were making:

> "it's always heartening to hear someone's success with TSM, especially after trying for a long time." (Vera, C2, 2)

Community

Anecdotes and stories in Group A were observed to reinforce the sense of community, as individuals shared a story whose significance would only be fully understood by other members: this may be in the sense of appreciating its humour, its significance or how annoying something had been. For example, when Michael told an anecdote about a work colleague who suggested he solved his drinking issue by buying more expensive wine and drinking less, he commented: "If only I'd been clever enough to think of that, eh? This is what we have to put up with." (Michael, A1, 10). This prompted sympathetic understanding from other members, one of whom recounted their own anecdote of annoying outsiders. There was less sense of community in Group B, and in Group C, the 'outsiders' tended to be the medical profession that were viewed as not understanding TSM and needing to be 'managed' to enable people to get access to the necessary medication. Stories of difficulties with the medical profession were frequent amongst treatment tales in this group.

5 Conclusion

This study identified the importance of story in three online non-12 step groups, and explored differences and similarities to the use of story to convey advice in face-to-face AA. In the non-12 step groups four types of story (drinking life-stories, moderate drinkers' tales, experimenters' tales and treatment stories) were identified. As well as advice-giving, five possible roles were noted: story can illustrate what is to come for the person entering recovery, provide hope, inspire, reduce loneliness and reinforce a sense of community.

References

1. American Psychiatric Association: Diagnostic and Statistical Manual of Mental Disorders (DSM–5), 5th edn. American Psychiatric Association, Arlington (2013)
2. Braun, V., Clarke, V.: Using thematic analysis in psychology. Qual. Res. Psychol. **3**(2), 77–101 (2006)
3. Cain, C.: Personal stories in Alcoholics Anonymous. In: Holland, D., Lachicotte Jr., W., Skinner, D., Cain, C. (eds.) Identity and Agency in Cultural Worlds, pp. 66–97. Harvard University Press, Massachusetts (1998)
4. Cain, C.: Personal stories: identity acquisition and self-understanding in Alcoholics Anonymous. Ethos **19**(2), 210–253 (1991)
5. Coulson, N.S.: Sharing, supporting and sobriety: a qualitative analysis of messages posted to alcohol-related online discussion forums in the United Kingdom. J. Subst. Use **19**(1–2), 176–180 (2014)
6. Coulson, N.S.: Problem drinking and peer support in cyberspace, small grant report. University of Nottingham, Nottingham (2011)
7. Hagger, M.S., Orbell, S.: A meta-analytic review of the common-sense model of illness representations. Psychol. Health **18**(2), 141–184 (2003)
8. Hanninen, V., Koski-Jannes, A.: Narratives of recovery from addictive behavior. Addiction **94**(12), 1837–1848 (1999)
9. Hoybye, M.T., Johansen, C., Tjornhoj-Thomsen, T.: Online interaction. Effects of storytelling in an internet breast cancer support group. Psycho-Oncology **14**, 211–220 (2005)
10. Lewis, S.C.: A grounded theory analysis of the forms of support on two online anorexia forums. Ph.D. thesis, Loughborough University, Leicestershire, UK (2014)
11. Lobban, F., Jones, S.: A review of the role of illness models in severe mental illness. Clin. Psychol. Rev. **23**, 171–196 (2003)
12. Lyytikainen, L.: Mutual support and recovery in the Russian Alcoholics Anonymous online community. Nord. Stud. Alcohol Drugs **33**(2), 151–172 (2016)
13. Nagy, J.: Online assistance for substance abuse and dependence: exploring the experience and dimensions of online self-help programs. Capella University, Minnesota (2015)
14. Petrie, K.J., Jago, L.A., Devcich, D.A.: The role of illness perceptions in patients with medical conditions. Curr. Opin. Psychiatry **20**, 163–167 (2007)
15. Riessman, C.K.: Narrative Analysis: Qualitative Research Methods, vol. 30. Sage, Newbury Park (1993)
16. Sandelowski, M.: Telling stories: narrative approaches in qualitative research. Image: J. Nurs. Scholarsh. **23**(3), 161–166 (1991)
17. Strobbe, S., Kurtz, E.: Narratives for recovery: personal stories in the 'Big Book' of Alcoholics Anonymous. J. Groups Addict. Recovery **7**(1), 29–52 (2012)

Ephemeral Communication
and Communication Places
What Influences College-Aged Negotiation of Instant Messaging Usage Within App Ecosystems?

Lauren Thomson, Adam J. Lee[✉], and Rosta Farzan

School of Computing and Information, University of Pittsburgh, Pittsburgh, USA
LET41@pitt.edu, adamlee@cs.pitt.edu

Abstract. In this paper, we present the preliminary results from an interview study of ten undergraduate students on instant messaging applications. We focus on how participants used both features of the applications and perceived atmosphere to determine how to manage their social network across multiple applications. Using qualitative methods, we identified factors of intimacy, playfulness, and ephemerality to play a key role in influencing the choice of messaging application.

1 Introduction

Since the migration of instant messaging to smartphones, there has been a proliferation of new applications dedicated to messaging, with social media platforms creating their own internal messaging systems that compete with both standard messaging and texting. All of this as messaging has grown in prominence as a mode of communication and users have defined their own social rules and structures within their application ecosystem.

Researchers have been studying how users utilize these technologies since early desktop instant messaging applications. Particularly, a recent work by Nouwens et al. [1] studied the ecosystem of instant messaging applications used by the individual user, and was one of very few that looked at how users manage multiple applications in concert, as the majority of users now do. They found that some users define a "communication place" with certain emotional connotations, a perceived purpose, and membership rules based upon an application's userbase, functionalities, and the communication patterns used in that space. The user's communication place informed how they used the application. Their usage patterns then cyclically lead to experiences that shaped the way they perceived the communication place.

The goal of this paper is to investigate what influences users' decisions in what applications to use for messaging and how they negotiate the use of those applications with their social network. We conducted an interview study with ten university students who considered themselves current users of both texting and instant messaging. This population group was selected as they represent the

© Springer International Publishing AG, part of Springer Nature 2018
G. Chowdhury et al. (Eds.): iConference 2018, LNCS 10766, pp. 132–138, 2018.
https://doi.org/10.1007/978-3-319-78105-1_17

highest rates of usage for instant messaging among the current university-aged demographic [2]. Focusing on this specific population also allowed us to reduce variance in the types of social networks between participants. In this paper, we will report on the details of our interview studies, the qualitative analysis of the interviews, and the results of our analysis. We end the paper with a discussion of how our results compared to prior work in this area and provide design implications based on our findings and avenues of future work.

In comparison to prior work [1], we found our participants far less likely to mention contact management and membership rules as factors that influenced their decision making. Instead, the consistent threads that showed up between users were the desire for or against ephemerality and emotional connotations generated by users developing their own private usages of application features.

2   Background

In the context of social use of messaging applications, much of the literature has focused on either current usage patterns or the connection between messaging behaviors and security decisions.

O'Hara et al. [3] looked at socialization on the instant messenger WhatsApp and identified what aspects of those conversations led to feelings of intimacy and more generally how users dwelled within the application. They investigated the way users utilized features such as read indicators, media messaging, groups, notifications in order to create a sense of continuity within a conversation in order to enact friendship. O'Hara et al. emphasized the importance of looking at messaging decisions in context of the social needs of the users, not just in the context of economics or technological features.

In investigating how users navigated the many functionalities of modern smartphones, Barkhuus and Polichar [4] looked into how users switch between communication channels. They found that convenience, urgency and pragmatic factors dominated the reasoning for choice of channel when initiating contact. Meanwhile, Ogara et al. [5] investigated factors that led to satisfaction with and continued use of instant messaging but did not differentiate between messaging applications. Wang and Datta [6] attempted to develop a theoretical model showing why users continued to use an application after initial adoption.

De Luca et al. [7] looked at what security knowledge users brought into their application usage decisions and whether that differed between normal and security expert users. Despite considering security important, they found that both groups did not make decisions primary along security lines. This was backed up by Abu-Salma et al. [8] who found that the primary drivers of application adoption were not usability, privacy of data or security concerns. All of these looked at what motivated use of and choice of applications and that was context we built off of. We've particularly focused on Nouwens et al. [1] as one of the most recent papers to address the same app ecosystem questions we're investigating.

3   Methods

3.1   Study Design

We designed the interview questions in an iterative process through several rounds discussions and revisions to narrow down the focus of the study and design our questions to best address the focus of the study. This process also involved two pilot interviews conducted by the first author. The pilot interview feedback was used to finalize question wording and determine question order. Interviews were semi-structured and took between 30 and 45 min. Questions covered a range of subjects related to the participants' use of instant messaging but only questions pertaining to negotiation of usage between applications were ultimately used in the analysis.

The final set of questions included four primary sections: (1) on the ways the participant used instant messaging, (2) on the applications the participant used for messaging, (3) on ranking and comparing the applications used, and (4) on demographics, comfort with technology, and user self-perception. Some examples of questions that became relevant during analysis were:

"Are there particular types of conversations you tend to have only via instant messaging?" (1)
"Do you still use this app for same types of social interactions?" (2)
"How do you choose which application to contact them [for contacts available on multiple channels] on?" (3)
"What access to or information about your messages would you be willing to share with a researcher in a future study?" (3)
"What features make this application work for you?" (4)

3.2   Procedure

Ten participants were recruited for this study, all university students between the ages of 18 and 23, 7 women and 3 men. Recruitment was conducted via posting flyers on campus and snowball sampling on social media. Interviews were conducted in person by the first author, recorded and then transcribed. The interviews were then coded through an iterative process. Using four of interviews, the first author conducted the first iteration of extracting themes and codes emerging from the interview data. All the emerging themes were discussed to refine the final set of codes, which were used to code the rest of the interviews.

4   Results

There was a range in how clearly participants could break down their own usage patterns and internal reasoning. Some users believed that the majority of their comfort with applications was due solely to familiarity (P1 and P7). Some could give no explanation for why a conversation would end up on a particular platform, while other users had extensive self-justifications for their application preferences and recognizable classification systems for conversations that broke down by application:

"I think that they're [the messaging applications used] all useful for the different purposes that they serve, and that most of the people that I know use them for the same reasons...we all understand which applications, yeah, which niche they serve and it helps us compartmentalize what we're doing on each one." (P4)

4.1 Perceived Atmosphere: Intimacy vs. Playfulness

One recurring explanation for participants favoring one application over another or how they decided which application to use in certain conversations was the perceived atmosphere of the application, which follows what Nouwens et al. referred to as emotional connotations [1]. This was framed by our participants in terms of applications that were either 'intimate' or 'fun'.

All of the participants that described an application as 'intimate' were referring to the default SMS application on their phone. P9 chose to use texting over other messaging applications when they were having conversations that they felt required greater privacy: "I guess it seems somewhat more private over texting...I guess it seems more secure to me." P5 cited the same feeling to describe why texting was their preferred messaging application: "I guess it feels like a little more, like, intimate in comparison to the other ones? Because usually it's one on one. And it's not in the context of something else. The sole purpose of the messaging application - of texting, is to text." P4 noted that "I know most people use Facebook Messenger, but I still use texts. It feels more authentic".

While participants did not have a specific justification for describing texting as more intimate, identifying an application as fun or playful was often accompanied by noting individual features. P6 favored Facebook Messenger and described it as fun, citing the way they used the feature of updating what emoji represented their conversation as a dialogue with friends. P2 also favored Facebook Messenger and described it as a "playful atmosphere", recounting a story where a group chat devolved into various members of the group ejecting members from the chat as a way of airing petty grievances. Several participants mentioned stickers, gifs and emoji both as reasons they favored a specific application and as contributing to a feeling of 'fun'.

4.2 Ephemerality

Another significant emerging theme from the interviews involved the ephemerality of messages in the messaging applications. Presence or absence of a permanent records of messages seemed to significantly influence the choice of which messaging applications to use. This tended to come up most often in the context of Snapchat Messenger, which automatically deletes instant messages after they've been read.

P1 mentioned appreciating having a permanent record when using texting "...you have a record. Like, I did type this things so you can't deny it" citing the ability to resolve disputes using their text archive as an 'alibi'. For P6, the lack of permanent messages on Snapchat caused it to rank last because

"I don't know what I was talking about." P4 described negotiating this challenge in the context of moving conversations off of Snapchat Messenger whenever they became something that they would need to remember, such as making dinner plans.

P4 described Snapchat Messenger as their favorite messaging application because of the lack of a permanent record.

"That I can say what I want to say without this fear that I'll go back on it and then say 'Ugh, what was I thinking? Like, I was so stupid'. Like, on Skype I can go back over three years of messages. Do you know how terrifying that is? If you right click on the computer you can jump back in time. You can jump back by a year." (P4)

P6 mentioned it as their application they'd use for "messaging for things I'm just a little bit more uncomfortable with", a step down in perceived security from talking on the phone. They also mentioned feeling generally uncomfortable with the permanent record of their messages: "It is kinda creepy sometimes when you scroll back up and it's like, we were talking about boys for like 20 min. Sometimes it's just kinda like, eeeh, I'd rather it not be on the record".

Whether or not a permanent record was accessible on their device, several users were concerned about the companies that run their messaging applications having permanent records of their messages. P6 believed that Facebook had human moderators that could be reading any messages stored on their servers for the purpose of generating targeted advertisements. P4 said, in reference to both Snapchat and Skype "But I feel like when I send it it goes to a server and then it sends it to somebody and I feel like when it's on the server, somebody could look at it...On Skype I'm convinced Microsoft has access to all the messages I've sent and they're stored somewhere and they hold them there".

5   Discussion and Future Work

5.1   Preliminary Results

Care should be taken extrapolating from the preliminary results of this study; we looked at a small sample group of the college-aged U.S. residents. However, our initial analysis is that at least some members of that group use various clues provided by their messaging applications to succeed in managing their messaging application ecosystems.

The framework that Nouwens et al. [1] sets out in their paper, of users developing communication places based upon the spaces and interactions provided for by an application, was backed up in our research by some of the participants. We did not find as strong of a focus on user management of their contact lists— when users mentioned managing contacts it was always in the context of initial avoidance. If they did not wish to include someone in the social network on a given application, they would not give their number, screen name or messaging access to the contact.

Within the population we interviewed, we did not see any evidence that users desired to reduce their number of messaging applications. While some users had more than five applications they used for instant messaging with largely overlapping groups of contacts, no one expressed a desire to streamline their instant messaging. Users that did desire to delete applications did so because of dissatisfaction with usability, the community of contacts on the application or the perceived tone of the application.

5.2   Future Work

There are a few essential unanswered questions about the framework of communication places. Presumably, all users have an internal conceptualization of an application as they use it to some extent, some are merely less able to explain. To what extent are those conceptualizations communication places? And then, how does a users's level of intentionality impact their behavior? Do users that are less able to describe why they make decisions about their messaging habits make different messaging decisions?

Our conclusion that the majority of application choices were navigated around ephemerality or perceived atmosphere is counter-intuitive. These seem like very small components of applications that can have a great many features. On the other hand, almost all of the applications used by our participants offered identical core features and largely overlapping userbases. This magnified the impact of small differences on participant's decision-making.

One potential design consideration brought up in this study is that features that can be repurposed have the potential to become communication methods in their own right. Features that Facebook Messenger intended to be used to customize a group message were used by our participants in ways that their group of contacts codified as communication styles. For instance, a participant who created a method of ephemeral conversation by chatting in the chat's title instead of the actual messages. Having created their own method of communication made the application seem more personal and more playful and was cited as a reason users favored an application.

References

1. Nouwens, M., Griggio, C.F., Mackay, W.E.: "Whatsapp is for family; Messenger is for friends": communication places in app ecosystems. In: CHI Conference on Human Factors in Computing Systems, pp. 727–735 (2017)
2. Jones, C., Ramanau, R., Cross, S., Healing, G.: Net generation or digital natives: is there a distinct new generation entering university? Comput. Educ. **54**, 722–732 (2010)
3. O'Hara, K., Massimi, M., Harper, R., Rubens, S., Morris, J.: Everyday dwelling with Whatsapp. In: ACM Conference on Computer Supported Cooperative Work & Social Computing, pp. 1131–1143 (2014)
4. Barkhuus, L., Polichar, V.E.: Empowerment through seamfulness: smart phones in everyday life. Pers. Ubiquit. Comput. **15**, 629–639 (2011)

5. Ogara, S.O., Koh, C.E., Prybutok, V.R.: Investigating factors affecting social presence and user satisfaction with mobile instant messaging. Comput. Hum. Behav. **36**, 453–459 (2014)
6. Wang, Y.K., Datta, P.: Investigating technology commitment in instant messaging application users. J. Organ. End User Comput. **22**, 70–94 (2010)
7. De Luca, A., Das, S., Ortlieb, M., Ion, I., Laurie, B.: Expert and non-expert attitudes towards (secure) instant messaging. In: ACM Symposium on Usable Privacy and Security, pp. 147–157 (2016)
8. Abu-Salma, R., Sasse, M.A., Bonneau, J., Danilova, A., Naiakshina, A., Smith, M.: Obstacles to the adoption of secure communication tools. In: IEEE Symposium on Security and Privacy, pp. 137–153 (2017)

An Upward Spiral Model: Bridging and Deepening Digital Divide

Biyang Yu[1]([⊠]), Ana Ndumu[1] [iD], Lorraine Mon[1], and Zhenjia Fan[2]

[1] Florida State University, Tallahassee, FL 32306, USA
{by13b, avg05d}@my.fsu.edu, lmon@fsu.edu
[2] Nankai University, Tianjin 30071, China
fanzhenjia@nankai.edu.cn

Abstract. The digital divide is a global problem that impacts an individual's ability to participate in society. To address disparate and conflicting theories on the dynamics of the digital divide, the researchers proposed an integrated upward spiral model that explains how digital divides are both alleviated and deepened. The researchers then utilized an existing 2014–2015 dataset comprised of 398 survey responses and nine interview responses from Chinese migrant workers to test the viability of this model. Two hypotheses suggested based on the upward spiral model were supported by path analysis and supplemental qualitative analysis of the data: 1. A path traced causal relationship exists among forces, resources, access, e-acceptance, and e-inclusion and 2. Situational e-inclusion initiates forces, which in turn facilitates resources and access, and prompts ongoing cycles of situational e-inclusion. The results support that a comprehensive upward spiral model can be utilized as an analytical framework to explain the reasons and extents to which the digital divide phenomenon exists in society.

Keywords: E-inclusion · Upward spiral model · Deepening digital divide

1 Introduction

Although there has been remarkable mobilization in global ICT investment and infrastructure, the digital divide problem has not been eradicated. Rather, it is widely accepted that this complex and dynamic issue continues to evolve, particularly as ICT advances [1]. The digital divide remains an important challenge for policy makers, practitioners, and researchers worldwide [2]. In order to investigate the complexities of the digital divide, a thorough and dynamic understanding of the problem is necessary.

The digital divide has been widely addressed by researchers from various disciplines. This interdisciplinarity has resulted in longstanding dichotomies and, thus, a cluttered field. As such, researchers have called for comprehensive theories on the ICT inequality [1, 3]. In response, we proposed an integrative model, based on a synthesis of literature spanning 20 years, that includes both measurements and causes of the digital divide [4]. To further explain our conceptualization of the digital divide, we designed an upward spiral model and then tested its viability using empirical data on Chinese migrant workers' ICT experiences.

© Springer International Publishing AG, part of Springer Nature 2018
G. Chowdhury et al. (Eds.): iConference 2018, LNCS 10766, pp. 139–144, 2018.
https://doi.org/10.1007/978-3-319-78105-1_18

2 An Integrative Model of Digital Inequality

Ongoing revisions of our original conceptualization [4], resulted in a more succinct model (as seen in Fig. 1), where digital divide and e-inclusion are regarded as juxtaposed concepts that represent actual and desired situations in terms of digital participation. E-inclusion is attained only when "the effective participation of individuals and communities in all dimensions of the knowledge-based society and economy through their access to ICT" is equally achieved [5]. However, as long as people are excluded from digital participation at any level (e.g., political, social, economic), a digital divide exists. While digital divide and e-inclusion constitute effect measurements of ICT use, e-acceptance is the behavioral measurement that influences elements of initial adoption and continuous use [6, 7].

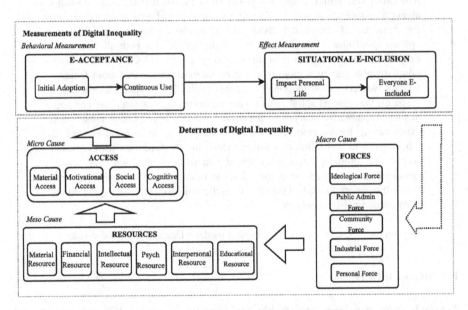

Fig. 1. An integrative model of digital inequality

Access, resource, and force describe micro, meso and micro determinants of digital inequality, respectively. Access denotes to the totality of an individual's ability to readily use certain technologies in specific scenarios [8]. Based on the research canon, the various types of access include material access (e.g., computing devices, Internet connectivity, software), cognitive access (i.e., ability to use technology for various tasks), motivational access (i.e., desire to adopt, purchase, use, or learn technology for specific situations), and social access (i.e., socially-constructed conditions necessary for task-specific use). In contrast to access, resource is defined as available assets (e.g., money, equipment, knowledge) that can be drawn on by end-users to achieve access and actualize general technology use. Six types of resources have been found in previous literature: financial (i.e., available monies for ICT use), material (i.e., available and affordable digital devices, infrastructure, and services for users), intellectual (i.e., general literacy, numeracy, and intellectual abilities related to ICT use), educational (external information, knowledge, and training materials or programs), psychological (i.e., psychological elements reifying motivational access), and interpersonal (i.e., interpersonal networks and social capital who promote ICT use). Different from access and resource, a force represents a higher order influential power that can directly or indirectly influence the structural, quality and quantity distribution of resources for ICT use and empowerments. Previous research substantiates that forces are ideological (i.e., influences from value systems or principles shared by mainstream society), industrial (i.e., influences from ICT vendors, ICT industries, and markets), public administrative (i.e., influences from municipalities, universities, libraries, etc.), community (i.e., influences stemming from local communities), and personal forces (i.e., influences associated with individual agency).

According to the model, forces distribute the necessary resources to supply individuals with multidimensional access, resulting in behavioral use of ICT (e-acceptance) as well as critical effects (e-inclusion). Those critical effects (e-inclusion) might reinforce the power of certain forces, resulting in another cycle of e-inclusion (as shown in the dotted lines in Fig. 1). Hindrances at either the force, resource, or access levels will lead to problems with e-acceptance and e-inclusion, resulting a digital divide.

3 An Upward Spiral Model of Digital Inequality

E-inclusion describes an ideal situation where all governing agencies support ICT use in all communities, granting each individual equal access to computing technologies and full participation in the digital society. The digital divide problem continues to deepen partly because e-inclusion is an ever-changing goal that coincides with the rapid evolution of computing technologies. Individuals may make adequate use of *specific* facets of ICT, which is referred to as *situational e-inclusion* (e.g., e-included in social media). However, as new technologies develop, new situations of e-inclusion sprout (e.g., e-included in virtual realities). The trajectory towards e-inclusion can be presented as an upward model as shown in Fig. 2. In the model, e-inclusion represents a phenomenon involving an infinite progression of forces, resources, accesses, e-acceptance and situational e-inclusion. The upward path denotes the ongoing levels of ICT engagement for individuals. However, individuals can either progress or become stagnant and eventually regress. According to the spiral model, situational e-inclusion is only achieved when everyone is e-included in specific technologies. Since technologies are evolving, there are infinite situational e-inclusion scenarios. Plus, people are situationally e-included at differing paces. Although a society may see gains in one type of situational e-inclusion, another aspect might remain unbridged. For example, although telecommunications infrastructure has promoted Internet use for millions of people in developing countries (e.g., one type of situational e-inclusion), poor economies and education inhibit the more advanced Internet use (e.g., another type of situational e-inclusion). Despite gains made related to bridging the divide, ICT continues to morph. This model helps to explain the ebbs and flows of the digital divide phenomenon.

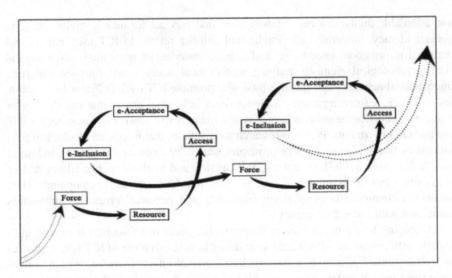

Fig. 2. An upward spiral model: bridging and deepening digital divide

4   Testing the Model

Based on the integrative model and the spiral model, the interactions among forces, resources, access, e-acceptance, and e-inclusion can be presented in the following two hypotheses:

Hypothesis I: A path trace causal relationship exists among force, resource, access, e-acceptance, and situational e-inclusion. Specifically, forces distribute resources, which impact access and facilitate e-acceptance and situational e-inclusion.

Hypothesis II: Situational e-inclusion can reinforce the power of forces, which in turn facilitates resources and access.

To test above two hypotheses, we used an existing dataset of computing technology experiences among Chinese migrant workers. Chinese migrant workers are those who temperately leave from rural regions to fulfill low-level jobs in urban areas. Since they are marginalized groups in China, they are considered more susceptible to the digital divide in comparison to dominant groups [9]. This dataset included 398 effective survey responses and 9 interview responses collected in 2014 and 2015 throughout China. Path analysis was applied to test the hypotheses and was analyzed using AMOS v.24, while content analysis was utilized to examine interview data that was organized using NVivo v.11. Codes were drawn from model constructs which were based on prior literature. We then investigated possible causal relationship between constructs. Two researchers achieved 0.71 Cohen's Kappa coefficient score for the qualitative analyses, and discrepancies were discussed with a third researcher until final agreement was achieved.

5 Preliminary Findings

The data supported Hypothesis I for all five forces. Various scenarios indicated a significant relationship linking forces to resource, and then from resources to access, e-acceptance, and situational e-inclusion. As demonstrated in Fig. 3, for instance, the public-administration force (i.e., influences stemming from governing bodies that effect changes in policy and public services) appeared to influence resources: Rural areas usually invest less and have inadequate broadband infrastructure. Poor ICT development negatively impacts ICT use and effects for local people. As seen in Fig. 3, path analysis results (df = 3, Chi-square = 3.758, RMSEA = 0.026, CFI = 0.998) suggest a trace path: big cities (i.e., public-administration force) provide better public broadband infrastructure (i.e., material resource), which led to suitable Internet connections (i.e., material access). This allowed migrant workers to significantly use ICT (i.e., e-acceptance), which positively impacted life domains (i.e., situational e-inclusion).

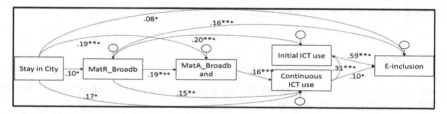

Fig. 3. Public administration force impacts preference between city or town and e-inclusion

Figure 4 showed the significant tracing path (df = 3, Chi-square = 2.315, RMSEA = 0, CFI = 1) of one type of personal force: monthly income of individuals. Likewise, higher incomes (i.e., personal force) allow for disposable income to purchase devices (i.e.,), which was in turn traced to the number of devices an individual owned (i.e., material access) along with their adoption rate (i.e., e-acceptance) and situational e-inclusion.

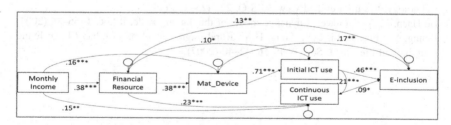

Fig. 4. The personal force impacts of monthly income on e-inclusion

According to Hypothesis II, situational e-inclusion can reinforce forces and subsequently advances situational e-inclusion. Therefore, e-inclusion is cyclical or iterative. Evidence of the spiral model was supported by the qualitative data; for example, when migrant workers positively rated the impacts of their basic ICT use (situational e-inclusion, e.g., look for health information online), they were more likely to upgrade their devices or explore advanced ways of using ICT, thus initiating another cycle of situational e-inclusion (e.g., use social media to defend for personal legal right).

6   Conclusion

In this preliminary study, we proposed an integrated upward spiral model representing the dynamics of deepening digital inequality problem. Digital inequality can be measured according to behavior (e-acceptance) and effect (e-inclusion) in regard to technology use, as suggested by a trace causal path of force, resource, and access. The evolving technologies and technology use scenarios create infinite goals of situational e-inclusions to be attained. Further examinations of issues involving forces, resources, and access will help to diagnose and rectify digital inequalities. Since the analysis is based on secondary analysis of one existing dataset, more empirical data needs to be collected to test the viability and applicability of the model.

References

1. van Dijk, J.A.G.M.: The Deepening Divide: Inequality in the Information Society. SAGE Publications, Thousand Oaks (2005)
2. Billon, M., Marco, R., Lera-Lopez, F.: Disparities in ICT adoption: a multidimensional approach to study the cross-country digital divide. Telecommun. Policy **33**, 596–610 (2009)
3. Yu, L.: The divided views of the information and digital divides: a call for integrative theories of information inequality. J. Inf. Sci. **37**, 660–679 (2011)
4. Yu, B., Ndumu, A., Liu, J., Fan, Z.: E-inclusion or digital divide: an integrated model of digital inequality. Proc. Assoc. Inf. Sci. Technol. **53**, 1–5 (2016)
5. eEurope Advisory Group: e-Inclusion: new challenges and policy recommendations. eEurope Advisory Group (2005)
6. Chen, I.Y.: The factors influencing members' continuance intentions in professional virtual communities - a longitudinal study. J. Inf. Sci. **33**, 451–467 (2007)
7. Venkatesh, V., Morris, M.G., Davis, G.B., Davis, F.D.: User acceptance of information technology: toward a unified view. MIS Q. **27**, 425–478 (2003)
8. De Haan, J.: A multifaceted dynamic model of the digital divide. It Soc. **1**, 66–88 (2004)
9. Keung, W., Fu, D., Li, C.Y., Song, H.X.: Rural migrant workers in urban China: living a marginalised life. Int. J. Soc. Welf. **16**, 32–40 (2007)

Exploration of Online Health Support Groups Through the Lens of Sentiment Analysis

Keyang Zheng[(✉)], Ang Li, and Rosta Farzan

School of Computing and Information, University of Pittsburgh, Pittsburgh, USA
KEZ20@pitt.edu

Abstract. Online health support groups have been gaining prominence in supporting patients and their caregivers. However, it stays as a challenge to understand the role they play in the life of their members. In this paper, we propose a novel approach in utilizing sentiment analysis to explore the dynamics and impact of online health support groups. We present our sentiment analysis model designed for social media support groups and our preliminary results in utilizing the model to understand a Facebook support group for patients with Sickle Cell Disease.

1 Introduction

Online health support groups are among the most popular Internet groups, being employed daily to share and seek health-related information, support, and advice. While there is an abundance of users' behavioral traces in the online communities, it has been an ongoing challenge to study the impact of online communities on their members beyond the online world since the offline traces are often invisible to researchers. In this work, we propose an approach to towards modeling the impact of health support groups through sentiment analysis of discussions in these groups. The sentiment of online discussions can be a reflection of users' offline state of mind and feelings at the time of posting online. Indeed discussions on the health support groups often carry strong sentiment, which may reflect the real-world challenges and experiences patients and their caregivers face. A patient who is in pain and suffering is likely to post a message containing negative sentiment representing their painful state. Similarly, a positive message can be an indication of something positive happening in their lives.

We have developed a sentiment analysis model to classify the sentiment of each Facebook posts and their comments with a high level of accuracy. The classifier allows us to study the group dynamics at a large scale to be able to identify patterns of sentiment changes across the discussion threads. By accurately modeling the sentiment of messages and interaction around messages, we can identify patterns of changes in sentiment and factors contributing to anomalies of sentiment changes. Changes in sentiment coupled with other online traces allow us

© Springer International Publishing AG, part of Springer Nature 2018
G. Chowdhury et al. (Eds.): iConference 2018, LNCS 10766, pp. 145–151, 2018.
https://doi.org/10.1007/978-3-319-78105-1_19

to connect online actions back to what a patient might be experiencing offline. At the same time, we can start analyzing what specific features and aspects of participation in online health support groups can lead to positive changes in patients' real lives. In this paper, we present the development of our sentiment classifier and examples of how sentiment analysis can represent the patterns of participation in online health support groups.

2   Background

The development of Internet has provided new ways to support patients and their caregivers by providing information [3,11] and social support. Research has shown that the support as a result of joining an OHC can reduce the stress level and depression among patients suffering from chronic diseases and help them and their caregivers to be more positive [1,2]. Qiu et al. also found that OHCs have positive impacts on their members' emotions and opinions [10].

Most previous studies of OHC have focused on observations, interviews, and surveys about the benefits of these communities. While such methods are crucial in understanding the impact of the OHC, they are limited in terms of number of people who can be studied and specific people who agree to participate in the studies. Moreover, these methods are limited in terms of real-time reaction to patients. To remedy some of these limitations, researchers have been investigating computational methods to analyze large amounts of online social interactions in an OHC. For example, Zhao et al. developed an approach in conducting sentiment analysis in an OHC for cancer survivors and used the changes in sentiment to identify influential members in the community [14].

We aim to advance the research on such computation models while focusing on a less studied group of patients. Specifically, our work has focused on studying an online health support groups dedicated to Sickle Cell Disease (SCD). SCD is a devastating genetic blood disease that affects millions worldwide but it has received much less support and attention in digital space. The goals of our research is to support patients with SCD by developing computational methods to better understand how and what kinds of participation lead into positive impacts on their lives. While our research currently focuses on SCD, we aim at designing models that can be easily adopted for other communities.

3   Sentiment Analysis

There are a large number of sentiment analysis approaches utilizing machine learning across different domains such as product reviews, news and blogs. However, as demonstrated in [7], sentiment analysis can often be domains dependent. Thus, approaches that are designed for one specific domain can perform poorly in another domain [10]. In case of SCD Facebook group, discussions are often informal and very specific to Sickle Cell and as a result an existing sentiment analysis does not perform accurately enough. We developed a sentiment analysis specific to our context inspired by [6,10].

3.1   Dataset

Our dataset includes data from a SCD group on Facebook, called Sickle Cell Unite, which started in 2009 by a patient living with sickle cell. It is a private Facebook group; i.e. membership request needs to be approved by the administrators, the messages are only visible to members, and only group members can post or comment [4]. We used Facebook Graph API to collect data from the group[1]. The data includes all the messages posted for a period of one year, from April 2016 until April 2017. In addition to the original messages, the data includes all the comments in response to each message. The dataset includes 4,862 posts and 26,057 comments associated with those posts.

3.2   Training Dataset

Our sentiment analysis model uses a supervised machine learning algorithm. Therefore, the first step involved creating labeled data. To do so, we randomly selected a set of 494 posts and comments from our dataset and used Amazon's Mechanical Turk crowdsourcing service to label each message in our training set into positive, negative or neutral class. Each message was labeled by five independent workers. We then aggregated the labels to determine the class of the message using majority class.

3.3   Iterative Development of Sentiment Analysis Model

Our first model of sentiment classification included a relatively small set of features: # of occurrences of proper names, # of occurrences of question marks or exclamation marks, the number of words in the message, the average length of words, the number of positive and negative words in BL lexicon[2] [6], and the strength of positivity and negativity in the message, as suggested by Thelwall et al. [13]. Using these features and our training dataset, we trained four different classifiers: SVM, logistic regression, AdaBoost and Neural Networks [9]. However, neither of the models resulted in acceptable accuracy. The best model achieved only 62% of accuracy and our qualitative assessment of messages identified important mis-classification.

Examination of the mis-classified cases by classification model showed that considering special lexicons is crucial to develop a context-specific sentiment classifier. Therefore, we added the Sent140 lexicon to address the specific language used in Facebook group discussions. Sent140 lexicon is an automatically generated word-sentiment association lexicon (Sent140) from Sentiment140 Corpus [5,6]. The Sent140 lexicon is generated from 1.6 million tweets that are labeled according to emoticons, which provide more specific coverage of words used in social media compared to more general purposed BL lexicon [6]. Using the

---

[1] Our data collection is approved by the University of Pittsburgh IRB and is with the permission of the owners of the group.

[2] A manually created lexicon (BL lexicon) for positive and negative word lists.

Sent140 lexicon, we added the number of words with positive scores or negative scores from Sent140 lexicon as well as the sum of scores of all the words with a score in Sent140 lexicon. We also considered the position of lexical features in the message as sentiment conveyed at the end of a message can have a bigger emphasis compared to the one occurs earlier in the message [8]. Additionally, we considered negation and reverted the lexical features in a negated context [12]. On the other hand, we removed the PosStrength and NegStrength features as they were not adding any values to our model after adding the Lexicon Score generated by Sent140 lexicon. We used the same four classification models with the new feature set and were able to improve the accuracy of our model by more than 10%. Our qualitative investigation of a set of messages further confirmed the improvement and exhibited satisfactory classification. The best accuracy was achieved using logistic regression classifier (accuracy = .73%).

4   Sentiment Analysis of Unite SCD Facebook Group

Using our sentiment classifier, we labeled the sentiment of the messages and their comments. Figure 1 shows the number of positive and negative original posts every month over the period of our data collection[3]. Overall, we observed that the majority of messages (65%) are positive and over time there is a significant drop of negativity.

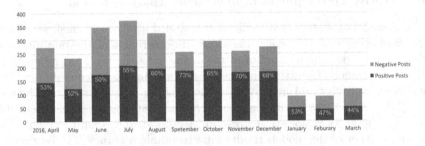

Fig. 1. Number of positive and negative messages over time

4.1   Community Responses in Unite SCD Facebook Group

In terms of community response to messages, overall, the majority of the comments in response to positive posts have a positive tone (86.5% positive vs. 13.4% negative). At the same time, the majority of responses to negative comments also have positive tone (62.6%); however, there are also a significant number of negative comments in response to negative posts (37.3%). Our analysis also

---

[3] The significant drop of activity is mostly due to the sad event of loss of one of the group leaders. The changes over time can be due to various internal and external factors that have not been necessarily considered in our study.

shows that the community provides a larger number of comments in response to negative messages. While positive messages receive an average of 5 comments (SD=9.07), negative messages receive an average of 23 comments (SD=34.66). These results highlight the supportive nature of these online health support groups that community members try to reinforce positivity in response to positive posts and cheer members up at their difficult moments.

Since the negative posts can particularly represent the struggles of the community and we observed a more even distribution of each sentiment in response to the negative posts, it is important to further investigate those cases. Our further investigation of responses to negative messages revealed two common patterns: (1) Responding positively using cheerful language such as *Get well sis* or *we love u*. These comments are often concise and short (average length of 16 words) and limited in numbers. Positive threads in response to negative responses rarely include more than 20 replies. (2) Responding negatively by sharing a similar negative experience to provide empathy. These comments are often longer (average length of 37 words) and also include informational support in addition to personal narratives of their experiences. For example, in response to: *Has this ever happen to anyone she is having pain in her leg, back, throat, head, and eyes. Her eyes are swollen shut with discharge*, other members respond with *Yes it has but it wasn't sickle cell it was a brain hemorrhage and my head was hurting really bad.*

4.2 Changes of Sentiment in Discussion Threads

The ability to automatically identify sentiment of messages most importantly allows us to study patterns of participation in discussion threads. We are particularly interested in identity distinct patterns of changes in the sentiment of comments within a discussion thread and assess whether such patterns can be the indication of the content and the impact of the discussions. Figure 2 presents two specific patterns of sentiment changes we observed in our analysis. Figure 2a presents a pattern of continuous change from positive to negative sentiment in response to a negative message. Our investigation of this thread highlights a common pattern of the community attempt to support a member going through a difficult time by either providing cheerful positive messages or providing empathy through sharing of their own negative experience (as discussed in the previous section as well). The continuous change of sentiment is an indication of the different style of individuals in providing such support. In comparison, Fig. 2b, presents a completely different pattern of a somewhat stable positive response which is followed by a complete change of patterns with a shift to a number of negative responses. Our investigation of this thread identifies a change of topic and deviation from the original topic.

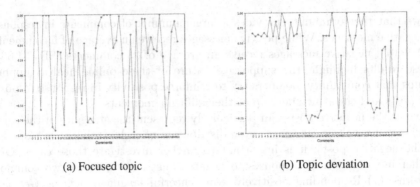

(a) Focused topic   (b) Topic deviation

Fig. 2. Patterns of sentiment changes

5   Discussion and Conclusion

In this preliminary work, we presented our model in accurately classifying the sentiment of messages in health support groups on social media and proposed a novel approach in utilizing sentiment analysis to understand the dynamics of such groups and the connection between online participation and patients' emotional status. We believe our approach can enable large scale and a more prompt analysis of online health support groups as it can complement qualitative content analysis without the intensive effort required for content annotation of each message. The approach is also sensitive to privacy of their members by focusing on the sentiment of messages as opposed to specific content of the message. The current work is the first step in developing a more comprehensive computational model to connect online participation to real-world impact of online health support groups.

References

1. Beaudoin, C.E., Tao, C.C.: Modeling the impact of online cancer resources on supporters of cancer patients. New Media Soc. **10**, 321–344 (2008)
2. Biyani, P., Caragea, C., Mitra, P., Yen, J.: Identifying emotional and informational support in online health communities. In: COLING, pp. 827–836 (2014)
3. Dunkel-Schetter, C.: Social support and cancer: findings based on patient interviews and their implications. J. Soc. Issues **40**, 77–98 (1984)
4. Farzan, R., Jonassaint, C.: Exploring dynamics of Facebook health support groups: a leadership perspective. In: Proceedings of the 50th Hawaii International Conference on System Sciences (2017)
5. Go, A., Bhayani, R., Huang, L.: Twitter sentiment classification using distant supervision. CS224N Proj. Rep. Stanf. **1**(12) (2009)
6. Kiritchenko, S., Zhu, X., Mohammad, S.M.: Sentiment analysis of short informal texts. J. Artif. Intell. Res. **50**, 723–762 (2014)
7. Pan, S.J., Ni, X., Sun, J.T., Yang, Q., Chen, Z.: Cross-domain sentiment classification via spectral feature alignment. In: Proceedings of the 19th International Conference on World Wide Web, pp. 751–760. ACM (2010)

8. Pang, B., Lee, L., Vaithyanathan, S.: Thumbs up?: sentiment classification using machine learning techniques. In: Proceedings of the ACL-02 Conference on Empirical Methods in Natural Language Processing, pp. 79–86 (2002)
9. Pedregosa, F., Varoquaux, G., Gramfort, A., Michel, V., Thirion, B., Grisel, O., Blondel, M., Prettenhofer, P., Weiss, R., Dubourg, V., Vanderplas, J., Passos, A., Cournapeau, D., Brucher, M., Perrot, M., Duchesnay, E.: Scikit-learn: machine learning in Python. J. Mach. Learn. Res. **12**, 2825–2830 (2011)
10. Qiu, B., Zhao, K., Mitra, P., Wu, D., Caragea, C., Yen, J., Greer, G.E., Portier, K.: Get online support, feel better - sentiment analysis and dynamics in an online cancer survivor community. In: Conference on Privacy, Security, Risk and Trust, pp. 274–281 (2011)
11. Rodgers, S., Chen, Q.: Internet community group participation: psychosocial benefits for women with breast cancer. J. Comput.-Mediat. Commun. **10**(4), 00–00 (2005)
12. Taboada, M., Brooke, J., Tofiloski, M., Voll, K., Stede, M.: Lexicon-based methods for sentiment analysis. Comput. Linguist. **37**(2), 267–307 (2011)
13. Thelwall, M., Buckley, K., Paltoglou, G., Cai, D.: Sentiment strength detection in short informal text. Am. Soc. Inf. Sci. Technol. **61**(12), 2544–2558 (2010)
14. Zhao, K., Yen, J., Greer, G., Qiu, B., Mitra, P., Portier, K.: Finding influential users of online health communities: a new metric based on sentiment influence. J. Am. Med. Inform. Assoc. **21**, e212–e218 (2014)

Mobile Information and Cloud Computing

'What Data?' Records and Data Policy Coordination During Presidential Transitions

Kristin B. Cornelius and Irene V. Pasquetto[⊠]

University of California, Los Angeles, Los Angeles, USA
irenepasquetto@ucla.edu

Abstract. The presidential transition in the United States takes place over the course of several years and involves the efforts of many different agencies and organizations. While it is standard practice for an incoming administration to change the content on government agencies' websites, the Trump administration pushed this practice beyond convention, even to alter the official narrative on climate change. Almost immediately after the inauguration, the official White House website deleted nearly all references to the phrase 'climate change,' and all online mentions of climate change on federal and government websites had been excised in the following months. Even if government data cannot be deleted completely, the manner in which they are preserved and made accessible, or hidden and obscured, is vitally important to the researchers and public that rely on this information. This project argues for the coordination of controls on this information: the policies, standards, and directives that regulate *both* the content accessed (e.g. the datasets) and the access points themselves, including the government agencies' websites that act as information sources and portals to the databases and repositories of publically funded research.

Keywords: Information policy · Open data · Record keeping
Knowledge preservation

1 Introduction

On Earth Day 2017, Saturday, April 22nd, 2017, more than 400 coordinated protests and marches took place across the United States under the banner "March for Science." These protests were a reaction, in part, to the recently elected Trump administration's agenda to support certain policies that seem to defy the findings of scientific data in relation to climate change research. Notably, President Trump publicly denied climate change science on several occasions, and, only few days after the new administration's inauguration, the head of the Environmental Protection Agency (EPA) was replaced with Scott Pruitt who previously stated that the debate on climate change is "far from settled" [14]. As a reflection of the Trump administration's attitude toward environmental research and transparency more generally, early in the transition process the official White House website deleted nearly all references to the phrase 'climate change,' and, in the following months, all online mentions of climate change on federal and government websites had been excised, buried or stripped of any importance [3, 13]. The EPA website was among the most targeted websites, with the entire climate

© Springer International Publishing AG, part of Springer Nature 2018
G. Chowdhury et al. (Eds.): iConference 2018, LNCS 10766, pp. 155–163, 2018.
https://doi.org/10.1007/978-3-319-78105-1_20

change section removed, only to be replaced by a static holding page (the section is still missing as of September 11th, 2017) [18]. These actions alarmed US environmental groups, archivists communities, and scientists, who worried not only for the change in the narrative by the science community, which has reached 97% consensus on agreement of manmade climate change [22], but also for the science data that is made available on those same websites. The activists' fear was confirmed by the fact that within the first few weeks of the inauguration, the Trump Administration removed dozens of data sets from openwhitehouse.gov [11].

The change from one presidential administration to another in the United States takes place over the course of several years and involves the efforts of many different agencies and organizations. It begins at least six months prior to the election, in accordance with the recently passed Presidential Transitions Improvements Act of 2015 that requires presidential candidates set up a team with agency leaders to smooth transition efforts [21]. While it is standard practice, to some extent, for an incoming administration to change the government agencies' output (e.g. content of websites) during a transition to reflect their own worldview and politics, generally, in addition to political ideology, transparency is the guiding principle, if not an achievable ideal, and public accessibility the aim. Alex Howard of the Sunlight Foundation, a think tank that influenced Obama's National Archives and Records Administration's (NARA) 2012 directive, referred to as the Managing Government Records Directive (M-12-18) [26], which supports public knowledge and transparency of government as its goal, for instance. Howard explains Obama's position: "They approached it from the default position that government data belongs to the public, and it should be (1) easily accessible and (2) machine-readable. They also tried to (3) put the data in formats that would easily allow software developers and researchers to use and analyze" [11]. In this observation, one can detect some trust placed in the ability of technology to make public information more accessible; however, even with the best intentions and clearest language, this goal requires much thought and coordination among several already existing processes and policies, as well as an evolving understanding of digital records. In explaining the need for a more efficient process to achieve a higher standard of accountability for users of data from publically funded research, former Chief Data Scientist for the White House, Dr. D.J. Patil notes how infrastructure changes can have an effect on the retrieval of datasets that are important to the public and how asking for datasets by FOIA is "an incredibly inefficient use of taxpayer dollars" [15]. Patil describes how the Obama administration dedicated "a lot of people" and "a tremendous amount of time [...] to streamline the process of requesting government data" [15]. And, how the motivation for this was "allowing what all administrations have typically provided, and that is transparency into who is using the White House and other datasets that people have a right to see" [17]. In other words, even prior to Trump taking office and promoting a radical overhaul of the information on and accessed from these sites, the processes by which these data were retrieved was complicated and already in need of revising. And now that it seems the current administration is not continuing to work toward transparency, but rather favoring "alternative facts" [1] and nondisclosure agreements [10]. These actions are *testing* our institutional procedures to see if the information provided to the public on these sites can uphold a certain amount of integrity through these transitions, and therefore it is time to look critically at the processes and policies whose job it is to do this vital work.

Even with the aim of being the primary archival institution for government records and public knowledge, NARA's strategies take coordinated effort and funding, which are two aspects that are subject to an administration's whims. For instance, reporters found that positions created under the Obama Administration to curate and protect data such as "chief digital officer" were eliminated [17]. Part of the response to this chain of events was the formation of the "Data Refuge" initiative, which saw the participation of data archivists, scientists, and volunteers from multiple North American universities, including, to mention just a few, UPenn, University of Toronto, UCLA, UCSD, MIT, and Harvard. Between December 2016 and April 2017, data archivists and information professionals selected, downloaded, and stored climate change-related datasets hosted on federal agencies' websites that were collected with public funding and in danger of disappearing or being deleted under the current administration's transition [7]. Thanks to the work of these activists and volunteers, these highly valuable "rescued datasets" are now safely stored, properly curated, and available to the scientific community, as well as to the general public [25]. The main outcome of these interventions is probably the foundation of the Environmental Data and Governance Initiative (EDGI), a non-profit international organization that has as a mission to preserve publicly accessible and potentially vulnerable scientific data and archive web pages from multiple agencies' websites, such as the Environmental Protection Agency (EPA), the Department Of Energy (DOE), the National Oceanic and Atmospheric Administration (NOAA), and the National Aeronautics and Space Administration (NASA).

However, much of this data rescue effort was more complicated than necessary. This was partly due to insufficient oversight over an administration that works tirelessly to subvert policies designed to ensure the integrity of information disseminated from government agencies. In particular, while much attention was paid to the data policies (e.g. open access, preservation, curation best practices), the policies that regulate the spaces where information is accessed, such as federal agencies' websites, failed to protect the preservation, access, and consistency of this data. This project argues that the policies (e.g. M-12-18 directive) that govern the platforms where government data is accessed should be coordinated with the open data policies (e.g. NSF/NIH data sharing policies for gov. 2013/2012, FAIR principles, codata, RDA) in order for there to be sufficient protection of and access to this information during presidential transitions.

2 Background

The background of this project looks at both policies and principles that govern the way data is presented to the public on government agency sites, as well as the directives and publishing regulations that control the way information is preserved in the case of change due to presidential transitions.

2.1 Data Policies

More than 30 DataRescue events, also called "archive-a-thons," occurred at cities across the U.S. and Canada during the first quarter of the Trump organization [25]. These events were mainly organized and coordinated by activists with the help of the EDGI, the Internet Archive, and the DataRefuge initiatives. Between Fall 2016 and Spring 2017, the activists archived over 200 TB of government websites and data. This includes over 100 TB of public websites and over 100 TB of public data from Federal FTP file servers totaling, together, over 350 million URLs/files. This includes over 70 million html pages, over 40 million PDFs and, towards the other end of the spectrum and, for semantic web aficionados, 8 files of the text/turtle mime type. The EDGI volunteer tech team of over 30 contributors has built open source and freely available tools and projects for grassroots archiving, and made all available to the public on their GitHub account. EDGI's efforts to archive, preserve, curate and make publicly available scientific data can be seen in the light of the expanding and increasingly influential "open data movement" in science [8]. Making scientific data open is a science policy priority in the US, Europe, and elsewhere. Typically, with the expression "open data" commentators refer to publicly funded research data that have been made openly available in digital repositories, archives, or databases. Openness is generally defined as "access on equal terms for the international research community at the lowest possible cost, preferably at no more than the marginal cost of dissemination" [19]. Multiple, but related, rationales for making science data open exist [2]. For instance, for the scientists, accessing and reusing each other's data can lead to faster discoveries and knowledge integration. Often, open data initiatives symbolize a reaction against the view of scientific knowledge production as an esoteric, technical, and overspecialized process – instead promoting the idea that scientific knowledge can and should be investigated as a whole. Finally, for policy makers, reusing data is a matter of return on investment, promoting economic innovation and enabling knowledge transfer to the industry. American funding agencies such as the National Science Foundation (NSF) and the National Institute of Health (NIH) commonly require scientists to deposit their data in open repositories as a condition of receiving funding [20]. A number of tools, standards, and conceptual models have been designed to enable scientists to work in "open science frameworks." Institutions and organizations worldwide are investing in infrastructures and policies to promote the centralization, access, and integration of scientific data. A promising new development to address the vagaries of open data is the FAIR standards – Findable, Accessible, Interoperable, and Reusable data. These standards apply to the repositories in which data are deposited. The FAIR standards were enacted by a set of stakeholders to enable open science, and they incorporate all parts of the "research object," from code, to data, to tools for interpretation [24].

2.2 Website Policies

Certain protections in the form of regulations are in place to preserve government information and records and to maintain the country's cultural record. The face of the agency's website provides information about both the agency's inner-activities, in addition to providing information about their work in the form of synthesized research data and official statements. EPA's website, for instance, is a place to find research data, but the website itself publishes information about both the environment and the work of the EPA. There are different standards and regulations that govern each of these types of information, in the form of record keeping practices and preservation strategies (like those outlined in [26]) and publishing regulations.

An awareness of the importance of record keeping in transparency efforts proved characteristic of the Obama administration's records policies; for instance, in 2012, a centralized records management program (M-12-18) [26] was put into place by a memorandum sent out from President Obama, Jeffrey D. Zients (Acting Director, Office of Management and Budget), and David S. Ferriero (Archivist, NARA) that aimed to ultimately increase transparency and accountability for the government by preserving records and making them accessible for the public. This was the stated goal of the memo, titled "Managing Government Records Directive," released on August 24, 2012:

> Records are the foundation of open government, supporting the principles of transparency, participation, and collaboration. Well-managed records can be used to assess the impact of programs, to improve business processes, and to share knowledge across the Government. Records protect the rights and interests of people, and hold officials accountable for their actions. Permanent records document our nation's history *(Managing Government Records Directive)* [26].

Here, Obama's strategy seemingly embraces the values of openness promoted by archivists and the open data community, even so far as to include a nod toward "collaboration," which can be used to subvert top-down policies. Certain mechanisms and practices began to be implemented as a result of this memo, including its request for each agency to assign a Senior Agency Official (SAO) to oversee their records management processes [26]. Agency SAOs continue to hold responsibility for records management practices such as M-12-18 makes it their charge to be "responsible for protecting the integrity of agency programs and trustworthiness of agency information" as they have "statutory responsibility" for the agency's records management program [5]. Further, the NARA "Guidance on Managing Web Records," released in January 2005, describes how the treatment of information on Federal agency websites is dictated by the head of the agency and that agencies cannot delete web records "related to the operation of Federal websites" without permission from NARA [15]. This leaves their entire official 'record' status up to NARA, placing a significant amount of trust in a system that is not yet entirely functional. Alex Howard, for instance, says he has only "low to moderate confidence" in the "completeness of the NARA archive," and, to compound these issues, the links pointing to the tools on NARA's White House portal were "simply broken" and the NARA couldn't guarantee API access would work for all the datasets [17].

As described in previous sections, certain mechanisms prevent the Trump administration from directly "go[ing] out and delet[ing] decades worth of information" entirely [17]. Howard notes how there is a difference between "retaining scientific data within the agencies and keeping things on the website" [17]. Spokeswoman Miriam Kleinman, for instance, said her agency primarily focuses on agencies' ability to preserve records, not whether they are "making them available to the public" [6]. Her full statement on this issue: "NARA's records management guidance mainly focuses on records creation, retention, and eventual deletion or transfer to NARA for permanent preservation. NARA has not issued specific guidance about large data sets being taken down from publicly-available websites" [6]. Therefore, while these policies are intended to ensure accountability, there are paths to circumvent them, some of which were utilized during the recent transition. For instance, the determination of which web records need to be retained as part of 'Federal agency operations' and for how long is ultimately left up to each agency's SAO's (who are put in place by the agency head appointed by the president) judgment—essentially, most agency records, including web records, need to be kept for a certain period to mitigate risk (in the business sense), and only records who hold "long-term historical value" should be transferred to NARA (at NARA's identification and discretion) [16]. Thus, in most cases, anything published on EPA's website besides datasets and records related to operations can be deleted once "old or when superseded, obsolete," and, minor upkeep and changes can be made without notification [16]. Even though several details are given as to how web records should be archived, including a suggestion to include contextual information, screenshots, code, and even website maps and all other documentation, the live site can change at the whim of the SAO under the guise of "standard practice" and normal upkeep; this was one of the explanations of the changes made by the Trump administration [23]. Moreover, at any time the current president could release a new directive to NARA that would overturn M-12-18 and its initiatives, and thus all of these regulations are only in place as long as this directive holds.

3 Discussion and Conclusion

The Trump administration's removal of information from its agencies' websites the weeks following its inauguration, including federal climate plans created under former President Obama, tribal assistance programs, and references to international cooperation on climate change efforts, reveals a shift in epistemological position. Transparency is not only *not* a priority for this administration, it might also be argued that secrecy is encouraged, as evidenced by the non-disclosure agreements asked to sign of all agency employees [10].

NARA's lack of distinction and the Trump administration's sense of 'comfort' in deleting this information could be from dealing with digitized documents (i.e. webpages), that seemingly possess immaterial qualities, rather than physical or paper documents, which could be seen as more difficult to alter or destroy. In other words, the ability to replace information on the websites because the very institutions that support their authority (i.e. NARA) seem to also support their immaterial, digital status, eases the path towards alteration and being ignored. Scholars have commented on the change from paper to electronic, including Drucker's [4] caution against the text's "(mis) perceived condition as immaterial in the electronic environment," or its ability to seem an "idea that appears to consciousness as a form but without materiality." In this view, and in line with NARA's lack of attention toward the display of information on website pages, it seems as though the pages of a website almost lose their status as document completely; this supports Levy's argument that digitized documents can "fail to register in a social space, to fail to have social identity, and thereby fail *to be* a document" [9]. This quality of 'immateriality' that exists in a digital space and attaches itself to electronic documents has been the concern of several activists, including Jefferson Bailey of the *Internet Archive,* who stated that with the recent transition, he was worried about "politically-driven ephemerality," or, in plain speak, "pages being shut down" [6]. He elaborates: "There's a lot more dynamic content on the web than there was four or eight years ago. Some of that is challenging to capture [...] There are sometimes FTP servers or other directories that a crawler might not discover because they're hidden [...] Subdirectories are very hard to find" [6]. Additionally, the authority of an institution, such as a federal agency, can imbue subversive acts like the removal of data with the qualities of benign, bureaucratic 'housekeeping'—such as combining the removal of climate science data and associated programs with the standard, basic functions of just 'updating' the websites. The authority of the data on these websites relies heavily, then, on their ability to perform as a record of evidence—not simply as a digital, immaterial document, or standard practice.

While current open data policies and principles that guided the Data Rescue efforts largely focus on identifying and describing what is necessary for ensuring the long-term preservation of the data themselves, little attention has been paid to the spaces in which the data are hosted and made available. Open access principles and policies apply to the datasets, to the databases that host and organize the data for retrieval, and, increasingly, to the code or software used to collect and analyze the raw data. The data archiving efforts from EDGI, for instance, brought attention to a new aspect of the open access challenge—one that, maybe, we never considered before: we can curate and make publicly available science data, databases, and code, but all these efforts are in vain if the federal websites that host, or point to, these resources can be taken down by new administrations at any time. Of course, by taking down EPA webpages, research data on climate change do not disappear. The science community is well equipped to ensure this would be a very unlikely outcome. In addition to being uploaded to agencies' repositories and NARA, research datasets exist in multiple copies, and whenever made available, these copies are safely stored in publicly funded data centers around the country. A recent white paper written by National Center for Atmospheric Research (NCAR) researchers rightfully pointed out that national research data centers have ad-hoc plans for data storage, migration, and rescue in place [12]. In the paper, the researchers also explained that research data are in need to be rescued all year around, not only during transition period, especially when data become obsolete (compared to the technologies available to analyze or manage them), or when there are types of data (e.g. small-scale datasets) that are not required to be shared by the scientists, but still of extreme importance to the science community at large, as well as to industries that rely on it for critical infrastructure projects. As the very history of our country relies on the effective implementation records keeping practices, and considering Orwell's ever-pervasive perception that "who controls the present controls the past," it is vital to consider how different administrations' policies and practices shape and control records as to maintain their version of truth, such as scientific research and data policies that affect how the story of climate change is told to the public and supported (or otherwise) by scientific research.

References

1. Blake, A.: Kellyanne Conway says Donald Trump's team has "alternative facts". Which pretty much says it all. Washington Post (2017)
2. Borgman, C.L.: Big Data, Little Data, No Data: Scholarship in the Networked World. MIT Press, Cambridge (2015)
3. Davenport, C.: With Trump in charge, climate change references purged from website. The New York Times (2017)
4. Drucker, J.: Performative materiality and theoretical approaches to interface. Digit. Humanit. Q. **7**, 1 (2013)
5. Duranti, L.: Luciana Duranti, Trusting Records and Archives in the Era of Alternative Facts and Misinformation, ILS Colloquium Speaker. IU Calendar (2017)
6. Gerstein, J.: Fears rise of Trump-era "memory hole" in federal data. POLITICO (2016)
7. Harmon, A., Fountain, H.: In age of Trump, scientists show signs of a political pulse. The New York Times (2017)
8. Leonelli, S.: Why the current insistence on open access to scientific data? Big data, knowledge production, and the political economy of contemporary biology. Bull. Sci. Technol. Soci. **33**, 1–2, 6–11 (2013). https://doi.org/10.1177/0270467613496768
9. Levy, D.M.: Scrolling Forward, Second Edition: Making Sense of Documents in the Digital Age. Skyhorse Publishing, Inc., New York (2016)
10. Marcotte, A.: Donald Trump is already trying to muzzle leakers—but government employees have broad free speech rights (2017). Salon.com
11. Maurielllo, T.: Data disappeared from Obama administration site promoting transparency. Pittsburgh Post-Gazette
12. Mayernik, M., et al.: Stronger together: the case for cross-sector collaboration in identifying and preserving at-risk data—ESIP (2017)
13. Milman, O., Morris, S.: Trump is deleting climate change, one site at a time. The Guardian (2017)
14. Mooney, C., et al.: Trump names Scott Pruitt, Oklahoma attorney general suing EPA on climate change, to head the EPA. Washington Post (2016)
15. NARA Guidance on Managing Web Records (2016). https://www.archives.gov/records-mgmt/policy/managing-web-records-index.html. Accessed 18 Sept 2017
16. NARA Guidance on Scheduling Web Records (2016). https://www.archives.gov/records-mgmt/policy/managing-web-records-scheduling.html. Accessed 18 Sept 2017
17. O'Brien, T.: Trump's quiet war on data begins. Engadget
18. Page being updated: https://www.epa.gov/sites/files/production/signpost/index.html. Accessed 17 Sept 2017
19. Pilat, D., Fukasaku, Y.: OECD principles and guidelines for access to research data from public funding. Data Sci. J. **6**, OD4-OD11 (2007). https://doi.org/10.2481/dsj.6.OD4
20. Ray, J.M.: Research Data Management: Practical Strategies for Information Professionals. Purdue University Press, West Lafayette (2014)
21. S.1172 - 114th Congress (2015–2016): Edward "Ted" Kaufman and Michael Leavitt Presidential Transitions Improvements Act of 2015 (2016). https://www.congress.gov/bill/114th-congress/senate-bill/1172. Accessed 17 Sept 2017
22. Scientific consensus: Earth's climate is warming: https://climate.nasa.gov/scientific-consensus. Accessed 17 Sept 2017
23. Sohn, T.: Leaked emails show what is wrong at the EPA 2017

24. Wilkinson, M.D., et al.: The FAIR guiding principles for scientific data management and stewardship. Sci. Data. **3**, 160018 (2016). https://doi.org/10.1038/sdata.2016.18
25. Archiving Data. EDGI
26. Memorandum for the Head of Executive Departments and Agencies and Independent Agencies (2012)

Limits to the Pursuit of Reproducibility: Emergent Data-Scarce Domains of Science

Peter T. Darch(✉) (iD)

School of Information Sciences, University of Illinois at Urbana-Champaign,
Urbana, IL, USA
ptdarch@illinois.edu

Abstract. Recommendations and interventions to promote reproducibility in science have so far largely been formulated in the context of well-established domains characterized by data- and computationally-intensive methods. However, much promising research occurs in little data domains that are emergent and experience data scarcity. This paper presents a longitudinal study of such a domain, deep subseafloor biosphere research. Two important challenges this domain faces in establishing itself are increasing production and circulation of data, and strengthening relationships between domain researchers. Some potential interventions to promote reproducibility may also help the domain to establish itself. However, other potential interventions could profoundly damage the domain's long-term prospects of maturation by impeding production of new data and undermining critical relationships between researchers. This paper challenges the dominant framing of the pursuit of reproducible science as identifying, and overcoming, barriers to reproducibility. Instead, those interested in pursuing reproducibility in a domain should take into account multiple aspects of that domain's epistemic culture to avoid negative unintended consequences. Further, pursuing reproducibility is premature for emergent, data-scarce domains: scarce resources should instead be invested to help these domains to mature, for instance by addressing data scarcity.

Keywords: Reproducibility · Data reuse · Little data · Open code
Open data

1 Introduction

Many key stakeholders (such as funding agencies, professional societies, researchers, and members of the information professions) regard pursuit of reproducibility as an urgent concern for all domains of science [1–4]. These stakeholders are concerned with promoting scientific integrity, and the ability to reproduce published scientific findings by replicating steps in the original analysis can detect error and malpractice.

To date, interventions and recommendations to promote reproducibility have largely been devised in the context of well-established data-intensive domains [5]. However, there are many other domains of science that are new and emergent, and that face a critical scarcity of data that hinders their prospects of maturation. These domains are culturally distinct from well-established data-intensive domains. Interventions to

© Springer International Publishing AG, part of Springer Nature 2018
G. Chowdhury et al. (Eds.): iConference 2018, LNCS 10766, pp. 164–174, 2018.
https://doi.org/10.1007/978-3-319-78105-1_21

advance reproducibility formulated in the context of well-established data-intensive domains may be unsuitable or even damaging if implemented in emergent data-scarce domains. Rather than investing their limited resources in interventions to promote reproducibility, emergent data-scarce domains should instead prioritize addressing data scarcity, for instance by investing in infrastructure for data production and reuse.

Through presenting a longitudinal case study of an emergent data-scarce domain, deep subseafloor biosphere research, this paper addresses the following questions:

(1) How feasible is pursuing reproducibility in emergent data-scarce domains?
(2) How desirable is pursuing reproducibility in emergent data-scarce domains?

2   Background

To frame subsequent discussions of reproducibility, this section first covers the concept of epistemic cultures, particularly in relation to data and software. Next, it considers efforts to promote reproducibility. This section concludes by discussing challenges facing deep subseafloor biosphere research as an emergent data-scarce domain.

2.1   Epistemic Cultures in Science

The *epistemic cultures* [6] of different scientific domains can vary in many ways, including how research activities are organized (such as the size of teams involved), and what counts as evidence of scientific phenomena. Domains also differ according to degree of institutionalization: markers of a well-established domain can include its own journals, conferences, professional societies, university departments or research institutes, and dedicated streams within funding agencies [7].

Other major differences between domains' epistemic cultures relate to data and software [1]. Some domains, such as astronomy and computational social science, are characterized by the use of highly standardized computationally- and data-intensive methods. Data and software sharing in these *big data* domains is typically supported by sophisticated digital infrastructure.

By contrast, *little data* domains are characterized by access to much smaller quantities of data that are often heterogeneous both in type and by method of production [1]. In these domains, such as ecology, data and software sharing is frequently inhibited by patchy or inadequate standards for data production, analysis, and management; inconsistent policies; and uneven provision of digital infrastructure [8]. Successful data sharing is often facilitated by personal contact between the original data producer, and the potential data user.

2.2   Computational Reproducibility: "Barriers" and Interventions

Stodden [9] distinguishes different types of reproducibility. *Empirical reproducibility* refers to provision of details about a non-computational experiment that allows another researcher to carry out the experiment. *Computational reproducibility* refers to availability of code and data used to produce a piece of research. As each type of reproducibility has different requirements and faces distinct challenges for its realization, this paper will focus on computational reproducibility.

The pursuit of reproducible science is often framed as a process of identifying and overcoming "barriers to reproducibility" [10, p. 73]. Frequently identified barriers include a lack of digital infrastructure for making code and data publicly accessible, and a lack of policies to encourage use of infrastructure where it exists [1]: these barriers can be addressed by building new infrastructure, and devising and enforcing new policies. Another barrier is use of proprietary software [11], which inhibits reproducibility for many reasons: its source code is often not publicly accessible; researchers are not able to extract and share workflows they produce using this software; and prospective reproducers may have to pay to use this software. Researchers are instead encouraged to use open source software, or to write and publicly share their own code [12]. Other scholars argue for new cultural norms to advance reproducibility, such as reproducibility "etiquette", where the prospective reproducer of a piece of research contacts the author who originally conducted that research [13, p. 310].

Interventions and recommendations to promote reproducibility often require substantial investments of resources in building infrastructure, devising policies, and changing practices. So far, these interventions and recommendations have been mainly formulated in the context of well-established big data domains [1]. Recently, attention has shifted to reproducibility in fields that are not usually considered big data, such as archaeology [14], although the focus is typically on the specific areas of those fields where computationally- and data-intensive practices are the norm [15].

2.3   Deep Subseafloor Biosphere Research: An Emergent Data-Scarce Domain

One type of little data domain is the *data-scarce* domain [16], characterized by not having enough data to pursue the domain's major objectives. Data scarce domains are often new and emergent, multidisciplinary, and struggle for resources as they attempt to establish themselves. Addressing data scarcity is a critical step for helping these domains to mature and raise their status. One example is deep subseafloor biosphere research, whose researchers integrate physical science and bioinformatics data to answer questions about relationships between microbial communities in the seafloor and the physical environment they inherit.

Since studies of the deep subseafloor biosphere began in the late 1990s, two infrastructures have been instrumental to this domain's emergence. One is the *Center for Dark Energy Biosphere Investigations* (*C-DEBI*), a ten-year NSF Science and Technology Center launched in 2010, providing short-term funding to over 150 researchers across the US and Europe. Since 2015, C-DEBI has operated an online data portal. C-DEBI requires recipients of its funding to upload data they produce to an openly-accessible public database or (where no relevant database exists) to its own portal.

The second infrastructure is the *International Ocean Discovery Program* (*IODP*), which operates five scientific ocean drilling cruises per year to procure physical samples (*cores*) of the seafloor for analysis. IODP serves multiple domains besides deep subseafloor biosphere research, such as studies of plate tectonics.

Besides C-DEBI and IODP, deep subseafloor biosphere research has little institutional strength: no journals exist that are dedicated to this domain, and its researchers are distributed across multiple university departments (including departments of biological sciences, of earth sciences, and of oceanography). A key objective of C-DEBI is to foster links between these researchers, and it provides significant funding to promoting research collaborations between distributed researchers.

The rarity of cruises, requirements to share IODP resources with other domains, and the domain's relative newness means deep subseafloor biosphere research has access to small quantities of data. This domain is data-scarce in that researchers wish to address the domain's research topics in a more statistically intensive manner than is afforded by current data [16]. Domain leaders seek to transition the domain from *discovery-driven* science, where researchers describe microbial communities in cores, to *hypothesis-driven* science, where researchers test statistical hypotheses about microbial activity. This transition would bring the domain in line with domains that study microbes in other environments. Domain leaders also hope deep subseafloor biosphere research contribute to key open questions in science through producing and integrating datasets about microbial communities in different geographic locations.

By addressing data scarcity, the domain's leaders seek not only to produce more and better science, but also to help the domain mature and increase its institutional strength [16]. Through shifting to hypothesis-driven science and addressing high profile questions, domain leaders hope the domain will become more credible and better-established. Thus, improving production of new data and encouraging circulation and reuse of extant data are critical priorities for the domain's leaders. C-DEBI also allocates a great deal of resources towards pursuing these priorities.

3 Methods

This paper presents findings from a longitudinal qualitative case study of deep subseafloor biosphere researchers, focussing on C-DEBI and IODP. Research methods comprised long-term participant observation, interviews, and document analysis, following standard ethnographic practices [17]. Fieldwork included eight months embedded in a laboratory headed by a leading figure in C-DEBI at a large US research university, weeklong observation trips to two other laboratories and to IODP headquarters, and observations of a research expedition and scientific conferences.

The interview sample comprises 55 people, including C-DEBI-affiliated scientists (n = 41), and curators and managerial staff involved in IODP (n = 14). Interviews ranged in length from 35 min to two hours and 30 min, with the majority being between one and two hours. Documents analysed include official C-DEBI documents such as Annual Reports, and documents about IODP operations.

4 Findings

This section presents a typical workflow in deep subseafloor biosphere research. Although domain researchers conduct a growing range of analyses, with different purposes, the workflow discussed here is widely used by researchers in many laboratories. This sections first describes key steps in this workflow, and the choices made by researchers during these steps, and then discuss the challenges that would be faced by a researcher seeking to reproduce a project incorporating this workflow.

4.1 A Typical Workflow in Deep Subseafloor Biosphere Research

The central aim of a project incorporating this workflow is to characterize the composition of the microbial community (type and quantity of microbes) in a particular part of the seafloor, and to understand this community's relationship to the physical environment it inhabits. The workflow is summarized in Fig. 1.

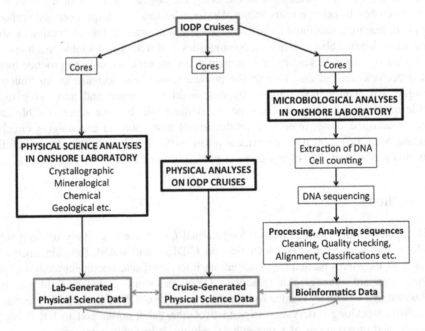

Fig. 1. A typical workflow in deep subseafloor biosphere research

The first step in this workflow is the collection of cores on IODP cruises. Some cores are subject to onboard analyses that yield baseline data of their physical characteristics. These data are made available through an online IODP database. Other cores are distributed among cruise participants, who take them to their onshore laboratories to analyze their physical characteristics, and the microbial communities they contain.

Here, we will focus more heavily on microbiological analyses. The first steps in a microbiological analysis are counting the number of cells and extracting DNA from cores. Researchers, even those in the same laboratory, display a high degree of methodological heterogeneity when conducting these steps (see [18] for more details). The reason for this heterogeneity is that, given the subseafloor biosphere is a low biomass environment, traditional methods for cell counting and DNA extraction do not work. Instead, researchers adapt methods they learned prior to embarking on deep subseafloor biosphere research. The type of method used, however, has implications for the bioinformatics data that is subsequently generated: some methods are biased in the sense they lead to overrepresentation of some types of microbes in the subsequent steps of the workflow, and some methods are more efficient than others, resulting in a greater yield of DNA.

Next, DNA is prepared for sequencing. Sequencing is carried out either in the laboratory itself or, more commonly, by an external sequencing facility. The outcome of sequencing is a file comprising a series of DNA sequences, representing the microbes in the core. Each sequence comprises a series of nucleotides, and the sequencing facility typically returns the sequences with probability estimates of how accurately they were able to identify each nucleotide (known as *quality scores*). Next, the researcher processes and analyzes these sequences. The first step is to use quality scores to check and clean sequences. Next, sequences are aligned. Similar sequences are clustered into *Operational Taxonomic Units*, which are then compared with publicly accessible bioinformatics databases of already-known microbes.

Researchers use a range of computational methods process and analyze sequences. Some researchers write their own code. Other researchers use a piece of open source software called mothur. Finally, researchers who are less comfortable with computational methods often choose to use proprietary software called Geneious, with a graphical user interface that researchers find intuitive and easy to use.

Next, the researcher correlates the microbial community's composition with certain characteristics (such as geochemical or mineralogical) of the physical environment it inhabits, with the aim of understanding how these physical characteristics shape the microbial community and vice versa. These physical science data may come from the IODP database, or from analyses of cores in onshore laboratories. Once the researcher has completed their analysis, they will prepare an article for publication. This article presents brief information about the methods used. Journals often require the researcher to upload supporting DNA sequences to a publicly accessible bioinformatics database before article publication: once uploaded, sequences are assigned accession numbers by the database, and these numbers are published alongside the journal article. C-DEBI also now requires all physical science data produced by its researchers to be uploaded to a relevant publicly accessible database.

However, not all research products resulting from the described workflow are made publicly accessible, such as pre-cleaned DNA sequences and quality scores, and code written by researchers. These research products often eventually got lost, for instance, when a graduating doctoral student takes up a position in industry.

4.2 Reproducing This Workflow: Accessing Data, Software, and Code

To reproduce this workflow in its entirety requires access to physical samples, data, and code and software. Reproducibility of the steps that involve handling core samples is highly infeasible: given the expense and rarity of IODP cruises, the IODP personnel interviewed explained that cores would only be given to researchers to produce new science, and not to reproduce previous analyses. Instead, the focus here is on later, post-sequencing, steps in the workflow.

A prospective reproducer of the workflow is likely to be able to access sequence data and physical science data used in the analysis, given the policies and digital infrastructure currently in place. However, the reproducer is unlikely to easily access data received from the sequencing facility (pre-cleaned sequences, and quality scores), posing a significant challenge in reproducing sequence-cleaning and quality-checking steps. Further, the reproducer may also lack the information necessary required to interpret sequence data, such as detailed accounts of the methods used to produce the sequences, to understand whether these data may contain biases.

The prospective reproducer may therefore need to contact the researcher who originally conducted the project for access to some data, and help in interpreting these data. However, a number of interviewed researchers expressed reservations about doing so, as they do not want to undermine relationships with their domain colleagues by implying they did not trust these colleagues' competence and honesty. The deep subseafloor biosphere domain is relatively small: maintaining good relationships is very important to researchers, particularly junior researchers who rely on senior researchers for patronage and employment opportunities.

A prospective reproducer may or may not be able to access the software or code necessary to reproduce the workflow, depending on the computing choices made by the researcher who conducted the original research. If open source software was used, the reproducer should be able to access this software. If the research was conducted using proprietary software, the prospective researcher is unlikely to be able to reproduce the workflow: the software costs money to use (an annual license for Geneious currently costs $395), its source code is not openly available, and it does not allow users to extract and share workflows.

Finally, if the research involved code written by the researcher themselves, the prospective reproducer may not be able to access this code. Occasionally, subseafloor biosphere researchers who produce their own code do make this code openly available, for instance via an online repository or their own website. Otherwise, the prospective reproducer would have to approach the researcher for the code: however, as with data, some subseafloor biosphere researchers expressed reservations about approaching colleagues for code for the purpose of reproducing research.

5 Discussion and Conclusions

In common with other emergent data-scarce domains, the deep subseafloor biosphere has two important objectives for establishing itself in the long-term. One objective is maintaining and deepening interpersonal relationships between domain researchers as a necessary precursor to increasing the domain's institutional strength. The second objective is addressing data scarcity to raise the domain's scientific profile. Although some proposed interventions to promote reproducibility may also aid pursuit of these two objectives, other commonly-proposed interventions are potentially fundamentally incompatible with these objectives. Emergent data-scarce domains should focus their scarce resources on addressing data scarcity rather than on pursuing reproducibility.

5.1   An Intervention that Promises to Benefit Emergent Data-Scarce Domains

While C-DEBI has made major strides in policy and infrastructure towards ensuring some data produced by its researchers are made openly accessible, other data and code necessary to fully reproduce deep subseafloor biosphere workflows remain inaccessible. Investing in better infrastructure for data and code is a key step in pursuing reproducible science, as is devising and enforcing policies that require researchers to use this infrastructure [1]. These steps are compatible with addressing data scarcity by promoting circulation and reuse of data and software.

5.2   Interventions that Risk Damaging Emergent Data-Scarce Domains

Some practices that are promoted as fundamental to reproducibility seem to be incompatible with the interests of emergent data-scarce domains. These practices have the potential to make data scarcity more acute or to undermine critical relationships between domain researchers.

Risk of Making Data Scarcity More Acute. A key requirement for promoting reproducibility is that code or software used in research should be openly accessible to others [12]. This requirement means researchers should avoid using proprietary software and instead either write and make openly available their own code, or use open source software. This requirement could conflict with production of new data and science in emergent data-scarce domains. In deep subseafloor biosphere research, computational skills are patchy. Researchers have experienced disparate amounts of computational training prior to joining the domain, depending on their disciplinary backgrounds. Researchers with lower levels of comfort with computational methods exhibited a strong preference for using a piece of proprietary software. The use of this software enables them to produce and process data more rapidly than the alternatives. Requiring these researchers to switch away from their preferred software would be likely to slow down production of new data, potentially exacerbating data scarcity.

In the long-term, this source of conflict between pursuing reproducibility and pursuing the domain's objectives is likely to lessen. As coding becomes more widespread in scientific curricula, more researchers are likely to enter the domain able to write their own code, or contribute to development of open source software. However, in the shorter term, demands of reproducibility will need to be balanced with the domain's critical need to produce new data and science.

Risk of Undermining Critical Interpersonal Relationships. Contact between the researcher who conducted the original research, and the prospective reproducer of that research, may be an integral part of reproducible science. Some advocates of reproducibility have argued that this contact is good etiquette and should become a cultural norm [13]. Even if this practice does not become an integral part of reproduction for the purposes of good manners, such contact may nevertheless be necessary when reproducing research in emergent data-scarce domains. However, such contact also risks undermining these domains' prospects of maturation.

Research on data and code sharing and reuse demonstrates that, in these domains, direct contact between the producer and potential reuser is often necessary so that the potential reuser can better understand and interpret a dataset or piece of code – even when this dataset or code is made openly accessible via a digital repository [8]. Likewise, a potential reproducer may well need to contact the researcher who conducted the original research for help in understanding data or code. For instance, the methodological heterogeneity in the deep subseafloor biosphere means that a prospective reproducer with a background in one scientific discipline may need help in understanding a dataset produced by a method that originated in another discipline.

However, contact between the researcher who conducted the original research, and the prospective reproducer risks damaging the strength of emergent data-scarce domains. Many deep subseafloor biosphere researchers expressed their concern at approaching a colleague for the resources necessary to reproduce this colleague's research, believing it would degrade their relationships. Unlike well-established big data domains, deep subseafloor biosphere research lacks institutional strength. Instead, the strength of the deep subseafloor biosphere domain relies on the strength of interpersonal relationships between researchers. Maintaining and deepening these ties is critical for the domain, and is a necessary precursor to increasing the domain's institutional strength. While sharing data and code for reuse can reinforce these ties by implying collegiality and forming the basis for future collaboration, sharing for reproducibility threatens instead to undermine these ties.

5.3   Implications for Pursuing Reproducible Science

This paper has two implications for pursuing reproducibility. One implication is to challenge the dominant framing of the pursuit of reproducibility as identifying, and then devising interventions to overcome, "barriers to reproducibility" [10]. This framing lends itself to a narrow focus on evaluating a possible intervention from the perspective of whether it advances reproducibility in a particular domain. However, this intervention could have far-reaching and harmful unintended consequences for the domain that go well beyond reproducibility.

Interventions devised in the context of established big data domains should instead only be rolled out to other domains with due care. The pursuit of reproducibility in a domain should involve understanding and analyzing that domain's epistemic culture [6] in its entirety, to better anticipate potential consequences of specific proposed interventions. The case study in this paper suggests that particularly relevant dimensions of an epistemic culture to consider include the domain's objectives, the domain's institutional strength, the role and scale of data in domain research, methodological heterogeneity in the domain, domain researchers' software/coding preferences, the disciplinary backgrounds and training of domain researchers, available digital infrastructure, the nature of relationships between domain researchers, and existing norms regarding sharing of data and software within the domain.

A second implication of this paper is that pursuing reproducibility should not be a priority for emergent data-scarce domains. C-DEBI focuses its scarce resources on addressing data scarcity and cultivating relationships between researchers, activities that help the domain to mature. Pursuing reproducibility prematurely could risk the long-term prospects of emergent data-scarce domains by directing scarce resources away from activities that help these domains establish themselves, and towards activities that instead hinder their maturation. Future work will examine the extent to which domains should mature before they pursue reproducibility. Reproducibility is important for scientific integrity, and its realization should be a major long-term goal for all scientific domains. However, its pursuit must not be at the expense of the development of promising emergent data-scarce domains.

Acknowledgements. This work is funded by the Alfred P. Sloan Foundation (Awards #20113194, #201514001). Thank you to current members of UCLA Center for Knowledge Infrastructures (CKI) for comments on earlier drafts of this paper (Christine L. Borgman, Bernie Boscoe, Milena S. Golshan, Irene Pasquetto, and Michael J. Scroggins), to past members of CKI (Ashley E. Sands and Sharon Traweek) for discussion of ideas, and to Rebekah L. Cummings for assistance with data collection. Thank you also to the C-DEBI and IODP personnel who were observed and interviewed.

References

1. Borgman, C.L.: Big Data, Little Data, No Data: Scholarship in the Networked World. The MIT Press, Cambridge (2015)
2. Vitale, C.R.: Is research reproducibility the new data management for libraries? Bull. Assoc. Inf. Sci. Technol. **42**(3), 38–41 (2016)
3. Baker, M.: 1,500 scientists lift the lid on reproducibility. Nat. News **533**(7604), 452 (2016)
4. Pellizzari, E., Lohr, K.N., Blatecky, A., Creel, D.: Reproducibility: A Primer on Semantics and Implications for Research, 1st edn. RTI Press/RTI International, Research Triangle Park (2017)
5. Stodden, V., Leisch, F., Peng, R.D. (eds.): Implementing Reproducible Research. CRC Press, Boca Raton (2014)
6. Knorr-Cetina, K.: Epistemic Cultures: How the Sciences Make Knowledge. Harvard University Press, Cambridge (1999)
7. Lenoir, T.: Instituting Science: The Cultural Production of Scientific Disciplines. Stanford University Press, Stanford (1997)
8. Wallis, J.C., Rolando, E., Borgman, C.L.: If we share data, will anyone use them? Data sharing and reuse in the long tail of science and technology. PLoS ONE **8**(7), e67332 (2013)
9. Stodden, V.: Resolving irreproducibility in empirical and computational research. IMS Bull. Online (2013)
10. Ram, K., Marwick, B.: Building towards a future where reproducible, open science is the norm. In: Kitzes, J., Turek, D., Deniz, F. (eds.) The Practice of Reproducible Research: Case Studies and Lessons from the Data-Intensive Sciences, pp. 69–78. University of California Press, Oakland (2018)

11. Ince, D.C., Hatton, L., Graham-Cumming, J.: The case for open computer programs. Nature **482**(7386), 485–488 (2012)
12. Stodden, V., et al.: Enhancing reproducibility for computational methods. Science **354** (6317), 1240–1241 (2016)
13. Kahneman, D.: A new etiquette for replication. Soc. Psychol. **45**(4), 310 (2014)
14. Marwick, B.: Computational reproducibility in archaeological research: basic principles and a case study of their implementation. J. Archaeol. Method Theory **24**(2), 424–450 (2017)
15. Kitzes, J., Turek, D., Deniz, F. (eds.): The Practice of Reproducible Research: Case Studies and Lessons from the Data-Intensive Sciences. Univ of California Press, Oakland (2018)
16. Darch, P.T., Borgman, C.L.: Ship space to database: emerging infrastructures for studies of the deep subseafloor biosphere. PeerJ Comput. Sci. **2**, e97 (2016)
17. Hammersley, M., Atkinson, P.: Ethnography: Principles in Practice, 3rd edn. Routledge, London (2007). Reprinted
18. Darch, P.T., Borgman, C.L., Traweek, S., Cummings, R.L., Wallis, J.C., Sands, A.E.: What lies beneath?: knowledge infrastructures in the subseafloor biosphere and beyond. Int. J. Digit. Libr. **16**(1), 61–77 (2015)

How to Assess Cloud Service Contracts?

A Checklist for Trustworthy Records in the Cloud

Marie Demoulin[1]([✉]), Jessica Bushey[2], and Robert McLelland[3]

[1] Université de Montréal, Montreal, Canada
marie.demoulin@umontreal.ca
[2] United Nations Framework Convention on Climate Change, Bonn, Germany
[3] Victoria, Canada

Abstract. How effective are cloud service providers' contracts at addressing the needs of records managers and archivists? Research undertaken by Inter-PARES Trust reveals that the ability to preserve the authenticity of the data and records throughout their life-cycle is not always clearly demonstrated in the contract terms, especially with regard to retention and disposition, ownership, location, preservation, and restitution of the data at the end of the service. This paper discusses the methodological approach taken by the authors to analyze the effectiveness of cloud service contracts from legal, archival and information management perspectives. The research is based on qualitative content analysis of selected boilerplate contracts in order to identify gaps or weaknesses regarding the concerns of records managers and archivists. It takes into account recordkeeping standards and principles, as well as legal issues such as data protection, freedom of information, national security, and data ownership. This interdisciplinary research has led to the elaboration of a *Checklist for Cloud Service Contracts*, presented in the paper. The primary goal of such a checklist is to help records managers and archivists gain an understanding of cloud contracts in order to verify if potential cloud contracts meet their concerns. Additionally, the *Checklist* may assist legal and IT departments as well as cloud service providers to understand and recognize the needs of the records management and recordkeeping community and to adequately address these needs during contract negotiations.

Keywords: Cloud computing · Cloud service provider · Contracts
Terms of service · Records · Archives · Recordkeeping · Records management

1 Introduction

The "cloud" is a term widely used to describe a broad array of scalable cloud computing services for the storage, access, and use of information. Apparently easy and cost-effective, these services appear as an increasingly attractive option for many organizations with limited information technology resources to store their records.

Yet, the risks associated with the storage of vital business records in the cloud are not always measured. Consequently, records might not be kept in accordance with legal requirements and best practices in the field of archives and records management. In the

© Springer International Publishing AG, part of Springer Nature 2018
G. Chowdhury et al. (Eds.): iConference 2018, LNCS 10766, pp. 175–184, 2018.
https://doi.org/10.1007/978-3-319-78105-1_22

process of selecting the appropriate cloud service, organizations of all kinds need the involvement and support of their records managers and archivists to ensure that records kept in the cloud will remain authentic, with all the required qualities.

The contract is a key element of the decision process, considering that it contains all the binding aspects of the provided service. However, cloud service contracts are comprised of a complex architecture of documents, policies, service level agreements (SLAs) and annexes, often written in complex and non-negotiable terms.

This research was conceived to assist information professionals and their organizations in the process of examining cloud service contracts to provide recordkeeping and long-term records preservation. The research outcome takes the form of a Checklist for Cloud Service Contracts, based on existing record-keeping standards and legal requirements for the purposes of ensuring the trustworthiness of digital records. The target audience of this Checklist is records managers, archivists, and others who are responsible for assessing cloud services for their organization. The aim of the checklist is to support organizations in:

- gaining an understanding of boilerplate cloud service contracts;
- verifying if potential cloud service contracts meet their organizational needs;
- clarifying recordkeeping and archival needs to legal and IT departments; and
- communicating recordkeeping and archival needs to cloud service providers.

It has to be noted that this *Checklist* is a tool for consideration only and does not constitute legal advice. Individuals and organizations should consult legal counsel if they want legal advice on a particular contract.

The research was conducted within the InterPARES Trust Project, a multi-national, interdisciplinary research project exploring issues concerning trust in digital records and data in the online environment.

2 Background

2.1 Cloud Service Contracts in the Recordkeeping Context

Amongst the various kinds and levels of cloud services offered, organizations need to select those which help them to comply with recordkeeping standards and meet legal requirements. Legal contracts reflect the fundamental basis for the services provided by cloud companies to their customers. Therefore, a cautious examination of the service contract is crucial before considering storing important or sensitive records and information in the cloud (Stiven 2014, pp. 423–424).

Cloud service contracts are often presented in 'boilerplate' format, written solely by the service provider, which can lead to an imbalance of power in business relationships. As such, customers may consent to such agreements without significantly understanding how the service will affect their recordkeeping and the legal or professional obligations therein. It is likely that larger organizations have the ability to negotiate their own contracts with service providers. However, some organizations do not have this capacity or cannot afford private corporate cloud services and rely on public cloud services aimed at individuals to meet their organizational needs. Moreover, the relevant literature suggests that there is very little standardization of terms across provider agreements (Baset 2012), but also that the manner in which such contracts are written make them "...incomprehensible to the vast majority of users" (Bradshaw et al. 2014, p. 71). In this context, there is a need for a tool that would help records managers and archivists to choose the appropriate service.

2.2 Literature Review

This study adopted an interdisciplinary approach, with a review of literature on cloud services from the fields of archival science, records management, and law (InterPARES Trust Project 2015). The review included professional standards and guidelines, such as ISO 15489, ISO 14721 (also known as OAIS), the ARMA International's Generally Accepted Recordkeeping Principles (2013) and the European Commission's MoReq2 (2008). Governance documents and recommendations regarding the adoption of cloud technologies were also examined, such as the European Commission's *Cloud Service Level Agreement Standardisation Guidelines* (2014; see also, inter alia, The National Archives, UK 2014), as well as academic papers discussing issues surrounding cloud technologies and the law (i.a. Ferguson-Boucher and Convery 2011; Baset 2012; Bradshaw et al. 2014; Stiven 2014; Reed and Cunningham 2014).

In spite of differences from one jurisdiction to another, the research highlighted some common legal concerns with regard to evidence law, copyright, privacy, personal data processing, rights to access to public documents, accountability and security. The research also built upon and expanded the results of another InterPARES Trust study that underlined gaps in boilerplate cloud service contracts with regard to records and information management concerns (InterPARES Trust Project 2014).

During this literature review, 7 key issues were identified for a recordkeeping system employing cloud technology: (1) data ownership; (2) availability, retrieval, and use; (3) data retention and disposition; (4) data storage and preservation; (5) data security, privacy, and confidentiality; (6) data location and cross-border data flow; and (7) issues related to end of service or contract termination (for a more detailed examination of each issue, see Bushey et al. 2015).

3 Methods

3.1 Qualitative Content Analysis

The first phase of the analysis involved drafting a series of questions that would guide organizations in the selection of a cloud service contract that could meet their recordkeeping needs. The questions were then tested on a selection of cloud-service contracts from 15 providers. The qualitative analysis focused on cloud services relevant for recordkeeping purposes. As many small organizations cannot afford private corporate services, a number of public cloud services aimed at individuals were also examined. In the interest of expediency, only publicly available boilerplate contracts from cloud service providers were selected. Moreover, only contractually binding documents such as terms and conditions, SLAs, privacy policies, acceptable use policies, etc. were taken into consideration. Marketing material or other information (such as white papers, guides, etc.) made available on the providers' websites were not analyzed, as these documents are not binding. These contracts spanned multiple jurisdictions, including Canada, the United States, Belgium, and Sweden. It should be noted that only English language contracts were selected, due to the level of analysis required.

The Qualitative Content Analysis was directed, as the codes were derived directly from the literature, with a particular focus on recordkeeping requirements. One of the researchers established the coding scheme and the analysis was then performed on the contracts to establish occurrence or absence of each code. Each of the 7 key issues represented a category with a range of 4 to 9 codes per category.

The final phase of the study involved the creation of a draft checklist that was presented to InterPARES Trust Project participants and made available to external reviewers from the records management and archival preservation community. Seven reviewers provided 45 comments that were used to create the final *Checklist*. The latter is available on the public area of the InterPARES Trust website (http://interparestrust. org/) and has been translated in Spanish, French and Dutch.

3.2 Terminology

As this study and the InterPARES Trust Project are both interdisciplinary research pursuits, the terminology used may be interpreted differently depending on the perspective of the reader. Additionally, the lack of standardization of terminology across cloud service contracts presented a number of challenges to researchers. For this reason, every effort has been made to utilize the InterPARES Trust Terminology Database for key terms. Accordingly, the following terms are operationalized as:

- "Record: a document made or received in the course of a practical activity as an instrument or a by-product of such activity, and set aside for action or reference";
- "Information: an assemblage of data intended for communication either through space or across time"; and
- "Data: the smallest meaningful units of information".

4   Results and *Checklist for Cloud Service Contracts*

4.1   Data Ownership

Legal principles and recordkeeping standards approach data ownership with the view that records may be physically stored with one organization even though the responsibility and management control may reside with either the creating organization or another appropriate authority. As a result, records stored in electronic systems require agreements that distinguish between the ownership of the records and the storage of the records. When reviewing the selected contracts for terms that declare ownership for customer information, it quickly became apparent that there is both a lack of consistency in terminology and in placement that could easily lead to confusion.

The issue is further complicated because an individual or organization may entrust their information to a cloud provider but also use the provider's platform and applications in the cloud to create further information. The provider might create a great deal of information related to these operations (such as data processing, management, marketing, etc.) that it might use for several purposes. Some have argued that information generated by the customer and stored in the cloud does not belong to the service provider but, rather, that the customer retains ownership and the provider is merely authorized to do specific operations with the data to provide the service (Reed and Cunningham 2014, p. 150). This is reflected by the *Checklist* in the following questions:

- Do you retain ownership of the data that you store, transmit, and/or create with the cloud service?
- Does the Provider reserve the right to use your data for the purposes of operating and improving the services or for the purposes of advertising?

The ownership of metadata generated by the service provider regarding the customer's information and operations in the cloud raises more questions. For the customer, metadata can be important to demonstrate that the security of the data has been preserved; however, it appears that metadata can be owned by the service provider who generated them for internal purposes such as managing the cloud and ensuring the use and quality of the service (Reed and Cunningham 2014, p. 150). Therefore, the *Checklist* invites customers to read and negotiate cloud service contracts with questions such as:

- Do the Provider's terms apply to metadata?
- Do you gain ownership of metadata generated by the cloud service system during procedures of upload, management, download, and migration?
- Do you have the right to access these metadata during the contractual relationship?

Beyond specifying ownership of metadata, the contract terms and conditions should determine both whether and how the customer has a right to access and use metadata for recordkeeping purposes either during the contractual relationship or at the end of service (see also below, Subsect. 4.7).

4.2 Availability, Retrieval and Use

The ability to have information and records immediately available to an organization to fulfill their current and future business needs is one of the driving forces behind organizations considering adopting the cloud. According to the InterPARES Trust Terminology Database, the term "availability" refers to the "capability of being accessed or used". Recordkeeping standards, such as ARMA International's Generally Accepted Recordkeeping Principles (2013) emphasize that records must be available for access and retrieval in a timely and efficient manner.

Analysis of the terms and conditions regarding availability, retrieval, and use of the customer contents reveals the use of SLAs to present monthly uptime percentages. Service credits are supplied in the event of failure to meet performance standards; however, the list of exceptions is long and it is the customer's responsibility to determine which types of outages, downtime, unavailability, losses, delays, or problems actually constitute a failure and quality for service credit. It is thus crucial for the organization to verify if precise indicators are provided regarding the availability of the service and if they meet its business needs. Furthermore, the organization should enquire about procedures, time, and cost for restoring the data following a service outage.

Availability and retrieval are also a legal issue given that they are closely linked to statutory or constitutional rights to have access to certain data, notably the right for individuals to access their own personal data, and the general right of access to information held by public bodies and government organizations. Availability is also crucial in case a governmental agency or an authorized control body requests access to the organization's information. These legal considerations are raised in the questions: Does the degree of availability of the data allow you to comply with freedom of information laws? …with the right of persons to access their own personal data? …with the right of authorities to legally access your data for investigation, control or judicial purposes?

4.3 Data Storage and Preservation

In the majority of the terms and conditions analyzed, the responsibility for backing up data rests with the customer. Although some providers admit creating backups of their systems on a regular basis, they do not necessarily guarantee customer access to them. Alternatively, others will provide data backup as a service. However, it is important to recognize that there can be a number of limitations listed in relation to backup services. Therefore, during the process of choosing a cloud service provider, one must carefully check if the provider creates backups of the organization's data and if the provider bears responsibility for data recovery in the event of accidental data deletion.

Organizations also need to consider how data will be preserved after they are no longer in use by the organization, considering that it impacts both the quality of the records and their capacity to be used for accountability purposes. Additionally, depending on the jurisdiction, evidence law can directly or indirectly impose certain requirements on the processing of the data to ensure a strong evidentiary value of the information. In turn, recordkeeping standards aimed at digital preservation state that systems selected by an organization for storing electronic records should ensure that the records held within the system remain accessible, authentic, reliable, and usable throughout any changes made to the system. Such a crucial requirement should be addressed in the cloud contract if the organization considers using the cloud for preservation purposes.

Maintaining information and records throughout changing technologies can be challenging for organizations. This is especially true if cloud providers are not transparent about the infrastructure and processes involved in providing cloud-based storage. To ensure that data preservation is managed in accordance with legal requirements and recordkeeping standards, precise questions can be formulated, such as: (1) Are there procedures to ensure file integrity during transfer of your data into and out of the system (e.g., checksums)? (2) Is there an explanation provided about how the service will evolve over time (i.e., migration and/or emulation activities)? (3) Does the system provide access to audit trails concerning activities related to evolution of the service? and (4) Will you be notified or can you request notification by the Provider of changes made to your data due to evolution of the service?

4.4   Data Retention and Disposition

"Retention" is defined by the InterPARES Terminology Database as "the act of keeping possession of something by preventing its disposal or alteration; preservation for a period of time". "Disposition" is defined as "records' final destruction or transfer to an archives as determined by their appraisal". Within organizations, records management and preservation activities rely on data retention and disposition schedules. Such schedules must remain compliant with increasingly complex legal and regulatory environments. Recordkeeping standards such as ISO 15489 suggest that decisions made by the organization on the subject of the retention and disposition of records should be carried out by the system. Authorized records destruction must be performed in a manner that preserves the confidentiality of the information. Additionally, the process should include all copies throughout the system and related metadata. Unfortunately, this can raise difficulties when the generated metadata are owned by the service provider in relation to the customer's data and operations in the cloud as the provider could refuse to destroy the metadata they have created if they are still considered useful for internal management purposes (for example, statistics or service improvement).

Despite its importance, the selected terms and conditions do not address data retention or deletion according to customer-stipulated schedules or recordkeeping requirements. In some cases, once the customer deletes their data (which are then no longer recoverable by the customer), the provider will delete these customer-deleted data later on, such as within a period of 180 days. If the destruction of data is required by law under a specific schedule, the organization would remain liable, as it is its legal duty to ensure the destruction of the data within the specified timeframe.

Therefore, cloud contracts should be checked with regard to the procedures for the destruction of the organization's data. The data and their copies (including backups) should be destroyed in compliance with the retention and disposition schedules. Information about the existence and nature of metadata generated by the provider's system should be included, and the eventuality to destroy them should be discussed as well. At the required moment, the data should be immediately and permanently destroyed in a manner that prevents their reconstruction, according to a secure destruction policy ensuring confidentiality of the data until their complete deletion. Audit trails of the destruction activity should be supplied, as well as a statement of deletion if required.

4.5   Security, Confidentiality, and Privacy

Issues of security, confidentiality, and privacy are exceptionally important for those wanting to contract in the cloud. Typically, the degree to which cloud providers will deliver security measures to customers appears to be reliant on the types of services being offered and whether or not the customer chooses to pay additional fees. Moreover, when the terms and conditions address controls on access and use of customer data, they focus on assigning responsibility to the customer for managing access restrictions to their account and their content.

According to the IPTrust Terminology Database, "security" is "the state of being protected from attack, risk, threat, or vulnerability"; "confidentiality" is "the expectation that private facts entrusted to another will be kept secret and will not be shared without consent"; and "privacy" is "control over access and use of one's personal information". From a legal perspective, the duty to ensure the confidentiality and privacy of the data is a very common legal requirement. When considering these broad issues, this research mainly focused on security conditions with regard to personal data.

The *Checklist* questions reflect a certain number of rules provided in ISO 15489 in terms of security, such as:

- Does the system prevent unauthorized access, alteration, or destruction of your data?
- Does the system provide and give you access to audit trails, metadata, and/or access logs to demonstrate security measures?
- Will you be notified in the case of a security breach or system malfunction?

Additional questions concern the existence of a disaster recovery plan and information regarding past performance with disaster recovery procedures. Finally, questions regarding the use of the services of a subcontractor are raised.

Privacy, confidentiality, and security policies should be communicated to the customer, especially for sensitive, confidential, personal, or other special kinds of data. Other questions on the *Checklist* relate to the collection of information about the customer, including the purpose of such a process and the potential sharing of this information with others.

The *Checklist* also encompasses "audit", defined as "a systematic assessment of compliance with established policies, procedures, laws, and standards" that govern the keeping of authentic records in a particular organization (InterPARES Terminology Database). The type of accreditation program, the frequency and independency of the audit process, the available documentation, and the expiration date of the certification are listed amongst the important aspects to be addressed.

4.6   Data Location and Cross-Border Data Flow

Given the nature of cloud computing, where the processing and storage services can be provided by using the cloud provider's resources throughout the globe, the issue of data location and cross-border data flow takes on increased importance. Legal concerns regarding cloud computing in this area focus on the issue that the customer's data may be stored or processed in different locations and unknown jurisdictions (Bradshaw et al. 2014, p. 55). From a legal perspective, this is mainly viewed as potentially problematic when data is stored outside the customer's jurisdiction because the customer might be subject to different laws and forced to appear in court in different jurisdictions if problems arise. Additionally, there is a concern about the customer being subject to foreign laws that allow investigation agencies access to any data stored in a provider's jurisdiction. In terms of recordkeeping standards, the discussion focuses mainly on location, with the imperative that electronic records system should be able to track the location of records as they move throughout the system (ISO 15489).

The above-mentioned concerns are translated into questions related to the presence of information (or the choice offered) about the location of the stored data, metadata and their copies; the compliance with location requirements that might be imposed to the customer's data by law; the possibility to be notified if the data location is changed and moved outside the customer's jurisdiction; the possibility of disclosure orders by national or foreign security authorities; and the legal jurisdiction governing the contract.

4.7 End of Service: Contract Termination

The issue of contract termination also requires consideration from both a legal and recordkeeping point of view. In the event that the relationship with a cloud provider ends, the organization needs assurance that it can gain access to the information and that any data left behind in the third-party system will be deleted by the cloud provider (Bradshaw et al. 2014, p. 66). Services might be terminated for several reasons, instigated by either party, or simply due to the scheduled end of the contract. Organizations should be aware of contract termination procedures before adopting cloud services. This can be particularly important when dealing with free services (Bradshaw et al. 2014, p. 45). When examining the selected terms and conditions, it became apparent that the contracts tended to deal with the termination of the service without explaining the process of restitution of the customer's data. However, this is a major concern with regard to the risk of discontinuation of a record system. Such a critical issue must be discussed at the negotiation stage of the contract, and not when the contract is terminated, in order to avoid unpleasant surprises.

According to ISO 15489 and ISO 14721, the termination of the service should not preclude ongoing access to those records formerly held by the system. More specific requirements are expressed in the *Checklist* through questions related to the procedure for the termination of the service by either party; the guarantee to return the data to the customer or to transfer them to another service provider in a usable and interoperable format; the cost, time, and period for returning or transferring the data; the right to access metadata generated by the provider after termination of the contract; the permanent destruction of the data and associated metadata after their restitution.

5 Conclusion

The analysis reveals that some contracts are ineffective at meeting the recordkeeping and legal needs of organizations. While other agreements do at least address some of them, they are generally written in favour of the service provider. Two conclusions can be drawn from these findings: first, records managers and archivists need to be included in the process of selecting a cloud service for their organization; secondly, due to the complexity of terms and agreements, there is a need for a tool to assess such services with regard to recordkeeping and legal requirements. It is the researchers' hope that the *Checklist for Cloud Service Contracts* will be used by records professionals as an assessment tool, but also as a tool to communicate their recordkeeping needs to their legal and information technology departments, as well as cloud service providers. The

Checklist therefore has the potential to foster the development of cloud services that support the management and preservation of trustworthy records for the long term.

Acknowledgements. Funding for the InterPARES Trust Project is provided by a SSHRC Partnership Grant. The authors would like to thank the reviewers who provided comments on the draft checklist for cloud service contracts, Elissa How for the annotated bibliography and Nadine Desrochers for her precious feedback on this paper.

References

ARMA International: Generally Accepted Recordkeeping Principles. Association of Record Managers and Administrators International (2013)

Baset, S.: Cloud SLAs: present and future. ACM SIGOPS Oper. Syst. Rev. **46**(2), 57–66 (2012)

Bradshaw, S., Millard, Ch., Walden, I.: Standard Contracts for Cloud Services. In: Millard, Ch. (ed.) Cloud Computing Law, pp. 39–72. Oxford Scholarship Online, Oxford (2014)

Bushey, J., Demoulin, M., McLelland, R.: Cloud service contracts: an issue of trust. Can. J. Inf. Libr. Sci. **39**(2), 128–153 (2015)

European Commission: Cloud Service Level Agreement Standardisation Guidelines. Cloud Select Industry Group (2014)

European Commission: Model Requirements for the Management of Electronic Records. Moreq2, Version 1.04 (2008)

Ferguson-Boucher, K., Convery, N.: Storing information in the cloud – a research project. J. Soc. Arch. **32**(2), 221–239 (2011)

InterPARES Terminology Database. http://arstweb.clayton.edu/interlex/en/

InterPARES Trust Project: Checklist for Cloud Service Contracts. Version 2.0 (2016). http://interparestrust.org/

InterPARES Trust Project: Contract Terms with Cloud Service Providers. Version 2 (2014). http://interparestrust.org/

InterPARES Trust Project: Trust in Cloud Service Contracts: Annotated Bibliography. Version 1.0 (2015). http://interparestrust.org/

ISO: ISO 15489-1. Information and documentation – records management. International Standards Organization (2001)

ISO: ISO 14721. Space data and information transfer systems – Open archival information system (OAIS). International Standards Organization (2012)

Reed, Ch., Cunningham, A.: Ownership of Information in Clouds. In: Millard, Ch. (ed.) Cloud Computing Law, pp. 144–164. Oxford Scholarship Online, Oxford (2014)

The National Archives, UK: The National Archives Guidance on Cloud Storage and Digital Preservation, 1st edn (2014)

Stiven, J.A.: The cloud: emerging issues in business and intellectual property law: preparing and advising your clients on cloud usage. DePaul Bus. Commer. Law J. **12**, 421–436 (2014)

Research on Fine-Grained Linked Data Creation for Digital Library Resources

Jing Huang[1]📷, Zhongyi Wang[2(✉)]📷, and Chunya Li[3]📷

[1] Wuhan Polytechnic, Wuhan City 430074, Hu Bei Province,
People's Republic of China
jianmo0320@hotmail.com
[2] School of Information Management, Central China Normal University,
Wuhan City 430079, Hu Bei Province, People's Republic of China
wzywzyl3579@163.com
[3] School of Business, Nantong Institute of Technology, Nantong 226002,
Jiang Su Province, People's Republic of China

Abstract. The best practices for publishing linked data have been adopted by an increasing number of libraries, leading to the creation of a global data space-the web of digital library data. However, in library linked data publishing, most of the existing researches mainly focus on structured and semi-structured digital library resources (for example catalogue data). Researches on publishing unstructured digital library resources (for example: contents of papers) are seldom. In order to overcome this problem, this paper proposes a fine-grained linked data creation method to publish the papers stored in digital libraries into linked data. At last, in order to evaluate this method, this paper conducted an experiment on the papers on "text segmentation". From the experiment results we find that our fine-grained linked data creation method is feasible and will promote the opening access to digital libraries resources.

Keywords: Linked data · Creation · Digital library · Fine granularity

1 Introduction

Technically, linked data refers to data published on the web in such a way that it is machine-readable. By publishing data on the web according to the linked data principles (Berners-Lee 2009), data providers can add their data to a global data space, which allows data to be discovered and used by various applications. Participants in the early stages of the research on publishing linked data were primarily researchers and developers in university research labs and small companies. Since that time the researches have grown considerably, to include significant involvement from large organizations such as the BBC, Thomson Reuters and the Library of Congress. With an imperative to support novel means of discovery, and a wealth of experience in producing high-quality structured data, libraries are natural complementers to linked data. This field has seen some significant early developments which aim at integrating library catalogs with third party information and at making library data easier accessible by relying on web standards. However, in library linked data publishing, most of the

© Springer International Publishing AG, part of Springer Nature 2018
G. Chowdhury et al. (Eds.): iConference 2018, LNCS 10766, pp. 185–194, 2018.
https://doi.org/10.1007/978-3-319-78105-1_23

existing researches mainly focus on structured and semi-structured digital library resources. Researches on publishing unstructured digital library resources are seldom. In order to overcome this problem, this paper proposes a fine-grained linked data creation method to publish the unstructured digital library resources into linked data to promote the opening access to digital library resources.

2 Related Work

Linked data is simply about using the web to create typed links between data from different sources. Since linked data was proposed, it has been adopted by an increasing number of data providers, leading to the creation of a global data space connecting data from diverse domains such as people, companies, books, scientific publications, films, music, online communities, and so on. In this paper, we concentrate on works on publishing liked data of digital libraries resources. Until now, works on library linked data publishing can be sectioned into three parts: library linked data projects, publishing methods and publishing tools.

2.1 Library Linked Data Projects

There are many projects on digital library linked data publishing. The American Library of Congress and the German National Library of Economics (Neubert 2009) publish their subject heading taxonomies as Linked Data. The Swedish Notional Union Catalogue is also available as Linked data. Similarly, the OpneLibrary publishes its catalogue in RDF, with incoming links from data sets such as ProductDB. Linked Data about scholarly publications is available from the L3S Research Center, which hosts a Linked Data version of the DBLP bibliography. The ReSIST project publishes and interlinks bibliographic databases such as the IEEE Digital Library, CiteSeer, and various institutional repositories. The RDF Book Mashup, a wrapper around the Amazon and Google Base APIs, provides Linked Data about books. The Open Archives Initiative has based its new Object Reuse and Exchange standard (OAI-ORE) on the Linked Data principles; this standard's deployment is likely to further accelerate the availability of Linked Data related to publications (Bizer 2009).

2.2 Publishing Methods

There are many practical recipes for publishing different types of information as linked data on the web. The simplest way to serve linked data is to produce static RDF files, and upload them to a web server. This approach is typically chosen in situations where the RDF files are created manually, and the RDF files are generated or exported by some piece of software that only outputs to files. However, if your data is stored in a relational database it is usually using D2R Server to publish a linked data view on your existing data base. D2R server relies on a declarative mapping between the schemata of the database and the target RDF terms. Based on this mapping, D2R Server serves a Linked Data view on your database and provides a SPARQL endpoint for the database. What's more, in view of data sources available on different kinds of Web APIs, it is often to implement linked data wrappers to publish linked data such as RDF Book Mashup which makes information about books, their authors, reviews, and online bookstores available as RDF on the Web (Bizer et al. 2007).

A variety of linked data publishing tools has been developed. The tools either serve the content of RDF stores as linked data on the web or provide linked data views over non-rdf legacy data sources. The tools shield publishers from dealing with technical details such as content negotiation and ensure that data is published according to the linked data community best practices (Sauermann and Cyganiak 2008; Berrueta and Phipps 2008; Bizer et al. 2007). All tools such as D2R Server (Bizer and Cyganiak 2006), Triplify (Auer et al. 2009), SparqPlug (Coetzee et al. 2008), etc. support dereferencing URIs into RDF descriptions. In addition, some of the tools such as Virtuoso Universal Server, Talis Platform, Pubby (Cyganiak and Bizer 2006) etc. also provide SPARQL query access to the served data sets and support the publication of RDF dumps.

From the above discussion we can see that in library linked data publishing, most of the existing researches mainly focus on structured and semi-structured digital library resources. However, besides these two kinds of digital library resources, digital library has more unstructured resources. Although most of the digital library resources are unstructured, there are seldom research works on publishing them as linked data, which prohibits library users to fully access and explore them dramatically. In order to overcome this problem, this paper proposes a fine-grained linked data creation method to publish the unstructured digital library resources into linked data.

3   Fine-Grained Linked Data Creation Method

In this paper, the procedure of fine-grained linked data creation can be considered as a process of the transformation from unstructured textual information to structured data. Steps of the fine-grained linked data construction process (see Fig. 1) include: "topic words extraction", "topic words normalization", "Relationship extraction between topic words", "topic words relationships normalization" and "Creating linked data based on D2R".

3.1   Topic Words Extraction

In this paper, topic words refer to nominal terms that can identify main themes in the document set. In order to realize the topic words extraction from digital libraries resources, text mining technique latent semantic analysis (LSA) is adopted. LSA is a technique in natural language processing of analyzing relationships between a set of documents and the terms they contain by producing a set of concepts related to the documents and terms. The basic idea of extracting topic words based on LSA is that: firstly topic information is gained by LSA statistical topic model; then words are graded according to this information, and at last words with high grade are selected as the topic words to identify documents. Specifically, the algorithm for extracting topic words based on LSA can be illustrated in Table 1. These extracted topic words will be used as entities in the next step of "3.3 relationship extraction between topic words".

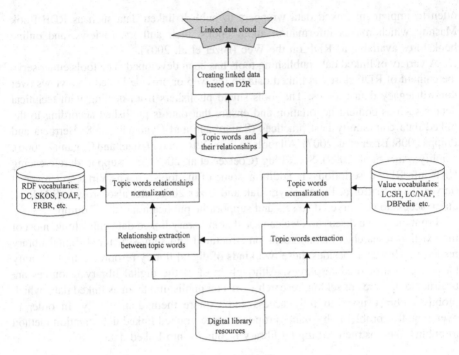

Fig. 1. The process of linked data construction

Table 1. The algorithm for words extraction based on LSA

Input: a set of documents
Output: topic words

1. Sentence splitting, break each document into a list of sentences using a heuristically-based approach on the basis of punctuation (".;/!/?/")

2. Word segmentation and POS-tagging, use the Stanford Segmenter to segment each sentence into a list of words which are parsed with POST tags

3. Words filtering, select noun words as candidate topic words, to generate $d = (w_1, w_2,..., w_n)$ where w_n is the tf-idf value of the nth word in the document d

4. Generate $D = (d_1,d_2,...,d_m)$ which is a collection of m documents

5. Singular value decompose, apply SVD to yield A according to the equation $A = U\Sigma V^T$, where X^T denotes the transposed matrix of X. The columns of U and V are the eigenvectors of AA^T and A^TA, respectively. The diagonal values of Σ are the corresponding singular values which are sorted in descending order

6. Extracting topic words, extract topic words from the first k columns of U according to the diagonal values of Σ. Because the eigenvectors in U are the principle axes for distinguishing the word feature vectors in AA^T which is a word similarity matrix where the meaning of a word w_i is expressed in terms of its dot-product with all other words $\{w_1, ..., w_n\}$, these extracted k words can be viewed as topic words to reveal the themes of documents in a k-dimensional space

3.2   Topic Words Normalization

Since topic Words extracted through the above process are uncontrolled words, it is common for the phenomenon of synonyms and homonyms to occur. In order to overcome these problems, there is a need to translate these extracted topic words into controlled words to achieve the purpose of topic words normalization. Therefore, translating topic words into thesauri is a good solution. In this paper, different kinds of value vocabularies (for example: LCSH, LC/NAF, DBPedia etc.) are used during the process of words normalization. Each of the above extracted topic words are covert to its corresponding thesauri through the projection between words and value vocabularies. However, since it is hard and laborious to ensure the currency of the thesaurus. Some new topic words may have no their corresponding thesauri in value vocabularies. In this case, experts are invited to assign thesauruses for them.

3.3   Relationship Extraction Between Topic Words

After topic words normalization, the next step is extracting relationship between them. A relationship extraction task requires the detection of semantic relationship between topic words from digital libraries resources. This paper extracts relationships between the above extracted topic words by using syntactic dependency patterns. The procedure of relationship extraction (see Fig. 2) is as follows.

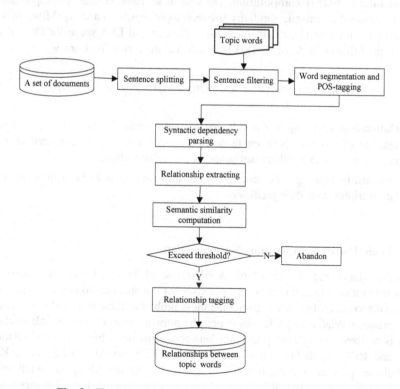

Fig. 2. The process of relationship extraction between words

Sentence splitting. As the task of sentence splitting has been done in the topic words extraction (see Sect. 3.1 Topic words extraction), we will not explain it in this part.

Sentence filtering. Irrelevant sentences which just contain one or null of the above extracted topic words are filtered out. And only sentences including two or more the above extracted topic words are selected as relevant sentences.

Word segmentation and POS-tagging. As the task of word segmentation and POS-tagging has been done in the topic words extraction (Sect. 3.1 Topic words extraction), we will not explain it in this part.

Syntactic dependency parsing. The task of syntactic dependency parsing is to encode syntactic structure with labeled directed arcs (dependencies) between the headwords of constituents and generate a dependency tree for each sentence, by using of the Stanford Parser.

Sentence skeleton extracting. The task of sentence skeleton extracting is to simplify dependency trees of sentences. As we focus on verb relationships, so in this paper the process of sentence skeleton extracting includes collecting for each verb its subject, object, preposition with arguments and auxiliary verb.

Relationship extracting. The task of relationship extracting is to extract relation triples from sentence skeleton based on their dependency relationships.

Semantic similarity computation. The task of semantic similarity computation is to calculate the semantic similarity between topic words w_i and w_j ($M(w_i, w_j)$) by use of the formula (1), where Λ_k is the k-dimensional LSA space for $D(d_1, d_2,\dots d_m)$, the i-th row in Λ_k, or $\Lambda_k(i)$ is the LSA feature vector for word w_i.

$$M(w_i, w_j) = \cos(w_i, w_j) = \Lambda_k(i) \times \Lambda_k(j) \Big/ \sqrt{\Lambda_k(i)^2 \times \Lambda_k(j)^2} \qquad (1)$$

Relationship selecting. If the value of semantic similarity exceeds the threshold level, the relationship between these two topic-words will be extracted as their semantic relationship, otherwise, abandon this relationship.

Relationship tagging. The task of relationship tagging is to label these selected relation triples with their predicates.

3.4   Topic Words Relationships Normalization

Since the relationships between topic words extracted through the above process are also uncontrolled terms, it is also very common for the phenomenon of synonyms and homonyms to occur. In order to overcome these problems, there is a need to normalize these extracted relationships. In this paper, the normalization of topic words relationships is realized through the projection between terms describing extracted relationships and RDF vocabularies (for example DC, SKOS, FOAF, FRBR, etc.). RDF vocabularies provide a controlled list of properties for describing the relationship between topic words. Since RDF vocabularies are also controlled vocabularies which need people to maintain them, it is hard to ensure the currency of them. Therefore, in this paper, experts are invited to assign a term to normalize the extracted relationships which are not included in the RDF vocabularies.

3.5   Creating Linked Data Based on D2R

Through the above steps, we have obtained topic words and their relationships, next we will create linked data based on them by using of the linked data construction tool: D2R. The procedure of linked data construction based on D2R (see Fig. 3) is as follows.

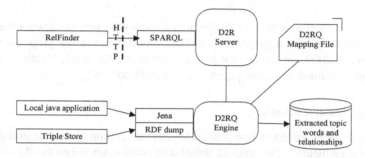

Fig. 3. Constructing linked data based on D2R

First, entity denomination, use the D2R Server to assign an URI to each topic words, which can be used to locate and search each entity. Second, constructing RDF, use the customizable D2RQ mapping to map each topic keyword and their relationships into RDF format. Third, publishing linked data, associate them with outside linked data cloud through D2R server to make full use of outside information resources revealing topic words' meanings. Last, linked data visualization, linked data is visualized by RelFinder which can be used to extract and visualize relationships interactively explorable. RelFinder is based on the open source framework Adobe Flex, easy-to-use and works with any RDF dataset that provides standardized SPARQL access.

4   Experiment

4.1   Data Source

In order to validate the fine-grained linked data creation method proposed in this paper, we conducted an experiment on papers of the "Linked data" research field which is used to describe a recommended best practice for exposing, sharing, and connecting pieces of data, information, and knowledge on the Semantic Web using URIs and RDF. We selected the "Linked data" as the test subject mainly for two reasons. First, as the "Linked data" is a new research field, the total number of related papers is not very big. So it is relatively easy for experts to evaluate the results of our experiment on this research field. Second, as the "Linked data" is an interdisciplinary research field, the semantic relationships between words are often very complex.

To ensure that all relevant papers can be collected as far as possible, this paper takes two mainstream databases (Web of Science, Engineering Index) as the data source. Web of Science Core Collection provides researchers, administrators, faculty, and students with quick, powerful access to the world's leading citation databases. Engineering Index (EI) was founded in 1884 by Dr. John Butler Johnson. EI is the broadest and most complete engineering literature database available in the world. It provides a truly holistic and global view of peer reviewed and indexed publications with over 17 million records from 73 countries across 190 engineering disciplines. By using EI, engineers can be confident information is relevant, complete, accurate and of high quality.

Then, the retrieval strategy: (Title = linked data) was used to conduct the retrospective searching in these two databases. Since linked data was first proposed by Tim Berners-Lee at 2009, we set the year in the retrieval as 2006–2015. Finally, removing the unrelated and non-academic papers, we got 1045 articles.

4.2 Experimental Results

According to the procedure of fine-grained linked data creation method proposed in this paper, we implemented a fine-grained linked data creation system on the Windows XP platform by means of JAVA, JSP development language. The entire system can be divided into two parts: linked data creation and linked data visualization. The function of linked data creation is to translate unstructured digital libraries resources into RDFs; and the job of linked data visualization is to provide users with a customizable interface to interact with our system. As shown in Fig. 4, users only need to click "add" button to add topic words into the input box in the upper part of the sidebar. These user-given topic words are then mapped to unique objects of the knowledge base by executing an automatic or manual disambiguation, and serve as starting nodes in a graph that is drawn in the presentation area of the user interface. The links between the topic words are visualized as labeled and directed edges in accordance with their representation in the knowledge base. Besides, the sidebar offer other sophisticated functionality for the interactive exploration of the found relationships. For example, the sidebar offers four types of filters (class filter, link filter, length filter and connectivity filter) that facilitate the exploration of the graph visualization by highlighting or removing certain elements.

Through the interface of linked data, users can explore any topic words and their relationships by entering them into the input box and clicking the "find relations" button. For example, if we add some topic words on "linked data" such as "semantic web" and "linked data" into the input box, then click "Find Relations", parts of linked data on "linked data" will be displayed (see Fig. 4).

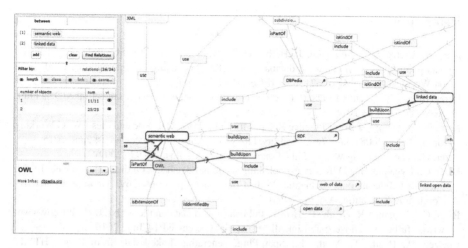

Fig. 4. Interface of linked data

5 Conclusion and Future Work

In order to publish the unstructured digital libraries resources as linked data based on the linked data principles and practices, this paper has done a lot of researches on it. Specifically, the main contributions of our study are threefold. First, we have analyzed limitations in library linked data publishing and pointed out that most of the existing researches mainly focus on structured and semi-structured digital library resources such as catalogue, subject heading taxonomies and so on, while researches on publishing unstructured digital libraries resources such as the text of digital books, papers are seldom. Second, this paper, in order to overcome this limitation, proposes a fine-grained linked data creation method to publish the unstructured digital library resources into linked data to promote the opening access to digital library resources. Third, using this method, the unstructured resources on the field of "linked data" is published as linked data. It is useful and meaningful to publish existing literatures in libraries as linked data. That is because most of library users have neither the time nor inclination to sift through long documents for small pieces of useful knowledge. While publishing the unstructured digital library resources into linked data can facilitate document fragment retrieval and support the delivery of the right knowledge in the right quantity.

Of course, with the application and development of library linked data, an increasing amount of libraries resources will be published and linked in the form of linked data. This trend certainly will bring new opportunities to libraries to improve their ability to serve their users.

Acknowledgment. This study is supported by MOE (Ministry of Education in China) Project of Humanities and Social Science: "Research on the Multi-granularity Hierarchical Topic-based Segmentation of the Digital Library Resources" (Project No. 16YJC870003).

References

Auer, S., Dietzold, S., Lehmann, J., Hellmann, S., Aumueller, D.: Triplify: light-weight linked data publication from relational databases. In: 18th Proceedings of International Conference on World Wide Web, pp. 621–630. IEEE, Madrid (2009)

Berners-Lee, T.: Linked Data (2009). http://www.w3.org/DesignIssues/LinkedData.html. Accessed 10 June 2015

Berrueta, D., Phipps, J.: Best Practice Recipes for Publishing RDF Vocabularies - W3C Working Group Note (2008). http://www.w3.org/TR/swbp-vocab-pub/. Accessed 14 June 2015

Bizer, C.: The emerging web of linked data. Intell. Syst. 24(5), 87–92 (2009)

Bizer, C., Cyganiak, R.: D2R server-publishing relational databases on the semantic web. In: 5th Poster of International Semantic Web Conference, pp. 360–369. Georgia Center for Continuing Education, Athens (2006)

Bizer, C., Cyganiak, R. Heath, T.: How to Publish Linked Data on the Web (2007). http://www4.wiwiss.fu-berlin.de/bizer/pub/LinkedDataTutorial/. Accessed 14 June 2016

Coetzee, P., Heath, T., Motta, E.: SparqPlug: generating linked data from legacy HTML, SPARQL and the DOM. In: 1st Proceedings of Workshop on Linked Data on the Web (LDOW 2008), Beijing, China (2008)

Cyganiak, R., Bizer, C.: Pubby - A Linked Data Frontend for SPARQL Endpoints. http://www4.wiwiss.fu-berlin.de/pubby/. Accessed 14 June 2016

Neubert, J.: Bringing the "Thesaurus for Economics" on to the web of linked data. In: Proceedings of WWW Workshop on Linked Data on the Web, Madrid, Spain (2009)

Potentials of Smart Breathalyzer: Interventions for Excessive Drinking Among College Students

Aehong Min$^{(\boxtimes)}$ (iD), Daehyoung Lee (iD), and Patrick C. Shih (iD)

Indiana University Bloomington, Bloomington, IN 47405, USA
aemin@iu.edu, {lee2055,patshih}@indiana.edu

Abstract. Excessive drinking among college students is a significant public health issue. Electronic Screening Brief Intervention (e-SBI) has been shown to be an effective prevention tool, and it has been implemented on personal computers, web, mobile phones and social networking platforms. In this research, we asked college students to discuss about their perception of BACtrack Mobile Pro, the FDA-approved and consumer-oriented smart breathalyzer. We recruited 15 college students who have consumed alcohol regularly, asked them to use the smart breathalyzer for two weeks, and conducted pre- and post-study surveys and interviews. We identified five barriers with design opportunities for the smart breathalyzer: (1) Support from immediate family members or close friends, (2) Personalized results, (3) Intuitive status display, (4) Accessorizing the form factor, and (5) Quicker access. Future mobile and smart wearable e-SBI interventions targeted at college students should take these design considerations into account.

Keywords: Smart breathalyzer · Screening and brief intervention
e-SBI · Excessive drinking · Alcohol consumption
Persuasive technology

1 Introduction

Excessive drinking among college students is a serious public health issue. A national survey shows that roughly 60% of college students between 18-to-22 years of age have consumed alcohol excessively in the previous month [30]. According to the Centers for Disease Control and Prevention, excessive drinking includes heavy drinking, which is defined as drinking 15 drinks or more per week for men and eight for women, and binge drinking, which is defined as a pattern of drinking that causes the blood alcohol concentration (BAC) level to rise over 0.08% [7, 26]. Excessive drinking could bring serious risks to students' health and safety that could result in car accidents, sexual assaults, bodily injuries, and long-term liver and kidney damage. About 1,800 students between 18 and 24 years old die annually from alcohol-related accidents [17]. Although problems

© Springer International Publishing AG, part of Springer Nature 2018
G. Chowdhury et al. (Eds.): iConference 2018, LNCS 10766, pp. 195–206, 2018.
https://doi.org/10.1007/978-3-319-78105-1_24

related to excessive drinking are well publicized, many college students perceive drinking as a part of their college life and subsequently establish drinking habits when they leave home to attend college after graduating from high school [27].

With recent advances in information and communication technologies (ICTs), electronic Screening Brief Intervention (e-SBI) has been found to have the potential of reducing the amount and frequency of drinking and is considered to be an effective prevention mechanism for young adults [21]. In spite of its importance and potential with current information technologies, little research has been conducted in the area of information science. In this paper, we first introduce existing literature on traditional and e-SBI studies. We then describe the results of our user study involving BACtrack Mobile Pro, which is a smart breathalyzer, as an intervention in a series of surveys and interviews with college students who consume alcohol regularly. We report five barriers and design opportunities related to current smart breathalyzers that have potential for providing a better user experience and more effective impacts on college students' perceptions on their drinking behavior.

2 Related Work

2.1 Screening and Brief Intervention

The screening and brief intervention (SBI) is a technique designed with the intent to assess a person's alcohol consumption behavior with a series of questions focusing on drinking patterns. Based on the SBI assessment score, feedback about various consequences of excessive alcohol consumption and suggestions of behavior change are then provided to raise awareness of the individual [8]. SBI has been conducted with various well-known, validated survey instruments, such as Alcohol Use Disorders Identification Test (AUDIT), Problem Oriented Screening Instrument for Teenagers substance use/abuse scale (POSIT), Cut, Annoyed, Guilty, Eye-opener (CAGE), Car, Relax, Alone, Forget, Friends, Trouble (CRAFFT), etc. [20]. Similarly, the brief interventions for excessive alcohol consumption could vary widely depending on the context of delivery (e.g., in the presence of a specialist, motivation of the targeted population, etc.) [15]. Although SBI researchers have focused on the research instruments and the context of delivery, there has yet to be a systematic review focusing on the form of delivery of technology-mediated SBI. Below, we provide a review of existing SBI methods and point to the potential of new forms of SBI using current technologies.

2.2 Face-to-Face SBI

Traditional SBI is typically provided by health care professionals in a face-to-face setting with in-person feedback, which includes information about one's alcohol consumption pattern, its risks, benefits of lower alcohol consumption, and suggestions for adjusting drinking patterns. If appropriate, referral to treatment could be included [6,8]. These traditional in-person and paper-based brief interventions have been found to be effective at reducing alcohol consumption and related problems in many studies. A meta-analysis study of 54 brief intervention trials shows positive evidence compared to the control group [25], and another meta-analysis study of 22 randomized control trials shows that after one year or longer, subjects who received brief interventions exhibited lower drinking levels compared to the control group [18].

Although research results focusing on SBI are generally positive, several studies have also pointed out limitations of utilizing it in the health care settings. A survey study of 282 general practitioners found that there is not adequate training and support for health care professionals to address alcohol-related issues [33]. Prior research has also found that the practitioners suffered from the lack of skills, knowledge, time, and resources for handling drinking problems [29]. Moreover, when it comes to the adoption of SBI among young people such as college students, research has shown that they are less receptive to being assessed by health care practitioners about drinking, and they tend to be more interested in receiving personalized feedback [21].

2.3   Electronic SBI

Unlike traditional SBI that typically accompanies face-to-face feedback, e-SBI could provide a personalized feedback about excessive drinking via digital medium such as web, text messages, mobile phone apps, and social network platforms. It could be fully automated and interactive [8], and it is possible to offer more anonymity and flexibility to the subjects. Instrumenting SBI using electronic medium is also relatively cheap to implement and deploy compared to paper-based and face-to-face mechanisms. In terms of reducing the time and cost, dissemination through digital medium has the potential of reaching more people who may benefit from SBI. Especially for young adults, e-SBI could mitigate concerns related to stigma in one's social circle [10]. Therefore, most health care professionals prefer e-SBI that offers anonymity. This anonymity can be provided by electronic alcohol risk assessment and feedback rather than face-to-face interaction [21,32].

Recent systematic reviews and meta-analysis studies show that e-SBI is effective for reducing alcohol consumption [12]. A systematic review of 31 e-SBI studies shows that a significant reduction in frequency and intensity of binge drinking were reported among participants who received e-SBI on regular intervals compared to the control group [32]. However, e-SBI studies have pointed out that the interventions may not be effective for long-term behavior changes beyond a period of three months [12,24].

Like traditional SBI that used various forms of interventions, e-SBI studies have experimented with various delivery platforms and feedback mechanisms. For example, computer-based interventions could involve a combination of web- and email-based interventions. Similarly, interventions on mobile platforms could involve text message prompts or native app notifications. We describe these electronic interventions in more detail below.

Computer-Based e-SBI. Research that analyzed 24 studies of online and in-person computer-based interventions found that the computer-based interventions are more effective at reducing the frequency drinking and binge drinking per week among college students compared to the control group [19]. Another computer-based intervention study shows a significant reduction in the students' drinking levels and drinking-related problems compared to the control group [16]. A review of 22 studies on social norm interventions that involve peer support, such as receiving notification messages from family and friends, showed that computer-based interventions are less costly, are more effective, and impacted across a broader set of outcomes for college students than mailed feedback, individual face-to-face feedback, and group face-to-face feedback for periods up to three months [24].

Although research shows that there are many positive potentials of e-SBI, some studies, particularly those that relied on personalized messages over emails, found that the interventions did not result in any significant effects to one's behavior. Several studies that utilized email interventions that contained personalized messages found that receiving those messages did not affect drinking patterns among college students [5,11,28]. Another email intervention study that provided personalized messages to college students found that only 8% of females and 3% of males believed that they would actually change their habits after receiving feedback [4].

Mobile Phone-Based e-SBI. Mobile phones are widely adopted in the young adult population. Mobile phones allow people to easily access text-messages, emails, and web contents. Research has found automated text messages to be an effective means for delivering alcohol-related interventions to college students [22,31]. Moreover, smartphones provide easier, wider, and faster access of the aforementioned services in addition to numerous other phone applications and connected devices. A current study in 2016 found 32 e-SBI apps on iTunes and Google Play that focused on drink monitoring [23].

In terms of the effectiveness of smartphone e-SBI, a randomized clinical trial study of 349 patients who suffered from alcoholism found that patients who used the e-SBI smartphone app reported significantly fewer risky drinking days than those in the control group [14]. However, for smartphone apps that calculate blood alcohol concentration (BAC), research found that using these apps tended to increase drinking frequency and BAC level among participants. Researchers attributed the increase to the fact that more male participants were represented in the study, and that they were more likely to treat the BAC level as a competitive social game [13].

Personal Smart Breathalyzer as New e-SBI. In general, although there are many studies that point to the positive impact of e-SBI for reducing alcohol consumption among young adults due to its ease of access and anonymity, there is very little research that involved the use of smartphone and wearable devices in both health- and information science-related areas. Also, little research has focused on the use of breathalyzer for e-SBI. One randomized clinical trial study focused on the effectiveness of a contingency management treatment on the mobile phone platform. The study used a breathalyzer to monitor breath alcohol concentration level (BrAC), but the study's primary focus was on the effectiveness of the contingency management treatment as opposed to using the breathalyzer as an intervention tool for drinking [1]. To our knowledge, there has been no prior reporting of consumer-oriented breathalyzer device usage. In this paper, we describe an exploratory study that involves the use of a personal smart breathalyzer device that can be paired to one's smartphone.

3   BACtrack Mobile Pro

Figure 1 shows BACtrack Mobile Pro with three mouthpieces and a pouch that was given to the participant for the research.

Fig. 1. BACtrack Mobile Pro

BACtrack Mobile Pro is a consumer breathalyzer. We selected this device as a tool to use for our research since BACtrack is the first, and currently the only, company to obtain FDA approval to manufacture and market breathalyzers for consumer use. Moreover, consumer reviews on Amazon.com also show higher user satisfaction than other competing products [2,3]. Therefore, we concluded that it is reliable to use for the study.

This breathalyzer is developed to monitor and manage one's BAC and drinking habits by linking to a smartphone or a smart watch. The device can connect to BACtrack app for a smartphone via Bluetooth. Through an attached mouthpiece of the device, a user could blow and check her/his BAC on the app. The app can record the BAC levels and GPS-based location with an additional comment area that allows the user to take notes. The user can retrieve and compare the information over time. Depending on the BAC level, the app also displays appropriate suggestions along with the BAC reading. In addition, the app provides the user an estimated time when her/his BAC level is expected to drop to 0. The app also contains convenience features such as calling Uber [3]. Figure 2 shows screenshots of the smartphone app.

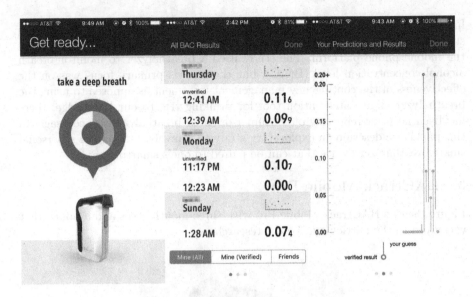

Fig. 2. Screenshots of BACtrack application

4   Methods

The goal of this research is to understand how the smart breathalyzer could influence college students' perceptions and behaviors on drinking, and how the design of the device and application could be potentially improved to prevent college students from excessive drinking.

We recruited undergraduate students by advertising the research through social media and snowball sampling. Our target population was college students who have consumed alcohol at least once a week. Participants were informed about the research process and signed an informed consent form approved by Institutional Review Board (IRB) at Indiana University. The participants were asked to fill out a basic demographics questionnaire. We then conducted an in-depth, one-hour interview asking about their current alcohol consumption perceptions, behaviors, and cultures. The participants were provided a short tutorial to learn how to use the breathalyzer device and the smartphone app. They then were given the breathalyzer with three mouthpieces, a pouch, and a charger for two weeks. At the end of each week, we sent short online surveys to query their usage experience in the previous week. At the end of the two-week period, the participants were required to fill out a post-study questionnaire about their overall user experiences. Finally, we conducted a follow-up interview to explore how the device had influenced the participant's alcohol consumption, perception, and behavior, and to uncover barriers related to device usage. All surveys were conducted via Qualtrics, and the interviews were audio-recorded and transcribed. We analyzed data by conducting open coding and iteratively refined the emerged themes [9].

5   Results

We recruited nine female and six male college students (mean age: 21.8 years old). They used the device between 2-to-7 times during the two-week period. From the follow-up surveys and interviews, we identified five main barriers with opportunities to improve the smart breathalyzer as a form of electronic intervention on drinking: *(1) Support from immediate family members or close friends, (2) Personalized results, (3) Intuitive status display, (4) Accessorizing the form factor, and (5) Quicker access.*

5.1   Support from Immediate Family Members or Close Friends

The functions of BACtrack Mobile Pro include not only BAC level calculation, but also calling Uber and simple sharing the BAC level online anonymously. At the beginning of the study, we expected that they might not want to share any alcohol-related information (e.g., BAC, status, or location) with other people they know. However, the college students said they want to share their drinking-related information with their immediate family members and close friends, mostly for safety. For instance, if a user registers their family members or friends on the app, the family or friends will receive notifications if the app detects an abnormally high BAC level. The family or friends could then provide any help to the user. Also, the participants wanted to help their family and friends if they become overly impaired.

P-02: "If I see one of my friends has a high BAC level, I will call and check on them to make sure they are ok."
P-11: "If I show my BAC level and status when I feel drunk, I can show it to my friends and let them know I should stop drinking. Then, they might not give me more shots."

A user can receive support by fending off peer pressure when the user shares BAC reading.

P-15: "I can share my BAC level with my friends when we drink together. Sometimes I may look fine to my friends, but I was actually drunk. So this BAC level would help me prove that I am drunk and that I won't be pressured into drinking more."

Our findings suggest that a closed peer support network system could be designed for those who want to share their states to get support from family members and friends.

5.2   Personalized Results

Participants also mentioned that they needed more meaningful representation of their BAC level; some of them have trouble understanding the meaning and difference between readings such as 0.08 and 0.12. A more meaningful visual representation is needed to help those participants understand their alcohol consumption habits.

Since each person is different and could react to alcohol differently, the BAC level, which is shown on the app, might not exactly indicate the precise risk level for each person. Although the color and value of BAC level could indicate the risk level to a certain degree, many of our participants reported that they did not feel drunk when their BAC level exceeded the legal threshold of 0.08. On the other hand, some participants reported feeling drunk despite the BAC level being far below the 0.08 threshold while the app shows a green color.

P-07 "I am a light weight compare to other people. When I began to feel a headache from drinking too much and blew the breathalyzer, the color of BAC level was green. The device stated that my status is OK, but I wasn't. So I felt this is not helpful for me."
P-10 "It would be good if the device knows my state and gives some alerts to prevent me from having bad symptoms."
P-11 "It should provide personalized information about my drinking in detail. You know, degree of excessive drinking might be different, so if I just get BAC level without any detailed information, it does not have enough value."

Future design could allow participants to annotate their BAC levels to indicate their personal comfort level, and that could be used to personalize the individual's status display. For example, the app could display a red color if a user sets the threshold to 0.05 as opposed to the normative 0.08. This feature could provide more effective personalized feedback as intervention.

5.3   Intuitive Status Display

The device shows BAC level, texts, and graph on the app. However, many participants stated that they were confused when they saw the results. For instance, they did not know the BAC level at which it becomes dangerous for operating a motor vehicle. Also, although the app displays what a BAC level means to a user's possible status and suggestions with texts, they said the messages were too small and lengthy to read and understand, especially when they were drinking or were already intoxicated. Thus, they suggested that if the results show visual images that correspond to someone's physical conditions, such as passing out or in a form of emoticon, it would help them understand the status much more intuitively.

P-02 "If the device shows pictures of someone who is passed out or police officer who hands out ticket, it would encourage me to stop drinking. If you are drunk, you might not be able to read the words, but you can see the pictures."
P-13 "I wanna see what each BAC status means. When I used the device and saw the value, I thought 'Is this BAC level enough for my body? Is this dangerous to drive?' I don't understand intuitively."

Thus, future design should consider a participant's cognition and their physical conditions while drinking. This could be understandable even for users who are already drunk. The addition of audio or haptic effects could provide a more noticeable and effective intervention for users.

5.4   Accessorizing the Form Factor

The size of BACtrack Mobile Pro is small enough to be held in one hand. It is convenient to carry in one's purse or bag, but almost every participant mentioned that they were worried about losing the device because of its size, especially when they were less cognizant of their surroundings when drinking. Also, some participants suggested different shapes of devices such as a watch, a neckless, or a bracelet that could better fit their lifestyle and aesthetic preferences.

P-01 "I had it in my purse, but I don't think it would be easy to carry for male students. It would be better if it could be attached to my cellphone."
P-05 "I don't wanna lose it, so I didn't bring it sometimes."
P-13 "At first time, I brought and used it. But the next day I was drunk, I almost could not find the device. Then I became really worried if I really lost it so I always leave the device at home."

Therefore, future designs that investigate different ways of accessorizing the appearance of the breathalyzer and how it can be worn or carried conveniently could significantly affect the wider adoption of the device.

5.5   Quicker Access

To retrieve the BAC level, the user must turn on Bluetooth, open the app, and click on the device to pair the app. When a connection is established, the user needs to wait for the device to 'warm up' before she or he can blow into it to get the BAC reading. The device needs to capture a large enough amount of air that contains alcohol before a reading can be registered. This process could take up to one minute. Some participants expressed that the process took too long and was inconvenient and burdensome to use.

P-09 "It was not easy to check my BAC because I was drunk. Why can't they monitor automatically?"
P-12 "I usually forgot to use it while I was drinking. It took quite a long time for me to set it up and check my BAC."
P-15 "You know, my device was really slow to turn on the app and Bluetooth. I was trying to check my level in the middle of drinking with my friends, but it took a long time. It was obvious that it disrupted our conversation."

Today's smartphone is capable of location detection. It may be possible to program the breathalyzer and the app to enter into a 'hibernation' mode so that it could be accessed quicker. For example, if the app detects that a user is located in the vicinity of a bar or any preset place where the user usually drinks, the app is automatically turned on in the hibernation mode. If automatic detection is not possible, it may be possible to create a manual mode that allows the user to set the connection state manually if they know when and where they plan to drink that evening.

6 Conclusion

This ongoing research has explored current college students' perceptions, behaviors, and cultures regarding drinking, and the issues of using a smart breathalyzer as a potential e-SBI device to prevent excessive drinking among college students. We have identified five current barriers and future design opportunities to improve the app interface and device form factor. Those promising features have potential for attracting college students and providing a better user experience to them for reducing risky drinking. Even though some limitations of the study include the short usage time (two weeks) and a relatively small number of users (15 college students), this study contributes to exploring potential of future e-SBI tools as an extension of previous SBI studies where few studies have focused on using up-to-date technology such as a smart breathalyzer. Also, we contribute to introducing a new, important role of information technology in the field of information science where little research has conducted for this significant role considering public health. Current information technology can be a more effective way of motivating and helping college students with preventing from drinking issues, which is a big problem that needs to be solved.

Future research should specifically consider how to design effective interventions for college students. We plan to design and implement a different smartphone app that integrates with the smart breathalyzer, and to conduct a longer-term deployment study to understand the potential impact on college students' perceptions and behaviors of alcohol consumption.

References

1. Alessi, S.M., Petry, N.M.: A randomized study of cell phone technology to reinforce alcohol abstinence in the natural environment. Addiction **108**(5), 900–909 (2013)
2. Amazon.com: BACtrack Mobile Smartphone Breathalyzer for iPhone and Android Devices (2017). https://www.amazon.com/BACtrack-Smartphone-Breathalyzer-Android-Devices/dp/B00CFN1HNY
3. BACtrack: BACtrack (2017). https://www.bactrack.com/
4. Bendtsen, P., Johansson, K., Åkerlind, I.: Feasibility of an email-based electronic screening and brief intervention (e-SBI) to college students in Sweden. Addict. Behav. **31**(5), 777–787 (2006)
5. Bernstein, M.H., Wood, M.D., Erickson, L.R.: The effectiveness of message framing and temporal context on college student alcohol use and problems: a selective e-mail intervention. Alcohol and Alcohol. **51**(1), 106–116 (2015)

6. Centers for Disease Control and Prevention: Planning and Implementing Screening and Brief Intervention for Risky Alcohol Use: A Step-by-Step Guide for Primary Care Practices. Atlanta, vol. 44. Centers for Disease Control and Prevention, National Center on Birth Defects and Developmental Disabilities, Georgia (2014)
7. Centers for Disease Control and Prevention: Alcohol & Public Health (2017). https://www.cdc.gov/alcohol/faqs.htm
8. Community Preventive Services Task Force: Preventing Excessive Alcohol Consumption: Electronic Screening and Brief Interventions (e-SBI). Technical report, U.S. Department of Health and Human Services (2013). https://www.thecommunityguide.org/topic/excessive-alcohol-consumption
9. Corbin, J., Strauss, A.: Basics of Qualitative Research. SAGE Publication, Inc., Thousand Oaks (2014)
10. Cunningham, J.A.: Internet evidence-based treatments. In: Miller, P.M. (ed.) Evidence-Based Addiction Treatment, pp. 379–397. Academic Press, Cambridge (2009)
11. Cunningham, J.A., Hendershot, C.S., Murphy, M., Neighbors, C.: Pragmatic randomized controlled trial of providing access to a brief personalized alcohol feedback intervention in university students. Addict. Sci. Clin. Practice 7, 21 (2012)
12. Donoghue, K., Patton, R., Phillips, T., Deluca, P., Drummond, C.: The effectiveness of electronic screening and brief intervention for reducing levels of alcohol consumption: a systematic review and meta-Analysis. J. Med. Internet Res. 16(6) (2014)
13. Gajecki, M., Berman, A.H., Sinadinovic, K., Rosendahl, I., Andersson, C.: Mobile phone brief intervention applications for risky alcohol use among university students: a randomized controlled study. Addict. Sci. Clin. Practice 9, 11 (2014)
14. Gustafson, D.H., McTavish, F.M., Chih, M.Y., Atwood, A.K., Johnson, R.A., Boyle, M.G.: A smartphone application to support recovery from alcoholism: a randomized controlled trial. JAMA Psychiatry 71(5), 566–572 (2014). http://archpsyc.jamanetwork.com/article.aspx?articleid=1847578
15. Heather, N.: Interpreting the evidence on brief interventions for excessive drinkers: the need for caution. Alcohol Alcohol. 30(3), 287–296 (1995). http://alcalc.oxfordjournals.org/content/30/3/287.short
16. Hester, R.K., Delaney, H.D., Campbell, W.: The college drinker's check-up: outcomes of two randomized clinical trials of a computer-delivered intervention. Psychol. Addict. Behav. 26(1), 1–12 (2012)
17. Hingson, R.W., Zha, W., Weitzman, E.R.: Magnitude of and trends in alcohol-related mortality and morbidity among U.S. college students ages 18–24, 1998–2005. J. Stud. Alcohol Drugs (Suppl. 16), 12–20 (2009). http://www.ncbi.nlm.nih.gov/pubmed/19538908
18. Kaner, F.S.E., Dickinson, H.O., Beyer, F.R., Campbell, F., Schlesinger, C., Heather, N., Saunders, J.B., Burnand, B., Pienaar, E.D.: Effectiveness of brief alcohol interventions in primary care populations. Cochrane Database Syst. Rev. (2) (2007)
19. Khadjesari, Z., Murray, E., Hewitt, C., Hartley, S., Godfrey, C.: Can stand-alone computer-based interventions reduce alcohol consumption? A systematic review. Addiction 106(2), 267–282 (2011)
20. Knight, J., Sherritt, L., Harris, S., Gates, E., Chang, G.: Validity of brief alcohol screening tests among adolescents: a comparison of the AUDIT, POSIT, CAGE, and CRAFFT. Alcohol Clin. Exp. Res. 27(1), 67–73 (2003). pm: 12544008

21. Kypri, K., Saunders, J.B., Gallagher, S.J.: Acceptability of various brief intervention approaches for hazardous drinking among university students. Alcohol Alcohol. **38**(6), 626–628 (2003)
22. Mason, M., Benotsch, E.G., Way, T., Kim, H., Snipes, D.: Text messaging to increase readiness to change alcohol use in college students. J. Primary Prev. **35**(1), 47–52 (2014). https://doi.org/10.1007/s10935-013-0329-9
23. Milward, J., Khadjesari, Z., Fincham-Campbell, S., Deluca, P., Watson, R., Drummond, C.: User preferences for content, features, and style for an app to reduce harmful drinking in young adults: analysis of user feedback in app stores and focus group interviews. JMIR mHealth uHealth **4**(2), e47 (2016)
24. Moreira, M.T., Smith, L.A., Foxcroft, D.: Social norms interventions to reduce alcohol misuse in university or college students. Evid.-Based Child Health **7**(2), 450–575 (2012)
25. Moyer, A., Finney, J., Swearingen, C., Vergun, P.: Brief interventions for alcohol problems: a meta-analytic review of controlled investigations in treatment seeking and non treatment seeking populations. Addiction **97**, 279–292 (2002)
26. National Institute on Alcohol Abuse and Alcoholism: NIAAA council approves definition of binge drinking. NIAAA Newslett. **3**, 3 (2004)
27. National Institute on Alcohol Abuse and Alcoholism: College Drinking. Technical report (2015)
28. Palfai, T.P., Winter, M., Lu, J., Rosenbloom, D., Saitz, R.: Personalized feedback as a universal prevention approach for college drinking: a randomized trial of an e-mail linked universal web-based alcohol intervention. J. Primary Prev. **35**(2), 75–84 (2014)
29. Shaw, S.J., Cartwright, A.K.J., Spratley, T.A., Harwin, J.: Responding to Drinking Problems. University Park Press, Baltimore (1978)
30. Substance Abuse and Mental Health Services Administration: 2014 National Survey on Drug Use and Health. Technical report (2014)
31. Tahaney, K.D., Palfai, T.P.: Text messaging as an adjunct to a web-based intervention for college student alcohol use: a preliminary study. Addict. Behav. **73**(November 2016), 63–66 (2017). https://doi.org/10.1016/j.addbeh.2017.04.018
32. Tansil, K.A., Esser, M.B., Sandhu, P., Reynolds, J.A., Elder, R.W., Williamson, R.S., Chattopadhyay, S.K., Bohm, M.K., Brewer, R.D., McKnight-Eily, L.R., Hungerford, D.W., Toomey, T.L., Hingson, R.W., Fielding, J.E.: Alcohol electronic screening and brief intervention: a community guide systematic review. Am. J. Prev. Med. **51**(5), 801–811 (2016). https://doi.org/10.1016/j.amepre.2016.04.013
33. Wilson, G.B., Lock, C.A., Heather, N., Cassidy, P., Christie, M.M., Kaner, E.F.S.: Intervention against excessive alcohol consumption in primary health care: a survey of GPs' attitudes and practices in England 10 years on. Alcohol Alcohol. **46**(5), 570–577 (2011)

Digital Nomads Beyond the Buzzword: Defining Digital Nomadic Work and Use of Digital Technologies

Caleece Nash$^{(\boxtimes)}$ ⓘ, Mohammad Hossein Jarrahi ⓘ,
Will Sutherland ⓘ, and Gabriela Phillips ⓘ

University of North Carolina at Chapel Hill, Chapel Hill, NC 27599, USA
caleecen@live.unc.edu

Abstract. Digital nomadicity has gained popularity in recent years as a fashionable lifestyle and as a way of challenging traditional work contexts, but there has been very little incisive empirical research on the lifestyle's characteristics, its implications for the future of work, or on the technology, which supports it. This paper describes the four key elements that constitute the work of digital nomads: (1) digital work, (2) gig work, (3) nomadic work, and (4) adventure and global travel. We present digital nomads as a community of workers situated at the confluence of these four elements and define how each of these are enabled by the use of digital technologies. This research serves as a foundation for information studies concerned with the dynamic and changing relationships between future of work, new population of workers (digital natives) and emerging digital platforms.

Keywords: Digital nomads · Gig work · Nomadic work · Digital work

1 Introduction

In the past few years, there has been a rise of digital natives with location-independent living and working styles [1]. The rise of digital nomads has been credited in popular media to a desire to escape the "rat race" of modern life, a dream to live in such a way that provides a withdrawal from "9-to-5 obligations." [2] Those who adhere to this style of life are "redefining…making a living" [3] by pursuing employment that allows for global travel, flexibility in work hours, and a departure from the traditional office environment. This romanticized image is one of "true freedom…[without] boundaries or borders…work[ing] from anywhere in the world." [2] The broader trend is often called the "digital nomads" movement, and arises from a combination of improved global access to information and information infrastructures, more flexible work arrangements, a preference for travel, as well as adventure and work flexibility among the younger generation of knowledge workers [4]. As perpetual travelers, many digital nomads have given up the idea of a permanent home and embark on extreme forms of remote and location-independent work; they may work from a coffee shop in Bali, Indonesia and the next month may be working from a co-working space in Berlin [5].

© Springer International Publishing AG, part of Springer Nature 2018
G. Chowdhury et al. (Eds.): iConference 2018, LNCS 10766, pp. 207–217, 2018.
https://doi.org/10.1007/978-3-319-78105-1_25

We argue that the digital nomads community is a fertile context for information research since it features a changing dynamic between people, information, and ICTs. Digital technologies play a critical role in the work practices of digital nomads, and these practices are therefore a useful context for studying the interplay between affordances of emerging technologies and organizational and location-independent work, which partly define the future of work and organization [6].

Digital nomadicity has been a popular topic for magazine articles and blog posts in both the world of management and amongst workers and avid travelers [5]. However, despite this surge in popularity of digital nomads, there is little empirical and academic research examining different aspects of this lifestyle such as the working arrangements of digital nomads, changing ties with organizations, new balance between work, personal life and travel, and the role of digital technologies [1, 7]. In particular, while the current characterizations of digital nomads invoke monikers such as remote workers, freelancers, location-independent workers, and online entrepreneurs, digital nomadic work tends to be different from these monikers[1].

These concepts only embrace certain aspects of the digital nomads community, and each falls short of providing a holistic perspective on the nuances of digital nomadic work. These labels are ill-equipped to accommodate the dynamic work arrangement of digital nomads. They are particularly less useful in adequately distinguishing digital nomadicity, which, in its current form, is a very recent phenomenon [2, 4], from more traditional forms of work that share some characteristics but are divergent along other dimensions (e.g., teleworkers).

Specifically, a key aspect of digital nomads work is the mediating roles played by a range of digital technologies and infrastructures. Although the current discussions on the topic (happening primarily in business press, websites, or blogs) are driven by excitement, they point to the digital nomad's savvy use of technology to accomplish work. As information researchers, we see this as an opportunity to explore the relationship between emerging forms of work and digital mediation. As a result, this paper is an attempt to address the gap in our understanding of digital nomads, common work practices, and the underlying role of digital technologies. In this paper, by building on analysis of digital nomads forums and interviews with twenty-two digital nomads, we seek to address the following questions: (1) What are the basic elements that define digital nomadic work? (2) How these elements are intertwined with the use of digital technologies?

2   Methods

Empirical data was gathered from two sources: an in-depth exploration of popular digital nomad forums and a series of 22 interviews with digital nomads. Forum posts were gathered from the/r/digitalnomad section of reddit.com, the Facebook group "Digital Nomads Around the World," and from nomadforum.io, a forum dedicated to digital nomadism. All three forums were chosen for their large, active populations, and

---

[1] See the Wikipedia entry for more information: https://en.wikipedia.org/wiki/Digital_nomad.

their focus on digital nomad topics. Interview participants were contacted based on their presence on the forums, through word of mouth, or because of other writings they had published on the topic of digital nomadism. The forum collection and subsequent interviews occurred from January to May of 2017.

While the broad forum collection provided empirical background for the community, analysis for this investigation focused primarily on a forum thread on nomadforum.io, in which digital nomads introduced themselves to the forums ("Introduce yourself"). Contributors gave their name, profession, and thoughts on digital nomadism, as well as a number of other self-identifying descriptions. In total, the analysis of this thread covered the introductions of 460 digital nomads and provided the basis for the researcher's initial characterizations of digital nomadic professional life. The posts collected from this thread spanned from December of 2013 to early 2017.

These initial characterizations were further explored through the interview process, which occurred concurrently with the forum analysis. Participants represented a variety of professional backgrounds but shared a nomadic, digital work situation, and associated themselves with the digital nomad community. Interview questions were developed based on initial exploration of the forums and developed as the interviews proceeded. Interviews were approximately one hour in length, were conducted through video conferencing software, and were transcribed verbatim.

3 Findings

Analysis of interview data and the digital nomads forum suggests that digital nomads' work is best described by the confluence of four key elements: digital work, gig work, nomadic work and global travel adventure. These interdependent characteristics can be collectively used to define who digital nomads are, and what important dimensions their work entail. In describing these elements, we also discuss how they are inseparable from various forms of digital technologies.

3.1 Digital Work

To maintain their lifestyle while constantly traveling the world, digital nomads engage with works that create digital goods using digital tools, what research has recently begun calling "digital work" [8]. Digital work is the essence of digital nomadic work since it is entwined with location-independent work practices and enables digital nomads to accomplish work while visiting different cities and countries. By using digital platforms to produce a digital product, digital nomads are able to travel light. Due to the frequency with which digital nomads relocate and the exotic locations they choose to explore, they also do not have access to machinery or the supplies to build a physical product. Digital devices and applications are the primary means through which digital nomads transform digital inputs to digital outputs, and this can be done virtually from any place where power and internet connectivity are available. In the NomadList forums, many digital nomads considered themselves minimalists. Thus, many choose to carry minimal or easily portable gear while traveling and completing work.

Transportable digital devices allow digital nomads to carry out an increasing variety of careers while traveling. The majority of digital nomads observed on the forum fall into the categories of programmers, developers, designers, or content creators. Out of the digital nomads who are considered programmers and developers, many have careers in software engineering and web development. However, digital nomads have also found work through a spectrum of careers including blogging, graphic design, translating documents, digital marketing, creating podcasts and YouTube videos as well as financial and business consulting. Over 15% of digital nomads from the NomadList forum thread "Introduce yourself" discussed starting their own business using their skills acquired from previous training or knowledge.

Digital nomads use many different technology platforms in order to conduct digital work and produce their digital products. It is quite common for digital nomads to find work on a third-party contracting website, work on a particular gig through an online application, store information on the cloud or their device, and send the final product to their contractor or employer digitally. The vast array of digital applications and programs used by digital nomads can be separated into two categories: (1) profession specific and (2) general tools. Profession specific tools support the work practices involved in specific sub-categories of digital work. For example, programmers use GitHub to write and share code whereas designers and creators often use Adobe Creative Cloud to format website layouts. These programs are generally only used by people in their same field of work. However, there are also certain technologies that are universal for all digital nomads, such as messaging applications, which are used for communication purposes. A popular messaging app amongst digital nomads in the forums is Slack, which allows the user to communicate with many different people and teams in one application. Digital nomads from all kinds of professions also described using communication applications like Skype to attend remote meetings with partners or clients.

Another essential component of digital work is that, regardless of the application, digital workers depend heavily on internet connectivity in order to work on applications and send their finished digital deliverables to their clients. Many digital nomads from the online forums inquired about the best way to get internet access in different countries. Some digital nomads discussed using public WiFi whereas others would their mobile data depending on several factors such as price, accessibility, and secure connection. However, the digital nomad's reliance on digital tools and services to conduct work means that having an internet connection is necessary.

3.2 Gig Work

Another critical aspect of digital nomads' professional situation is reliance on gig work. Gig work allows people to work short term as independent contractors with flexible work arrangements on demand [9]. The combination of gig and digital work creates the opportunity of working online freelance jobs that can be completed using digital platforms and technologies remotely and untethered from specific locations. Participant 8 described how switching to gig work has rendered her work location-independent: "*Changing the kind of work I do changed everything; I was very much tied to Los Angeles; now that most of my work is online I can be anywhere in the world.*"

Digital nomads can find gigs that allow them to work anywhere in the world as long as there is a demand for their particular set of skills and they can find a contractor. Depending on the type of skills needed and the amount of time spent on the gig, income levels vary between digital nomads. There is an increasing trend amongst firms that outsource projects to gig workers since they may not need to pay for health insurance or other firing benefits [10]. However, this often creates issues for digital nomads since they do not have the accessibility to the resources a business generally provides its employees, and may result in precarious work situations.

Since digital nomads (often as soloworkers) do not have access to the large and expensive resources of a firm, they must rely on an array of web services and freelance marketplaces in order to conduct work. Unlike an employee working for an organization, gig workers must search to find jobs in order to make a steady income. Many digital nomads who have experience with gig work will market themselves to employers online using various online vehicles [11]. For example, participant 17 created advertisements that sent interested clients to a website in order to bring awareness of the services their start-up offered. Participant 20 used LinkedIn and Medium to maintain connections with other professionals in a similar field. Some digital nomads see such a web presence as an effective way to promote their reliability to potential clients. Others may choose websites such as Upwork and Remoteok to find location-independent gigs.

Not only are there many technologies available to help digital nomads find and complete gigs, but also to help them perform a wide variety of tasks that are important for any business. For example, since digital nomads use PayPal and Transferwise as a way of receiving payment digitally. This allows them to bypass having a physical mailing address and keep record of transactions. As another example, participant 18, discussed his use of software called Groove, which helped manage his customer service. By using these technologies, doing gig work and tasks associated with it becomes more feasible for digital nomads and allows them to spend more time on the core project activities.

3.3 Nomadic Work

Perhaps the most conspicuous aspect of the digital nomad lifestyle is its constant movement, not only from country to country, but also from workspace to workspace. This presents the digital nomad with not only the problem of mobility, of moving between spaces and finding locations, but also the more complicated problem of nomadicity, which requires the mobilization of resources, and the navigation of local infrastructures [12]. A significant amount of research from the field of computer-supported cooperative work (CSCW) and information systems has already labored to articulate the concept of nomadicity, and a number of candidate definitions have emerged. This research specifically describes the process of leveraging technology to accomplish work across a variety of locations and local infrastructures [13]. Many participants from the forums feel that nomadicity allows them to have experiences outside of a regular routine and gain freedom from the corporate world, but it also requires them to find or assemble their workspace themselves rather than relying on the stable office environment provided by an organization. Digital nomads look for many of the resources described by Pinatti de Carvalho et al. [13, p. 2]: "space, time, privacy, silence, and other people." From the NomadList thread, "Introduce yourself", a nomadic couple discussed their need to find a "comfortable working space in order to get any work done." Without this space, the couple feels their work productivity would be limited.

It is important to note that even though digital nomads share some important characteristics of nomadic workers commonly studied in the previous research, their career aspiration and motivation for constant mobility may differ from most nomadic workers (who are also rising in numbers in the corporate world). What makes digital nomads distinct is their length of travel and decision not to have a home base [7]. In addition, while nomadic workers typically travel *for* their work, the digital nomad travels *while* working. While the nomadic worker is often drawn to various locations and spaces *by* their work, the digital nomad's work must be flexible around whatever spaces they can find in the locations they choose to travel. One member of NomadList named Zbynek discusses how he quit his IT career in the banking industry to become a self-employed android developer in order to live as a digital nomad. This change in career allows Zbynek to work remotely, unlike a career in corporate IT support that may be location-bound. Similarly, participant 12 discussed the transition from a career in legal services to becoming a food and travel blogger. In a similar manner to Zbynek, participant 12 now enjoys the world travel, and as a blogger, she can do work anywhere in the world as long as there is internet access and a properly working device (as opposed to her previous career as a lawyer). It is quite common for many digital nomads to completely change career paths in order to make an income while traveling. While this may require acquiring more knowledge or a different set of skills, digital nomads make necessary preparations before becoming location independent.

The use of portable technologies and personal cloud services facilitates nomadic work of digital nomads across different places. Given the knowledge-heavy varieties of digital nomad work, it is of utmost importance for such workers to maintain a large, stored collection of information. By transferring their relevant information to cloud storage, where it can be accessed anywhere with an internet connection, digital nomads can maintain the necessary knowledge base without the struggle of packing, storing, and carrying more things. Most interviewed digital nomads noted they accomplish work across various devices, and portable devices provide them with the flexibility to work from different spaces or while in transit. Additionally, digital nomads use cloud services to share information or collaborate on a document with clients or peers. Through these services, digital nomads assemble a kind of movable office, which allows them to reach their professional materials from anywhere.

Evident from interviews and discussion on online forums was the fact that one of the largest challenges of constant nomadicity is loneliness, since most digital nomads are unable to maintain long-term relationships and are confined to whatever spaces and people they can find in their location. A user on reddit described the problem: "...*there are profound psychological factors in remote work. They can be obstacles to overcome or job/mood killers if not. Also, I fear 'cabin-fever' may be added to the list as you sleep and work in the same place. Not very stimulating.*" A number of online communities and social programs like Hacker Paradise have developed around the digital nomad community in order to partially address this negative consequence of nomadism. Through these online communities and interaction on online social platforms like Twitter and meetup.com, digital nomads sympathize and connect to others that are dealing with the same difficulties, or find meetups and events near where they are traveling. Founder of NomadList forum, Pieter Levels, is looked up to by many in the digital nomad community for creating the digital platform that allows digital nomads to share not only their travel advice but also to meet others in the digital nomad community.

3.4 Global Adventure Travel

For digital nomads, work and life blur together because of the choice to travel and work nonstop simultaneously. Digital nomads are also different from many forms of nomadic workers studied in the previous literature [e.g., 12, 13] because they are global travelers with a passion for continuously visiting new places. Digital nomads choose to travel to exotic locations around the globe, such as Chiang Mai, Ubud, and Phuket. Since digital nomads choose their lifestyle, most of them opt for tropical areas or places that are known to be ideal areas for hobbies like surfing, hiking, backpacking, or skiing. From nomads forums, we observed some digital nomads embark seasonal travel styles that more closely resemble the true traditional nomadism. For example, participant 19 spends winters in tropical regions, and returns to Northern Europe during summers. There are a number of digital nomad meetups, such as the travel program Hacker Paradise and the Digital Nomad Conference, which are often marketed for the variety of its destinations, allowing the digital nomad to "travel the world."[2]

Some digital nomads find traveling partners or arrange to room with other digital nomads in order to reduce costs. Nomad-specific online communities provide essential hubs for finding important information about places to visit and people to travel with. Digital nomads use Facebook as a way to connect with people in order to find housing, and connect with other digital nomads through NomadList and the slack channel #digitalnomad. On these forums, digital nomads make recommendations to each other, offer advice, and rate different aspects of a travel destination, such as its internet connectivity, cost of living, and fun. For example, one commenter on NomadList discussed how he would negotiate with Airbnb hosts to obtain lower rates for long-term housing.

Unlike tourists, digital nomads work continually while traveling and must therefore constantly balance their travel and professional productivity. Conflation of perpetual travel and work imposes non-trivial challenges; productivity for digital nomads is a critical issue that many deal with on a daily basis because of their constant state of 'workation.' A commenter on Reddit described the problem of avoiding productivity loss while travelling: "*Keeping a schedule ensures that doesn't happen and also helps with motivation. Here where it's warm and sunny, and the cool people you meet tell you about all the awesome things they are going to do, it's a lot harder to motivate yourself to work.*" In many cases, enforcing the boundary between personal and professional life involved digital nomads setting aside time to be available to their team

---

[2] http://www.hackerparadise.org/.

members on chat programs, and using productivity applications to keep track of work schedules. Additionally, part of the digital nomad's productivity problem is due to constantly switching time zones or working in a different time zone than their client or employer. A contributor to the NomadList forum described the obstacle of working with employers across time zones and how he dealt with it by changing his work schedule for different clients and by making himself available to collaborators through messaging apps. Such messaging applications like Slack, as well as team management applications like Asana or Trello, helped digital nomads maintain work schedules for themselves and for their team members. Similarly, applications, which keep track and compare time zones were a common subject of discussion on the forums. Digital nomads use these digital applications to stay on top of their work hours and manage productivity.

While digital nomads travel to likely tourist destinations, they differ from tourists in that they seek out resources, which allow them to accomplish nomadic work. In both the forums and interviews, many digital nomads discussed frequenting co-working spaces, which are specially designed for remote workers; these spaces offer a temporary office and a more predictable work environment. Tourists are much less likely to leverage such work-related resources while visiting new places.

4   Discussion

Digital nomadicity can be seen as a hybrid of four concepts described above and is complicated by the compound problems of mobility and professional flexibility (See Fig. 1). Digital nomads share commonalities with other non-traditional work settings such as remote or nomadic work. However, as an emerging community of digital workers, digital nomads exhibit characteristics that make them distinct from these categories and descriptors. Although digital nomads inherit characteristics from all the four labels, people categorized under one label are not necessarily digital nomads.

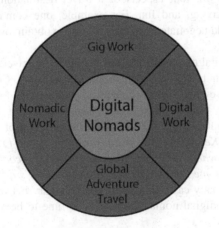

Fig. 1. Digital nomads at the confluence of four concepts

There are groups and professions that fit each label but are not necessarily considered digital nomads such as: (a) stationary corporate IT support (digital workers), (b) Amazon Turkers (gig workers), (c) tourists (global travelers), and (d) itinerant salespeople (nomadic workers). Borrowing the essential aspects of these different labels, we can gain some insight into the dynamics of digital nomadicity, and into the enabling roles of technology in their work life.

The work practices and work life of digital nomads signal the declining roles of organizations and the fixed notion of workplace. This trend also highlights the agentic power of individual digital workers who increasingly act as "free agents" [6] and enjoy the benefit of choosing where and when to accomplish work. This sociotechnical change can be associated with changing norms of work (e.g., looser ties to organizations among new generations of workers and desire for benefits like "flexworking") and the proliferation of ubiquitous personal technologies and services.

Research findings also make it clear that in order to arrive at a holistic perspective on digital nomads and their digitally mediated work practices, there is a need for a more nuanced understanding of the core elements of their work such as gig work and digital work. Current conceptions of digital work as a distinct subcategory of knowledge work are in their infancy [8]. As evident in the context of digital nomads, the nature of digital work lends itself to virtualization, liberating workers from specific workspaces and therefore enabling location-independent work. Research on gig work is also in its developing stages and lacks conceptual clarity about online freelancing, which constitutes the type of gig work digital nomads engage with, is little taken up in the current bulk of information research. A vast majority of current research has directed attention to microtasking via platforms such as Amazon Mechanical Turk or more idealized forms of gig work such as those taking place around ridesharing applications.

Because of its focus on the digital nomad's work situation and the imperative roles played by digital technologies, this research has a number of contributions to the ongoing discourse on digitally mediated work and future of work. Specifically, in answer to our second research question concerning the role of digital technologies, we can see that various digital technologies play an essential supporting role regarding all the four categories. These technologies therefore mediate all aspects of the digital nomad's professional life: from marketing and acquiring clients to conducting work and communicating with clients. For example, cloud services provide access to information from different places, algorithms on websites such as Upwork matches them with potential clients, and as their work and personal life blends together, their devices can assist in both completing work and being productive. The entanglement of digital technologies in how digital nomads achieve work epitomize what Orlikowski and Scott recently noted about digital workers: *"specific materializations of work today include digital platforms operated by complex algorithms and continual streams of data"* [14, p. 5].

These technologies provide a mobile and flexible work environment, but they also require a significant amount of expertise from the worker. Digital nomads typically demonstrate a substantial level of literacy for information applications and tools, and confidence in choosing configuring or even developing them to solve their particular problems. These understandings are not solely personal but developed and passed along via community channels for information sharing (e.g., nomads forums).

5 Conclusion

The ubiquity of personal digital technologies and pervasive information infrastructures across the globe together with changing norms of work has resulted in a surge in popularity of digital nomadicity. Beyond the hyperbole, it is now critical to study characteristics of this community of digital workers as it exemplifies problems of nomadicity and flexibility of work, which may pervade the future of work. As such, the digital nomad community provides a window into changing dynamics of digitally mediated work practices and therefore presents a valuable context for the study of digital technologies and information resources in the work practices of the new generation of workers. We argue information researchers are well posited to study these new dynamics given their focus on technology, information and work.

This paper should be seen as an exploratory engagement with the digital nomad community, and a number of factors could improve future investigations of the topic. Our research was limited by the lack of breadth of information on digital nomads, and a more formalized survey of the digital nomad community could provide valuable insights on the people and professions represented there. Additionally, more developed conceptualizations of underlying concepts such as gig work and digital work would provide a better analysis of the practices involved in digital nomadicity.

References

1. Müller, A.: The digital nomad: Buzzword or research category? Transnational Soc. Rev. **6**, 344–348 (2016)
2. Forbes. https://www.forbes.com/sites/robertadams/2017/01/20/how-to-become-a-digital-nomad-and-travel-the-world/#219d8f781ae4
3. Forbes. https://www.forbes.com/sites/julesschroeder/2016/03/17/what-digital-nomads-know-that-you-dont-yet/#33a0e08f34bd
4. Dal Fiore, F., Mokhtarian, P.L., Salomon, I., Singer, M.E.: "Nomads at last"? A set of perspectives on how mobile technology may affect travel. J. Transp. Geogr. **41**, 97–106 (2014)
5. Spinks, R.: Meet the 'digital nomads' who travel the world in search of fast Wi-Fi. Guardian 2017 (2015)
6. Barley, S., Bechky, B., Milliken, F.: The changing nature of work: careers, identities, and work lives in the 21st century. Acad. Manag. Discov. (2017). Published online before print
7. Sutherland, W., Jarrahi, M.H.: The gig economy and information infrastructure: the case of the digital nomad community. Proc. ACM Hum.-Comput. Interact **1**, Article No. 97 (2017)
8. Durward, D., Blohm, I., Leimeister, J.M.: Crowd work. Bus. Inf. Syst. Eng. **58**, 281–286 (2016)
9. De Stefano, V.: The rise of the 'just-in-time workforce': on-demand work, crowd work and labour protection in the 'gig-economy'. Comp. Labor Law Policy J. **37**, 471–503 (2015)
10. Torpey, E., Hogan, A.: Working in a gig economy. Career Outlook, U.S. Bureau of Labor Statistics, May 2016
11. Gandini, A.: The Reputation Economy: Understanding Knowledge Work in Digital Society. Springer, London (2016)

‌

12. Jarrahi, M.H., Nelson, S.B., Thomson, L.: Personal artifact ecologies in the context of mobile knowledge workers. Comput. Hum. Behav. **75**, 469–483 (2017)
13. Pinatti de Carvalho, A.F., Ciolfi, L., Gray, B.: Detailing a spectrum of motivational forces shaping nomadic practices. In: Proceedings of the 2017 ACM Conference on Computer Supported Cooperative Work and Social Computing, CSCW 2017, pp. 962–977. ACM (2017)
14. Orlikowski, W.J., Scott, S.: Digital work: a research agenda. In: Czarniawska, B. (ed.) A Research Agenda for Management and Organization Studies. Edward Elgar Publishing, Cheltenham (2016)

Adoption of Cloud Computing in Hotel Industry as Emerging Services

Elaine Vella[1] , Longzhi Yang[2] , Naveed Anwar[2] , and Nanlin Jin[2(✉)]

[1] Distribution, Loyalty, Partnerships and MIS, Corinthia Hotels International,
Floriana, Malta
elaine.vella@corinthia.com
[2] Department of Computer and Information Sciences, Northumbria University,
Newcastle upon Tyne NE1 8ST, UK
{longzhi.yang,naveed.anwar,nanlin.jin}@northumbria.ac.uk

Abstract. The hotel industry is experiencing forces of change as a result of data explosion, social media, increased individualized expectations by customers. It is thus appealing to study the cloud computing adoption in the hotel industry to respond such changes. This paper reported an investigation on such topic by identifying the cloud computing services and summarising their benefits and challenges in organization, management and operation. The research findings were comparatively studied in reference to the results appeared in the literature. In addition, recommendations were made for both cloud service providers and hotels in strategic planning, investment, and management of cloud-oriented services.

Keywords: Cloud computing · Cloud service adoption · Hospitality

1 Introduction

The core requirements for a hotel to be successful were to be affiliated to a hotel group and to have a good quality product in terms of rooms and facilities before the age of computer networks and cloud services [4]. This success dependency has shifted in recent years to a hotel's ability to provide customers a personalized service offering comfortable home-like environment. This need has created a very hungry hotel industry for data about customer habits, desires and preferences. To gather, analyze and make use of such data, translate this into customer services, and deliver tailor services to the finest detail in an age of increased mobility, hotel groups required to become more dynamic and efficient in the way they make use of technology.

Information technology (IT) can help in this case, which allows hotels to become globally competitive and present wherever their guests are. This is key to the success of a hotel group in a market where (1) mobile booking on travel websites are increasing at a faster rate (20% annually) than desktop bookings (2% annually), (2) 21% of bookings are originating from smart phones and tablets, and (3) 12% of mobile bookings are implemented by Apps [2]. For hotel groups,

G. Chowdhury et al. (Eds.): iConference 2018, LNCS 10766, pp. 218–228, 2018.
https://doi.org/10.1007/978-3-319-78105-1_26

maximizing the use of IT could mean freeing themselves of physical infrastructure, associated maintenance and risk to have unrevealed access to their mission critical hotel property management and reservation systems, customer relationship management systems, business intelligent reporting as well as reservation channel management.

Cloud computing [6] has demonstrated the potential to fulfill such demands. The cloud phenomenon brings about a change in the way IT is devised, developed, implemented, extended, improved, maintained and sold [3,11]. Cloud computing has been used for tourism management, for example to rank popular tourism destinations in cities [22], to support distributed big data analysis for smart tourism [10]. Limited research has been done in how cloud computing can benefit to hotel industry. A study has showed that excluding the hotel chain which use clouding partially, the franchise or local do not implement this technology [15]. Our paper investigates the level of cloud adoption, and the cloud service models on the basis of over 300 hotels.

This paper studies how and why hotel groups need to operate in the cloud, in specific with relation to the service and deployment models implemented by these enterprises, and benefits and challenges encountered through their adoption. Case studies have been undertaken with four hotel groups representing 306 hotels, of which data gathered were analyzed and presented in the format of a cross case analysis.

2   Background

Cloud computing is a technology that allows the provision and utilization of resources over the internet in lieu of installations on a desktop computer [6]. Information Systems (IS) can be consumed as utilities like water and electricity through cloud computing [5]. Four deployment models are specified in the National Institute of Standards and Technology (NIST) cloud computing definition: Private, Public, Community and Hybrid clouds. Adoption of cloud computing brings about technological, economical and environmental benefits to an organization, which is also the case for hospitality industry. New technologies and competitive marketing strategies available through the cloud such as the use of social media, channel management, online reservation streams, hotel review portals and increased use of mobile technology for improved customer service have significantly changed the way hotels interact with their customers and will still change for a long time to come [16].

After the 2008 recession, when lowering costs was a key objective for hotels, PAR Springer-Miller, introduced ATRIO as the Next Generation Hospitality Management Software[1] into the market. An application in the cloud, on Windows Azure, ATRIO allows hotels around the world to perform reservations, billing and other guest related transactions. Through such deployments hotel groups are able to lower the Total Cost of Ownership (TCO) as it reduced the amount of investment needed in purchasing, maintaining and updating hardware [13].

---

[1] http://www.atrio.com/.

In this context, research has been carried out widely in this field. The work of [21] discussed how cloud computing is utilized in the hospitality and travel industry. This work particularly describes how a Quality of Service (QoS) ranking mechanism enables cloud applications such as airline ticketing systems, hotel booking services and car rental services to interact with each other to deliver services to their customers. The Falkensteiner Hotel Schladmig, in Austria is an example of a hotel that has moved from the traditional telephone system to a cloud based VoIP solution which is integrated to their SaaS hotel management system solution provided by Protel [16].

The hospitality industry is one where budgets are limited and whose market is highly dynamic. Cloud computing enables organizations within this sector to extend the life of their existing systems with new innovations, improve time to market through affordable pricing, and ultimately gain competitive advantages [9]. Reservation booking centralization and electronic distribution was one of the key factors to implement this. For instance, motivated by this, the Louvre Hotel Group to deploy OPERA property management system cloud application in over 850 of their hotels. The hotel management system is no longer maintained on the hotel premises and storage of their data is outsourced (MICROS Systems Inc., 2013). InterContinental Hotels Group were able to eliminate hardware infrastructure costs and centralize management activities such as updating prices, at the touch of a button across sixty one of their UK properties by adopting a cloud solution for their restaurant point of sale systems called SIMPHONY. As a result the hotel group is making use of improved business intelligence reporting through detailed sales tracking as well as improved customer relationship management by means of targeted marketing [12].

Ian Miller from the Ecole de hoteliere Lausanne states that Cloud computing is the only way forward for hospitality. It offers better uptime, flexibility and security than installed software and allows hoteliers to concentrate on being hoteliers [16]. Various could services for hospitality industry have been developed. Oracle has acquired hospitality solutions provider MICROS in September 2014, and launched its Hospitality Global Business Unit in February 2015. Carlin, VP for Hospitality Strategy and Solutions Management at Oracle states that the benefits that hospitality industry can reap through cloud adoption are mainly through the agility these services bring. Rapid technology deployment in his view tops the benefit list through faster introduction of new functionality and latest release deployment. Ability is given to the hotel operator to become more responsive through Oracle's cloud, mobile and guest experience solution [7].

3   The Methodology - Case Study

It is difficult to find existing databases detailing the cloud usage and its impact in the hotel industry. Therefore, case study is used in this work to sample the industry in an effort to understand: (i) how ICT solutions are delivered by some main players in the hotel industry to their businesses when cloud computing is in use; (ii) what are the most used services and deployment and why are they favored over others by hotels; and (iii) the most significant impact, positive or negative, of cloud computing experienced by this industry and how that compares to the findings reported in the literature.

3.1 Case Specification

This research took multiple cases for facilitating cross-case analysis. A basic data set relating to the way that cloud computing is utilized by hotel group establishments was collected in advance of a in depth analysis to realize the research goal. Questionnaires were identified as the most appropriate way in the case study, in addition to in-depth interviews. In order to guarantee the quality of this research, tests for construct validity, external validity and reliability were adapted as proposed by [19]. In particular, the validity tests used for this research are summarized in the Table 1. Both the questionnaires and interviews were reviewed by specialists from the cloud computing and hospitality field to check adequacy.

Table 1. Quality tests employed in this case study research (Adapted from Case Study Tactics for Four Design Tests [20])

Validity test	Selected case study tactic for this research	Research phase in which tactic is employed
Construct	Data collection using multiple evidence sources	Data collection phase
External	Replication logic was used in multiple case study design	Research design phase
Reliability	Utilizing a case study protocol	Data collection phase

3.2 The Participants

The units of analysis were determined ahead of the research study commencing. Each of the case study units of analysis consisted of a hotel group, representing hotels in Europe, Middle East and Africa (EMEA) at regional level, of which some already started adopting cloud computing technology. Note that hotels are usually organised in hierarchy from hotel group, to hotel brand and finally individual hotels. It is assumed that all hotels are managed, franchised, leased or owned under the brand, depending on the hotel group's business model. The units of analysis in this study were the hotel groups, as it is often the case that decisions or negotiations with suppliers are made at this level, on behalf of their hotels to leverage economies of scale. Profiles of the studied hotel groups are listed in Table 2 which details their geographical presence, number of hotels for the hotel group, respective number of rooms, as well as profit for each hotel group in 2014. One survey participant and one interviewee per hotel group were selected in collecting the required data.

Table 2. Profiles involved in the case study units of analysis (The Profit figures are based on Consolidated Income Statement Reported figures for 2013; Hotels are EMEA Only; the No. of rooms are worldwide figure)

Hotel group	Hotels	Brands	Hotel locations	No. of rooms	Profit (€ Million)
Hotel group 1	54	1	Europe, Africa, Middle East	22,582	Data not available
Hotel group 2	14	3	Europe, Africa and Middle East	4,343	26,24
Hotel group 3	38	3	Europe, Middle East	8,300	26,117
Hotel group 4	200	14	Europe, Africa and Middle East	675,623	528

The survey partakers, identified to collect basic operational data, needed to be in a lead position, closely involved in daily cloud computing operations. Also, the interview participants, with whom the more in depth interviews were held, needed to be in a managerial position, and were either decision makers in key aspects relating to cloud computing implementation or had a high level of influence in this decision making process. Participants included this study were all Senior IS Directors, Regional IT Managers and Senior Application Managers.

3.3 Data Collection

The questionnaire was applied to collect data about the cloud computing service and deployment models in use by hotel groups to run industry specific ICT solutions. In addition data was also requested about challenges and benefits of cloud computing from a hotel group operational perspective. In the format of a structured questionnaire, the survey was composed of in total 11 questions (provided in the Appendix[2]). A multiple choice type question was utilized for the respondents to select one of three service models and one of the three deployment models in use in their properties. The participants were also asked to indicate if each IS listed was in use, and if so whether it was only running on-premise, only on cloud or both across hotels. Rating questions were then used to ask the respondents to rate cloud computing benefits and challenges in order based on their importance.

The purpose of the interview was to obtain a more in-depth perspective on why specific cloud computing deployment and service models are used, and what drives such decisions in addition to the insight of hotel groups future cloud related plans. An interview schedule was prepared in advance by the researcher to ensure key points for which data collection was necessary were not missed. A semi-structured interview design was utilized as this type of interview combines the structure of a list of issues to be covered together with the freedom to follow up points as necessary.

---

[2] http://computing.unn.ac.uk/staff/kwff2/interviewandsurvey.pdf.

3.4   Data Analysis and Analytics

Date cleansing and data reduction took place which summarized the collected raw data to a manageable set followed by data interpretation. Triangulation of perspectives was achieved by comparing responses of questions in the interview and questionnaire. This procedure was initially performed per case, followed by a cross case analysis by comparing data across the four cases.

4   Cross Case Synthesis

4.1   Cloud Computing Usage

The distribution of the usage of cloud information system (IS) or on-premise IS in the studied hotel groups shows that the majority of IS used by hotel groups were running on the cloud, and that the smallest (in terms of number of rooms) hotel groups' (group 2) level of cloud adoption is equivalent to that of the largest (group 4). The volume of those running on cloud supersedes in each of the case studies than those running on premise as well as those running partially on premise and partially on cloud.

For those solutions identified as running on cloud, further investigation was made to uncover which service and deployment models were being used. In particular, 82.43% of the investigated hotel groups applied Saas; 14.86% employed Iaas; and the remaining 2.70% used Paas. 89.19% hotel groups used public cloud deployment modes; 8.11% employed hybrid models; and 2.7% used private models. These numbers imply that SaaS and Public solution were the mostly adopted service and deployment models. This research findings suggest that there are industry specific variations to cloud service and deployment models used. The paper [18]'s survey was performed across multiple industries. The results conflict with this research's findings in that [18] reports 94% of surveyed organizations are currently running or experimenting with IaaS and 74% considering Hybrid model as the preferred deployment choice.

4.2   Service and Deployment Model Selection

Five out of thirteen interview questions provided answers in the reason of service and deployment model selection. The most pronounced reason provided by the researched hotel groups, in justifying the combination of a SaaS and Public deployment cloud solution, was connected to the participants core business. There was an emphasis identified during the interviews that outsourcing the maintenance of the necessary service and software delivery in order to allow the hospitality groups to concentrate on customer service and hotel management. An additional factor mentioned by Hotel Groups 2 and 3 is the change driven by their operation in critical application providers. There were scenarios where the software vendor, moved away from providing thick client software to a SaaS cloud delivered solution. In that case, the participants naturally followed the move of their service providers.

PaaS was mostly discarded due to the lack of developers employed by the participants. It was commonly argued that there was a general unwillingness to invest in in-house infrastructure as well as the supporting human resource element to maintain the system. These thoughts emerged when discussing with the participants reasons for not using IaaS or Private cloud solutions. Some contributors acknowledged that even though at times cloud solutions may be more expensive, the reality is that an inferior service would be provided in-house for critical tasks such as the provision of regular useable backups as well as adequate and functional redundancy.

4.3 Impacts of Cloud Computing Adoption

The hotel group representatives, were asked in both the interview and survey, to list the five most important cloud computing challenges and benefits to their organization, and the results are listed in Tables 3 and 4. The most common two benefits identified are: (1) solving the problem of lack of hardware on site, and (2) transferring the risk relating to security and PCI/PA-DSS requirements to the cloud service suppliers. Not having hardware on site alleviates finance, skill and resource pressure from the hotel groups who do not require to purchase hardware and recruit personnel that have the required skills to maintain such an important component of their operations service delivery. The transfer (or sharing) of risk, time and effort to ensure that data security and PCI/PA-DSS compliance is also another benefit that the hotel groups value greatly, as having to look after the latter individually at their properties can potentially result into a costly, lengthy exercise with inconsistent results.

The cloud related challenges that have stood out from the hotel groups responses were (a) the increase in Opex (OPerating EXpense), (b) restricted access to the environments and (c) concerns about information security. The increase in Opex comes as a result of the cloud financial model which moves away from the typical initial capital expenditure involved. Higher operating expenses put a strain on hotels to meet budgets, on which management key performance indicators (and in turn bonuses) are usually based. There are concerns about information security possibly arise from lack of transparency provided by cloud vendors on the methods used to ensure the required measures are in place and available at all times. The reason for hotel groups listing limited cloud environment access as a challenge could emerge from one of the two factors. The hotel groups may not feel satisfied enough with the support quality or speed provided by the cloud provider. Alternatively, it could be due to the change in process experienced by IT Managers and now having to depend on a third party for issues which previously could be quickly checked and resolved with servers being on site.

The challenge which received the highest average rank (12.38 points) by the participants was the Dependency on bandwidth whilst that of least significance was the issue of Software licensing (3.38 points). [8] mentioned of the cost of

Table 3. Respondent rank of cloud benefits based on the role each had during the cloud implementation process

Rank/role	Consultative	Influencer	Decision maker and influencer
1	Security, less headaches in maintaining hardware	No on-site hardware to maintain; work from anywhere; flexibility in moving from one application solution to another, data security, PCI & PA-DSS	Round the clock support based on SLA; application and field expertise
2	Compliance; less human resources required	No need to worry about software upgrades; reduced capital cost; scalability; support and maintenance being outsourced to guarantee system availability	Standard conformity (HW, versioning); reduces hardware that we need on site
3	Speed of Implementation; PCI/PA-DSS compliancy	Available redundancy; scalability; moving from Capex to Opex; ongoing stability and system monitoring services	Information sharing across estate; speed of delivery
4	Reduction of capex; unlimited redundancy	Data backup looked after. Transfer risk to vendor; easier for vendor maintenance due to access; access control and data security; ease of system upgrades and security patches	Minimal downtime and controlled upgrades; scalability
5	Focus and resolution as all in one environment; physical data security	Ability to have SLAs; no need to manage the environment; obtaining latest available software in the market with least effort; changes in system standards are applied with minimal effort	Focus and resolution as all in one environment

bandwidth but not the dependency on it, as a challenge in a study. However internet access dependency is validated as a challenge that could hinder cloud computing accessibility by [14]. Dependency on bandwidth is of so much concern for the respondents possibly due to the fact that it is hard to find the right balance between cost and performance whilst depending on third parties. Business continuity in contrast, was the cloud computing benefit uncovered as most important in the research with an average rank of 11.38 points. Greener IT was the least ranked (3.13 points) in value by the research contributors. This result is challenged by business continuity being included in a top ten list of obstacles to cloud computing growth ranked by [1] but supported by [17] study uncovering reliability as the highest ranked benefit in that study for SaaS. One reason of this discrepancy is that some of the benefits and challenges appeared in this study were not presented in reviewed literature.

Table 4. Respondent rank of cloud challenges based on the role each had during the cloud implementation process

Rank/role	Consultative	Influencer	Decision maker and influencer
1	Increased opex; limited environment, accessibility	Capex to Opex, information security, system stability and availability is not always guaranteed or per SLA, data security	Restricted access, reliance on network availability
2	Impact of issues (global issue); dependance on internet, connectivity	Challenges in exiting; connectivity issues due to internet problems; one issue can impact the entire hotel estate; data privacy and storage location	Reliance on third party; performance latency
3	Reliance on vendors (reputation); increase in bandwidth requirement	Difficult to see financial viability of vendor; data privacy protection; dependency on network connectivity; internal training for users to keep up with changes to cloud computing	Issue impacts all estate; having to have the right processes to ensure access levels etc
4	Central management team needed; not knowing where data is	Location of own data; issues due to lack of customer specific testing; identifying vendors that have cloud computing compatible software	Level of impact in case of issue
5	Central management cost; switching providers not easy	Maintenance schedules according to vendor availability; lack of single sign on solution across cloud vendors; Cloud based solutions are mostly for consumer not enterprise world	

Table 5. Criteria for cloud vendor selection

Hotel Grp 1	Vendor expertise in the field; alignment of vendor's strategic direction with that of the hotel group
Hotel Grp 2	Level of adoption of same solution; vendor by other hotel groups
Hotel Grp 3	Vendor reputation; operational and functional requirements
Hotel Grp 4	Vendor competency; vendor ability to meet todays and future requirements; balance of the above two criteria against cost

4.4 Service Vendor Selection

The most important criteria in selecting cloud service vendors is shown in Table 5. This question was included in both the research questionnaire and interview. In addition, the reasons driving the selection were also listed in the table.

5 Conclusions

The paper investigated the cloud computing adoption specifically in the hotel industry. In particular, it identified what kind of cloud computing combinations hotels have adopted; investigated the reasons of such decisions; and analyzed the benefits and challenges that cloud computing could offer in the hotel industry. The work therefore provides insights in the adoption of cloud computing that will assist hotel groups making strategic system development plan. The information is also useful for cloud provides to understand their customers experiences and better address the challenging they may have, which eventually helps to improve their services and open more business opportunities. Discrepancies between this research findings and the reported results in the literature suggest the future work, which will consolidate the results documented herein.

References

1. Armbrust, M., et al.: Above the clouds: a Berkeley View of Cloud Computing (2009). Accessed 10 Mar 2014
2. Beccari, D., Maillard, F.: Travel Flash Report: Online travels never looked so mobile (2012). Accessed 8 Dec 2014
3. Botta, A., de Donato, W., Persico, V., Pescap, A.: Integration of cloud computing and internet of things: a survey. Future Gener. Comput. Syst. **56**(Suppl. C), 684–700 (2016)
4. Buhalis, D., Law, R.: Progress in information technology and tourism management: 20 years on and 10 years after the internet the state of etourism research. Tourism Manag. **29**(4), 609–623 (2008)
5. Carr, N.G.: The Big Switch: Rewiring the World, from Edison to Google. WW Norton & Company, New York City (2008)
6. Cecowski, M., Becker, S., Lehrig, S.: Cloud computing applications. In: Becker, S., Brataas, G., Lehrig, S. (eds.) Engineering Scalable, Elastic, and Cost-Efficient Cloud Computing Applications, pp. 47–60. Springer International Publishing, Cham (2017). https://doi.org/10.1007/978-3-319-54286-7_3
7. Fox, J.T.: How Oracle is leveraging the cloud for hotels (2015). Accessed 19 May 2015
8. Ghanam, Y., Ferreira, J., Maurer, F.: Emerging issues & challenges in cloud computing a hybrid approach. J. Softw. Eng. Appl. **5**(11), 923 (2012)
9. Hopkins, G.: Why the Cloud is Right for Hospitality (2011)
10. Li, Y., Hu, C., Huang, C., Duan, L.: The concept of smart tourism in the context of tourism information services. Tourism Manag. **58**(Suppl. C), 293–300 (2017)
11. Marston, S., Li, Z., Bandyopadhyay, S., Zhang, J., Ghalsasi, A.: Cloud computing the business perspective. Decis. Support Syst. **51**(1), 176–189 (2011)
12. MICROS Systems Inc.: Louvre Hotels Group renews its OPERA cloud contract with MICROS Systems for additional five years [Press release] (2013)
13. Microsoft: ISVersus Cloud Solution Helps Cut Costs, Transform Business in the Global Hospitality Industry (2014). Accessed 7 Apr 2014
14. Mladenow, A., Kryvinska, N., Strauss, C.: Towards cloud-centric service environments. J. Serv. Sci. Res. **4**(2), 213 (2012)

15. Musab, A.K., Li, C.L., Naji, H.A.: Cloud services for hotel industry. In: Advances in Applied Materials and Electronics Engineering III. Advanced Materials Research, vol. 905, pp. 693–696. Trans Tech Publications (2014)
16. Protel hotelsoftware GmbH: Top Four Indicators it's Time to Change a Running [Property Management] System (2012)
17. Quinstreet: Cloud Computing Outlook: Private Cloud Expected to Grow at Twice the Rate of Public Cloud (2009). Accessed 12 Mar 2014
18. RightScale: State of the Cloud Report (2014). Accessed Oct 2014
19. Yin, R.K.: Case Study Research: Design and Methods. Sage Publications, Thousand Oaks (2013)
20. Yin, R.K.: Case Study Research: Design and Methods, Fifth edn. SAGE Publications, Thousand Oaks (2014)
21. Zheng, Z., Wu, X., Zhang, Y., Lyu, M.R., Wang, J.: QoS ranking prediction for cloud services. IEEE Trans. Parallel Distrib. Syst. 24(6), 1213–1222 (2013)
22. Zhou, X., Xu, C., Kimmons, B.: Detecting tourism destinations using scalable geospatial analysis based on cloud computing platform. Comput. Environ. Urban Syst. 54(Suppl. C), 144–153 (2015)

Privacy Attitudes and Data Valuation Among Fitness Tracker Users

Jessica Vitak[1]([⊠]) [iD], Yuting Liao[1] [iD], Priya Kumar[1] [iD],
Michael Zimmer[2] [iD], and Katherine Kritikos[2]

[1] University of Maryland, College Park, MD 20742, USA
{jvitak,yliao598,pkumarl2}@umd.edu
[2] University of Wisconsin—Milwaukee, Milwaukee, WI 53211, USA
{zimmerm,kritikos}@uwm.edu

Abstract. Fitness trackers are an increasingly popular tool for tracking one's health and physical activity. While research has evaluated the potential benefits of these devices for health and well-being, few studies have empirically evaluated users' behaviors when sharing personal fitness information (PFI) and the privacy concerns that stem from the collection, aggregation, and sharing of PFI. In this study, we present findings from a survey of Fitbit and Jawbone users (N = 361) to understand how concerns about privacy in general and user-generated data in particular affect users' mental models of PFI privacy, tracking, and sharing. Findings highlight the complex relationship between users' demographics, sharing behaviors, privacy concerns, and internet skills with how valuable and sensitive they rate their PFI. We conclude with a discussion of opportunities to increase user awareness of privacy and PFI.

Keywords: Fitness tracking · Privacy · Fitbit · Jawbone · Quantified self
Smartphones

1 Introduction

Fitness trackers are increasingly popular. A 2012 Pew Research Center survey found that 60% of Americans track their diet, weight, or exercise; of these, 21% used some form of technology, such as fitness trackers [13]. And demand has only increased in recent years, with companies shipping 71.5 million fitness-tracking watches and wristbands in 2015; by 2020, that number is predicted to reach 172 million [30].

These devices are part of a larger movement to capture and analyze metrics about one's health and behaviors, the so-called "quantified self" [23]. Designed to be worn unobtrusively on the body, fitness trackers collect data in an ambient manner with little effort from the user. The miniaturization and ubiquity of sensors in smartphones and fitness trackers enable people to track several aspects of their bodies with one device [23]. These data points, known as "personal fitness information" (PFI), may seem innocuous, but when collected over time or combined with other data, they can reveal detailed insights about people's health and habits [6, 27, 28].

This paper explores how people who use fitness trackers value the PFI they generate, how much they know about the data collection policies of fitness tracking companies, and how their sharing behavior compares to their overall privacy concerns and protection strategies. Our conceptualization of value encompasses several factors, including how sensitive people perceive their PFI to be, how concerned they would be if it were compromised, and how they compare their PFI to other types of personal data.

Our findings highlight how users' perceptions of PFI and their knowledge of fitness tracking companies' data collection policies are similar to and different from other types of information. We discuss the findings in light of the privacy paradox, or the idea that people express privacy concerns about certain activities but behave in ways that appear to undermine their privacy [31]. We conclude by discussing opportunities to increase user awareness of privacy and PFI.

2   Related Work

2.1   Fitness Trackers and Ubiquitous Data Collection and Sharing

Prior research has evaluated how people embed activity and fitness trackers into their personal and professional lives [14, 16, 29]—or why they do not [7]—with a recent focus on ubiquitous data collection and privacy [2, 6, 8, 27, 28]. The mobile and networked nature of fitness trackers means that they automatically and persistently collect data, which companies share with or sell to third parties [12, 19, 20].

The intersection of fitness trackers and ubiquitous data collection poses three main privacy problems [7]. First, people who use fitness trackers often lack awareness about how PFI feeds into larger infrastructures of data collection. This hinders informed decision making about sharing their PFI. Second, the dynamic nature of ubiquitous data collection means that data used for one purpose today may be used for another in the future. Analysis of PFI can be used to infer other characteristics that people have not directly shared [28]. Third, seemingly anonymous user data can be re-identified with increasing ease. Sensor data, for example, is granular enough "that each individual in a sensor-based dataset is reasonably unique" [27, p. 38].

While studies reveal that people are broadly concerned with the collection of location data [21, 25, 26], data about their mood or stress level [26, 28], conversational behavior [28], and detailed health information like glucose level or blood pressure [26], users of fitness trackers do not express specific privacy concerns about data collection on their devices [15, 21, 25]. Motti and Caine [25] surmise that users' lack of concern stems from a lack of awareness of how privacy can be compromised when companies collect granular data about users over a long time.

2.2   The Privacy Paradox and Mismatch in Users' Attitudes and Behaviors

Prior work illustrates that while people express concerns about privacy, they continue to behave in ways that undermine it [31]. This concept, known as the privacy paradox, has been studied extensively in relation to social media use [1, 3, 5]. Such work attributes the paradox to users' lack of awareness of privacy issues associated with use of such platforms and lack of knowledge of ways to protect privacy. As mobile computing reaches greater ubiquity and internet-enabled devices such as fitness trackers gain popularity, privacy concerns are becoming more salient.

Hargittai and Marwick [18] note that behaviors often presented as a "privacy paradox" can be more accurately attributed to a sense of apathy or cynicism about online privacy. Even when they engage in privacy-protective behaviors, users recognize that these measures are likely insufficient in the face of online data mining, widespread data aggregation, and confusing privacy settings. This leads to a belief that privacy violations are inevitable. Considering the privacy paradox as a response to online apathy may yield a more nuanced explanation of why people share PFI.

2.3 Current Study

We offer the following research questions to study users' knowledge of how fitness-tracking companies use PFI and how much users value their PFI. First, we consider if the privacy paradox applies to PFI and empirically analyze Motti and Caine's [25] suggestion that users lack concerns because they are unfamiliar with companies' data use policies. If the paradox exists, we would expect a person's general internet skills, privacy concerns, and knowledge of the fitness tracking company's privacy policies would be unrelated to their usage of the device. If no paradox exists, we would expect to see a positive correlation between people's knowledge and skills and their usage of their device and a negative correlation between privacy concerns and device usage.

RQ1: What differences—if any—exist between users who have a high understanding of fitness tracking companies' data policies and those who have little to no understanding of these policies?

Second, we empirically examine how much value users place on their PFI. Even though fitness trackers increasingly collect data that people perceive as sensitive, qualitative research suggests users do not have significant privacy concerns [15, 21, 25]. We believe one reason is because data collection happens largely in the background and the primary data point for most fitness trackers—steps taken—is innocuous on its own. To investigate this, we compare the perceived value users place on their PFI with other types of personal information like financial data.

RQ2: How do users view the value of PFI compared to other types of personal information?

Finally, a goal of this paper is to understand how to help people embed privacy considerations in their decision-making processes around whether and how to use fitness trackers. To do this, we must parse the inter-relationships between various factors that influence a users' valuation of their PFI.

RQ3: How are individual characteristics and privacy attitudes associated with users' perception of the sensitivity of PFI?

3 Method

In January 2017, we invited two random samples of 3000 employees from two American public universities to participate in an online study if they were at least 18, owned a smartphone, and currently used a Fitbit or Jawbone device—which were most popular fitness trackers at the time. Respondents completed an online survey and were invited to enter a raffle for one of five USD$50 gift cards. We received 361 usable responses. Respondents were generally female (75%), age 38 (median = 34, SD = 13.1), and highly educated (69% had an advanced degree). The vast majority (96%) used a Fitbit device, and most (71%) reported wearing it every day.

3.1   Measures

Perceptions of personal fitness information. Respondents were asked to think about the various types of data their fitness tracker generated and to respond to four original questions with a 0–100 slider scale they could move.

- **Data Sensitivity:** "How concerned would you be if your [Fitbit/Jawbone] data were compromised, such a through a security breach at the company?" (0 = Not at All Concerned, 100 = Very Concerned; $M = 54.44$, $SD = 29.26$).
- **Personal Data Value:** "Compared to other types of personal information about you —like financial information—how valuable is your [Fitbit/Jawbone] data to you?" (0 = Not That Valuable, 100 = Very Valuable; $M = 43.94$, $SD = 26.92$).
- **Advertisers' Data Value:** "Compared to other types of personal information about you—like financial information—how valuable do you think that your [Fitbit/Jawbone] data is to third-party advertisers?" (0 = Not That Valuable, 100 = Very Valuable; $M = 52.60$, $SD = 27.13$).
- **Black Market Data Value:** "Compared to other types of personal information about you—like financial information—how valuable is do you think that your [Fitbit/Jawbone] data is on the black market?" (0 = Not That Valuable, 100 = Very Valuable; $M = 35.66$; $SD = 27.85$).

Privacy and mobile concerns. Two measures were included to assess respondents' general and mobile-specific concerns about the privacy of their data. General privacy concerns [32] is an 11-item scale ($\alpha = .93$; $M = 3.72$; $SD = 0.98$) that asks respondents to "indicate your level of concern about the following scenarios that might happen when you use communication technologies" (scale: 1 = Not at all concerned to 5 = Very concerned). Mobile users' information privacy concerns (MUIPC) [33] is an eight-item scale ($\alpha = .93$; $M = 4.20$, $SD = 0.82$) measuring respondents' concerns related to personal data sharing via mobile apps (scale: 1 = Strongly Disagree, 5 = Strong Agree).

Perceived internet skills. Internet skills are an often-used measure to gauge a person's baseline knowledge about the internet. This measure is often used as a proxy to capture a broad understanding of a person's technical skills. We used Hargittai and Hsieh's [17] 10-item version of their internet skills scale ($\alpha = .91$; $M = 3.72$; $SD = 0.98$).

Knowledge of fitness tracking companies' data collection policies. To measure the extent to which people's practices and concerns matched their knowledge of company data policies, we asked respondents a series of questions about what data Fitbit or Jawbone collect, who owns their data, how it is stored, and with whom companies share the data. Respondents' knowledge scores were calculated based on how their answers reflected the company's publicly stated privacy policies.

Respondents were first asked about nine pieces of information—IP address, full name, email address, home address, birthdate, height, weight, smartphone operating system, and GPS/location information—and whether that data is "Not Collected," "Automatically Collected/Required," "Optional Information Requested by Company," or "I Don't Know/Not Sure" by the company. For example, because Fitbit requires users to provide their email address, respondents who correctly selected "Automatically Collected or Required" received five points toward their knowledge score. Those who said the email address is optional received one point, and those who said the email address is not collected or said they did not know received zero points. Eight open-ended questions were coded in a similar fashion. The knowledge score was derived by summing scores from each item ($M = 30.07$, $SD = 14.09$; range: 0–72).

Fitness tracker sharing activities. We asked three Yes/No questions about whether respondents had (1) shared fitness stats online, (2) joined a group or competed with other users, and (3) configured their device to automatically post stats online. These items were averaged based on the number of "Yes" responses to create an index of sharing activities; 62% of respondents engaged in at least one activity ($M = .79$, $SD = .74$; range: 0–3).

4   Findings

4.1   Factors Associated with Knowledge of Fitness Data Privacy Policies

Our first research question explored whether specific factors are associated with users' knowledge of what Fitbit and Jawbone do with user-generated data (i.e., their "knowledge score"). Echoing other research on privacy policies, respondents had very limited knowledge of the policies of fitness tracking companies: 73% did not know whether Fitbit/Jawbone sold their data, and 66% were not sure who owned their data. Regarding data retention, 85% of respondents did not know how long companies stored the data, and 89% were unsure where their data was stored besides the device.

To determine factors associated with a respondent's knowledge of the privacy policies, we first ran an OLS regression with the knowledge score as the dependent variable (DV) and demographic variables, internet skills, and privacy concerns as independent variables (IVs). Although the overall model was significant, the adjusted R-square was very low, with IVs explaining just 2.3% of the variance. This lack of significant IVs provides preliminary support for the existence of a privacy paradox, since privacy concerns and internet skills were similar across all levels of knowledge.

We also explored whether sex and perceived internet skills interacted in predicting respondents' knowledge. Results showed a significant main effect of sex on respondents' knowledge, $F(1, 236) = 4.22$, $p < .05$. Pairwise comparisons indicated a significant difference in knowledge scores between females ($M = 50.80$, $SD = .95$) and males ($M = 46.61$, $SD = 1.71$). There was no evidence of a main effect of perceived internet skills on respondents' knowledge; however, there was a significant interaction between sex and perceived internet skills on knowledge, $F(2, 237) = 3.04$ $p < 0.05$.

In other words, males scored higher on the knowledge test when they reported the highest level of perceived internet skills, while females scored higher when reporting lower levels of internet skills. After controlling for age and education, the main effect of sex and the interaction effect remained significant.

4.2   Users' Attitudes Toward the Value of Their PFI

To address RQ2, we used Personal Data Value, Advertisers' Data Value, and Black Market Data Value as DVs in a series of OLS regressions to identify differences in respondents' perceptions of the personal and financial value of PFI (see Table 1).

Table 1. OLS regressions predicting three measures of users' valuation of their PFI.

	Personal value	Third-party value	Black market value
	Standardized betas reported		
Sex	−.06	.14	.02
Age	.14*	−.02*	−.01
Education	−.14*	.07	.06
Internet skills	.01	−.03	.02
Privacy concerns	.06	−.10	−.07
Mobile data concerns	−.04	.18*	.18**
Data Sensitivity	.51***	.43***	.50***
Sharing activities	.02	.01	.01
$F(8,180) =$	11.87***	7.10***	10.59***
R^2	**.312**	**.213**	**.298**

$* \ p < .05 \ ** \ p < .01 \ *** \ p < .001$

Depending on the audience for their PFI, different factors emerged as significant predictors of respondents' data valuation. For example, age was positively correlated with how valuable PFI was to an individual ($\beta = .14$, $p < .05$), while education was negatively correlated with this assessment ($\beta = -.14$, $p < .05$). On the other hand, age was negatively correlated with the perceived value of PFI to third parties like advertisers ($\beta = -.02$, $p < .05$). For both third parties and the black market, mobile data concerns positively correlated with how valuable respondents perceived their PFI was to other groups ($\beta = .18$, $p < .05$ in each model). This was not the case in determining the value of PFI to the individual. Finally, respondents' level of concern about their PFI being compromised was positively correlated with all three valuations.

4.3   Predicting Users' Perceived Sensitivity of Their PFI

Our final RQ uses structural equation modeling (SEM) to build on the prior analyses to consider the inter-relationships between demographic factors, privacy and skills factors, and tracker-specific factors in explaining respondents' overall valuation of their data. We used Data Sensitivity as the primary dependent variable, asking respondents to indicate how concerned they would be if their PFI were compromised, as in the case of a data breach.

The proposed model was not a good fit to the data, $X^2(14,201) = 28.04$, $p = .01$; CFI = .79, RMSEA = .07. Therefore, we removed non-significant relationships between variables (including sex and knowledge of the company's privacy policies) and retested the model. The final model (see Fig. 1), provided a strong fit to the data, $X^2(13,201) = 15.77$, $p = .28$; CFI = .97, RMSEA = .03. We found a positive correlation between respondents' privacy concerns and the value they place on their fitness data. These variables alone explain 22% of the variance in a person's PFI valuation.

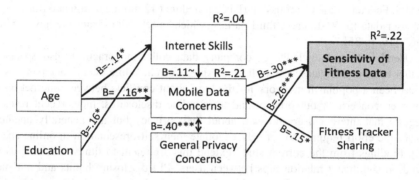

Fig. 1. Final path model addressing RQ3. All paths are significant. $\sim p < .07$, $* p < .05$, $** p < .01$, $*** p < .001$

5   Discussion

Fitness trackers are an increasingly popular gadget. In this study, we moved beyond the health factors that drive people to use these devices and focused on how users conceptualize the privacy concerns that may arise from the creation and sharing of the data these devices generate. Through a survey of Fitbit and Jawbone users, we examined how users' attitudes and beliefs influence their use of fitness trackers, their concerns about PFI, and the value they place on this data when compared to other forms of personal information. Below, we discuss how our findings extend existing knowledge and theories about ubiquitous data collection and privacy.

5.1   New Platforms, Same User Practices

While researchers have not yet delved deeply into users' perceptions of PFI, this study's findings are largely consistent with how users think about sharing other types of information online. The general lack of knowledge about how fitness tracking companies collect, store, and share data is unsurprising in light of prior research that has found that users generally do not read company privacy policies [24] and—even when they do—they are unlikely to understand or remember all the details [10, 22].

For example, Fitbit's privacy policy states, "We don't sell data that could identify you to anyone, anywhere, anytime. Ever. Period." It then states that it "may share or sell aggregated, de-identified data" but does not explain what data this includes or how the company de-identifies it [12]. This is important because PFI is particularly challenging to de-identify [27]. Likewise, Jawbone's policy states, "We do not rent, sell or otherwise share your individual personal information with third parties, except as follows" and lists six cases in which it may share information [20]. These statements apply to identifiable data (Fitbit) and "individual personal information" (Jawbone), but it is not clear whether these terms encompass data that fitness trackers generate. This echoes the lack of definitional clarity found in other privacy policies [22]. Research confirms that fitness companies share the data their devices generate. A 2014 study by the U.S. Federal Trade Commission (FTC) found that 12 mobile health and fitness apps sent user data to 76 different third parties, which raises "significant privacy implications" [19, p. 35].

Users' lack of knowledge of company data collection practices also speaks to another trend in this dataset, as well as in prior research. While the privacy paradox [1, 3] has been a popular framework for thinking about conflicts between internet users' professed concerns about privacy and their online disclosures, more recent research suggests that internet users do care about their privacy but are generally apathetic toward the effort required to actively negotiate their self-presentation in online spaces [18]. Findings from the current study extend this argument to fitness trackers, as we found no significant relationships between users' PFI disclosure habits and our measures of privacy concerns. Future research should explore the underlying reasons for this seeming lack of concern to determine whether it stems from apathy, lack of knowledge of potential harms, or something else.

5.2 Opportunities for Increased User Awareness of Privacy and PFI

Findings from our study identify more opportunities for cross-sector partnerships, such as the one between Fitbit and the Center for Democracy & Technology [9], to approach this privacy challenge. First, our analyses revealed a strong positive correlation between users' general privacy concerns, their mobile data concerns, and how sensitive they rate their PFI. Likewise, users who publicly shared PFI expressed greater concerns about how their mobile data is used. Thus, the more users care about privacy in general —and the more they engage in sharing activities that might jeopardize their privacy— the more concern they have about PFI. Fitness tracking companies must find ways of easing anxiety over privacy if they wish to have users increasingly engage in information sharing activities on their platforms. Partnering with organizations that focus on privacy research is one way for them to do so.

Few regulations exist to constrain companies from sharing PFI with third parties. While the EU's General Data Protection Regulation explicitly protects health data [11], U.S. law does little to regulate or protect the collection and use of PFI [6, 26]. Companies view this data as valuable from a monetary and research perspective and use it accordingly. People who use fitness trackers and seek to protect their privacy may wrongly assume that the law protects it. Our analyses of users' (lack of) privacy policy knowledge suggest a need for greater education and outreach to users. This may include a more robust explanation of user-controlled privacy settings during onboarding; contextual explanations of how adjustments to device settings might affect data collection and flows; or regular communication to users reminding them of their current privacy settings.

6 Limitations and Conclusion

We must note some limitations to this research. First, while recruitment methods (random sampling at public universities) were designed to minimize response bias, the sample is significantly more educated than the general population and likely more than the population of fitness tracker users. This could introduce bias related to data valuation and internet skills. The sample was also significantly skewed toward female users, and existing research has found that women both share more online than men and have greater privacy concerns. Finally, this data collection comes from a one-time survey, meaning our analyses can only identify correlations between variables and not causation. That said, because of the lack of empirical research on the privacy and security issues around fitness trackers, we believe the findings presented here provide useful insights to guide future theoretically driven and design-based studies.

Emerging technologies provide new opportunities for users to learn about themselves, meet and interact with new and existing friends, and explore ways to enhance their well-being. However, these technologies—and the associated data generated from their use—also bring challenges to managing individual privacy. In this paper, we argue that more attention should be devoted to considering the privacy implications of fitness trackers and other wearable devices that collect large amounts of data about users' movement and health. As Boyd and Crawford [4] note in their work on the challenges of big data, PFI is neither objective nor a "fix" for health-related problems. We are entering a time when PFI will be used to evaluate healthcare incentives, court cases, and more. Users must recognize how this data can be used against them, and companies should be more proactive in educating users on strategies to more easily access and manage their data.

References

1. Acquisti, A., Gross, R.: Imagined communities: awareness, information sharing, and privacy on the Facebook. In: Danezis, G., Golle, P. (eds.) PET 2006. LNCS, vol. 4258, pp. 36–58. Springer, Heidelberg (2006). https://doi.org/10.1007/11957454_3
2. Ball, K., Di Domenico, M.L., Nunan, D.: Big data surveillance and the body-subject. Body Soc. 22(2), 58–81 (2016). https://doi.org/10.1177/1357034X15624973
3. Barnes, S.D.: A privacy paradox: social networking in the United States. First Monday 11(9) (2006)
4. Boyd, D., Crawford, K.: Critical questions for big data: provocations for a cultural, technological, and scholarly phenomenon. Inf. Commun. Soc. 15(5), 662–679 (2012). https://doi.org/10.1080/1369118X.2012.678878
5. Boyd, D., Hargittai, E.: Facebook privacy settings: who cares? First Monday 15(8) (2010)

6. Christovich, M.: Why should we care what Fitbit shares: a proposed statutory solution to protect sensitive personal fitness information. Hastings Commun./Entertain. Law J. **38**, 91–116 (2016)
7. Clawson, J., et al.: No longer wearing: investigating the abandonment of personal health-tracking technologies on Craigslist. In: Proceedings of UbiComp 2015, pp. 647–658. ACM, New York (2015). https://doi.org/10.1145/2750858.2807554
8. Crawford, K., Lingel, J., Karppi, T.: Our metrics, ourselves: a hundred years of self-tracking from the weight scale to the wrist wearable device. Euro. J. Cult. Stud. **18**(4–5), 479–496 (2015). https://doi.org/10.1177/1367549415584857
9. De Mooy, M., Yuen, S.: Toward privacy aware research and development in wearable health. Center for Democracy and Technology, Washington (2016)
10. Earp, J.B., Anton, A.I., Aiman-Smith, L., Stufflebeam, W.H.: Examining internet privacy policies within the context of user privacy values. IEEE Trans. Eng. Manag. **52**(2), 227–237 (2005). https://doi.org/10.1109/TEM.2005.844927
11. European Union: Regulation (EU) 2016/679 of the European Parliament and of the Council of 27 April 2016 on the protection of natural persons with regard to the processing of personal data. Off. J. Eur. Union **119**, 1–88 (2016)
12. Fitbit: Fitbit Privacy Policy (2016). http://www.fitbit.com/legal/privacy-policy
13. Fox, S., Duggan, M.: Tracking for Health. Pew Research Center, Washington (2013)
14. Fritz, T., Huang, E.M., Murphy, G.C., Zimmermann, T.: Persuasive technology in the real world: a study of long-term use of activity sensing devices for fitness. In: Proceedings of CHI 2014, pp. 487–496. ACM, New York (2014). https://doi.org/10.1145/2556288.2557383
15. Gorm, N., Shklovski, I.: Sharing steps in the workplace: changing privacy concerns over time. In: Proceedings of CHI 2016, pp. 4315–4319. ACM, New York (2016). https://doi.org/10.1145/2858036.2858352
16. Gorm, N., Shklovski, I.: Steps, choices and moral accounting: observations from a step-counting campaign in the workplace. In: Proceedings of CSCW 2016, pp. 148–159. ACM, New York (2016). https://doi.org/10.1145/2818048.2819944
17. Hargittai, E., Hsieh, Y.P.: Succinct survey measures of web-use skills. Soc. Sci. Comput. Rev. **30**(1), 95–107 (2012). https://doi.org/10.1177/0894439310397146
18. Hargittai, E., Marwick, A.: "What can I really do?" Explaining the privacy paradox with online apathy. Int. J. Commun. **10**, 3737–3757 (2016)
19. Ho, J.-J., Novick, S., Yeung, C.: A snapshot of data sharing by select health and fitness apps. Federal Trade Commission, Washington (2014)
20. Jawbone: Jawbone UP Privacy Policy (2014). https://jawbone.com/up/privacy
21. Klasnja, P., Consolvo, S., Choudhury, T., Beckwith, R., Hightower, J.: Exploring privacy concerns about personal sensing. In: Tokuda, H., Beigl, M., Friday, A., Brush, A.J.B., Tobe, Y. (eds.) Pervasive 2009. LNCS, vol. 5538, pp. 176–183. Springer, Heidelberg (2009). https://doi.org/10.1007/978-3-642-01516-8_13
22. Kumar, P.: Privacy policies and their lack of clear disclosure regarding the life cycle of user information. In: FS-16-04, pp. 249–256. AAAI, Palo Alto (2016)
23. Lupton, D.: The Quantified Self: A Sociology of Self-Tracking. Polity, Cambridge (2016)
24. McDonald, A.M., Cranor, L.F.: The cost of reading privacy policies. ISJLP **4**, 543–568 (2008)
25. Motti, V.G., Caine, K.: Users' privacy concerns about wearables: impact of form factor, sensors and type of data collected. In: Brenner, M., Christin, N., Johnson, B., Rohloff, K. (eds.) FC 2015. LNCS, vol. 8976, pp. 231–244. Springer, Heidelberg (2015). https://doi.org/10.1007/978-3-662-48051-9_17
26. Patterson, H.: Contextual expectations of privacy in self-generated health information flows. In: TPRC 41, pp. 1–48. SSRN, Rochester (2013). https://doi.org/10.2139/ssrn.2242144

27. Peppet, S.R.: Regulating the internet of things: first steps toward managing discrimination, privacy, security and consent. Tex. Law Rev. **93**, 85–178 (2014)
28. Raij, A., Ghosh, A., Kumar, S., Srivastava, M.: Privacy risks emerging from the adoption of innocuous wearable sensors in the mobile environment. In: Proceedings of CHI 2011, pp. 11–20. ACM, New York (2011). https://doi.org/10.1145/1978942.1978945
29. Rooksby, J., Rost, M., Morrison, A., Chalmers, M.: Personal tracking as lived informatics. In: Proceedings of CHI 2014, pp. 1163–1172. ACM, New York (2014). https://doi.org/10.1145/2556288.2557039
30. Shirer, M., Llamas, R., Ubrani, J.: IDC Forecasts Wearables Shipments to Reach 213.6 Million Units Worldwide in 2020. IDC (2016)
31. Taddicken, M.: The "privacy paradox" in the social web. J. Comput.-Mediat. Commun. **19**, 248–273 (2014). https://doi.org/10.1111/jcc4.12052
32. Vitak, J.: A digital path to happiness? In: Reinecke, L., Oliver, M.B. (eds.) Routledge Handbook of Media Use and Well-Being, pp. 274–287. Routledge, New York (2016)
33. Xu, H., Gupta, S., Rosson, M.B., Carroll, J.M.: Measuring mobile users' concerns for information privacy. In: Proceedings of ICIS 2012, pp. 1–16. AIS, Atlanta (2012)

Data Mining and Data Analytics

Identifying the Affective Dimension of Data Mining Practice: An Exploratory Study

Jo Bates$^{(\boxtimes)}$ ⓘ and Jess Elmore ⓘ

Information School, University of Sheffield, Sheffield, UK
jo.bates@sheffield.ac.uk

Abstract. The paper aims to illuminate how feeling, emotion and affect influence the practice of data mining. While data mining is sometimes presented as an objective and neutral technique by which to rationally understand and predict phenomena, we observe that there is an important affective dimension in how people understand, engage in and respond to data mining practices. We report the findings of a small exploratory pilot study conducted in 2016 in which we used ethnographic methods to observe the culture of a collaborative project between data scientists and a small digital marketing company. The project aimed to explore potential uses of data mining techniques in the process of telesales lead generation. Thematic analysis of collected data indicates that even in the case of a small scale project, the practice of mining data is deeply influenced by an underlying affective dimension. While these affective dynamics rarely surfaced explicitly in discussions between team members, it is clear from our interview data that feelings and emotions had a significant impact on how participants experienced and engaged with the practice of data mining. Our findings point to the necessity for a much deeper understanding of, and reflexivity in relation to, the affective dimension of data mining practice and how it emerges in the cultures and practices of data science projects. We argue that a deeper awareness of, and openness about, this affective dimension could benefit practitioners' understanding of their own practice and motivations in decision making, and thus has the potential to improve data science practice.

Keywords: Data mining · Data science · Data practices · Emotion
Affect

1 Introduction

Data mining in many ways can be understood as a provocation to relate to the world around us in a different way – to see, and thus interact with, phenomena differently [14]. Unsurprisingly then, the inputs, outputs and practices of data mining provoke emotional responses. This affective dimension[1] can be observed in the response of 'data

---

[1] Definitions of affect, emotion and feeling are contested within the literature. Following common usage in psychology, we here use the term 'affective' to refer in general to experiences of feeling and emotion. In terms of specific affective dynamics, we draw upon Shouse's [26] distinction that feelings are personal responses to sensations that we label on the basis of experience, emotions are social in that they are projections of feelings, and affects are non-conscious experiences of intensity that cannot be fully realised in language.

© Springer International Publishing AG, part of Springer Nature 2018
G. Chowdhury et al. (Eds.): iConference 2018, LNCS 10766, pp. 243–252, 2018.
https://doi.org/10.1007/978-3-319-78105-1_28

subjects' to particular data mining practices, for example, discourses of "creepiness" in response to personalised advertising. It can also be observed in some of the popular and academic discussion about controversial data mining and machine learning practices and outputs, and it can be seen in the attraction of becoming a data scientist – "the sexiest job of the 21st century". Thus, while data mining is sometimes presented as an objective and neutral technique by which to rationally understand and predict phenomena, there appears to be an important affective dimension in how people understand, engage in and respond to data mining practices.

We currently have little understanding of the affective dynamics of data mining practice, whether in terms of the feelings and emotions of data mining practitioners and customers, or those of 'data subjects' and wider publics. Yet, if we are to influence the development of data mining as an ethical and socially beneficial practice, it is important that we develop a much deeper understanding of such dynamics. In doing so, we aim to advance our understanding of both the cultural politics of emergent forms of "data power" [10] and contribute to ongoing efforts to illuminate the "social life of methods" [25].

To this end, this paper presents a subset of findings from a small exploratory pilot study about cultures of data science practice in which we observed the important role of feeling, emotion and affect in how practitioners relate to the inputs, outputs and practices of data mining. The study is based on an ethnography of a small-scale collaboration between academic data scientists and a small digital marketing firm that took place in 2016.

2   Theorizing Data Mining Practice

Traditionally, the term data mining refers to a stage of the Knowledge Discovery in Databases (KDD) process, which also involves the stages of data pre-processing, cleaning, visualisation and analysis [6]. According to this definition, data mining refers to the practice of using algorithms in order to discover hidden patterns in complex datasets, often with the intention of training a machine learning classifier to automatically predict output variables. More recently, as interest in the power of algorithms has spread to non-computational disciplines, the term data mining has been used in a much looser way in order to describe both practices of harvesting data from e.g. social media sites, and to describe the whole of the Knowledge Discovery in Databases (KDD) workflow (e.g. Kennedy [12]). In this paper, we are particularly interested in practices related to data mining for the purpose of supervised machine learning.

Early developments in data mining were concentrated in the computational and physical sciences, and industries such as advertising and pharmaceuticals; however, in recent years we can observe what Mackenzie [18] terms an "unruly generalization" of such techniques across different settings. Advocates are enthusiastic about the insights and value that might be uncovered from illuminating hidden patterns within the increasing volume of data that is becoming available to analysts. However, there is also significant evidence accumulating about the social biases embedded in the data and algorithms used in data mining e.g. [5, 23], and growing concerns about the influence of data-driven algorithmic processes on the cultural, political and economic wellbeing of societies e.g. [3, 8, 22, 23].

The important role of emotion in shaping information behaviour has been observed by a number of scholars e.g. [2, 21], however this research tends to focus on the role of emotion as people go about identifying and satisfying their information needs. As Kennedy and Hill [11] observe, the nature of the relationship between data and emotion has rarely been examined. Only the work of Ruckenstein [24] and Kennedy and Hill [11] draws attention to the importance of understanding the emotional dynamics of how people make sense of data. However, as Kitchin [15] identifies, subjectivities – and thus feelings, emotions and affects – are a key component in the complex data assemblages that frame "what is possible, desirable and expected of data" (p. 24). While other research has tended to focus on other components of the data assemblage such as infrastructure, political economy, finance, regulations and data ideologies, the affective dimension has, as yet, been largely overlooked.

Much of the popular and academic literature on the role of feeling, emotion and affect in human responses to events, practices and so on, depends on a sharp distinction between affective and cognitive modes of processing information. For example, Nobel Prize winning social psychologist Kahneman [9] posits that humans rely on two separate thought systems, the first being intuitive and emotional, and the second being conscious, logical and calculating. Similar frameworks are often assumed in disciplines at the heart of data mining practice (e.g. computer science, information science). Accordingly, data mining, as a computational technique, is often understood by these disciplines as being firmly situated within the more logical and rational domain of information processing. However, as cultural theorist Andrejevic [4] observes, data mining can also be understood as a technique for enabling pre-rational forms of "thoughtless thought". In an era of information overload, he argues, people are "enjoined to rely on their emotions, their gut instinct, and their thoughtless thoughts, to anchor themselves in a flood of information" (p. 47). For Andrejevic data mining – specifically sentiment mining – is merely another method for coming to conclusions with minimal engagement in more discursive, deeper forms of reasoning.

As many social and cultural theorists have observed, the drawing of a sharp distinction between affective and cognitive processes is problematic at both the ontological and analytical levels. Rather, such theorists argue that we ought to understand affective and cognitive dynamics as being complexly interrelated, and therefore much more difficult to distinguish analytically than is often assumed [1]. In this study, we adopt such a position, understanding the affective dynamics we observe to be complexly interrelated with cognitive processes.

3   Methodology

Our project ran from April-July 2016, and involved two social scientists based at the University of Sheffield (the authors), two academic data scientists (an academic [DS2] and a postgraduate student [DS1]), and a small digital marketing company that provides services to a range of well-known national firms (main contact: B1). Other than the two female social scientists, all members of the project team were male. At the time the collaboration was set up, an initial discussion between the firm and one of the data scientists about a possible collaboration had already taken place, and the rest of the team 'piggy-backed' onto this emerging collaboration. The technical aim of the project was for the data scientists to use data mining techniques in order to predict positive and negative outcomes of telesales calls. To this end, the firm provided the data scientists with a dataset of 600,000 records of calls made to households, and the outcome of the call. The dataset included a range of attribute data about the person called and nature of the call, including time, date, gender, and region.

The social scientists (the authors of the paper) conducted a small scale ethnographic study of this project. There has been little research of this type in the field of emergent data mining practices. Most ethnographic work examining data work has been conducted in the relation to research data practices e.g. [7] or public services e.g. [12, 16], rather than in commercial or hybrid commercial settings, and has not focused specifically on data mining as a practice.

Data were collected via two interviews with each project member, observations of all project meetings, and email communications. Data have been analysed thematically using Nvivo. In this paper, we discuss our findings related to the role of emotion, feeling and affect in shaping data mining practices. Emerging from the coding, a number of affective themes are apparent: (1) Anticipation and hope for the project, (2) Anxiety about data mining practices, (3) Tensions, uncertainties and confusion about data mining, (4) Disappointment, (5) Thrill of the game, (6) The pressure of the promise of data mining, (7) Feelings influencing judgement, (8) Empathy with data subjects, (9) Embodied practice, and (10) The pleasure/pain of data mining.

Ethical approval for the project was gained from the University of Sheffield's Research Ethics Committee.

4   Findings

In general, we observed few explicitly affective statements during group interactions between project members. Email communication tended to be concise and to the point. Only one email message from DS2 to the company representative demonstrated any emotions in relation to the task, expressing excitement about the project in an email encouraging the firm to get the (at this point delayed) data ready for sharing: "I hope you can get something to us as it sounds a pretty exciting project for us!" (DS2-email). The final written report was also free of any affective content, demonstrating no feelings towards the human subjects and focusing entirely on the data analysis. Similarly, in group meetings the dynamic was largely free of emotional statements and affect. Other than friendly utterances about football, discussion was focused on the analysis of the data and opportunities for collaboration. This dynamic was suggestive of a performance of masculinity not only in relation to the topics of conversation, but also with regard to the affective dynamics of interpersonal communications within the project team. In contrast, while a lot of the conversation during interviews was similarly focused on the detail of the data mining task, we also observed a higher emotional content as participants expressed more of their internal feelings about the project in these discussions.

All members of the project team were interviewed prior to the transfer of data from the company to the data scientists. In these interviews, we observed an interesting mix of feelings and emotions in relation to the forthcoming project. There was a strong sense of anticipation from the two data scientists. One spoke of his excitement about seeing the data, and finding out how far they would be able to push the quality of predictions (DS2-1). Both were looking forward to getting their "hands dirty on the data" (DS1-1); a phrase which suggests data mining was experienced as an embodied practice (something lived and experienced through the perceptions, emotions and movements of the body). This observation is echoed in the use of other figures of speech by team members such as "eyeballing the data" (DS2; B2) and references to the "painful[ness]" (DS2) of some of the more boring data mining tasks.

For DS2, his excitement was grounded in the forthcoming opportunity to "play". The anticipation of building an accurate classifier was perceived as a challenging game: "I think there is some sort of gamification. I'm trying to reach a higher score at the end" (DS2-1). However, this excitement was checked with a sense of realism about what were perceived as the more arduous data mining practices, such as data cleaning: "I mean on one hand it's super exciting to try these models, on the other it's probably also painful to deal with all this data for months and data quality issues at the beginning, so it's mixed feelings" (DS2-1). In this sense, there was both a pleasure and pain in data mining, however the draw of the 'game' seemed to outweigh the more laborious, "painful" tasks. Here, we can understand these pleasures and pains to be both feelings and sensations; the pain of data cleaning is both experienced mentally and physically.

For, DS1 there was a sense of anticipation about the positive feelings that he expected to get from seeing the data mining outputs: "So the way when you visualise the output of the classification or testing or techniques that you apply, it makes me happy" (DS1-1). However, for this project member there were also various anxieties in relation to the project. This was his first experience of a "real-world" project, and there was a sense of worry about the pressure to generate "real value" from the data mining process: "with a real company, they want you to get real value from their data. So this sometimes you know, make me afraid. [Laughs]" (DS1-1). There was also a tension and confusion about how the individual's ethical beliefs about mining personal data might be brought into conflict with the needs of the company and project:

> "It may be we don't have the right to search for this [personal] data or to analyse this data without permission from the people whose data we are analysing. So it's confusing.... It's my moral, the way that I have been taught by my family to always respect others and always respect the privacy of others. This also affect me and I believe it will affect me dealing with this data" (DS1-1).

In contrast to this concern, for the participant based at the digital marketing company, the aim of the project was to help data subjects rather than invade their privacy. He spoke of hoping to "make a genuine sort of difference with it" (B1-1). He spoke empathetically of the data subjects, emphasizing that they were "human beings with emotions, thoughts" (B1-1). From his perspective a more accurate prediction model would help to rid these consumers of unwanted sales calls: "annoying calls that people get or emails and anything else, we'd just eradicate all of that" (B1-1).

Following the transfer of data from the business to the data scientists, we began to observe a shift in the affective dynamics of the project. For the data scientists, the data was not as detailed as they had hoped; while there were a large number of call records

($\sim$ 600,000) there were few attributes about the call that could be used to train the classifier. For the novice data scientist, this was disappointing and made him concerned about whether he would be able to build an accurate model: "It was small. I expected it to have been more–, more bigger.... I believe it will affect [the accuracy of the model]" (DS1-2). However, for the more experienced data scientist the lack of detail in the dataset was perceived as a challenge: "It's a nice challenge, right.... I think the prediction for me is very, very interesting" (DS2-2). His excitement about getting access to the data was not dampened: "So their data is honestly extremely exciting. I think having this outcome variable for 600,000 phone calls, that's really gold data...we are kind of lucky to have this opportunity to have the data" (DS2-2).

As anticipated by the experienced data scientist, the data needed a lot of cleaning before it could be mined. The novice data scientist who undertook this work spoke of the process he went through to deal with missing values: "I have to deal with what I have, but...if I'm working, for example, on [a different project mining] medical data, I will always be cautious about how to deal with the missing data because it's sensitive data" (DS1-2). This was an interesting observation in the sense that it demonstrates how data scientists' personal feelings about the sensitivity and value of the mining exercise can impact upon the care taken in critical data cleaning exercises.

The practice of mining data results in the production of a numerical value that represents the accuracy of the classifier when run on a test dataset. As mentioned above, for DS2 the "game" of data mining was to get this number as high as possible. In our interviews, we observed how feeling, emotion and affect framed this number. For DS1, a good number meant success and thus happiness: "I see...success or failure as the accuracy of my model, and how much the accuracy of my model - that much I will be happier" (DS1-2). The definition of a good result for a particular project was seen as something that could be agreed within the project team. However, this also brought pressure: "We expect that 70/80 per cent will be good accuracy for this one. Q: Okay. And do you think you'll get to that? A: I hope [laughs]" (DS1-2). DS2 similarly recognized this demand for a high number, and while he was curious about how high they could push the accuracy, he was fairly relaxed about the tension between the desires of the firm and his perhaps more realistic expectations: "I think they will be looking for a high number...Given the not so rich data we have, I expect it to be low, in the 60 s, probably. But I think if you push it to the 80 s, that would be extremely good...We'll see how it goes" (DS2-2).

In the end, the outputs of the data mining exercise were perceived as "inconclusive" by the representative of the business. He recognized that there was limited time for the project and that the results were influenced by the limitations of the data that was made available to the data scientists. Nonetheless, he observed: "I think, er, it wasn't fudged but it was sort of hashed so that a result could be found in it" (B1-2). B1 here seems to be referring to a decision made by the data scientists to oversample the small number of calls with successful outcomes, which increased the accuracy of the model in predicting the success or failure of a call from 52% to 93%; a decision B1 was concerned was a matter of "just applying brute force" to the data (Obs. Notes). When this decision and outcome was reported to other company representatives in the final meeting it similarly appeared to be met with some skepticism: "DS2 picks up the report again, and all three of them look at it...There is then a pause and B2 says 'it would be interesting to have more data"' (Obs. notes). This was an interesting observation and, given the above discussion, questions emerge about how the affective dimensions of data mining practice might in some cases contribute to decision making that "forces" a desired result through crude methods. In this way the methods would produce apparently good numbers that nevertheless have little relation to reality. In response to this concern, DS2 acknowledged that it was important to have "a balanced model", and while the numbers couldn't be "trust[ed]", he believed they looked "promising" (Obs. Notes).

In our final interview with the business representative, we began to see the emergence of some uncertainty around data mining practices. While he perceived that this was the direction the business ought to go, there was also a sense that the business was being driven by external pressures to mine data: "you know, you have–, you've got to stay with the times and the times are driven by data science, a lot of things now" (B1-2). This comment echoes a similar statement made in a project meeting: "we have realized data science is huge for us, it's a necessity...it's gone from interesting to imperative" (B1: Obs. Notes – final meeting). However, despite these perceived drivers, in his final interview the participant also reflected on and expressed some anxieties regarding the potential social implications of mining data about people. He began to frame data mining practices such as those in the project in terms of the wider practices of data mining:

> "the way [people's] lives are being run from a data perspective...you basically just reinforce everything that you already believe and so all you're doing is–, it's like self-justification endlessly back to yourself, which is dangerous I think, it's not good... if you apply it to advertising, which is what we would be doing, you're removing people's hope for aspirations because all they can ever do is be exposed to things that would only ever be applicable to them as they exist at the moment...".

This quotation reflects an emerging tentativeness that was also expressed more directly by the participant:

> "So is it depriving, you know – Strange"; "sorry if I'm going on but yeah—"; "I–, 'cause I–, for me personally, I like deeply disagree with the way those companies run their – I–, I didn't–, I've never actually thought about it until fairly recently"; "So yeah, it's a strange one really...".

These emotions demonstrate this participant's deepening awareness about some of the negative social implications of particular applications of data mining, and his position within these emerging developments. There was a clear uneasiness that began to come through, yet also a sense that he and the business was compelled to follow this path. Similar to the ethical concerns of DS1, it was interesting to see that these concerns never emerged within the group communications that we observed between project members.

5   Discussion

The findings from our study demonstrate that even in the case of a small scale project, the practice of mining data is deeply influenced by an underlying affective dimension. While these affective dynamics rarely surfaced explicitly as emotions in discussions between team members, it is clear from our interview data that the project members nonetheless experienced many complex feelings related to their work that impacted upon how they engaged with the practice of mining data. Echoing observations in other domains of scientific practice e.g. [13, 17], these findings contradict common understandings of data mining and other computational methods as being solely the expression of logic and rational cognition; as practices devoid of an affective dimension.

Our findings resonate with Kennedy and Hill's [11] observation that people respond emotionally to data visualization. DS1, for example, spoke of how the visual outputs of data mining made him "happy". Yet, the affective dynamics went much deeper and broader than simply responding to the visualization of data. We observed complex affective dynamics in relation to every stage of the data mining process: data acquisition, data cleaning, building a classifier, and the numerical and visual outputs. We also observed how feeling and emotion framed the practitioners' understanding and empathy with the people behind the data – the data subjects. Interestingly, we also observed that these affective dynamics tended to emerge only in the interview setting – in one to one conversations with the interviewer. Within project meetings, email communications and project reports participants' feelings and emotions were largely hidden from others. This suggests team members may have had limited awareness and understanding of the underlying affective dynamics that were shaping other team members' activity and engagement with the project. It is likely that the affective dynamics shaping data scientists' engagement with different stages of the data mining process may have influenced decisions made during the project. For example, their feelings about the accuracy of their prediction - the final "score" of the project – may have influenced the decision to oversample successful call data in order to achieve a high, but ultimately for the end-users implausible, level of predictive accuracy. This points to a critical need for those engaged in data mining projects to have a deeper awareness about how affective factors may be influencing their own and others' decision making.

As Andrejevic [14] observes, rather than the data deluge we are currently experiencing leading necessarily to an increase in accurate information about phenomena, people are seemingly still dependent upon "their emotions, their gut instinct, and their thoughtless thoughts, to anchor themselves in [the] flood of information" (p. 47). And just as he suggests, practices of data mining are not independent of this dynamic; rather, data mining can be enabling of particular forms of "thoughtless thought". Yet, data mining is also a powerful means of illuminating hidden patterns in data, and it would be facile to dismiss it as a method on the basis that there is an affective dimension to data mining practice. Similarly, there is nothing to be gained from the impossible task of striving to rid data mining of this affective dimension. Rather, our findings point to the necessity for a much deeper understanding of, and reflexivity in relation to, the affective dimension of data mining practice and how it emerges in the cultures and practices of data mining projects.

6 Conclusion

Given the pilot nature of the project, our research is limited in scope and we experienced practical restrictions on being able to conduct further follow up interviews (e.g. one member of the team left the country and we lost contact). However, through this small exploratory study, we have identified that there is an important affective dimension to data mining practice. We have also suggested that a deeper awareness of, and openness about, this affective dimension could benefit practitioners' understanding of their own practice and motivations in decision making, and thus has the potential to improve data mining practices. Following on from this exploratory study, suggestions for further research include (1) systematic investigation of the affective dynamics of data mining practice in various contexts through adoption of a model of affect in the data collection and analysis stages, (2) further investigation into the gendered nature of affective dynamics in data mining practice, and (3) expansion of the study of affective dynamics into other domains of data science practice.

References

1. Ahmed, S.: The Cultural Politics of Emotion. Edinburgh University Press, Edinburgh (2004)
2. Albright, K.: Psychodynamic perspectives in information behaviour. Inf. Res. **16**(1), 9 (2011)
3. Amore, L.: Biometric borders: Governing mobilities in the war on terror. Polit. Geogr. **25**(3), 336–351 (2006)
4. Andrejevic, M.: Infoglut: How Too Much Information is Changing the Way We Think and Know. Routledge, New York (2013)
5. Barocas, S., Selbst, A.D.: Big data's disparate impact. Calif. Law Rev. **104**, 671 (2014)
6. Coenen, F.: Data mining: past, present and future. Knowl. Eng. Rev. **26**(1), 25–29 (2011)
7. Edwards, P., Mayernik, M., Batcheller, A., Bowker, G., Borgman, C.: Science friction: data, metadata, and collaboration. Soc. Stud. Sci. **41**(5), 667–690 (2011)
8. Gillespie, T.: The relevance of algorithms. In: Media Technologies: Essays on Communication, Materiality, and Society. MIT Press, Cambridge (2014)
9. Kahneman, D.: Thinking, Fast and Slow. Penguin, London (2012)
10. Kennedy, H., Bates, J.: Data power in material contexts: introduction. Telev. New Media **18**, 701–705 (2017)
11. Kennedy, H., Hill, R.: The feeling of numbers: emotions in everyday engagements with data and their visualisation. Sociology (2017)
12. Kennedy, H.: Post, Mine, Repeat: Social Media Data Mining Becomes Ordinary. Palgrave, London (2016)
13. Kerr, A., Garforth, L.: Affective practices, care and bioscience: a study of two laboratories. Sociol. Rev. **64**(1), 3–20 (2016)
14. Kirschenbaum, M.: The Remaking of Reading: Data Mining and the Digital Humanities (2009). https://www.csee.umbc.edu/~hillol/NGDM07/abstracts/talks/MKirschenbaum.pdf. Accessed 6 Sept 2017
15. Kitchin, R.: The Data Revolution: Big Data, Open Data, Data Infrastructures and Their Consequences. SAGE, London (2014)

16. Kitchin, R., Lauriault, T.P.: Towards critical data studies: charting and unpacking data assemblages and their work. The Programmable City Working Paper 2; pre-print version of chapter to be published in Eckert, J., Shears, A., Thatcher, J. (eds.) Geoweb and Big Data. University of Nebraska Press (2014), Forthcoming. SSRN: https://ssrn.com/abstract= 2474112
17. Lorimer, J.: Counting corncrakes: the affective science of the UK corncrake census. Soc. Stud. Sci. **38**(3), 377–405 (2008)
18. Mackenzie, A.: Machine Learners: Archaeology of a Data Practice. MIT Press, Cambridge (2017)
19. Mackenzie, A.: The production of prediction: what does machine learning want? Eur. J. Cult. Stud. **18**(4–5), 429–445 (2015)
20. Mittelstadt, B.D., Allo, P., Taddeo, M., Wachter, S., Floridi, L.: The ethics of algorithms: mapping the debate. Big Data Soc. **3**(2), 1–21 (2016)
21. Nahl, D., Bilal, D. (eds.): Information and Emotion: The emergent Affective Paradigm in Information Behavior Research and Theory. Information Today, Medford (2007)
22. Neyland, D.: On organising algorithms. Theory Cult. Soc. **32**(1), 119–132 (2014)
23. O'Neil, C.: Weapons of Math Destruction: How Big Data Increases Inequality and Threatens Democracy. Crown, New York (2016)
24. Ruckenstein, M.: Visualized and interacted life: personal analytics and engagements with data doubles. Societies **4**(1), 68–84 (2014)
25. Savage, M.: The 'social life of methods': a critical introduction. Theory Cult. Soc. **30**(4), 3–21 (2013)
26. Shouse, E.: Feeling, emotion and affect. Media Cult. J. 8(6) (2005). http://journal.media-culture.org.au/0512/03-shouse.php

Data Retrieval = Text Retrieval?

Maryam Bugaje(✉) and Gobinda Chowdhury

Faculty of Engineering and Environment, iSchool,
Northumbria University, Newcastle, UK
{maryam.bugaje,gobinda.chowdhury}@northumbria.ac.uk

Abstract. Due to the comparatively more recent emergence of data retrieval systems than text-based search engines, the former have still yet to achieve similar maturity in terms of standards and techniques. Most of the existing solutions for data retrieval are more or less makeshift adaptations of text retrieval systems rather than purpose-built solutions specially designed to cater to the particular peculiarities, subtleties, and unique requirements of research datasets. In this paper we probe into the key differences between text and data retrieval that bear practical relevance to the retrieval question; these differences we demonstrate by evaluating some representative examples of research data repositories as well as presenting findings from previous studies.

Keywords: Data retrieval · Text retrieval · Research data management
Research data repositories

1 Introduction

Among the more comprehensive definitions of research data is that they are "entities used as evidence of phenomena for the purposes of research or scholarship", which may range in form from digital records (e.g. text, audio, video, spreadsheets, etc.) to physical objects (e.g. laboratory specimens, historical artefacts, soil samples, etc.) [1]. A stricter definition, however, stipulates that in addition, research data must be associated with useful metadata, or "information describing its creation, transformation, and/or usage context" [2]. Research data repositories perform various useful functions, among the first of which is storage/curation of research datasets, and not the least of which is enabling the discoverability of the same by authorized parties. The latter function is primarily fulfilled by the retrieval system via (a) a search interface by means of which the underlying database may be queried; (b) a browsing interface through which the same may be accomplished in a structured way; or (c) a URL that links directly to the resource itself. Data retrieval systems are still at a relatively early stage of development, and most of the data repositories currently in use are essentially text-based in their methods of metadata indexing, query processing, and retrieval; and as well in the way that their search results are presented. Superficially, this fact may hardly be regarded as constituting a definite issue in itself, until the question is considered whether we interact differently with data than with publications; and, if so, whether there may not be better advantage, then, in modelling data retrieval systems specially to reflect the unique requirements and opportunities indicated by these

© Springer International Publishing AG, part of Springer Nature 2018
G. Chowdhury et al. (Eds.): iConference 2018, LNCS 10766, pp. 253–262, 2018.
https://doi.org/10.1007/978-3-319-78105-1_29

differences. This is an important question retrieval-wise, partly because the task of tagging research datasets with metadata, which is the central component that powers the retrieval engine, is often complex; and partly because unlike the indexing of research papers by services like Web of Science, the indexing of research datasets is not standardized or controlled [3]. This paper recognizes the need to not only identify existing problem areas in data retrieval, such as the aforementioned; but as well the relationships of these problems to one another, in order that they may be traced to, and addressed at the root. There is need, also, to ascertain the requirements of a proper data retrieval system in order that appropriate means may be devised for the achievement of that end. It is not our object in this paper to expound on the theoretical differences between text retrieval and data retrieval; but rather, to investigate on the more evident and frequently encountered differences that bear practical relevance to retrieval. The particular aims of this paper form a part of an ongoing research, and have been tailored expressly with this purpose in mind; they are:

To –

1. Review the currently supported features and functionalities of RDM repositories as pertains retrieval. It is not part of our aim to critique these services from a usability perspective, nor to compare their general features, but to provide a snapshot of the standard search and retrieval features available;
2. Assess the degree to which these services cater and are adapted to the special requirements of data retrieval as distinguished from text retrieval (i.e. research publications);
3. Ascertain as to the existence of any marked improvements in retrieval performance and output, between services that support only simple-keyword searches and those that support more advanced querying options; and
4. Establish, via an exploratory study, the differences, as specially pertains retrieval, between the requirements of research data content and text content.

This paper addresses points 1 and 4 above.

2   Appraisal of Repositories in Current Use

As of date re3data.org lists upwards of 900 research data repositories in its directory. For better manageability of this mammoth number, and for the purpose of giving structure to our review we have organized these into 6 broad, non-mutually exclusive groups viz. disciplinary, institutional, publisher-service, location-based, dedicated content-type, and commercial/general purpose repositories. For each group, we have hand-picked a few representative examples for evaluation against the following yard-sticks which have special relevance to the retrieval question:

1. *Metadata.* The method by which the metadata associated with each dataset is extracted and used for indexing; and the degree to which this metadata appears to be exploited to provide features for browsing, searching/querying, filtering and result presentation;

2. *Querying facility.* The level of expressiveness allowed in searching/querying the repository; which, in addition, further enhances discoverability; and

3. *Result filtering.* The availability of options for filtering down search results, and the furthest granularity to which this is possible.

Our choices of data repository examples were guided by the combined recommendations of re3data.org and Nature[1].

Disciplinary Repositories. These are dedicated repositories housing research data from a specific disciplinary branch or sub-branch; e.g. Dryad[2] for the Biosciences, and the Virtual Solar Observatory (VSO)[3] for Solar Physics data. Figure 1. shows the search interface of the VSO, where metadata can evidently be seen to be made ample use of to enable searches by an extensive range of variables. To be sure, solar data is a highly standardized, machine-collected data; and it is exhaustively machine-tagged to a metadata schema standard to the discipline. The latter affords immense potential for building, on the strength of it, functionalities capable of supporting very expressive search queries, as well as result filtering to a fine granularity. It also allows for better indexing methods, and, consequently, more efficient retrieval.

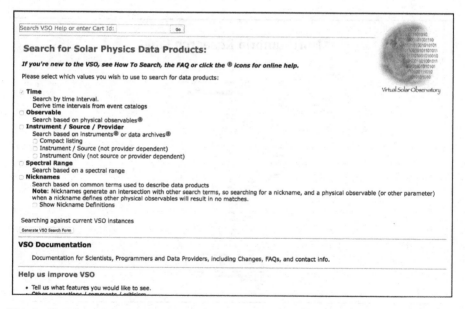

Fig. 1. The bounded domain of disciplinary repositories affords scope for exploiting disciplinary metadata to improve query expressiveness, indexing techniques, and retrieval efficiency among others

---

[1] https://www.nature.com/sdata/policies/repositories.

[2] datadryad.org/.

[3] https://sdac.virtualsolar.org/cgi/.

Publisher-service Repositories. These are provided by journal publishers, some of whom conduct peer reviews on research data and publish them as regular scholarly outputs; e.g. Nature's Scientific Data[4]. Publisher-service repositories are mostly optimized for linking research data with the publications that they underlie; and, as journals generally publish around specific subjects/topics, their repositories may share some of the aforementioned advantages of disciplinary repositories; these services, however, are few.

Institutional Repositories. Institutions of higher learning may make available repositories for the exclusive use of their research communities; e.g. Oxford University's Research Data Oxford[5]. These repositories are usually hidden behind a login, and many universities outsource the provision of this service to third-party vendors. Furthermore, the repositories are built such that they could as well house other research outputs, including books, patents, reports, and theses among others. All these combine to ultimately give very little scope for specially adapting their retrieval systems to work well for research datasets. As could be seen in Fig. 2, however, institutional repositories may have a modest provision of options for advanced searching and for filtering search results.

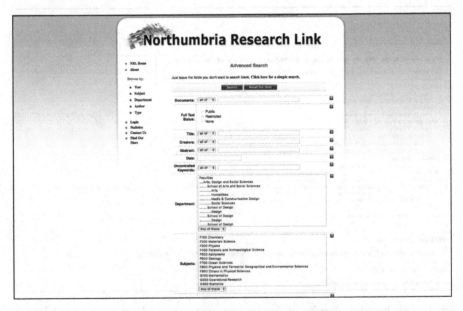

Fig. 2. Institutional repositories are designed, generally, to accommodate other research outputs in addition to datasets. Consequently there is little scope for data-centric features.

---

[4] https://www.nature.com/sdata/.

[5] http://researchdata.ox.ac.uk.

Location-based Repositories. Research Data housed in these repositories are generally accessible to anyone globally, but submissions are solicited and accepted only from researchers within a specified geographical area; e.g. ANDS Research Data Australia, and the European Union Open Data Portal (EU ODP)[6]. These repositories are generally more data-centric than institutional repositories, and feature advanced search options that are more pertinent to research data (e.g. Fig. 3); but, in their attempt to accommodate all data that falls within their geographical boundaries, they sacrifice much of the benefits, such as have been previously mentioned under the example of disciplinary repositories, of well-exploited metadata which come with having a more streamlined content.

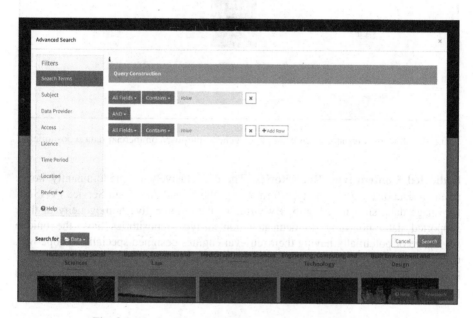

Fig. 3. Advanced search options by Research Data Australia

Commercial Service-provider & General-purpose Repositories. These place little to no restrictions on research data submitted to them; e.g. Figshare[7]. They tend to house multidisciplinary data, as well as data from niche disciplines that do not have dedicated repositories. As shown in Fig. 4, general-purpose repositories, by the mere fact of their being general-purpose, find it harder to achieve any fine-grained filtering of search results, to say nothing of forming expressive queries. This is because the metadata that is needed to support such functionalities is, in the interest of inclusivity, kept superficial at best; and, as such, the retrieval mechanism is essentially very text-like.

---

[6] https://data.europa.eu/euodp/en/data.
[7] https://figshare.com.

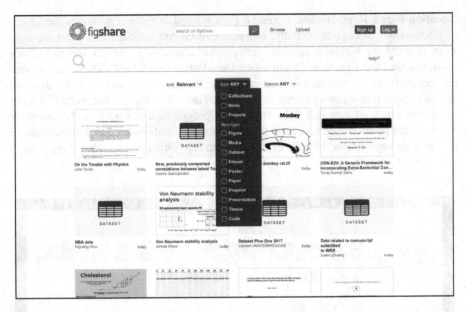

Fig. 4. Showing Figshare as an example of general-purpose/commercial data repositories.

Dedicated Content-type Repositories. These exclusively or predominantly house research data of a certain file type/format; e.g. the Visual Arts Data Service (VASD)[8] for image data, shown in Fig. 5. By virtue of the comparative homogeneity of their supported data, not only do dedicated content-type repositories have the unique advantage of potentially having their retrieval engines designed specially to cope with their content type and support interaction possibilities unique to it, but also their search interfaces to be designed around ideas and principles as best suit or express the special properties of their content.

2.1   Section Summary

While in the preceding sections we have dwelt on the strengths and advantages that purpose-built data retrieval systems promise, we have not sufficiently touched on the disadvantages and consequences of settling for a text-based system for data retrieval. Unlike research publications (text), data may be said to entail an active interaction: researchers do not "read" datasets in the passive sense that they do publications; rather, they "use" it by visualizing, combining, or manipulating it among other things. In the section that follows we briefly present the findings of a previous exploratory study that argues a strong case in favor of retrieval solutions designed purposely for use with data [3].

---

[8] https://vads.ac.uk.

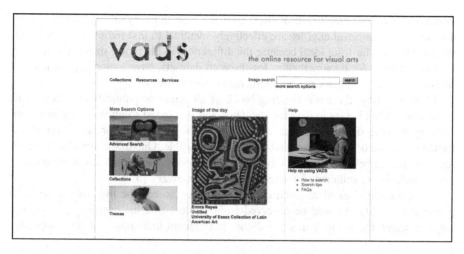

Fig. 5. Showing VADS as an example of dedicated content-type data repositories.

3   Comparison-in-Action Between Text & Data Retrieval

Figure 6 shows the search interface of the popular Web of Science[9], a text-based search engine for research publications. It can be observed that the search options it provides do not decidedly differ from those previously seen of data repositories. In fact, the

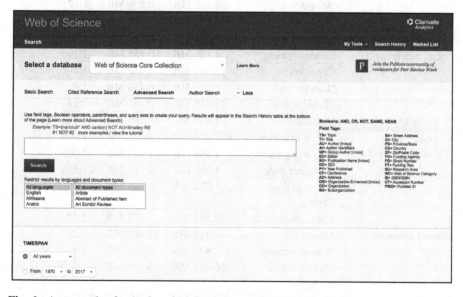

Fig. 6. An example of a text-based retrieval system, Web of Science, showing advanced search options.

---

[9] https://apps.webofknowledge.com/.

resemblance is not superficial: at their core the vast majority of currently-available data-repository retrieval engines are effectively identical to text retrieval engines. This state of affairs is far from ideal because the differences in file types, size, and format, as well as the need for documentation for research datasets, have major implications for search efficiency and resource requirements of data retrieval.

Fundamentally, the basic building block of all scientific publications is text. This uniformity makes it easy to develop standards and fine-tuned solutions. Data, however, even by its mere definition indicates variability. The sheer variation in file types and formats of datasets makes any standardization unfeasible. One of the key challenges of data retrieval arises from the lack of use of standard metadata and documentation to contextualize data sufficiently for re-use [4] and discovery [5, 6].

Also, the file sizes of research datasets typically exceed the file sizes of research publications (text). It could be observed from Table 1 that the average file size of a single research dataset may in some disciplines amount to as much as 900 times over

Table 1. Average sizes of files retrieved for research datasets and research publications.

Discipline	Keywords	Data retrieval[a]	Text retrieval[b]	Approx. ratio of text to data
Arts & Humanities	Art museums	6.205 MB	0.820 MB	1:8
	Nineteenth century	2.898 MB	1.042 MB	1:3
	"World war"	6.158 MB	0.508 MB	1:12
	Medieval	5.158 MB	1.091 MB	1:5
	Popular music	9.334 MB	1.000 MB	1:9
Social Sciences	Unemployment	4.729 MB	0.455 MB	1:10
	Cognition	13.340 MB	1.612 MB	1:8
	"Labour law"	2.827 MB	0.410 MB	1:7
	"Trade union"	15.939 MB	0.748 MB	1:21
	Imprisonment	2.444 MB	0.503 MB	1:5
Computer & Information Science	Search behavior	657.707 MB	0.731 MB	1:900
	Face recognition	**1.394 GB**	1.535 MB	1:908
	Computer vision	**1.339 GB**	2.782 MB	1:481
	Research data sharing	1.574 MB	0.521 MB	1:3
	Social media data	19.597 MB	1.078 MB	1:18
Natural Sciences	Marine life	32.318 MB	1.491 MB	1:22
	"Climate change"	2.808 MB	2.497 MB	1:1
	"Renewable energy"	766.432 MB	3.606 MB	1:213
	"Ultraviolet light"	496.745 MB	1.991 MB	1:250
	"Oxidative phosphorylation"	41.177 MB	1.895 MB	1:22

[a]*Average File Size, inclusive of documentation.*
[b]*Average File Size.*

the average file size of a single research publication. The ordinary web browser, consequently, cannot support the preview of datasets online as it does research publications; and consequently in turn, datasets must necessarily be downloaded before even a glimpse of them could be had [3]. These false downloads of large files result in considerable processing overhead, and it is more advisable that the retrieval system returns a manageable subset of the data so that the user may view it beforehand and be able make an informed decision as to whether to download it.

Research shows that energy consumption increases with increase in server load because energy is consumed during both phases: while doing computing work and while waiting for database data to arrive [7]. Hence, a reduction in the volume of data downloaded will reduce the energy consumption of IT infrastructure of data services as well as the universities and research institutions, thereby reducing the environmental costs of research data management.

4   Conclusion

With special reference to retrieval, this paper has expounded on some key differences between research data and publications (text), and urged the development of data retrieval systems that are modelled around requirements and opportunities unique to data. The current state of affairs in which data retrieval and text retrieval are equated and dealt with interchangeably is unsatisfactory, unsustainable (for details on sustainability of information see [8, 9]) and results in an unnecessarily high consumption of network, computing, and storage resources. Most of the current data retrieval systems offer features that are based on keyword searches and are appropriate for text retrieval, but they seldom meet the specific requirements of data retrieval.

References

1. Borgman, C.: Big Data, Little Data, No Data: Scholarship in the networked world. MIT Press, Cambridge (2015)
2. Weber, A., Piesche, C.: Requirements on long-term accessibility and preservation of research results with particular regard to their provenance. ISPRS Int. J. Geo-Inf. **5**, 49 (2016)
3. Bugaje, M., Chowdhury, G.: Is data retrieval different from text retrieval? An exploratory study. In: Choemprayong, S., Crestani, F., Cunningham, S.J. (eds.) ICADL 2017. LNCS, vol. 10647, pp. 97–103. Springer, Cham (2017). https://doi.org/10.1007/978-3-319-70232-2_8
4. Borgman, C.L.: The conundrum of sharing research data. J. Am. Soc. Inf. Sci. Technol. **63**(6), 1059–1078 (2012)
5. Borgman, C.L., Wallis, J.C., Mayernik, M.S.: Who's got the data? Interdependencies in science and technology collaborations. Comput. Support. Coop. Work **21**(6), 485–523 (2012)
6. The data harvest: how sharing research data can yield knowledge, jobs and growth. An RDA Europe report, December 2014. https://rd-alliance.org/sites/default/files/attachment/The% 20Data%20Harvest%20Final.pdf. Accessed 06 Nov 2017

7. Boru, D., Kliazovich, D., Granelli, F., Bouvry, P., Zomaya, A.Y.: Energy-efficient data replication in cloud computing datacenters. Clust. Comput. **18**(1), 385–402 (2015)
8. Chowdhury, G.G.: Sustainability of Scholarly Information. Facet Publishing, London (2014)
9. Chowdhury, G.G.: How to improve the sustainability of digital libraries and information services? J. Assoc. Inf. Sci. Technol. **67**(10), 2379–2391 (2016)

Information and Knowledge Based Conceptual Study of 2008 Financial Crisis

Josep Cobarsí-Morales[1](✉) and Agustí Canals[2]

[1] Computer Science, Multimedia and Telecommunication Studies,
Universitat Oberta de Catalunya, Rambla de Poblenou 156, 08018 Barcelona,
Catalonia, Spain
jcobarsi@uoc.edu
[2] Economics and Business Management Studies,
Universitat Oberta de Catalunya, Av. Tibidabo 39-43,
08035 Barcelona, Catalonia, Spain

Abstract. Although a proper and wide diffusion of information and knowledge is acknowledged by economic theory as a necessary condition for a perfect functioning of markets, there are some weaknesses of conceptualization of information and knowledge applied to economics. As a contribution to fill this gap, the purpose of this paper is to set up a conceptual analysis and discussion of 2008 Great Financial Crisis (GFC) in terms of information and knowledge. As theoretical basis for this discussion we have selected the Boisot's framework of Information Space (I-Space) [1, 2] which we relate with the proposal of Van den Berg [3] about encapsulated knowledge. This enhances us to discuss two key elements concerning the 2008 GFC: securitization and qualifications of rating. Our analysis shows how the sociotechnical innovations concerning financial markets in the years previous to GFC, contributed to create or increased information and knowledge asymmetries. These asymmetries impacted the risk management by the stakeholders implied in financial markets and eroded the correct function of these markets until the 2008 collapse.

Keywords: Information Space · Encapsulated knowledge
Market asymmetries · Great Financial Crisis · Knowledge management
Economics of information

1 Introduction

Financial crises are a recurrent phenomenon along human history. Economists Reinhardt and Rogoff [4], made an exhaustive study of financial crises worldwide since XIIth century to 2008 events, the so called 2008 Great Financial Crisis (GFC). Suddenness, dimensions and global impact of GFC have made of it a critical and controversial incident for economic science [5, 6] and also for other social sciences [7, 8]. Technical reports by official institutions or by think-tanks have compiled and discussed the events [9–11]. Academic literature has analyzed different aspects of GFC, such as [12–14].

© Springer International Publishing AG, part of Springer Nature 2018
G. Chowdhury et al. (Eds.): iConference 2018, LNCS 10766, pp. 263–271, 2018.
https://doi.org/10.1007/978-3-319-78105-1_30

In this paper we propose a new approach to study of GFC: an information and knowledge based conceptual study. Our approach builds upon two key concepts of knowledge management literature: Information Space (I-Space) defined by Boisot [1, 2] and encapsulated knowledge defined by Van den Berg [3].

In the next sections we set up objectives (Sect. 2), then we expose the concepts of I-Space and encapsulated knowledge and relate with asymmetries in financial markets (Sect. 3). In Sect. 4 we apply this conceptual framework to the analysis and discussion of two key aspects of GFC: the role of securitization and the role of rating qualifications. Finally, in Sect. 5 we finish with a conclusion and hints for future research.

2 Objectives

Since the origins of economic science to present time, economic thinking has not clearly articulated the concept of information nor others related, such as knowledge and data [15, 16], although the importance of information for a correct function of the markets has been acknowledged by important streams of economic thinking, such as behavioral economics [17], and new institutional economics [18]. New institutional economics consider information asymmetries a common element related to market imperfections [19]. As first objective for our study we address: to propose a conceptual framework based on a selection of knowledge management literature and relate with economic theory about information asymmetries in markets, in order to enhance the analysis of GFC.

On the other hand, technical reports and papers we have mentioned in the previous section point at the importance in this GFC of two sociotechnical novelties of the years previous to this crisis. One novelty is the apparition and generalization of new financial products, the so called securities, of great complexity during the years previous to GFC [20]. Also, during the decades previous to GFC, there are growing trends of globalization and intermediation in financial markets, so that investors rely growingly on qualifications of rating agencies to take their decisions [21]. Then, as second objective for our study we address: to test the framework established in Objective 1 for the analysis and discussion of the role of securitization and the role of qualifications of rating in GFC.

In order to achieve both objectives, a selection of bibliography has been consulted and analyzed, taking into account three main topics: economic theory about information asymmetries in markets, knowledge management literature related to economic science, technical reports and scientific papers about GFC.

3 Conceptual Framework: I-Space, Encapsulated Knowledge and Asymmetries in Financial Markets

With the objective of shedding some light on the role of information and knowledge in financial markets, we will rely on the I-Space conceptual framework, developed by Boisot [1, 2]. The I-Space is aimed at understanding knowledge flows in social systems. It is built on the premise that structured knowledge flows more easily than unstructured knowledge. For instance, the highly situated and tacit knowledge possessed by a Zen master can only be transferred through prolonged face-to-face interactions with a small number of disciples. Contrarily, the completely structured information used by a bond trader, i.e. the price, reaches all the world market in a matter of seconds.

Based on the idea that human knowledge uses categories to make sense of the world and is built up through the two processes of discrimination and association [22], the I-Space takes information structuring as being achieved through two cognitive activities: codification and abstraction. *Codification* articulates and helps to distinguish from each other the different categories we use. The higher the degree of codification of any phenomenon, the fewer amount of data processing will be needed to categorize it. When a phenomenon is complex or vague, or when the categories we use to apprehend it are not clear-cut, the amount of processing effort needed will be higher. *Abstraction* reduces the number of categories that we need to draw upon to capture a phenomenon by treating things that are different as if they were the same [23]. When two categories are highly correlated, one can be used in lieu of the other. Thus, the more abstract a phenomenon, the fewer the categories we will need to make sense of it.

Codification and abstraction act reinforcing one another. Codification facilitates the association of categories required to achieve abstraction, and abstraction, in turn, reduces the amount of data processing needed to categorize by keeping the number of categories needed down to a minimum. Working together, they allow us to have better structured data, and therefore to reduce encoding, transmission, and decoding efforts. Therefore, the more structured is knowledge, the easier is for it to be diffused. Structured knowledge flows quite easily and impersonally between the agents in a population while tacit, highly unstructured knowledge, is difficult to transfer, and often requires face-to-face communication.

Figure 1 represents the I-Space in a graph showing two dimensions: structuring (a combination of codification and abstraction) and diffusion [24]. At point A knowledge is unstructured and undiffused, while at point B it has been completely structured and, thanks to that, diffused. Knowledge is valuable when it has utility and at the same time is scarce. Therefore, the high value region of the I-Space is its higher left part, but the nature of the structuring process and diffusion pushes knowledge to the right once it is structured following the diffusion curve.

Van den Berg [3] notes that Boisot [2, pp. 12–13] describes three repositories of knowledge: (1) residing in individual brains, (2) codified as information, (3) embodied in physical artifacts. Building upon this Van den Berg [3] proposes the concept of encapsulated knowledge, which may be defined as the value endowing meta-resource originating from thought, reflection, or experience that is embedded in an artifact's design and functionality. As an example of encapsulated knowledge he proposes software. We must note that encapsulated knowledge is a kind of structured knowledge in terms of I-Space. Also, we remark this kind of structured knowledge is not explicit for the users, who don't understand how the software is coded, how it accomplishes its tasks, or the language used in this development. In lots of cases, encapsulation of knowledge is a suitable mechanism of knowledge diffusion and enables getting from it the proper value for all the participants in a market. We may think for instance of office automation software. But in other cases encapsulation may be related to market

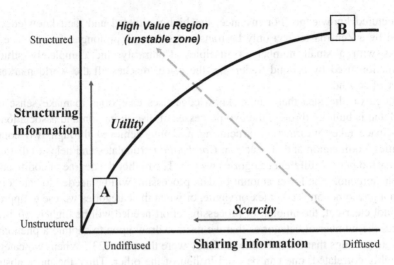

Fig. 1. The Information-Space (adapted from Ihrig and Child [24])

problems, for example we will see further on how encapsulation of knowledge plays a role in financial markets and their disfunctions.

As information and knowledge are key elements in financial markets, it makes sense to look at financial crises through the I-Space lenses. For instance, it is clear financial markets are only perfect markets when they work at the B area of the I-Space. Indeed, when knowledge is completely diffused and all agents have access to it, markets are efficient and work for everyone. However, when one moves to the left and information has not been diffused to all players, there is room for inefficiencies [25].

Information asymmetries may explain many of the financial market failures. When one of the intervening parts in a deal knows more or has better information than the other one, it will use this circumstance to its advantage, making the transaction inefficient and capturing most of the value generated in it.

In some occasions some of the knowledge may be 'encapsulated' in some products [3], giving the impression that this knowledge can be used by anyone able to buy those products without understanding its foundations, and making the market work. However, without a complementary knowledge on the intricacies of those financial products, which often resides in the left part of the I-Space, agents may use them inadequately.

In economic bubbles, some (wrong) information implying the soundness of the market is shared and agreed among agents, what increases their level of trust. Being that information at the higher right part of the I-Space, all agents act as if it is right. The fact that it promises to generate a lot of value being far away from the high value region of the I-Space does not seem to worry them. Until the bubble explodes and suddenly everyone realizes that the information was not right.

In some occasions, information asymmetries are combined with the principal-agent problem, giving rise to different harmful situations. This may happen when there is one part that has some objectives (the 'principal'), but that needs to rely on another part (the 'agent') that acts in its name for a compensation. In *moral hazard* problems the agent engages in a behavior which is not aligned with the principal's interests; for instance, not working hard enough. In hidden information problems, the agent uses its better knowledge of the situation to make decisions in its advantage and not in the advantage of the principal [19: p. 477]. In financial markets where different kinds of players coexist (e.g. customers, traders, financial products designers, bank managers and bank shareholders) and technical complexity is high, these kind of problems appear. Information is only shared within one or some kinds of players (i.e., resides on the middle-left part of the I-Space) and they take advantage of this fact to try and capture its value. And often these actions that seem to be rational from an individual point of view turn into something harmful from a collective standpoint.

When information is not shared among everyone, agents in a market resort to trust to guide their actions. But trust cannot be built in financial markets where transactions are often anonymous or happen only once with each counterpart. As game theory shows us, one of the few ways to build trust is through repeated interactions [26], and that does usually not happen in financial markets.

4 Applied Analysis and Discussion: Securities and Rating Qualifications

We will apply the conceptual framework in the previous section to the role of two key elements regarding GFC: securities and rating qualifications.

4.1 Securities

Since the decade of 1980, several sociotechnical innovations impacted financial markets [9, 27]. In this sense, a major innovation at early 2000 decade was the creation and widespread use of new financial derivative products of high conceptual and mathematic complexity. The most representative of this type were the so called securities, which aggregated individual debts (typically subprime mortgage loans) of different individual risk and commercialized them as a packet [20]. These products obtained a quick acceptation and were widely diffused. In this sense, we may think of this diffusion as a case of encapsulation, a type of structuration of information which allows a wide diffusion across the participants of a market.

Buyers readily accepted the idea of creating an aggregated product made of smaller products of different individual risks. Securities encapsulated the knowledge of the designers about the calculation of the risk of these products, whose details were not understood or even known by potential buyers and sellers. But this was not seen as a problem before 2008, as participants in financial markets trusted on designers' knowledge about calculation of their risk. In fact, the calculation of risk of these products was of high mathematical complexity, so that even the designers were not completely aware of the risk when these products were extensively commercialized, repacked and resold. Thus, this encapsulation of knowledge contributed to the diffusion of positive information across the participants of the markets, and enhanced optimistic behavior about it which contributed to the financial bubble. Therefore, there was an information asymmetry, as investors had a very superficial knowledge about these new financial products and the risk associated to them.

We may ask ourselves why such novel and complex financial products were so quickly and widespread accepted by the participants in financial markets. The qualifications of risk made and published by the agencies of rating were a key point about this, as we expose in the next subsection.

4.2 Rating Qualifications

According to Rajan [27], a major change in the decades previous to 2008 GFC is a gradual shift from very direct and personalized relationship between lenders and borrowers, were they exchange confidentially very concrete and low structured (so to speak in the A zone in terms of I-Space), to a much more globalized, depersonalized and intermediated market environment. This new market environment needs to work in the B zone of the I-Space, and accordingly requires highly structured information, which is highly codified and abstract, and therefore easy to diffuse.

In this context, investors rely increasingly for their decisions upon the qualifications of risk made and published by a very small set of rating agencies (such as Moody's or Standard and Poors). These agencies categorize the products according to the risk they calculate for the potential investors who may buy these products. This categorization is highly structured and abstract, as applies to all kind of financial products, such as securities, sovereign debt of countries, etc., the same set of categories. In a perfect financial market, interest offered to potential investors must be proportional to the risk of not payment that they assume. Thus, qualifications of rating encapsulate the knowledge of the rating agencies about risk of financial products, and have high influence over the interest offered for each product. Increasing scarcity of information compelled investor to rely almost exclusively upon rating qualifications, which are in B zone of I-Space highly structured and diffused. But knowledge of this very small set of agencies about risk calculation is partly tacit and they are not at all interested to disclose it unless they receive incentives, therefore it remains in A zone of I-Space.

On the other hand since the decade of 1970s there was an important change about the system of payment to the agencies of rating: they shifted from being paid by subscription by the users of information, that is the potential investors, to being paid by the institutions which offered the financial products [28]. Also, some of these rating agencies started to offer consultancy and software models to the institutions which offered financial products, so they disclosed to them part of their knowledge, but not to the potential investors. Therefore, designers of products could know what to do to obtain the maximum qualification for their products, but this knowledge remained closed for the potential investors, the ones who used this qualifications as key point for their decisions. On the other hand these rating agencies functioned as an informational oligopoly, under recognition and protection of regulators with no chance for users of qualifications to ask from them any responsability [29].

Thus, the sociotechnical evolution of financial markets favored not just information asymmetries, but also principal-agent problems as explained in Sect. 3. Even so, investors kept their trust on rating qualifications until the very beginning of the 2008 GFC.

In this context, securities used to receive until the beginning of 2008 GFC the maximum qualification, the same qualifications received by the debt of countries or corporations considered of maximum solvency. Now it could seem to us surprising that these securities offered a rate of interest to investors bigger than the other products with the same qualifications of rating and similar conditions. This could have hinted to the investors that something did not match about the qualifications of rating. But we must also note that there were not historical precedents of such looses as securities suffered in 2008 GFC, which had affected to financial products with similarly good rating qualification. Thus, information asymmetries and principal agent problems we have analyzed and discussed had brought no significant effects for investors until 2008 GFC, so their trust in the system of financial markets until that time may be understood with the information and knowledge that was widespread available in the B zone of I-Space.

5 Conclusion

We have proposed in this paper an information and knowledge analysis and discussion about 2008 GFC, based on Boisot's I-Space conceptual framework and Van den Berg's concept of encapsulated knowledge. We have shown, with its application to financial markets, that the combination of both is a valid conceptual tool for the analysis of information asymmetries and principal agent problems in a market, which are key issues in a market according to economic theory.

In particular, we have pointed that encapsulation of knowledge, being an efficient way to diffuse knowledge in a market environment, must be considered cautiously, because it may create or increase information asymmetries which may damage the capability of participants in a market to properly take decisions.

Anyway, our paper is just a first step to apply I-Space and encapsulation of knowledge to the study of market functioning. This first step constitutes a useful base to enhance needed future research. For instance, changes in financial regulations after 2008 GFC could be analysed and discussed with the same framework we have proposed in this paper, which may be a conceptual alternative to examine regulation policies not just for financial markets but also for other knowledge intensive and complex environments. Also, our conceptual approach could be useful to enhance future empirical studies about impact of information and knowledge difussion in markets, a promising research topic as showed in [30].

References

1. Boisot, M.H.: Information Space: A Framework for Learning in Organizations, Institutions and Culture. Routledge, London (1995)
2. Boisot, M.H.: Knowledge Assets: Securing Competitive Advantage in the Information Economy. Oxford University Press, New York (1998)
3. Van den Berg, H.A.: Three shapes of organizational knowledge. J. Knowl. Manag. **17**(2), 159–174 (2013)

4. Reinhart, C.M., Rogoff, K.S.: This Time is Different: Eight Centuries of Financial Folly. Princeton University Press, Princeton (2011)
5. Lane, J.E.: The crisis from the point of view of evolutionary economics. Int. J. Soc. Econ. **37** (6), 466–471 (2010)
6. Krugman, P.: How Did Economists Get It So Wrong? The New York Times, 2 September 2009. http://www.nytimes.com/2009/09/06/magazine/06Economic-t.html?pagewanted=all. Accessed 12 Sept 2017
7. Patterson, L.A., Koller, C.A.: Diffusion of fraud through subprime lending: the perfect storm. In: Deflem, M. (ed.) Economic Crisis and Crime, pp. 25–45. Emerald, Bingley (2011)
8. Munir, K.: Financial crisis 2008–2009: what does the silence of institutional theorists tells us? J. Manag. Inq. **20**(2), 114–117 (2011)
9. Financial Crisis Inquiry Comission: The Financial Crisis Inquiry Report. US Government Printing Office, Washington, DC (2011). https://www.gpo.gov/fdsys/pkg/GPO-FCIC/pdf/GPO-FCIC.pdf?utm_source=rss&utm_medium=rss. Accessed 12 Sept 2017
10. Russo, T.A., Katzel, A.J.: The 2008 Financial Crisis and Its Aftermath: Addressing the Next Debt Challenge. Group of Thirty, Washington, DC (2011). http://group30.org/images/uploads/publications/G30_2008FinancialCrisisAftermathDebtChallenge.pdf. Accessed 12 Sept 2017
11. De la Roisière, J. (ed.): The High Level Group on Financial Supervision in the EU Report. European Commission, Brussels (2009). http://ec.europa.eu/internal_market/finances/docs/de_larosiere_report_en.pdf. Accessed 12 Sept 2017
12. Calomiris, C.W., Haber, S.H.: Fragile by Design: The Political Origins of Banking Crises and Scarce Credit. Princeton University Press, Princeton (2014)
13. Sikorski, D.: The global financial crisis. In: Batten, J.A., Szilagyi, P.J. (eds.) The Impact of the Global Financial Crisis on Emerging Financial Markets, pp. 17–90. Emerald, Bingley (2011)
14. Ivashina, V., Scharfstein, D.: Bank lending during the financial crisis of 2008. J. Financ. Econ. **97**(3), 319–338 (2010)
15. Boisot, M., Canals, A.: Data, information and knowledge: have we got it right? J. Evol. Econ. **14**(1), 43–67 (2004)
16. Stiglitz, J.E.: The contributions of economics of information to twentieth century economics. Q. J. Econ. **140**, 1441–1478 (2000)
17. Tversky, A., Kahneman, D.: Judgment under uncertainty: heuristics and biases. In: Went, D., Vlek, C. (eds.) Utility, Probability and Human Decision Making, pp. 141–162. Springer, Cham (1975). https://doi.org/10.1007/978-94-010-1834-0_8
18. Williamson, O.E.: Markets and Hierarchies: Analysis and Antitrust Implications. Free Press, New York (1975)
19. Mas-Colell, A., Whinston, M.D., Green, J.R.: Microeconomic Theory. Oxford University Press, New York (1995)
20. Mizruchi, M.S.: The American corporate elite and the historical roots of the financial crisis of 2008. In: Lounsbury, M., Hirsch, P.M. (eds.) Markets on Trial: The Economic Sociology of the U.S. Financial Crisis: Part B, pp. 103–138. Emerald, Bingley (2010)
21. Blöchlinger, A., Leippold, M., Maire, B.: Are ratings the worst form of credit assessment apart from all the others? (2012). http://www.efaw012.org/papers/f2h1.pdf. Accessed 12 Sept 2017
22. Thelen, E., Smith, L.B.: A Dynamic System Approach to the Development of Cognition and Action. The MIT Press, Cambridge (1994)
23. Dretske, F.I.: Knowledge and the Flow of Information. CSLI Publications, Stanford (1981)

24. Ihrig, M., Child, J.: Max Boisot and the dynamic evolution of knowledge. In: Child, J., Ihrig, M. (eds.) Knowledge, Organization and Management: Building on the Work of Max Boisot. Oxford University Press, Oxford (2013)
25. Tirole, J.: Économie du bien commun. Presses Universitaires de France, Paris (2016)
26. Gibbons, R.: Game Theory for Applied Economists. Princeton University Press, Princeton (1992)
27. Rajan, R.G.: Has financial development made the world riskier? National Bureau of Economic Research, Working Paper No. 11728 (2005), http://www.nber.org/papers/w11728. Accessed 12 Nov 2017
28. Bullard, J., Nelly, C.J., Wheelock, D.C.: Systemic risk and the financial crisis: a primer. Fed. Reserve Bank St. Louis Rev. **91**, 403–417 (2009)
29. De la Dehesa, G.: Twelve Market and Government Failures Leading to 2008–2009 Financial Crisis. Group of Thirty, Washington, DC (2010). http://www.group30.org/images/PDF/ReportPDFs/OP80.pdf. Accessed 12 Sept 2017
30. Jackson, R.J., Jiang, W., Mitts, J.: How quickly do markets learn? Private information dissemination in a natural experiment. Columbia Business School Research Paper No. 15-6 (2016). https://ssrn.com/abstract=2544128. Accessed 12 Dec 2017

All the Homes: Zillow and the Operational Context of Data

Yanni Loukissas(✉)

Georgia Institute of Technology, Atlanta, GA 30308, USA
yanni.loukissas@lmc.gatech.edu

Abstract. Zillow, an online real estate marketplace that seeks to make information available about "all the homes" in the United States, tells us that "data want to be free". But a close analysis reveals that Zillow works to ground data: to put data into an operational context. I use the phrase "operational context" to denote a setting in which data—for real estate: current listings, tax assessments, and other digital property records—are meant to be fully understood. This paper examines the design of operational contexts for data as well as their cultural and political significance, using Zillow as a case. Zillow was founded in 2006, at the height of the housing bubble. Although practices with real estate have been under scrutiny ever since, the treatment of real estate data has not. This paper examines how Zillow operationalizes data for the housing market through a combination of analytical, discursive, and algorithmic devices. These dimensions of operational context are less about establishing the truth of data than a level of tractability for prospective buyers and sellers. The operational context for data is not derived from a neutral retrospective view (i.e. where the data come from). Rather, it is a matter of connecting data to an existing cultural system, defined by inherited practices, concepts and affordances that support specific use cases. Operational context can enable interpretation and action based on data, but it can also reify the power of a dominant culture.

Keywords: Data · Context · Housing

1 Introduction

Whether you are looking for a place to live, a good meal, upcoming events in your area, or a ride to work, a new economy of apps stands ready to serve, through interactions that can be carried out on any networked computing device. The data that enable these transactions are created at the local level, collected by civic institutions or crowd-sourced from the users themselves. However, beginning in the United States, they have been rapidly mobilized by data brokers [1, 2], who build and maintain national- or international-scale data infrastructures for profit. The boosters of this new "smart" lifestyle are ushering in a new kind of individualism tailored for affluent and tech-savvy urban dwellers. Yelp, an online directory of restaurants, shopping, and personal services, can make sure you "connect with great local businesses" [3]. Nextdoor, a place-based social media platform, invites you to "discover your neighborhood" [4]. Uber, a networked car service, equates "getting there" with personal

© Springer International Publishing AG, part of Springer Nature 2018
G. Chowdhury et al. (Eds.): iConference 2018, LNCS 10766, pp. 272–281, 2018.
https://doi.org/10.1007/978-3-319-78105-1_31

freedom: "your day belongs to you" [5]. Zillow, the real estate website, will help you "find your way home" [6]. These information systems promise not only access to data, but also the *operational context* to act on them.

By operational context, I mean the analytical, discursive, and algorithmic systems that connect abstract streams of zeros and ones—the bare-bones definition of contemporary digital data—to the concepts and resources that support their effective use. Analytical elements, such as a map, graph, or timeline, help users see meaningful patterns in data. Discursive elements offer you ready-made narratives with which to frame these data. Algorithmic elements enrich data, by generating new value from existing inputs. I call all these elements of context *operational* because they transform data from simple representations of the city—in terms of prices, distances, and rankings, for instance—into drivers for local and highly personalized behavior. Data, as well as the proper context to use them, are increasingly desirable for affluent consumers in cities across the United States and in many places abroad.

In this paper, I bring an interpretive approach to the question: what does it mean to put data in context? This entails a cultural analysis of the interfaces, discourses and processes that shape information systems, such as those described above. The question of context is of deep relevance for those who study and design systems that mediate relationships between people and data. Although the term *context* is widely used in both academic and popular writing, its relationship to data is not well understood [7]. I argue that scholars and designers of information should see context in operational terms. On the face of it, connecting data to an operational context is a pragmatic problem of supporting data use. However, establishing operational context is also a problem with important social and even political consequences: who can use data? how they can use data? and what they can use data for? Indeed, operational contexts establish the subject positions that users of data are expected to adopt. In the case of Zillow, which will be my main focus throughout the paper, you can be a prospective home buyer, renter, or seller; or you can be a relator. No homeowner or resident, according to Zillow, is outside of the market. As I will show, the potential operational contexts for data are always local and always multiple; they enable different forms of engagement and interpretation, with implications for what data appear to say and who they are made to speak to.

In order to elucidate this point, I examine the concrete problem of putting housing data into operational context. The values of homes in the United States, and other countries where property is on the market, have long been determined, in large part, by context. The perceived worth of a home is not determined solely based on its age, square footage, or the number of bedrooms and bathrooms it contains. Home values fluctuate based on comparable sales in the area, changes in the neighborhood itself, interest rates, and even the time of year. What counts as context when it comes to pricing a home? The seller and the buyer are the ultimate arbitrators of that. However, professionals—including realtors, lenders, researchers, developers, and, more recently, information technologists and designers—seek to influence perceptions of context in housing.

Today, context in housing is increasingly assessed through data. But although the housing crisis of 2007 raised important questions about the way we finance housing in the United States, it has not raised parallel, and necessary, questions about the way we use housing data. I intend to address some of those questions here, asking: how are housing data put in context, and how does this context then shape perception and action in public life? Zillow, a prominent example of information design applied to housing data, takes input from public and private sources, such as tax assessments and sales records, in nearly every municipality in the United States. It has used these resources to shape—as much as any other information system—the context in which non-experts understand housing through a combination of analytical, discursive, and algorithmic choices. Zillow demonstrates a range of ways for putting data in operational context and the stakes in doing so. In fact, the frames through which we examine housing data —specifically the operational context as defined herein—impact access to affordable housing on the market. For this reason, it is necessary to reconsider the settings through which we look at, talk about, and calculate with housing data. However, before I delve into the specific elements of operational context cultivated by Zillow, I would like to distinguish operational context from other models of context used in the study and design of information systems.

2   Data in Context

My operational perspective on context differs substantially from the dominant modes of accounting for context in information systems. Theorist Paul Dourish sums up the prevailing views in his article "What We Talk about When We Talk about Context" [8]. He specifically addresses definitions of context in ubiquitous computing, an area of research that explores the potential for computers to be distributed throughout the range of human environments. Dourish juxtaposes a "representational" model of context, pursued by the majority of researchers in computing, with an "interactional" model, grounded in phenomenological inquiry—an area of philosophical thought focused on understanding individual human experience.

Dourish explains that in the representational model, context "consists of a set of features of the environment surrounding generic activities" [8]. Representational context is easily delineable, stable, and separable from the subject itself. Meanwhile, in an interactional model, writes Dourish, "context isn't something that describes a setting. It is something that people do" [8]. As such, the context of any event or object can vary enormously depending on whom you talk to and when. Interactional context is relative, dynamic, spontaneous, and arising from activity. However, in order to avoid further confusion over the term, Dourish suggests that we leave aside the notion of context altogether. Instead, why not think about "practices" as the forming the settings for human interactions with computers?

However, the term context is not disappearing from use. As we seek more generalized solutions for managing human relationships with data, the concept will need further refinement. Representational context is certainly inadequate. But neither can context be summarized as something determined spontaneously, in an unselfconscious moment— what Dourish terms interactional context. Rather, I argue, context should be understood as a "cultural system" [9], composed of inherited practices, concepts, and affordances. Although an operational context for data does not determine the way data are used, it provides a setting that shapes the roles and forms of reasoning adopted by users.

The operational context of data is the setting in which participants are equipped with the resources and subject roles necessary to access, interpret, and take action on predetermined objects of attention. However, to put it that way is to suggest that operational context is something settled and uncontested. That is not the case. Contexts that operationalize data are always under construction. Moreover, disputes over operational context are common, sometimes with striking significance, as the case of Zillow reveals.

In a domain like housing, operational context can have the highest stakes. Thus, we must ask, what does operationalizing data enable? For operational context is not just an issue of knowledge, but of use. Scholars and designers of information systems should consider how operational contexts are rooted in normative cultural assumptions about what data can and should do.

Zillow operationalizes data through a context that combines analytical, discursive, and algorithmic elements. The analytical setting of Zillow is defined by the functionality of its map. Placing data on a map enables comparative reasoning, but only about things that have a geographic dimension. Zillow's main discursive setting is that of "public data." Data in the public realm are increasing accessible, but at what cost? Finally, Zillow uses an automated valuation model, the "Zestimate," to contextualize data. This algorithmic setting offers an interpretation of data, but through a set of opaque and speculative rules. These three dimensions of operational context are less about establishing the (capital "T") truth of data on property values than creating traction with a community of users. In the case of Zillow, the users are expected to be buyers, renters, or sellers engaged in the housing market. Kitchin has used the term "assemblage" to describe the many facets of such interactions with data [1]. But operational context is much more precise and structured than the term assemblage suggests.

3   The Case of Zillow

Zillow is a leading online real estate marketplace seeking to redefine the context in which we understand housing through access to and analysis of data. The name is a portmanteau created by combining the words zillion and pillow (where you rest your head). The company was founded in 2006 by Rascoff and Humphries with the goal of estimating the value of every home in the United States. It is not a licensed real estate firm, which would require that the company submit to licensing rules and regulations in every state that Zillow practices. However, it has strategically intervened into the real estate market in a way that has changed the work of realtors and other professionals in the industry. Zillow is not the first web company to tread into real estate. It is just one of the many data brokers that seek to produce surplus value from available data on housing [10]. Moreover, Zillow's way of operationalizing data is not original or unique. However, its recent purchase of Trulia—another major platform for home listings focused more on user experience than analytics—has consolidated Zillow's position as the market leader in the United States.

"Data want to be free," explains a representative of Zillow during a routine webinar. Setting data free sounds like a laudable, emancipatory goal. However, much of what Zillow does is to ground data in existing systems: analytical, discursive, and algorithmic. Indeed, Zillow offers important lessons on how to put data into operational context. But their approach should also give us pause, for they demonstrate that operational contexts are not neutral. They make data available to specific groups and support targeted actions. I will discuss three elements of Zillow's operational context. Each of these elements establishes relations that are important for working with data: access, interpretation, and action. These strategies for operationalizing data were not invented by Zillow. They are cultural forms that exist independently of the platform. However, Zillow assembles its operational context in a way that has significant implications for the way we understand housing data. For Zillow is invested in furthering the consumer culture of property, by creating a seemingly classical economic setting in which individuals are given access to information and encouraged to make rational choices based on their own self-interests. But the effects of this setting are damaging in ways that Zillow obscures. For although users may believe they are independent actors, the demand they place on the market works to increase the value of all property in an area, and limit the availability of affordable options. Zillow not only supports this system, but increases anxiety about its instability through the introduction of its Zestimate algorithm. In the sections that follow, I will unpack all three dimensions of Zillow's operational context, by explaining how they are constructed and by reflecting on their effects on data and housing.

3.1 Analytics

For Zillow, putting data in context starts with positioning it on a map. Zillow data—listings of properties for sale, for rent, or otherwise of interest (i.e., foreclosure or a category simply labelled "make me sell")—appear as colored dots outlined in white and placed on a grey background. The uniform setting for listings data is marked only by a faint network of streets, parks, bodies of water, and place names. Hovering over a dot brings up a price tag, including the number of bedrooms and bathrooms, the square footage, and a small thumbnail image. This intentionally generic setting—the same everywhere across the geography where Zillow lists properties—frames our understanding of housing data, not by showing the conditions of their production (representational context) or how they might have been used in the past (interactional context), but by suggesting what can be done with them today. The map is analytical and operational.

A venerable technology for visual reasoning, maps are recognizable and accessible to most of Zillow's users [11]. They offer a structure for making sense of data through spatial patterns; they show where the listings are located. This enables comparative readings of listings (i.e., "these listings are close to one another") as well as readings of each data point within a matrix of surrounding features (i.e., "these listings are close to a park"). These are operational relationships—they can serve as the basis for consumer decisions about real estate, a domain in which it is said that the three most important indicators of value are location, location, and location [12]. But the map does not merely register the locations of real estate in the real world [13]. Rather, the map produces a reading of location using a narrow set of visible relationships (i.e., to select streets, bucolic parks, and highly ranked schools). In this way, the map participates in the production of reality for real estate, by establishing or confirming conceptions about what conditions of location determine value [13, 14]. Thus, putting data in the operational context of the map is not a retrospective practice. The map does not reunite data with some preexisting setting. Zillow's map is operational because it stimulates actionable interpretations of location and its relationship to home value.

But maps do not "unfold" in isolation [15]. Zillow's map is framed by other media and modes of access to the underlying data. Above the map is a search bar, with filters for listing type, price, number of beds, and more that can be applied to further narrow the number of listings displayed. To the right of the map is a column of property images, mostly facades. Each is annotated with further details about an individual listing such as the number of days on Zillow, the name of the listing agent, and the type of sale (house for sale, pre-foreclosure, lot/land for sale). These images in turn can act as links to a full-screen view of an individual listing.

The additional elements of the Zillow interface serve to put the map itself in relief. They help users interpret the map as a collection of commodities: locations valued because of their potential to be bought and sold, not because of their historical significance as places or the significance of the people who live there. Thus, the analytical elements of context illuminate a number of things: which data points matter, the relationship between the points, the meaning of the space in between them, and the connection between data and any secondary media.

3.2   Discourse

Beyond the setting established by Zillow's map interface, the company offers a discursive component of operational context. It serves to establish and stabilize Zillow's use of data as a legitimate representation of the world of real estate. Among the most important discourses that Zillow invokes is that of *public data*. In a list of frequently asked questions on their website, Zillow explains *public information* (a related but more expansive term than *public data*) as the way and the reason it knows about your house:

> Zillow receives information about property sales from the municipal office responsible for recording real estate transactions in your area. The information we provide is public information, gathered from county records [6].

The term *public* tells us that Zillow's map is based on data from an open and authoritative source: the municipal office in "your area." This legitimizes both the data and Zillow's use of them. For although Zillow operates outside of the boundaries of any particular municipality (remember it is not licensed anywhere), it is making fair use of data created by and for the people. Moreover, invoking the public context of their data protects Zillow from requests by homeowners to have it removed from the site. Their reasoning: it is not private data. And although Zillow acknowledges that municipally created data may contain errors, the company takes no responsibility for them. After all, the data are not created by Zillow. It is up to homeowners to show proof of errors that might affect public perceptions of the value of their house. Ironically, all these assertions about Zillow's rights with respect to the data are wrapped in the language of public empowerment:

Our mission is to empower consumers with information and tools to make smart decisions about homes, real estate, and mortgages. For this reason, we do not remove public record property data from Zillow unless it is shown to be erroneous [6].

Beyond their use of public sources, Zillow also cultivates a perception of their map as a virtual public space in which data from private sources might be made broadly accessible. There are two ways this can happen: realtors can contribute their own listings—and pay a fee to have their profiles promoted in association with those listings —or owners can contribute "house facts" in order to improve the online image of their property. A former employee of Trulia explains, "if you are able to give people a real-time value of their home, they are going to check that value and ask: what can we do to update that value? The Zestimate is a powerful consumer engagement instrument" [16]. By making their database open to public reading as well as public writing, Zillow fashions itself as the "Wikipedia of housing": a democratic, free, and transparent context for sharing data publically [16].

In tension with the discourse of public data is that of the personal journey. "Find your way home" is the welcoming message on the Zillow front page. "You are in the driver's seat," we are told. The implication is that Zillow is a powerful vehicle that we can use in our travel towards homeownership. This second discourse positions the platform as a navigational aid in an individualized search for *home*—a term used as a synecdoche for personal comfort, security, and belonging—through a bewildering landscape of consumer options. While the space of data on Zillow is public, the journey through that space is private and the implication is that it should be guided by individualized interests, as opposed to the public good. The result is the creation of a public space in which everyone has access, but no one is equal. Everyone comes to the map with different resources for buying or selling and Zillow lets you know right where that places you. Thus, the discursive elements of context define the relationships between people and data: who owns it, manages it, or uses it, and who doesn't? and what stories about the nature of the data justify these attachments or exclusions?

The map, its media annotations, and an overarching discursive framing put Zillow's data in context, a context that isn't a reconstruction of the origins of data, but rather an operational setting that makes the data actionable. But the context marshaled by Zillow extends beyond these analytical and discursive elements. Zillow has been successful in large part because of an additional computational layer of operational context that it brings to the existing set of housing listings.

3.3 Algorithms

Zillow's "rules of real estate" establish the final dimension of operational context I will discuss [17]. The company not only accumulates data from a variety of sources but also extracts surplus value from those data—in the form of computationally generated predictions. Using the data that Zillow has assembled on sales and historic valuations of homes in a particular area, the company is able to produce estimated values for properties that are not currently on the market. This process of triangulating property values is called an automated valuation model. The results of Zillow's model, comically called "Zestimates," can be applied to nearly every home in the United States. Today, in 2017, a Zestimate is calculated for about 100 million homes nationwide using public data as well as data contributed by relators or homeowners. The physical characteristics of a home, such as its location, square footage, number of bedrooms and bathrooms, as well as past sale prices of the home and comparable homes nearby, are analyzed using proprietary valuation rules. Instead of relying on a single complex model of the entire United States market, Zillow relies on simpler, localized models (sometimes at the scale of a single street) to account for different market situations [17]. Moreover, their models are dynamic. Home values are discarded every night and built again in the morning using fresh data that incorporate changing conditions and new information from local sources.

Highlighting the operational context they bring to existing data, Rascoff and Humpharies, the founders of Zillow, argue that it is not their data, but the Zestimates they extract from those data that differentiates them from other online real estate sites. Indeed, Zillow claims it has a pulse on market conditions in local areas across the country, and, moreover, that it can make accurate predictions on where the market is headed in the near future. For Zillow, the future is just another discursive element to be marshaled in operationalizing housing data.

Such algorithmic elements of operational context are a form of what Janet Murray and other digital media scholars call procedurality, "the computer's defining ability to execute a series of rules" [18]. More specifically, the Zestimate might count as a form of what Ian Bogost terms "procedural rhetoric" [19]. To adapt this framework, we might say that the Zestimate makes claims about how property values operate. It claims that not only square footage or the number of bathrooms and bedrooms, but a host of other, sometimes specifically local characteristics are intertwined with value. But we shouldn't see this as simply a representational system, as in the case of the persuasive games that Bogost studies. Rather, Zillow is an operational part of the way that the housing market works today. Zillow's rules form a system that homeowners can interact with by updating their home facts or simply checking their Zestimate regularly.

The Zestimate is an "algorithmic system," an arrangement code and people [20]. Understanding such systems means examining not only the technical details, but also the cultural practices of its creators and users. Such efforts are further complicated by the fact that the Zesimate, like many commercial algorithms, is a closely guarded secret and requires insider knowledge to be decoded. However, we can learn much from simply looking at how the Zestimate is discursively framed.

Like the map, the Zestimate has its own discursive elements. Buyers and sellers are encouraged to put the Zestimate itself into context using feelings, facts, comps, pop psychology, and the general economic climate. After all, Zestimates may be wrong; the company acknowledges that they are within 5% of the actual value (sale price) of the home just half of the time. Ultimately it may not matter, if they lure you into a conversation with realtors and other professionals who pay Zillow to stay in business.

Indeed, Zillow doesn't depend on the accuracy of its Zestimates to make money. It thrives on subscriptions from realtors and other related professionals. This is an advertising model of revenue, not unlike those used by other web platforms that host social media, such as Facebook and Twitter. From an operational perspective, the algorithm is good enough if it catalyzes a certain kind of social relation between subscribing real estate professions and potential clients. Zillow is concerned less about the truth of data than its tractability: the holding power it exerts on users.

4 Conclusion

The purpose of this paper has been to make the possible contexts for data more visible. But this requires a clear understanding of what context can mean. The case of Zillow demonstrates that the context for data need not be simply representational: an account of the setting in which the data were made. Nor is context exclusively interactional: the spontaneous result of an engagement with data. Rather, putting data in context can be operational: a matter of connecting data to an existing cultural system, defined by a combination of practices, concepts, and affordances that are meant to support data's use. Through analytical, discursive, and algorithmic devices, Zillow has constructed a captivating operational context that supports the use of data to buy, rent, or sell housing. But the context that Zillow has assembled also reifies dominant and deeply problematic relationships inherent to our market-based culture of property.

While technologists and designers at Zillow are working to establish operational contexts in which consumers might make the best personal choices based on housing data, others, community organizers for instance, may seek to reveal another operational context: one that calls the market into question. For example, by: 1. using a timeline as the main analytical setting, to illuminate the chaotic history of market values; 2. invoking the discourse of gentrification, to call attention to the damage caused by rapid market change; and 3. calling for regulatory rules rather than only the rules of the market to set home values. Conflicting contexts enable different ways of imagining and enacting the future of housing through data. They both implicitly accept that data are now a necessary tool for addressing the problem of housing, which has reached a scale that would be difficult to contemplate otherwise. Indeed, the operational context of housing data has become a site of contestation, which will determine how housing evolves and for whose benefit.

Although this paper is illustrated by examples from the domain of housing, where the stakes for accessibility, interpretation, and action are high, there are many other domains from which important examples of operational context might be drawn: health, crime, and climate change, to name a few. In any of these areas, practitioners who design for information do not act autonomously. Rather, they must connect with existing communities of use to support data-based action. For contexts are not merely representative or interactional; they are deeply rooted in operational cultural systems.

References

1. Kitchin, R., Lauriault, T.P.: Towards critical data studies: charting and unpacking data assemblages and their work. Social Science Research Network, Rochester (2014)
2. Small, B.: FTC report examines data brokers. Federal Trade Commission (2014)
3. Yelp Homepage. https://www.yelp.com. Accessed 15 Dec 2017
4. Nextdoor Homepage. https://nextdoor.com. Accessed 15 Dec 2017
5. Uber Homepage. https://uber.com. Accessed 15 Dec 2017
6. Zillow Homepage. https://www.zillow.com. Accessed 15 Dec 2017
7. Seaver, N.: The nice thing about context is that everyone has it. Media Cult. Soc. **37**(7), 1101–1109 (2015)

8. Dourish, P.: What we talk about when we talk about context. Pers. Ubiquit. Comput. **8**(1), 11–30 (2004)
9. Geertz, C.: The Interpretation of Cultures: Selected Essays. Basic Books, New York (1973)
10. Federal Trade Commission: Data Brokers: A Call for Transparency and Accountability. Government of the United States (2014)
11. Crampton, J.W.: Mapping: A Critical Introduction to Cartography and GIS. Wiley, Hoboken (2011)
12. Pearson, D.: Location, location, location. The New York Times (2009). http://www.nytimes.com/2009/06/28/magazine/28FOB-onlanguage-t.html. Accessed 13 Nov 2017
13. Robinson, A.H.: The Look of Maps. University of Wisconsin Press, Madison (1952)
14. Baudrillard, J.: Simulations and Simulacra. Sheila Glaser (trans). University of Michigan Press, Ann Arbor (1984)
15. Kitchin, R., Gleeson, J., Dodge, M.: Unfolding mapping practices: a new epistemology for cartography. Trans. Inst. Br. Geogr. **3**(3), 480–496 (2013)
16. From an interview by the author (2016)
17. Rascoff, S., Humphries, S.: Zillow Talk: Rewriting the Rules of Real Estate. Grand Central Publishing, New York (2015)
18. Murray, J.: Hamlet on the Holodeck. MIT Press, Cambridge (1998)
19. Bogost, I.: Persuasive Games: The Expressive Power of Videogames. MIT Press, Cambridge (2007)
20. Seaver, N.: Algorithms as culture: some tactics for the ethnography of algorithmic systems. Big Data Soc. **4**(2) (2017)

The Development of an Undergraduate Data Curriculum: A Model for Maximizing Curricular Partnerships and Opportunities

Angela P. Murillo(✉) and Kyle M. L. Jones

Indiana University – Purdue University Indianapolis,
Indianapolis, IN 46202, USA
apmurill@iu.edu, kmlj@iupui.edu

Abstract. The article provides the motivations and foundations for creating an interdisciplinary program between a Library and Information Science department and a Human-Centered Computing department. The program focuses on data studies and data science concepts, issues, and skill sets. In the paper, we analyze trends in Library and Information Science curricula, the emergence of data-related Library and Information Science curricula, and interdisciplinary data-related curricula. Then, we describe the development of the undergraduate data curriculum and provide the institutional context; discuss collaboration and resource optimization; provide justifications and workforce alignment; and detail the minor, major, and graduate opportunities. Finally, we argue that the proposed program holds the potential to model interdisciplinary, holistic data-centered curriculum development by complimenting Library and Information Science traditions (e.g., information organization, access, and ethics) with scholarly work in data science, specifically data visualization and analytics. There is a significant opportunity for Library and Information Science to add value to data science and analytics curricula, and vice versa.

Keywords: Curriculum · Undergraduate education · Data studies
Data science · Data analytics · Library and Information Science
iSchool

1 Introduction

Our data-intensive world requires individuals to build data-specific skill sets to participate in the workforce and society. In recent years, we have seen the value of data skills increase in academia, business, and government. Additionally, we have seen the emergence of data-focused programs to provide students the skills needed to succeed in nearly all domains and disciplines. The current situation for employers is dire with an estimated dearth of nearly 200,000 laborers needed with "deep analytical skills" and 1.5 million employees who lack the knowledge to make effective decisions using data-driven insights [1].

As a discipline, Library and Information Science (LIS) has developed theories, practical frameworks, and critical perspectives centered around data. And while modern LIS curricula have largely concentrated on graduate education, there is

© Springer International Publishing AG, part of Springer Nature 2018
G. Chowdhury et al. (Eds.): iConference 2018, LNCS 10766, pp. 282–291, 2018.
https://doi.org/10.1007/978-3-319-78105-1_32

potential to translate data-focused curricula for the education of undergraduate students. Data organization and representation, data curation and management, and data policy and ethics are all perspectives and skill sets that would benefit undergraduates. With these opportunities in mind, the Department of Library and Information Science (DLIS) at Indiana University–Purdue University Indianapolis (IUPUI), began its Data Studies Minor program and developed the Applied Data and Information Science (ADIS) undergraduate major in 2017.

The department's motivation was to provide students across the campus access to a data-focused curriculum that would provide students skills necessary to enter the data workforce and analyze data practices. This minor and major provides students the opportunity to learn how to manage data, curate data, as well as understand the policy and governance issues associated with data work—all things the workforce increasingly needs as it seeks to maximize value from big and small data practices alike. Perhaps more importantly, it provides students a set of skills and critical perspectives that are valuable for participating in our information society. As one of three interdisciplinary departments in the School of Informatics and Computing (SoIC), DLIS was well positioned to accomplish these goals.

For this paper, we will use the term "data-focused" to discuss in general data-related curricula. Additionally, we will use the term "data studies" to discuss the original vision for the data studies minor. Data Studies "combines data acquisition, management, analysis, and use of data…with an understanding of the nature of data and its broader implications for society" [2]. Lastly, we will use the term "data science" to described curriculum "more associated with data analytics and computer science which implies a specific set of content that is more technical in nature" [2].

Moving forward, we analyze current LIS curricula and explore data-focused curricula. Next, we describe the development of the undergraduate minor and major program developed at IUPUI, and we cover the institutional and labor contexts that informed the program development. Finally, we argue that the proposed program holds the potential to model interdisciplinary, holistic curriculum development at the undergraduate level.

2 Undergraduate Curricula

2.1 Trends in Library and Information Science

Library and Information Science (LIS) educators have historically focused on graduate education; however, in recent years we are seeing a resurgence of undergraduate curriculum development with a focus on preparing students for careers in information industries. Modern undergraduate program development began in the 1990s. Florida State University's undergraduate program, for instance, began in 1996 with 91 students and by 2002 had over 600 enrollments. Undergraduate enrollment at Syracuse and Rutgers saw similar upward enrollment trends from the late 1990s to the early 2000s [3]. Non-United States undergraduate LIS programs include Australia [4], Latin America and the Caribbean [5], and Europe where there are more undergraduate programs available than graduate programs [6].

In the early 1990s, the demand for students who understood emerging information and communication technologies in a variety of contexts motivated many institutions to create undergraduate programs. For example, the Rutgers and University of Washington undergraduate programs focused on informatics, the University of Wisconsin-Milwaukee and Emporia State program focused on information resources, and the Pittsburgh, SUNY, and Southern Mississippi programs focused on information science [3]. The LIS community continued to create new undergraduate programs throughout the 2000s with the University of North Carolina in 2003 [7] and University of Texas-Austin, which created a minor in 2005 [8]. All of this activity points towards changes in the scope of LIS education outside of graduate programs, indicating that there is a path for curricular influence by LIS educators in undergraduate programs when new opportunities emerge.

2.2   The Emergence of Library and Information Science Data Curricula

Outside of creating undergraduate programs, LIS educators have created certificate programs and specializations to consider the many facets of data labor. From 2006–2010, UNC-Chapel Hill, the University of Illinois at Urbana Champaign, University of Arizona, and the University of Michigan at Ann Arbor developed Digital Curation Education certificate programs [9, 10]. These programs focus on skills needed for digital or data curation including digital presentation, curation, records management, digital collections, and data manipulation. Other universities developed similar programs with specific subject foci, including eScience at Syracuse and Cultural Heritage at Pratt Institute [9].

The LIS community has seen a rise in curriculum development with other data related or technology related skill sets, as well as domain-specific skill sets. These included addressing the curriculum gap between LIS education and intelligence analysis. As described in Jin and Bouthillier [11] and Wu [12], while LIS programs provide education in computer skills for information collections, geographic information systems, and information security, there is a lack of programming in science and technology intelligence. Additionally, there have been several efforts to develop LIS curriculum and eScience and/or scientific data management; however while this curriculum is in place to educate students and there is demand for experts, there is still yet to be a unified title for the scientific data specialization [13]. Domain science educators have indicated that the majority of the work in data literacy has focused on graduate students, while there is a real need for similar data literacy instruction to include undergraduate students [14].

As described above, LIS curricula already include courses that are specific for data professionals. In a study by Varvel Jr. et al. (2012) 475 courses in 158 programs at 55 schools contained at least some aspects of data education [15]. These courses included data-centric courses related to data curation, data management, or data science topics, data inclusive courses related to e-science or e-research, digital courses including digital libraries, collections, and preservation; they also included traditional LIS courses, which introduced important topics to be developed further in data inclusive or data-centric courses [15]. There has been a steady growth in data related curriculum in LIS schools to educate the future data workforce and to provide students the skills needed to work in data-intensive environments. Tonta provides an overview of the major developments in LIS education from 1887–1963 (the first period), 1994–1993 (the second period), and 1994-the present (the third period). As described by Tonta, the third period is shifting curriculum to information science, information systems, technologies, as well as overlapping some with computer science in certain topics such as information retrieval, social informatics, and infometrics [16]. All of this activity points towards an increasing growth of data related curricula in LIS graduate programs.

2.3 Interdisciplinary Opportunities

While the LIS community has been developing data-focused curricula, and LIS research has become interdisciplinary, there has also been a significant development in data science undergraduate curricula. Studies have analyzed the differences between undergraduate data analytics programs and undergraduate data studies programs with data science programs. Data science often requires more mathematical and programming courses than data analytics and data studies programs. Data analytics programs emphasize the use of case studies and evaluations of tools, while data science programs emphasize the implementation of tools, techniques, and visualization strategies [17]. There has also been a history of establishing undergraduate data science programs through interdisciplinary collaborations, resulting in joins of curricula from multiple disciplines. As shown in Anderson, 2014, three undergraduate programs often inform interdisciplinary efforts in data science: (1) computer science and mathematics, (2) computer science, business informatics, and statistics, and (3) computer science, mathematics, and economics [18]. The study of data science programs has also indicated that data science mirrors the interdisciplinary nature of data, and that curricula should balance theory and concepts, tools and techniques, and should include contributions from computer science, artificial intelligence, mathematics, statistics, data mining, communication, and discussion of social and ethical issues [19]. Other studies indicate the need to include specific skill sets including data visualization, data manipulation/data wrangling, computational statistics, and machine learning in data science curricula [20]. Lastly, the six main subject areas of data science are data description and curation, mathematical foundations, computational thinking, statistical thinking, data modeling, and communication, reproducibility, and ethics [21].

While LIS has traditionally taught subjects important to data science curriculum including data description, curation, representation, management, policy, and ethics —among other things—certain topics are more typically taught in other departments such as data manipulation, visualization, and analytics. With this in mind, DLIS along with DHCC at IUPUI can provide the full spectrum of data-related curriculum, providing SoIC the unique opportunity to create a data-focused curriculum for undergraduates.

3 Developing an Undergraduate Data Curriculum

3.1 Institutional Context

The IUPUI Department of Library and Information Science (DLIS) is within the School of Informatics and Computing (SoIC), which also contains the Human-Centered Computing (DHCC) and BioHealth Informatics departments (DBHI) [22]. SoIC's mission is to excel in education, research, and civic engagement in the field of informatics, an integrative discipline which advances knowledge in: (1) computing, information, and media technologies, (2) the implication those technologies have for individuals and society; and, (3) their application to any field of study adapting to the challenges of the Information Age and fosters a broad and interdisciplinary view [23]. It is with this mission in mind DLIS partnered with DHCC to create the programs described below.

3.2 Disciplinary Collaborations and Resource Optimization

DLIS saw an opportunity to develop a complete undergraduate curriculum as the structure of SoIC provided the unique opportunity for DLIS to leverage already existing resources and make strategic partnerships with research and teaching faculty in DHCC. The collaboration between DLIS and DHCC focused on providing a holistic approach to a data-focused curriculum. Together, they proposed a major with two specializations. The program is titled Applied Data and Information Science (ADIS), and its specializations include Applied Data Science (ADS) and Information Science (IS). The departments worked together incorporating courses from both departments to create the major curriculum. Additionally, the departments worked together to update already existing courses for the major and created new courses as necessary.

The DHCC faculty provides courses in informatics, visualization, cloud computing, and data analytics and DLIS faculty provides courses in data representation, organization, preservation, curation, policy and ethics, and socio-technical analysis. Since DLIS and HCC have collaborated on this program together, we are financially benefiting each other but not competing with each other. At SoIC, the instructor of record's home department receives the funds from the courses taught. Additionally, technology and staff resources are shared at SoIC, providing shared support for the program regardless of departmental affiliation.

3.3 Justifications and Workforce Alignment

Data Labor

Data labor skill sets have been well-documented in data science and data lifecycle workflows such as the OSEMN taxonomy of data science which provides the types of data skills needed by data scientists, including obtaining data from multiple sources, scrubbing data, exploring data using visualization techniques, modeling data, and interpreting data [24]. Additionally, the DataONE lifecycle has provided an understanding of the data lifecycle, as well as the various skills needed for successful management, curation, and preservation of data. These skill sets include creating data plans, collecting data, assuring the quality of data, describing data, understanding data preservation, discovering data, integrating data from multiple data sources, and lastly understanding various data analysis techniques [25]. While each of these models describes the skill sets needed for data labor and the activities involved in data labor, there is some overlap. Additionally, nearly every field needs these skill sets, and the proposed program provides students a unique opportunity by ensuring that students can gain experience in the entire spectrum of data labor skill sets.

Indianapolis and Indiana

This new program is serving the needs of the state and community. As a public university, our role is to provide education that is beneficial to our community. Indiana and Indianapolis have been working to promote the technology industry, and by training students in data, we are assisting in developing a data-savvy workforce for Indiana.

Trends related to high-tech labor highlight Indiana and Indianapolis as a thriving market, a standout in fact when compared to other so-called "flyover" regions of the country [26]. According to Moody's data, as analyzed by the Brookings Institute, the Indianapolis area created around 5,000 high-tech jobs between 2013 and 2015, which marked a 13.9% increase and even beat San Francisco's growth rate [27]. In July 2016, former governor Mike Pence pledged a total of $1 billion "to advance innovation and entrepreneurship in Indiana," out of which the governor's office directed $300 million to the 21 Fund for research and technology and $100 million to "further advance innovation and entrepreneurship education" [28]. Even after a transition in the governor's office, the funding commitments remain, and the state is on track to attract innovative talent and educate the next leaders in information technology. Investments by the state have started to pay off. According to the Central Indiana Corporate Partnership report, "since 2007, 12 tech community companies in Central Indiana have either been acquired or have gone public, generating $4.5 billion in market value and creating more than 3,700 Indiana jobs, demonstrating the momentum of the tech sector and the continued need for top talent" [29]. Indiana higher education institutions, including IUPUI, contribute to the labor workforce of these companies and the economic programs the state deeply supports.

3.4   The Minor

The initial program development began with the creation of a 15 credit hour Data Studies minor [30]. The minor was created to provide a humanistic approach to data—both big and small—and to train students on data management and curation, and to introduce students to data analysis, manipulation, organization and representation, and policy. The minor was created to make students more marketable in any field. We created several new undergraduate courses for this minor and pulled from already existing LIS areas of study, including: data organization and representation, data curation and management, and data policy and governance. The foundational course, Foundations in Data Studies, provides students an overview of the many topics of the minor and prepares the students for the program. From this program, students will be able to apply principles of representation and organization, understand and apply data curation processes, and develop data policy. Additionally, a minor focused on applied data science was created and focuses on data analytics and technical aspects of working with data [31]. These minors are currently available to all students at IUPUI and stand alone as complimentary curricular additions to any student's major.

3.5 The Major

After developing the Data Studies minor, DLIS and DHCC together proposed the 120-credit hour ADIS undergraduate major. This major provides students an additional avenue to learn more extensive data skill sets, as well as prepare them for graduate studies in data-focused or LIS programs if they so choose. ADIS students earn a bachelor of science degree with one of two specializations: Applied Data Science (ADS) and Information Science (IS). The purpose of having these two specializations is to encompass the entire spectrum of data labor skill sets. The ADS specialization focuses on aspects of data labor involved with data analysis, visualization, and the more technical aspects of data labor, which is a good fit for students comfortable in mathematics and computing. The IS specialization focuses on data curation, organization, and management, which is a good fit for students who are less comfortable in mathematics, but still interested in learning the technical skills needed to work with data. All students have to take courses in the other specialty. For example, all ADS students will take data curation and all IS students will take data visualization, as well as policy and ethics courses to provide them holistic knowledge of data skills.

Additionally, students in both specializations take courses regarding societal implications of data labor including courses related to ethics, policy, surveillance, and privacy. Furthermore, we are creating a wide variety of elective courses for students including courses focused on specific types of data (business data, scientific data, social science data), as well as specific relevant topics (data and society, data archives, data of social media). These courses will help provide students a more refined study of data labor of interest to them or their future employment. Students will also be involved in internships to provide them real-world experience and will have a capstone experience as they complete their studies.

3.6 Graduate Opportunities

The program holds the excellent potential to bridge students into graduate programs at IUPUI, especially within SoIC. The workforce data supports our argument that ADIS students will be employable with respectable salaries, but we do not deny that the same data also shows even greater potential to make marked salary jumps if ADIS students pursue a graduate degree. Should students seek a master or doctoral-level degree, a background in ADIS from either proposed specialization will surely benefit students. SoIC currently offers the following graduate degree options that align with the ADIS curriculum, many of which provide flexible learning arrangements:

- Library and Information Science (M.L.S.)
- Bioinformatics (M.S. and Ph.D.)

- Applied Data Science (M.S.)
- Sports Analytics (M.S.)
- Data Science (Ph.D.)

Students coming from a health background who pursue a minor in ADIS will also be more prepared for these SoIC programs:

- Bioinformatics (M.S.)
- Health Informatics (M.S.)
- Health/Biomedical Informatics (Ph.D.)

All of the above programs require a statistical foundation, technical skill sets, and sensitivity to the social, legal, and ethical implications related to implementing data-driven technologies and building socio-technical infrastructures—all of which ADIS provides.

Given how the proposed ADIS program will prepare students to pursue related graduate degrees, there existed an excellent opportunity to develop the program into a 4 + 1 model (four years to earn a bachelor degree, one year to earn a master degree). We developed two 4 + 1 options for students to enter into the Applied Data Science or Library and Information Science SoIC master programs. That said, we are currently pursuing opportunities to work with other departments within and outside of SoIC to co-develop more 4 + 1 degree options. The creation of this undergraduate program completed the educational pipeline into SoIC's master and doctoral-level programs focused on data, as well as into the master of library science program.

4 Conclusion

Library and Information Science programs are already well-established in educating in specific areas of data labor skill sets, including data curation, preservations, representation, organization, and research data management. While these skill sets do not encompass the entire spectrum of data labor, they do encompass a rather substantive portion. With this in mind, the Department of Library and Information Science (DLIS) at IUPUI was in the unique and promising position to collaborate with the Department of Human-Centered Computing (DHCC) to create a data program that encompasses the majority of data skills needed in today's data-intensive world.

With the ever-changing and transforming world of technology and data, we envision these types of curricular collaborations to become more relevant and necessary to ensure that our students have the education and skills they need to enter the emerging data-driven workforce. As discussed, the LIS community already has a well-established history of teaching data and information literacy-related courses and the expertise in specific data topics. However, with other important data topics such as data analytics, data mining, and visualization; it is sensible to partner with related disciplines. We envision our model for program development as an innovative and inspiring way to conceptualize LIS undergraduate education.

References

1. Brown, M.S.: What analytics talent shortage? How to get and keep the talent you need. Forbes, 27 June 2016. https://www.forbes.com/sites/metabrown/2016/06/27/what-analytics-talent-shortage-how-to-get-and-keep-the-talent-you-need/. Accessed 18 Sept 2017
2. UNC Chapel Hill Faculty Working Group on Data Studies Curriculum: Developing data-literate students acquiring, managing, analyzing, and using data in societal context. Report and Recommendations (2014). http://innovate.unc.edu/wp-content/uploads/2016/10/Data-Studies.pdf
3. McInerney, C., Delay, A., Vandergrift, K.E.: Broadening our reach: LIS education for undergraduates. Am. Libr. **33**(2), 40–43 (2002). https://www.jstor.org/stable/25646224?seq=1#page_scan_tab_contents
4. Sanders, R.: Current demand and future need for undergraduate LIS education. Aust. Libr. J. **57**(2), 102–127 (2008)
5. Gallardo, A.R.: Library education in Latin America and the Caribbean. New Libr. World **108** (1/2), 40–54 (2007)
6. Borrego, A.: Library and information education in Europe: an overview. BiD: Textos universitaris de biblioteconomia i documentació 35 (2015)
7. UNC Bachelor of Science in Information Science (BSIS). https://sils.unc.edu/programs/undergraduate/bsis. Accessed 1 Sept 2017
8. Roy, L., Simmons, R.N.: Tradition and transition: the journey of an iSchool deep in the heart of Texas. J. Libr. Inf. Technol. **37**(1), 3–8 (2017)
9. Fulton, B., Botticelli, P., Bradley, J.: DigIn: a hands-on approach to a digital curation curriculum for professional development. J. Educ. Libr. Inf. Sci. **52**(2), 95–109 (2011)
10. Murillo, A.P., Barnes, H.L., Poole, A.H., Uckum, T.: Digital curation education programs in the United States. In: DCC 7th International Digital Curation Centre Conference, Bristol, England (2011)
11. Jin, T., Bouthillier, F.: The integration of intelligence analysis into LIS education. J. Educ. Libr. Inf. Sci. **53**(2), 130–148 (2012)
12. Wu, Y.: A preliminary study on the curriculum overlap and gap between LIS education and intelligence education. J. Educ. Libr. Inf. Sci. **54**(4), 270–285 (2013)
13. Li, S., Xiaozhe, Z., Wenming, X., Weining, G.: The cultivation of scientific data specialists: development of LIS education oriented to e-science service requirements. Libr. Hi Tech **31** (4), 700–724 (2013)
14. Reisner, B.A., Vaughan, K.T.L., Shorish, Y.L.: Making data management accessible in the undergraduate chemistry curriculum. J. Chem. Educ. **91**, 1943–1946 (2014)
15. Varvel Jr., V.E., Bammeril, E.J., Palmer, C.L.: Education for data professionals: a study of current courses and programs. In: Proceedings of iConference 2012, pp. 527–529. ACM, Toronto (2012)
16. Tonta, Y.: Developments in education for information: will "data" trigger the next wave of curriculum in LIS schools? Pak. J. Inf. Manag. Libr. **17**, 2–4 (2016)
17. Aasheim, C.L., Williams, S., Rutner, P., Gardiner, A.: Data analytics vs. data science: a study of similarities and differences in undergraduate programs based on course descriptions. J. Inf. Syst. Educ. **26**(2), 103–115 (2015)
18. Anderson, P., McGoufee, J., Uminsky, D.: Data science as an undergraduate degree. In: Proceedings of SIGCSE 2014, pp. 705–706. ACM, Atlanta (2014)
19. Anderson, P., Bowring, J., McCauley, R., Pothering, G., Starr, C.: An undergraduate degree in data science: curriculum and a decade of implementation experience. In Proceedings of SIGCSE 2014, pp. 145–150. ACM, Atlanta (2014)

20. Baumer, B.: A data science course for undergraduates: thinking with data. Am. Stat. **69**(4), 334–342 (2015)
21. De Veaux, R.D., Agarwal, M., Averett, M., Baumer, B.S., Bray, A., Bressoud, T.C., Bryant, L., Cheng, L.Z., Francis, A., Gould, R., Kim, A.Y., Kretchmar, M., Lu, Q., Moskol, A., Nolan, D., Roberto, R., Raleigh, S., Sethi, R.J., Sondjaja, M., Tiruviluamala, N., Uhlig, P.X., Washington, T.M., Wesley, C.L., White, D., Ye, P.: Curriculum guidelines for undergraduate programs in data science. Ann. Rev. Stat. Appl. **4**, 15–30 (2017)
22. Indiana University – Purdue University Indianapolis, School of Informatics and Computing Departments. https://soic.iupui.edu/departments/. Accessed 2 Sept 2017
23. Indiana University – Purdue University Indianapolis, School of Informatics and Computing Mission. https://soic.iupui.edu/about/mission/. Accessed 2 Sept 2017
24. Dataists: A Taxonomy of Data Science. http://www.dataists.com/tag/osemn/. Accessed 12 Sept 2017
25. DataONE: The Data Life Cycle. https://www.dataone.org/data-life-cycle. Accessed 12 Sept 2017
26. Muro, M.: Tech jobs are spreading into 'Flyover Country'. Wall Str. J. (2016). https://blogs.wsj.com/experts/2016/09/18/tech-jobs-are-spreading-into-flyover-country/
27. Muro, M., Liu S.: Tech in metros: the strong are getting stronger. Brookings, 8 March 2017. https://www.brookings.edu/blog/the-avenue/2017/03/08/tech-in-metros-the-strong-are-getting-stronger/
28. Indiana Economic Development Commission: Governor Pence announces plan to invest $1 billion in Hoosier innovation and entrepreneurship, 14 July 2016. http://www.in.gov/activecalendar/EventList.aspx?fromdate=1/1/2016&todate=12/31/2016&display=Month&type=public&eventidn=249728&view=EventDetails&information_id=247868&print=print
29. Central Indiana Corporate Partnership: TechPoint workforce report: demand for computer-related jobs grows in Central Indiana as tech sector gains momentum, 14 March 2014. https://www.cicpindiana.com/techpoint-workforce-report-demand-computer-related-jobs-grows-central-indiana-tech-sector-gains-momentum/
30. Indiana University – Purdue University Indianapolis, School of Informatics and Computing, Data Studies Minor. https://soic.iupui.edu/undergraduate/degrees/data-studies-minor/. Accessed 2 Sept 2017
31. Indiana University – Purdue University Indianapolis, School of Informatics and Computing, Applied Data Science Minor. https://soic.iupui.edu/undergraduate/degrees/data-science-minor/. Accessed 2 Dec 2017

Data Visualization Revisited

Kai A. Olsen[1,2], James G. Williams[3],
and Michael B. Spring[3(✉)]

[1] Molde University College, Molde, Norway
[2] Department of Informatics, University of Bergen, Bergen, Norway
[3] School of Computing and Information,
University of Pittsburgh, Pittsburgh, USA
spring@pitt.edu

Abstract. More than 25 years ago we developed a data visualization system called Vibe. During this same period we developed a system for collaborative authoring – CASCADE – that made heavy use of visualization. These were but a few of many efforts at that time to develop new methods for understanding data, stimulated by improved hardware - faster CPUs, more memory and high resolution graphical displays that made it possible to perform advanced visualization on ordinary PCs. In this paper we revisit some of these efforts and then discuss where visualization is today. We briefly examine big data and scientific visualization where many of the issues we explored 25 years ago are being revisited. Our focus however is on general visualization. What we find is that advanced visualization systems for data presentations have not come into general use. We explore some of the reasons this may be the case.

Keywords: Visualization · Systems · Data analysis

1 Introduction

Through the 80's and 90's, Vibe, CASCADE, and many other systems, introduced novel and advanced visualization techniques for what we would call general visualizations, i.e., where the idea is to present the data in meaningful ways. Our objective was to extend the traditional range of visualization techniques beyond such techniques as time series, bar code diagrams, pie charts, etc., i.e., visualization methods that have been here for hundreds of years.

While our focus is on general visualization techniques we see that scientific visualization and visualization of c data continue to receive attention [1]. We are in a highly data-driven environment, in which data are acquired on a continuous basis for a variety of purposes. The ability to make accurate and timely decisions based on available data is crucial for business decisions, medical treatments, national security, crime resolution, disaster management and many other areas. The traditional statistical and visualization techniques used to extract knowledge from these large and complex datasets have not developed significantly.

Visualization has proven effective not only for presenting essential information in vast amounts of data but also for driving complex analyses. Big data exploration/analytics and

G. Chowdhury et al. (Eds.): iConference 2018, LNCS 10766, pp. 292–302, 2018.
https://doi.org/10.1007/978-3-319-78105-1_33

presentation create new research issues for the computer graphics and visualization community. Big data characteristics such as volume, velocity, variety, value and veracity require quick decisions for implementation, as the information can lose value very fast. Such fast data expansion will result in challenges related to a human's ability to manage the data, extract information and gain knowledge from it using traditional statistical and visualization methods. Current activity in the field of Big data visualization is focused on the invention of tools that allow a person to produce quick and effective results working with large amounts of data. Big data related visualization challenges are based on an understanding of human perception and the correlation between Augmented Reality and Virtual Reality that are suitable for the perception capabilities of humans. To visualize Big data, feature extraction and geometric modeling can be implemented. A visual representation is more likely to be accepted by a human in comparison with unstructured textual information or statistics. Likewise, an analyst is likely to find relationships in data using advanced visualization tools such as Vibe that would not be discovered otherwise.

While scientific visualization, geo-coded visualization and big data may provide us with many new and advanced visualization techniques, which may be introduced into mainstream data visualization sometime in the future, we shall concentrate here on general visualization. Here the objective of visualization is to present the data to the reader. The idea is to show the information that may be hidden in the data in a way such that the reader gets an immediate understanding. While the traditional visualizations are a part of most reader's vocabulary, the aim of many of the visualization methods and their prototypes developed in the early nineties, such as Vibe and CASCADE, was to extend this vocabulary with more advanced methods.

2 General Data Visualization – The Vibe System

Vibe is a multidimensional visualization system [2, 3]. With Vibe the users define POIs (points of interest). These work similar to axes in a two dimensional visualization, however, in a Vibe display one could have many POIs. Data objects are attracted to POIs. If an object has a value on only one POI a symbol for the object will be placed on top of the POI. If it has an equal value for two POIs it will be placed between these, etc.

Figure 1 shows a VIBE diagram with four POIs, each shown as a small circle. One data object has only values on POI A, and the icon representing this object is placed on top of A. We see two objects that have a value on POIs A and B, one with a stronger value on A than B, and another with a stronger value on B and A. The objects in the middle have a value on all POIs. Vibe allows the user to reposition the POIs and to block the influence from one or more POIs. The system can then visualize how the data objects move by drawing a line from the former to the new position. The user can click on any object and will then get additional information on this data object. There are functions for zooming in and out and to use color, for example to distinguish different types of data objects.

The user interface is shown in Fig. 2. In the example shown here the POIs are data types that characterize countries, such as life expectancy, literacy and infant mortality. Each is offered in two variations, one that attracts higher than average values, and one

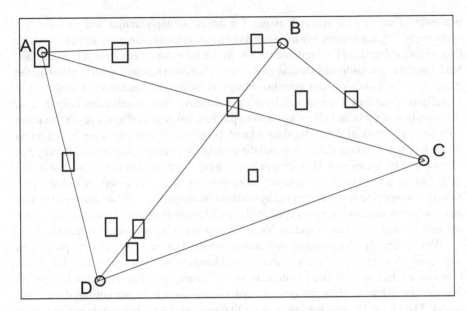

Fig. 1. A VIBE diagram with four POIs

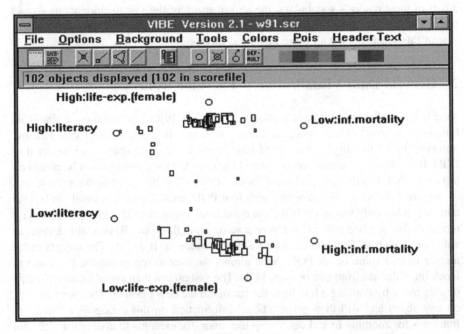

Fig. 2. VIBE user interface, here displaying countries of the world

that attracts lower than average values. The data objects are the countries of the world. We see that these fall into two groups, the ones that have positive values on these POIs and the others. Some countries fall outside of these groups.

In another visualization of the data on all the countries of the world (Fig. 3) we also introduced POIs for GDP (Gross Domestic Product). Back in 1991 we were able to show that there were two countries that fell outside of the "normal" groups: Cuba had a low GDP per person but scored well on the POIs for literacy, life expectancy and infant mortality while Kuwait had a high GDP but scored low on these POIs. That is, by visualizing these data one was able to see combinations that were not apparent from the data directly.

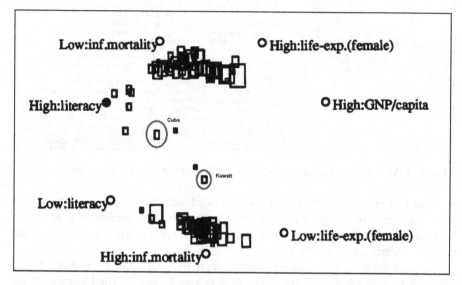

Fig. 3. Countries of the world fall into one of two groups

3   Document Visualization: CASCADE

During this same period we worked on the development of a collaborative authoring software system called CASCADE – "Computer Aided Support for Collaborative Authoring and Document Editing" [4, 5]. The system made heavy use of visualization to augment the authoring and editing process.

Figure 4 shows a document with comments. In the upper left corner, is a dialog box that controls how comments are rendered within the document. The classification of comments and the colors associated with them can be set per project. In this case, comments are rendered and shown in the document and the "mural" based on the status of the comment. The comment dialog appears when the user clicks on the document and allows the user to make a comment and classify it – in this case over three dimensions. The "mural" appears to the right of the scroll bar which shows a thumb proportional to the amount of the document displayed. Three comments are visible in the portion of the document displayed, one pending, one open, and one settled. Four comments are shown in the mural. The user can see that there is another open comment towards the end of the document as depicted in the mural.

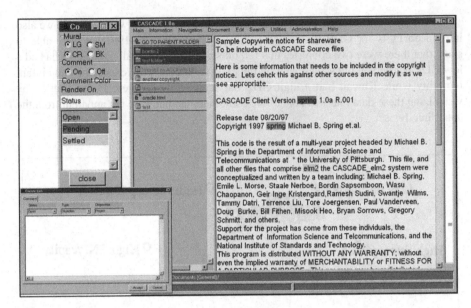

Fig. 4. CASCADE showing comments, comment control, and mural (Color figure online)

Note that the folder listing is also color coded with files shown as dark type on pastel backgrounds – yellows for text, blues for images, etc. and folders displayed as light type on dark backgrounds. Folders could be of various types as well – ordered versus unordered as an example.

Figure 5 shows a visualization of the activity of five users over a period of 29 days. The lines in each white bar show when the user was logged in. The histogram at the bottom shows times when the users were concurrently logged on over the period of

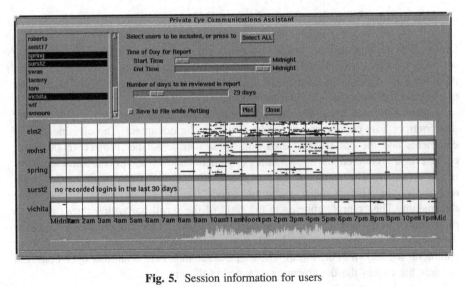

Fig. 5. Session information for users

review. The visualization shows the overall work effort of team members and may be used to find the best time to schedule synchronous meetings. Similar visualizations were developed to track keystrokes and mouse actions that could inform decisions about accelerator buttons that would ease editing and authoring activity.

CASCADE had a variety of static and dynamic hypertext displays. For example, a set of documents could be analyzed generating an ad hoc hypertext structure that could be used to access some or all of the comments on a set of documents. (One motivation for the development of CASCADE was the authoring of standards documents which involved tens to hundreds of editors working on large complex documents over a significant period of time). CASCADE was designed to make the processing of such documents more efficient. Figure 6 shows one of the more ambitious navigation tools – called "Docuverse". Docuverse was designed to show attributes of a large set of documents. In this case, it is displaying the size of about 400 documents. Beginning at the root, the user can choose any subdirectory on the left side to drill down. Docuverse had a half dozen attributes that could be visualized – age, size, number of comments, last access, last modification, etc. Double clicking on a folder would exit Docuverse into a more traditional directory listing.

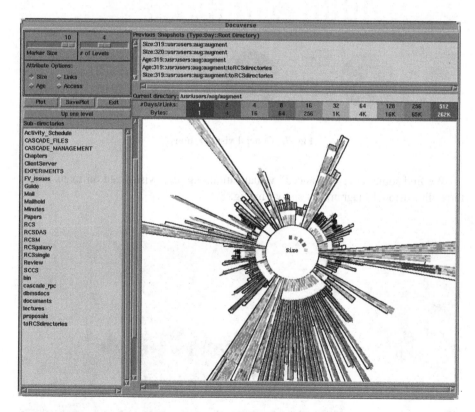

Fig. 6. Docuverse

4 Visualization Today

Novel visualization methods dedicated to abstract data have decreased in recent years. If we examine the visualizations that are used today in newspapers, reports and scientific papers we find only standard data visualizations as illustrated in Fig. 7. That is, two, perhaps three, dimensional figures, and charts. We find the traditional pie and bar diagrams. In practice, these are the type of diagrams that can be made by an Excel spreadsheet.

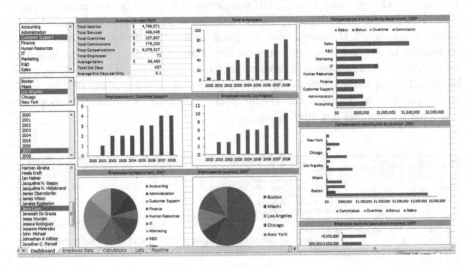

Fig. 7. General visualizations

We find some more "advanced" visualization, e.g. data visualized on maps and in three dimensional diagrams as shown in Fig. 8.

Fig. 8. Geocoding information

A particularly interesting geocoded example of a large data set visualization also makes use of a timeline as shown in the visualization of a distributed denial of service attack that took place on August 31, 2013 (Fig. 9). See www.digitalattackmap.com for more.

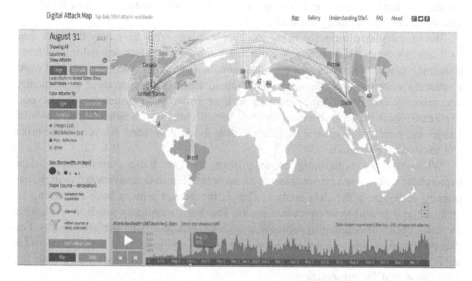

Fig. 9. DDOS attack on the US, China and others August 31, 2013

However, geocoding of data is nothing new. Minard's famous visualization of Napoleon's disastrous campaign in Russia is a well-known example. It was drawn in 1869. Today we may find more visualizations than at that time, since they both are easier to produce and easier to disseminate, but in practice there has been little development for abstract data visualizations – today we find, for the most part the same techniques used 150 years ago. The interesting question then is, why haven't Vibe, CASCADE and other experimental systems evolved?

5 Why Did General Visualization Tools Not Evolve?

One reason for not using advanced visualization methods is surely that in many cases the data will speak for itself. If the median income in the US is $865 per week for a full time worker there is no need for any visualization. If 33% of the population surveyed supports the president no visualization is needed. The number says everything, but instead of presenting the raw data that 330 out of a 1000 people surveyed confirmed that they supported the president, we offer the result as a percentage. In many cases it is sufficient to present the data as numbers or with simple diagrams.

However, if we want to study how income changes from year to year a time diagram will show this. With more advanced visualizations it is possible to see relationships not as apparent in multi-dimensional data sets. For example, using VIBE on the countries of the world we were able to find many facts that were not apparent from the data directly. One example was Cuba and Kuwait, another was how countries at war fell from the "good" group to the "bad" group, and how they managed to get back as soon as a war ended. We saw this when we visualized the Balkan countries over the years of conflict and peace. With other advanced visualization techniques it was possible to draw interesting information out of complex data. Still, nearly all the visualizations we see today are traditional.

We may criticize users for being too conservative – that they only do what they have always done. However, past experience shows that users are willing to learn something new if the advantages are high enough. Typewriters were replaced by word processing systems, users have been willing to learn how to produce high quality document layouts, PowerPoint presentations have grown in sophistication well beyond overheads, snail mail has been replaced by email that may include various kinds of emojis and pictures. In general users are willing to use computers for very many tasks and to develop new skills.

When working with complex data there are two basic considerations; data exploration/analysis and presentation to an audience. For data analysis/exploration, the primary audience is the data analyst. This is the person who is both attempting to analyze the data and to interpret the results. This person typically needs to work with feedback cycles of defining hypotheses, analyzing data, and visualizing the results. For data presentation, the audience is typically a group of end-users such as the readers of a publication. As far as we can see the novel and advanced methods failed both for exploration and for presentation.

Independent of the technique used the main idea of an abstract visualization is to translate numbers into graphical presentations. When communicating to a general audience it will be necessary for the visualizations to be intuitive. Traditional visualization techniques are intuitive. A pie chart shows part of the whole and connects to, yes, pies. Time series gives us the impression of something that goes up and down, such as a country road. Similarly, a bar chart may connect to the skyline of a large city, with high and low buildings. The more advanced visualization, especially the multi-dimensional, are less intuitive.

The visualizations for data exploration need to be easy to create and may often show multiple dimensions to unearth complex patterns. Many of the advanced data exploration tools require more hypothesis formation and concept creation than simpler visualization techniques such as a line graph or bar chart or basic statistical methods. For data presentation, it is critical that visualizations be simple and intuitive. The audience doesn't have the patience to decipher the meaning of complex presentations. For instance, presenting data in a chart as a visualization cannot stand-alone without an explanation to readers. With more complex visualizations produced by tools such as VIBE the users have a difficult time understanding the presentation without a comprehensive explanation of how to use them.

Tools such as Vibe for data exploration offer function over form where analytical, programming, data management, and business intelligence skills are more important than the ability to create presentable visualizations which may be why these tools are not used frequently. For visualizations, most users can understand the simple diagrams. These are used so many times that users get experience. There is no need to explain the basics of existing visualization techniques to readers. While VIBE, along with all the other advanced and novel methods, would need an explanation of how the visualizations are produced, this is not needed for simple charts. By using traditional visualizations we speak a language that the user knows, with the new advanced methods we introduce new "terms" and "concepts" that needs an explanation. The cost-benefit analysis may not favor new advanced visualizations.

6 Discussion

General visualization tools, tools that can be used on a wide range of data, are often favored over specialized tools, even if the specialized tools may be better for a specific application. That is, when we write reports, books or scientific papers we try to use the same tools all the time. This makes the production of the visualizations very effective. We also avoid the need for explaining the technique as long as we keep to visualizations that the readers have seen before. This holds true for general use of a technique. If we move into special areas such as scientific visualization users may find it worthwhile to invest in learning to use more advanced methods. In these cases the visualization is often used to let the researcher explore complex data to find correlations, and perhaps not to explain these to a general public. It is interesting to note the similarities between Spring and Jennings [6] and Olshannikova et al. [1]. Both look to rules for the use of virtual and augmented reality. On the other hand, with the type of visualizations that we consider here the goal is to communicate information clearly and effectively [7]. The basic rationale is to explain data to readers, the methods used are time series, ranking different values, showing correlation and deviation and methods to compare values.

The fact that general, simple techniques often are preferred over the more special and complex is seen in other areas as well. At one time there were expectations that 3D movies would conquer the market. While there have been some successful examples in few selected genres, 2D seems to do the job. Similarly, there may be interesting applications for virtual reality and augmented reality, but it seems that it is difficult to get these systems used generally. Speech recognition may be another example. There are applications where it is needed, for example where the user's hands are tied up, but it seems that most of us would still choose a keyboard for entering data. In general, reliability and simplicity seem to be what we want.

References

1. Olshannikova, E., Ometov, A., Koucheryavy, Y., Olsson, T.: Visualizing Big Data with augmented and virtual reality: challenges and research agenda. J. Big Data 2, 1–27 (2015)
2. Olsen, K.A., Hirtle, S.C., Sochats, K.M., Williams, J.G.: Ideation through visualization: the VIBE system. Multimed. Rev. 3(3), 48–59 (1992)
3. Olsen, K.A., Korfhage, R.R., Sochats, K.M., Spring, M.B., Williams, J.G.: Visualization of a document collection: the VIBE system. Inf. Process. Manag. 29(1), 69–82 (1993)

302   K. A. Olsen et al.

4. Sapsomboon, B., Spring, M.B.: Computer based collaborative authoring for standards development. Open Syst. Stand. Track. Rep. **5**(8), 4–6 (1996)
5. Spring, M.B., Vathanophas, V.: Peripheral social awareness information in collaborative work. J. Am. Soc. Inf. Sci. Technol. **54**(11), 1006–1013 (2003)
6. Spring, M.B., Jennings, M.C.: Virtual reality and abstract data: virtualizing information. Virtual Real. World **1**(1), c–m (1993)
7. Friedman, V.: Data visualization and infographics. In: Graphics, Monday Inspiration (2008)

Mining Open Government Data Used in Scientific Research

An Yan[✉] and Nicholas Weber

The Information School, University of Washington, Seattle, USA
{yanan15,nmweber}@uw.edu

Abstract. In the following paper, we describe results from mining citations, mentions, and links to open government data (OGD) in peer-reviewed literature. We inductively develop a method for categorizing how OGD are used by different research communities, and provide descriptive statistics about the publication years, publication outlets, and OGD sources. Our results demonstrate that, 1. The use of OGD in research is steadily increasing from 2009 to 2016; 2. Researchers use OGD from 96 different open government data portals, with data.gov.uk and data.gov being the most frequent sources; and, 3. Contrary to previous findings, we provide evidence suggesting that OGD from developing nations, notably India and Kenya, are being frequently used to fuel scientific discoveries. The findings of this paper contribute to ongoing research agendas aimed at tracking the impact of open government data initiatives, and provides an initial description of how open government data are valuable to diverse scientific research communities.

Keywords: Open data · Literature mining · Research policy
E-government

1 Introduction

The release of public sector information (PSI) has traditionally been motivated by democratic ideals related to representative governance, accountability, and transparency. Over the last decade, governments around the world have greatly expand the scope of PSI accessibility through their participation in e-democracy and e-government initiatives [1]. Most notably, there is a global movement towards publishing openly licensed, machine-readable data, known as Open Government Data (OGD), from transportation, budgeting, agricultural, and public health agencies [2].

While much of the public support for open government data remains focused on increasing government transparency, public officials have also begun to recognize the value of open data for the private sector [3]. Thus, much of the existing research into open government data initiatives has focused on two questions: First, how does open government data affect government accountability and transparency ? [1]; and, Second, in opening up government data to entrepreneurs,

© Springer International Publishing AG, part of Springer Nature 2018
G. Chowdhury et al. (Eds.): iConference 2018, LNCS 10766, pp. 303–313, 2018.
https://doi.org/10.1007/978-3-319-78105-1_34

what economic impact does open government data create? [4]. In this paper, we seek to expand current efforts in tracking the impact and value of open data initiatives by exploring the use of OGD in scientific research. By mining citations, mentions, and links to open government data found in a broad collection of peer-reviewed literature, we present empirical evidence about which scientific research communities are using OGD, and for what purposes. In the following section, we situate our work amongst previous studies of OGD users, and then present the research design for this study.

2   Related Work

Although OGD has sparked a growing level of interest among researchers, there is little empirical work that focuses explicitly on how these resources are used, in practice, by the public [5]. Notable exceptions include, Bright et al. [6] who analyzed downloads of data hosted by data.gov.uk. They found that a majority of OGD has never been accessed, and the most frequent use of OGD was for commercial purposes. Similarly, Young and Yan [7] examined the challenges and expectations of civic hackers using open government in developing new technologies. They found that this community expressed a desire for higher quality data, and that issues related to the functionality of an open data portal greatly limited OGD use.

There are few studies that have examined OGD and its potential use in scientific research. Safarov et al. [8] conducted a systematic literature review examining the utilization of open government data through peer-reviewed publications. These authors categorize open government data use based on the type, condition, effect, and users of open data. They argue that OGD could allow researchers to form new analysis based on OGD, but note that there is little evidence suggesting that scientific communities are interested in this data source. In one of the few targeted studies looking into how open government data is actually being used in scientific research, Martin et al. [9] examined the requirements for and potential uses of the New York State's open health data portal. Collecting data through surveys and focus groups, they argue that obstacles to OGD use in research include low awareness of data availability and limited engagement with government data producers.

This paper seeks to better understand the use of open government data for scientific research by answering the following research questions:

- How are OGD used in academic research?
- What sources of OGD do researchers use?
- What fields of academic research are using OGD?

In the following sections, we describe the methods used for identifying and analyzing citations, mentions, and links to open government data in peer reviewed literature published between January 2009 and July 2017. We summarize our findings through descriptive statistics, and preliminary observations about how open data are used by different scientific research communities.

3   Methods

We developed a systematic review protocol to identify, select, and categorize published literature where open government data was explicitly used as a research input. By following a systematic review protocol this study is replicable, in that our results can be reproduced by following the steps outlined below, and exhaustive, as our search for relevant literature makes use of all potential sources currently indexed by three major publication databases [10]. In the following sections, we describe the systematic protocol used for identifying and selecting relevant literature, and the methods used for mining this literature for evidence of OGD use.

Search Terms: We first obtained a list of open government data portals from data.gov[1]. We chose to remove portals from this list that were not specific to one particular government or agency (e.g. The World Bank), and we also added well-respected international OGD sources that were absent from the initial list (e.g. Taiwan - data.gov.tw). In total, there were 302 unique URLs representing sources where researchers might obtain open government data. Table 1 provides a summary of the types of OGD portals included in this study.

Table 1. Summary of OGD portals used as search terms

Type	Count	Examples
International Regional	155	Victoria (http://www.data.vic.gov.au/)
International Country	54	Australia (http://data.gov.au/)
US City or County	46	Seattle (http://data.seattle.gov/)
US State	38	Hawaii (http://data.hawaii.gov/)
Other State Related	8	NY Department of health (https://health.data.ny.gov/)
US	1	Data.gov (https://www.data.gov/)

Article Retrieval: We constructed a query combining the 302 data portal URLs described above, and used this query to search the Scopus, Springer, and IEEE databases in July, 2017. Queries were limited, by date, to January 2009 to July 2017 in order to align with the establishment of major open data initiatives, such as the launch of data.gov in 2009. In total, 2486 articles were identified.

Next, we removed duplicate publications that appeared in multiple databases. We then further refined the study sample by selecting only peer-reviewed full-text journal articles or conference papers (i.e. we did not include abstracts, chapters, or books). We only selected publications that were written in English, had full-text accessible to our research team, and in which OGD was actually used by the authors, and not simply mentioned as being a relevant topic or phenomena of interest. To determine which papers should remain in the sample using

---

[1] https://www.data.gov/open-gov/.

this selection criteria, the two authors of this paper individually examined 170 articles selected randomly from the initial sample of 2039 publications. Cohen's Kappa was calculated to determine selection agreement, and Landis and Koch's guideline was used to interpret the kappa statistics [11]. The authors achieved substantial agreement for both inclusion and exclusion of relevant papers. The first author then applied the selection criteria to the remaining papers in the initial sample. This process yielded a study sample of 1229 papers (Fig. 1).

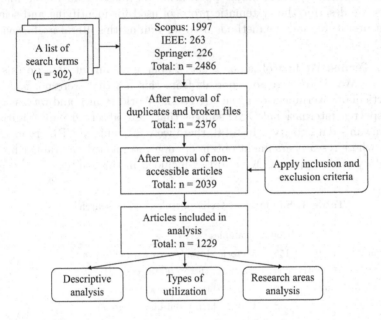

Fig. 1. The process of literature mining

Determination of Usage Types: Using the study sample (n = 1229), the two authors read through the full text of a randomly selected subset of 63 papers. While reading the two authors inductively developed separate codebooks to categorize different ways that the publications described using OGD. The authors then met, combined their codebooks, and recoded an additional 200 articles. Seven usage types emerged from this inductive coding: OGD were used (1) As the main data source for new analysis, (2) As ancillary data source for new analysis, (3) For result evaluation, (4) To demonstrate the effectiveness of a proposed new method, (5) To develop information services or new platforms, (6) To create a combined or composite dataset, and (7) To provide a broader context for a study's subject or topic. We noted that the categories were not mutually exclusive; an author may use multiple OGD sources in a single publication, or may use a single OGD source for multiple purposes in the same publication. To ensure our shared understanding of the merged codebook, Cohen's Kappa was calculated in a final round of coding (n = 50 articles). Nearly perfect agreement was achieved for usage types (1), (2), (5), (6), and (7), and substantial agreement was achieved for usage types (3) and (4). The first author then coded the rest of the samples based on the mutual understanding of the codebook.

Additional Analysis of Sample: We analyzed publications in our sample based on publication year, in order to understand the trend of OGD usage over time, as well as the source of OGD, in order to understand which data portals were most popular. We also analyzed the publication outlets (e.g. journal, conference, etc.) to gain an understanding of how various research fields engage with OGD. We associated each outlet with its research area using Scopus source title list[2] which provided information of each publication outlet indexed by Scopus. We discuss these results below.

4   Results

Descriptive Analysis: Figure 2 shows the number of articles that used OGD from January 2009 to July 2017. There is an upward trend of publications using OGD over time, implying the increasing attention to OGD in scientific research. This is consistent with previous findings that as open data initiatives mature, portals are more frequently used by diverse stakeholders [12].

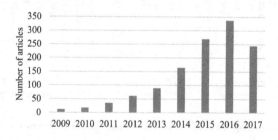

Fig. 2. Number of articles using OGD by year

The sources of OGD research are provided in Fig. 3. Data from 96 different Open Government Data Portals were used by publications in our sample. Notably, the United Kingdom's OGD portal (data.gov.uk) was used by 25.5% of all papers in our sample. This is more than twice the number of articles (11.6%) that used the United States OGD portal (data.gov). It is not surprising that national portals are more frequently used than state, province, city or county portals due to the fact that both the UK and USA portals have more data available. National OGD portals, such as data.gov, also harvest data from sub-national portals at the city and state level. However, it is surprising that Chicago is ranked as the sixth most frequent source of OGD (3.6%). Chicago is the most popular OGD portal among all US city or county level portals. This is

---

[2] https://www.elsevier.com/solutions/scopus/content.

also surprising as other major USA cities such as New York City, Seattle, and Boston have more data available for download, and have holdings which are more extensive than those of Chicago [13]. Among international regions, Amsterdam (3.8%) and Queensland (2.6%) received the most use. This result is in line with Safarov et al.'s [8] findings that OGD-related studies were most active in developed countries with the Netherlands, the United States, the United Kingdom as the most researched countries. However, OGD in two developing countries, India (7.0%) and Kenya (6.3%), notably appear in the top 5 of all sources found in our study. This is a significant finding, as it suggests that although these two nations have relatively new OGD programs, they are a unique and valuable source of data for researchers working on topics related to these countries.

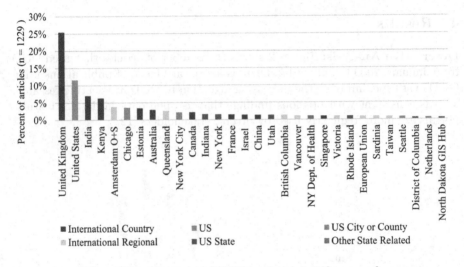

Fig. 3. Top 30 sources of OGD used in scientific research

Research Areas That Use OGD: We examined the publication outlets for the selected articles in our sample (n = 1229). Among the 815 different publication outlets, PloS ONE produced the most (32) articles, followed by BMC Public Health (14), Science of the Total Environment (12), Sustainability (Switzerland) (11), BMJ Open (11), and Scientific Reports (9). Notably, all of these journals, with the exception of Science of the Total Environment, are open-access publications. This suggests that authors who use open data may be more likely to publish in open-access venues, or that these publication outlets have more strict standards about data source citation. However, further research is required to validate this observation.

We also associated the title of each publication in our sample with a corresponding field of research as defined by the Scopus database. Table 2 shows that Medicine, Environmental Sciences and Social Sciences occupy the top three fields that use OGD in publications, suggesting that OGD is playing the role of advancing both natural science and social science discoveries. Computer Sciences and Engineering also rank high in the list (No. 4 and No. 6), suggesting that OGD is also contributing to technical innovations. Noticeably, OGD was used by all available Scopus research fields, including Dentistry and Chemistry. We caution that the research area of a publication outlet does not necessarily represent the research areas of a paper published in it, but we do argue that these labels are a strong proximate indicator of the topic of the article. Thus, the breadth and diversity of research fields using OGD demonstrates that these PSI are indeed a valuable source for scientific research.

Table 2. Top 10 research areas that use OGD

Research areas	Count
Medicine	557
Environmental science	448
Social sciences	412
Computer science	242
Agricultural and biological sciences	178
Engineering	145
Earth and planetary sciences	144
Biochemistry, genetics and molecular biology	80
Energy	76
Business, management and accounting	45

OGD Usage Types: Through inductive coding, seven major OGD usage types were identified. OGD were used (1) As the main data source for new analysis, such as being a variable in regression or a parameter in a mathematic model; (2) As ancillary data source for new analysis, such as the base map upon which newly collected data are plotted; (3) For result evaluation, such as to validate or verify a research claim, or to benchmark the quality of an existing dataset; (4) To demonstrate the effectiveness of a proposed new method (e.g., an innovative statistical model); (5) To develop information services or new platforms (e.g., a semantic web browser); (6) To create a combined or composite dataset; and (7) To provide study context, such as describing the motivation for a study. Figure 4 illustrates the distribution of OGD uses from our study sample. Over half of the publications used OGD as data sources for new research: 33.4% used OGD as main source and 19.5% as an ancillary source. In our sample, 33.2% of the articles cited OGD to provide background context for the study, including demographic information about a population of study, or as validation for a chosen sampling method. Less then 5% of the articles belong to other usage types that were unclear from the text of the article.

Limitations: There are several limitations to this study. First, and most significantly, our search only retrieved articles that explicitly cite, mention, or link to

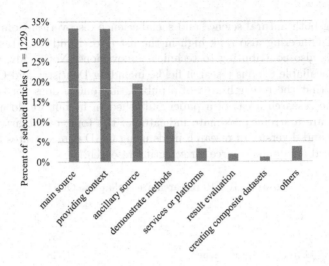

Fig. 4. Percentage of usage types by article

an open government data portal. Many researchers likely use OGD, but do not explicitly document the source. We present these results as preliminary findings about how OGD are used, and discuss future ways in which implicit OGD use could be identified below. Second, we only considered OGD sources retrieved from an initial list of 302 portals. Although we believe this list to be extensive, there are certainly sources of OGD that were not included in our search. Third, we only included three databases in our analysis and most selected articles were retrieved from Scopus, therefore our results relied heavily on the content coverage of the Scopus database. Our categorization of research areas is also constrained by the way that Scopus assigns research areas to each publication outlet. In the future, we hope estimate the impact of OGD on academic research by incorporating journal impact factors, and citation counts of selected articles into our analysis. We also hope to understand researchers' practices with OGD by conducting surveys and interviews. By combining the literature mining approach described here with survey and qualitative methods, we believe these results could be improved. Below, we restate the key findings of this initial work.

5   Discussion and Conclusion

This paper is one of the first empirical examinations of how OGD are being used in scientific research. By mining a total of 1229 research articles that used OGD, we found that 1. The use of OGD in research is steadily increasing from 2009 to 2016; 2. Researchers use OGD from 96 different open government data portals in their publications, with data.gov.uk and data.gov being the most frequent sources; 3. Contrary to previous findings, we provide evidence that OGD from developing nations, notably India and Kenya, are popular amongst OGD users; 4. OGD has been used by nearly all research fields, with Medicine,

Environmental Science, and Social Sciences being the most active fields that engage with OGD; and 5. Researchers mainly use OGD as data sources for new analysis and to provide context for a research finding. OGD was also used for testing new methods, providing new services or systems, result evaluation, and creating composite datasets.

Popular OGD Sources: We discovered in our results that United Kingdom, Kenya, and Chicago ranked high in our sources of OGD. Looking further into the use of these sources, we found out that each of the three portals had one particular type of dataset that had been used most frequently. For example, in the United Kingdom, an "index of deprivation"[3] dataset was used frequently as an ancillary source for Medicine and Public Health research [14]. For Kenya, demographic data was often used to describe the study setting for research on poverty in developing countries [15]. For Chicago, crime data[4] was the most used source for social, urban, and computer science studies [16]. The frequent use of a particular dataset from a particular data portal requires further consideration: First, as official data published by a government entity, these datasets may be the only authoritative sources for certain types of information, such as demographic characteristics of a population. This would explain why, for example, the city of Chicago appears high in our rankings of ODG sources. Researchers interested in crime may find this the best, or only source to answer a research question. Second, these key sources of data can help answer questions that are of great local interest, but the remaining datasets published by a government may be of limited use to researchers outside of a particular topic. For example, if we removed poverty data from the Kenya portal we would get substantially different results as to the popularity of developing nations ODG source. But, these results imply that governments should seek to identify highly unique data, and promote their use amongst research communities. In turn, this could spur further engagement with a data portal. Further, governments should consider prioritizing the release of datasets that satisfy the above-mentioned conditions in order to maximize the utilization of their investment in open government data initiatives.

Research Areas: Finally, we highlight our finding that nearly all scientific fields are using OGD. Previous studies [17] have shown that OGD may be used by researchers to investigate education, policies, health-care, and government activities. But, our results suggest that OGD can also be applied to broad research areas such as chemistry [18] and Dentistry [19] that seem less likely to use OGD and that OGD has exhibited more potential use for research than reflected in exiting literature.

Acknowledgement. This research was supported in part by IMLS grant # RE-40-16-0015-16. Supporting data and in-depth explanation of the methods used in this study can be found at https://github.com/OpenDataLiteracy/iConference_2018.

---

[3] https://data.gov.uk/dataset/index-of-multiple-deprivation.

[4] https://data.cityofchicago.org/public-safety/crimes-2001-to-present/ijzp-q8t2.

References

1. Jaeger, P.T., Bertot, J.C.: Transparency and technological change: ensuring equal and sustained public access to government information. Gov. Inf. Q. **27**(4), 371–376 (2010). https://doi.org/10.1016/j.giq.2010.05.003
2. Davies, T.: Open data, democracy and public sector reform. A look at open government data use from data.gov.uk (2010)
3. Zuiderwijk, A., Marijn, J.: Open data policies, their implementation and impact: a framework for comparison. Gov. Inf. Q. **31**(1), 17–29 (2014). https://doi.org/10.1016/j.giq.2013.04.003
4. Gruen, N., Houghton, J., Tooth, R.: Open for business: how open data can help achieve the G20 growth target (2014)
5. Zuiderwijk, A., Marijn, J., Yogesh, K.D.: Acceptance and use predictors of open data technologies: drawing upon the unified theory of acceptance and use of technology. Gov. Inf. Q. **32**(4), 429–440 (2015). https://doi.org/10.1016/j.giq.2015.09.005
6. Bright, J., Margetts, H.Z., Wang, N., Hale, S.A.: Explaining usage patterns in Open Government Data: the case of data.gov.uk. Social Science Research Network, Rochester, NY, SSRN Scholarly Paper ID 2613853 (2015). https://doi.org/10.2139/ssrn.2613853
7. Young, M., Yan, A.: Civic hackers user experiences and expectations of Seattle's open municipal data program. In: Proceedings of the 50th Hawaii International Conference on System Sciences (2017). https://doi.org/10.24251/HICSS.2017.324
8. Safarov, I., Meijer, A., Grimmelikhuijsen, S.: Utilization of open government data: a systematic literature review of types, conditions, effects and users. Inf. Polit. **22**(1), 1–24 (2017). https://doi.org/10.3233/IP-160012
9. Martin, E.G., Helbig, N., Birkhead, G.S.: Opening health data: what do researchers want? Early experiences with New York's open health data platform. J. Public Health Manag. Pract. **21**(5), E1–E7 (2015). https://doi.org/10.1097/PHH.0000000000000127
10. Fecher, B., Friesike, S., Hebing, M.: What drives academic data sharing? PloS ONE **10**(2), e0118053 (2015). https://doi.org/10.1371/journal.pone.0118053
11. Landis, J.R., Gary, G.K.: The measurement of observer agreement for categorical data. Biom. **33**(1), 159–174 (1977). https://doi.org/10.2307/2529310
12. Thorsby, J., Stowers, G.N., Wolslegel, K., Tumbuan, E.: Understanding the content and features of open data portals in American cities. Gov. Inf. Q. **34**(1), 53–61 (2017). https://doi.org/10.1016/j.giq.2016.07.001
13. Kassen, M.: A promising phenomenon of open data: a case study of the Chicago open data project. Gov. Inf. Q. **30**(4), 508–513 (2013). https://doi.org/10.1016/j.giq.2013.05.012
14. Evans, J., Kaptoge, S., Caleyachetty, R., Di Angelantonio, E., Lewis, C., Parameshwar, K., Pettit, S.J.: Socioeconomic deprivation and survival after heart transplantation in England an analysis of the United Kingdom transplant registry. Circ. Cardiovasc. Qual. Outcomes **9**(6), 695–703 (2016). https://doi.org/10.1161/CIRCOUTCOMES.116.002652
15. Okotto, L., Okotto-Okotto, J., Price, H., Pedley, S., Wright, J.: Socio-economic aspects of domestic groundwater consumption, vending and use in Kisumu, Kenya. Appl. Geogr. **58**, 189–197 (2015)

16. Zheng, Y., Liu, T., Wang, Y., Zhu, Y., Liu, Y., Chang, E.: Diagnosing New York city's noises with ubiquitous data. In: Proceedings of the 2014 ACM International Joint Conference on Pervasive and Ubiquitous Computing, pp. 715–725. ACM, New York (2014). https://doi.org/10.1145/2632048.2632102

17. Graves, A., Hendler, J.: A study on the use of visualizations for open government data. Inf. Polit **19**, 73–91 (2014). https://doi.org/10.3233/IP-140333

18. Croft, B., Wentworth, G.R., Martin, R.V., Leaitch, W.R., Murphy, J.G., Murphy, B.N., Kodros, J.K., Abbatt, J.P., Pierce, J.R.: Contribution of Arctic seabird-colony ammonia to atmospheric particles and cloud-albedo radiative effect. Nat. commun. **7**, 13444 (2016). https://doi.org/10.1038/ncomms13444

19. de Silva, A.M., Gkolia, P., Carpenter, L., Cole, D.: Developing a model to assess community-level risk of oral diseases for planning public dental services in Australia. BMC Oral Health **16**(1), 45 (2016). https://doi.org/10.1186/s12903-016-0200-5

Information Retrieval

Metadata versus Full-Text: Tracking Users' Electronic Theses and Dissertations (ETDs) Seeking Behavior

Daniel Gelaw Alemneh$^{(\boxtimes)}$ and Mark Phillips

University of North Texas, Denton, TX 76201, USA
Daniel.Alemneh@unt.edu

Abstract. This presentation provides data from a recent research project at the University of North Texas (UNT) Libraries to better understand how users are discovering the electronic theses and dissertations (ETDs) in the UNT Libraries. To extract the specific requests for ETDs in the UNT Digital Library, the data was obtained from a server log-that contained more than 178 million lines of requests. From these requests, the search query was executed in an ambiguous way (not specific fielded searches) queries were extracted to create a dataset of item-query pairs. These item-query pairs were presented to the Solr full-text indexer that powers the search and retrieval side of the UNT Digital Library to report back on statistics, and help to explain whether a specific query was satisfied by either the ETDs full-text, metadata, or by both fields. The resulting data helps us understand how our users are arriving at a given ETD in the collection. Among other speculations, the role of metadata for the discovery process, and the possible overlap that is present between metadata and the full-text of the ETD itself will be analyzed and discussed.

Keywords: Electronic theses and dissertations · ETD discovery
Metadata

1 Introduction

1.1 Metadata vs. Full-Text Controversy

Successful retrieval of information resources that are useful to a user relies on the quality of the information representation [1]. One of the things that comes up from time to time in discussions of library cataloging and metadata is whether our users are in fact making use of the metadata records we create for them or if they are able to find the resources they want with just the full-text of the item they are seeking. This conversation of course is only relevant when we are talking about open access resources that have full-text associated with them [2].

Considering the resource-intensive process of original cataloging and metadata creation processes, a group of UNT faculty members set out to get a better sense of whether users were arriving at our digital resources from searches that were answered by an items' descriptive metadata or by parts of the full-text of the item. In addition, when a resource was found with metadata, we tried to identify fields being used to

© Springer International Publishing AG, part of Springer Nature 2018
G. Chowdhury et al. (Eds.): iConference 2018, LNCS 10766, pp. 317–322, 2018.
https://doi.org/10.1007/978-3-319-78105-1_35

retrieve that item. Results may, among other things, help to identify or justify resources needed for metadata/Catalog creation [3]. We approached this problem by looking at a specific collection in the UNT Digital Library. In this case we were interested in understanding how users arrived at electronic theses or dissertations (ETDs) in our system.

1.2 ETD at UNT

Over the last two decades, colleges and universities have been transitioning from physical (paper and microfilm) to electronic submission and management processes for student theses and dissertations [4]. UNT was one of the first three American universities to require ETDs for graduation, and by 1999 all theses and dissertations submitted by students in pursuit of advanced degrees were digital. In addition we retrospectively digitized earlier analog these and dissertations [5]. The UNT ETD collection consists of more than 18,000 items and more than 2 million pages or files.

All of these documents share the characteristics that they are full-text searchable and have metadata records created for them as part of inclusion to our Digital Library. Currently, more than 90% of UNT's ETDs are freely accessible full-text to the public via the UNT Digital Library, while less than 10% have been restricted by their authors for use by the UNT community only and via metadata for the rest of the world. UNT tracks the use of its ETDs, as well as the use of other digital collections hosted by UNT Libraries. The ETD Collection is heavily used, ranging between 2,000 and over 5,000 uses per day from 200+ countries.

2 Method

This analysis used Web server logs from the application server that provides access to the UNT Digital Library, occurred between May and January 2015. The log files were limited to discoveries of items in the UNT ETD collection – 11,873 unique items available with metadata at the time this research was conducted. The raw dataset contained 172,115,682 lines during that timeframe, in the standard Extended Log File Format. Further limitations removed requests made by known robots, or without known search queries, resulting in a two-column intermediary dataset that contained 84,837 item-query pairs (i.e., a local identifier for each discovered item and the request used). Following normalization, the final dataset contained 46,366 unique item-query pairs.

The UNT Digital Library uses the Solr full-text indexer, which can provide explanatory information noting why a query yielded certain results, if a specific document would be returned by a query, and in which specified fields the terms appear. To utilize this, the item-query pairs were fed to the Solr search system. The final dataset used in the remainder of this paper lists the percentage of each search query that was found in the metadata (full descriptive record), full text, and four specified fields – title, subject, agent (both creator and contributor values) and description. The dataset has 43,420 unique query results; 2,946 samples were combined during processing because after further normalization they were no longer unique samples (Table 1).

Table 1. Example dataset entries for three search queries.

Dataset field	Example 1	Example 2	Example 3
Item	Metadc129697	Metadc146510	Metadc155618
Query	Susan cheal	Human trafficking	Article writing
Query tokens	2	2	2
Metadata	100%	100%	50%
Page text	0%	100%	100%
Title	0%	100%	50%
Subject	0%	100%	0%
Agent	100%	0%	0%
Description	0%	100%	0%

3 Findings

First, some basic analysis revealed statistical facts about the data collected. For example, the dataset represented **9,794** unique items, comprising 82% of the UNT ETD collection. Items in the dataset were queried an average of 1.62 times during the time period, however, the actual rate ranged from a single query to 15 queries for a specific item (see Table 2).

Table 2. Statistics for the number of queries per unique item and tokens per query.

Total no.	Min	Median	Max	Sum	Mean	Stddev
9794 Query per unique item	1	2	24	43420	4.43	2.92
43420 Tokens per query	1	2.5	31	104102	2.40	1.59

Although queries varied in length, they were analyzed as individual words (or tokens) rather than phrases. This allowed for partial matches in a given field, resulting in percentages less than 100. The distribution of tokens across queries ranged from 1 to 31 tokens (see Table 2). At this point, the analysis turned toward answering the research question. Table 4 gives a breakdown of the total number of queries found in the metadata and full-text including partial and full matches. The numbers overlap in cases where tokens appeared in both indexes. A number of record discoveries were dependent entirely on the full-text (9463) or metadata (1,723). For the subset of record discoveries with token matches in both indexes (32,056), Table 4 shows how many items could be found using either index equally, how many had a partial match in one index, with a full match in the other index, and the number of queries (1376) that could be found *only* through the combination of metadata and full-text versus either index alone (Table 3).

Table 3. Record discoveries based on matches in metadata and full-text (n = 43420).

Matches found in	Total queries found
Both metadata and full-text	32,056
Any part of query in full-text	41,519
100% of query in full-text	36318
Queries ONLY in full-text	9463
Any part of query in metadata	33,779
100% of query in metadata	29661
Queries ONLY in metadata	1723
Both metadata and full-text	32,056
Any part of query in full-text	41,519

Table 4. Record discoveries categorized for discoveries in both metadata and full-text (n = 32056).

Overlapping matches found in	Number of queries
Metadata/full-text equally (m = 100/p = 100)	23,935
ONLY with metadata/full-text combined (m < 100/p < 100)	1,376
Metadata/partial full-text (m = 100/p < 100)	5,726
Partial metadata/full-text (m < 100/p = 100)	12,383

At a more granular level, Table 5 displays average query matches by field: title, subject/keyword, agent, or content description. Most terms were found in the agent and subject fields. Table 6 shows the match percentage by field for the subset of 1723 items discovered through metadata-only retrieval. Most query matches were in the agent fields, followed by subject with few matches coming from description or title.

Table 5. Average percentage of query found for each record discovery (n = 43420).

General location						
Location of query match	PageText	Metadata	Title	Subj.	Agent	Descr.
Average % of each query by field	90.24	72.52	16.60	29.42	31.95	23.77

Table 6. Number of record discoveries per field from queries only found in metadata (n = 1723).

	0%	≥1%	% ≥ 1% found in field
Title	1715	8	0%
Subj.	1499	224	13%
Agent	809	914	53%
Description	1689	34	2%

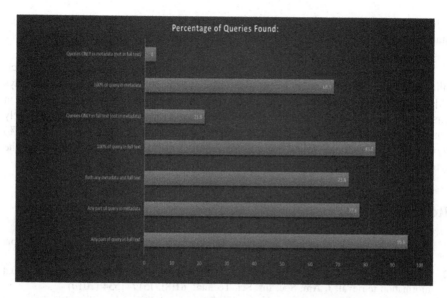

Fig. 1. Percentage of queries found

4 Summary

Arguably, there has been a shift in the way users search, access, and use information resources. Although the starting point for new research is increasingly digital, the challenge yet to be overcome in the provision of access to digital contents is achieving

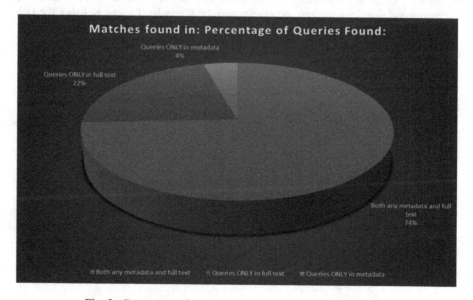

Fig. 2. Percentage of queries found in metadata and/or full-text

a level of description sufficient to ensure success in information retrieval. Our usage statistics show that users from more than 200 countries around the world visit the UNT Digital Libraries' diverse collections.

Effective metadata and taxonomies add value and amplify the mostly interdisciplinary ETDs – allowing users to explore and delve deeper in multi-dimensional ways [6]. Figures 1 and 2 reveal the value of both metadata and full-text approaches in answering users' queries. Based on the matches found only in metadata, we can safely conclude that had it not been for the rich metadata, more than 800 UNT's ETDs (4%) would have never been found by some of our global ETDs users. Enhancing the retrieval quality or ETDs discoverability is worth considering, regardless.

References

1. Alemneh, D., et al.: Guidance documents for lifecycle management of ETDs. Educopia Institute (2014). https://educopia.org/publications/gdlmetd. Accessed 15 Dec 2017
2. Jansen, B.J., Rieh, S.: The seventeen theoretical constructs of information searching and information retrieval. J. Am. Soc. Inf. Sci. Technol. **61**(8), 1517–1534 (2010)
3. Ramirez, M., et al.: Do open access electronic theses and dissertations diminish publishing opportunities in the social sciences and humanities? Findings from a 2011 survey of academic publishers. Coll. Res. Libr. **74**(4), 368–380 (2013)
4. Fyffe, R., William, C.W.: ETDs, scholarly communication, and campus collaboration. Coll. Res. Libr. News **69**(3), 152–155 (2008)
5. Alemneh, D., Ralph, H.: Theses and dissertations from print to ETD: the nuances of preserving and accessing those in music. In: Krueger, Janice M. (ed.) Cases on Electronic Records and Resource Management Implementation in Diverse Environments, pp. 41–60. IGI Global, Information Science Reference, Hershey (2014)
6. Alemneh, D., et al.: Knowledge representation and subject access in ETDs: analysis of creators' and users' assumptions and expectations. In: Watanabe, T., Seta, K. (eds.) The 11th International Conference on Knowledge Management, Osaka, Japan (2015)

"What was this Movie About this Chick?"
A Comparative Study of Relevance Aspects in Book and Movie Discovery

Toine Bogers[1(✉)], Maria Gäde[2], Marijn Koolen[3], Vivien Petras[2],
and Mette Skov[4]

[1] Science, Policy and Information Studies,
Department of Communication and Psychology,
Aalborg University Copenhagen, Copenhagen, Denmark
toine@hum.aau.dk

[2] Berlin School of Library and Information Science,
Humboldt-Universität zu Berlin, Berlin, Germany
{maria.gaede,vivien.petras}@ibi.hu-berlin.de

[3] Huygens ING, Royal Netherlands Academy of Arts and Sciences,
Amsterdam, The Netherlands
marijn.koolen@huygens.knaw.nl

[4] Department of Communication and Psychology,
Aalborg University, Aalborg, Denmark
skov@hum.aau.dk

Abstract. In recent decades, information retrieval research has slowly expanded its focus to address the wealth of complex search requests present in our work and leisure environments. A better understanding of such complex needs could aid in the design of more effective, domain-specific search engines. In this paper we take a first step towards such domain-specific understanding. We present an analysis of a random sample of 1000+ complex book and movie search requests posted in the LibraryThing and Internet Movie Database forums. A coding scheme was developed that captures the 29 different relevance aspects expressed in these requests. We find that while the identified relevance aspects are remarkably similar for complex book and movie requests, their relative occurrence does vary considerably from domain to domain.

Keywords: Query analysis · Book search · Movie search
Information need categorization · Relevance aspects

1 Introduction

The increasing popularity and presence of computers, smartphones and tablets in our daily lives have a correspondingly strong influence on our information seeking behavior. With their use no longer confined to the work environment

© Springer International Publishing AG, part of Springer Nature 2018
G. Chowdhury et al. (Eds.): iConference 2018, LNCS 10766, pp. 323–334, 2018.
https://doi.org/10.1007/978-3-319-78105-1_36

only, searching for leisure has become a major part of the way we use web search engines [19,28]. As a result, the past decade has seen a steady increase in the amount of research dedicated to different aspects of everyday-life information seeking behavior. Savolainen [26], for example, proposed a typology of different types of leisure searchers, while McKenzie [16] introduced a general model of the entire everyday-life information seeking process.

The question of what people search for and what aspects of the desired resources they mention in their requests remains vague in many domains, however, even though this information is crucial for building successful search and discovery systems. For instance, despite the popularity of movie discovery services such as Netflix, our understanding of how people search for and discover, which movies to watch next, is still underdeveloped. Moreover, we lack a good understanding of how relevance aspects across different domains compare to each other. In this paper, we take a first step towards answering these questions and addressing this research gap by comparing two domains: books and movies. We focus on requests that elaborate a searcher's information need more than simple web search queries do, in order to elicit more details about their relevance aspects. Discussion forums are places where we can expect to find people expressing such complex requests. Considering this context, our study is not only related to everyday-life information seeking, but is also part of a growing research community in information retrieval that focuses on complex search tasks [4]. We collected over 120,000 discussion threads from the LibraryThing and IMDB discussion forums and annotated a random sample of 503 book and 538 movie search requests expressed in these threads. We developed a coding scheme for the relevance aspects expressed in these requests and present here an analysis of the results for both domains. Finally, we compare the relevance aspects and the relative distributions of the categories in both domains.

We find that requests in forum posts reveal several relevance aspects related to content and user experience that are rarely considered in system design, but could be addressed using appropriate search functionalities and data sources— e.g., book text, movie subtitles, and user reviews. In this sense, our analysis provides pointers for future system development.

2   Related Work

Query intent, query categorization and relevance aspects. Researchers have previously studied the content of and intent behind queries in order to improve the performance and relevance decisions of search engines. Although relevance is a fundamental concept in information science, very different viewpoints and characteristics evolved over the years. In this study, we use the broader phrase 'relevance aspect' to encompass subject and cognitive relevance expressions in search requests [24]. For web search, query intent analysis has long focused on the three goals (informational, navigational and transactional) first identified by Broder's [6] now classic study. Automatic query classification algorithms are commonly based on these goals [29]. Other studies have broadened the spectrum of relevance aspects by further specifying the intents [22] or analyzing the content of the query [11]. Studies on academic search engines have adopted Broder's goals to make results comparable [12,15]. They found that searchers generated a lot more informational requests in academic contexts in contrast to web search. This demonstrates that while almost all search environments are now web-based, the domain of inquiry affects the relevance aspects. In everyday-life information seeking, television [8] and music [10,14] are domains where relevance aspects have also been studied.

Relevance aspects in book search. In comparison to other information seeking domains, book search has been studied more extensively. Some studies focus on book selection [18,21,23,27] rather than on book searching. Other studies focus on search strategies in physical bookshops [7] or libraries [17,20] rather than online. Despite the differences, some of the identified relevance aspects are similar to this study.

Our categorization scheme is based on and adapted from relevance aspects in previous studies in the domain of books [13,21,23], but with the aim to cover multiple, related domains. The eight relevance aspects identified by Koolen et al. [13] were elicited from LibraryThing book requests, just as in our study. There is strong overlap with the coding scheme for books by Mikkonen and Vakkari [18], which is based on selections from library catalogs, using four simulated search tasks. Similarly, there is an overlap with the classification scheme reflecting users' multifaceted reading goals developed by Pejtersen [20], based on user-librarian conversations. We base our coding scheme on naturally occurring search requests in forums to avoid the constraints introduced by existing systems and simulated tasks. This resulted in additional aspects compared to Mikkonen and Vakkari [18], as well as different choices in grouping aspects. Our coding scheme also led to a category for search task type.

Relevance aspects in movie search. Movie information needs have not been given the same level of attention as books. In media studies and psychology, the relationship between watchers and movie choices has been studied, for example, the role of age or gender in movie genre selection [3]. For movie selection, Austin [1,2] found that high school students choose movies first based on plot, followed by the actors and then based on friend recommendations. A first categorization of complex requests was performed by Bogers [5], who annotated 400 IMDB forum threads into eight broad relevance categories with 30 sub-level categories. Bogers' study and categorization scheme served as a motivation and background for our analysis of movie requests here.

3   Methodology

In order to conduct a comparative analysis of the aspects that make books and movies relevant to searchers, we collected a representative sample of book and movie search requests. We first describe the data collection process, then the development of our coding scheme for relevance aspects in the book and movie domains.

3.1 Data Collection

Books. We collected examples of book requests from the online discussion forums on LibraryThing (LT), one of the major social cataloging websites[1]. Currently, there are over 196,000 threads in the LT forums[2], many of which are dedicated to book clubs and reading challenges. The starting point of the data collection process was a 2012 crawl of the first 131,000 LT forum threads posted up to that point. All threads without any empty or hidden first posts were converted to XML, resulting in 115,858 XML threads. As part of the work by Koolen et al. [13], a focused sample of 1,461 threads were manually classified as book search requests, after having been pre-filtered using a simple regular-expression-based classifier, which removed all posts not containing one or more 'trigger' expressions, such as '*suggest*', '*looking for*' and '*which books*'. For the purpose of our analysis, we only extracted the 1,461 first posts in each thread that contain the original requester's book search request[3].

Movies. In order to collect examples of movie requests, the Internet Movie DataBase (IMDB) message boards were chosen. IMDB shut down its message boards on February 20, 2017, so it was not possible to get an exact overview of its size at the time of writing, but in 2015 they contained over 1.19 million threads [5]. Discussion on the IMDB message boards covered a wide variety of topics, but for the work described in this paper, we restricted ourselves to threads where users were most likely to describe their movie-related information needs. Threads that covered movie news, reviews, or discussion of specific movies, actors, director or other aspects were not considered. We restricted ourselves to two message boards in particular: (1) "*I need to know*" (INTK), which typically (but not exclusively) contained known-item requests, where user are interested in re-finding a specific movie already known to them with the purpose of determining the title, using descriptions of the plot or other aspects of the movie; and (2) "*Lists & recommendations*" (L&R), which contained explicit requests for movie recommendations or lists of similar movies with a particular theme.

We combined two different non-overlapping crawls of all threads posted to these two message boards, one originally documented by Bogers [5] and conducted in June 2014, and the second conducted between February 15–17, 2017. The combination of these crawls resulted in 6,320 INTK threads and 634 L&R threads for a total of 6,954 threads. Although the exact proportion of known-item threads in the INTK message board is hard to determine without coding them, the majority consists of known-item threads, which suggests a strong skew

---

[1] http://www.librarything.com/, last visited December 5, 2017.

[2] According to http://www.librarything.com/zeitgeist, last visited December 5, 2017.

[3] Available at http://toinebogers.com/?page_id=779.

in the distribution of information need types already before coding. Again, all threads without any empty or hidden first posts were converted to XML, resulting in 6,879 XML threads[4]. For the purpose of this paper, we only extracted the 6,879 first posts in each thread that contained the original requester's movie search request. In contrast to the book requests, these movie requests were not pre-annotated as requests or non-requests, resulting in a mix of both types.

3.2 Coding

Development of initial coding schemes. The first phase in analyzing the relevance aspects was the development of initial coding schemes for both domains separately. These initial coding schemes were based on an open coding approach. All five authors acted as annotators and developed their own individual coding on the same development set of book and movie posts. The size of this initial development set had to be large enough to ensure that even infrequent relevance aspects had a decent chance of occurring in that set. Based on the coding frequencies from an earlier book coding scheme [13], we set the size of the development set at 50 posts, as the least frequent coding category occurred once every 27 posts on average. For movies, we set the size of the development set to 75 posts to take into account that two-thirds of all threads from the INTK and L&R messages boards were movie search requests according to Bogers [5]. For each thread in the development and final coding sets, annotators were shown the title and full text of the initial post as well as the group it was posted in.

Calibration of the final coding scheme. The development phase resulted in 10 different initial coding schemes, five for each domain. In total, initial coding resulted in 89 different relevance categories for books and 82 for movies. To arrive at a single coding scheme for each domain, we used card sorting to split, merge, and label the initial categories into a smaller set of unique categories, one for each domain. All grouping or merging decisions where made on the premise to inform information systems that support heterogeneous real-life user requests with different strategies.

After this initial phase, we grouped related categories into top-level aspects. Next, the individual coding schemes were sent around for discussion by all five authors until agreement was reached about the aspects and their labels. The book coding scheme was calibrate *before* the movie coding scheme, which meant that the latter was influenced by our experiences with the former.

In our final discussion round, we attempted to identify similar aspects in both domains and unify the names and descriptions of these aspects so that a unified coding scheme for books and movies could be developed, although some aspects only occur for one domain. Textual descriptions of the different aspects were then added for each aspect along with prototypical examples of each aspect to aid in the final annotation process. None of these aspects are mutually exclusive.

---

[4] Available at http://toinebogers.com/?page_id=779.

Actual coding process. After calibrating our coding scheme for both domains, each annotator was tasked with annotating 120 book requests and 120 movie requests and provided with a random selection of posts. Posts from the development sets were not re-used for the final annotation. Because not every post was a search request—especially for the movie threads, which had not been pre-filtered—annotators kept annotating until they reached 120 true requests. In practice, this meant between 123–126 book and between 181–218 movie posts were annotated in total. After the first round of final coding, all annotators discussed their experiences. This led to the addition of a Dialogue aspect to the coding scheme as well as clearing up any possible confusion about specific aspects, after which every annotator revisited their 120 requests to harmonize their annotations. Coding agreement is reported in Sect. 4.3.

4   Book and Movie Requests

The final coding scheme (see Fig. 1) includes four top-level categories—Content, Metadata, Context, and Experience—and an other category, which was used to annotate aspects not already covered. The four main categories are further divided into sub-categories. While there is a great deal of overlap, each domain does have unique aspects. For each request, the type of Information Need was categorized as Discovery, Known-item, Sequence & Series or Similarity. None of the categories are mutually exclusive; requests could be assigned to more than one category and information need, although at least one information need had to be assigned to each request.

4.1   Books

In total, 503 unique posts were annotated for the book domain. The majority of requests are long and complex, containing inquiries related to more than one category. For example, the following post includes details about the topic, author background, recency as well as the perspectives used: *"Can someone suggest a book [on Climate change] that's relatively up to date and 'fair to both camps'? ... One, preferably by an actual, reputable scientist, not someone pretending to be a scientist (not making any claims; I can only imagine)? And I would consider myself a fairly dumb layman." (ID 73244).* Requesters mostly asked for Metadata aspects (80.5%), followed by Content (77.9%), mainly including topical and plot information, and Experience (23.1%) or Context (17.1%) aspects. More than half of the threads were discovery-type requests (53.5%), where the searcher is not aware of any books that match the specified relevance criteria. Similarity-type requests were the second-most frequent information need at 39%. Also, requesters often remember when they read a book: *"I read it in the 1960's but it may have been published much earlier." (ID 36142).* Although this information might not be consistent with the publication date, we still decided to classify these requests with the Release date aspect, since it might help provide the system with an approximate time frame. In known-item requests (where the purpose is to re-find

Top-level aspect	Sub-aspect		Description	Books	Movies
What should it be about?	Content	Characters	Books/movies with specific characters or organizations, types of characters or character development	✓	✓
		Design	Books/movies with a particular design, layout, structure or cinematography	✓	✓
		Dialogue	Movies that contain a particular phrase or style of dialog	✓	✓
		Plot	Books/movies with specific plot or narrative elements or scenes	✓	✓
		Setting	Books/movies set a specific location or near distinct geographical landmarks	✓	✓
		Time	Books/movies that are set in a particular time period or around a specific historical event	✓	✓
		Topic	Books/movies that cover one or more specific topics	✓	✓
What kind of properties should it have?	Metadata	Audience	Books/movies that are aimed at a specific audience	✓	✓
		Contributors	Books/movies that have a particular contributor involved (e.g., author, actor, cinematographer, director, illustrator, etc.)	✓	✓
		Format	Books that come in a specific format	✓	
		Filming location(s)	Movies that were recorded in a specific location		✓
		Genre	Books/movies that fall in one or more specific genres	✓	✓
		Language	Books/movies in a particular language	✓	✓
		Properties	Movies with specific characteristics		✓
		Publisher	Books from a particular publisher	✓	
		Release date	The date/period a book/movie was released	✓	✓
		Soundtrack	Movies with a particular soundtrack or sound design.		✓
		Title	Books/movies that have specific (words in the) title	✓	✓
		Version	Specific versions of a book/movie	✓	✓
How will it be used?	Context	Context	Books/movies that describe the context in or purpose for which they will be used	✓	✓
What kind of experience should it provide?	Experience	Comprehensiveness	Books that cover their topic with a certain level of detail	✓	
		Mood	Books/movies that evoke a certain mood, tone or reading/viewing experience	✓	✓
		Novelty	Books/movies that are unusual or quirky, or have novel content	✓	✓
		Impact	Books/movies that have a specific impact on the consumer or that motivate them in a certain way	✓	✓
		Perspective	Books/movies presenting a story from a particular perspective	✓	✓
What type of need is it?	Information need	Discovery	Books/movies that match relevant aspects, where the searcher is not aware of any books/movies that match their search criteria	✓	✓
		Known-item	Describing books/movies already known to the user with the purpose of re-finding them	✓	✓
		Sequence & series	Requests for a set or sequence of related books/movies	✓	✓
		Similarity	Books/movies that mention other items that the requested item should (or should not) be similar to (in some aspect)	✓	✓

Fig. 1. The coding scheme derived for the book and movie domains. The two right-most columns show, which aspects apply to which domain(s).

a book), traditional metadata elements such as title or author are often forgotten, yet design elements are present: *"Can't remember anything about the author or title, and while I can't quite remember I'm pretty sure it was a chapter book, softcover, with a kind of creepy cover illustration."* (ID 72482). Requests like these resulted in adding a Design sub-category for both domains covering these expressions. This relevance aspect is typically not included in traditional book metadata, but could be extracted from cover images by future search systems. We note that our coding scheme covers most of the book appeal elements (pace, storyline, frame and tone) of Saricks [25, Chap. 3], which are based on reference interviews in libraries. We did not encounter explicit mentions of pace, although qualifications such as 'pageturner' can be interpreted as indirectly referring to pace.

4.2   Movies

In total, 538 posts were annotated for the movie domain. Requesters most frequently asked for Content (95.4%) and Metadata (76.6%) aspects. The other categories played only minor roles (Experience 4.1% and Context 1.9%). A clear dominance of Known-item type requests (86.4%) was observed. Often, requesters remembered plot elements up to specific dialogue or sentences: *"I can only remember: (1) Someone ends up mutilated in a bathtub. (1) The villain was an old Italian mafioso complete with hat and suit. One line he said has stuck with me: "What the sh-t is this?" That's all I remember".* (ID 225359993). As the example shows, plot elements are often complemented with a description of characters. Within the Metadata category, 53.2% of all requests reported a Release date, varying from very specific dates—*"I saw an animated Japanese movie in the summer of 1984"* (ID 227693731)—to more vague descriptions, such as *"I saw a movie or TV show at least 15 or 20 years ago"* (ID 228781692).

Some requests expressed movie-specific relevance aspects. For example, posts sometimes mentioned aspects belonging to Properties, such as a particular format (black & white), a specific type of end credits, movie budget, etc. Another example are movie requests that address the Soundtrack or sound design of one or more movies.

4.3   Inter-annotator Agreement

In order to calculate inter-annotator agreement, we arranged for an overlap of 25 posts between successive annotators. Finally, inter-annotator agreement was calculated over a total of 100 overlapping posts. We calculated Fleiss' kappa, because agreement was calculated between different pairs of annotators [9][5]. In the book domain, agreement on whether a post contains a search request is $\kappa = 0.65$, for movies it is $\kappa = 0.83$. The lower agreement for books is probably due to the fact that they were pre-filtered, creating a stronger skew between requests

---

[5] Agreement scores for all aspects available from http://toinebogers.com/?page_id=779.

and non-requests. With 94 agreed requests and three agreed non-requests, the three disagreements have a large impact on overall agreement. The eight disagreements in the 100 movie posts have a much smaller impact, because the numbers of requests and non-requests are more balanced.

For the relevance aspects, we computed agreement based only on the posts that both annotators labeled as requests. In general, the top-level aspects show substantial agreement ($\kappa > 0.6$) apart from Metadata in the book domain ($\kappa = 0.32$) and Experience and Context (both have $\kappa = -0.03$) in the movie domain. The latter two rarely occur—respectively in 5% and 7% of the requests at least one annotator considers these aspects to be present—so more double annotations are needed to reliably determine agreement.

For the sub-aspects, agreement is substantial ($0.6 \leq \kappa < 0.8$) or strong ($\kappa \geq 0.8$) for several of the Content and Metadata sub-aspects, such as Plot, Dialogue and Publication date or Release date. Agreement on the type of information need is even higher: it ranges from $\kappa = 0.64$ for Sequence & Series to $\kappa = 0.91$ for Known-item in the book domain, and between $\kappa = 0.78$ (Discovery) to $\kappa = 0.82$ (Known-item and Similarity) in the movie domain. Many other sub-aspects in these top-levels have moderate agreement ($\kappa > 0.4$). Experience sub-aspects are rare and have no or slight agreement ($-0.2 \leq \kappa < 0.2$), except Impact and Perspective in the book domain ($\kappa > 0.6$). Across the two domains, 12 sub-aspects have below moderate agreement ($\kappa < 0.4$, most of which occur in less than 5% of requests), 15 have moderate agreement ($0.4 \leq \kappa < 0.6$), 11 have substantial agreement ($0.6 \leq \kappa < 0.8$) and 10 have strong agreement ($\kappa > 0.8$), and 4 sub-aspects do not occur at all. In general, our annotations are reliable for high-level aspects and specific aspects that are very concrete (plot, dialogue, publication date), but reliability drops with increasingly specific and affective aspects.

5   Comparison

Our results indicate that for both domains, relevance aspects are very often Content- or Metadata-related. Book requests include the Metadata aspect more often (80.5%) than movie requests (76.6%), while movie requests mention the Content more often (in 95.4% of all annotated requests) than book requests (77.9%) (see Fig. 2). More significant differences occur for the Experience (in 23% of the book and only 4% of the movie requests) and the Context aspects (in 17.1% of the book and only 1.9% of the movie requests). Such differences are also observable for the sub-categories. For example, twice as many movie requests include Character information (47% vs. 20%) and almost three times as many requests are for Plot elements compared to the book posts (85% vs. 31%). For book requests, Topic is much more common (43%) than for movie requests (8%).

A striking difference that might have influenced our results is the high proportion of Known-item information needs for movies (86.3%) in comparison to Discovery- (53.5%) and Similarity-related (39.0%) book inquiries (see Fig. 3). This was undoubtedly influenced by known-item requests being more common in the

IMDB message boards, although this could very well be a reflection of movie information needs in general.

The next analysis step would be to compare relevance aspects per information need type. For example, comparing Discovery and Known-item book requests, a remarkable difference between the occurrence of Experience aspects (33.5% in comparison to 6.4%) is observable. The same is true for movie requests. For Known-item book and movie requests, the Content aspect (99.4% and 92.7% respectively) is frequently included because of Plot descriptions (81.4% and 92.7%). In contrast, for Discovery book and movie requests, Topic is the most prevalent aspect. Characteristic for Known-item requests in both domains are Publication Date (74.4%) for books and Release Date (58.7%) for movies compared to Discovery requests, where these aspects occur with less than 4%. These preliminary findings of information need characteristics suggest considerable variations in relevance aspects.

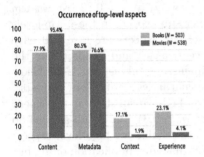

Fig. 2. Occurrence of the top-level aspects in both domains.

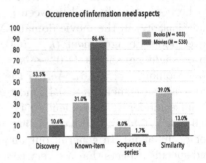

Fig. 3. Occurrence of the information need aspects in both domains.

6   Discussion and Conclusions

Through an analysis of 1041 complex search requests from online discussion forums, we have presented an overview of the different relevance aspects that are prevalent in such requests, but currently not well-supported by search systems. System design for Known-item requests typically considers cases where the user knows important metadata aspects such as title and author, but the forum posts show a different type of Known-item request that require different data sources, such as plot description, movie scripts and book covers to satisfy them. As future work, we would also like to expand our analysis to other domains such as music and game requests. In addition, we would like to evaluate the proposed coding frameworks using content from different forums. This would allow for further validation of our coding framework, especially by focusing on evaluating highly specific sub-categories and affective aspects related to requester's experience where inter-annotator agreement in this study is challenged.

References

1. Austin, B.A.: Motion picture attendance and factors influencing movie selection among high school students. In: Proceedings of 33rd Annual University Film Association Conference (1979)
2. Austin, B.A.: Motivations for movie attendance. In: Proceedings of the 76th Annual Meeting of the Eastern Communication Association, pp. 3–34 (1985)
3. Banerjee, S.C., Greene, K., Krcmar, M., Bagdasarov, Z., Ruginyte, D.: The role of gender and sensation seeking in film choice: exploring mood and arousal. Media Psychol. 20(3), 97–105 (2008)
4. Belkin, N., Bogers, T., Kamps, J., Kelly, D., Koolen, M., Yilmaz, E.: Second workshop on supporting complex search tasks. In: CHIIR 2017, pp. 433–435 (2017)
5. Bogers, T.: Searching for movies: an exploratory analysis of movie-related information needs. In: Proceedings of iConference 2015. iDEALS (2015)
6. Broder, A.: A taxonomy of web search. ACM SIGIR Forum 36(2), 3–10 (2002)
7. Buchanan, G., McKay, D.: In the bookshop: examining popular search strategies. In: JCDL 2011, pp. 269–278 (2011)
8. Elsweiler, D., Mandl, S., Kirkegaard Lunn, B.: Understanding casual-leisure information needs: a diary study in the context of television viewing. In: IIiX 2010, pp. 25–34 (2010)
9. Fleiss, J.L.: Measuring nominal scale agreement among many raters. Psychol. Bull. 76(5), 378–382 (1971)
10. Inskip, C., Butterworth, R., MacFarlane, A.: A study of the information needs of the users of a folk music library and the implications for the design of a digital library system. IPM 44(2), 647–662 (2008)
11. Jansen, B.J., Spink, A., Bateman, J., Saracevic, T.: Real life information retrieval: a study of user queries on the web. ACM SIGIR Forum 32(1), 5–17 (1998)
12. Khabsa, M., Wu, Z., Giles, C.L.: Towards better understanding of academic search. In: JCDL 2016, pp. 111–114 (2016)
13. Koolen, M., Bogers, T., van den Bosch, A., Kamps, J.: Looking for books in social media: an analysis of complex search requests. In: Hanbury, A., Kazai, G., Rauber, A., Fuhr, N. (eds.) ECIR 2015. LNCS, vol. 9022, pp. 184–196. Springer, Cham (2015). https://doi.org/10.1007/978-3-319-16354-3_19
14. Lee, J.H.: Analysis of user needs and information features in natural language queries seeking music information. JASIST 61(5), 1025–1045 (2010)
15. Li, X., Schijvenaars, B.J., de Rijke, M.: Investigating queries and search failures in academic search. IPM 53(3), 666–683 (2017)
16. McKenzie, P.J.: A model of information practices in accounts of everyday-life information seeking. J. Doc. 59(1), 19–40 (2003)
17. Mikkonen, A., Vakkari, P.: Readers' search strategies for accessing books in public libraries. In: IIIX 2012, pp. 214–223 (2012)
18. Mikkonen, A., Vakkari, P.: Readers' interest criteria in fiction book search in library catalogs. J. Doc. 72(4), 696–715 (2016)
19. Pass, G., Chowdhury, A., Torgeson, C.: A picture of search. In: InfoScale 2006 (2006)
20. Pejtersen, A.M.: New model for multimedia interfaces to online public access catalogues. Electron. Libr. 10(6), 359–366 (1992)
21. Reuter, K.: Assessing aesthetic relevance: children's book selection in a digital library. JASIST 58(12), 1745–1763 (2007)

22. Rose, D.E., Levinson, D.: Understanding user goals in web search. In: WWW 2004, pp. 13–19 (2004)
23. Ross, C.S.: Finding without seeking: the information encounter in the context of reading for pleasure. IPM **35**(6), 783–799 (1999)
24. Saracevic, T.: Relevance: a review of the literature and a framework for thinking on the notion in information science. Part II: nature and manifestations of relevance. J. Am. Soc. Inf. Sci. Technol. **58**(13), 1915–1933 (2007)
25. Saricks, J.G.: Readers' Advisory Service in the Public Library, 3rd edn. American Library Association, Chicago (2005)
26. Savolainen, R.: Everyday life information seeking: approaching information seeking in the context of 'way of life'. Libr. Inf. Sci. Res. **17**, 259–294 (1995)
27. Serantes, L.C.: "I'm a marvel girl": exploration of the selection practices of comic book readers. In: Proceedings of Annual Conference of the Canadian Association of Information Science (2009)
28. Waller, V.: Not just information: who searches for what on the search engine Google? JASIST **62**(4), 761–775 (2011)
29. Zhou, S., Cheng, K., Men, L.: The survey of large-scale query classification. In: AIP, vol. 1834, no. 1 (2017)

Position Bias in Recommender Systems
for Digital Libraries

Andrew Collins[1,2](✉) ⓘ, Dominika Tkaczyk[1] ⓘ, Akiko Aizawa[2],
and Joeran Beel[1,2] ⓘ

[1] School of Computer Science and Statistics, ADAPT Centre,
Trinity College Dublin, Dublin, Ireland
{Andrew.Collins,Dominika.Tkaczyk,
Joeran.Beel}@adaptcentre.ie
[2] National Institute of Informatics (NII), Tokyo, Japan
aizawa@nii.ac.jp

Abstract. "Position bias" describes the tendency of users to interact with items on top of a list with higher probability than with items at a lower position in the list, regardless of the items' actual relevance. In the domain of recommender systems, particularly recommender systems in digital libraries, position bias has received little attention. We conduct a study in a real-world recommender system that delivered ten million related-article recommendations to the users of the digital library Sowiport, and the reference manager JabRef. Recommendations were randomly chosen to be shuffled or non-shuffled, and we compared click-through rate (CTR) for each rank of the recommendations. According to our analysis, the CTR for the highest rank in the case of Sowiport is 53% higher than expected in a hypothetical non-biased situation (0.189% vs. 0.123%). Similarly, in the case of Jabref the highest rank received a CTR of 1.276%, which is 87% higher than expected (0.683%). A chi-squared test confirms the strong relationship between the rank of the recommendation shown to the user and whether the user decided to click it ($p < 0.01$ for both Jabref and Sowiport). Our study confirms the findings from other domains, that recommendations in the top positions are more often clicked, regardless of their actual relevance.

Keywords: Recommender systems · Position bias · Click-through rate

1 Introduction

Position bias is a commonly observed phenomenon in Information Retrieval. It describes a tendency of people to notice or interact with items in certain positions of lists with higher probability, regardless of the items' actual relevance. Eye tracking studies demonstrate that users are less likely to look at lower ranking items in vertical lists, typically only examining the first few entries [7]. Furthermore, 65% of users

This publication has emanated from research conducted with the financial support of Science Foundation Ireland (SFI) under Grant Number 13/RC/2106. This work was also supported by a fellowship within the postdoc-program of the German Academic Exchange Service (DAAD).

© Springer International Publishing AG, part of Springer Nature 2018
G. Chowdhury et al. (Eds.): iConference 2018, LNCS 10766, pp. 335–344, 2018.
https://doi.org/10.1007/978-3-319-78105-1_37

interact with lists in a depth-first fashion, clicking on the first item which seems relevant, without evaluating the entire list in a holistic fashion [10].

Position bias creates challenges in evaluating recommender systems based on users' interaction with recommendations. The relevance of sets of recommendations is often implicitly inferred by tracking clicks by a user on a set. The effectiveness of a recommender system can therefore be evaluated using this click data. Due to position bias, however, the probability of a user interacting with an item might not indicate that item's absolute relevance within the set. Evaluations which rely on click data, but which don't take bias into account, may be misleading.

There is little research that tests for the existence of position bias in recommender systems, and no research on position bias in recommender systems for digital libraries, to the best of our knowledge. Recommender system studies do not usually assess bias using click data from typical real-world system, and particularly not with click data which reflects typical digital library usage. A small number of user studies and offline evaluations exist, however it is not certain that the results from offline studies will be generally applicable to real-world digital library recommender systems [3]. Consequently, it remains uncertain if, and to what extent, position bias exists for recommender systems in the real-world.

Our research goal is therefore to assess if position bias exists in real-world recommender systems, in the context of digital libraries.

2 Related Work

Existing research into position bias in recommender systems tends to either: test for its existence through small user studies [17, 19], model or simulate biased user behavior based on past data [5, 15], or account for biased click behaviour with the possible goal of training a system [8, 13, 14, 18]. In search engine research, robust eye tracking studies have also been conducted which assess its effects [6, 7].

A common approach to testing position bias without the need for eye tracking interventions, in both recommender systems and search engine research, is to alter the order of ranked recommendations or search results in some manner. Users' interactions with altered orderings are then compared to that of non-altered orderings. Some studies randomly shuffle each set of items and compare them to non-shuffled sets [16, 17, 19]. Other studies re-order results in a specific, non-random way. For example, results are presented to users in a reverse ordering in several studies, and clicks on reversed sets compared to those of non-reversed sets [7, 9].

In the case of both random shuffling, and reversed orderings, inferences about biased behaviour can be made from comparison to the correct ordering. For example, if users click the first rank of a list with similar probability when it has either a highly relevant item, or irrelevant item, position bias may be evident. Keane et al. [9] and Joachims et al. [7] each used reversed-set comparisons and found that position bias was evident in search engine usage; the percentage of clicks on the highest rank remained higher than the lowest rank with reversed rankings (40% vs 10% [9], 15% vs 5% [7]). However in both cases, the percentage of clicks on the lowest ranking items increased in the reversed state (0% to 10% [9], 2% to 5% [7]). This suggests that, despite the effects of position bias, some users are perhaps systematic in their browsing behaviour, and will examine lists of results more thoroughly before clicking on an item.

Results from recommender system user studies are inconsistent with findings from search engine research however. Through random shuffling, Teppan and Zanker found that the position of an item in a recommender system is less important that the desirability of an item to a user, as assessed by clicks, specifically when encouraged to examine lists closely [17]. Zheng et al. found that recommendation relevance was the sole determinant of click rates, and that position bias had *no* impact on behaviour [19].

Position bias is not only tested through shuffling recommendations, but its negative effects can also be countered by taking advantage of it. Pandey et al. promote random items to the top of recommendation sets to account for position bias, which acts against new items in systems which make recommendations based on item popularity [13].

Finally, reordering has been recently used to estimate the strength of position bias in a given scenario, and derive click propensity scores for ranks within recommendation sets. These propensity scores can then be used to train performant learning-to-rank using biased feedback [8, 18].

Joachims et al. suggest that the effect of position bias may be more of a problem in systems which do not assess user judgments of relevance explicitly [7]. Implicit data such as clicks on recommendations are used to approximate relevance for a user, because they are cheap to collect and analyse. For such approximation to be useful, however, there must be strong correlation between the item's relevance and clicks. The effects of position bias, therefore, may be an important consideration for digital libraries that employ recommender systems but do not require explicit ratings of recommendations by users.

3 Methodology

In order to assess position bias in recommender systems, we examined data from the digital library Sowiport, and reference manager Jabref. Both Sowiport and Jabref use Mr. DLib, a recommendation-as-a-service provider, to recommend documents to users [2, 4]. Sets of recommendations were chosen and ranked by the Mr. DLib recommender system based upon users' actions on Sowiport and in Jabref. The recommendations are presented to users in a vertical list format, and subsequent user-interactions with each set are tracked [1].

In total, approximately 1.6 m sets, each containing 6 recommendations, were delivered to users during the course of the study. The study was run over a period of 5 months beginning in March 2017. In total 10 m recommendations were delivered to users and 12,543 clicks were logged. Click-through Rates (**CTR**) – the ratio of clicked recommendations to delivered recommendations – were established for each rank of the vertical lists of recommendations. "Highly ranked" items are those that appear towards the top of lists (Fig. 1).

Of the sets of recommendations which receive clicks, most receive just one click (Fig. 2). We expect that any tendency for users to pay more attention to highly ranked items in a set should manifest as a disproportionately high number of clicks for those ranks on average, when compared to lower ranks.

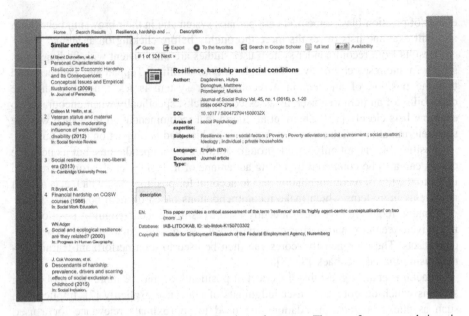

Fig. 1. Recommendations displayed for a Sowiport document. The set of recommendations is highlighted for this figure, with each rank of the list numbered

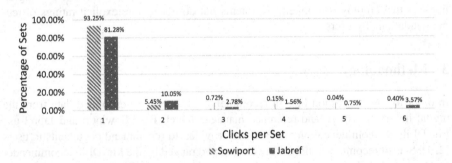

Fig. 2. A vast majority of recommendation sets that receive at least one click, receive only one click (93% of Sowiport sets, 81% of Jabref sets)

Of the 10 million recommendations delivered, approximately half were delivered in sets whose rankings were shuffled before being presented to users. Furthermore, 1% of recommendations were chosen randomly from the entire corpus, to act as a baseline.

Due to the large amount of randomly shuffled data available, it was possible to retrospectively conduct several analyses of the click data, based upon other author's analyses.

The first analysis aims to verify the results of user studies that test for bias through random shuffling of sets of recommendations [17, 19]. To do this we simply compared the total average CTR for each rank in non-shuffled data, to that of shuffled data. A Chi-squared test is used to determine if, in the shuffled data, there is a significant relationship between the rank of the recommendation and whether it was clicked by the user. A significant relationship suggests the existence of position bias. Shuffling sets of recommendations should not drastically affect click rates; all sets in this experiment were limited to six items and all items within each set will typically be somewhat relevant.

A post hoc examination showed that ∼40,000 randomly shuffled recommendations were shuffled into an approximately reversed ordering within their respective sets. Consequently, we also want to verify the results of offline studies that evaluate bias through purposeful perturbations of items presented to users, specifically, studies which compare reversed sets to non-reversed sets [7, 9].

Lastly, the randomly shuffled data allows for an assessment of bias which is similar to propensity estimation as described by Joachims et al. [8], and by Wang et al. [18], in building their click propensity models. In our study, we aggregate the sets of randomly shuffled recommendations according to the rank, in which the user saw the most relevant item. We analyse the CTRs for these aggregated subsets separately.

All data of our study is be available at http://data.mr-dlib.org to enable other researchers to replicate our calculations, and use the data for extended analyses beyond the results we present.

4 Results

Click-through rates for non-shuffled sets appear as would be expected in an appropriate recommender system. The highest ranks experience the highest CTR (0.243% on average for Sowiport, 1.281% for Jabref), with a decreasing CTR by rank (Fig. 3). Users *should* expect that an effective recommender system is delivering results in a sequentially relevant manner, so it is not surprising to see a decreasing CTR by rank when the system delivers recommendations in accordance with these expectations.

If a large number of recommendation sets are uniformly shuffled, and users assess lists in a rational, unbiased manner, it might be expected that CTR for each rank would be approximately equal. This expected CTR for each rank in shuffled sets, given

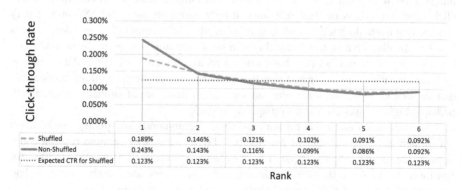

Fig. 3. Users of the digital library Sowiport appear to exhibit bias in choosing items, following a random shuffling of recommendations

unbiased behaviour on Sowiport (0.123%) and Jabref (0.683%) is shown in Figs. 3 and 4. It is calculated as total clicks on recommendations divided by the total number delivered. Some small user studies of position bias in recommender systems do find that, following uniform shuffling, CTR for each rank is approximately equal [19]. However in our online evaluation, the data resulting from shuffling sets of recommendations shows a significant relationship between the rank of the recommendation and whether the user decides to click it (Chi-squared test, p < 0.01). CTR for shuffled sets decreases at approximately the same rate as that of non-shuffled, rank to rank (Fig. 3).

Similar results can be seen for users of Jabref (Fig. 4), with a significant difference between shuffled CTR and that of a uniform distribution (Chi-squared test, p < 0.01).

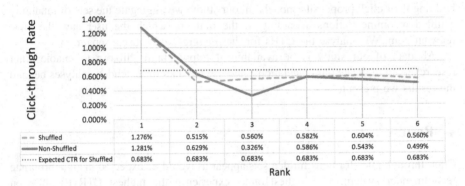

Fig. 4. Users of reference manager Jabref also appear to exhibit position bias, following random shuffling of recommendations

In both cases, significant position bias seems evident in users' clicking behavior. With no meaningful difference in CTR between non-shuffled and shuffled sets on average, it seems as if users do not interact with recommendations in a rational manner.

A decreasing CTR by rank for shuffled recommendations may suggest several things. First, it may tell us that users do not care about recommendation quality and will click items regardless of their relevance simply based on their rank. Second, it may suggest that users do interact with lists in a "depth-first" manner [10], and don't assess lists holistically. That is, they may choose a poor recommendation in the second rank, because they have not noticed that there's a relatively better recommendation in e.g. rank six. Finally, it may suggest that the system is not discretely ranking recommendations well enough, and that users can see that all items are of similar relevance and, perhaps, higher ranks are more convenient to click.

The suggestion that users do not care about recommendation quality can be ruled out immediately: in the case of Mr. DLib, CTR for arbitrarily random recommendations is miniscule when compared to ranking algorithms (0.012% vs 0.130% for Sowiport, 0.012% vs 0.683% for Jabref) (Fig. 5). Users are keenly aware of bad recommendations and will generally refuse to interact with them.

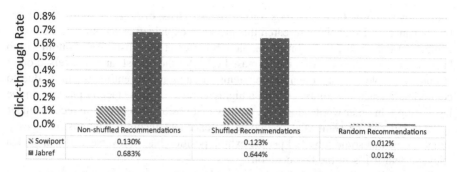

Fig. 5. CTR for non-shuffled, shuffled, and random recommendations

The second and third suggestions – "depth first" searching, and insufficiently discrete ranking – require further analysis:

When rankings are displayed in reverse ordering, the least relevant items are placed into the highest ranks. Comparing non-shuffled sets to reverse-ordered sets produces results in-line with Keane et al. [9], and Joachims et al. [7], who evaluated bias in a similar manner (Fig. 6). On average, highly ranked items maintain a high CTR despite their lower relevance. Similarly, the most relevant items being placed into the lowest ranks incurs a lower CTR than when they're left in the highest rank. As seen in the above studies, despite position bias still being evident here, the distribution of CTR seems to shift to lower ranks, with a significantly reduced CTR for the highest rank, and a significantly increased one for the lowest.

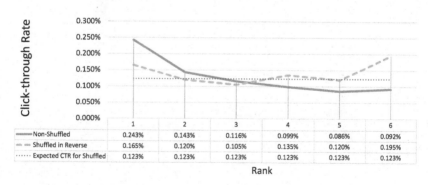

Fig. 6. CTR by rank for non-shuffled sets on Sowiport versus sets which were shuffled into an approximately reverse ranking

This suggests that, although people are biased on average, sometimes recommendation relevance is deduced by users in a way which seems to agree with the ranking algorithm used. It is not clear whether this is due to characteristics of some subset of recommended items, which encourage searching, or characteristics of a subset of users. It is known in position bias research, for example, that users are better able to remember the first and last items in lists when compared to middle items [12]. It is also commonly seen that CTR increases for last items in lists, even when items are ordered by relevance. In Psychology research this has been explained as 'contrarian' behavior, exhibited by a small proportion of people who interact with lists from bottom to top [11]. It is unclear then whether the increased CTR for the lowest rank in reversed order is due to people seeking out relevant items throughout the entire list, or is due to contrarian interactions combined with a highly attractive item – luckily placed – in the last position. In other words, does Fig. 6 show that position bias exists in recommender systems but can be somewhat overcome by excellent recommendations, or does it simply show that some subset of people exhibit position bias in reverse, and will click a relevant item if it's in the last position?

When uniformly shuffled data is analysed according to where the ranking algorithm's *most relevant* recommendation is placed, user behavior is more clear (Figs. 7 and 8). Every analyses still seems to show position bias: higher ranks still receive a higher average CTR, and lower ranks a smaller one, despite recommendations being shuffled randomly. However, on average, regardless of rank, people seek out and are able to discern the most relevant items. CTR increases for all ranks which have the most relevant item shuffled to it, with an average increase of 29%. This suggests that increases in CTR for the lowest rank of reversed sets, as shown in Fig. 6 and by Keane et al., are likely *not* due to 'contrarian' click-behavior. This seems to mirror Joachims et al.'s eye-tracking study which shows that users are more likely to examine lower ranks when presented with less relevant items in higher ones, and that they do so in a sequential fashion [7].

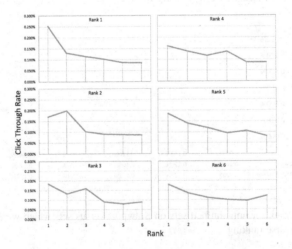

Fig. 7. Effect on click-through rate seen when aggregating shuffled Sowiport data according to where the highest recommendation has been shuffled to. For instance, the top-right graph shows average CTR by rank when the most relevant item was randomly shuffled to rank 4 (all other ranks are randomly shuffled, too). The most relevant recommendation results in an outlying average CTR for its rank. Some portion of users seem to seek out relevant information to an equal degree at all ranks.

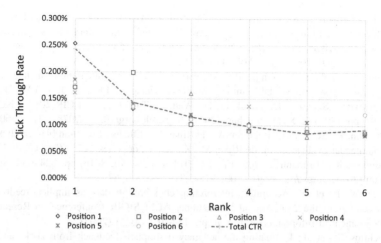

Fig. 8. Figure 7 combined into one graph. Each symbol represents the average CTR-by-rank for each aggregation of Sowiport shuffled data, e.g. the circle symbol shows the average CTR-by-rank for sets whose most relevant recommendation was shuffled to rank six. CTR is increased for all ranks containing the most relevant recommendation, by an average of 29.07%

5 Conclusion and Future Work

Our research confirms that position bias exists for recommender systems in digital libraries. The analysis shows that articles recommended at higher positions received significantly higher click-through rates than expected, regardless of their actual relevance. The CTR for the highest rank in the case of Sowiport is 0.189%, which is 53% higher than expected (0.123%). In the case of Jabref the highest rank received a CTR of 1.276%, which is 87% higher than expected (0.683%). A chi-squared test confirms the strong relationship between the rank of the recommendation shown to the user and whether the user decided to click it ($p < 0.01$ for both Jabref and Sowiport). However, our research also shows that a significant number of users look at all recommended items. Ranking recommendations in a reverse order shows click-through rates which mirror this reversal, although bias is still apparent. More distinctly, in shuffled recommendation lists, ranks containing the most relevant recommendation have a higher average CTR (29.07%) than the average CTR for shuffled recommendations on that position.

In future work, it should be determined how to quantify position bias given different modes of user interaction with recommender systems within digital libraries, as opposed to other domains. The effectiveness of unbiased learning-to-rank may then be tested for digital libraries with comparison to classical recommendation algorithms.

References

1. Beel, J., et al.: Introducing Mr. DLib, a machine-readable digital library. In: Proceedings of the 11th ACM/IEEE Joint Conference on Digital Libraries (JCDL 2011) (2011)
2. Beel, J., et al.: Mr. DLib: Recommendations-as-a-Service (RaaS) for academia. In: 2017 ACM/IEEE Joint Conference on Digital Libraries, JCDL 2017, Toronto, ON, Canada, 19–23 June 2017, pp. 313–314 (2017)

3. Beel, J., Langer, S.: A comparison of offline evaluations, online evaluations, and user studies in the context of research-paper recommender systems. In: Kapidakis, S., Mazurek, C., Werla, M. (eds.) TPDL 2015. LNCS, vol. 9316, pp. 153–168. Springer, Cham (2015). https://doi.org/10.1007/978-3-319-24592-8_12
4. Feyer, S., Siebert, S., Gipp, B., Aizawa, A., Beel, J.: Integration of the scientific recommender system Mr. DLib into the reference manager JabRef. In: Jose, J.M., Hauff, C., Altıngovde, I.S., Song, D., Albakour, D., Watt, S., Tait, J. (eds.) ECIR 2017. LNCS, vol. 10193, pp. 770–774. Springer, Cham (2017). https://doi.org/10.1007/978-3-319-56608-5_80
5. Hofmann, K., Schuth, A., Bellogín, A., de Rijke, M.: Effects of position bias on click-based recommender evaluation. In: de Rijke, M., Kenter, T., de Vries, A.P., Zhai, C., de Jong, F., Radinsky, K., Hofmann, K. (eds.) ECIR 2014. LNCS, vol. 8416, pp. 624–630. Springer, Cham (2014). https://doi.org/10.1007/978-3-319-06028-6_67
6. Joachims, T., et al.: Accurately interpreting clickthrough data as implicit feedback. In: Proceedings of the 28th Annual International ACM SIGIR Conference on Research and Development in Information Retrieval, pp. 154–161. ACM (2005)
7. Joachims, T., et al.: Evaluating the accuracy of implicit feedback from clicks and query reformulations in web search. ACM Trans. Inf. Syst. (TOIS) 25(2), 7 (2007)
8. Joachims, T., et al.: Unbiased learning-to-rank with biased feedback. In: Proceedings of the Tenth ACM International Conference on Web Search and Data Mining, pp. 781–789 ACM (2017)
9. Keane, M.T., et al.: Are people biased in their use of search engines? Commun. ACM. 51(2), 49–52 (2008)
10. Klöckner, K., et al.: Depth-and breadth-first processing of search result lists. In: CHI 2004 Extended Abstracts on Human Factors in Computing Systems, p. 1539. ACM (2004)
11. Lerman, K., Hogg, T.: Leveraging position bias to improve peer recommendation. PLoS ONE 9(6), e98914 (2014)
12. Murphy, J., et al.: Primacy and recency effects on clicking behavior. J. Comput.-Mediat. Commun. 11(2), 522–535 (2006)
13. Pandey, S., et al.: Shuffling a stacked deck: the case for partially randomized ranking of search engine results. In: Proceedings of the 31st International Conference on Very Large Data Bases, pp. 781–792. VLDB Endowment (2005)
14. Schnabel, T., et al.: Recommendations as treatments: debiasing learning and evaluation. In: Proceedings of the 33nd International Conference on Machine Learning, ICML 2016, New York City, NY, USA, 19–24 June 2016. pp. 1670–1679 (2016)
15. Schuth, A.: Search engines that learn from their users. SIGIR Forum 50(1), 95–96 (2016)
16. Serenko, A., Bontis, N.: First in, best dressed: the presence of order-effect bias in journal ranking surveys. J. Informetr. 7(1), 138–144 (2013)
17. Teppan, E.C., Zanker, M.: Decision biases in recommender systems. J. Internet Commer. 14 (2), 255–275 (2015)
18. Wang, X., et al.: Learning to rank with selection bias in personal search. In: Proceedings of the 39th International ACM SIGIR Conference on Research and Development in Information Retrieval, pp. 115–124. ACM (2016)
19. Zheng, H., et al.: Do clicks measure recommendation relevancy?: an empirical user study. In: Proceedings of the Fourth ACM Conference on Recommender Systems, pp. 249–252. ACM (2010)

Rules for Inducing Hierarchies
from Social Tagging Data

Hang Dong[1,2]($\boxtimes$), Wei Wang[2], and Frans Coenen[1]

[1] Department of Computer Science, University of Liverpool, Liverpool, UK
{HangDong,Coenen}@liverpool.ac.uk
[2] Department of Computer Science and Software Engineering,
Xi'an Jiaotong-Liverpool University, Suzhou, China
Wei.Wang03@xjtlu.edu.cn

Abstract. Automatic generation of hierarchies from social tags is a challenging task. We identified three rules, set inclusion, graph centrality and information-theoretic condition from the literature and proposed two new rules, fuzzy set inclusion and probabilistic association to induce hierarchical relations. We proposed an hierarchy generation algorithm, which can incorporate each rule with different data representations, i.e., resource and Probabilistic Topic Model based representations. The learned hierarchies were compared to some of the widely used reference concept hierarchies. We found that probabilistic association and set inclusion based rules helped produce better quality hierarchies according to the evaluation metrics.

1 Introduction

Tagging is a popular functionality on many social media platforms. Users can add "free" words (tags) to describe shared resources to facilitate searching and recommendation. These user-generated tags form a taxonomy of users' terminologies called folksonomy. There have been great interests and motivation to automatically induce knowledge structures from social media data. The most challenging issue is the intrinsic difficulties (e.g., sparse data, weak context, polysemy, concatenated tags and typos [10]) to learn large-scale concept hierarchies in various domains. Even for human being this requires considerable cognitive work [19]. Although there have been some general guidelines to associate semantics to tags [7], no theoretical consensus were reached on the rules and assumptions to determine semantic relations among tags.

There have been methods using different rules to derive hierarchical structures from social tags. However, there is no comprehensive research on analysis and comparison of these rules in a rigorous manner. The work in [16] compared four clustering and generality based techniques and found that generality-based methods in general outperform the clustering based ones. It primarily focused on evaluation techniques and did not analyse how the underlying rules and their assumptions affected the results. Furthermore, other important rules such as set inclusion and information-theoretic condition were not discussed.

© Springer International Publishing AG, part of Springer Nature 2018
G. Chowdhury et al. (Eds.): iConference 2018, LNCS 10766, pp. 345–355, 2018.
https://doi.org/10.1007/978-3-319-78105-1_38

A rule in the context of this work is defined as certain conditions that need to be satisfied to determine whether a pair of words (tags) has a directed hierarchical or subsumption relation. We summarise existing rules used in learning hierarchical relations from social tagging data and propose two new rules: probabilistic association and fuzzy set inclusion based rules. Then we evaluate the performance of these rules in learning relations and compare the results to three well-know reference hierarchies. We aim to conduct an in-depth study for the following two questions:

Q1. Which rule can effectively capture the hierarchical relations between social tags?

Q2. How do rules and data representation techniques affect the quality of the induced concept hierarchies?

Our contributions can be summarised as follows. First, we performed a thorough analysis on the existing rules and proposed two new rules. Second, we designed an algorithm that can accommodate different rules to iteratively learn a knowledge hierarchy. The algorithm ranks all pairwise tag pairs by similarity in descending order, and passes the tag pairs to a rule to determine their relations. Third, we used three reference knowledge hierarchies (DBPedia, Microsoft Concept Graph and ACM Computing Classification System) to evaluate the quality of the learned hierarchies based on standard metrics (taxonomic precision, recall and F-measure). To our best knowledge, this is the first comprehensive study on the rules for learning knowledge hierarchies from social tagging data.

2   Hierarchical Relation: Definitions and Rules

Creation of concept hierarchies representing the world knowledge is a difficult cognitive task that requires lot of effort [19, p. 139]. Hierarchical relation is a paradigmatic relation, which means that two words should fit into the same grammatical slot or be of the same semantic type [3]. It is different from syntagmatic relations which exist between concepts in specific documents or other contexts [15]. In this way, co-occurrence of tags is syntagmatic relation, but provides great source for paradigmatic relations, as stated in [14, p. 223]. Hierarchical relations can be divided into hyponymy and meronymy. In some ontology models, they are merged and referred to as broader/narrower relations (e.g., SKOS[1]).

We take a mixed view of hierarchical relations, with a focus on hyponymy. Although it seems intuitive to tell whether there is a hierarchical relation between two words, the idea of hyponymy is not straightforward. In the linguistic domain, Cruse [3] gave three definitions of hyponymy and proposed a prototype-theoretical characterisation to derive hyponymy. In the first definition, hyponymy was conceptualised in a **logical** way both extensionally and intensionally. Extensionally, X is a hyponym of Y iff the form $\forall x[X'(x) \rightarrow Y'(x)]$

---

[1] https://www.w3.org/TR/skos-primer/.

is satisfied, but none of the form $\forall x[Y'(x) \rightarrow X'(x)]$ holds, where X' and Y' are the logical constants corresponding to the concepts X and Y, and x can be understood as an instance object. This is equivalent to say that the extension of X' should be included in the extension of Y'. Intensionally, "X is a hyponym of Y iff F(X) entails, but is not entailed by F(Y)", where F(-) is a sentential function satisfied by X or Y. The second definition utilises the **collocational** property. The more restricted a word is through the collocational normality, then the more specific it is, or more formally, "X is a hyponym of Y iff the normal context of X is a subset of the normal context of Y". The third idea for defining hyponymy is **componential**. "X is a hyponym of Y iff the features defining Y are a proper subset of features defining X". Based on this idea, to analyse the degree of inclusion between X and Y, "prototypes" of characterisation of hyponymy were proposed [3]. Stock also pointed out a case that holds in most occasions: there is reciprocity between the extension and intension of concepts in a hierarchical chain [15], in other words, specific terms, with further restrictive properties, tend to have less number of objects than general terms.

Moving from linguistic definitions to machine computation, we summarised the main rules found in literature below. We adapted the fuzzy set theory with probabilistic topic representation and named it fuzzy set inclusion. We also proposed another new rule called probabilistic association, which has a strong probabilistic foundation. We use **R1** to **R5** to refer to these rules.

Data Representation. A tag can be represented as a vector over all resources. Let $v[R_i]$ refer to the number of times the tag used to annotate the resource R_i, and i be the index for resources. This **resource-based representation** can capture co-occurrence of tags and is usually high dimensional and sparse. Another representation is based on a Probabilistic Topic Model (**PTM**), representing a tag as a vector over latent (or hidden) topics. PTM is generally a dimension reduction technique and each topic can be represented as a probabilistic distribution of the vocabulary. We used the standard Latent Dirichlet Allocation (LDA) [8] for PTM representation. With LDA inference, we can obtain two matrices, the distribution of hidden topics for each document, p(Topic|Doc) and the distribution of tags for each hidden topic p (Tag|Topic). Using the Bayesian's Theorem, we can estimate p(Topic|Tag).

R1: Set Inclusion. The logical extension of a tag can be quantified using its contexts, i.e., the set of resources it annotated or the set of users who used it for annotation. Through measuring the degree of inclusion between the contexts of two tags, Mika [13] generated a lightweight taxonomy from social tags. De Meo [12] defined this formally as Inclusion measure, set-inc$(A, B) = \frac{|R_A \cap R_B|}{|R_A|}$, where R is the set of resource annotated by the tag A or B. Formally, **tag A is a hyponym of tag B if set-inc$(A, B) \geqslant p \wedge$ set-inc$(B, A) < p \wedge$ sim$(A, B) >$** s, where p is experimentally set as 0.5. For all the rules R1–R5, the function $\text{sim}(A, B)$ measures the similarity (cosine similarity in this study) between A and B; and s is a similarity threshold to be determined by the researcher (see **Data Collection** in Sect. 4).

R2: Graph Centrality. Graph centrality measures the influence or popularity of an object in a social network. The work in [9] assumed that there is a latent taxonomy underlying the similarity graph of social data, and centrality can be used to mine the taxonomy. A *tag similarity graph* is generated through linking each pair of tags having similarity greater than a threshold. It is assumed that in such a graph, nodes with higher centrality are more popular and thus are more general. Both degree and betweenness centrality can be used [1,9]. The rule states that **tag A is a hyponym of tag B if graph-cent(A) < graph-cent(B) $\wedge$ sim$(A, B) > s$**, where *graph-cent()* computes the centrality of a node, we used degree centrality in this study.

R3: Fuzzy Set Inclusion. We propose this rule adapting the set inclusion rule to the PTM representation. We define a fuzzy set of a tag A as a pair (U, m), where U is the set of topics for the tag and $m: U \rightarrow [0, 1]$ is a membership function defined by p(Tag|Topic): for each topic $z \in U$, $m(z) = p(A|z)$. Therefore, the inclusion degree [17] of a fuzzy set S_A of S_B for a pair of tags A and B is defined as fuzzy-set-inc$(S_A, S_B) = \frac{\sum_i \min(S_{Ai}, S_{Bi})}{\sum_i S_{Bi}}$. Instead of measuring the resource set inclusion between a pair of tags, the fuzzy set inclusion rule measures the topic set inclusion in a low dimensional space. We assume that **tag A is a hyponym of tag B if fuzzy-set-inc$(S_A, S_B) \geqslant p \wedge$ fuzzy-set-inc$(S_B, S_A) < p \wedge$ sim$(A, B) > s$**, where p is set as 0.5.

R4: Information-Theoretic Condition. The hierarchical relations between tags were captured using the information-theoretic principle which measures the difference of relative entropy, i.e., Kullback-Leibler (KL) Divergence, from one tag topic distribution to another [18]. KL Divergence is defined as $D_{\mathrm{KL}}(P_A \| P_B) = \sum_i P_{Ai} \log \frac{P_{Ai}}{P_{Bi}}$, where P_A and P_B are probabilistic distributions of hidden topics for a pair of tags A and B, based on the PTM representation. It represents the information wasted by encoding events with one distribution P_A with a code based on another distribution P_B. It is elaborated as the average "surprise" received from a tag A, when it is expected to receive B. The information-theoretic condition [18] is constructed as follows, **tag A is a hyponym of tag B if $D_{KL}(P_B \| P_A) - D_{KL}(P_A \| P_B) < f \wedge$ sim$(A, B) > s$**, where f is a noise factor with a very small value (0.05 in this study).

R5: Probabilistic Association. We propose another rule called probabilistic association, which quantifies the (relative) componential features (in this case, topics) of a tag. Based on the PTM-representation, the probabilistic association [8], p(A|B), can be computed by marginalising over topics, $p(A|B) = \sum_z p(A|z)p(z|B)$, where $p(z|B) \propto p(B|z)p(z)$. Based on the fact that tag A and B are conditionally independent given a topic z, $p(z)$ can be estimated using either uniform distribution or the fraction of tag annotations assigned to the topic z to all tag annotations. The rule is defined as: **tag A is a hyponym of tag B if** $p(A|B) < p(B|A) \wedge \mathbf{sim}(A, B) > s$. This measures the relative topic components of a tag given another tag. If a tag A is highly associated by the topics contained in another tag B, while B is less associated from the topics contained in tag A, then tag B tends to be more general.

3   Methodology: Algorithm for Hierarchy Generation

To facilitate comparison of the rules R1–R5, we designed an algorithm for hierarchy generation. A hierarchy in this work is defined as a Directed Acyclic Graph G, $G = \{V, E\}$, where V is a set of vertices (tags) and $E \subseteq V \times V$ is a set of edges. Algorithm 1 incorporates a rule to select candidate hierarchical tag pairs whose similarity exceeds the threshold. Starting from tag pair with highest similarity, an edge is iteratively added to the graph G if the rule is satisfied. The algorithm assumes the learned hierarchies have a single parent tag for each tag (i.e. mono-hierarchies) and all established relations are direct and transitive.

Algorithm 1. Hierarchy generation algorithm using *any* rules.

Input: $L_{PairSim}$ is a pre-computed list of tag pairs $< t_i, t_j >$ ranked in descending order by similarity. s is a similarity threshold for a tag pair. $sim(t_i, t_j)$ computes the cosine similarity between t_i and t_j; $hasParent(t, G)$ returns a boolean indicating whether tag t has a parent node in G; $isHypo(t_i, t_j)$ determines whether t_i is a hyponym of t_j.

Output: G, an induced hierarchy as a directed graph.

```
 1  Initialise G;
 2  for i ← 1 to |L_PairSim| do
 3  |    < t_i, t_j > ← L_PairSim[i];
 4  |    if sim(t_i, t_j) < s then
 5  |    |    continue to the next i;
 6  |    end
 7  |    if NOT hasParent(t_i, G) then
 8  |    |    if isHypo(t_i, t_j) then
 9  |    |    |    G ← G ∪ < t_i, t_j >;
10  |    |    end
11  |    end
12  end
```

To answer Q1, we replaced the $isHypo(t_i, t_j)$ with different rules to generate different hierarchies. To answer Q2, we represented tags using resource-based and PTM representations respectively to generate two different sets of $L_{PairSim}$. Different s for the two representations were used to ensure the same number of tag pairs passed to a rule. The set inclusion rule is based on resource-based representation; fuzzy set inclusion, information-theoretic condition and probabilistic association rules are based on the PTM representation; and graph centrality can be based on any of the two representations.

4 Experiments

In this section, we present the experiments and evaluation results and discuss our findings in relation to the two research questions.

Data Collection. The academic social bookmarking data Bibsonomy was used. The whole dataset[2] comprises 3,794,882 annotations, 868,015 distinct resources, 283,858 distinct tags annotated by 11,103 users. We followed the steps in [6] to clean the dataset and further removed resources annotated with less than 3 tags. The cleaned dataset contains 7,846 tags and 128,782 resources. Each resource is a bag-of-tags, to represent tags using PTM, we set the number of topic as 1000 minimising perplexity of LDA model. The similarity threshold s were set as 0.2 and 0.038 for PTM and resource-based representation resp. to control same number (2.3 million) of pairwise tag pairs passed to a rule. For reference-based evaluation, we chose three gold-standard hierarchies of different nature, the crowd-sourced DBpedia, the web-mined Microsoft Concept Graph (MCG) and the expert-crafted ACM Computing Classification System (CCS). DBpedia[3] is a knowledge base containing structured information from Wikipedia. MCG[4] is a knowledge base mined from billions of web pages. ACM computing classification system (CCS)[5] is a classification system to organise ACM publications by subjects and support retrieval. In Bibsonomy, there are 6,616 common concepts overlapped with DBpedia, 6,029 with MCG and 691 with CCS.

Evaluation Metrics. With the cleaned dataset, we used Algorithm 1 to generate several hierarchies based on rules R1–R5 and different data representations. A number of proposals on evaluation metrics for this purpose are available, see [4,5,11]. We chose the *taxonomic precision* (TP), and *taxonomic recall* (TR) [4]. The basic idea for these metrics is to find common concepts presented in both hierarchies, and then for each common concept to extract a set of concepts that characterises it, termed as *characteristic excerpt*. The similarity of hierarchies is then computed based on the similarity of these characteristic excerpts.

The common semantic cotopy was proposed to define the characteristic excerpt in [5]. However, it cannot judge the direction of hierarchical relations. Thus, we adopted the direct common subconcepts, by traversing from the common concept to all subconcepts until a subconcept is found, which is contained in both hierarchies. We restricted this search to one level only in the hierarchy. This is because that the study requires evaluating the rules' ability to capture

---

[2] http://www.kde.cs.uni-kassel.de/bibsonomy/dumps/.
[3] http://downloads.dbpedia.org/2015-10/core/.
[4] https://concept.research.microsoft.com/Home/Download.
[5] http://www.acm.org/about/class/class/2012.

direct relations and the reference ontologies are generally sparse (especially for DBpedia and MCG). We named this new characteristic except as common direct subsumption (cdsub). The taxonomic precision is defined in Eqs. 1 and 2, where L is the learned hierarchy and G the referenced one. The taxonomic recall is computed as $TR(L, G) = TP(G, L)$. Similar to the standard F-measure, the taxonomic F-measure is the harmonic mean of taxonomic precision and recall $TF(L, G) = \frac{2 * TP(L,G) * TR(L,G)}{TP(L,G) + TR(L,G)}$. The metrics are defined for non-leaf nodes ensuring $|cdsub(c, L, G)|$ above zero; leaf concepts (have no direct subconcepts) in L or G have tp_{cdsub} as zero.

Another two metrics were also used: *taxonomic overlap* (TO) [11] measuring the quality of hierarchies and *taxonomic F'-measure* $(TF'$, note that it is different from $TF)$ [2,5] measuring the overall quality of the lexical and relation levels. TO is a symmetric measure and is calculated with Eqs. 3 and 4. As cdsub only concerns common concepts, TF and TO are not affected by non-common concepts in both hierarchies. Thus, to include lexical coverage into evaluation, *taxonomic F'-measure* (TF') is introduced, computed as the harmonic mean of Lexical Recall (LR) and TF, $TF'(L, G) = \frac{2 * LR(L,G) * TF(L,G)}{LR(L,G) + TF(L,G)}$. LR is defined as $LR(L, G) = \frac{|V_L \cap V_G|}{|V_G|}$, where $|V|$ is the size of vocabulary in a hierarchy.

$$tp_{\text{cdsub}}(c, L, G) = \frac{|\text{cdsub}(c, L, G) \cap \text{cdsub}(c, G, L)|}{|\text{cdsub}(c, L, G)|} \tag{1}$$

$$TP(L, G) = \frac{1}{|L \cap G|} \sum_{c \in L \cap G} tp_{\text{cdsub}}(c, L, G) \tag{2}$$

$$to_{\text{cdsub}}(c, L, G) = \frac{|\text{cdsub}(c, L, G) \cap \text{cdsub}(c, G, L)|}{|\text{cdsub}(c, L, G)| \cup \text{cdsub}(c, G, L)|} \tag{3}$$

$$TO(L, G) = \frac{1}{|L \cap G|} \sum_{c \in L \cap G} to_{\text{cdsub}}(c, L, G) \tag{4}$$

Results and Discussion. From Fig. 1 it can be seen that in terms of the quality of hierarchies (measured by TF and TO, left column), with PTM representation, the set inclusion rule (set-inc) outperformed the others. With resource-based representation, the results were rather inconsistent. Probabilistic association rule (prob-asso) had comparable performance to set inclusion rule with DBpedia and MCG. The results obtained on CCS were more inconsistent compared to the other two due to the low overlapping with the learned hierarchy. For CCS, information-theoretical condition (info-theo) and fuzzy set inclusion (fuzzy-set-inc) with resource-based representation performed the best.

In terms of overall quality of the learned hierarchies (measured by TF'), due to the huge size of DBpedia, there is little difference among rules. Notable difference was found with MCG: using the PTM representation, the set inclusion rule showed the best TF'; with the resource-based representation, prob-asso has the best TF'; fuzzy-set-inc performed well with both representation techniques.

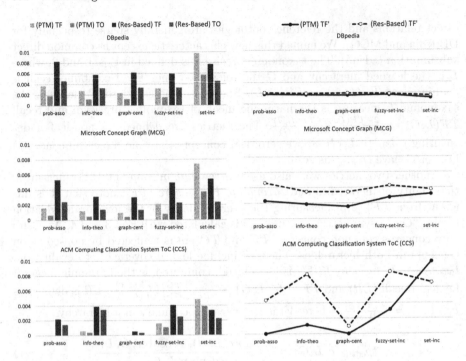

Fig. 1. Results of the reference-based evaluation. The figures illustrate the quality of each learned hierarchical structure based on its similarity to three gold-standard taxonomies (rows: DBpedia, Microsoft Concept Graph (MCG) and the ACM Computing Classification System ToC (CCS)), with different rules and data representation techniques (PTM and Resource-based). Three metrics were used for evaluation: in left column, *taxonomic F1-measure* (TF), *taxonomic overlap* (TO) that measure the quality of concept hierarchies; and in right column *taxonomic F'-measure* (TF') that measures the overall lexical and relational quality of the learned hierarchy.

Again, the results using CCS demonstrated considerable inconsistency, with the PTM representation, the set inclusion performed quite well, while graph centrality rule has the lowest TF'. With the resource-based representations, information theoretic condition and fuzzy set inclusion rule performed almost equally well, both slightly better than the set inclusion rule. The hierarchy learned using set inclusion rule showed high overall quality with both representations.

With regard to **Q1** and **Q2**, the set inclusion rule generated the best result with PTM representations, while the probabilistic association and fuzzy set inclusion rules with the resource-based representation generated competitive results. This finding is interesting as the simplest rule produced the best result. It is probably because the set theory provides the most precise simulation to the extension of a concept. The probabilistic association rule simulated the semantic association of concepts and achieved best results when the resource-based representation is used. In terms of the overall quality of hierarchy taking into consideration lexical coverage, results were considerably inconsistent. This can

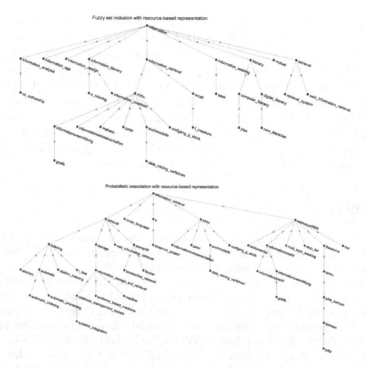

Fig. 2. Hierarchies learned with the two proposed rules. (We suggest to view the figures by zooming in on the digital version of this paper.)

be attributed to different nature of reference hierarchies and also demonstrated the usefulness of different rules for this task. There might be issues with the reference-based evaluation, as it only measures the global similarity between the learned hierarchy to the reference hierarchy. However, it is possible that some branches of the learned hierarchy were very similar to the reference hierarchy [16]. Two excerpts (due to the limited space) of the learned hierarchies are illustrated in Fig. 2 with fuzzy set inclusion and probabilistic association rule.

We also realised that the current evaluation strategies might not be perfect due to the significantly different nature of the datasets. In general, quality of the learned hierarchies from social data cannot be compared to those created by human beings or learned from sentential data using lexico-syntactic patterns. Nevertheless, useful and unseen concepts and relations can still be discovered.

5   Conclusion and Future Study

Hierarchical relations are essential to Knowledge Organisation Systems and research has shown these relations can be learned from folksonomies. This work summarised the representative rules used to induce such relations and conducted

an in-depth comparison on these rules. We believe that with a deeper understanding of the rules, it is possible to design methods to extract valuable information even from low-quality social data to enrich existing knowledge bases.
The reference-based evaluation showed that with the proposed hierarchy generation algorithm, the set inclusion rule and probabilistic association rule can
derive useful hierarchical knowledge with resource-based and PTM representations. For future studies, we plan to include more fine-grained rules and evaluate
them with other folksonomies. We are also combining these rules with machine
learning approaches to generate hierarchies with higher quality. Other representations, such as neural word embeddings, are also to be explored.

References

1. Benz, D., Hotho, A., Stumme, G., Stützer, S.: Semantics made by you and me: Self-
   emerging ontologies can capture the diversity of shared knowledge. In: Proceedings
   of the 2nd Web Science Conference (WebSci10) (2010)
2. Cimiano, P., Hotho, A., Staab, S.: Learning concept hierarchies from text corpora
   using formal concept analysis. J. Artif. Intell. Res. (JAIR) **24**(1), 305–339 (2005)
3. Cruse, D.A.: Hyponymy and its varieties. In: Green, R., Bean, C.A., Myaeng, S.H.
   (eds.) The Semantics of Relationships: An Interdisciplinary Perspective, pp. 3–21.
   Springer, Dordrecht (2002). https://doi.org/10.1007/978-94-017-0073-3_1
4. Dellschaft, K., Staab, S.: Measuring the similiarity of concept hierarchies and its
   influence on the evaluation of learning procedures. Master's thesis (Diplomarbeit),
   University of Koblenz-Landau (2005)
5. Dellschaft, K., Staab, S.: On how to perform a gold standard based evaluation
   of ontology learning. In: Cruz, I., Decker, S., Allemang, D., Preist, C., Schwabe,
   D., Mika, P., Uschold, M., Aroyo, L.M. (eds.) ISWC 2006. LNCS, vol. 4273, pp.
   228–241. Springer, Heidelberg (2006). https://doi.org/10.1007/11926078_17
6. Dong, H., Wang, W., Frans, C.: Deriving dynamic knowledge from academic social
   tagging data: a novel research direction. In: iConference 2017 Proceedings (2017)
7. García-Silva, A., Corcho, O., Alani, H., Gómez-Pérez, A.: Review of the state of
   the art: discovering and associating semantics to tags in folksonomies. Knowl. Eng.
   Rev. **27**(1), 57–85 (2012)
8. Griffiths, T.L., Steyvers, M.: Prediction and semantic association. In: Proceedings
   of the 15th International Conference on Neural Information Processing Systems,
   pp. 11–18. MIT Press (2002)
9. Heymann, P., Garcia-Molina, H.: Collaborative creation of communal hierarchical
   taxonomies in social tagging systems. Technical report, Stanford University (2006)
10. Jabeen, F., Khusro, S.: Quality-protected folksonomy maintenance approaches: a
    brief survey. Knowl. Eng. Rev. **30**(5), 521–544 (2015)
11. Maedche, A., Staab, S.: Measuring similarity between ontologies. In: Gómez-Pérez,
    A., Benjamins, V.R. (eds.) EKAW 2002. LNCS (LNAI), vol. 2473, pp. 251–263.
    Springer, Heidelberg (2002). https://doi.org/10.1007/3-540-45810-7_24
12. Meo, P.D., Quattrone, G., Ursino, D.: Exploitation of semantic relationships and
    hierarchical data structures to support a user in his annotation and browsing activ-
    ities in folksonomies. Inf. Syst. **34**(6), 511–535 (2009)
13. Mika, P.: Ontologies are us: a unified model of social networks and semantics. Web
    Semant.: Sci. Serv. Agents World Wide Web **5**(1), 5–15 (2007)

14. Peters, I., Becker, P.: Folksonomies: Indexing and Retrieval in Web 2.0. De Gruyter/Saur, Berlin (2009)
15. Stock, W.G.: Concepts and semantic relations in information science. J. Am. Soc. Inf. Sci. Technol. **61**(10), 1951–1969 (2010)
16. Strohmaier, M., Helic, D., Benz, D., Körner, C., Kern, R.: Evaluation of folksonomy induction algorithms. ACM Trans. Intell. Syst. Technol. **3**(4), 1–22 (2012)
17. Tho, Q.T., Hui, S.C., Fong, A.C.M., Cao, T.H.: Automatic fuzzy ontology generation for semantic web. IEEE Trans. Knowl. Data Eng. **18**(6), 842–856 (2006)
18. Wang, W., Barnaghi, P.M., Bargiela, A.: Probabilistic topic models for learning terminological ontologies. IEEE Trans. Knowl. Data Eng. **22**(7), 1028–1040 (2010)
19. Weller, K.: Knowledge Representation in the Social Semantic Web. De Gruyter Saur, Berlin/New York (2010)

Giveme5W: Main Event Retrieval from News Articles by Extraction of the Five Journalistic W Questions

Felix Hamborg[✉] ⓘ, Soeren Lachnit, Moritz Schubotz ⓘ,
Thomas Hepp ⓘ, and Bela Gipp ⓘ

University of Konstanz, Konstanz, Germany
{felix.hamborg,soeren.lachnit,moritz.schubotz,
thomas.hepp,bela.gipp}@uni-konstanz.de

Abstract. Extraction of event descriptors from news articles is a commonly required task for various tasks, such as clustering related articles, summarization, and news aggregation. Due to the lack of generally usable and publicly available methods optimized for news, many researchers must redundantly implement such methods for their project. Answers to the five journalistic W questions (5Ws) describe the main event of a news article, i.e., who did what, when, where, and why. The main contribution of this paper is Giveme5W, the first open-source, syntax-based 5W extraction system for news articles. The system retrieves an article's main event by extracting phrases that answer the journalistic 5Ws. In an evaluation with three assessors and 60 articles, we find that the extraction precision of 5W phrases is $p = 0.7$.

Keywords: News event detection · 5W extraction · 5W question answering

1 Introduction and Background

Extraction of a news article's main event is a fundamental analysis task required for a broad spectrum of use cases. For instance, news aggregators, such as Google News, must identify the main event to cluster related articles, i.e., articles reporting on the same event [5, 15]. News summarization extracts an article's main event to enable users to quickly see what multiple articles are reporting on [16, 25]. Other disciplines also analyze the events of articles, e.g., in so called frame analyses researchers from the social sciences identify how media reports on certain events [31].

Though *main event extraction from news* is a fundamental task in news analysis [16, 27], no method is publicly available that extracts *explicit descriptors* of the main event. We define explicit event descriptors as properties that occur in a text that is describing an event, e.g., text phrases in a news article that enable a news consumer to understand what the article is reporting on. Explicit descriptors could be used by various news analysis tasks, including all of the previously mentioned news analysis tasks, e.g., clustering, summarization, and frame analysis. State-of-the-art methods that extract events from articles suffer from three main shortcomings. Most approaches either (1) detect events only *implicitly* or are (2) *highly specialized* for the extraction of

© Springer International Publishing AG, part of Springer Nature 2018
G. Chowdhury et al. (Eds.): iConference 2018, LNCS 10766, pp. 356–366, 2018.
https://doi.org/10.1007/978-3-319-78105-1_39

task-specific event properties. Some approaches extract explicit event descriptors, but (3) are *not publicly available.*

Approaches of the first category detect events only implicitly, e.g., they find groups of textually similar articles by employing topic modeling or other clustering methods [32]. Some approaches afterward compute cluster labels that describe what is common to the group of related articles, typically the shared event or topic [2, 16, 27]. However, none of these approaches extract descriptors of a single article's main event to enable further analysis using these descriptors. The second category of approaches is highly specialized on task-specific event properties, such as the number of dead or injured people for crisis monitoring [32] or the number of protestors in demonstrations [26]. Approaches of the third category extract explicit event descriptors but are not publicly available [29, 34–36].

These shortcomings result in two disadvantages to the research community. First, researchers need to redundantly perform work for a task that can be well addressed with state-of-the-art techniques, due to the non-availability of suitable implementations. Second, non-optimal accuracy of produced results, since for many projects the extraction of explicit event descriptors is only a necessary task but not their actual contribution.

The main objective of our research is to devise an automated method that extracts the main event of a single news article. To address the three main shortcomings of state-of-the-art methods, our method needs to *extract explicit main event descriptors* that are *usable* by later tasks in the analysis workflow. The approach must also be *publicly available* and *reliably extract* the main event descriptors by exploiting the characteristics of news articles.

Journalists typically answer the five journalistic W-questions (5W), i.e., *who did what, when, where,* and *why,* within the first few sentences of an article to quickly inform readers of the main event. Figure 1 shows an excerpt of an article reporting on a terrorist attack in Afghanistan [1]. The highlighted phrases represent 5W main event properties. Due to their descriptiveness of the main event, we focus our research on the extraction of the journalistic 5Ws. Extraction of event-describing phrases also allows later analysis tasks to use common natural language processing (NLP) methods, such as

---

Taliban attacks German consulate in northern Afghan city of Mazar-i-Sharif with truck bomb

> *The death toll from a powerful Taliban truck bombing at the German consulate in Afghanistan's Mazar-i-Sharif city rose to at least six Friday, with more than 100 others wounded in a major militant assault.*

The Taliban said the bombing late Thursday, which tore a massive crater in the road and overturned cars, was a "revenge attack" for US air strikes this month in the volatile province of Kunduz that left 32 civilians dead. [...]

Fig. 1. News article [1] with title (bold), lead paragraph (italic), and first of remaining paragraphs. Highlighted phrases represent the 5W event properties (who did what, when, where, and why). (Color figure online)

TF-IDF and cosine similarity including named entity recognition (NER) [12] to assess the similarity of two events.

Section 2 discusses 5W extraction methods that retrieve the main event from news articles. Section 3 presents Giveme5W, the first open-source 5W extraction system. The system achieves high extraction precision, is available under an Apache 2 license, and through its modular design can be efficiently tailored by other researchers to their needs. Section 4 describes our evaluation, and discusses the performance of Giveme5W with respect to related approaches. Section 5 discusses future work.

2   Extraction of Journalistic 5Ws from News Articles

This section gives a brief overview of 5W extraction methods in the news domain. The task is closely related to closed-domain question answering, which is why some authors call their approaches *5W question answering* (QA) systems. Systems for 5W QA on news texts typically perform three tasks to determine the article's main event: (1) *preprocessing*, (2) *phrase extraction*, and (3) *candidate scoring* [34, 35]. The input data to QA systems is usually text, such as a full article including headline, lead paragraph, and main text [30], or a single sentence, e.g., in news ticker format [36]. Other systems use automatic speech recognition (ASR) to convert broad casts into text [35]. The outcomes of the process are five phrases, one for each of the 5W, which together represent the main event of a given news text, as exemplarily highlighted in Fig. 1. The *preprocessing task (1)* performs sentence splitting, tokenizes them, and often applies further NLP methods, including part-of-speech (POS) tagging, coreference resolution [30], NER [12], parsing [24], or semantic role labeling (SRL) [8].

For the *phrase extraction task (2)* various strategies are available. Most systems use manually created linguistic rules to extract phrase candidates from the preprocessed text [21, 30, 35]. Noun phrases (NP) yield candidates for "who", while sibling verb phrases (VP) are candidates for "what" [30]. Other systems use NER to only retrieve phrases that contain named entities, e.g., a person or an organization [12]. Others approaches use SRL to identify the agent ("who") performing the action ("what") and location- and temporal information ("where" and "when") [36]. Determining the reason ("why") can even be difficult for humans because often the reason is only described implicitly, if at all [13]. The applied methods range from simple approaches, e.g., looking for explicit markers of causal relations [21], such as "because", to complex approaches, e.g., training machine learning (ML) methods on annotated corpora [4]. The clear majority of research has focused on explicit causal relations, while only few approaches address implicit causal relations, which also achieve lower precision than methods for explicit causes [6].

The *candidate scoring task (3)* estimates the best answer for each 5W question. The reviewed 5W QA systems provide only few details on their scoring. Typical heuristics include: shortness of a candidate, as longer candidates may contain too many irrelevant details [30], "who" candidates that contain an NE, and active speech [35]. More complex methods are discussed in various linguistic publications, and involve supervised ML [19, 36]. Yaman et al. use three independent subsystems to extract 5W answers [36]. A trained SVM then decides which subsystem is "correct" using features, such as the agreement among subsystems, or the number of non-null answers per subsystem.

While the evaluations of the reviewed papers generally indicate sufficient quality to be usable for news event extraction, e.g., the system from [36] achieved $F_1 = 0.85$ on the Darpa corpus from 2009, they lack comparability for two reasons: (1) There is no gold standard for journalistic 5W QA on news; even worse, evaluation data sets of previous papers are no longer available publicly [29, 35, 36]. (2) Previous papers use different quality measures, such as precision and recall [11] or error rates [35].

3   Giveme5W: System Description

Giveme5W is an open-source main event retrieval system for news articles that addresses the objectives we defined in Sect. 1. The system extracts 5W phrases that describe the generally usable properties of news events, i.e., who did what, when, where, and why. This section describes the processing pipeline of Giveme5W as shown in Fig. 2. Giveme5W can be accessed by other software as a Python library and via a RESTful API. Due to its modularity, researchers can efficiently adapt or replace components, e.g., use a parser tailored to characteristics their data or adapt the scoring functions if their articles cover only a specific topic, such as finance.

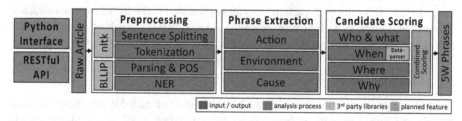

Fig. 2. Shown is the three-tasks analysis pipeline as it preprocesses a news text, finds candidate phrases for each of the 5W questions, and scores these.

3.1   Preprocessing of News Articles

Giveme5W can work with any combination of the following input types, where at least one must be provided: (1) *headline,* (2) *lead paragraph,* and (3) *main text.* If more than one type is given, Giveme5W appends them to one document, but keeps track of the individual types for later candidate scoring. Optionally, the article's publishing date can be provided, which helps Giveme5W to parse relative dates, such as "today at 12 am". Giveme5W integrates with the news crawler and extractor *news-please* [17].

During preprocessing, we use the Python NLP toolkit nltk [7] for sentence splitting, tokenization, and NER (with the trained seven-class model from Stanford NER [12]). For POS-tagging and full-text parsing we use the BLLIP parser [9]. To parse dates, we use parsedatetime [28]. For all libraries, we use the default settings for English.

3.2 Phrase Extraction

Giveme5W performs three independent extraction chains to extract the article's main event: (1) the *action* chain extracts phrases to the journalistic "who" and "what" questions, (2) *environment* for "when" and "where", and (3) *cause* for "why".

The *action extractor* identifies who did what in the article's main event, analyzing named entities (NE) and POS-tags. First, we look for any NE that was identified as a person or organization during preprocessing (cf. [12, 30]). We merge adjacent tokens of the same type within one NP to phrases (agent merge range $r_a = 1$ token), and add them to a list of "who"-candidates. We also add a sentence's first NP to the list if it contains any noun (NN*)[1] or personal pronoun (PRP) (cf. [30]). For each "who"-candidate, we take the VP that is the next right sibling in the parse tree as the corresponding "what"-candidate (cf. [7]).

The *environment extractor* identifies the temporal and local context of the event. Therefore, we look for NE classified as a location, date, time, or a combined datetime (cf. [36]). Similarly to "who"-candidates we merge tokens to phrases, using a temporal range $r_t = 2$ and locality range $r_l = 2$. This is necessary to handle phrases that do not purely consist of NE tokens, such as "Friday, 5th".

The *cause extractor* looks for linguistic features indicating a causal relation. The combined method consists of two subtasks, one analyzing POS-patterns, the other tokens. First, we recursively traverse the parse-tree to find the POS-pattern NP-VP-NP, where often the last NP is a cause [13]. We then check if a pattern contains an action verb, such as "allow" or "result", by using the list of verbs from [21]. If an action verb is used, the last NP of the POS-pattern from above is added to the list of cause candidates. The second subtask looks for cause indicating adverbs (RB) [3], such as "therefore", and causal conjunctional phrases [3], such as "because" or "consequence of".

3.3 Candidate Scoring

The last analysis task is to determine the best candidate of each 5W question. To score "*who*"-candidates we define three goals: the candidate shall occur in the article (1) *early* (following the inverse pyramid concept [10]) and (2) *often* (a frequently occurring candidate more likely refers to the main event), and (3) contain an *NE* (in news the actors involved in events are often NEs, e.g., politicians). The resulting scoring formula is $s_{who}(c) = w_0(d - p(c)) + w_1 f(c) + w_2 NE(c)$, where the weights $w_0 = w_1 = w_2 = 1$ (cf. [30, 35]), d the document length measured in sentences, $p(c)$ the position measured in sentences of candidate c within the document, $f(c)$ the frequency of phrases similar to c in the document, and $NE(c) = 1$ if c contains a NE, else 0 (cf. [12]).

To measure $f(c)$ we initially counted only exact matches, but we achieved better results with a simple *distance measure* for which we compute the normalized Levenshtein distance lev_{ij} between any candidate pair $c_i c_j$ of the same 5W question and increase the frequency of both c_i and c_j if $lev_{ij} < t_w$, where t_w is defined for each

---

[1] We use the POS-tag abbreviations from the Penn Treebank Project [33].

question w. We achieve the best results with $t_{who} = 0.5$. Due to the strong relation between agent and action, we rank the VPs according to the scores of their NPs. Hence, the most likely VP is the sibling in the parse tree of the most likely NP: $s_{what} = s_{who}$.

We score *temporal* candidates according to three goals: (1) occur *early* in the document, (2) *accuracy* (the more accurate, the better, i.e., instances including date and time are preferred over only date over only time), and (3) *parsable* to a datetime object [28]. Hence, $s_{when}(c) = w_0 \frac{d-p(c)}{d} + w_1 DT(c) + w_2 TM(c) + w_3 TP(c)$, where $w_0 = 10$, $w_1 = w_2 = 1$, $w_3 = 5$, $DT(c) = 1$ if c is a date instance, else 0, $TM(c) = 1$ if c is a time instance, 0.8 if c is a date instance, in which an adjacent time instance was merged, 0 else. $TP(c) = 1$ if c can be parsed into a datetime object, else 0.

The scoring of *location* candidates follows two simple goals: the candidate shall occur (1) *early* and (2) *often* in the document. $s_{where}(c) = w_0(d - p(c)) + w_1 f(c)$, where $w_0 = w_1 = 1$. The distance threshold to find similar candidates is $t_{where} = 0.6$. Section 4 describes how we plan to improve the location scoring.

Scoring *causal* candidates turned out to be challenging, since it often requires semantic interpretation of the text and simple heuristic may fail [13]. We define two objectives: (1) occur *early* in the document, and (2) the *causal type*. $s_{why}(c) = w_0 \frac{d-p(c)}{d} + w_1 CT(c)$, where $w_0 = w_1 = 1$, and $TC(c) = 1$ if c is a bi-clausal phrase, 0.6 if it starts with a causal RB, and 0.3 else (cf. [21, 22]).

3.4 Output

The highlighted phrases in Fig. 1 are the highest scored candidates extracted by Giveme5W for each of the 5W event properties of the sample article. If requested by the user, Giveme5W enriches the returned phrases with additional information that the system needed to extract for its own analysis. The additional information types for each token are its POS-tags, syntactical role within the sentence, which was extracted using parsing, and NE type if applicable. Enriching the tokens with this information increases the efficiency of the overall analysis workflow in which Giveme5W may be embedded since later analysis tasks can reuse the information.

Giveme5W also enriches "when"-phrases by attempting to parse them into datetime objects. For instance, Giveme5W resolves the "when"-phrase "late Thursday" from Fig. 1 by checking it against the article's publishing date, Friday, November 11, 2016. The resulting datetime object represents 18:00 on November 10, 2016.

4 Evaluation and Discussion

We performed a survey with three assessors (graduate IT students). We created an evaluation dataset by randomly sampling 60 articles (12 for each category) from the BBC corpus described in [14]. Instructions to recreate the dataset are available in the project's repository (see Sect. 5). The BBC corpus consists of 2,225 articles in the categories business (*Bus*), entertainment (*Ent*), politics (*Pol*), sport (*Spo*), and tech (*Tec*).

We presented all articles (one at a time) to each participant. After reading an article, we showed them Giveme5W's answers. We asked them to judge the relevance of each answer on a 3-point scale: *non-relevant* (if an answer contains no relevant information, score $s = 0$), *partially relevant* (if part of the answer is relevant or information is missing, $s = 0.5$), and *relevant* (if the answer is completely relevant without missing information, $s = 1$).

Table 1 shows the *mean average generalized precision* (MAgP), a precision score suitable in multi-graded relevance assessments [20]. The MAgP over all categories and questions was 0.7. Excluding the "why"-question, which also the assessors most often disagreed on (discussed later and in Sect. 5), the overall MAgP was 0.76.

Table 1. ICR and generalized precision of Giveme5W.

Property	ICR	Bus	Ent	Pol	Spo	Tec	Avg.
Who	.87	.92	.94	.84	.74	.74	.87
What	.90	.90	.91	.81	.87	.70	.84
When	.76	.77	.77	.65	.51	.87	.72
Where	.75	.73	.52	.76	.56	.52	.62
Why	.63	.48	.62	.42	.44	.34	.46
Avg.	.78	.76	.75	.70	.66	.63	**.70**

Compared to the fraction of "correct" answers by the best system in [29], Giveme5W achieves a 0.05 higher MAgP. The best system in [36] achieves a precision of 0.89, which is 0.19 higher than our MAgP and surprisingly even better than the ICR of our assessors. However, comparing the performance of Giveme5W with other systems is not straightforward for several reasons: other systems were tested on non-disclosed datasets [29, 35, 36], were translated from other languages [29], or used different evaluation measures, such as error rates [35] or binary relevance assessments [36], which are both not optimal because of the non-binary relevance of 5W answers (cf. [20]). Finally, none of the related systems have been made publicly available, which was the primary motivation for our research as described in Sect. 1. For this reason, comparing the evaluation results of our system and related work was not possible.

Using the *intercoder reliability* (ICR) as a very rough approximation of the best possible precision that could be achieved (cf. [18]), we conclude that Giveme5W comes very close to the current optimum (ICR = 0.78, MAgP = 0.7).

We found that different forms of journalistic presentation in the five news categories led to different QA performance. Business and entertainment articles, which yielded the best performance, mostly reported on single events, while the sports and tech articles, on which our system performed slightly weaker, contained more non-event coverage, e.g., background reports or announcements.

Before we conducted the survey, we conducted a pre-survey to verify sufficient agreement among the assessors. We let the assessors rate ten articles and measured the overall ICR of the assessors' ratings using the average pairwise percentage agreement. We also let users fill in a questionnaire, asking how they understood the rating task. The pre-survey yielded an $ICR_{pre} = 0.65$. We found that some questions, specifically the "why"-question, required further explanation so that we added examples and clarified the assessment rules in the tutorial section of our survey application.

The ICR was 0.78 in the final survey, which is sufficiently high to accept the assessments (cf. [23]). While assessors often agreed on "who" and "what", they agreed less often on "when" and "where" (see Table 1). Similarly to Parton et al. [29], we found that lower ICR for "when" and "where" were caused by erroneous extractions of the "who" and "what" question, which in turn also yielded wrong answers for the remaining questions. "Why" had the lowest ICR, which is primarily because most articles do not contain explicit causal statements reasoning the event (see also Sect. 5). This increases the likelihood that assessors inferred different causes or none, and hence rated Giveme5W's answers discrepantly (see Sect. 5).

5   Future Work

We plan to investigate three ideas, from which all 5W-questions may benefit: (1) *coreference resolution* and (2) *semantic distance measure*, which will both allow Giveme5W to better assess the main agent (including the main action), and potentially also the cause. We plan to use WordNet or Wikidata to measure how two candidates are semantically related, and we will replace the currently used Levenshtein distance, which cannot handle synonyms. (3) Introduce *combined scoring* (see Fig. 2), which uses features of other Ws to score one W. For instance, if the top candidates for "who" and "what" are located at the beginning of the article, "when" and "where" candidates that are likewise at the beginning should receive a higher rating than others further down in the article. In our dataset, we found that this idea would particularly improve the performance of "where" and "why".

We also plan to improve the individual 5W extractors and scorers. For "where"-extraction we will replace the current accuracy estimation with a method that uses reverse geocoding, and prefer locations, e.g., a restaurant, over small regions, e.g., San Francisco, over larger regions, e.g., California, since the former are more accurate. The poor performance and rather low ICR of "why" require further investigation, especially when compared to evaluations of other systems, which have higher ICR and better performance. Some evaluations are biased, e.g., the dataset used in [36] was specifically designed for 5W QA. Such datasets may contain more explicit causal phrases than our randomly sampled articles that often only implicitly describe the cause. We plan to use the sophisticated list of rules suggested in [22] to further improve our cause extraction. We also plan to add an extractor for "how"-phrases (cf. [30, 34]).

Finally, we think that the creation of a gold standard dataset containing articles with manually annotated 5W phrases will help to advance research on main event retrieval from articles.

6   Conclusion

The main contribution of this paper is the first open-source system for retrieving the main event from news articles. The system, coined *Giveme5W*, extracts phrases answering the five journalistic W-questions (5W), i.e., *who* did *what, when, where,* and *why*. Giveme5W also enriches the phrases with POS-tags, named entity types, and parsing information. The system uses syntactic and domain-specific rules to extract and score phrase candidates for each 5W question. In a pilot evaluation, Giveme5W achieved an overall, mean average generalized precision of 0.70, with the extraction of "who" and "what" performing best. "Where" and "why" performed more poorly, which was likely due to our use of real-world news articles, which often only imply the causes. We plan to use coreference resolution and a semantic distance measure to improve our extraction performance. Since answering the 5W questions is at the core of any news article, this task is being analyzed using different approaches by many projects and fields of research. We hope that redundantly performed work can be avoided in the future with Giveme5W as the first open-source and freely available 5W extraction system.

The code of Giveme5W and the evaluation dataset used in this paper are available under an Apache 2 license at: https://github.com/fhamborg/Giveme5W.

References

1. Agence France-Presse: Taliban attacks German consulate in Northern Afghan city of Mazar-i-Sharif with truck bomb. The Telegraph (2016)
2. Allan, J., et al.: 1998 Topic detection and tracking pilot study: final report. In: Proceedings of the DARPA Broadcast News Transcription and Understanding Workshop, pp. 194–218 (1998)
3. Altenberg, B.: Causal linking in spoken and written English. Studia Linguistica 38(1), 20–69 (1984)
4. Asghar, N.: Automatic extraction of causal relations from natural language texts: a comprehensive survey. arXiv preprint arXiv:1605.07895 (2016)
5. Best, C., et al.: Europe media monitor (2005)
6. Bethard, S., Martin, J.H.: Learning semantic links from a corpus of parallel temporal and causal relations. In: Proceedings of the 46th Annual Meeting of the ACL on Human Language Technologies, pp. 177–180 (2008)
7. Bird, S., et al.: Natural Language Processing with Python: Analyzing Text with the Natural Language Toolkit. O'Reilly Media, Inc., Sebastopol (2009)
8. Carreras, X., Màrquez, L.: Introduction to the CoNLL-2005 shared task: semantic role labeling. In: Proceedings of the Ninth Conference on Computational Natural Language, pp. 152–164 (2005)
9. Charniak, E., Johnson, M.: Coarse-to-fine n-best parsing and MaxEnt discriminative reranking. In: Proceedings of the 43rd Annual Meeting on ACL, pp. 173–180 (2005)
10. Christian, D., et al.: The Associated Press Stylebook and Briefing on Media Law. Associated Press, New York (2014)
11. Das, A., Bandyaopadhyay, S., Gambäck, B.: The 5W structure for sentiment summarization-visualization-tracking. In: Gelbukh, A. (ed.) CICLing 2012. LNCS, vol. 7181, pp. 540–555. Springer, Heidelberg (2012). https://doi.org/10.1007/978-3-642-28604-9_44
12. Finkel, J.R., et al.: Incorporating non-local information into information extraction systems by gibbs sampling. In: Proceedings of the 43rd Annual Meeting on ACL, pp. 363–370 (2005)
13. Girju, R.: Automatic detection of causal relations for question answering. In: Proceedings of the ACL 2003 Workshop on Multilingual Summarization and Question Answering, vol. 12, pp. 76–83 (2003)

14. Greene, D., Cunningham, P.: Practical solutions to the problem of diagonal dominance in kernel document clustering. In: Proceedings of the 23rd International Conference on Machine Learning, pp. 377–384 (2006)
15. Hamborg, F., et al.: Identification and analysis of media bias in news articles. In: Proceedings of the 15th International Symposium of Information Science (2017)
16. Hamborg, F., et al.: Matrix-based news aggregation: exploring different news perspectives. In: Proceedings of the ACM/IEEE Joint Conference on Digital Libraries, p. 10 (2017)
17. Hamborg, F., et al.: news-please: A generic news crawler and extractor. In: Proceedings of the 15th International Symposium of Information Science, pp. 218–223 (2017)
18. Hripcsak, G., Rothschild, A.S.: Agreement, the F-measure, and reliability in information retrieval. J. Am. Med. Inform. Assoc. 12(3), 296–298 (2005)
19. Jurafsky, D.: Speech and Language Processing. Pearson Education India, New Delhi (2000)
20. Kekäläinen, J., Järvelin, K.: Using graded relevance assessments in IR evaluation. J. Am. Soc. Inform. Sci. Technol. 53(13), 1120–1129 (2002)
21. Khoo, C.S.G., et al.: Automatic extraction of cause-effect information from newspaper text without knowledge-based inferencing. Lit. Linguist. Comput. 13(4), 177–186 (1998)
22. Khoo, C.S.G.: Automatic identification of causal relations in text and their use for improving precision in information retrieval (1995)
23. Landis, J.R., Koch, G.G.: The measurement of observer agreement for categorical data. Biometrics 33(1), 159–174 (1977)
24. Manning, C.D., et al.: Foundations of Statistical Natural Language Processing. MIT Press, Cambridge (1999)
25. McKeown, K.R., et al.: Tracking and summarizing news on a daily basis with Columbia's Newsblaster. In: Proceedings of the 2nd International Conference on Human Language Technology Research, pp. 280–285 (2002)
26. Oliver, P.E., Maney, G.M.: Political processes and local newspaper coverage of protest events: from selection bias to triadic interactions. Am. J. Sociol. 106(2), 463–505 (2000)
27. Park, S., et al. NewsCube: delivering multiple aspects of news to mitigate media bias. In: Proceedings of SIGCHI 2009 Conference on Human Factors in Computing Systems, pp. 443–453 (2009)
28. parsedatetime - Parse human-readable date/time strings. https://github.com/bear/parsedatetime. Accessed 21 Aug 2017
29. Parton, K., et al.: Who, what, when, where, why?: comparing multiple approaches to the cross-lingual 5W task. In: Proceedings of the Joint Conference of the 47th Annual Meeting of the ACL and the 4th International Joint Conference on Natural Language Processing of the AFNLP, vol. 1, pp. 423–431 (2009)
30. Sharma, S., et al.: News event extraction using 5W1H approach & its analysis. Int. J. Sci. Eng. Res. – IJSER 4(5), 2064–2067 (2013)
31. Stemler, S.: An overview of content analysis. Pract. Assess. Res. Eval. 7(17), 137–146 (2001)
32. Tanev, H., Piskorski, J., Atkinson, M.: Real-time news event extraction for global crisis monitoring. In: Kapetanios, E., Sugumaran, V., Spiliopoulou, M. (eds.) NLDB 2008. LNCS, vol. 5039, pp. 207–218. Springer, Heidelberg (2008). https://doi.org/10.1007/978-3-540-69858-6_21
33. Taylor, A., et al.: The Penn treebank: an overview. In: Abeillé, A. (ed.) Treebanks. TLTB, vol. 20, pp. 5–22. Springer, Dordrecht (2003). https://doi.org/10.1007/978-94-010-0201-1_1

34. Wang, W., et al.: Chinese news event 5W1H elements extraction using semantic role labeling. In: 2010 Third International Symposium on Information Processing (ISIP), pp. 484–489 (2010)

35. Yaman, S., et al.: Classification-based strategies for combining multiple 5-W question answering systems. In: INTERSPEECH, pp. 2703–2706 (2009)

36. Yaman, S., et al.: Combining semantic and syntactic information sources for 5-W question answering. In: INTERSPEECH, pp. 2707–2710 (2009)

Opportunities for Computer Support for Systematic Reviewing - A Gap Analysis

Linh Hoang$^{(\boxtimes)}$ (iD) and Jodi Schneider (iD)

University of Illinois at Urbana-Champaign, Champaign IL 61820, USA
{lhoang2,jodi}@illinois.edu

Abstract. Systematic review is a type of literature review designed to synthesize all available evidence on a given question. Systematic reviews require significant time and effort, which has led to the continuing development of computer support. This paper seeks to identify the gaps and opportunities for computer support. By interviewing experienced systematic reviewers from diverse fields, we identify the technical problems and challenges reviewers face in conducting a systematic review and their current uses of computer support. We propose potential research directions for how computer support could help to speed the systematic review process while retaining or improving review quality.

Keywords: Systematic review · Meta-analysis · Gap analysis
Interview study

1 Introduction

A systematic review is a type of literature review designed to provide all available evidence on a given question. Systematic reviews can support translation of research into practice, when the underlying research has concordant findings; and they can also draw attention to gaps in the evidence, such as discordant findings that need further investigation. Despite their importance, systematic reviews require great amount of human effort: a mean of 67 weeks from deposit of a protocol to publication of the review [1], with a mean of 1000 hours of person time [2]. To address this, informatics and methodology researchers are working to minimize the effort required to complete systematic reviews [3]. Already, several commercial software packages have been designed as end-to-end tools to support the reviewing process. Dissemination of tools and methods is an ongoing effort (for instance by the Medical Library Association and by Cochrane [4]) and there are some large-scale efforts to transform the production of systematic reviews (e.g. Cochrane's Project Transform [5]). However, the gap between reviewers' current practices and existing computer support is not well understood. Through interviews with systematic reviewers, we seek to identify the gaps between the computer support available and what reviewers actually use, at a Research I university without an academic medical center. Our two main research questions are:

R1. What technical problems and challenges do reviewers face in conducting a systematic review?

R2. What current computer support technology are reviewers using?

© Springer International Publishing AG, part of Springer Nature 2018
G. Chowdhury et al. (Eds.): iConference 2018, LNCS 10766, pp. 367–377, 2018.
https://doi.org/10.1007/978-3-319-78105-1_40

2   Background

The process of conducting a systematic review includes a series of steps designed to locate and synthesize all available evidence on a specific research question. Figure 1 shows the typical steps as described in [6]: after identifying relevant studies, reviewers extract data from these studies and evaluate and interpret the evidence. While the typical methodological challenges [7] and methodologies are well-documented (e.g. PRISMA[1], Cochrane Handbook[2], among many others), review takes varied forms [8]. Since the reliability of a systematic review hinges on the completeness of the information used, a systematic search [9] is of key importance, though this work can come at a cost: In a typical systematic review, over 2000 abstracts need to be reviewed in order to find 15 relevant studies [10].

This intense cost in time and effort has led to the development of computer support tools. Previous survey research has found that reviewers typically use software such as EndNote, Reference Manager, RefWorks, and Excel to manage references [11]. Some commercial products are designed as end-to-end support tools: DistillerSR[3] and Covidence[4] primarily provide an integrated environment for data capture and management, for tasks such as harvesting search results from databases, screening studies, and providing questionnaires for manual data extraction. Another end-to-end tool, EPPI-Reviewer[5], provides (and continues to develop) advanced features such as automatic term reorganization, and document clustering and classification, using machine learning and data mining. The Systematic Review Toolbox[6] collects and describes relevant tools. Currently, research prototype systems are in development to support or automate each of the steps shown in Fig. 1. A 2014 review [3] listed fourteen tasks that could potentially be automated, and identified more than 10 applications being developed to assist different phases of the review process, including search engines (Quick Clinical and Metta); and data extraction support tools using machine learning and natural language processing (ExaCT and RobotReviewer). Yet to understand whether and how reviewers are actually using these tools, and how well the current and emerging technologies fulfill reviewers' requirements, a gap analysis is needed.

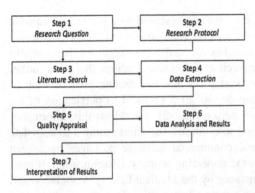

Fig. 1. Steps in a systematic review process according to [6]

[1] Preferred Reporting Items for Systematic Reviews http://prisma-statement.org/

[2] http://training.cochrane.org/handbook

[3] https://www.evidencepartners.com/

[4] https://www.covidence.org/

[5] https://eppi.ioe.ac.uk/cms/

[6] http://systematicreviewtools.com/

3 Methods

We conducted a series of semi-structured interviews with 16 systematic reviewers who had co-authored at least one published systematic review. We used interviews in order to investigate the technologies reviewers use and why, based on our interviewees' detailed explanations [12]. Potential interviewees were initially identified by searching for "systematic review" in publication databases (e.g., Scopus, limited by affiliation) and university websites. Our email invitation and our interviews both ended by asking who else we should consider interviewing; this led us to add publications with "meta-analysis" in the title. After a number of interviews, we focused our recruiting on maximizing the diversity of interviewees fields and career stage since, for instance, faculty were far less likely to accept interview invitations than graduate students.

Our data analysis was rooted in thematic analysis [13]. We recorded and transcribed interviews, then coded transcripts using ATLAS.ti 7, starting with 4 preliminary codes related to our research questions: systematic reviews in practice; difficulties and challenges; current technology support; and opinions and suggestions about technology support. We iteratively coded transcript segments, allowing more specific sub-codes to emerge within the initial coding framework. After several rounds, we identified two themes and collected sub-coded data to support these two themes described next.

4 Interview Analysis

We first report interviewee demographics and then describe two prominent themes:

(1) Technical challenges in the current practice of conducting a systematic review.
(2) Limitation of technological support in the systematic review process.

4.1 Interviewee Demographics

Our interview study comprised sixteen interviewees associated with a Research I university without an academic medical center. Figure 2 summarizes interviewees' fields and positions. Overall our 16 interviewees had published 25 reviews, 55% had published 1 systematic review and the remaining 45% had published at least 2 systematic reviews. Half (50%) of our interviewees were also actively working on a new systematic review project.

4.2 Interview Results

Theme 1: Technical problems and challenges in the current practice of conducting a systematic review

Our interviewees described multiple technological problems and challenges they face in the current practice of systematic reviewing, summarized in Table 1.

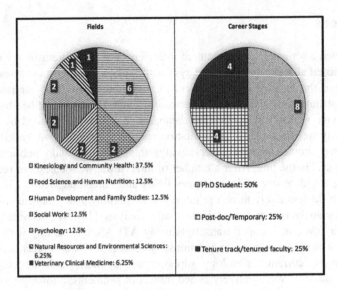

Fig. 2. Interviewees' demographic information

Table 1. List of technical problems and challenges in each phase

Phase	Technical problems and challenges
Research protocol	• Lack of a collaborative platform
Literature searching	• Lack of comprehensive search strategy • Varied vocabulary • Database coverage • Manual screening process
Data extraction	• Manual data extraction process

Problems and challenges in the Research Protocol phase

The lack of a collaborative platform: During the research protocol phase, reviewers needed to decide how to communicate with each other and how to share data. Many of our interviewees were hampered by the lack of a collaborative platform for sharing data and communicating with the team. The most common methods for sharing data were either to manually copy data and send it to other team members or to copy into a cloud storage space (e.g. Box or Dropbox) that the review team could access at the same time. Reviewers often described spending a huge amount of time figuring out how to share their work together during the process.

> *"I then have the students go back to that link where we can find the full text and save a copy of the full text in a folder that we use on Box."(P15)*

The team size averaged five people for a small to medium systematic review and the average time to complete was about one year. This raised a real difficulty of how team members communicated efficiently during the reviewing process.

"The other two studies we had everybody in the same department, and we were meeting on a weekly basis. So, it was kind of easy to coordinate meetings, and to motivate each other to keep going. With this particular one, where you have three or more institutions involved and everybody having different time commitments, I think it will take longer." (P18)

This communication problem not only exists across reviewers from different institutions, but also between the review team members who regularly meet face-to-face throughout the project.

"That actually is very difficult to get everyone on the same page to have them all understand what's going on." (P16)

While multiple software is used throughout a systematic review, even in the same step, most of this software works separately. The lack of streamlined connections between this software creates a serious threat to data integration. It leads to a potential data loss problem when users try to transfer data from one software to another or when multiple users working on the same articles at the same time.

"When we got down to have 34 articles left. My advisor and I were both reading articles so if I could've went in and logged in and seen, all right he's read these first 10. I could've probably read those too and then we could've talked about them. But if he was updating one and I was working on opposite ones then we weren't kind of getting to a point where we should sync together." (P8)

Problems and challenges in the Literature Searching phase

The literature search is one of the most difficult and time-consuming steps in the whole review process.

The lack of comprehensive search strategy: Our interviewees often start the literature search without a consistent, well-designed strategy. Interviewees normally start by identifying simple keywords which they use to pull out "potentially relevant" studies from online databases. Then they quickly scan through the initial search results —normally up to thousands of papers for the first round—to determine whether the studies may actually be relevant. Interviewees keep revising the search algorithms by using alternative keywords and repeat the "search - screen" tasks multiple times until they "feel" that all studies are captured correctly.

"I remember one time when I selected some kind of keywords… Traditionally, I applied maybe the first attempt and then I would read some of the titles to see what I missed something that worrisome, my keywords. So, I need to do some refine of the algorithm. Maybe 4–5 times." (P7)

Determining whether all potential relevant studies have been captured is also another concern. Oftentimes, the reviewers' biggest fear is that they do not know whether they got everything from the search.

"The searching, I never knew if I got everything or I did it right, I never knew if my search terms are good enough. I could have had search terms that never turned anything out, I never knew if I was searching the right databases." (P3)

It takes time, and requires adequate knowledge of the review topic, for reviewers to figure out which terms should be used in their searches, and to identify useful keywords and variants.

Varied vocabulary: Interviewees repeatedly mentioned that it is common for people from different fields, or even in the same field but doing research from different angles, to use different terminologies to describe the same thing within the same narrow topic. Thus, the process often requires extra time for reviewers to read through the search results, identify alternative keywords, and then revise the search terms accordingly.

"People use different phases to describe one same thing. So, when you started to search for related studies, you only start with one phrase, and then you realize that they use different phrases, so you need to revise all the time in order to search all of the relevant studies." (P5)

Varied vocabulary is a core and enduring issue in library science that especially impacts multi-disciplinary work [14]. Articles may mention the keyword reviewers search on without talking about the same topic or analyzing it in a way reviewers find relevant. Not all interviewees seem familiar with the techniques of using a controlled vocabulary such as MeSH as an efficient alternative to keyword search.

"Different fields looked at the same construct in different ways, and so you had to make sure you were capturing it by using all the keywords possible for that construct you're interested in investigating." (P6)

Database coverage: Another long-recognized problem, database coverage and information scattering [15], also poses challenges according to our interviewees.

"We have the problem of all the journals that are not available. Even smaller journals that are not available when we're doing the search terms. So, good studies were just not coming up. They're not indexed in the places where we're searching, so we're not finding them..." (P15)

Manual screening process: One of the most critical problems in the screening phase is its manual nature, and the lack of trusted technical support for this process. Our interviewees typically export search results from online databases to an application (usually EndNote) in order to perform screening tasks including title, abstract, and full-text screening. The average number of studies screened in each review as reported by our interviewees is approximately 4000 studies. Due to the large number of search results, the screening process is considered one of the longest steps to complete.

"I think once you're screening, you're screening everything. You go title, then you go abstracts, then you go full studies. That takes a lot of time and a lot of understanding, and your part about everything and how everything's interconnected. ... Sometimes you have to be very strategic because titles may not necessarily really imply, looking at it, so maybe you hold off on taking it on." (P6)

"The quality checking and the inclusion/exclusion criteria, the abstract, pulling out... that stuff is so time-consuming when you do it by hand and there is no need for that to be done by hand, but that's the only option you have." (P2)

Limitations of current support tools will be discussed in more detail under Theme 2.

Problems and challenges in the Data Extraction phase

Manual data extraction process: Data extraction is another time-consuming, highly manual phase, in part because data is normally extracted separately by at least two reviewers, who then come to an agreement about which information and how much of it should be used for the subsequent synthesizing stage.

"It's totally a manual process and you need to be very careful because the results will be published in public. So, I think each of the article I need to go through maybe 3–5 times." (P7).
"What I did was I extracted the data. I actually manually entered it on an Excel, whatever data is available from the studies." (P12)

Our interviewees describe being accustomed to reading the studies manually by themselves without any advanced technology support. Some interviewees even printed out articles and performed the data extraction manually with pen and highlighter.

"I downloaded all the papers for, well, it probably took a long time. I'm not very good about reading on the computer, so I actually printed them all out. I started organizing them just briefly by heading, like the subject... Then essentially, I went through and I read every one. While I was reading them, I took notes for myself. Just on a paper, on each of them." (P10)

Theme 2: The limitations of technology support

The second theme that emerged from the interviews is the limitations of technology support in systematic review. Despite a large amount of commercial software, we notice a gap between the technology available and what our interviewees are using. Figure 3 summarizes the technology support our interviewees used in the review process. The most common applications that are used in the process are Excel and EndNote, which are not designed specifically for systematic review, and in some ways, they do not meet all reviewers' requirements.

Excel was the most common software package our interviewees reported using. Excel was especially used in the data extraction process and sometimes for copying and pasting reference lists during searching and screening. Excel is popular among our interviewees because it allows users to organize data in tabular format. Nevertheless, the software is not specifically designed for bibliographic purposes. It has limitations especially for organizing a large number of publications. The most commonly used version of Excel (version 2013) is an offline application, which leads to data integration problems when users need to export data from one package to another manually.

"This is what it looks like [showing the Excel spreadsheet used for [screening]. This is horrible. We ended up color-coding it. It's horrible. It's based off what we included or exclude. This is the abstract. That is the title. We ended up with putting the abstracts in and then need to dump everything in the Excel file." (P2)

EndNote[7], the second most popular systematic review support software among our interviewees, has somewhat similar data integration issues, but is specifically designed for publishing and managing bibliographies. It is popular in the systematic review community because of the tool's affordances for performing screening tasks. However, our interviewees also reported a number of significant problems when using EndNote. Losing data seems to be the most serious problem.

---

[7] http://endnote.com/

"I'm not sure how reliable it [EndNote] is. The very first obstacle you have is that... I don't know, sometimes I feel I have 7,000, and then the next day, I have 6,500, and I'm like where did my 500 go? If we do the search with [EndNote] the same exact terms, I won't find the same 7,000. That is one of my main fears." (P9)

Moreover, reviewers reported that it was not straightforward to share an EndNote library (especially version 6 backwards) between collaborators. In order to do so, users either needed to use EndNote Web in an online environment, or to export the EndNote library file locally and then copy it for other team members. This is inconvenient and time-consuming, and espe-cially within a large group of reviewers and with a large number of studies, data loss became a common problem.

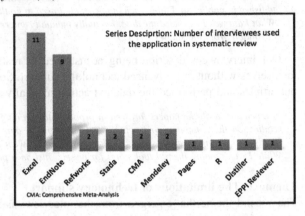

Fig. 3. Current applications used by reviewers

"We use EndNote Web, it ended up deleting all the information at some point because we were sharing it. One day we woke up, there was nothing on it." (P9)

Some reviewers are aware of or use meta-analysis software such as Stata[8], R[9], and Comprehensive Meta-Analysis[10]. Even though some software is specifically designed to support the systematic review process, they are not popular with our interviewees. Only two of our 16 interviewees mentioned using more advanced end-to-end appli-cations. Particularly, P17[11] mentioned using EPPI-Reviewer for a published review and P18 mentioned using Distiller for a future review.

Steep learning curve was one reason mentioned for software avoidance.

"I used formulas to convert them into mean and standard deviation. I could have used Stata or whatever but I did it manually. It would take more time to figure out how to do in that software rather than do it manually." (P12)

The size of review also impacted the decision to use software.

"For the smaller sample of studies, when we had between 10 and 15, it was doable manually. But when we're looking at 130 studies, I'm hoping that Distiller is going to cut short some time, at least by half if not more. Just so that we can get this process completed in a timely fashion." (P18)

---

[8] Data Analysis and Statistical Software http://www.stata.com/

[9] The R Project for Statistical Computing https://www.r-project.org

[10] Comprehensive Meta-Analysis https://www.meta-analysis.com

[11] We report 16 interviews with systematic reviewers; we exclude from our report 2 interviews with librarians who support and conduct systematic reviews.

5 Gap Analysis, Discussion and Future Work

Our interview results indicate a gap between the technology support available and what technology is being used by our reviewers. Despite the existence of advanced technology support (e.g. end-to-end applications or automation programs discussed in the background section), most steps are still done manually, making the review process more time-consuming and inefficient than it needs to be. There seem to be four potential explanations: first, reviewers might not be aware of these technologies; second, reviewers might have limited access to these technologies due to cost; third, reviewers might be stymied by actual or perceived learning curve and may prefer simple, familiar tools that require less training (e.g. the preferences of using such tools like EndNote and Excel); and fourth, tool features and availability may have changed since interviewees started their reviews.[12]

We also acknowledge the limitations of our study. Our conclusions about methodological problems may not be applicable for the whole population of reviewers since we had a small sample that may not have been representative beyond the large Research I university where we conducted our work. Future work should seek an even more diverse sample, with the awareness that multiple aspects may impact reviewers' practices and propensity towards computer support.

These interview results open up multiple directions for future research. Automation is not the only opportunity. Facilitating communication between team members could help make reviewing faster and more efficient, because according to interviewees, the more they communicated, the faster review tasks could be done. Bridging between low-tech and high-tech solutions, or integrating smaller tools into a custom pipeline might also help. Dissemination work is also needed, especially beyond the clinical medicine community, to help reviewers become more familiar with these existing applications as well as with co-evolving methodologies. A comprehensive review of what applications are available with detailed analysis of their costs, availabilities, feature advantages and disadvantages could help. One of our interviewees specifically called for cross-pollination between evidence synthesis methodologies in different fields.

Trust and accountability of software is another area that needs further development. For instance, automatic data extraction is one of the newest focus areas for systematic review automation research, often involving machine learning and natural language processing. However, our interview findings show that, once they reach the data extraction step, our interviewees prefer to read and extract data from included studies themselves. Being able to check machine results in a natural way (such as RobotReviewer's inline annotation of extracted data [16]) could help reviewers gain trust and identify further development needs for specific software. The ability to experiment with tools and observe their results is likely to increase reviewers' acceptance of new technologies [17].

---

[12] The three end-to-end systematic review tools were commercially available circa 2002 (EPPI-Reviewer v2), 2010 (Distiller), and 2013 (Covidence). For comparison, the oldest systematic review authored by our interviewees was published in 2012.

Further research is also needed to address the enduring vocabulary and scatter problems which heavily impact the systematic review community (e.g. retrieval of ~2000 references in order to find ~15 relevant studies [9]). One underexplored approach is to use science mapping tools, ranging from visualization to automatic citation network generation. Another idea is to develop a vocabulary mapping mechanism, which could collect keywords from scientific studies across fields, then identify the term definitions in order to map related terms with the same meanings together. By doing that, once reviewers search for studies that include a term, the system would be able to identify which other terms potentially have the same meaning. We believe these future directions for computer support could help to speed the systematic review process while retaining or improving review quality.

Acknowledgments. We would like to show our gratitude to all of the interview participants for sharing their experiences and also the pearls of wisdom that allowed us to complete this study. We would also like to thank our colleagues Lori Kendall and Peter Darch for discussions about qualitative research methodologies; Susan Lafferty who provided expertise that greatly assisted in the IRB process; and Katrina Felon for comments that greatly improved the manuscript. Research reported in this publication was supported in part by the National Library of Medicine of the National Institutes of Health under grant number R01LM010817, "Text Mining Pipeline to Accelerate Systematic Reviews in Evidence-based Medicine". The content is solely the responsibility of the authors and does not necessarily represent the official views of the National Institutes of Health.

References

1. Borah, R., Brown, A.W., Capers, P.L., Kaiser, K.A.: Analysis of the time and workers needed to conduct systematic reviews of medical interventions using data from the PROSPERO registry. BMJ Open 7(2), e012545 (2017)
2. Allen, I.E., Olkin, I.: Estimating time to conduct a meta-analysis from number of citations retrieved. J. Am. Med. Assoc. 282(7), 634–635 (1999)
3. Tsafnat, G., Glasziou, P., Choong, M.K., Dunn, A., Galgani, F., Coiera, E.: Systematic review automation technologies. Syst. Rev. 3(1), 74–88 (2014)
4. Turner, T., Green, S., Tovey, D., McDonald, S., Soares-Weiser, K., Pestridge, C., Elliott, J.: Producing Cochrane systematic reviews—a qualitative study of current approaches and opportunities for innovation and improvement. Syst. Rev. 6(1), 147–157 (2017)
5. Thomas, J., Noel-Storr, A., Elliott, J.: Human and machine effort in project transform: how intersecting technologies will help us to identify studies reliably, efficiently and at scale. Cochrane Methods Suppl. 1, 37–41 (2015)
6. Wright, R.W., Brand, R.A., Dunn, W., Spindler, K.P.: How to write a systematic review? Clin. Orthop. Relat. Res. 455, 23–29 (2007)
7. Anderson, N.K., Jayaratne, Y.S.: Methodological challenges when performing a systematic review. Eur. J. Orthod. 37(3), 248–250 (2015)
8. Grant, M.J., Booth, A.: A typology of reviews: an analysis of 14 review types and associated methodologies. Health Inf. Lib. J. 26(2), 91–108 (2009)
9. Bartels, E.M.: How to perform a systematic search. Best Pract. Res. Clin. Rheumatol. 27(2), 295–306 (2013)

10. Ross-White, A., Godfrey, C.: Is there an optimum number needed to retrieve to justify inclusion of a database in a systematic review search? Health Inf. Libr. J. **34**(3), 217–224 (2017)
11. Lorenzetti, D.L., Ghali, W.A.: Reference management software for systematic reviews and meta-analyses: an exploration of usage and usability. BMC Med. Res. Methodol. **13**(1), 141–145 (2013)
12. DiCicco-Bloom, B., Crabtree, B.F.: The qualitative research interview. Med. Educ. **40**(4), 314–321 (2006)
13. Braun, V., Clarke, V.: Using thematic analysis in psychology. Qual. Res. Psychol. **3**(2), 77–101 (2006)
14. Svenonius, E.: The Intellectual Foundation of Information Organization. MIT Press, Cambridge (2000)
15. Sutton, S.: Encyclopedia of Library and Information Sciences. Taylor and Francis, Abingdon (2009)
16. Marshall, I.J., Kuiper, J., Wallace, B.C.: RobotReviewer: evaluation of a system for automatically assessing bias in clinical trials. J. Am. Med. Inform. Assoc. **23**(1), 193–201 (2015)
17. Thomas, J.M.: Diffusion of innovation in systematic review methodology: why is study selection not yet assisted by automation? OA Evid. Based Med. **1**(2), 12–17 (2013)

Music Artist Similarity: An Exploratory Study on a Large-Scale Dataset of Online Streaming Services

Xiao Hu[1]($\boxtimes$) , Ira Keung Kit Tam[1] , Meijun Liu[1] ,
and J. Stephen Downie[2]

[1] University of Hong Kong, Pokfulam Road, Hong Kong, Hong Kong S.A.R.
xiaoxhu@hku.hk
[2] University of Illinois, 501 Daniel Street, Champaign, IL 61820, USA

Abstract. In supporting music search, online music streaming services often suggest artists who are deemed as similar to those listened to or liked by users. However, there has been an ongoing debate on what constitutes artist similarity. Approaching this problem from an empirical perspective, this study collected a large-scale dataset of similar artists recommended in four well-known online music steaming services, namely Spotify, Last.fm, the Echo Nest, and KKBOX, on which an exploratory quantitative analysis was conducted. Preliminary results reveal that similar artists in these services were related to the genre and popularity of the artists. The findings shed light on how the concept of artist similarity is manifested in widely adopted real-world applications, which will in turn help enhance our understanding of music similarity and recommendation.

Keywords: Music Artist Similarity · Online music services
Large-scale dataset · Genre · Artist popularity

1 Introduction

Online music streaming services have been playing an increasingly important role in helping people access music. According to IFPI (2016), 45% of the revenues of the global recorded music industry in 2016 came from digital services. Available in all major services is the function of similar artist recommendation. However, there has been a long-time debate on how artist similarity is defined. In other words, by which criteria can a set of artists be deemed as similar (Ellis et al. 2002; Oramas et al. 2015). Is artist similarity related to the genres and styles of the music the artists usually play, the popularity level of the artists, or other factors? Interestingly, artists recommended as similar to one particular artist often differ across online music services, yet all services claim effective in recommending similar artists (Echo Nest 2016; Zax 2011). Therefore, an empirical study on similar artists recommended on the most well-adopted online music streaming services can help shed light on how artist similarity is manifested in the real-world, which in turn can contribute to the literature of music similarity and recommendation.

© Springer International Publishing AG, part of Springer Nature 2018
G. Chowdhury et al. (Eds.): iConference 2018, LNCS 10766, pp. 378–383, 2018.
https://doi.org/10.1007/978-3-319-78105-1_41

In this paper, the "recommendation of similar artists" function of four popular online music streaming service providers, Spotify, last.fm, KKBOX, and the Echo Nest, are examined. As none of these commercial services published their recommendation mechanism, this study aims to analyze the relationships among recommended artists with regard to the genre of the music they play and their popularity. A large dataset of recommended artists was collected from these four services, on which a preliminary quantitative analysis was conducted, to answer the research questions:

1. To what extent is artist similarity related to music genre played by the artists?
2. To what extent is artist similarity related to popularity level of the artists?

2 Related Work

Artist is an important and universal access point of music information, on both traditional music catalogs and emergent music streaming services. Crosslinks of similar artists are often provided to facilitate browsing and seeking for music information (Lee and Waterman 2012). However, how best similarity among artist can be defined has been an ongoing debate (Ellis et al. 2002; Oramas et al. 2015), with some arguing that artists playing the same genre of music are similar (Bonnin and Jannach 2015), and others taking popularity level of the artists into consideration (Pucihar et al. 2017). Notwithstanding the importance of theoretical conceptualization of artist similarity, empirical evidences from online music streaming services are also invaluable in discovering how artist similarity is manifested in the real-world, given the fact that they strive to satisfy music needs of large quantities of users on a daily basis.

Prior studies have analyzed recommendation of similar artists in different online music services, for the purpose of improving recommendation performances (Celma 2010; Celma and Cano 2008; Jacobson 2011; Koenigstein et al. 2011). With the growth of the streaming music industry, many online music services emerged and expanded in the last few years. To help users find songs that match their needs, virtually all streaming music services provide recommendations based on artist similarity. These recommendations form connections of artists who are regarded as similar to one another. However, little research has systematically examined the characteristics of similar artists recommended by multiple services, partially because this would involve collecting and analyzing large-scale datasets (Celma 2010). This paper thus aims to explore possible missing links between artist similarity and artistic characteristics, namely music genre and popularity levels, based on a large-scale dataset collected from four most popular online music streaming services.

3 The Dataset

The dataset analyzed in this study was collected from four popular streaming music services, Spotify, Last.fm, KKBOX, and the Echo Nest. Launched in 2008, Spotify is a global music streaming services where a list of related artists is provided for each artist.

The web application program interface (API) provided by Spotify allows registered developers to access these profiles. Last.fm is an online music database which aims to create a recommendation system based on users' listening histories (Pálovics and Benczúr 2013). The company provides an API for developers to obtain similar artists to each given artist. KKBOX is also a music streaming service and is well adopted in the market of Asia. The profiles of artists in its music catalog include lists of related artists and can be viewed on the web interface. As the company does not provide any API, artist profiles were obtained by a web crawler and then parsed with scripts. The Echo Nest also provides similar artists in an artist's profile (Zax 2011), and makes them available through its API. All the data were collected between September 2015 and February 2016. The collected data will be made available for further research.

As there was no complete list of artists provided by any of the services, snowball sampling was used to obtain artist profiles from each of them. Starting from a randomly selected artist, we collected the profiles of all artists connected to the initial one. The process was repeated on each of the obtained artists until a preset sample size was reached. It was suggested that such a sampling method would bias towards artists with many incoming connections (Lee et al. 2006), and thus a large sample size was necessary to approximate the structure of the complete databases. Therefore, over 100 K artists were sampled from each of the services. It is noteworthy that the similarity relationship obtained in recommendation services can be non-symmetric (Ellis et al. 2002). That is, artist A can be recommended as similar to artist B, but sometimes artist B may not be recommended as similar to artist A. Therefore, the similarity connection between each pair of artists is directed, pointing from the source artist (for whom similar artists are recommended) to the recommended artist.

To answer the research questions, we collected artist attributes including the genres of music he/she often plays, and his/her popularity level. Genre refers to a class, type or category of music, sanctioned by convention (Oxford Music Online n. d.). Usually an artist is associated with one or more genres (Mauch et al. 2015), and genres are regarded as being related to artist grouping (Oramas et al. 2015). The tags of artists from Last.fm were collected as the source of genre information of artists in this study. To simplify the problem, when an artist was associated with multiple genre labels, the first genre appeared in the list of tags (i.e., being tagged most often) was chosen as the dominant genre of the artist. In this study, we adopt the 13 genres suggested in (Celma 2010) which are popularly used across the four services under study.

Artist popularity was measured by the number of users who listened to an artist's work (Cillessen and Rose 2005). As Last.fm provides software to collect listening history of users in major music streaming platforms, we obtained the number of listeners for sampled artists via the Last.fm API and used it to represent artist popularity. Since a small portion of sampled artists did not have their profiles included in Last.fm, we removed them from the dataset. Statistics of the resultant dataset is shown in Table 1.

Table 1. Statistics of the dataset.

Size	Echo Nest	KKBOX	Last.fm	Spotify
Genre				
No. of artists	58,927	72,875	355,543	128,029
No. of connections between artists	1,489,805	303,196	1,512,138	2,057,834
Popularity				
No. of artists	99,807	11,0342	472,790	199,179
No. of connections between artists	2,669,482	513,873	2,209,871	3,650,175

4 Data Analysis and Results

We calculated the distributions of similar artist connections across different genres and popularity levels which were defined in a log-linear scale due to the power-law distribution of music listening activities (Koch and Soto 2016). By comparing the percentage of pairs of similar artists across genres and popularity levels, we can observe whether genre and popularity played a role in artist similarity in the four online services.

4.1 Distribution of Genres Among Similar Artists

Table 2 shows the percentage of similar artist pairs across all 13 genres. The rows are genres of the source artists to whom other artists were recommended as similar. The columns are genres of the recommended artists who were deemed as similar to the source artists (denoted as "similar artists" in Table 2). It is noteworthy that the percentages were calculated separately for each online service. As the patterns across services were similar, the percentages averaged across services are reported in Table 2.

On average, 43% to 84% similar artists were in the same genre as the source artists, as demonstrated by the percentages (bolded) on the diagonal line of Table 2, indicating a fairly strong relationship between genre and artist similarity. Among all genres, Classical had the highest percentage (84%) on the diagonal line, meaning that 84% of similar artists recommended to Classical artists were also Classical artists. This seems to be related to the uniqueness of Classical music among the 13 genres. In contrast, R&B had the lowest percentage (43%) on the diagonal line, meaning less than half of the artists who were recommended as similar to R&B artists also played R&B as their dominant genre. Notable portions of similar artists of R&B artists were Pop and Hip-hop artists (16% each). The distribution of similar artists across genres seems in accordance to the relationships among genres. For instance, 18% of similar artists of Pop artists were Rock artists, whereas 14% of artists similar to those in the genre of Country were mainly playing Folk music. These two pairs of genres do have common origins (Oxford Music Online n. d.).

Table 2. Percentage of similar artist pairs across genres.

Similar artists Source artists	Blues	Classical	Country	Electronic	Folk	Hip-hop	Jazz	Metal	Pop	Punk	R&B	Reggae	Rock
Blues	**62%**	0%	4%	1%	5%	1%	7%	2%	2%	2%	1%	1%	13%
Classical	0%	**84%**	0%	4%	3%	0%	3%	1%	1%	0%	0%	0%	2%
Country	4%	0%	**65%**	1%	14%	1%	1%	1%	3%	1%	0%	0%	9%
Electronic	0%	1%	0%	**75%**	2%	3%	2%	2%	4%	2%	0%	1%	6%
Folk	2%	1%	5%	4%	**62%**	1%	2%	2%	7%	2%	0%	0%	11%
Hip-hop	0%	0%	0%	5%	1%	**81%**	2%	2%	3%	1%	1%	2%	3%
Jazz	3%	2%	0%	6%	3%	2%	**72%**	1%	3%	1%	0%	1%	5%
Metal	1%	0%	0%	3%	2%	1%	1%	**79%**	1%	4%	0%	0%	9%
Pop	1%	1%	1%	8%	7%	3%	3%	2%	**52%**	3%	1%	1%	18%
Punk	1%	0%	1%	4%	2%	2%	1%	5%	3%	**67%**	0%	1%	15%
R&B	5%	0%	1%	4%	1%	16%	7%	1%	16%	1%	**43%**	1%	5%
Reggae	1%	0%	0%	3%	1%	6%	2%	1%	2%	4%	0%	**76%**	4%
Rock	2%	0%	1%	6%	5%	2%	2%	5%	9%	8%	0%	1%	**58%**

4.2 Distribution of Popularity Levels Among Similar Artists

Calculated as averages across all four online services, the distribution of similar artists across different popularity levels is reported in Table 3 where the highest percentage in each row (popularity level of the source artists) is bolded. As it can be seen, the percentage of similar artists with higher popularity increases as the popularity level of the source artists does. In other words, artists with higher popularity have higher chances to be recommended as similar to artists who are equally popular. On the other hand, artists with low popularity have slim chances to be regarded as similar to artists with high popularity (as shown by the underscored percentages in Table 3).

Table 3. Distribution of pairs of similar artists across popularity levels.

Popularity of source artists	Popularity level of similar artists						Total
	0–10	10–100	100–1K	1K–10K	10K–100K	>100K	
0–10	20%	**25%**	22%	18%	10%	4%	100%
10–100	6%	26%	**38%**	22%	6%	2%	100%
100–1K	2%	8%	**43%**	39%	7%	2%	100%
1K–10K	1%	2%	16%	**56%**	22%	4%	100%
10K–100K	1%	1%	2%	23%	**56%**	17%	100%
>100 K	1%	0%	1%	3%	31%	**64%**	100%
Total	31%	62%	122%	161%	131%	93%	600%

5 Conclusion and Future Work

In this paper, we analyzed similar artists as recommended by four widely adopted online music streaming services, with regard to the genres of music they play and their popularity levels. Preliminary results show that artist similarity, as manifested in these online services, is related to the genre and popularity of the artists, with certain recognizable patterns. The dataset can support further in-depth analyses (e.g., using network metrics) in the future, to find out more patterns that will enhance our understanding of artist and music similarity. The study also exemplifies the emerging trend of quantitative analysis of concepts in information science with large-scale empirical datasets.

References

Bonnin, G., Jannach, D.: Automated generation of music playlists: Survey and experiments. ACM Comput. Surv. (CSUR) **47**(2), 26 (2015)

Celma, Ò.: Music Recommendation and Discovery: The Long Tail, Long Fail, and Long Play in the Digital Music Space. Springer, Heidelberg (2010). https://doi.org/10.1007/978-3-642-13287-2

Celma, Ò., Cano, P.: From hits to niches?: or how popular artists can bias music recommendation and discovery. In: Proceedings of the 2nd KDD Workshop on Large-Scale Recommender Systems and the Netflix Prize Competition, pp. 5. ACM (2008)

Cillessen, A.H.N., Rose, A.J.: Understanding popularity in the peer system. Curr. Dir. Psychol. Sci. **14**(2), 102–105 (2005)

Echo Nest: our company (2016). http://the.echonest.com/company/. Accessed 09 Aug 2017

Ellis, D.P., Whitman, B., Berenzweig, A., Lawrence, S.: The quest for ground truth in musical artist similarity. In: Proceedings of International Society for Music Information Retrieval, Paris, France (2002)

Jacobson, K.: Connections in music. Ph.D. thesis, Queen Marry University of London, London, U.K. (2011)

Koch, N.M., Soto, I.M.: Let the music be your master: power laws and music listening habits. Musicae Scientiae **20**, 193–206 (2016). European Society for the Cognitive Sciences of Music

Koenigstein, N., Dror, G., Koren, Y.: Yahoo! music recommendations: modeling music ratings with temporal dynamics and item taxonomy. In: Proceedings of the 5th ACM conference on Recommender systems, pp. 165–172 (2011)

Lee, J.H., Waterman, N.M.: Understanding user requirements for music information services. In: Proceedings of International Society for Music Information Retrieval, Porto, Portugal, pp. 253–258 (2012)

Lee, S.H., Kim, P.-J., Jeong, H.: Statistical properties of sampled networks. Phys. Rev. E. Stat. Nonlinear, Soft Matter Phys. **73**(1), 016102 (2006)

Mauch, M., Maccallum, R.M., Levy, M., Leroi, A.M.: The evolution of popular music: USA 1960–2010. R. Soc. Open Sci. **2**(5), 150081 (2015)

Oramas, S., Sordo, M., Anke, L.E., Serra, X.: A semantic-based approach for artist similarity. In: Proceedings of International Society for Music Information Retrieval, Malaga, Spain, pp. 100–106 (2015)

Oxford Music Online: genre. http://www.oxfordmusiconline.com/subscriber/article/grove/music/40599. Accessed 23 Aug 2017

Pálovics, R., Benczúr, A.A.: Temporal influence over the Last.fm social network. In: IEEE/ACM International Conference on Advances in Social Networks Analysis and Mining (ASONAM), pp. 486–493 (2013)

Pucihar, A., Borštnar, M.K., Kittl, C., Ravesteijn, P., Clarke, R., Bons, R.: Music recommender systems challenges and opportunities for non-superstar artists. In: 30th Bled eConference, Slovania (2017)

Zax, D.: The Echo Nest makes pandora look like a transistor radio (2011). http://www.fastcocreate.com/1679062/the-echo-nest-makes-pandora-look-like-a-transistor-radio. Accessed 23 Aug 2017

Unsupervised Citation Sentence Identification Based on Similarity Measurement

Shiyan Ou[(⊠)] and Hyonil Kim

School of Information Management, Nanjing University, Nanjing, China
oushiyan@nju.edu.cn, kimhyonil@126.com

Abstract. Citation Context Analysis has obtained the interest of many researchers in the field of bibliometrics. To do this, the first step is to extract the context of each citation from a citing paper. In this paper, we proposed a novel unsupervised approach for the identification of implicit citation sentences without attaching a citation tag. Our approach selects the neighboring sentences around an explicit citation sentence as candidate sentences, calculates the similarity between a candidate sentence and a cited or citing paper, and deems those that are more similar to the cited paper to be implicit citation sentences. To calculate text similarity, we proposed four methods based on the Doc2vec model, the Vector Space Model (VSM) and the LDA model respectively. The experiment results showed that the hybrid method combing the probabilistic TF-IDF weighted VSM with the TF-IDF weighted Doc2vec obtained the best performance. Compared against other supervised methods, our approach does not need any annotated training corpus, and thus can be easy to apply to other domains in theory.

Keywords: Citation sentence identification · Word embedding
TF-IDF

1 Introduction

Citation is a very common but important phenomenon in academic articles, which reflects the author(s) of an article how to reuse, improve and evaluate other researchers' related work. Thus citation analysis has been used for a long history to investigate the impact of an article or a scholar in academic communities. However, traditional citation analysis focuses mainly on citation frequency and does not consider the motivation, objective and sentiment of a citation, which makes it impossible to deeply discover the real value of a cited work. With the rapid growth of online full-text articles and the development of text processing techniques, it becomes possible to analyze citation content and explore the meaning of each citation in depth. This new citation analysis method is called Content-based Citation Analysis or Citation Context Analysis (CCA), and has obtained the interest of many researchers in the field of bibliometrics [4].

To do citation context analysis, the first step is to extract the context of a citation from a citing paper. Citation context refers to the pieces of text fragments that mention a cited paper. At sentence level, citation context can be divided into two categories: explicit citation sentences and implicit ones. The former refers to the sentences that

© Springer International Publishing AG, part of Springer Nature 2018
G. Chowdhury et al. (Eds.): iConference 2018, LNCS 10766, pp. 384–394, 2018.
https://doi.org/10.1007/978-3-319-78105-1_42

attach one or more citation tags, whereas the later refers to those that do not attach any citation tag but provide additional interpretation to the content of a cited paper. The following shows an example of explicit and implicit citation sentences that refer to the same cited paper, in which the first is an explicit one whereas the rest is implicit ones.

> "A FrameNet semantic parser usually follows a three-step process (Das et al., 2014). The first step is .... This step is usually .... The second step is .... The final step is .... This step identifies and finds...."

Most of studies on citation context analysis either explored explicit citation sentences only [1] or used a fixed-size text window to recognize citation context [9]. It is not a problem to identify explicit citation sentences because an article usually has its own fixed citation format. Thus, this paper focuses mainly on the identification of implicit citation sentences. Although the fixed-size window methods can be used to identify implicit citation sentences more or less, they also create lots of noises [3]. Among the small number of studies on implicit citation sentences identification, supervised learning methods were often used [2, 3]. However, as the articles in different domains usually have different citation styles, different training corpus need to be prepared for them, which is very time consuming. Instead, in this paper we propose a novel unsupervised learning approach for identifying implicit citation sentences from a citing paper. In the rest of this paper, we first review the existing methods for citation context identification, and then present our novel similarity-based citation sentence identification approach and report the experiments and their results.

2 Related Work

The previous studies on citation context identification can be divided into two categories: clause-level and sentence-level identification. The former is to identify the clause(s) corresponding to a reference within an explicit citation sentence, whereas the latter is to distinguish a whole implicit citation sentence. Compared to the clause-level identification, the sentence-level identification is a more popular research spot. Various approaches were developed by using CRF, HMM, SVM and so on. In 2009, Kaplan et al. proposed an identification method based on coreference chains [5]. They first trained a SVM coreference resolver based on the MUC-7 corpus, then applied it to look for the antecedents corresponding to the noun phrases in an explicit citation sentence from its surrounding sentences, and deemed those that contain an antecedent to be implicit citation sentences. However, in their experiments, there was a big difference between the macro-averaged F1-score (84%) and the micro-averaged one (69.3%), which means that their method was not stable. In 2010, Angrosh et al. proposed a CRF-based method [2]. They manually extracted word sequence patterns from the sentences in the "related work" section, and developed a CRF classifier based on 13 features selected from them to predict the category (explicit citation, implicit citation, or others) of a new sentence in this section. However, it is not clear whether the classifier can be used in other sections. In 2011, Athar used a SVM classifier with 12 features to identify implicit citation sentences [3]. The important features include lexical hooks, acronyms, formal citations, author's names, beginning with a pronoun, work nouns occurring in a candidate sentence. However, the F1-score of the categorization result was only 51.3%, which is not promising. Recently, Sondhi and Zhai proposed a HMM-based method [11]. They trained Hidden Markov Model (HMM) based on a human-annotated corpus to estimate the word generation probability from each of the two states (i.e. a citation or a non-citation sentence). The experiment results showed that its precision was very high (98.7%) but the recall was very low (50.3%). It seemed that HMM was not good at distinguishing citation sentences since the state sequences are too simple for this issue.

In addition to supervised methods, some unsupervised methods were also developed, most of which were based on rules or statistics. In 1999, Nanba and Okumura proposed a rule-based method [8]. They extracted the most frequent N-grams from a citation-annotated corpus to discover cue phrases and created 100 rules based on these cue phrases (e.g. anaphors, negative expressions) to extract reference areas. The experiment showed a relatively good result with a F1-score of 77.9%. However, it is very difficult to create rules and also difficult to avoid the interferences among the rules as the number of the rules grows. In 2010, Qazvinian and Radev treated citation sentence identification as a Markov process and built MRF (Markov Random Field) based on a sentence's lexical features and its similarity with neighboring sentences to determine whether it is a citation sentence [10]. However, according to their experiment, the performance of this method was not stable with the F1-scores ranging from 34.1% to 88.9% for different test data. The reason is that the method is under their supposition that the citation sentences for the same reference are usually similar each other, but this may not always be true especially for a pair of explicit and implicit citation sentences.

3 Similarity-Based Citation Sentence Identification

In this section, we propose to identify implicit citation sentences based on their similarity with the citing and cited paper. A citation sentence usually summarizes the main content of a cited paper or mentions some key points of the paper, rather than focuses on the current work in the citing paper. Thus, it may be more closely related to the cited paper. Therefore, we assumed that a citation sentence should be more similar to the cited paper than to the citing paper.

There are various approaches for calculating text similarity. The most common one is the cosine similarity based on the Vector Space Model (VSM). However, the VSM-based measures have the limitation of only considering word occurrence and ignoring polysemys, synonyms and related words. This problem becomes more serious while calculating the similarity between a citation sentence and its corresponding reference because this sentence usually summarizes or rephrases the content of the reference in a very compressed way.

With the advent of deep learning methods, two word vector models (CBOW and Skip-gram) proposed by Mikolov et al. [7] made a breakthrough in measuring word similarity by "calculating" their semantics. In this study, we intended to use word embedding to improve the classical VSM-based similarity measures. Two novel measures were proposed by representing a document based on the combination of word vectors and TF-IDF weights. In addition, a third method was also proposed based on the LDA topic model by indirectly measuring text similarity with text generation probability.

3.1 Measuring Document Similarity Based on Doc2vec

In 2014, Le and Mikolov derived a document vector model PV-DBOW from the word vector models to learn continuous distributed vector representations for pieces of texts [6]. In PV-DBOW, a document is treated as a special word, which is represented as a bag of words occurring in it without word ordering [6]. However, this model only considers the TF of each word rather than the TF-IDF while representing a document. To solve this problem, we intended to improve it using a TF-IDF weighted linear model of word vectors of distributed bag of occurrence words. To construct this model, we used the corpus which contains multi-sense words and their annotated senses (each sense can be regarded as a virtual word) to explore the relationship between the vector representation of a multi-sense word and the vector representation of its bag of virtual words.

Multi-sense Word Representation. To discover the proper vector representation of a multi-sense word, we used a sense-tagged corpus SENSEVAL[1] as the source of the training corpus. Although SENSEVAL is not a corpus of scientific articles, it does not matter since our goal is to explore the relationships between word vectors rather than obtain word vectors only. To prepare the training corpus, we duplicated each sentence in SENSEVAL by replacing each multi-sense word with a corresponding virtual word. Table 1 shows some sentences in which the original word *line* is replaced with different virtual words.

Table 1. The example corpus of multi-sense words for training word vector representation

He hung on to his **line_cord** *and landed the fish*
Further, blur the legal **line_division** *separating commercial and investment banking*
Correspondent said in the passport **line_formation** *at Moscow's Sheremetyevo airport*
He made another call and came back on the **line_phone** *with the news that ...*
In addition, Mr. Frashier will push for development of a **line_product** *of protein-based adhesive....*
Clients reportedly get a one-page bill on which is written a single **line_text**

As shown in Table 1, for the word *line* having six senses, *line_cord*, *line_division*, *line_formation*, *line_phone*, *line_product* and *line_text* are the virtual words that respectively represent its different senses in the sentences. By using the Skip-gram word embedding model, we obtained the word vectors of a multi-sense word and its

---

[1] SENSEVAL is a English corpus used in a word sense disambiguation evaluation exercise, see https://raw.githubusercontent.com/nltk/nltk_data/gh-pages/packages/corpora/senseval.zip.

virtual words respectively from the training corpus. To explore how to represent a multi-sense word with a bag of its virtual words, we defined two average word vectors of the virtual words and then compared them with the word vector of the multi-sense word.

Given a multi-sense word w, let $U = \{u_1, u_2, \cdots, u_i, \cdots, u_m\}$ be the set of its virtual words, V_{u_i} is the trained word vector of a virtual word u_i. Then the average word vector of the virtual words (AWV) is calculated from Eq. 1 and the TF weighted average word vector (TF-AWV) is calculated from Eq. 2.

$$AWV(U) = \frac{1}{m} \sum_i V_{u_i} \tag{1}$$

$$TF - AWV(U) = \frac{1}{z} \sum_i f(u_i) V_{u_i} \tag{2}$$

where m is the total number of the virtual words of the word w, $f(u_i)$ is the TF of a virtual word u_i in the corpus, and z is the sum of $f(u_i)$ as a normalization factor.

To test whether the above-mentioned two average word vectors can represent a multi-sense word properly, we calculated the cosine similarity between the word vector of the multi-sense word and the two average word vectors of its virtual words respectively. Four multi-sense words *line*, *serve*, *interest*, and *hard* were tested, and the results are shown in Table 2.

Table 2. The comparison between the word vector of a multi-sense word and the two average word vectors of its virtual words

Real word	Virtual word	Similarity	Real word	Virtual word	Similarity
line	line_cord	0.45	interest	interest1	0.59
	line_division	0.54		interest2	0.62
	line_formation	0.48		interest3	0.53
	line_phone	0.57		interest4	0.49
	line_product	0.92		interest5	0.57
	line_text	0.46		interest6	0.86
	AWV	0.74		**AWV**	0.78
	TF-AWV	**0.96**		**TF-AWV**	**0.92**
server	server2	0.79	hard	hard1	0.98
	server6	0.62		hard2	0.81
	server10	0.79		hard3	0.61
	server12	0.78		**AWV**	0.94
	AWV	0.91		**TF-AWV**	**0.99**
	TF-AWV	**0.93**			

As shown in Table 2, the TF weighted average of the virtual word vectors (TF-AWV) is the most similar to the word vector of a multi-sense word for all the four tested words, whereas the average of the virtual word vectors (AWV) is less similar than some of the individual virtual word vectors in some cases. Thus, we can use TF-AWV to represent a multi-sense word.

Doc2vec-based Document/Paragraph Representation. By regarding a document as a multi-sense word and its occurrence words as its virtual words, thus we also can use TF-AWV to represent a document. However, TF-AWV has the same limitation as the PV-DBOW model because each occurrence word in a document is only weighted with TF. Therefore, we improved the Eq. 2 to Eq. 3 by replacing the TF weight with the TF-IDF weight to obtain the vector representation of a document, namely the TF-IDF weighted average word vector (TFIDF-AWV).

$$TFIDF - AWV(\boldsymbol{d}) = \frac{1}{z}\sum\nolimits_{w\in d} tfidf(w,\boldsymbol{d}) \bullet V_w \qquad (3)$$

where d is a document that can be a piece of text of any length, V_w is the word vector of a word w occurring in the document d, and $tfidf(w, \mathbf{d})$ is its TF-IDF weight in this document, z is a normalization factor as the sum of the TF-IDF weights of all the words occurring in the document d.

Based on the document vectors of each candidate citation sentence, the cited paper and the citing paper, we can calculate their cosine similarity to determine which candidate sentences are more similar to the cited papers than to the citing paper.

3.2 Measuring Document Similarity Based on Probabilistic TF-IDF

In this section, we intended to improve the TF-IDF based text similarity measure using word embedding from another perspective different from Le and Mikolov's. Here, we represented a document still using the traditional TF-IDF weighted VSM. But we solved the problems of synonyms, polysemys and related words in text as a probabilistic issue.

For example, the two sentences "*SVM shows the best performance in this test.*" and "*The result of their classifier is good.*" have very similar meaning. If we calculate the VSM-based cosine similarity, the value is 0 because there is no common non-stop word between these two sentences. Actually, the word *best* in the first sentence is closely related with the word *good* in the second. Although it is possible to find related words with the help of some semantic dictionaries such as WordNet, it is hard to measure their relatedness quantitatively and also requires to do word-sense disambiguation first. To measure the mutual impact of such closely related words, we used a fuzzy value (0–1) to quantitatively represent the occurrence probability of a word which does not really occur in a document. In this study, the fuzzy value was calculated as the cosine similarity between two word vectors built using word embedding. Meanwhile, we ignored the words that did not occur in both documents, since they are apt to make noise.

Let $V_{\mathbf{d}}$ be the vector of a document d based on VSM, i.e. $V_{\boldsymbol{d}} = \{v_1, v_2, \cdots, v_i, \cdots, v_n\}$. Here, the ith element v_i refers to the TF-IDF weighted occurrence probability of the ith word in a vocabulary. If the ith word really occurs in the document d, its occurrence probability value p_i is equal to 1; otherwise, p_i is calculated from Eq. 4 as the maximum cosine similarity between the word and the other real-occurrence words.

$$p_i = \begin{cases} 1, & w_i \in \boldsymbol{d} \\ \max_{W_j \in d} sim(V_{w_i}, V_{w_j}), & w_i \notin \boldsymbol{d} \end{cases} \tag{4}$$

Then, each element v_i in the document vector V_d is calculated from Eq. 5.

$$v_i = p_i \bullet TFIDF(w_i, \mathbf{d}) \tag{5}$$

In this way, we can measure the cosine similarity between a candidate citation sentence and the citing or cited paper based on their probabilistic TF-IDF weighted VSM-based document vectors.

3.3   Measuring Document Similarity Based on LDA

In this section, we proposed a method for measuring the similarity between two documents based on the LDA topic model, since LDA is a real generative model and more effective than other non-generative topic models (e.g. LSI and PLSI). Compared against VSM, LDA can cluster related words into a meaningful group (i.e. topic) and represent a document as the distribution of a set of topics. Instead of directly calculating the similarity between a candidate citation sentence and a paper, we assumed that if a candidate sentence has a higher generation probability under the condition of a document (i.e. the cited or citing paper), it is more similar to the document. The generation probability of a candidate sentence can be calculated from Eq. 6.

$$sim(s, D) \approx P(s|D) \approx \prod_{w_i \in s} P(w_i|d) \tag{6}$$

where s refers to a candidate citation sentence, and d refers to a document (i.e. citing or cited paper), w_i refers to the ith non-stop word occurring in the candidate sentence s, $P(w_i|d)$ refers to the occurrence probability of the word w_i given the document d.

The occurrence probability of a word in a document can be calculated based on LDA. We first extracted the topic distribution of a document and the word distribution of each topic using LDA and then calculated the occurrence probability of a word in a document from Eq. 7.

$$P(w_i|d) = \sum_{t_j} P(w_i|t_j) \bullet P(t_j|d) \tag{7}$$

where t_j refers to the jth topic of the document d, $P(w_i|t_j)$ refers to the occurrence probability of the word w_i under the topic t_j, and $P(t_j|d)$ refers to the occurrence probability of the topic t_j in the document d.

Then we can compare the two generation probabilities of a candidate sentence under the condition of the cited paper or citing paper respectively to measure which paper the candidate sentence is more "similar" to.

4 Experiments

4.1 Test Corpus for Citation Identification

We selected 7 academic papers in the field of computer science as citing papers from some Elsevier journals published in HTML and collected the full texts and abstracts of the references (i.e. cited papers) for each citing paper. There are 164 references in total for the 7 citing papers, among which the full texts of 84 references and the abstracts of 164 references are available. We only selected 84 references whose full texts and abstracts are both available as the test cited papers, and then manually annotated citation sentences referring to them in each citing paper and found 158 explicit citation sentences and 98 implicit citation sentences in total from the 7 papers.

4.2 Experiments and Results

In this study, we proposed four novel methods to measure the similarity between a candidate citation sentence and the cited or citing paper, i.e. TF-AWV, TFIDF-AWV, PTFIDF-VSM and LDA, based on the Doc2vec model, the VSM model and the LDA model respectively. The candidate sentences which are more similar to the cited paper were deemed to be real citation sentences. The neighboring sentences around each explicit citation sentence in the test corpus were selected as candidate sentences. To determine a proper range of candidate sentences, we tested the F1-scores of the abovementioned four methods on different ranges using the full texts of citing and cited papers, and the results are shown in Fig. 1.

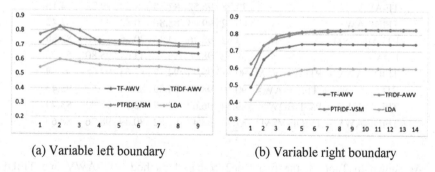

(a) Variable left boundary   (b) Variable right boundary

Fig. 1. The F1-scores of the four methods on different candidate sentence ranges.

Figure 1 shows the F1-score curve of the four methods on different candidate sentence ranges by changing the left or right boundary respectively. As the left boundary changing from 1 to 9 sentences before an explicit citation sentence whereas the right boundary is fixed to 10 sentences after the explicit one, the best performance was obtained when the left boundary is 2 sentences (as shown in Fig. 1(a)). As the right boundary changing from 1 to 14 sentences whereas the left boundary is fixed to 2, the best performance was obtained when the right boundary is 10 sentences (as shown in Fig. 1(b)). Finally we selected 2 sentences before an explicit citation sentence and 10 sentences after it as candidate citation sentences.

Among the four proposed methods, the two Doc2vec-based methods (TF-AWV and TFIDF-AWV) and the probabilistic VSM-based method (PTFIDF-VSM) require a pre-trained Word2vec model. To obtain it, we downloaded 23,500 ACL academic papers[2] and converted them from PDF to plain text using Apache PDFBox[2] as a training corpus to train word vectors. Then we evaluated the identification performance of the four methods with precision, recall and F1-score based on two test sets, i.e. the papers' abstracts or full texts in the test corpus. The similarity measurement based on the traditional TF-IDF weighted VSM (referred as TFIDF-VSM) and the PV-DBOW document vector model proposed by Le and Mikolov (referred as PV-DBOW) were both used as baselines. Furthermore, we also tested the hybrid methods by combining any two individual methods, in which the second method was used to further judge a non-citation sentence deemed by the first method as its complement to improve the recall. Table 3 shows the performance of the six individual methods and top-four hybrid methods on the abstract and full-text test set respectively.

Table 3. The performance of the different methods on two test sets.

Method	Abstract test set			Full-text test set		
	R	P	F1	R	P	F1
TFIDF-VSM	69.33	97.25	80.95	57.11	100.00	72.70
PV-DBOW	63.06	84.96	72.39	54.28	97.66	69.77
TF-AWV	79.78	96.52	87.36	59.20	99.25	74.16
TFIDF-AWV	80.32	99.43	**88.86**	70.82	98.57	**82.42**
PTFIDF-VSM	73.62	98.76	84.36	70.65	100.00	**82.80**
LDA	39.52	98.70	56.44	43.64	95.80	59.96
TFIDF-AWV + PTFIDF-VSM	90.51	99.45	**94.77**	87.63	99.05	**92.99**
PTFIDF-VSM + TFIDF-AWV	90.10	98.90	**94.30**	88.04	99.52	**93.43**
TFIDF-AWV + PV-DBOW	89.54	96.67	92.97	80.73	97.92	88.49
TFIDF-AWV + TFIDF-VSM	87.78	98.47	92.82	80.49	98.76	88.69

As shown in Table 3, the two Doc2vec-based methods (TF-AWV and TFIDF-AWV) and the probabilistic VSM-based method (PTFIDF-VSM) got the better performance than the others among the six individual methods on both test sets. Especially, TFIDF-AWV obtained the highest F1-score of 88.86% on the abstract set, whereas PTFIDF-VSM obtained the highest 82.80% on the full-text set. That means that it is very effective to use a TF-IDF weighted average of a bag of word vectors to represent a document vector. Surprisingly, the generation probability method based on LDA got the worst performance on the two sets and was even worse than the traditional

---

[2] Apache PDFBox is an open source Java PDF library, see https://pdfbox.apache.org/.

VSM-based method. Among all the methods, the combination of the top-two individual methods (TFIDF-AWV and PTFIDF-VSM) got the highest F1-scores (94.77%, 93.43%) on both sets. Although the order of the two methods has little effect on the performance, there is no significant difference. It is also surprising that all the methods showed better performance on the abstract set than on the full-text set except the LDA-based method. This finding is very promising since paper abstracts are usually easier to get than full texts, which makes our approach easy to implement.

5 Conclusions

This paper reported our work on identifying implicit citation sentences by comparing the impact of a citing paper and a cited paper on a candidate sentence. The impact of a paper on a sentence was measured using their similarity. We proposed four novel methods for measuring the similarity between a document and a candidate citation sentence in a citing paper based on the Doc2vec model, the VSM model and the LDA model respectively. The experiment results showed that the hybrid method, which combines the probabilistic TF-IDF weighted VSM and the TF-IDF weighted average word vector, obtained the best performance with a F1-score of 94.77% based on the abstracts of citing and cited papers. The advantage of our approach lies in that it is unsupervised without requiring any annotated training corpus and thus can be extended to other domains easily in theory. A limitation of our work is that the experiment data is very small. In the future, we will increase the size of our test corpus by adding the papers from multiple domains, and thus verify the portability of our approach across domains. Furthermore, we will also explore the difference between explicit and implicit citation sentences in expressing citation motivation, sentiment, and the content of a cited paper.

Acknowledgement. This paper is one of the research outputs of the project supported by the State Key Program of National Social Science Foundation of China (Grant No. 17ATQ001).

References

1. Abu-Jbara, A., Radev, D.: Reference scope identification in citing sentences. In: Proceedings of the 2012 Conference of the North American Chapter of the Association for Computational Linguistics: Human Language Technologies, pp. 80–90. Association for Computational Linguistics (2012)
2. Angrosh, M.A., Cranefield, S., Stanger, N.: Context identification of sentences in related work sections using a conditional random field: towards intelligent digital libraries. In: Proceedings of the 10th Annual Joint Conference on Digital Libraries, pp. 293–302. ACM (2010)
3. Athar, A.: Sentiment analysis of citations using sentence structure-based features. In: Proceedings of the ACL 2011 Student Session, pp. 81–87. Association for Computational Linguistics (2011)
4. Ding, Y., Zhang, G., Chambers, T., et al.: Content-based citation analysis: the next generation of citation analysis. J. Assoc. Inf. Sci. Technol. **65**(9), 1820–1833 (2014)

5. Kaplan, D., Iida, R., Tokunaga, T.: Automatic extraction of citation contexts for research paper summarization: a coreference-chain based approach. In: Proceedings of the 2009 Workshop on Text and Citation Analysis for Scholarly Digital Libraries, pp. 88–95. Association for Computational Linguistics (2009)
6. Le, Q., Mikolov, T.: Distributed representations of sentences and documents. In: Proceedings of the 31st International Conference on Machine Learning (ICML-14), pp. 1188–1196 (2014)
7. Mikolov, T., Chen, K., Corrado, G., et al.: Efficient estimation of word representations in vector space. arXiv preprint arXiv:1301.3781 (2013)
8. Nanba, H., Okumura, M.: Towards multi-paper summarization using reference information. IJCAI **99**, 926–931 (1999)
9. O'Connor, J.: Citing statements: computer recognition and use to improve retrieval. Inf. Process. Manag. **18**(3), 125–131 (1982)
10. Qazvinian, V., Radev, D.R.: Identifying non-explicit citing sentences for citation-based summarization. In: Proceedings of the 48th Annual Meeting of the Association for Computational Linguistics, pp. 555–564. Association for Computational Linguistics (2010)
11. Sondhi, P., Zhai, C.X.: A constrained hidden Markov model approach for non-explicit citation context extraction. In: Proceedings of the 2014 SIAM International Conference on Data Mining, pp. 361–369. Society for Industrial and Applied Mathematics (2014)

Using Full-Text of Research Articles to Analyze Academic Impact of Algorithms

Yuzhuo Wang🆔 and Chengzhi Zhang$^{(\boxtimes)}$🆔

Department of Information Management,
Nanjing University of Science and Technology, Nanjing 210094, China
{wangyz, zhangcz}@njust.edu.cn

Abstract. Top-10 algorithms in data mining voted by experts were widely used in various domains. How about the academic impact of these algorithms in a special domain, e.g. Natural Language Processing (NLP)? To answer this question, this paper uses full-text corpus of research articles published in ACL conference to explore influence of the Top-10 data mining algorithms in NLP domain. Academic influence of algorithms is analyzed according to three aspects: number of papers which mention algorithm, mention frequency, and mention location of algorithm. What's more, we find the most popular algorithm in a particular task via correlation coefficient between algorithm and task. This research offers a new way for evaluating influence of algorithms quantitatively. Results show that there are obvious differences of influences among algorithms. Specifically, impact of SVM algorithm is significantly higher than the other algorithms. Moreover, the most related task resolved by each algorithm is different.

Keywords: Influence of algorithm · Full-text content · Citation features

1 Introduction

In 2006, ICDM (http://www.cs.uvm.edu/~icdm/) launched a poll to choose the classical algorithms of data mining. After an initial nomination and screening, organizers invited 145 experts to vote and select the "Top Ten Algorithms in Data Mining" [1]. These 10 algorithms cover the most important topics in data mining, and each of them plays a directive role in the field of data mining and artificial intelligence. It should be noted that these algorithms were voted by experts from a qualitative perspective. This method has two limitations: the assessment process is based on experts' experience and it could not avoid their subjectivity; it is a general result and can't present algorithms' impacts in a specific domain, e.g. NLP. Besides, are there any differences among influences of these algorithms? Which kind of topic or task in a specific domain are these algorithms used to solve? We have to find other approaches to answer these two questions.

Currently, data mining algorithms are broadly used in NLP. For beginners, they are so needy to know application of different algorithms in their research. So, it is very important for them to select an appropriate algorithm for their topic or task. This paper firstly uses full-text corpus to investigate mention times and location of the Top-10 data

© Springer International Publishing AG, part of Springer Nature 2018
G. Chowdhury et al. (Eds.): iConference 2018, LNCS 10766, pp. 395–401, 2018.
https://doi.org/10.1007/978-3-319-78105-1_43

mining algorithms in a specific domain. Then, we analyze academic influence of algorithms in the domain according to their usages information.

2 Methodology

We use NLP as case and investigate applications of Top-10 data mining algorithms in this domain. We analyze full-text of NLP articles, extract sentences containing one of the 10 algorithms. Then, we assess academic impact of these algorithms.

2.1 Data Collection and Labeling

(1) Sources of raw data

We download all ACL (The Association Computational Linguistics) annual conference papers between 1979 and 2017 from the ACL Anthology (http://www.aclweb.org/anthology). This meeting is one of the top conferences in NLP domain, and the conference papers reflect the most cutting-edge topic. We obtain 5,212 main conference articles containing 3,824 long papers and 1,488 short papers.

(2) Algorithm sentences extraction

To label the top-10 data mining algorithms in all the ACL articles, we use a dictionary to exact match each algorithm. The dictionary contains all algorithms' names from "The Top Ten Algorithms in Data Mining" [1]. Moreover, we use these standard names as query to search Google Scholar and Wikipedia, according to description of algorithms in related papers and interpretation in Wikipedia, alias of each algorithm are acquired. The algorithms' names and their alias are listed in Table 1.

Table 1. Names of top10 algorithms in data mining

No.	Standard name	Alias
1	C4.5	
2	K-Means	k means
3	Support vector machines	Support vector machine, svms, svm
4	Apriori	
5	EM	Expectation-maximization, expectation maximization
6	PageRank	Pr
7	AdaBoost	Adaptive Boosting
8	K-Nearest Neighbor	Knn, k-nn, k nearest neighbor, k nearest neighbour, k nearest neighbors, k nearest neighbours, k-nearest neighbors
9	Naive Bayes	Naïve-bayes, naïve bayes, naive-bayes, nb
10	CART	Classification and regression trees

Then, we extract algorithm sentences from articles, and record information such as title, section etc. After manual filtering, we get 6,341 sentences which mention one of the Top-10 algorithms. Brief descriptions of labels are shown in Table 2.

Table 2. Meaning of labels in the annotation corpora

Label	Meaning
No	Sequence number of an algorithm sentence
Id	Unique identifier of a monograph or an article
Section_type	Type of the section where an algorithm locates
Section_title	Title of the section where an algorithm locates
Algorithm	Name of the algorithms which an algorithm sentence contains
Content	Content of an algorithm sentence
Task	Task of article which contains the algorithm

(3) Task classification

A professor and a PhD student who are familiar with NLP are invited to classify task of each article which contains algorithm sentences. They label tasks according to *The Oxford Handbook of Computational Linguistics* [2]. The professor reviews the results. Finally, 40 kinds of tasks are obtained, 37 of them come from the handbook, i.e. *anaphora resolution, corpus linguistics, disambiguation, discourse, evaluation, finite state technology, formal grammars and language, information extraction, information retrieval, lexical knowledge acquisition, lexicography, machine learning, machine translation, morphology, multilingual on-line natural language processing natural language generation, natural language in multimodal and multimedia system, natural language interaction, natural language processing, ontology, parsing, part of speech tagging, phonology, pragmatics and dialogue, question answering, segmentation, semantics, speech recognition, statistical methods, sublanguage and controlled languages, syntax, term extraction and automatic indexing, text data mining, text summarization, text to speech synthesis, tree adjoining grammars, word sense disambiguation. OCR, machine reading comprehension and cognitive linguistics* are added by us because these tasks are not introduced in the handbook.

2.2 Analyzing Academic Impact of Algorithms

The 6,341 algorithm sentences are classified into ten categories by name of algorithms. Then their impact in the ACL articles are analyzed.

(1) Impact measurement of algorithms

We measure the impact of different algorithms in NLP from three perspectives.

Number of papers: "Count One" [3] is frequency of papers which have mentioned each algorithm.

Frequency of mention: "Count X" [4] is frequency of an algorithm appearance in papers. Sum of sentences of each algorithm is total frequency of algorithms mentioned.

Location of algorithms: According to the findings of An et al. [5], all sections are classified into 8 categories: *abstract, background, introduction, related work, method, evaluation, discussion and conclusion.* We explore distribution of each algorithm in various section. No matter how many times that an algorithm appears in a section, we only count it one time.

(2) Impact measurement of algorithms in different tasks

In order to know which one is the most popular algorithm in a particular task, we measure correlation between algorithms and tasks. After computing Chi-square value (χ^2) [6] between each algorithm and task, the most correlated task of each algorithm is obtained.

3   Experimental Results Analysis

3.1   Comparing Top-10 Data Mining Algorithms Based on Number of Papers

This paper assumes that the more papers an algorithm is mentioned, the wider influence it has. As shown in Table 3, SVM has a wider influence compared with other algorithms and it is one of the most stable and precise methods of all well-known algorithms [1].

Table 3. Number of papers of each algorithm

No.	Algorithm	# papers (Ratio)	No.	Algorithm	# papers (Ratio)
1	SVM	774 (44.33%)	6	KNN	67 (3.84%)
2	EM	403 (23.0%)	7	C4.5	57 (3.26%)
3	Naive Bayes	190 (10.88%)	8	AdaBoost	21 (1.20%)
4	K-Means	115 (6.59%)	9	Apriori	14 (0.80%)
5	PageRank	92 (5.27%)	10	CART	13 (0.74%)

3.2   Comparing Top Ten Data Mining Algorithms Based on Frequency of Mention

Table 4 illustrates some differences in rank order according to algorithms. SVM still has the highest frequency of mention. We calculate average frequency by the formula "frequency of mention/number papers". Table 5 indicates some changes in impacts of different algorithms. We propose that average frequency of mention represents depth of influence. As can be seen from the Table 5, the influence of PageRank is the deepest.

Table 4. Mention frequency of algorithm

No.	Algorithm	Freq.
1	SVM	3,000
2	EM	1,606
3	Naive Bayes	575
4	PageRank	417
5	K-Means	320
6	KNN	185
7	C4.5	116
8	AdaBoost	73
9	CART	32
10	Apriori	18

Table 5. Avg. mention frequency of algorithm

No.	Algorithm	Avg. Freq.
1	PageRank	4.51
2	EM	3.99
3	SVM	3.88
4	AdaBoost	3.48
5	Naive Bayes	3.03
6	K-Means	2.78
7	KNN	2.76
8	CART	2.46
9	C4.5	2.04
10	Apriori	1.29

3.3 Comparing Top Ten Data Mining Algorithms Based on Location of Algorithm

McCain and Turner [7], Maričić et al. [8] suggested that sections of *"method"* and *"results"* in papers are more important than *"introduction"* and *"conclusion"*. Therefore, this paper mainly compares usages of different algorithm in "method" and *"results"*, namely *"method, evaluation & discussion"*. As Table 6 shown, the most influential algorithm is still SVM in these three sections. It is obvious that algorithms appearing in the *"method"*, *"evaluation"* and *"discussion"* are more likely to be used as a method. Thus, the most comprehensive being used algorithm is SVM, while the least one is CART.

Table 6. Distribution of each algorithm in different section

Rank	Algorithm	Method section (#/ratio)		Evaluation section (#/ratio)		Discussion section (#/ratio)	
1	SVM	329	37.69%	56	51.85%	482	54.46%
2	EM	235	26.92%	21	19.44%	139	15.71%
3	Naive Bayes	86	9.85%	16	14.81%	93	10.51%
4	K-Means	59	6.76%	6	5.56%	58	6.55%
5	PageRank	58	6.64%	2	1.85%	39	4.41%
6	KNN	40	4.58%	4	3.70%	29	3.28%
7	C4.5	35	4.01%	2	1.85%	28	3.16%
8	AdaBoost	13	1.49%	1	0.93%	14	1.58%
9	Apriori	9	1.03%	0	0.00%	0	0.00%
10	CART	9	1.03%	0	0.00%	3	0.34%
Sum		873	100%	108	100%	885	100%

3.4   Comparing Top Ten Data Mining Algorithms Based on Task

According to χ^2 value, we obtain the task which has the highest correlation with each algorithm. As Table 7 shown, almost each algorithm is suitable for different tasks except SVM and EM, both of which have the highest correlation with machine translation (MT). There is a typical article entitled "*Soft Syntactic Constraints for Word Alignment through Discriminative Training*", in which SVM is mentioned 19 times. A max-margin syntactic aligner is created with SVM to resolve word alignment in MT.

Table 7. The most relevant task of each algorithm

Algorithm	Task	Algorithm	Task
Adaboost	Finite state technology	K-Means	Corpus linguistic
Apriori	Natural language interaction	KNN	Pragmatics and dialogue
C4.5	Anaphora resolution	Naive Bayes	Natural language processing
CART	Text to speech synthesis	PageRank	Text summarization
EM	Machine translation	SVM	Machine translation

4   Discussion and Conclusion

Using the full text of ACL conference articles, this paper analyses impact of Top-10 data mining algorithms in a specific domain. We know the difference of the algorithms in number of papers, frequency of mention, location and tasks. The results indicate that although the Top-10 data mining algorithms seem to play an equal role in NLP, the applications of them in specific areas are still significantly different. In a short, in NLP domain, SVM algorithm has the widest influence while PageRank is the most effective. Comparison between our result and votes of experts suggests that influence of Top-10 algorithms reflected by its practical application in a specific domain is different from the overall assessment. Moreover, our research answers which kind of task these algorithms used to solve.

In the future, we can extend top ten data mining algorithms into datasets, models, tools and other aspects, and construct a complete method system. After that, in the view of accessing impact of various methods for different disciplines, we can provide a reference of research methods for scientific researchers in different discipline.

Acknowledgement. This work is supported by Major Projects of National Social Science Fund (No. 17ZDA291) and Qing Lan Project.

References

1. Wu, X., et al.: Top 10 algorithms in data mining. Knowl. Inf. Syst. **14**(1), 1–37 (2008)
2. Mitkov, R.: The Oxford Handbook of Computational Linguistics. Foreign Language and Res. Oxford University Press, Oxford (2012)

3. Ding, Y., Liu, X., Guo, C., et al.: The distribution of references across texts: some implications for citation analysis. J. Informetr. **7**(3), 583–592 (2013)
4. Wan, X., Liu, F.: WL-index: leveraging citation mention number to quantify an individual's scientific impact. J. Assoc. Inf. Sci. Technol. **65**(12), 2509–2517 (2014)
5. An, J.Y., Kim, N., Kan, M.Y., et al.: Exploring characteristics of highly cited. J. Assoc. Inf. Sci. Technol. **68**(8), 1975–1988 (2017)
6. Pearson, K.: On the criterion that a given system of deviations from the probable in the case of a correlated system of variables is such that it can be reasonably supposed to have arisen from random sampling. Philos. Mag. Ser. **50**(5), 157–175 (1900)
7. McCain, K., Turner, K.: Citation context analysis and aging patterns of journal articles in molecular genetics. Scientometrics **17**(1–2), 127–163 (1989)
8. Maričić, S., Spaventi, J., Pavičić, L., et al.: Citation context versus the frequency counts of citation histories. J. Assoc. Inf. Sci. Technol. **49**(6), 530–540 (1998)

Can Word Embedding Help Term Mismatch Problem? – A Result Analysis on Clinical Retrieval Tasks

Danchen Zhang and Daqing He[✉]

University of Pittsburgh, Pittsburgh, USA
{daz45, dah44}@pitt.edu

Abstract. Clinical Decision Support (CDS) systems assist doctors to make clinical decisions by searching for medical literature based on patients' medical records. Past studies showed that correctly predicting patient's diagnosis can significantly increase the performance of such clinical retrieval systems. However, our studies showed that there are still a large portion of relevant documents ranked very low due to term mismatch problem. Different to other retrieval tasks, queries issued to this clinical retrieval system have already been expanded with the most informative terms for disease prediction. It is therefore a great challenge for traditional Pseudo Relevance Feedback (PRF) methods to incorporate new informative terms from top K pseudo relevant documents. Consequently, we explore in this paper word embedding for obtaining further improvements because the word vectors were all trained on much larger collections and they can identify words that are used in similar contexts. Our study utilized test collections from the CDS track in TREC 2015, trained on 2014 data. Experiment results show that word embedding can significantly improve retrieval performance, and term mismatch problem can be largely resolved, particularly for the low ranked relevant documents. However, for highly ranked documents with less term mismatching problem, word emending's improvement can also be replaced by a traditional language model.

Keywords: Clinical Decision Support · Word embedding · Term mismatch

1 Introduction

During their clinical decision making process, doctors often consult external literature for reference. The published biomedical literature, which contains expert written materials on nearly all topics in the medical area, are the most common source of reference [1]. TREC has hold Clinical Decision Support (CDS) track since 2014 to support medical text retrieval, based on which we proposed a diagnosis prediction enhanced retrieval model (MRF-Wiki) [3, 4], which outperforms the state-of-art models.

However, our MRF-Wiki model still has room to improve, because many relevant articles are either lowly ranked or not returned at all. Different to other retrieval tasks, queries in disease prediction-based retrieval systems, such as ours, have already included the most informative terms with the help of predicted diseases. It is hard for

© Springer International Publishing AG, part of Springer Nature 2018
G. Chowdhury et al. (Eds.): iConference 2018, LNCS 10766, pp. 402–408, 2018.
https://doi.org/10.1007/978-3-319-78105-1_44

traditional Pseudo Relevance Feedback (PRF) model to find new and more informative words to expand the original query, not to mention its topic drift problem [7].

In this paper, we will firstly examine the failure cases in the current model and particularly explore the effects from term mismatch, which is a common problem in retrieval tasks [5, 6]. In medical domain, the term mismatch problem can appear like this. Disease in the query might not appear in the relevant document, and the virus causing the disease could be an important evidence for making the document relevant. But they cannot be matched with traditional language models.

In this situation, the word embedding model, trained on the large collections, can identify words that are used in similar contexts with respect to a given word [6]. It is expected that word embedding could introduce a full list of reasonably weighted new words closely relevant to the query terms, which might help in resolving term mismatch problem in medical domain.

Consequently, we try to answer the following research questions in this study: (1) To what extent does term mismatch problem affect the diagnosis-based clinical text retrieval models? (2) In what situation can word embedding model solve term mismatch problem? And (3) What are the problems still limiting the system enhanced by word embedding?

2   Related Works

Pseudo Relevance Feedback extracts new informative terms from top ranked documents, and it is one of the traditional ways to resolve word mismatch problem in information retrieval. In CDS task, majority previous studies utilized PRS to enhance the original queries. For example, Limsopatham et al. [2] explored collecting terms from different knowledge sources to expand the query. Choi and Choi [8], the best run in CDS 2014, utilized the most frequent Medical Subject Heading label terms inside the PRF documents to expand the original query. Balaneshin-kordan et al. [9] expanded the queries with terms selected from both PRF documents and Google search results. All these methods of using PRF significantly improved the retrieval performance. However, different to these systems, queries in our disease prediction based clinical retrieval system have already included the most informative terms (i.e., predicted disease), which makes it challenging for PRF to find new and more informative terms.

Word embedding models, which can leverage the underlying word semantic similarities, have been widely used in information retrieval [5, 6, 10, 11]. Zhou et al. [5] demonstrated that word embedding can significantly improve the performance of a question-answer system by alleviating term mismatch problems. Ganguly et al. [6] proposed a word embedding-based word transformation model to address the term mismatch problem. In this study, we want to explore, after the most informative words have already existed in the query, whether word embedding can further improve the retrieval performance by solving the remaining term mismatch problems.

3 Methods

To answer the above-mentioned research questions, we conducted retrieval experiments using TREC CDS 2014 and 2015 collections. The three retrieval models employed in the study are presented below.

3.1 Baseline: Markov Random Field with Wikipedia Based Diagnosis Prediction (MRF-Wiki) Model

MRF-Wiki was a model we proposed in [3, 4]. The patient's disease related information is extracted from the topic, and a Wikipedia based disease predictor model is called to predict the patient's disease diagnosis, which is used to expand the query generated by Markov Random Field (MRF). The query can be written in the form of Indri query language as in Formula (1). This model is the baseline in this study.

$$\#weight\ ((1 - \alpha)\ \#combine\ (MRF\ query)\ \alpha\ \#combine\ (predicted\ diagnosis))\quad(1)$$

3.2 PRF Enhanced Document Ranking (PRF-DR) Model

The PRF model used in this study is Relevance Model 3 (RM3), a classic PRF model presented in [12]. RM3 selects the most informative terms form topK documents, and each term is weighted by their importance. It can be written in Indri query language:

$$\#weight\ ((1 - \beta)\ \#combine\ (MRF - WIKI\ query)\ \beta\ \#combine\ (weighted\ terms))\quad(2)$$

3.3 Word Embedding Enhanced Document Ranking (WE-DR) Model

Trained on large collections, word embedding models can learn high-quality dense word vector representations from the contextual information of the word. These dense word vectors keep the semantic relationships, which provide us the basis for resolving the term mismatch problem.

In our WE-DR model, only the title and keywords parts are used to represent the whole document. This is because these two parts contain the most informative terms and disclose the document's main topics. Through analyzing MRF-WIKI queries, we found that patient's diagnosis information is more important than symptom information because nearly all relevant documents contain the diagnosis but usually do not mention the symptoms. Thus, predicted diagnosis terms were used as the surrogate of the query in the enhancement with word embedding. For a text (i.e., query or document) with n terms, vectors are calculated as the averaged accumulated word vectors:

$$text\_vec = \frac{1}{n}\sum_{term \in text} word\_vec\quad(3)$$

Cosine similarity is commonly chosen to evaluate the association between two vectors [10, 11]. We used it here for calculating the similarity between query and document. The relevance score of the document is combined by the score in MRF-Wiki model and the cosine similarity, which are combined with a parameter γ:

$$Score(d) = (1 - \gamma) MRF - WIKI(d) + \gamma Cos(doc\_vec, query\_vec) \qquad (4)$$

We used a collection of pre-trained word vectors of 200 dimensions that were generated using skip-gram model with a window size of 5 on PubMed and PMC texts [13]. The collection contains vectors for 2,515,686 words.

4   Experiments and Discussions

4.1   Dataset and Metrics

In this study, the target collection is a corpus of 744,138 PubMed articles, published in TREC 2014 CDS track. It was preprocessed with stop word removal and Porter stemming, and was indexed with Indri. We used the 30 topics from TREC 2014 CDS track to train the models, and used 30 topics from TREC 2015 CDS track for testing. In this study, α *is set 0.5;* β *is set 0.5, and* γ *is set 0.25. For RM3 model,* 3 most important terms from top 5 retrieved documents are expanded to MRF-WIKI.

Following TREC CDS track, the evaluation metrics used include infNDCG (inferred Normalized Discounted Cumulative Gain), P@10, and MAP.

4.2   Results: Impacts of Word Embedding

WSU-IR [14] was the best performed model in CDS track 2015, and the three methods mentioned in Sect. 3 (i.e., MRF-WIKI, PRF-DR and WE-DR) all achieved better infNDCG than it. But only WE-DR has higher P@10 and MAP that WSU-IR (see Table 1). As only a final performance is provided for WSU-IR [14], we cannot conduct significant test for further comparation. However, using Wilcoxon Signed Ranks Test to examine among our three models, we find that WE-DR significantly outperforms MRF-WIKI on infNDCG, and significantly outperforms both MRF-WIKI and PRF-DR on P@10 and MAP (p-value < 0.05). PRF-DR shows no significant difference from the baseline MRF-WIKI in all three metrics.

Table 1. Performance comparison on CDS 2015 task. * indicates significantly outperform MRF-WIKI; ** means significantly outperform MRF-WIKI and PRF-DR;

	infNDCG	P@10	MAP
WSU-IR [4]	29.39%	46.67%	18.64%
MRF-WIKI	31.04%	42.33%	18.61%
PRF-DR	32.71%	44.67%	17.74%
WE-DR	32.26%*	49.67%**	19.52%**

4.3   Results: Analysis of Term Mismatch Problem

We performed manual analysis on the results of six topics to further explore the effect of word embedding model, and the six topics are randomly selected from the topics with correct diagnosis prediction. During the analysis, we selected three groups of documents. Firstly, we selected top ranked relevant documents using those relevant documents appearing within the top 10 ranks. Secondly, we then selected low ranked relevant documents by identifying the last 5 relevant documents from ranks 500 to 1000. Finally, for each topic, we randomly selected 5 relevant but not returned (i.e., false negative) documents. There are totally 98 documents selected from these topics, as shown in Table 2.

Table 2. Selected 98 documents in result analysis

	Doc count	Term mismatch affected Docs
Top relevant documents	28	2
Low relevant documents	35	14
False negative documents	35	10
Total documents	98	26

To what extent does term mismatch problem affect the diagnosis based clinical text retrieval system (baseline)?
In the selected 98 documents, if a document does not contain the query terms, it is labeled as a document affected by term mismatch. From Table 2 we can see that the number of highly ranked documents affected by this problem is small, but the lowly ranked relevant documents and false negative ones are much commonly affected by term mismatch frequently appears. Totally we collected 26 term mismatch cases.

In what situation can word embedding model resolve term mismatch problem?
Highly ranked documents. P@10 is significantly improved in WE-DR, implying word embedding helps highly ranked documents. In our selected document set, half of top relevant documents ranking are boosted, while most of the other half ranking stay at the same. After exploration, we find that those boosted documents usually have short title/keywords but the query terms appear several times. In contrast, those few declined documents usually have long title/keywords and the query terms only appear one time. This implies that embedding model boosts the documents with more query terms, so it works like a traditional language model in highly ranked documents, where term mismatch seldom appears.

Lowly ranked relevant documents. Table 2 shows that, among the 14 lowly ranked relevant documents suffering term mismatch problem, 13 of them have their ranks boosted by the word embedding model, The only document with declined ranking has a rhetoric title "How 40 kilograms of fluid retention can be overlooked: two case reports", even though its main topic is about the diagnosis of "heart failure". This relevant document is even hard to identify using manual methods. In addition, P@1000 of WE-DR is 8.84%, which significantly outperforms MRF-Wiki's 8.68% (p-value < 0.05). This indicates that the embedding model can improve the lowly ranked document ranking by resolving the word mismatch problem.

What are the problems still limiting the system enhanced with word embedding?
We further analyzed the non-relevant documents ranked within the top 10, and identified three main reasons. First, **documents discussing irrelevant patient situations**. For example, topic 11 is related to a 56-year-old lady, but some non-relevant articles talk about patients as pregnant female, male, adolescent, or even animals. Second, **document concerns another disease**. For example, topic 3 seeks documents of "Pulmonary embolism", and some top ranked documents talk about "Pulmonary hypertension", which is a different disease. The last one is **different aspects of disease.** For example, topic 17 seeks for information about what test cervical cancer patient should receive, but some non-relevant articles talk about treatment plan, or study people's attitude towards cervix cancer, which make them non-relevant.

5 Conclusion

In this paper, we presented and examined a diagnosis prediction-based clinical decision support system with a word embedding model. The embedding model aims to resolve the term mismatch problem. Our results show that for highly ranked documents, word emending's improvement can also be replaced by a traditional language model, however, for the lowly ranked documents, improvement comes from overcoming the term mismatch problem. Overall, our system outperforms the state-of-the-art performance. In next step, we will explore ideas on how to filter out top non-relevant documents.

References

1. Roberts, K., et al.: Overview of the TREC 2016 clinical decision support track. In: TREC (2016)
2. Limsopatham, N., et al.: Modelling the usefulness of document collections for query expansion in patient search. In: Proceedings of the 24th ACM International on Conference on Information and Knowledge Management. ACM (2015)
3. Zhang, D., He, D.: Enhancing clinical decision support systems with public knowledge bases. Data Inf. Manag. **1**, 49–60 (2017)
4. Zhang, D., et al.: Wikipedia-based automatic diagnosis prediction in clinical decision support systems. In: iConference 2017 Proceedings (2017)
5. Zhou, G., et al.: Learning continuous word embedding with metadata for question retrieval in community question answering. In: ACL, vol. 1 (2015)
6. Ganguly, D., et al.: Word embedding based generalized language model for information retrieval. In: Proceedings of the 38th International ACM SIGIR Conference on Research and Development in Information Retrieval. ACM (2015)
7. Carpineto, C., Romano, G.: A survey of automatic query expansion in information retrieval. ACM Comput. Surv. (CSUR) **44**(1) (2012)
8. Choi, S., Choi, J.: SNUMedinfo at TREC CDS track 2014: medical case-based retrieval task. Seoul National Univ (Republic of Korea) (2014)

9. Balaneshin-kordan, S., Kotov, A., Xisto, R.: WSU-IR at TREC 2015 clinical decision support track: joint weighting of explicit and latent medical query concepts from diverse sources. In: Proceedings of the 2015 Text Retrieval Conference (2015)
10. Gurulingappa, H., et al.: Semi-supervised information retrieval system for clinical decision support. In: TREC (2016)
11. Mitra, B., et al.: A dual embedding space model for document ranking. arXiv preprint arXiv: 1602.01137 (2016)
12. Lv, Y., Zhai, C.X.: A comparative study of methods for estimating query language models with pseudo feedback. In: Proceedings of the 18th ACM Conference on Information and Knowledge Management. ACM (2009)
13. Pyysalo, S., Ginter, F., Moen, H., Salakoski, T., Ananiadou, S.: Distributional semantics resources for biomedical text processing (2013)
14. Balaneshin-kordan, S., Kotov, A., Xisto, R.: WSU-IR at TREC 2015 clinical decision support track: joint weighting of explicit and latent medical query concepts from diverse sources. Wayne State University, Detroit, US (2015)

Research on the Semantic Measurement in Co-word Analysis

Liqin Zhou[1] , Zhichao Ba[1(✉)] , Hao Fan[1] , and Bin Zhang[2]

[1] Center for the Studies of Information Resources, Wuhan University,
Wuhan 430072, China
zhoulq92@163.com, bazhichaoty@126.com, hfan@whu.edu.cn
[2] Center of Traditional Chinese Cultural Studies,
Wuhan University, Wuhan 430072, China
zb0205@126.com

Abstract. Aiming at problems of the "same amount with different qualities" phenomenon and the lack of semantics in co-occurring terms, this paper proposed a new semantic measurement method in co-word analysis. The method firstly gave different weights to document units based on the Pointwise Mutual Information (PMI) method, and then extended them to the generation process of the Latent Dirichlet Allocation (LDA) model to extract core keywords. Then the word-2vec model was used to transform the Top-N keywords into low-dimensional value distributions, and the semantic correlation among keywords were calculated based on the length of windows. Finally, data from the domain of "deep learning" was used to verify the scientificity and effectiveness of the method. Comparing the results of general co-word analysis with our proposed method in terms of clustering analysis, network parameters, distribution structures and other aspects, we can find that our method is scientific and effective in considering different feasibilities of terms and their semantic correlations.

Keywords: Co-word analysis · Keyword selection · Semantic measurement
LDA · Word-2vec · Deep learning

1 Introduction

As one of the major research methods of content analysis, co-word analysis mainly reveals relationships among words, semantic associations between topics, and knowledge network structures within a subject, through exploring the statistical characteristics of co-occurring keywords or subject terms. At present, the method has been widely used in artificial intelligence, information retrieval, scientific metrology, biological information engineering, and other research fields.

Common co-word analysis in the choice of etymology generally draws from keywords, titles, and abstracts. Owing to the indexing and convenience features, researchers usually preferentially use keywords as co-word analysis unit. But with a certain randomness and habitual element, the indexing keywords will sometimes lead to the "indexing effect" (Ding et al. 2001). Then relevant scholars (Guo et al. 2015) proposed to extract core terms from titles and abstracts to replace keywords, which can

© Springer International Publishing AG, part of Springer Nature 2018
G. Chowdhury et al. (Eds.): iConference 2018, LNCS 10766, pp. 409–419, 2018.
https://doi.org/10.1007/978-3-319-78105-1_45

avoid the subjectivity of selection keywords and solve the problems of missing keywords. However, it is obviously unreasonable to treat terms equally without considering their weights and believe that they are the same important. Existing scholars rarely studied semantic relationships between co-occurring terms. They just intuitively assumed that co-occurring terms were bound to be related and their correlation intensity were exactly the same. But from the perspective of a single study or the whole literature sets, there exist a direct co-occurrence correlation or an indirect semantic association between co-occurring terms (Wang et al. 2012). Ignoring their semantic relationships will inevitably lead to a distortion in the final co-word analysis.

The purpose of this study is to solve the problems of the "same amount with different qualities" phenomenon and the lack of semantics in co-occurrence terms in correlation calculation. We consider the weight of each attribute selected from papers, and expand them to the Latent Dirichlet Allocation (LDA) model to extract core keywords with a strong ability of characterization. Then the word-2vec model is used to transform the Top-N keywords into low-dimensional value distributions to calculate the sematic correlation between keywords. To illustrate the process of the method, data from the domain of "deep learning" is taken as an example. The constructed method can also be applied to other disciplines or other types of research entities, such as experts and research teams.

2 Related Work

Since the co-word analysis method first proposed by Callon et al. in 1983, it has been an important research method to reveal the subject and content of research fields. Previous studies mainly focused on the following two aspects.

2.1 Selection of Core Terms

In co-word analysis, analysis units were usually obtained from keywords, unified indexing subject terms, titles, abstracts, and other means. Several related scholars standardized the treatment of keywords using a dictionary or classification vocabulary. Ding et al. (2001) used keywords, titles, and abstracts as co-word analysis units, and integrated the plurality and unity to reduce the influence of domestic terms. The other etymology choice was by means of subject terms, which attached importance to the logic of semantic distribution and performed more powerfully in clustering results (Guardiola et al. 2013). However, indexing keywords and subject terms only recreated the content of literatures, they cannot reflect the core subject accurately and fully. In this paper, we used the full text automatic indexing method to extract high quality terms with the machine learning algorithm, which is used less in practical research.

2.2 Semantic Measurement of Co-occurring Terms

Existing methods had three main kinds of implementations: one was based on the literature content by virtue of the statistic law of literature sets to indirectly reflect the relationship between terms (Li et al. 2016). Other implementation was based on ontologies, which realized the explanation of keyword concepts through external existing knowledge resources. And utilized a general ontology library (e.g., DBpedia, Cyc, HowNet, WordNet) and knowledge hierarchy of a domain dictionary (e.g., MeSH, OpenGALEN etc.) to realize the quantitative calculation of keyword semantic relevance (Tsatsaronis et al. 2010). The last implementation was based on the large-scale corpus method, which measured the correlation of terms through large-scale data (Zhang and Zhu 2015). In the co-word analysis method, considering the semantic connection among keywords through the above methods can further improve the scientific and validity of co-word analysis results.

3 Methodology

We proposed a new method of semantic measurement in co-word analysis in virtue of semantic modeling and deep learning. The basic process is shown in Fig. 1.

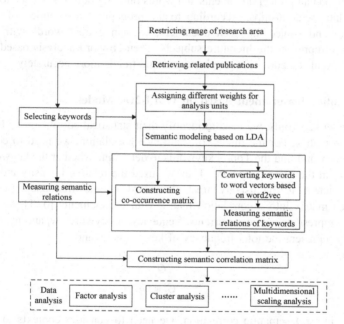

Fig. 1. Basic process of keyword selection and semantic measurement method

3.1 Keywords Selection Strategy Based on Weighted LDA Model

Traditional LDA model treats each keyword equally without considering their weights. But related scholars indicated that reasonable weighting strategies can make high frequency words naturally distributed without being assigned to subjects randomly (Wilson and Chew 2010). Therefore, this paper proposed to assign different weights to keywords extracted from different documents based on Pointwise Mutual Information

(PMI) method, which has been widely used in feature selection. Then we extended them to the LDA model to construct a new Gibbs sampling, as shown in Eq. (1).

$$p(z_i = k, w_i = t \mid z_{\neg i}, w_{\neg i}, \alpha, \beta)$$

$$= \frac{w(t,d)n_{k,\neg i}^{(t)} + \beta_t}{\sum_{t=1}^{V} \left(w(t,d)n_{k,\neg i}^{(t)} + \beta_t \right)} \cdot \frac{w(t,d)n_{m,\neg i}^{(k)} + \alpha_k}{\sum_{k=1}^{K} \left(w(t,d)n_{m,\neg i}^{(k)} + \alpha_k \right)} \tag{1}$$

Compared with traditional LDA model, the weighted LDA model assumed that the generation probability of keywords not only related with the polynomial weighting $\phi_{k,t}$, but also related with their weights $w(t, d)$, as shown in Eq. (2).

$$p(w \mid \theta, \phi) = \frac{w(t,d) \cdot \phi_{k,t}}{\sum_{t \in V} w(t,d)} \tag{2}$$

The method can project documents and words onto a group of subjects, to mine the latent semantic relationships. According to the probability distribution of words on each subject and subject on each document, we can extract words with a higher probability to represent the literature subjects. Then co-word analysis based on these words can reveal the current research subject and trends more accurately.

3.2 Semantic Measurement Based on Word-2vec Model

After selecting keywords, we need to identify their statistical correlation and construct a correlation matrix. For the direct co-occurrence correlation, we need to construct a co-word matrix and find the Top-N keywords to determine whether the keywords were co-occurring in the same document. Then we used the relative intensity index equivalence coefficient to inclusively treat the word couple frequency to turn the multi-valued matrix into a correlation matrix with the elements [0, 1], as shown in Eq. (3). $G_{i,j}$ represents the co-occurrence frequency of keywords w_i and w_j; G_I and G_j respectively represent the total frequency of keywords w_i and w_j.

$$E_{i,j} = \frac{G_{i,j}^2}{G_i * G_j} \tag{3}$$

For the indirect semantic correlation, we need to consider contexts to mine the grammar and semantic information. The word2vec model (Mikolov et al. 2013) was used to turn the Top-N keywords into a low-dimensional real value distribution, such as by taking the keyword "deep learning" as [0.734, 0.726, 0.642, 0.618, ..., 0.127], in which each real value represents the Cosine value or Euclidean distance between keywords. Through training the model, we can effectively abandon the traditional *0–1* sparse representation method and make up for the defects of keywords independence hypothesis to a certain extent. What's more, the model provides an effective Continuous Bag-of-Words (CBOW) and Skip-gram implementation method for calculating the word vector. The framework is shown in Fig. 2.

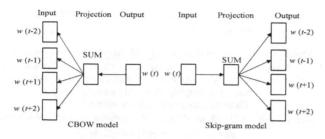

Fig. 2. Principle diagram of CBOW and the Skip-gram model

We mainly used the Hierarchical Softmax method based on the CBOW model to optimize training processes. The conditional probability function p (w | Context(w)) is shown as follows in Eq. (4).

$$p(v^w \mid context) = \prod_{j=1}^{L} p(v_j^w \mid v_1^w, v_3^w, \ldots, v_{j-1}^w, context)^{1-v_j}$$
$$(1 - p(v_j^w \mid v_1^w, v_3^w, \ldots, v_{j-1}^w, context))^{v_j} \tag{4}$$

Among them, $v^w = (v_1^w, v_2^w, \cdots v_L^W) \in (0,1)$ represents the Huffman encoding of the current word, and $(w_{t-n+1}, \cdots w_{t-1}, w_{t+1}, w_{t+n-1})$ represents the context of word w, abbreviated as *context*. Through the CBOW model, we can obtain the word vector length and then use it to calculate the semantic similarity of the keyword couples.

In terms of keyword w_i, the vector is represented as $w_i = (S_{i,1}, S_{i,2}, \cdots S_{i,k})$, where k represents the keywords most similar with w_i, and $S_{i,k}$ represents the cosine between the first k keywords with w_i. We applied the Pearson correlation coefficient (PCC) to calculate indirect semantic correlations between Top-N keywords. The indirect correlation value $\rho(w_i, w_j)$ between the word vector of keywords w_i and w_j is calculated as follows in Eq. (5).

$$\rho(w_i, w_j) = \frac{\sum_k (S_{i,k} - \bar{S}_i)(S_{j,k} - \bar{S}_j)}{\sqrt{\sum_k (S_{i,k} - \bar{S}_i)^2} \sqrt{\sum_k (S_{j,k} - \bar{S}_j)^2}} \tag{5}$$

Among them, $\bar{S}_i$ and $\bar{S}_j$ respectively represent the average value of cosine between keyword w_i, w_j. When the calculated $\rho(w_i, w_j)$ value is larger, the keywords w_i and w_j are more related. Through calculating the indirect semantic correlation of keywords, we can fully reveal the semantic correlation among co-occurring keywords, thus providing adequate semantic support for the analysis results.

3.3   Construction of the Co-word Correlation Matrix

Since the direct co-occurrence relationship only measures the correlation of keywords from the perspective of co-occurrence frequencies, we need to further analyze the semantic correlation between keywords to effectively reveal the characteristics of network knowledge and micro-evolution. The final co-word correlation matrix is constructed as follows in Algorithm 1.

Algorithm 1: Construction algorithm of the semantic correlation matrix
---
Input: (1) Top-N keyword set D^k, (2) Limited domain data set D, (3) Context window size parameters -*window*, (4) the most similar word dimension -*topNSize* and high-frequency sampling threshold parameter -*sample*;

Output: Semantic correlation matrix Θ

Step 1: Train set D with word2vec model to obtain $X_{(w_i)}$ of Top-N keywords;

For $t \leftarrow 1$ to $T = N(N-1)/2$ **do**

Step 2: Construct co-occurrence $\mho$ based on (w_i, w_j) and calculate direct co-occurrence intensity $E_{i,j}$ using Eq. (3);

Step 3: Calculate indirect correlation intensity $\rho (w_i, w_j)$ between $X(w_i)$ and $X(w_j)$

Step 4: Calculate $S(w_i, w_j) = \lambda E_{i,j} + (1-\lambda) \rho(w_i, w_j)$ as the correlation intensity of (w_i, w_j);

End Step 5: Output semantic correlation matrix Θ

---

4 Results Analysis and Discussion

4.1 Data Collection and Preprocessing

In order to verify the scientificity and effectiveness of our proposed method, this paper used the search strategy "TS = deep learning or KY = deep learning" in CNKI, Wanfang and Chongqing VIP to backtracking, retrieval period limited to 2006–2015. After removing the comments, notices, news, uncorrelated and repetitive literatures, we finally obtained 187 articles. Then titles, abstracts, and full texts were segmented based on the ICTCLAS segmentation system of Chinese Academy of Sciences (Zhang et al. 2003), except the self-indexing keywords. Then the segmentation results were applied to different extraction algorithms to obtain Top-N core keywords with a strong representation ability, N was set as 30.

Next, we used the word2vec model to train the document sets. The parameters were set as follows: $-topNSize = 40$, $-window = 10$, $-sample = 1e-3$, $-hs = 1$, $-cbow = 0$. Finally, we compared the results of general co-word analysis with our proposed method in terms of clustering analysis, network parameters, distribution structures and other aspects.

4.2 Clustering Effects Analysis

From the perspective of Top-N keyword selection, we can find that the effects of general co-word analysis method based on frequency interception is worse than our proposed weighted LDA method. When considering the number of clusters, we set the value of the calibration shaft to 20.5. Our proposed weighted LDA method classified the top 30 keywords into seven clusters, while the general co-word analysis method formed 4 clusters, as shown in Figs. 3 and 4.

We can find that the effect of the general co-word analysis method is not really well. For example, in Cluster 3, the clustering granularity cannot identify the specific research topics, such as "image recognition," "speech recognition," "target detection,"

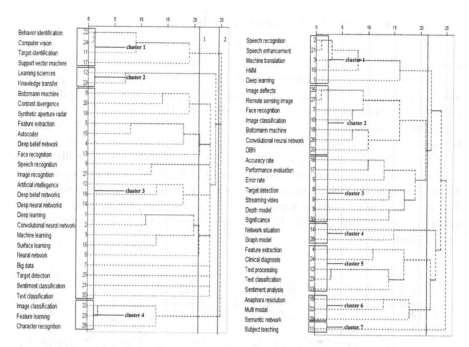

Fig. 3. Clustering of general co-word analysis   **Fig. 4.** Clustering of our proposed method

and "sentiment classification". These keywords should be divided into different clusters. In addition, it is more reasonable to classify the keywords "face recognition" and "image recognition" into Cluster 4, because they are more similar with the keyword "image classification". What's more, the keyword "learning science" belongs to the teaching research field, since the keyword "knowledge transfer" belongs to cross-disciplinary learning and transfer learning of text classification. It is obviously not reasonable to classify the two keywords in the same cluster.

In the weighted LDA model, the seven clusters are relatively clear. For example, Cluster 1 contains four keywords, which is mainly about the application of deep learning thought in "speech recognition and machine translation"; Cluster 2 contains keywords like "image deflects," "remote sensing image," "face recognition," and so on, which is mainly about applications in "image classification and recognition"; Cluster 3 puts the keywords "streaming video," "accuracy," and "performance evaluation" into the same cluster, which is not appropriate; Cluster 4 describes the application of deep learning in the "analysis of network situation awareness"; Cluster 5 contains "sentiment analysis," "clinical diagnosis," and other keywords, which are mainly about the text type data and application in "text mining"; Cluster 6 contains three keywords. The expressed topic is not as obvious as in the former five clusters, but there also exist strong semantic relationships. For example, the keywords "multi-modal" and "semantic web" are about research methods, which can be effectively applied to "anaphora resolution" research.

4.3   Semantic Measurement in Co-word Analysis

Figure 5 shows the measurement relationship of keywords based on the general co-word analysis method. We can find that the keyword "target identification" co-occurred twice with "deep learning", but did not co-occurred with "image recognition". The keyword "image classification" co-occurred four times with "deep learning" and three times with "image recognition". This indicates that there is no correlation between the keywords "target detection" and "image recognition", while the keywords "image classification" and "deep learning" have a higher relationship. However, it is difficult to truly reflect the interdependence degree without considering the semantic correlation among keywords. Otherwise, the frequency disparity data and more zeroes in multi-valued matrix would also impact the final statistic results. The general co-word analysis method simply assumed that literatures as a "lexical package" can be used to quantify the relationships among terms by the two- or multi-valued matrix.

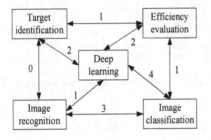

Fig. 5. Relational graph of co-occurrence   **Fig. 6.** Relational graph of semantics

Figure 6 shows the semantic measurement of keywords based on our proposed method. We can find that the correlation intensity between "image recognition" and "target detection" is 0.126, which indicates that there exists an indirect semantic relationship rather than a direct co-occurrence. Moreover, the correlation intensities with "deep learning" and "image classification" are 0.219 and 0.445, this indicates that they are stronger correlated with "image classification". Compared with general co-word analysis method, our proposed semantic measurement method can more clearly reveal semantic relationships among keyword and can provide more adequate support for analysis results.

4.4   Comparative Analysis of Basic Network Parameters

Table 1 shows the characteristics of basic network parameters in three schemes. For the keyword networks obtained by the LDA model or weighted LDA model, if the threshold value ξ is set as 0.05 and $S(w_i, w_j) < 0.05$, we identify that there is no correlation between keywords. Then, we select same keywords to construct three networks.

Table 1. Keywords network parameters of the three schemes

	Scheme 1	Scheme 2	Scheme 3
	Co-word analysis	LDA model	Weighted LDA model
Network density	0.19	0.63	0.71
Point central potential	0.86	0.25	0.29
Central potential	0.54	0.27	0.10
Closeness centralization	0.90	0.32	0.40
Cohesive subgroup density	−0.87	−0.72	−0.94

We can find that there are significant differences in the characteristics of three networks. Scheme 2 and Scheme 3 have significantly greater network density than Scheme 1, which indicates that the connections between network members are closed. The point central potentials of Scheme 2 and Scheme 3 are in the range of 0.0247– 0.0954, and significantly lower than in Scheme 1, this indicates that the central node aggregation ability of the two schemes is weak. The network centralization index of Scheme 3 is the minimum, this means the network members are less dependent on the nodes with transitive relations, and also reflects that the current deep learning field does not form the core research content. The depth of research is not sufficient, and this is consistent with the current status. In addition, the closeness centralization of the three kinds of networks is between 0.3218–0.9032, which shows that the difference of network nodes is bigger. The density of the condensing subgroup is between −0.721– −0.942, and it is the least for Scheme 3. This means the fragmented degree is the minimum. Therefore, from the characteristics of the basic parameters of the three networks, the co-word analysis effect of Scheme 3 is the best, and that of Scheme 1 is the worst.

As seen in Table 2, the average degree and clustering coefficient of network are larger than in the general co-word analysis method, which shows that the network has stronger diffusion performance.

Table 2. Basic data of the node degree distribution

	Minimum	Maximum	Average	Clustering coefficient
General co-word analysis	1	81	8.290	0.253
Weighted LDA model	7	100	67.62	0.758

For a more intuitive display and study of the internal relationship of the co-word networks, we used the network analysis software Gephi to analyze their differences. As shown in Fig. 7, we can see that the network based on the general co-word analysis method is present as the star topology, which completely focuses on deep learning but does not reflect well the relationship with other keywords. The number of graph nodes maximally connected is four. Because of the larger dependence on the central node, when the keyword "deep learning" is deleted, the other keywords almost become isolated. Therefore, a network with poor connectivity cannot really reflect the internal

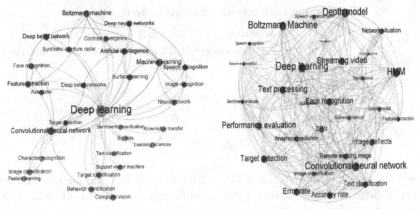

(a) Network based on co-word analysis   (b) Network based on our proposed method

Fig. 7. Network knowledge graph of the deep learning field

structure of the research field. The semantic co-word network based on the weighted LDA model is present as a mesh topology, which can better reflect the semantic relations between keywords. Further, the network structure formed has a higher reliability and connectivity, which truly reflects the characteristics of the network and provides full semantic support for the further interpretation of the co-word analysis.

5   Conclusion

The main contributions of this study are threefold. First, we find that considering textual semantic structures and the phenomenon of "the same amount with different qualities" by a weighted mechanism to obtain the normalized words from the title, abstract, and full text can effectively improve the quality of co-word analysis.

Second, in order to overcome the mentioned limitations, this paper proposed a new method of semantic-based co-word analysis, and its performance is well proved. On the one hand, the proposed method introduces semantic modeling and deep learning thought, not only considering differences of vocabulary and lack of self-indexing keywords, and weighting the keywords in the title, abstract, and full text, but also extending the weighted strategy to the feature word formation process to mine the core keywords with a strong representation capability. On the other hand, it also uses the word2vec model to transform keywords into a feature vector at a semantic level, and combines the direct co-occurrence relation with indirect semantic relation intensity as the semantic correlation intensity value in order to realize the semantics of extracted keywords.

Third, we use domestic deep learning research as the application background and verify the proposed method from many angles. This analysis proves that the method has scientific value and effectiveness, and here we point out several applications of domestic deep learning, such as synthetic speech recognition and machine translation, image classification and recognition, video classification and behavior recognition, and text data processing and mining.

6 Limitation and Future Work

This study has two limitations. First, this paper only adopts a word model to measure the relations among keywords and compares it with the general co-word analysis method without considering their different feasibilities and adaptabilities. Second, it is difficult to keep abreast of new developments in corresponding fields for semantic measurement. In the future, we will further consider semantic measurements in scientific research cooperation network and citation networks, and select an appropriate index to further improve the effectiveness of the semantic-based co-word analysis.

Acknowledgment. This paper is supported by the Chinese NSFC International Cooperation Program. Research on Intelligent Home Care Platform based on Chronic Disease Knowledge Management (71661167007). It is also partially sponsored by the project by the National Natural Science Foundation of China (71420107026) and National Nature Science Foundation of China (Grant No. 71704138).

References

Callon, M., Courtial, J.P., Turner, W.A., et al.: Form translations to problematic networks: an introduction to co-word analysis. Soc. Sci. Inf. **22**(2), 191–235 (1983)

Ding, Y., Chowdhury, G.G., Foo, S.: Bibliometric cartography of information retrieval research by using co-word analysis. Inf. Process. Manag. **37**(6), 817–842 (2001)

Guo, S., Zhang, G.Z., Ju, Q.H., et al.: The evolution of conceptual diversity in economics titles from 1890 to 2012. Scientometrics **102**(3), 2073–2088 (2015)

Guardiola, R., Sanz, J., Wanden, C.: Medical subject headings versus psychological association index terms: indexing eating disorders. Scientometrics **94**(1), 305–311 (2013)

Li, S., Sun, Y., Soergel, D.: Erratum to: a new method for automatically constructing domain-oriented term taxonomy based on weighted word co-occurrence analysis. Scientometrics **103**(2), 1023–1042 (2016)

Mikolov, T., Sutskever, I., Chen, K., et al.: Distributed representations of words and phrases and their compositionality. In: Advances in Neural Informational Processing Systems, pp. 3111–3119. Neural Information Processing Systems Foundation, US (2013)

Tsatsaronis, G., Varlamis, I., Vazirgiannis, M.: Text relatedness based on a word thesaurus. J. Artif. Intell. Res. **37**(1), 1–40 (2010)

Wang, Z.Y., Li, G., Li, C.Y., Li, A.: Research on the semantic-based co-word analysis. Scientometrics **90**(3), 855–875 (2012)

Wilson, A.T., Chew, P.A.: Term weighting schemes for latent dirichlet allocation. In: Human Language Technologies: The 2010 Annual Conference of the North American Chapter of the Association for Computation Linguistics, pp. 465–473. Association for Computational Linguistics, Stroudsburg (2010)

Zhang, H.P., Yu, H.K., Xiong, D.Y., et al.: Chinese lexical analyzer using hierarchical hidden Markov model. In: Sighan Workshop on Chinese Language Processing, vol. 17, no. 8, pp. 63–70 (2003)

Zhang, K.Y., Zhu, K.Q.: An association network for computing semantic relatedness. In: Proceedings of the 29th AAAI Conference on Artificial Intelligence, pp. 593–600 (2015)

Information Behaviour and Digital Literacy

Factors Influencing Emoji Usage
in Smartphone Mediated Communications

Jiaxin An, Tian Li, Yifei Teng, and Pengyi Zhang

Peking University, 5 Yiheyuan Rd, Haidian District, Beijing, China
{jiaxin.an, tianlee, yifeiteng, pengyi}@pku.edu.cn

Abstract. Emojis have become more and more popular in text-based online communication to express emotions. This indicates a potential to utilize emojis in sentiment analysis and emotion measurements. However, many factors could affect people's emoji usage and need to be examined. Among them, age, gender, and relationship types may result in different interpretations of the same emoji due to the ambiguity of the iconic expression. In this paper, we aim to explore how these factors may affect the frequency, type, and sentiment of people's emoji usage in communications. After analyzing 6,821 Wechat chatting messages from 158 participants, we found people between 26–35 had lowest frequency of emoji usage; younger and elder groups showed different sentiment levels for the same emojis; people chose emoji types based on relationships. These findings shed light on how people use emojis as a communication tool.

Keywords: Emoji usage · Factors · Smartphone mediated communication

1 Introduction and Related Research

Emojis, "picture" (e) + "characters" (moji)", are pictures used in online text-based communications. The emoji "face with tears of joy" (😂) was chosen as "the word of the year" in 2015 by Oxford Dictionaries. People interpret emoji sentiment (from strongly positive to strongly negative) differently within or across platforms [1], while they seem to agree on the general attitude of emotions (positive, neutral, and negative) expressed through emojis [2]. Research on emoticon (a pictorial representation of a facial expression using texts, such as ":-)") found that factors such as knowledge background [3], culture [4] and gender [5] could affect the position, frequency, and sentiments of emoticons in Instant Massaging (IM). These factors may have similar effects on emoji usage.

The popularity of computer-mediated communication has prompt the need for nonverbal cues to express emotions [6–8]. People first use emoticons, typographic symbols that appear sideways as resembling facial expressions [9], for emphasis, assuagement, conversion and addition [10]. In late 1990s, emoji was introduced into instant messaging, which represent more emotions [11] and various objects, and gradually replace emoticons [6, 7].

Research found that people use emojis in different frequencies [6, 12], types [12] and may interpret the same emojis differently [1, 8, 13–15]. However, relatively less is

© Springer International Publishing AG, part of Springer Nature 2018
G. Chowdhury et al. (Eds.): iConference 2018, LNCS 10766, pp. 423–428, 2018.
https://doi.org/10.1007/978-3-319-78105-1_46

known about the factors influencing the interpretation of emojis. Research found that emoji styles in different platforms [1, 15], gender [6], countries and areas [12, 13] could affect people's emoji usage. Even in the same culture background and platform, people could interpret emoji differently [1, 8]. In general, people could understand an emoji's overall positive or negative attitudes [2], Barbieri et al. reported that the overall semantics of emoji did not largely vary across four countries. Prior research revealed many potential factors that might affect emoji usage such as the context surrounding emojis [1, 8, 14], shared knowledge between communicators [15], familiarity with emojis, social-demographic and behavior factors [14]. Emojis could be rich resources for sentiment analysis and emotion measurement [2, 11], and used to improve user experience [16] and so on.

In this research, we analyzed messages from users of Wechat, a popular social networking and IM APP in China, aiming to understand the differences in frequency, type, and sentiment of emoji usage in smart-phone mediated communications. We aim to explore the influences of factors including age, gender, and relationship types.

2   Methods

2.1   Data Collection

We recruited 31 participants and asked them to collect the latest 50 chatting messages from 4–6 Wechat contacts of various relationship types. A total of 6,821 chatting messages from 127 communications were collected. All participants are Chinese. Table 1 summarizes their characteristics.

Table 1. Participant characteristics.

		16–25	26–35	36–50	>50	M	SD	Total
Participants	Male	7	0	1	2	30.20	14.65	10
	Female	13	4	2	2	27.43	10.84	21
Communication counterparts	Male	16	10	7	2	30.74	11.12	35
	Female	32	24	24	12	34.61	13.79	92
Total		68	38	34	18	32.52	13.09	158

In addition to demographic background information, we also asked participants to identify the age differences in the same vs. different generations. In average, participants think that people belong to the same generation if their age difference is within 11.7 (SD = 10.5, SK = 2.5, K = 6.9) years, whereas they belong to different generations if their age difference is over 15.6 years (SD = 7.7, SK = 3.0, K = 13.0).

2.2   Data Analysis

We analyzed WeChat's emojis that are both available and same-styled in Android and IOS platforms. After anonymizing personal information, we counted the types and frequencies of emojis in all 127 communications. We examined the sentiments of five most frequent emojis. Two researchers separately coded the sentiments of each occurrence of the emojis on a 7-likert scale ranging from −3 (very negative) to 3 (very positive). They reached moderate consistency when considering three categories (negative, neutral, and positive) (Kappa = .38, P = .04), one coder rates all emojis more negatively than the other. We calculated the average sentiment score for each emoji occurrence, then conducted statistic tests to compare the types and frequency of emoji usage, and sentiment levels expressed by the emojis across different age, gender, and relationship types. We divided the relationship types by two dimensions:

Primary vs. secondary. Primary groups (such as families) "tend to be in small size, informal, intimate and enduring", while secondary groups (such as colleagues) tend to be larger, formal, less personal and temporary [17].

Same-generation vs. cross-generation. People in same generations have similar age and cultural identification to each other [18].

3   Results

3.1   Overall Emoji Usage

A total of 1,103 emojis (72 emoji types) were used in the 6,821 messages, one out of six messages had an emoji in it. However, only a few emoji types were frequently used, and 15 types of emojis had only one occurrence (Fig. 1).

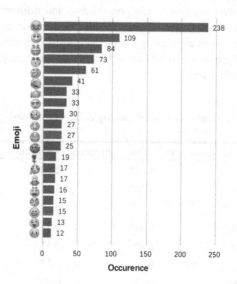

Fig. 1. Most frequently used 20 emojis (# of occurrences ≥ 12).

3.2 Emoji Frequency

People of different age used different number of emojis in their communications. K-Wallis Test shows significant difference among age groups ($\chi^2 = 17.2$, $p < .01$). Table 2 shows that participants between 16–25 and 36–50 had similarly high average emoji frequencies; elder participants (over 50) used the least number of emojis. Surprisingly, participants between 26–35 used less emojis; perhaps because their conversations were more serious than other age groups. Gender and relationship types have no effect on number of emojis used.

Table 2. Average emoji occurrences in different age groups.

	16–25	26–35	36–50	>50	Total
Mean	5.68	3.02	5.56	1.54	4.54
N	68.00	38.00	34.00	18.00	158.00
SD	5.87	4.28	7.78	2.17	5.88
Median	3.63	1.00	3.00	0.88	2.75

3.3 Emoji Type

Analysis show that participants of different age groups used different types of emojis (K-Wallis Test, $p < .05$). Elder people used more positive emojis (such as "thumbs up" (👍) and "hug" (🤗)), while younger people used more emojis expressing complex feelings (such as "facepalm" (🤦) and "face with tears of joy" (😂)).

Participants also used different emojis based on their relationships (see Table 3, *$p < .05$). We compared same vs. cross generations, and primary vs. secondary relationship types. When chatting with friends in cross generation or secondary relationships, they used more emojis expressing simple and positive meanings, with less risk of misunderstanding. There is no significant difference in frequency and types of emoji among male and female users.

Table 3. Average occurrences of emojis among different relationship types. (*$p<0.05$)

	Same-generation	Cross-generation	Secondary	Primary
😂	2.89*	0.77*	2.69	1.12
🤗	0.61*	0.02*	0.26	0.38
😢	0.21*	0.02*	0.13	0.11
👍	0.08*	0.46*	0.31	0.21
😜	0.2*	0.3*	0.31	0.21
😎	0*	0.11*	0.07	0.05
🤦	0.26	0.72	0.69*	0.29*
😳	0.11	0.10	0.18*	0.03*

3.4   Emoji Sentiment

We chose five types of emojis that occur more than 30 times and compared their average sentiment scores (see Table 4, *p < .05). We found that younger people used some emojis with different emotional connotations comparing to the elderly. For example, T-test (p < .01) shows that people in 16–25 age group expressed negative or neutral sentiment with "smile" (😊) (Mean sentiment = −.2), while people in 36–50 group expressed positive sentiment (Mean = .9). This could be a result of generation gap.

Table 4. Average sentiment scores of emojis in different age groups. (*p<0.05)

	16-25	26-35	36-50	>50
😁	1.55	1.33	1.75	1.80
😂	1.50	1.32	1.61	1.08
😆	0.32	-0.25	-	-
😊	-0.20*	0.38*	0.85*	-
😖	-2.33	-1.71	-1.33	-1.00

4   Conclusion and Discussion

This paper presents exploratory results of how age and relationship could affect people's emoji usage:

(1) People chose emojis having simple and positive meanings when chatting with friends in secondary or cross-generation relationships. They use more emojis chatting with secondary ones, perhaps using emojis as a way to bind them closer.

(2) For some emojis such as "smile" (😊), elders expressed positive sentiments, while young people expressed negative ones, perhaps picking up the unhappy connotation of looking downward [19].

(3) Gender has no effect on emoji usage, which is different from previous research [6]. It could be a result of cultural difference or difference in communication contexts.

This exploratory study provides some initial insights into factors influencing peoples' emoji use and the nuanced differences in emoji sentiments, and may have implications for improving user experience in emoji design, and using emojis for sentiment analysis. Future research can verify these results in larger samples, different cultural backgrounds and communication contexts. By observing emoji using behavior for a prolonged period, future research can reveal that how emoji using habits change over time due to social interaction with a particular person.

References

1. Miller, H., et al.: "Blissfully happy" or "ready to fight": varying interpretations of emoji. In: Proceedings of ICWSM (2016)
2. Novak, P.K., et al.: Sentiment of emojis. PLoS ONE **10**(12), e0144296 (2015)
3. Garrison, A., et al.: Conventional faces: emoticons in instant messaging discourse. Comput. Compos. **28**(2), 112–125 (2011)
4. Hautasaari, A.M., Yamashita, N., Gao, G.: Maybe it was a joke: emotion detection in text-only communication by non-native english speakers. In: Proceedings of the 32nd Annual ACM Conference on Human Factors in Computing Systems. ACM (2014)
5. Ogletree, S.M., Fancher, J., Gill, S.: Gender and texting: masculinity, femininity, and gender role ideology. Comput. Hum. Behav. **37**, 49–55 (2014)
6. Chen, Z., et al.: Through a gender lens: an empirical study of emoji usage over large-scale android users. arXiv preprint arXiv:1705.05546 (2017)
7. Kelly, R., Watts, L.: Characterising the inventive appropriation of emoji as relationally meaningful in mediated close personal relationships. In: Experiences of Technology Appropriation: Unanticipated Users, Usage, Circumstances, and Design (2015)
8. Tigwell, G.W., Flatla, D.R.: Oh that's what you meant!: reducing emoji misunderstanding. In: Proceedings of the 18th International Conference on Human-Computer Interaction with Mobile Devices and Services Adjunct. ACM (2016)
9. Walther, J.B., D'Addario, K.P.: The impacts of emoticons on message interpretation in computer-mediated communication. Soc. Sci. Comput. Rev. **19**(3), 324–347 (2001)
10. Yamamoto, Y., Kumamoto, T., Nadamoto, A.: Role of emoticons for multidimensional sentiment analysis of Twitter. In: Proceedings of the 16th International Conference on Information Integration and Web-Based Applications & Services. ACM (2014)
11. Jaeger, S.R., et al.: Can emoji be used as a direct method to measure emotional associations to food names? Preliminary investigations with consumers in USA and China. Food Qual. Prefer. **56**, 38–48 (2017)
12. Lu, X., et al.: Learning from the ubiquitous language: an empirical analysis of emoji usage of smartphone users. In: Proceedings of the 2016 ACM International Joint Conference on Pervasive and Ubiquitous Computing. ACM (2016)
13. Barbieri, F., et al.: How cosmopolitan are emojis?: Exploring emojis usage and meaning over different languages with distributional semantics. In: Proceedings of the 2016 ACM on Multimedia Conference. ACM (2016)
14. Jaeger, S.R., Ares, G.: Dominant meanings of facial emoji: insights from Chinese consumers and comparison with meanings from internet resources. Food Qual. Prefer. **62**, 275–283 (2017)
15. Miller, H.J., et al.: Understanding emoji ambiguity in context: the role of text in emoji-related miscommunication. In: ICWSM (2017)
16. Kaye, L.K., Malone, S.A., Wall, H.J.: Emojis: insights, affordances, and possibilities for psychological science. Trends Cogn. Sci. **21**(2), 66–68 (2017)
17. Thoits, P.A.: Mechanisms linking social ties and support to physical and mental health. J. Health Soc. Behav. **52**(2), 145–161 (2011)
18. Aroldi, P., et al.: Generational belonging between media audiences and ICT users. Broadband Soc. Gener. Changes **5**, 51–67 (2011)
19. Ekman, P.: Emotions Revealed: Recognizing Faces and Feelings to Improve Communication and Emotional Life. Macmillan, Basingstoke (2007)

Domestic Migrant Workers in Israel: The Strength of Weak Ties

Jenny Bronstein[✉]

Bar-Ilan University, 52900 Ramat-Gan, Israel
jenny.bronstein@biu.ac.il

Abstract. This paper presents an ongoing exploratory study examining the role that weak ties play in the information behaviour of domestic migrant workers living in Israel. Weak ties are social acquaintances that provide varied information and social support. The study used the narrative inquiry method that allows the researcher to study and understand information behaviours intrinsically related to the life stories of the population studied. The interviews looked for narratives that described their interactions with different information sources, and the role that weak ties play as sources of information and social support that help them make sense of their lives in Israel. Findings revealed that weak ties fulfilled four functions: extending access to information, fostering social interactions with dissimilar others, facilitating low-risk discussion of high-risk topics, and fostering a sense of belonging.

Keywords: Migrant workers · Weak ties · Information seeking
Information sources · Migration

1 Introduction

The growing pace of economic globalization, higher rates of unemployment, increasing poverty, as well as climate change and armed conflicts, have forced millions of people in developing countries to seek work elsewhere. At the same time, developed countries have increased their demand for labour, especially unskilled labour. At present, there are an estimated 150 million migrant workers, of which 11.5 million are domestic workers. These workers experience social exclusion characterized by discrimination and exploitative working and living conditions that are often exacerbated by the lack of access to information sources, to economic resources, and to the educational skills needed to adapt to life in a new country [1].

Access to information is crucial for migrants at all stages of the settlement process [2]. Past studies have revealed that migration disrupts the individual's information landscapes by disconnecting them from the information sources and the social networks they knew and rendering the information practices used in their country of origin irrelevant in their host country. That is, their information landscapes are fractured because of migration [3]. This disruption, hinders the migrants' decision-making, restricts their capacity to satisfy basic needs (i.e., employment, education, housing, health care), to learn a new language, and to adopt new social norms and understandings [4–7]. How do migrant workers manage to navigate new and complex

© Springer International Publishing AG, part of Springer Nature 2018
G. Chowdhury et al. (Eds.): iConference 2018, LNCS 10766, pp. 429–434, 2018.
https://doi.org/10.1007/978-3-319-78105-1_47

information landscapes and find the information they need? Preliminary findings of this study show that acquaintances or weak ties have a significant role in helping migrants rebuild their fractured information landscapes by functioning as an important source of information and social support and helping them learn new "ways of knowing" [3].

The strength of weak ties is a social network theory formulated by Granovetter. This theory defines the strength of a social tie as the combination of the amount of time, emotional intensity, and level of reciprocity and intimacy that characterize the tie. Weak ties, then, are relationships formed with individuals outside our immediate social network. They are much more significant as information sources than strong ties because our friends or relatives tend to circulate in the same social circles as us and the information they have to share is to a large extent the same as we encounter [8]. Contrarily, weak ties provide access to information that is more varied. As Granovetter explained, "individuals with few weak ties will be deprived of information from distant parts of the social system and will be confined to the provincial news and views of their close friends" [8]. Furthermore, weak ties often provide support during times of crisis when strong ties are disrupted such as (e.g., death of a family member, divorce, long-term illness [9] or, as in the case of this study, migration). Prior studies on migration have emphasized the significance that social networks have for migrants since they bridge social distance, bringing together people from different social locations [10–12] and helping them become resilient and adapt to their new country [13]. Resilience refers to positive adaptation despite adversity [14]. Hence, the purpose of this study is to understand the role that weak ties play as sources of information and social support in the settlement process of domestic migrant workers in Israel, as shown through their life stories.

2 Research Approach and Methodology

The study uses narrative inquiry as a research method. Narrative inquiry is a qualitative method based on the notion that we obtain understanding of and provide meaning to our lives through narrating our life stories. It investigates the stories people tell about themselves, their inner thoughts, states of mind, and how they perceive their own reality [15]. This method of inquiry was chosen because narratives or stories "represent the character or lifestyle of specific subgroups in society, defined by their gender, race, religion, and so on. From a social, cultural or ethnic point of view, these groups frequently are discriminated against, minorities whose narratives express their unheard voices" [16]. Because of its naturalistic character, narrative inquiry is a natural and intuitive methodology for eliciting and examining human behaviour [17]—in this case information behaviour. Narratives have been used in past studies dealing with migrant populations such as Polish migrants in Britain [11], Latinos in the US [18], Chilean immigrants in New Zealand, [19] and Andalusian migrants in Spain [20]. Although it is widely used in the social sciences, this has been scarcely applied to the study of information behaviour [21, 22].

Data was collected through 20 narrative interviews with Spanish-speaking domestic migrant workers living in Israel. During the interviews, participants were asked to talk about their emigration to Israel and their lives as migrant workers in the country. The study looked for narratives that describe their interactions with information sources, and their views and perceptions of the social role of information.

The information behaviour of migrants has been investigated in studies that have focused on the use of information sources and the information literacy skills needed to fulfil their information needs during the different stages of the settlement process [2, 23–26]. The current study examined the role that weak ties play in the information behaviour of domestic migrant workers by applying Adelman, Parks and Albrecht's theoretical framework to the analysis of the data. This framework proposes that the distinctive features of weak ties result in four different functions: (1) extending access to information, (2) fostering social interactions with dissimilar others, (3) facilitating low-risk discussion of high-risk topics, and (4) fostering a sense of belonging [9].

3 Preliminary Findings

First function: Extending access to information
Weak ties represent a diverse and unique set of informal information sources that can provide the individual with experiential information and social support not always provided by strong ties. While the number of strong ties is rather small, the number of weak ties can be large; therefore, they provide extended access to information [27]. These weak ties were sometimes strangers who helped them in time of need:

> Well I think ... I do not know .. But God puts like angels in our way for us to find, look many times I've been lost in a train, on a bus, in a city and I always find someone who speaks Spanish and helps me.

Adelman, Park, and Albrecht refer to some of these weak ties as "community agents" [9], people like clergy or teachers that play a specific role as information sources. For participants, lawyers and volunteers at different NGOs functioned as community agents by helping them solve issues related to their visas, for example:

> There is an NGO, called "Israel children", and there are volunteers who also speak Spanish. There was this lady who spoke Spanish, she helped us a lot, translations, messages, she used to call me, let's do this, we want to collaborate, we want to help. This is how we arranged my daughter's visa.

Second function: Fostering social interactions with dissimilar others
Weak ties tend to be people from different backgrounds that provide distinctive perspectives and reference points; the low levels of intimacy and reciprocity in the relationship tend to ease the need for similarity [9]. Employers were revealed in the content analysis as important sources of information, oftentimes using their own social networks to help the workers:

> [when I need to solve a problem] I'll sometimes ask my employers, and if they don't know they'll ask their friends or search the internet for me.

The employers also provided instrumental help that was perceived as social support:

I have excellent employers ... all of them ... they helped me set up my internet connection, my contract with the cable company ... they are not my bosses, I tell you, I do not know ... they are like my guardian angels in this country.

Third function: facilitating low-risk discussion on high risk subjects

Most weak ties are restricted to specific temporal and situational contexts, and the interactions are limited to a narrow range of subjects (i.e., doctors, clergy, and people on the bus). This temporality "provides a sense of freedom and anonymity that often allows individuals to disclose far more than they otherwise would" [9]. One participant relates how she confided in a stranger on a bus who gave her the information she needed:

When my son was born I had to take him to Jerusalem to see a doctor, I needed to find a way to see a doctor closer [to home]. One of those things in life happened; I met an Argentinian lady on the bus. We started talking and I told her about my problem. She worked in a ... what was this called? NGO. I did not know anything about rights but she told me how to get a better health insurance for my son.

Fourth Function: fostering a sense of belonging

Weak ties foster a sense of belonging because they connect people from different backgrounds that eventually become a support network, a group of people to turn to in time of need. Building relationships with people outside their social environment gave participants a sense of belonging and connection to Israel:

I want to stay here, I have a child who was born here and he loves Israel, he likes everything here, I also like all the Jewish holidays, I like going to the synagogue, I like everything about Israel.

This sense of belonging helped participants become resilient and adapt to their new country:

For me Israel is my place even if I was not born here. I respect the Jewish traditions, I try not to offend other people, and I always respect their traditions.

The settlement process can be a difficult experience for migrant workers who immigrate to a different country looking for a better quality of life; but it is this promise that helps them develop the resilience needed.

I came here twelve years ago with a tourist visa looking for a better life; I decided to stay here in the country, because the situation in Venezuela was very bad at the time. Nowadays the situation is even worse. It has not been easy, but I feel relieved ... I feel the peace of mind that I am giving my daughter a future a little different from what I could have [back home] and from what I know I can give her in Venezuela.

4 Conclusion

Migrant workers come to their host country to escape conflict and poverty, looking for a better life. During their settlement process, they encounter social, cultural and linguistic barriers that greatly hinder their process of social inclusion. Weak ties in the form of social acquaintances or community agents can provide them with invaluable information and expose them to new information skills that their strong ties within the migrant community cannot always offer. Moreover, because the information provided comes from people with whom migrant workers do not have a reciprocal or intimate bond, this information is perceived as social support that fosters a sense of belonging and helps them develop the resilience needed to confront the challenges they face during the settlement process.

References

1. International Labour Organization: ILO global estimates of migrant workers and migrant do mestic workers: results and methodology. http://www.ilo.org/wcmsp5/groups/public/dgreports/dcomm/documents/publication/wcms_436343.pdf
2. Shankar, S., O'Brien, H.L., How, E., Lu, Y.W., Mabi, M., Rose, C.: The role of information in the settlement experiences of refugee students. Proc. Assoc. Inf. Sci. Technol. **53**(1), 1–6 (2016)
3. Lloyd, A.: Researching fractured (information) landscapes: implications for library and information science researchers undertaking research with refugees and forced migration studies. J. Doc. **73**(1), 35–47 (2017)
4. Aspinall, P.J.: Language ability: a neglected dimension in the profiling of populations and health service users. Health Educ. J. **66**(1), 90–106 (2011)
5. Caidi, N., Allard, D.: Social inclusion of newcomers to Canada: an information problem? Libr. Inf. Sci. Res. **27**(3), 302–324 (2010)
6. Khoir, S., Du, J.T., Koronios, A.: Everyday information behaviour of Asian immigrants in South Australia: a mixed-methods exploration (2015). http://InformationR.net/ir/20-3/paper687.html
7. Lloyd, A., Lipu, S., Kennan, M.A.: On becoming citizens: examining social inclusion from an information perspective. Aust. Acad. Res. Libr. **41**(1), 42–53 (2010)
8. Granovetter, M.: The strength of weak ties: a network theory revisited. Sociol. Theory **1**, 202–233 (1983)
9. Adelman, M.B., Parks, M.R., Albrecht, T.L.: Beyond close relationships: support in weak ties. In: Albrecht, T.L., Adelman, M.B. (eds.) Communicating Social Support, pp. 126–147. Sage, Newbury Park (1987)
10. Awumbila, M., Teye, J.K., Yaro, J.A.: Social networks, migration trajectories and livelihood strategies of migrant domestic and construction workers in Accra, Ghana. J. Asian Afr. Stud. (2016). https://doi.org/10.1177/002190961663474313
11. Ryan, L.: Migrants' social networks and weak ties: accessing resources and constructing relationships post-migration. Sociol. Rev. **59**(4), 707–724 (2011)
12. Ryan, L., Sales, R., Tilki, M., Siara, B.: Social networks, social support and social capital: the experiences of recent polish migrants in London. Sociology **42**(4), 672–690 (2008)
13. Rashid, R., Gregory, D.: 'Not giving up on life': a holistic exploration of resilience among a sample of immigrant Canadian women. Can. Ethn. Stud. **46**(1), 197–214 (2014)
14. Bandura, A.: Self-efficacy: the exercise of control. In: Vilanayur, R.S. (ed.) Encyclopedia of Human Behaviour, pp. 71–81. Academic Press, New York (1997)
15. Riessman, C.K.: A short story about long stories. J. Narrat. Life Hist. **7**(1–4), 155–159 (1997)
16. Lieblich, A., Tuval-Mashiach, R., Zilber, T.: Narrative Research: Reading, Analysis, and Interpretation. Sage, Thousand Oaks (1998)

434   J. Bronstein

17. Spector-Mersel, G.: Narrative research: time for a paradigm. Narrat. Inq. **20**(1), 204–224 (2010)
18. Courtright, C.: Health information-seeking among Latino newcomers: an exploratory study. Inf. Res. **10**(2) (2005). http://www.informationr.net/ir/10-2/paper224.html
19. Smythe Contreras, K.C.: "Maybe because we are too Chilean": stories of migration from Hispanic women living in New Zealand. Massey University, Manawatū, New Zealand (2015)
20. Macías-Gómez-Estern, B.: Narrative as a sense-making tool in the construction of migrants' identities. Apprehending emotions. Procedia-Soc. Behav. Sci. **173**, 168–175 (2015)
21. Bates, J.A.: Use of narrative interviewing in everyday information behavior research. Libr. Inf. Sci. Res. **26**(1), 15–28 (2004)
22. Eckerdal, J.R.: Empowering interviews: narrative interviews in the study of information literacy in everyday life settings. Inf. Res.: Int. Electron. J. **18**(3), 3 (2013)
23. Fisher, K.E., Durrance, J.C., Hinton, M.B.: Information grounds and the use of need-based services by immigrants in Queens, New York: a context-based, outcome evaluation approach. J. Am. Soc. Inf. Sci. Technol. **55**(8), 754–766 (2004)
24. Khoir, S., Du, J.T., Koronios, A.: Study of Asian immigrants' information behaviour in South Australia: preliminary results. In: iConference 2014 Proceedings, pp. 682–689 (2014). https://doi.org/10.9776/14316. https://www.ideals.illinois.edu/handle/2142/47274
25. Lingel, J.: Information tactics of immigrants in an urban environment (2011). http://InformationR.net/ir/16-4/paper500.html
26. Lloyd, A.: Stranger in a strange land; enabling information resilience in resettlement landscapes. J. Doc. **71**(5), 1029–1042 (2015)
27. Rubenstein, E.L.: "They are always there for me": the convergence of social support and information in an online breast cancer community. J. Assoc. Inf. Sci. Technol. **66**(7), 1418–1430 (2015)

Serendipity with Music Streaming Services: The Mediating Role of User and Task Characteristics

Ying-Han Chang and Muh-Chyun Tang[✉]

National Taiwan University,
No. 1, Sec. 4, Roosevelt Road, Taipei 10617, Taiwan (R.O.C.)
d04126002@ntu.edu.tw, muhchyun.tang@gmail.com

Abstract. An experimental study was conducted to test the feasibility of using the construct of "serendipity" to evaluate the performance of two music streaming services, Spotify and KKBOX. The impact of search tasks (goal-oriented vs. exploratory) and users' psychological traits—the degree of "music involvement" and "openness to novelty"—on system performance was explored. Four dimensions of serendipity, "introducing the unexpected," "accessibility," "navigability," and "enabling connection" were used as the performance criteria along with usability. The study employed a Latin square experimental design, in which 32 participants were asked to perform goal-oriented vs. exploratory tasks alternately with the two music streaming services. The main effects of music involvement were identified for three out of four serendipity dimensions. An interaction effect of tasks and systems on performance was also found. The implications of our results on the evaluation of music discovery tools were discussed.

Keywords: Music involvement · Openness to novelty
Streaming music service · Serendipity · Web leisure

1 Introduction

Online music streaming services provide novel ways of music recommendation and navigational features that greatly expand users' opportunities to come across previously unknown music. It has been pointed out that nonobviousness criteria such as "novelty" and "serendipity" should be used to complement traditional accuracy-based measures to system evaluation [1]. In the context of information behavior, serendipity usually occurs when people are looking in "likely" sources or searching by "chance" [2]. The construct of serendipity has been explored in studies of information seeking behaviors, and attempts have been made to create serendipity scales in both physical [3] and digital environments [4]. We believe that serendipity is especially important when users are exploring a music site without a specific search request [5, 6]. It was also hypothesized that psychological traits such as "music involvement" and "openness to novelty" play a mediatory role in serendipity. Involvement denotes the degree of affective investment users have in a product. In a music experience sampling study,

© Springer International Publishing AG, part of Springer Nature 2018
G. Chowdhury et al. (Eds.): iConference 2018, LNCS 10766, pp. 435–441, 2018.
https://doi.org/10.1007/978-3-319-78105-1_48

highly engaged music listeners demonstrated markedly different music seeking and listening behaviors [7]. Novelty refers to a system's ability to recommend previously unknown or serendipitous items to users [8]. Individuals with high openness to novelty might welcome more novel or serendipitous results. In summary, the purpose of this study is to investigate the feasibility of using the construct of serendipity as the evaluation criteria in online music finding. In addition to using an evaluation methodology, we investigate the impact of users' psychological traits and task types on different dimensions of serendipity.

2 Research Design

This study employed a 2 (systems) × 2 (tasks) Latin square designed (within-subject) experiment, and multiple methods were adapted to collect data, including questionnaires, screen logging, and interviews. Two music stream services, KKBOX and Spotify, were chosen as the test sites because of their popularity and richness in music discovery tools. The population we aimed to study were mostly young listeners who are Web-savvy to utilized these music discovery tools.

A revised serendipity scale consisting of 15 items representing the dimensions of serendipity was adopted [3, 4]. To access the two psychological traits, namely, music involvement and openness to novelty, we adapted the Personal Involvement Inventory from Zaichkowsky [9] and the novel recommendations scale from Chang [10], respectively, indicating users' preference characteristics. In addition, system usability assessment employed the System Usability Scale (SUS) [11] was used for global assessments of system usability. The participants were asked to perform two music searching tasks with the two online music streaming services. Before performing the music finding tasks, participants were introduced to the concept of serendipity (i.e., surprising valuable finds) and asked to complete a questionnaire regarding music involvement and openness to novelty. As the experiment started, each participant was randomly assigned into one of the four groups, and they were asked to perform exploratory and goal-oriented music searching tasks alternately. The tasks were described in as follows: "Exploratory task": "Find some music for relaxing: You're so tired today, and you want to listen to some music for relaxing," and "goal-oriented task": "Find some music for singing: You're going to a Karaoke Bar with friends, and you want to find songs for practice."

No time limit was set for each task, they could stop whenever they could no longer find interesting songs. When they completed a task, they were asked to complete questionnaires for the serendipity scale and SUS, both on 1–5 scale. They were rewarded with an honorarium of 300 NTD (10 USD) for the time of approximately 2 h required to complete the study.[1]

[1] This research was sponsored in part by the Ministry of Science and Technology of Taiwan under Grant No: 105-2410-H-002 -119.

3   Preliminary Result

Each of the 32 participants performed two search tasks using two music streaming services, resulting in 64 observations. The participants are comprised of 20 females and 12 males; 7 were undergraduate students, 15 were graduate students, and 10 were full-time professionals. A manipulation check was performed for the music searching tasks to test whether participants' recognition of exploratory and goal-oriented tasks in the main experiment corresponded with the pretest. Results indicated that finding relaxing songs was perceived as significantly more exploratory ($T(31) = 10.06$, $p < .000$). A reliability test was performed for the two psychological traits. The Cronbach's α were 0.708 and 0.804, respectively. The average scores of the items in each construct were used to establish the two psychological variables.

3.1   Serendipity Factors of Music Streaming Services

An exploratory factor analysis was then performed to examine the dimensionalities and validities of the serendipity scales. The Principal Component Analysis was then performed using the diagonal rotation extraction method. Four factors were extracted from the 15 items (Table 1). Four factors accounted for 66.52% of the total variance, and the Cronbach's α was ranged from 0.63 (factor 4) to 0.84 (factor 1).

Interpretive labels were then added to the four factors as described as follows:

- *Factor1: Introducing the unexpected* consists of five items, representing the dimension that provides a way of exploration or browsing (S5, S7, S11) and facilitates unexpected music or topics (S6, S8). These items converge on the ability of the system to make connections with other content, especially unexpected connections.
- *Factor 2: Accessibility* consists of four items related music accessibility (S1, S2, S12) and the provision of diverse content (S3). These items all associated with ease of content exploration.
- *Factor 3: Navigability* consists of three items, related to simple and intuitive interaction with the system (S13, S14, S15).
- *Factor 4: Enabling connection* consists of three items, focus on connections between contents, such as content diversity (S4) and establishing linkages between different music or topics (S9, S10).

3.2   Influence of Serendipity

Regression analysis was conducted to study the main effects of users' psychological traits, the systems, and the task types, as well as their interactions, on the four dimensions of serendipity (See Table 2). Standardized regression coefficients (β) are the estimates resulting from regression analyses, which can be used to interpret the relative importance of various factors.

Table 1. Principal component analysis for serendipity scale (N = 64).

No	Items	Factors				h²
		1	2	3	4	
S06	Unexpected words and phrases caught my eye	**.862**	−.120	.027	.159	.784
S07	Unexpected words and phrases sparked my thinking	**.787**	.104	.124	−.302	.737
S05	I wanted to click on things to see where they would take me	**.786**	−.064	.103	.360	.763
S11	Exploring one topic unexpectedly led me to other	**.668**	.305	.101	.469	.769
S08	I found interested music/content by misclassification	**.587**	.359	−.061	.228	.529
S03	I was able to see music in a range of formats	.113	**.747**	−.081	−.058	.580
S02	The system will not overburden me to listen, explore or access music	−.033	**.744**	.132	−.039	.574
S01	I was able to explore music that interested me when using the system	.212	**.630**	.309	.323	.641
S12	I could find music in several alternative ways	−.041	**.589**	.374	.284	.569
S15	I could return to topics that I had explored earlier	−.028	.040	**.843**	−.153	.736
S14	I could easily explore many topics without getting lost	.187	.125	**.809**	.192	.742
S13	The system encouraged me to browse and explore	.086	.531	**.604**	.012	.654
S04	I explored many topics that normally I do not examine	.113	−.096	−.139	**.799**	.680
S09	The system enabled me to make connections between different music	.420	.258	.187	**.600**	.638
S10	The system presented content in ways that invited me to explore across topics	.134	.483	.375	**.551**	.696
Eigenvalues		3.22	3.02	1.88	1.86	
Variance (%)		21.44	20.13	12.52	12.4	
Cronbach's α		0.84	0.71	0.74	0.63	

Firstly, music involvement was shown to have a significant positive effect on "introducing the unexpected," "accessibility," and "enabling connection." Conversely, individuals with high openness to novelty were found to appreciate more the dimension of navigability. One of the reason that highly involved users were more likely to embrace all the dimensions of serendipity apart from "navigability," probably because of their strong willingness to seek out new music also being equipped with more music knowledge [12]. Secondly, the nature of tasks only had a significant positive effect on the dimension of navigability (T = 2.34, p = .023), showing that users were more likely to experience the navigability dimension of serendipity when conducting exploratory tasks. Thirdly, a significant effect of system was found on "navigability"

Table 2. MANOVA analysis result for tasks, systems, and user preferences with serendipity factors.

	Introducing the unexpected		Accessibility		Navigability		Enabling connection	
	β	T	β	T	β	T	β	T
Task								
Exploratory(E)	.323	1.20	.118	.453	.519	2.34*	.217	.939
Goal-oriented(G)	0	–	0	–	0	–	0	–
System								
KKBOX	−.014	−.053	.305	1.17	.686	3.10**	−.075	−.326
Spotify	0	–	0	–	0	–	0	–
Involvement	.514	2.61*	.624	3.28**	.078	.480	.381	2.25*
Openness	.061	.362	−.036	−.220	.276	1.98*	.235	1.62
KKBOX×E	−.522	−1.36	−.376	−1.01	−.810	−2.56*	−.433	−1.32
KKBOX×G	0	–	0	–	0	–	0	–
Spotify×E	0	–	0	–	0	–	0	–
Spotify×G	0	–	0	–	0	–	0	–

Note: 1. $*p < .05$, $**p < .005$.

2. R^2 Introducing the unexpected $= .186$, R^2 Accessibility $= .188$, R^2 Navigability $= .243$, R^2 Enabling connection $= .238$.

3. "–" indicates null (default) and means that the independent variable has no effect; it is usually accompanied with a β coefficient of 0.

($T = 3.10$, $p = .003$); KKBOX scored better on navigability than Spotify. Some participants mentioned that the interface design of KKBOX is more akin to a collection management system, enabling them to grasp the current path without being overwhelmed by heterogeneous music items. Conversely, Spotify's strengths lie in its ability to facilitate more exploration of related music through building lots of "connecting bridge" or "shortcuts" for users to link across different music genres or styles, which is more effective for discovering new music.

The interaction effects between systems and tasks also revealed that users experienced significantly lower "navigability" when conducting the exploratory task with KKBOX ($T = -2.56$, $p < .05$). It was found that the majority of participants relied heavily on previous known artists works and their connections to other artists and works to explore new works, which was predictable given the difficulty of query-based search in non-textual materials. Only few participants (2 out of 32) ventured into entirely new domains. For exploratory-minded users, recommendations and linkages of contents to traverse the information space were heavily relied in order to discover novel and desirable items. A similar negative interaction was observed on the SUS. The result shows that SUS metrics were significantly lower when the exploratory task was performed with KKBOX ($T = -2.06$, $p = .044$), with seems to lead support to the observation that KKBOX is superior for organizing known items, but lacking in terms of facilitating exploration. Based both on our comparison of music discovery tools on the two platform and participants' feedback from our interview, it seems clear that more features for exploring and discovering new music are available in Spotify. Therefore, when exploring known territory, KKBOX performed better. However, the advantage of Spotify is clear with the exploratory task.

4 Conclusion

With increasingly many interactive features now available in today's cue-rich information environments, traditional accuracy oriented criteria are no longer able to faithfully reflect the value generated by the system to the users. This study demonstrated that it is feasible to use serendipity-related constructs as performance criteria in highly interactive information environments such as music streaming platforms. To the best of our knowledge, this study is the first to explore serendipity-related criteria in online music finding. Four core dimensions of serendipity were found to present in music streaming services environments: "introducing the unexpected," "accessibility," "navigability," and "enabling connection." Another novel aspect of this study was the assessment of the effects of user preference characteristics [12] and task nature [5] on serendipity criteria. Our results point to the need to apply recommendation strategies adaptively to users with different types of characteristics. For example, for highly involved listeners, the balance between accuracy and serendipity might tip toward the later. It was also shown that the impact of task types on the effectiveness of music discovery tools. Systems might perform quite differently when different types of tasks are used as the evaluation instrument. Beyond simple system comparison, future studies can identify search or discovery features that might improve performance for users with different preference characteristics when conducting different tasks.

References

1. Konstan, J.A., Riedl, J.: Recommender systems: from algorithms to user experience. User Model. User-Adap. **22**(1–2), 101–123 (2012). https://doi.org/10.1007/s11257-011-9112-x
2. Foster, A., Ford, N.: Serendipity and information seeking: an empirical study. J. Doc. **59**(3), 321–340 (2003)
3. Björneborn, L.: Serendipity dimensions and users' information behaviour in the physical library interface. Inf. Res. **13**(4) (2008)
4. McCay-Peet, L., Toms, E.: Measuring the dimensions of serendipity in digital environments. Inf. Res. **16**(3) (2011)
5. White, R.W., Roth, R.A.: Exploratory search: beyond the query-response paradigm. Synth. Lect. Inf. Concepts, Retr. Serv. **1**(1), 1–98 (2009)
6. Laplante, A., Downie, J.S.: Everyday life music information-seeking behaviour of young adults. In: ISMIR, pp. 381–382 (2006)
7. Greasley, A.E., Lamont, A.: Exploring engagement with music in everyday life using experience sampling methodology. Music Sci. **15**(1), 45–71 (2011). https://doi.org/10.1177/1029864910393417
8. Sternberg, R.J.: Images of mindfulness. J. Soc. Issues **56**(1), 11–26 (2000). https://doi.org/10.1111/0022-4537.00149

9. Zaichkowsky, J.L.: The personal involvement inventory: reduction, revision, and application to advertising. J. Advert. **23**(4), 59–70 (1994)

10. Chang, M.-M.: The development and validation of preference diversity and openness to novelty scale for movie preference structure. National Taiwan University, Taipei City, Taiwan (2015)

11. Brooke, J.: SUS: a quick and dirty usability scale. Usability Eval. Ind. **189**(194), 4–7 (1996)

12. Tang, M.C., Sie, Y.J., Ting, P.H.: Evaluating books finding tools on social media: a case study of aNobii. Inf. Process. Manag. **50**(1), 54–68 (2014). https://doi.org/10.1016/j.ipm. 2013.07.005

Affective, Behavioral, and Cognitive Aspects of Teen Perspectives on Personal Data in Social Media: A Model of Youth Data Literacy

Yu Chi[1], Wei Jeng[2(✉)], Amelia Acker[3], and Leanne Bowler[1]

[1] University of Pittsburgh, 135 North Bellefield Avenue, Pittsburgh, PA, USA
yuc73@pitt.edu, lbowler@sis.pitt.edu
[2] National Taiwan University, 1, Sec 4, Roosevelt Road, Taipei, Taiwan
wjeng@ntu.edu.tw
[3] University of Texas at Austin, 1616 Guadalupe Street, Austin, TX, USA
aacker@ischool.utexas.edu

Abstract. In this study, we explored the interplay between teens' *A*ffective states (A), *B*ehavioral states (B), and *C*ognitive states (C) in relation to the personal data they generate in social media, applying the "ABC model" from the social psychology domain. The data was collected from semi-structured interviews with 22 US teens in three library branches of the Carnegie Library of Pittsburgh, USA. Results from content analysis suggest that: (1) Young people are positive about their data skills, while feeling negative or insecure about data privacy issues; (2) young people with negative affective states related to data privacy are more likely to make an effort to secure their social media accounts and profiles. Given the results, we suggest librarians, educators and software developers apply a range of strategies in reaction to teens' different ABC states to the design of data literacy programs, services, and software applications.

Keywords: Data literacy · Affect · Behavior · Cognition · Teens

1 Introduction

Today's young people have grown up in a world of digital technology, including both software (e.g., social networking and video games) and hardware (e.g., smartphones and wearable devices), coupled with an increase in the generation of personal data about users. These so-called "digital natives", however, are not natural born experts in navigating the digital world, as some assume. In Plowman and McPake (2013)'s observation, children need guided interactions from parents and educators before they are fully competent users. Related work also shows that teens are unaware of the privacy and security issues around personal data (Madden et al. 2013).

To help with this situation, we need knowledge about how teens think, feel, and behave around data. What is their attitude towards data and the associated issues, such as data privacy, data rights, data subjectivity, etc.? The answer to these questions might help predict and explain teens' behavior vis à vis technology.

This study adopts Ostrom's *ABC model* (1969) of attitudes from the domain of social psychology, which defines the three components of attitudes as: *A* (affect),

© Springer International Publishing AG, part of Springer Nature 2018
G. Chowdhury et al. (Eds.): iConference 2018, LNCS 10766, pp. 442–452, 2018.
https://doi.org/10.1007/978-3-319-78105-1_49

B (behavior), and *C* (cognition). We employ the *ABC model* because it serves as a theoretical perspective that help explain the relationship between teens and their personal data, meanwhile allowing an exploration of possible interplay between affect, cognition, and behavior. Specifically, the research questions are the following:

RQ1: What are teens' "ABC" – their affective (how they feel), behavioral (how they act or react), and cognitive (how they think) states about digital data in their daily lives?

RQ2: How are teens' affective and cognitive states associated with their behaviors toward data?

Having presented young people's attitudes towards data, this study discusses the ABC model with regard to youth data literacy services in public libraries, i.e., the role that libraries can be expected to play in supporting young people in the digital age.

To answer the questions above, we use qualitative data from semi-structured interviews with 22 teens. This study is part of the research project *Exploring Data Worlds at the Public Library*, whose broader goal is to examine young people's data awareness, knowledge, and practices in order to propose ways that the public library can support the development of youth data literacy. In earlier work, the project focused on young people's data awareness (Bowler et al. 2017), e.g., their understandings about the rhetoric of data, and their basic knowledge of data flows and infrastructures. As a contrast, this study focuses on teens' affective, behavioral, and cognitive states.

2 Related Work

2.1 Young People and Their Data Worlds

Growing up in the networked digital world, young people today are more than passive users; they are also active creators, adding content to the growing collections of data that are aggregated through digital platforms, services, and applications. Teens' data footprints are unobtrusively tracked and added to their "digital dossier" (Montgomery 2015) that could be used to track, profile, and shape young people throughout their lives. Young people, however, are generally unaware of the data they generate and how the ubiquitous collection of data collection takes place (Deahl 2014), thus making them particularly vulnerable to the potential risks. According to the Pew Research (Madden et al. 2013), young people are sharing more personal data than before: 92% of teen social media users post their real names and 91% post a photo of themselves. The personal data they share also includes real address, birthdate, etc.

Though there exists a wide body of research on information literacy, research that has helped libraries design services to better support information interaction, there is as yet, little research in the emerging field of data literacy, especially research related to teens. Deahl (2014) proposed the definition of "data literacy" and also established design principles that would guide the data literacy initiatives. In this paper, we argue that it is critical to know how the teens themselves talk and think about data and how it associates with their behavior. Knowing the answers might help researchers, educators and practitioners understand how best to serve teens in our data driven world.

2.2 Affect, Behavior and Cognition Studies in LIS

As a central topic in the domain of social psychology, the concept of "attitude" is seen as a result of the interaction between three components: affect, behavior, and cognition (hereafter referred to as ABC, a concept based on the work of Ostrom 1969). The adoption of the ABC model of attitude allows researchers to investigate how people feel, think and interact with the attitude object, which in this case is digital data (Mizokawa and Hansen-Krening 2000).

In the Library and Information Science domain (LIS), scholars consider affect and cognition as important factors in the study of human information behavior (Kuhlthau 1991; Julien et al. 2005; Nahl and Bilal 2007). For example, Martzoukou (2005) critiqued the literature on web information seeking research arguing that this body of work should be more holistic, concentrating on not just on behaviors, but also the interplay of behavior with cognition and affect. We suggest that our understanding of teens and their interactions with data needs to be built upon a similar holistic view, rather than being confined to one dimension of the human experience.

3 Methodology

3.1 Data Collection

This study uses a dataset collected in the project of "*Exploring Data Worlds at the Public Library*," in which we interview 22 young people (age range 11–18) in three urban library branches in Pittsburgh Area, USA. The interviews were conducted in "The Labs," a technology-enhanced teen space in a public library where teens have access to advanced hardware and software (e.g., 3D printers and music composition toolkits). Teens can also hang out together to work on projects, homework, or just play games and socialize while they are at The Labs. The space is facilitated by library staff trained in the technologies available.

A semi-structured protocol was used to guide the interview process. The participants were allowed to be interviewed individually or in groups. As a result, we conducted 5 individual interviews, 7 groups of two interviews and 1 group of three. In total, we conducted 13 interviews with 22 participants. After the interviews were transcribed, twelve base codes are eventually developed to identify the essential themes or components in interview data. Each code can be link back to quotes from actual conversations. The full coding scheme is reported in (Bowler et al. 2017).

3.2 Data Analysis-Coding Process

Codes Identified as Affective-Feelings

In a second level analysis, the four researchers built out the *Affect* theme, two researchers assigned a qualifier to the data coded for Affect, capturing the nature of affect, e.g., surprised or scared. As well, the "affect" data was coded in terms of positive attitude, negative attitude, or neutral. The extended coding structure for affect was then reviewed and discussed by all authors in multiple meetings.

Codes Identified as Behavioral and Cognitive

We added two new base codes into the pre-existing coding framework: *cognitive states* and *behavioral states*. Cognitive states capture teens' thoughts and beliefs as they relate to digital data. Behavior states refers to actions or decisions to act. We thoroughly checked the documents tagged by "affective characteristics," and then we re-examined the transcripts again to tag the incidents that suggest "cognitive states". In total, 53 quotes were yielded with an affective state, a cognitive state, or both. For these 53 quotes, we went through adjacent quotes to find out if the respondent also mentioned how they behave or they decide to behave in the future. Table 1 provides the definitions of the ABC codes and the definition.

Table 1. Base codes and the definition

Base codes	Definitions
Affective states	Respondents' feelings and emotions about data
Cognitive states	Respondents' thoughts and beliefs about data
Behavioral states	Respondents' practices or decisions associated with their affects or cognitions

4   Results

4.1   Teen's Affective States About Data in Their Daily Life

After extracting all the affective quotes and assigning qualifiers, the data was grouped into the following categories: (1) positive affect, (2) negative affect, and, (3) affect that appeared to be neither positive nor negative. Among the 42 quotes suggesting the interviewees' affective states, we found that nearly half of them are positive (N = 20). The second popular states are negative (N = 12). Besides, there is a fair amount of affective states suggesting neither positive nor negative feelings (N = 10).

A-1. Positive Affective States

Confidence is one frequently found positive affective state in the interview. There were two contexts where the teens would express their confidence about the data and technology. Firstly, when talking about who controls their data, T3 (age: 15), T5 (age: 14) and T9 (age: 14) all reported that they were sure that the data they created were definitely controlled by themselves, demonstrating a positive sense of agency. As said by T9, *"Mine [data] says nice things"* and *"seems pretty controlled at the moment"*. Secondly, we found that teens are confident about their skills and aptitudes relate to data (Note, however, that this paper does not assess their actual skill level). Confidence is associated with a general feeling of liking:

> *"I like it, but I like technology and stuff. It comes, all the software stuff, especially, comes really easily to me… when I'm doing stuff on the computer, it's really fun. I like coding. Coding is fun, because I get to make the computer do stuff, which is cool."* (T19, age: 14)

Interest and curiosity were commonly expressed as positive affects, and they are also considered as positive cognitions:

"this [the interview] is making me want to go in deeper into learning more about different types of data." (T17, age: 17)

This might because, at that moment, after talking about so many issues regarding their digital data, teens got the feeling that data is interesting and they were eager to know more. Other positive affective states include pride, relief and ease.

A-2. Negative Affective States

Young people in the interviews showed strong negative feelings related to the fact that their data is being tracked and recorded. If data they created or the data about them was published online, they couldn't control who would get access to it and how long this data would exist. Teens expressed a sense of a loss of empowerment and this made them feel angry, sad, and scared. T11 (age: 17) shared a real experience to us:

T11: If you Google "[school name]," this horrible picture of me comes up...And so that picture comes up because it was on my profile on the [website name]. And it's such a bad picture.
Interviewer: And it follows you?
T11: Every time... We had to do a [school name] iMovie so people looked up [school name] to find pictures, and people would come up to me in the hallway and be like, "I saw a picture of you on Google!" Oh, it's so bad.

T11 is not the only teen in this study who was bothered by the digital identity projected through data. The situation seemed worse when teens were feeling confusion and uncertainty at the same time: They are not sure exactly how the data they post online will affect them in the future.

T22 (age: 14): "I think it starts a lot of drama sometimes, or it starts a lot of rumor in a lot of ways, just because of too much that you put out there. Teens, if they try to avoid it, or if they just wish that it wasn't there, you can't do anything about it."

A-3. Neither Positive nor Negative Affective States

While we identified both positive and negative affect, representing both the pleasant and the negative aspects of teens' feelings, we also found that, along the spectrum of feelings, some of the participants reported neither positive nor negative feelings (i.e. seemingly neutral) – a paradox that we feel should be further explored because there could be many reasons behind this observation.

Though many teens strongly conveyed negative feelings about the notion of being tracked, T13 (age: 13) held an indifferent and unmindful attitude, and replied: *"I just don't feel like it's such a big deal if privacy's being invaded."* And T13 further explained: *"As long as they don't take any severe action towards me, who cares what they see? That's how I feel."*

When being asked about their feelings about data, T4 (age: 15) was neutral: *"I don't know, it's kind of both. Positive and negative."* T6 (age: 15) and T9 (age: 14) simply answered that they didn't know, which might have implied evasive, indifferent, or just unaware attitude.

4.2   Teen's Cognitive States About Data in Their Daily Life

Teens' cognitive states were discovered in the interview transcripts, with at least 19 quotes from the transcripts speaking to the teens' knowledge, beliefs, and thought processes with regard to data. As with the analysis of affective states, cognitive states were grouped into three categories: (1) self-awareness of data and its consequences (related to metacognitive states), (2) belief that there is no absolute right or wrong and (3) belief that there are no consequences with regard to the use of their data by others (the latter two categories related to moral judgement and decision making).

C-1. Self-awareness of Data and Its Consequences

Half of the cognitive states suggest that teens *believe* they are aware of what happens with their data (Note that we did not assess the validity of this belief in this paper). Some of these quotes also contain positive feelings of confidence.

> *"Aware. It makes me feel aware of what's going on and how it affects our society in different ways." (T20, age: 16)*

Some teens expressed an awareness that their digital data traces were being watched and associated that knowledge with feelings of constraint and suspicion. For example, T2 (age: 14) believed that *"Somebody keeps a record of everything that you do and...Feels like you're tied down to something."* Similarly, T19 (age: 14) said *"just makes me feel like I'm always being watched."*

C-2. Sophisticated but Complicated: No Absolute Right or Wrong About Data

Online data such as one's social media profile promotes communication between teens and their social world. People, including teens, can easily reach friends and family through the data world. Even strangers can easily connect through online identities. Despite the benefits of data, there are disadvantages, according to some teens in this study. In the interview, we found that some teens had an ambiguous notion of right or wrong in terms of their own data, seeming to believe that there is no absolutely right or wrong regarding data creation, gathering, and use.

T15 (age: 18) and T14 (age: 16) admitted the advantages of data but were conscious about the bad sequences at the same time.

> *T15: "I see all the good it does, but I also just see how I think it... I think it kind of makes us less human in a way. It's weird to say, but it's how I feel about it."*
> *T14: "When someone goes to a concert and they'd rather take a Snapchat about the stuff instead of enjoying the moment."*
> *T15: "...You lose the awareness that you have with the things that are actually going on around you. And that really affects you as a human."*

C-3. Belief that There are no Consequences

For some teens in this study, awareness of *"being tracked"* or *"being watched"* was not accompanied by any concern or worry. Although some teens might believe their data doesn't belong to them (or, that others have access to it), they also view this as inconsequential: Nothing severe will happen and it's simply not worth their concern.

As replied by T11 (age: 17): *"I mean, honestly, nothing's going to happen to me. It's not like the government is going to smash into my house..."*

T12 (age: 16): *"Personally, I feel like if they're trying to collect all this data for safety purposes, as long as you're not doing anything wrong online, I don't see anything wrong with having it."*

T13 (age: 13) thought that data rights are not important and *"People who cry about it are stupid."*

4.3 Behaviors Corresponding to Affective and Cognitive States

Table 2 summarizes the young people's behaviors and their corresponding affect and cognition. As shown in the first column, there are five major types of behaviors referred

Table 2. Behaviors corresponding to affective and cognitive states and the number of reported incidents (N.B., darker color indicates more incidents)

Behaviors	Example Behavior Quotes (ID, Age)	Corresponding Affects and No. of reported incidents			Corresponding Cognitions and No. of reported incidents		
		A-1	A-2	A-3	C-1	C-2	C-3
B-1. Active — Hide personal information, e.g., use fake names; hide address, birthday, etc.	*"...Don't use your full name. And you don't give it to strangers."* (T9, 14)	3	3	2	4	0	1
B-2. Active — Increase security settings, e.g., use incognito mode, etc.	*"...you can add a password or a fingerprint...I change it [password] once a month"* (T4, 15)	0	4	2	1	1	0
B-3. Passive — Anticipate for more knowledge or training, e.g., expect for awareness training, skill training, etc.	*" since we're young, we don't have all that information, all that knowledge about data in particular, and so we don't have the right knowledge to really understand..."* (T17, 17)	7	0	1	2	0	0
B-4. Passive — Reduce Usage, e.g., abandon accounts; post less, etc.	*"Maybe when I was young and I just posted little... You know, stupid pictures or stupid posts. I'll just leave the account, don't use it anymore. "* (T22, 14)	0	4	2	1	1	0
B-5. Passive — Maintain current settings, e.g., don't use any tricks to protect data; don't anonymize anything, etc.	*"...I've never actually worried about having my data be private, like, ever. So no, not specifically. No tricks."* (T1, 11)	3	0	1	1	0	4

to. The five types of behaviors are divided into active behavior and passive behavior according to the required effort of the subject. Therefore, B-1 and B-2 are active behaviors as the subjects are actively updating their settings or adopting tools, while B-3 to B-5 are passive because no extra effort is put in. An example quote of each type of behaviors is displayed in the second column. We also report the number of incidents discovered with certain affective states or cognitive states. When the teens talked about how they feel or how they think, they did not necessarily mention how they behaved or how they would behave in the future. But whenever they expressed an action after they answered the question about affective states and cognitive states, the incident is counted as a *behavior corresponding to that affective state*.

B-1. Hide Personal Information

Hiding personal information is a popular behavior adopted by some teens who consciously protect their data. It includes use fake information such as fake name, address, birthday on their profiles, and clear personal traces online.

T8 replied that a digital ID is different from the real person. Though believing that there is no need to worry too much about it, T8 still preferred to partially hide the personal information online. T18 believed that if avoiding putting middle initials on the Internet, others would not be able to locate him.

Teens who are *self-aware of data and its consequences (C-1)* are more likely to hide personal information comparing to other cognitive states.

B-2. Increasing Security Settings

Some teens have more skills and knowledge on how to increase the security of their accounts and devices. T6 changed password once a month. T15 used Duck Duck Go instead of Google as the former one claimed to track no user data. T20 was cautious when using public devices: *"But outside of home-wise, I just make sure I log out."*

We were surprised to find that teens who hold negative feelings about data tend to consciously increase security settings. This might because with the negative feeling, these teens are doubtful about the data security and thus are willing to actively improve the security level of their online accounts and profiles.

B-3. Anticipating More Knowledge or Training

Young people's expectation for more knowledge or training on data, or, the behavior they *anticipate* - is associated with positive feelings. In other words, some teens reported that they wanted to learn more about data in the future. This might be due to one of the commonly found positive feelings of curiosity. Curiosity drives T17 to expect to *"go in deeper into learning more about different types of data."*

We also found that some teens have ideas about what kind of training or data-related knowledge should be delivered to them. For example, T19 is very interested and confident in coding and technology, thus expected training in coding.

Talking about who should offer the training, T5 believed that a conversation led by the libraries could be helpful: *"They [libraries] could possibly do a meeting or have something that... Young adults or younger kids know what it is and how they could and should use it, and what an impact it has on everybody, each individual's life."* While, T16 thought it should be parent's responsibility to teach their children about the necessary information for using the technologies.

B-4. Reducing Usage

When teens have extreme negative feelings about digital data about themselves, they reduce their usage of some online services or even abandon some accounts.

T11, whose picture was captured by Google search results, reported: *"I used to use Instagram and Twitter and stuff. I don't really use those anymore...I just didn't want to anymore. They're just a distraction and I wanted to focus on other things."* Similarly, T22 also said *"I'll just leave the account, don't use it anymore."*

B-5. Maintaining Current Privacy Settings

Some participants reported that they prefer to take no actions and they believe there is no need to make data private.

For example, T12 had a positive feeling, believing that nothing dangerous will happen to his data and it should not be individual's responsibility to protect personal data: *"I feel like if they're trying to collect all this data for safety purposes, as long as you're not doing anything wrong online, I don't see anything wrong with having it. But if you're doing something wrong, then I feel like it's the government's responsibility to be able to..."* T13 has a very similar opinion: *"If it's necessary for people to view what I'm doing, I don't have to hide much."*

5 Discussion and Conclusion

Young People are Positive About Their Data Skills while Negative About their Data Privacy

In our analysis of teens' affective states associated with their data in their daily life, it is not surprising to find that young people appear to be very confident about their data related skills, such as coding. On the other hand, though several teens believed that they had control over the data they created, most teens expressed negative feelings when the conversation was about data privacy issues. What made the feeling worse was their lack of knowledge about what data was released to other entities or to the Web and how exactly how that data might affect them.

Teens with Negative Affective States are more Likely to Adopt Effortful Behaviors to Protect the Data Privacy

By analyzing the relationships between teens' behavior and their associated affects, we found that affective states may influence the teens' behavioral strategies. To be specific, teens with negative affects tend to adopt active behaviors to deal with the potential problematic situations, such as *B-1 hiding personal information* and *B-2 increasing security settings*. On the contrary, the teens who perceive current situation as a positive environment are more like to passively rely on the existing routines and adopt no actions to protect themselves *(B-5 remaining current settings)*.

This finding aligns with Schwarz (2000)'s argument that negative affective states foster the use of "effortful, detail-oriented, analytical processing strategies." It implies that educators should try their best to evaluate teens' data confidence, because over-confidence may negatively influence the teens' behaviors regarding data security.

Librarians, Educators and Software Developers can Apply Different Strategies in Reaction to Different ABC States

We suggest librarians, educators and software developers incorporate implications from this study about ABC states of teens with regard to data into the design of data literacy programs, services, and software applications. For example, as implied by the interplay between *A-1. positive affective states* and *B-3. expect for more knowledge or training*, if librarians observe the teens showing increasing interests about the data, it may be a good time to push more knowledge and technical skills. Likewise, for the teens who are *not aware of the consequence of data privacy C-3*, there is a high chance that they adopt no actions to protect their data. In this case, it is recommended that librarians show the teens the potential risk of, for instance, personal data leaks or a compromised password, perhaps through the use of videos or news clips. Libraries can also encourage teens to share their own experiences in peer-to-peer teaching.

6 Future Work

While the interview sample size in this study aligns with general practices in qualitative research, the number of incidences regarding teens' *ABC states* is relatively small, making it difficult to draw wide generalizations across the population of all teens. A core contribution of this work is the development of a new analysis framework for investigating how young people interact with digital data in their daily lives. Our analysis focused on three aspects: (A) affect, (B) behavior, and (C) cognitive states. Almost a quarter of teens in this study expressed indifferent opinions with regard to data, a finding worth further investigation. It is difficult to know why, based on the data we had available. Is it because the teens didn't want to expose their feelings to the researchers or, that they simply felt nothing about data? Future research is needed to fill in this gap.

References

Bowler, L., Acker, A., Jeng, W., Chi, Y.: "It lives all around us": aspects of data literacy in teen's lives. Proc. Assoc. Inf. Sci. Technol. **54**(1), 27–35 (2017)

Deahl, E.S.: Better the data you know: developing youth data literacy in schools and informal learning environments. Unpublished master's thesis, Massachusetts Institute of Technology (2014)

Julien, H., McKechnie, L.E., Hart, S.: Affective issues in library and information science systems work: a content analysis. Libr. Inf. Sci. Res. **27**(4), 453–466 (2005)

Kuhlthau, C.C.: Inside the search process: information seeking from the user's perspective. J. Am. Soc. Inf. Sci. Technol. **42**, 361–371 (1991)

Madden, M., Lenhart, A., Cortesi, S., Gasser, U., Duggan, M., Smith, A., Beaton, M.: Teens, social media, and privacy. Pew Res. Center **21**, 2–86 (2013)

Martzoukou, K.: A review of web information seeking research: considerations of method and foci of interest. Inf. Res. **10**(2), Paper 215 (2005)

Mizokawa, D.T., Hansen-Krening, N.: The ABCs of attitudes toward reading: inquiring about the reader's response. J. Adolesc. Adult Lit. **44**(1), 72–79 (2000)

Montgomery, K.: Children's media culture in a big data world. J. Child. Media **9**(2), 266–271 (2015)

Nahl, D., Bilal, D. (eds.): Information and Emotion: The Emergent Affective Paradigm in Information Behavior Research and Theory. Information Today, Inc., Medford Township (2007)

Ostrom, T.M.: The relationship between the affective, behavioral, and cognitive components of attitude. J. Exp. Soc. Psychol. **5**(1), 12–30 (1969)

Plowman, L., McPake, J.: Seven myths about young children and technology. Child. Educ. **89** (1), 27–33 (2013)

Schwarz, N.: Emotion, cognition, and decision making. Cogn. Emot. **14**(4), 433–440 (2000)

Analyzing Political Information Network
of the U.S. Partisan Public on Twitter

Miyoung Chong[(⊠)]

University of North Texas, Denton, TX 76203, USA
chong.miyoung@gmail.com

Abstract. The growing significance of social media among potential voters has been recognized by politicians because social media provides a direct method for political actors to connect with their citizens and organize them into online clusters through their use of hashtags. However, with few exclusions, most of the former studies stressed on the identification of personal tweets or cumulative properties of a mass of tweets and political fondness of discrete users, not on partisan public in the U.S. Thus, there is a lack of complete understanding about online social network of politically conflicting public and the public discourse in the network. Therefore, the purpose of this study is to investigate how people adopt political information on Twitter via hashtag as a networked public and how people facilitate political communication among users with similar or disparate political orientations. This study confirmed the theory of homophily in adopting political hashtags on Twitter network. The referred media and highly mentioned domains for each network also support the concept of homophily. The manually examined users with top betweenness centralities were identified as opinion leaders and their tweeting patterns provide evidences that they play key roles in disseminating information through eWOM by occupying an important relational spot in the network.

Keywords: Twitter · Political information network · Homophily

1 Introduction

The growing significance of social media among potential voters has been also recognized by politicians because social media provides a direct method for political actors to connect with their citizens and organize them into online clusters through especially their use of hashtags (Bode et al. 2015). Many U.S. presidential candidates, including Barack Obama, Hillary Clinton, and Donald Trump, launched their presidential campaigns on social media to reach a younger population and create a more welcoming impression among the general voting public by avoiding media gatekeepers. As politicians increasingly rely on social media to communicate their messages, the political impact of social media has been the focus of many research studies.

Among social media, Twitter emerged as the most popular micro-blogging platform, where information proliferates rapidly, and posted information and actions cause instantaneous responses from users. These characteristics are ideal to promote political viewpoints, particularly during contentious election campaigns (Makazhanov et al.

© Springer International Publishing AG, part of Springer Nature 2018
G. Chowdhury et al. (Eds.): iConference 2018, LNCS 10766, pp. 453–463, 2018.
https://doi.org/10.1007/978-3-319-78105-1_50

2014). Political impact on social media has been examined through political discourses, and the political discourses on Twitter have been explored during the past several years by researchers. The emphasis on those studies were analyzing online networks of candidates and active users to forecast the results of the elections (Makazhanov et al. 2014). Moreover, with few exclusions, most of those former studies regarding the political discourses on Twitter stressed the identification of personal tweets or the cumulative properties of a mass of tweets and the political fondness of discrete users (Makazhanov et al. 2014). Little is known about how the partisan public in the U.S. interacts on Twitter, and thus, there is a lack of complete understanding in the body of knowledge about information behaviors of politically conflicting publics in online social networks and the public discourse in the networks. One ignored area of Twitter is the adoption of the political hashtag, user-created keywords prearranged with the # symbol. Twitter users adopt hashtags to gather around certain issues, which fundamentally are used to generate conversational groups around a public interest. Based on this rationale, the study argues that Twitter contributes the generation of manifold public spheres among the politically driven via hashtag adoption, and the users in these configurations are identified by shared interests and concerns, social and political identities, and communication sources and strategies.

This study employs a targeted and unique sample that applied the pro-Trump #MAGA and anti-Trump #Resist in order to investigate Twitter users' adoption of the political hashtag and its distributional force on the networked platforms. The hashtags were selected because they respectively represent those who support and those who oppose Trump and his agenda. Tweets were collected through Twitter application programming interface (API) on 10 am, April 22, 2017. The collected data was curated by a combination of network clustering algorithms and investigated by applying social network analysis and manual examinations of selected data to discover the answers to the research questions concerning the user behaviors and disseminations of political communication in the opposing networks.

2 Literature Review

In *The structural transformation of the public sphere*, Habermas (1962) developed the idea of a public sphere where people convene to discuss issues, establish problems, and tried to arrange a course of political action. Recent studies discovered that the public sphere has increasingly been fragmented and polarized, which is attributed to the growing dominance of digital communication (Dahlgren 2005; Habermas 2006; Papacharissi 2002). But much disagreement exists regarding the degree of this polarization (Neuman et al. 2011). Many researchers claimed that social media boosts polarization (Baum and Groeling 2008) and online users bisect along a conventional Right and Left political split (Adamic and Glance 2005; Farrell and Drezner 2008; Hindman 2008; Tremayne et al. 2006). Based on these viewpoints, social networking services (SNSs) and online news platforms either nurture diverse public arenas or support and intensify factional divides, or they demonstrate a little mixture of the two (Baum and Groeling 2008; Robertson et al. 2010). Regardless of these arguments, digital technologies reinforced the public's capacity to link to each other while forming a spectrum of collective and connected entities (Shah et al. 2005).

This study is related to the body of research analyzing political communication on Twitter. In light of the arguments about the Internet media's contribution to political fragmentation and polarization, along with the fact that a number of U.S. politicians, including candidates for the U.S. Congress and President who adopted Twitter for their election campaigns, few studies have investigated information behaviors of like-minded publics in the polarized political networks. Most studies focused on the strategic application of Twitter, emphasizing the behaviors of the candidates while encouraging them to adopt Twitter with helpful tips for effective applications (Lassen and Brown 2011; Gulati and Williams 2010).

Other research studies explored how Twitter is applied within the electoral context to forecast electoral results (DiGrazia et al. 2013) by discovering candidates' patterns of political practice (Bruns and Highfield 2013; Graham et al. 2013). These investigations stressed the behaviors of the candidates, paying less attention to the behavior and flocking of the political public. Though SNSs provide a channel for political candidates to link to the public, these public spheres also give channels for the online public to connect with each other, self-establish, and get involved with antagonistic politics. Adamic and Glance (2005) discovered that interactive patterns online demonstrated conspicuous conservative and liberal groupings in blogs, such as book recommendations on Amazon.com. This discovery supports the concept of homophily, which is the inclination of people to search for and befriend others who have similar characteristics including physical attributes, beliefs, religion, and political tendencies (McPherson et al. 2001). The principle of homophily has been identified as a primary mechanism in social institutions in both physical and online environments (Thelwall 2009).

Drawing from the Diffusion of Innovation theory (Rogers 1962), many studies have investigated people's power to influence other people. Rogers (1962) defined an individual's asymmetrical influence on others' mindsets or actions as opinion leadership. This theory forecasts that, by focusing on these influencers, a large-scale series of reactions driven by word-of-mouth (WOM) can occur (Katz and Lazarsfeld 1955). Currently, substantial knowledge is lacking in the study of how influencers relate to electronic-word-of-mouth (eWOM), yet a greater knowledge of eWOM structures in SNSs can improve our understanding of promoters of eWOM and give us meaningful insights into online political communication.

3   Research Questions

Tweets are considered relevant when they include a term from a list of devised keywords, comprised manually or semi-automatically (Conover et al. 2011). Hashtags are also a primary feature of Twitter because the users can annotate tweets with metadata establishing the subject or gathering like-minded individuals across the network. In other words, they are applied "to bundle together tweets on a unified, common topic," which makes it easy to identify and characterize the discursive clusters with certain hashtags (Bruns and Burgess 2011, p. 5). For instance, #MAGA stands for "Make America Great Again!" and #tcot stands for "Top Conservatives on Twitter."

Individual hashtag determines the stream of content when participants tag selections, indicating engagement in diverse information channels (Conover et al. 2011). Via hashtags, users can engage with a certain issue or topic, and their tweets belong to an extensive communication among disconnected individuals, which results in a significant structure of online political conversation and behavior (Bode et al. 2015).

Approaching the hashtag networks of #MAGA and #Resist as homophily clusters, this study examines the following research questions:

- RQ 1: How do #MAGA and #Resist networks demonstrate their political attributes on the Twitter?
- RQ 2: How are the shared information sources characterized within the Twitter network of #MAGA and #Resist?

Also, by drawing from the diffusion of Innovation theory (Roger 1962) in conjunction with social network analysis (SNA) approach (Otte and Rousseau 2002), this study investigates the Twitter network of #MAGA and #Resist to discover influencers in transmitting information. Thus, the following research question will be examined:

- RQ 3: Who are the influencers on the Twitter network of #MAGA and #Resist?

To discover the answers to the research questions, this study applies social network analysis (SNA) method. This study improves upon past efforts to examine Twitter network disseminating political information in an online community via hashtags. In addition, this study compares the Twitter network of the partisan public in the U.S., and through this approach, we can better explore the theory of homophily and diffusion of innovation applied in hashtag network on the Twitter.

4   Methods

4.1   Data Collection

Tweets were collected by applying #MAGA and #Resist through Twitter application programming interface (API) on April 22, 2017. Theoretically, NodeXL Pro version allows researchers to gather the last 18,000 tweets on a certain hashtag through the Twitter Search network function. However, generally, not quite that many tweets are collected because of Twitter's age screening policy. Twitter.com clarifies, "Age screening is a way for brands and others to determine online whether a follower meets a minimum age requirement, in a way that is consistent with relevant industry or legal guidelines. This makes it easier for advertisers and others with content not suitable for minors (e.g. alcohol advertisers) to advertise on Twitter." In this study, a total of 5,287 vertices (tweets, retweets, mentions, and replied to) generated a total of 10,781 edges (relations between tweets) in #MAGA network, and a total of 6,682 vertices (tweets, retweets, mentions, and replied to) generated a total of 10,567 edges (relations between tweets) in #Resist network.

4.2   Data Analysis

To investigate the proposed research questions, Social Network Analysis (SNA) was conducted using NodeXL (Hansen et al. 2011). Four different types of Twitter edges, including retweets, replies- to, mentions, and tweets, as well as following and follower relationships among users, were extracted. To visualize interpretable data, the data has been calculated and processed with calculating metrics, including indegree, outdegree, betweenness centrality, and page rank among the sampled tweets. During this process, isolates, which are not connected with any other vertices within the network, were removed because they do not present clear relationships with other users. A total of 307 groups were discovered in #MAGA network, and a total of 448 groups were discovered in #Resist Twitter network. Clauset-Newman-Moore algorithm was applied to create these clusters. This algorithm defines the main clusters in a network by placing vertices into the best fitting cluster depending on the patterns of interconnectedness, and this clustering method generally forms a few dominant groups and several very small ones. (Wakita and Tsurumi 2007).

Visual network diagrams of collections of actors (vertices) were created, the network impact (e.g., betweenness centrality or page rank) of a single actor on others was estimated, and significant information, such as top-word pairs and the most frequent domains in tweets in the entire network on the #MAGA and #Resist networks, was retrieved. For each hashtag, ten major clusters were identified and several iterations were conducted to condense sub-groups. To closely examine the influencers of the two networks, the Twitter accounts of the high betweenness centralities were manually examined. Betweenness centrality is a measure of how often a given vertex lies on the shortest path between two other vertices and how a vertex connects groups by bridging the gap in the global network (Hansen et al. 2011). High betweenness centrality implies that it connects the major groups otherwise they are fragmented or incoherent, and it also indicates the elevated level of influence and connectivity (Freeman 1978). Some vertices have high betweenness centralities, which implies that they are closely connected with the major groups in the network.

5   Findings

Figures 1 and 2 present the top ten groups from the entire network of #MAGA and #Resist, respectively. In Fig. 1, the groups were shown with the top keywords next to the number of the group name. The top key words are the most frequently used terms in the cluster. These key words, which include maga (6629), Trump (1968), POTUS (1041), america first (933), president (412), made_usa (362), tcot (362), and conservative (241), clearly demonstrate that #MAGA network supports Trump, his agenda, and the Republican party. For the first research question, the network connectedness and word frequency were examined. The two network graphs are highly reciprocal and actively tied together in their conversations through Twitter activities such as tweets, retweets, mention, and reply to. The top keywords in the entire #Resist network are Resist (8119), trump (2076), trumprussia (1815), the Resistance (1411), funder (1020), russiagate (812), trumpleaks (550), and impeachtrump (221). The keywords used in the

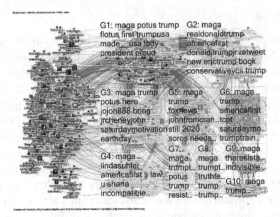

Fig. 1. The top 10 group of the #MAGA network on Twitter with top key words

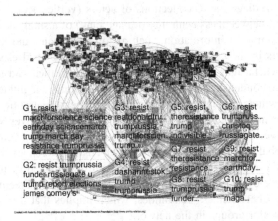

Fig. 2. The top 10 group of the #Resist network on Twitter with top keywords

#Resist network also represent that the network is a strong adversarial to Trump and his agenda. The most frequently used word pairs in the entire network are present in Table 1. This also solidifies the argument that content of communication within the networks dominantly support their political side, respectively.

The shared word pairs within the networks reveal extremely polarized conversation of #MAGA and #Resist because while the #MAGA network resonates the important agenda of the Trump administration, the #Resist network promotes to Resist his agenda, to raise concerns about his relationship with Russia during the presidential campaign, and even to impeach Trump.

Information sources of the social media network are very important because more than half of the U.S. population obtain news through social media, and around 50% of these social media users get information about the 2016 presidential election via social media websites (Gottfried and Shearer 2016). The sources of information can also

Table 1. Top word pairs in #MAGA and #Resist networks

Top word pairs in the #MAGA network				Top word pairs in the #Resist network			
Word1	Word 2	Count	Salience	Word1	Word 2	Count	Salience
maga	trumptrain	442	0.007	resisit	theResistance	844	0.010
maga	americafirst	430	0.007	trumprussia	Resist	616	0.008
americafirst	maga	407	0.007	russiagate	Resist	604	0.008
maga	trump	303	0.005	trumprussia	russiagate	600	0.008
u	s	290	0.005	theResistance	indivisible	571	0.008
sharia	law	287	0.005	marchforscience	Resist	418	0.006
trump	maga	270	0.005	indivisible	scrotus	397	0.006
s	constitution	259	0.005	scrotus	peeotus	337	0.005

indicate the political inclinations of the shared news and conversations in the network. Table 2 describes the most frequently appearing domains in the entire #MAGA and #Resist networks. These domains illustrate the most used and referred websites in the networks. The shared domains among the hashtag users clearly show their political alikeness. Truthfeed.com, breitbart.com, and americanthinker.com are the examples of conservative media, which is arguably called the right extreme media. On the other hand, top domains in tweets shared in the #Resist network reveal that they obtain information from the progressive or liberal media, such as huffingtonpost.com and washingtonpost.com. In addition, the top urls in tweets also came from these top shared domains. Therefore, this also bolsters the findings of the RQ1while supporting the principle of homophily.

Table 2. Top domains in tweets of #MAGA and #Resist networks

Top domains in the #MAGA network	Top domains in the #Resist network
twitter.com	twitter.com
truthfeed.com	instagram.com
comicallyincorrect.com	cnn.com
reddit.com	huffingtonpost.com
israelvideonetwork.com	co.uk
youtube.com	moveon.org
facebook.com	pfaw.org
breitbart.com	youtube.com
americanthinker.com	dailykos.com
thehill.com	washingtonpost.com

To answer the third research question, degree centralities and betweenness centralities were examined between the two networks. Table 3 presents the users with the highest betweenness centrality, and tweets by POTUS (President of the United States) and Trump were the most popular and important position in the #MAGA network.

POTUS had dominant impact on the entire network, and its tweets were most frequently retweeted and mentioned in the network.

Table 3. Top 10 vertices ranked by betweenness centrality

#MAGA	Betweenness centrality	#Resist	Betweenness centrality
potus	6453489.678	funder	8050720.433
realdonaldtrump	6274745.945	realdonaldtrump	5588982.278
lindasuhler	3427726.595	dashannestokes	4181448.956
mcspocky	1663081.129	mcspocky	3877107.458
drumpfshit360	1390032.349	immigrant4trump	1250191.559
jimrobinsonsea	1036666.227	potus	1233574.705
jali_benz	976978.64	fmoniteau	1140418.018
uncletony52	823659.5114	altstatedpt	989964.7122
lorihendry	768630.0174	badhombrenps	883408.129
johnfromcranber	757015.8872	indivisibleteam	841818.4517

POTUS also demonstrates high betweenness centrality in the #Resist network with 1233574.705. However, when compared with 6453489.678 of the #MAGA network, it represents that POTUS is not the primary network gap bridger in the #Resist network. Most vertices with high betweenness centralities in #MAGA's network were identified as right-wing or far-right conservatives. For example, lindasuhler describes her profile as "I support PRESIDENT Donald Trump AMERICA FIRST Christian supports Family ~ Constitution ~ Capitalism ~ 1A ~ 2A ~ 10A ~ NRA ~ Military ~ Police ~ Israel".

In the case of the #Resist network, funder, the top influencer, is identified as Scott Dworkin, and he describes himself as "Dem Campaigner since '04; Co-Founder-@TheDemCoalition aka Dems Against Trump; Obama Alum; '09 Inaug/'12 DNCC" and promotes hashtags such as #TrumpLeaks, #TrumpRussia, and #RussiaGate, which are prevalent in the entire #Resist network, as previously examined. Other users with high betweenness centrality in #Resist network also coherently expose their anti-Trump stance through their posted tweets, retweeted information, and linked media sources. For example, dashannestokes describes himself as "sociologist, author, speaker, pundit. Fighter for equality & justice" and tweets along with #trumprussia, #TheResistance, #trumpleaks, #russiagate, and #impeachtrump in many cases.

6   Discussion and Conclusions

This study discovered that the #MAGA network is conservative, and the users of #MAGA were identified as nationalists or ultraconservatives. The users of the #MAGA employ anti-liberal hashtags and express antagonistic views and emotions by sharing certain hashtags, including #obamadisaster, #arresthillary, and #hillaryforjail. Interestingly, anti-Democratic hashtags were primarily focused on attacking Democratic politicians while the anti-Trumpers focused on the political issues and events, such as

#russiagate, #Marchforscience, and #trumprussia. The major influencers on Twitter were @realDonaldTrump and @POTUS with the highest betweenness centrality, and this confirms that Trump is the nucleus of the #MAGA network.

On the other hand, liberals, activist groups, and anti-Trump organizations adopted #Resist along with other anti-trump hashtags, such as #trumprussia, #russiagate, and #impeachtrump. #Marchforscience and #earthday were also shared by these same users because the analyzed data set were collected on the Earth Day and there were global rallies with the slogan of March for Science. This illustrates that #Resist is related to the exogenous hashtag, which captures activities or incidents resulting from outside of the Twitter system (Papacharissi 2015). The most frequently appearing domains were democratic movement organizations such as moveon.org (democracy in action) and pfaw.org (People for the American Way). Unlike the #MAGA network, top consulted media includes major mainstream media outlets such as cnn.com, huffingtonpost.com, and washingtonpost.com.

Among top influencers of both hashtag users, #MAGA users chiefly concentrated on retweeting pro-Trump tweets and information, while #Resist users focused on creating tweets to post information, thoughts, and action guides, which implicates a dissimilar pattern between the grassroots who employed the hashtags. This pattern explains that the users of #Resist more creatively and pro-actively adopted Twitter to distribute political information and facilitate the Twitter platform for grass-root activism.

Therefore, this study confirmed the theory of homophily in adopting political hashtags on the Twitter network. The referred media and highly mentioned domains for each network also support the concept of homophily. The manually examined users with top betweenness centralities were identified as opinion leaders and their tweeting patterns provide evidences that they play key roles in disseminating information through eWOM by occupying an important relational spot in the network. This study also established the methodological implication by implementing the concept of betweenness centrality as criteria of influencers in social network analysis.

This study also identified significant political polarization along with these hashtags among the U.S. online public, which confirms the previously examined literature regarding political polarization of political communication among Americans. Some users combined several hashtags with #MAGA or #Resist while others rarely integrated other related hashtags with those two. This study reveals that layperson users or bot Twitter account can also be a powerful influencer depending on their position and connectivity on the Twitter network. The study also revealed that Twitter contributes the creation of various public spheres among the politically oriented through hashtag use, and the users in these configurations are recognized as homophily in terms of political viewpoints.

Acknowledgement. I would like to thank Dr. Tracy Everbach for assistance with her expertise and for comments that greatly improved the manuscript.

References

Adamic, L.A., Glance, N.: The political blogosphere and the 2004 US election: divided they blog. In: Proceedings of the 3rd International Workshop on Link Discovery, pp. 36–43. ACM, August 2005

Baum, M.A., Groeling, T.: New media and the polarization of American political discourse. Polit. Commun. 25(4), 345–365 (2008)

Bode, L., Hanna, A., Yang, J., Shah, D.V.: Candidate networks, citizen clusters, and political expression: strategic hashtag use in the 2010 midterms. Ann. Am. Acad. Polit. Soc. Sci. 659 (1), 149–165 (2015)

Bruns, A., Burgess, J.E.: New methodologies for researching news discussion on Twitter (2011)

Bruns, A., Highfield, T.: Political networks on Twitter: tweeting the Queensland state election. Inf. Commun. Soc. 16(5), 667–691 (2013)

Conover, M., Ratkiewicz, J., Francisco, M.R., Gonçalves, B., Menczer, F., Flammini, A.: Political polarization on Twitter. ICWSM 133, 89–96 (2011)

Dahlgren, P.: The Internet, public spheres, and political communication: dispersion and deliberation. Polit. Commun. 22(2), 147–162 (2005)

DiGrazia, J., McKelvey, K., Bollen, J., Rojas, F.: More tweets, more votes: social media as a quantitative indicator of political behavior. Plos One 8(11), e79449 (2013)

Farrell, H., Drezner, D.W.: The power and politics of blogs. Public Choice 134(1–2), 15 (2008)

Freeman, L.C.: Centrality in social networks conceptual clarification. Soc. Netw. 1(3), 215–239 (1978)

Gottfried, J., Shearer, E.: News Use Across Social Media Platforms 2016, vol. 26. Pew Research Center (2016)

Graham, T., Broersma, M., Hazelhoff, K., van't Haar, G.: Between broadcasting political messages and interacting with voters: the use of Twitter during the 2010 UK general election campaign. Inf. Commun. Soc. 16(5), 692–716 (2013)

Gulati, J., Williams, C.B.: Communicating with constituents in 140 characters or less: Twitter and the diffusion of technology innovation in the United States Congress (2010)

Habermas, J.: Political communication in media society: does democracy still enjoy an epistemic dimension? The impact of normative theory on empirical research. Commun. Theory 16(4), 411–426 (2006)

Habermas, J.: The Structural Transformation of the Public Sphere. Polity, Cambridge (1962)

Hansen, D.L., Shneiderman, B., Smith, M.A.: Analyzing Social Media Networks with NodeXL: Insights from a Connected World. Morgan Kaufmann, Boston (2011)

Hindman, M.: The Myth of Digital Democracy. Princeton University Press, Princeton (2008)

Katz, E., Lazarsfeld, P.F.: Personal Influence: The Part Played by People in the Flow of Mass Communications. Transaction Publishers, New Brunswick (1955)

Lassen, D.S., Brown, A.R.: Twitter: the electoral connection? Soc. Sci. Comput. Rev. 29(4), 419–436 (2011)

Makazhanov, A., Rafiei, D., Waqar, M.: Predicting political preference of Twitter users. Soc. Netw. Anal. Min. 4(1), 1–15 (2014)

McPherson, M., Smith-Lovin, L., Cook, J.M.: Birds of a feather: homophily in social networks. Ann. Rev. Sociol. 27(1), 415–444 (2001)

Neuman, W.R., Bimber, B., Hindman, M.: The Internet and four dimensions of citizenship. In: The Oxford Handbook of American Public Opinion and the Media, pp. 22–42 (2011)

Otte, E., Rousseau, R.: Social network analysis: a powerful strategy, also for the information sciences. J. Inf. Sci. 28(6), 441–453 (2002)

Papacharissi, Z.: Affective Publics: Sentiment, Technology, and Politics. Oxford University Press, Oxford (2015)

Papacharissi, Z.: The virtual sphere: the internet as a public sphere. New Media Soc. **4**(1), 9–27 (2002)

Rogers Everett, M.: Diffusion of Innovations, vol. 12, New York (1962)

Robertson, S.P., Vatrapu, R.K., Medina, R.: Online video "friends" social networking: overlapping online public spheres in the 2008 US presidential election. J. Inf. Technol. Politics. **7**(2–3), 182–201 (2010)

Shah, D.V., Cho, J., Eveland Jr., W.P., Kwak, N.: Information and expression in a digital age: modeling Internet effects on civic participation. Commun. Res. **32**(5), 531–565 (2005)

Thelwall, M.: Homophily in myspace. J. Am. Soc. Inf. Sci. Technol. **60**(2), 219–231 (2009)

Tremayne, M., Zheng, N., Lee, J.K., Jeong, J.: Issue publics on the web: applying network theory to the war blogosphere. J. Comput.-Mediat. Commun. **12**(1), 290–310 (2006)

Wakita, K., Tsurumi, T.: Finding community structure in mega-scale social networks: [extended abstract]. In: Proceedings of the 16th International Conference on World Wide Web, pp. 1275–1276. ACM, May 2007

Comparing Information Literacy Levels of Canadian and German University Students

Maria Henkel(✉) , Sven Grafmüller, and Daniel Gros

Heinrich Heine University, 40225 Düsseldorf, Germany
maria.henkel@hhu.de

Abstract. The objective of this study is the assessment and comparison of information literacy among Canadian and German students from informational cities. 892 students from Berlin, Munich, Frankfurt, Montreal, Toronto and Vancouver completed our multiple-choice questionnaire. In most cases, a significant difference between Canadian and German students is confirmed. In both countries surveyed, the majority of students reach only the beginner level.

Keywords: Information literacy · Information literacy assessment
Informational city · Questionnaire · University students
International comparison

1 Introduction

Today, modern information and communication technology (ICT) in omnipresent and increasingly affects our daily lives. Due to its wide distribution, many people have constant access to the great stock of information available on the internet and elsewhere. But to be able to really take advantage of information as a resource, one needs information literacy. By investigating different definitions and models of information literacy, Stock and Stock [1] identify two threads: The first focuses on skills for information retrieval. "It starts with the recognition of an information need, proceeds via the search, retrieval and evaluation of information, and leads finally to the application of information deemed positive." The second puts emphasis on skills for knowledge representation. It includes the "creation of information", "representation and storage of information" and issues of information ethics, law and privacy. No matter what definition of information literacy you look at, it becomes obvious that information literacy is a core competence for both social and economic participation in the information age. This becomes especially clear at urban level in so-called informational world cities. These "prototypical cities of the knowledge society" [2] are characterised by their "space of flows (flows of money, power, and information) [that] tend to override space of places" [2]. Compared to traditional industries, especially the creative industries and the knowledge economy take on greater significance in informational cities, which leads to a so-called job polarisation: Routine tasks that used to be done by employees are now executed by computers with increased regularity, leading

© Springer International Publishing AG, part of Springer Nature 2018
G. Chowdhury et al. (Eds.): iConference 2018, LNCS 10766, pp. 464–475, 2018.
https://doi.org/10.1007/978-3-319-78105-1_51

to the loss of jobs in the middle class. This results not only in "a gap between rich and poor" but also between "educated and uneducated people" [3] – the digital divide. To manage the flows that define informational cities, companies and public authorities, citizens must be able use technologies appropriately to search for, produce and use needed information. Here, information literacy plays a major role and enables people to participate socially and professionally, giving them an advantage at school, at work and in their everyday lives [4]. It must be said, however, that most people today never had any information literacy education. And although the importance of information literacy is widely recognised on an academic level, there is plenty of research showing "evidence that many students are information illiterate when they enter institutions of higher education." [5] Furthermore, "despite clear evidence that sophisticated information literacy skills are beneficial to academic success, students are generally unsophisticated information seekers in academic contexts." [6].

The purpose of this study is not only to assess the status of information literacy among students, but also to attempt an international comparison. By the means of a multiple-choice questionnaire, we assess the level of information literacy among university students of informational cities in Canada and Germany, allowing a comparison between the two countries for the different competence areas of information literacy. After presenting our results, it is necessary to discuss what can be learned from this approach and whether such a comparison can be beneficial to improve information literacy education or if a comparison is even possible.

Different tools to assess the state of information literacy, especially among students, already exist. The *Information Literacy Test* (ILT), developed at James Madison University, is one of them [7]. It is based on and covers four of the five aspects presented in the ALA standards [8]. The actual use of information is excluded, as it cannot be covered in a multiple-choice test. Regarding the total score, the student is classified as "below proficient" ($< 65\%$), "proficient" ($\geq 65\%$) or "advanced" ($\geq 90\%$). Smith et al. used the ILT at high-schools in Canada and revealed that 80 out of 103 students of the 12th grade were classified as "below proficient" [9]. Another method is the *Standardized Assessment of Information Literacy Skills* (SAILS) [10]. SAILS utilises eight skill sets, based on the ALA standards. Beutelspacher [11] developed another assessment tool, a multiple-choice questionnaire available for the following target groups: "7th grade", "10th grade", "high-school graduates and students", "teachers" and "scientists". It is based on 62 indicators for information literacy, divided into seven spheres of competence:

I. to identify an information need
II. to search for and find information
III. to evaluate information
IV. to use information

V. to organise information
VI. to communicate and publish information
VII. responsible handling of information

These indicators which represent a "generic list of skills which should be mastered in order to persist in a knowledge society" [11] were collected by evaluating contemporary definitions, models and standards of information literacy. It is important to note that Beutelspacher's questionnaire tests skills in information retrieval, similar to the ILT and SAILS, but also includes skills in knowledge representation. This second thread of information literacy has become more and more important and should not be missing in any assessment tool. It is the main reason this tool was chosen for our study.

2 Methods

To test information literacy skills, Beutelspacher's questionnaire version for high-school graduates and students was used. It consists of 41 different multiple-choice questions leading to positive and negative scores. As an example, question 10 of the test is shown below. A complete list of all questions and possible answers can be found in the appendix.

Question 10: If a search engine retrieves too many web pages, what should you do?

- Use advanced search.
- Only use one search engine.
- Only look at the first ten search results.
- Use the "help"-function.

- Add further search terms.
- Delete some search terms.
- I don't know.

Checking the answer "I don't know" leads to 0 points. The maximum score is 69 points. Participants are classified as "not information literate" if the total score is below 50% (34.5 points). With a total score of at least 50% they count as a "beginner". The "advanced" level starts at a total score of at least 75% (51.75 points). Our target groups were students attending universities located in informational world cities [2]. We further limited the first round of our survey to two countries: Canada and Germany. In each of those two countries, there are currently 3 cities identified as informational world cities by Mainka [12]: Montreal, Toronto, Vancouver and Berlin, Munich, Frankfurt. There are 14 universities located in those cities. An online survey (English and German) was set up and the link to the questionnaire was distributed among Facebook groups associated with those universities. Literature shows that many students are using Social Networking Sites (SNSs) on a regular basis. Facebook is one of the most popular SNSs [13], especially for students [14, 15]. We identified Facebook groups for this study by searching groups containing the university's name in its group title. Beforehand, the administrators of the groups were asked for permission. The survey link was posted in 128 different Facebook groups. The distribution started in February 2014 and ended in October 2014. Due to the long processing time of the voluntary questionnaire, a low participation rate was expected [16]. A raffle (gift cards) was added to the survey as incentive to raise the participation rate and to finish the questionnaire.

To test Beutelspacher's questionnaire in terms of internal consistency, Cronbach's Alpha (α) was calculated [17]. In addition to that, a t-test shows whether differences between the total score of Canadian and German students are significant.

3 Results

In total, 892 students participated in the survey. 291 Canadian (109 male; 175 female; 7 preferred not to say; average age: 21.3 years) and 601 German students (203 male; 398 female; average age: 23.3 years). 154 of the 291 Canadian students were based in Montreal (52.92%), 74 in Vancouver (25.43%), 63 in Toronto (21.65%). 395 of the German participants were studying in Berlin (65.72%), 151 in Frankfurt (25.12%), 55 in Munich (9.15%). Since Berlin and Montreal offer more universities than the other cities, their strong participation was predictable. Most of the participants were aiming for a bachelor degree or state examination (Canada: 83.85%; Germany 75.04%). 16.15% of the Canadian and 24.96% of the German students were in a master or PhD program at the time of the survey. Over 40 different major subjects were represented. On average, German students scored 48.62 (70.46%) and Canadian students scored 44.63 (64.68%) out of 69 points (maximum score). A significant difference between the two groups was verified ($p < 0.001$). 13.06% of the Canadian and 4.83% of the German students were judged to be "not information literate", while the greatest share of both groups (Canada: 65.64%; Germany: 56.24%) reached the "beginner"-level. Only 21.31% of Canadian and 38.94% of German participants were classified as "advanced". Table 1 in the Appendix lists all items as well as the arithmetic mean of point scores for both countries and the significance value (p) of the t-test. A significant difference ($p < 0.05$) between the results was found in 25 cases. It should be noted that an equal variance is given in items 2, 9, 10, 13, 15, 17, 19, 23, 26, 30, 33c, 37 and 38 only. All other p-values were calculated with the total score of the students.

According to the six spheres of competence tested, it is observed that German participants scored higher in every sphere (Fig. 1). Compared to the other spheres, the

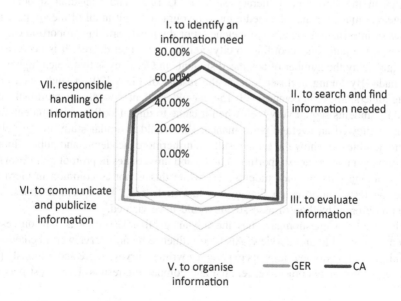

Fig. 1. Average results for each sphere of competence (Canada vs. Germany)

results of both groups in sphere V ("to organise information") are noticeably low. The distribution of information literacy skill level by gender showed that in both countries, male participants had more members in both the "advanced" and the "not information literate" category. On average, however, female participants scored slightly better. When comparing students by desired degree, it stands out that "Bachelor of Science" and "Master of Arts" students had the best results, also, no master student from Canada was classified as "not information literate". This improvement cannot be observed for German students. Here, the best results were achieved by "Master of Arts" and "Bachelor of Arts" students. Comparing Canadian and German students who aim for the same degree, significant differences could be found within the groups "Bachelor of Arts" (p ≤ 0.001), "Master of Arts" (p ≤ 0.001) and "Master of Science" (p = 0.033). An equal variance is given in each of these groups.

For all test items Cronbach's Alpha (α) was 0.814, which is an indicator for a "good" internal consistency and a "reasonable goal" [18].

4 Discussion

By means of a multiple-choice questionnaire, we are able to take a glimpse at the current status of information literacy among young citizens of informational cities in Canada and Germany. Overall, the results are in conformity with other studies assessing student's information literacy [5, 19], which means that measured information literacy levels were relatively low. The fact that students in a master program achieved noticeably better results than their colleagues aiming for a bachelor degree, indicates that students at least improve their information literacy skills during their academic career. The results of the comparison indicate that there are noticeable differences in the information literacy skills of German and Canadian students. On average, German students obtained a more favourable result in all of the six measured spheres of information literacy competence. For the most part, this proportion can also be seen in the numbers according to city, gender and target degree. It is necessary to investigate why the number of advanced students in Germany is that much higher than in Canada. By taking a closer look at the results of PISA [20], a study measuring, among others, the competences of 15-year-old students on an international scale, Canada's students scored very well when it came to digital skills, while students from Germany showed an average performance. But would a similar study in the field of information literacy show the same results? Furthermore, academic and public libraries in informational cities are supporting schools and universities in promoting information literacy among citizens and students [21] while this is not as common in Germany, where the term "information literacy" is known to few. The question arises, what results a different method of assessment would have yielded.

The use of a questionnaire has the advantage that less time and resources are needed, compared to an interview. Also, no influence by an interviewer's behaviour is possible. Additionally, participants experience written surveys more anonymously [22]. A questionnaire yields objective, reliable and comparable results. Every test person is given the same questions and answer options, which are explicitly right or wrong. Moreover, the results of this survey can be compared with future surveys of the same kind [11]. While a multiple-choice questionnaire has advantages, it is also limiting the assessment of competences, workflows and other aspects. Especially now, that the definition of information literacy is shifting from a catalogue of standards to a framework of "core ideas" [23], it might not be as easy to create questionnaires, which are able to asses this "new" definition of information literacy. In general, it is difficult to measure information literacy skills in a holistic way, since these are higher-order skills much more complex than assessible by a short questionnaire [24]. Since students were not monitored while filling in the questionnaire it is possible that participants were looking for answers with help of a search engine. Most students filled in the survey in the presumed time which leads us to believe that students were usually not using any help. However, the possibility that a student is guessing or picking any answer randomly is still given.

Although almost 900 students participated in our survey, it is not possible to draw general conclusions yet. A greater number of students — from different major subjects and faculties, and with different degrees — is needed, to get results that are more representative. Also, an equal distribution of participants from each city or university is needed, to draw a more detailed analysis. Up to now, none of these assessment tools have been used on a national range. Luckily, we may soon be able to see results of the *International Computer and Information Literacy Study* (ICILS), a computer-based international assessment and comparison of eighth-grade students' computer and information literacy [25]. These results could provide valuable information, for example on when and how to promote information literacy skills among students. Different institutions could learn from each other. If a real difference existed, what could be reasons for those? Furthermore, results could be analysed regarding correlations with programs offered by universities and libraries to promote information literacy skills. Does the availability of such programs lead to better results?

While comparing results from different countries, this is by no means seen as a competition. It is rather an opportunity to learn about differences and to teach each other. But first, to find out more about the origin of the differences in results, further information is needed. For example, personal interviews at the participating universities, not only with students but also with teaching faculty, could help us to gain further insight. We chose Canada and Germany for this study, because we deemed them to be relatively similar. But when comparing different countries, cultural differences, linguistic peculiarities, distinctions in school systems and infrastructure have to be taken into account as well. These and other factors can turn a simple comparison into a challenge. And if this challenge were mastered, we still had to ask ourselves whether our definition of information literacy is the same of our neighbours. And does it have to be?

Appendix

Table 1. Questionnaire items (1–41), average results (Canada, Germany) and p-value (t-test).

#	Question	Ø CAN	Ø GER	p
1	True or false? The first search result a search engine lists is always the best one. (*"True"*, *"False"*, *"I don't know"*) 1pt	0.928	0.958	0.077
2	True or false? All search engines give out the same results. (*"True"*, *"False"*, *"I don't know"*) 1pt	0.928	0.942	0.422
3	When researching a topic that you don't know anything about, what is the best place to start looking? (*"In a journal"*, *"In an encyclopaedia or dictionary"*, *"In a library catalogue"*, *"I don't know"*) 1pt	0.680	0.760	0.014
4	Which statement is true? (*"In an internet research you should check as many web pages as possible"*, *"You should only use a single search engine"*, *"You should compare different websites"*, *"You should only look for information that supports your personal viewpoint"*, *"I don't know"*) 2pt	1.478	1.827	<0.001
5	You have performed a search in a library catalogue and were not able to find any documents. What is the most likely reason for this? (*"The wrong search terms were used"*, *"All documents on this topic are borrowed at the moment"*, *"The system is defective"*, *"I don't know"*) 1pt	0.918	0.968	0.004
6	You must write a paper comparing schools in Germany to ones in Switzerland. Which words would you use in your web research? (*"Germany, Switzerland, Europe, Schools"*, *"Europe, Germany, Switzerland"*, *"Schools, Switzerland, Germany"*, *"Schools, Europe"*, *"I don't know"*) 1pt	0.986	0.972	0.064
7	*You must discuss a certain topic in a paper. You have already found a book on this topic. Which section of the book will you consult if you wish to find further documents on the same topic?* (*"Glossary"*, *"Table of contents"*, *"Bibliography"*, *"Index"*, *"I don't know"*) 1pt	0.777	0.684	0.003
8	You are looking for information on the social integration of foreigners, but you may not use the word "integration." Which word would you use instead? (*"Migration"*, *"Immigration"*, *"Assimilation"*, *"Foreigner"*, *"I don't know"*) 1.5pt	1.015	1.273	<0.001
9	Which two terms are synonymous? (*"Blue (colour)"* – *"Blues (music)"*, *"Tree – apple tree"*, *"Eggplant – aubergine"*, *"Dead – alive"*, *"I don't know"*) 1pt	0.869	0.887	0.451
10	Which query will retrieve more documents? (*"Dog AND cat"*, *"Dog OR cat"*, *"Both queries above will yield the same amount of results"*, *"I don't know"*) 1pt	0.601	0.576	0.465

(*continued*)

Table 1. *(continued)*

#	Question	Ø CAN	Ø GER	p
11	You would like to research the following recipe using a search engine: Cookies, either with nuts or with almonds, but definitely without cinnamon. Which of the queries below (including operators) would you use to retrieve the recipe? *("Cookies AND (nuts OR almonds) NOT cinnamon", "(Nuts OR almonds) (AND cookies NOT cinnamon)", "NOT cinnamon AND cookies (nuts OR almonds)", "Cookies AND almonds AND nuts NOT cinnamon", "I don't know")* 2pt	1.505	1.344	0.012
12	Which words are retrieved when you search for Science* in a scientific search engine or in a library catalogue with truncation? *("Science", "Scientific", "Sciences", "Scientist", "Science project", "Conscience", "I don't know")* 3pt	1.399	1.474	0.396
13	If you search for "Shores in Germany" using a search engine, which results will you get? *("All documents containing the word ,shore'", "All documents containing the word ,Germany'", "All documents whose full text contains the phrase ,shores in Germany'", "No documents", "I don't know")* 2pt	1.574	1.544	0.617
14	If a search engine retrieves too many web pages, what should you do? *("Use advanced search", "Only use one search engine", "Only look at the first ten search results", "Use the "help" function", "Add further search terms", "Delete some search terms", "I don't know")* 3pt	1.395	1.118	<0.001
15	If your library does not have a certain book, how can you borrow it anyway? *("Via inter-library loan", "By going to another library", "It's impossible", "I don't know")* 1.5pt	1.246	1.191	0.092
16	Choose a broader term, a narrower term, and a related term (in that order) for the word "tree". *("Spruce, apple, trunk", "Trunk, plant, flower", "Plant, trunk, spruce", "Spruce, flower, spruce", "Plant, spruce, flower", "I don't know")* 1pt	0.426	0.719	<0.001
17	*Which pages are in the Deep Web? ("Pages that can only be found by one search engine", "Government pages", "Pages in special databases", "All pages that can be found by Google", "I don't know")* 1pt	0.519	0.463	0.115
18	What is a meta search engine? *("A search engine that searches for other search engines", "A search engine that searches in social networks", "A search engine that searches through data from search engines", "I don't know")* 2pt	1.155	1.481	<0.001
19	To find the most up to date information, you should check: *"A printed encyclopaedia", "A book", "A newspaper", "The internet", "I don't know")* 2pt	1.543	1.484	0.112
20	Current scientific studies are first published in: *"Books", "Encyclopaedia entries", "Articles in scientific journals", "Conference papers", "I don't know")* 2pt	1.326	1.484	0.001

(continued)

Table 1. (*continued*)

#	Question	Ø CAN	Ø GER	p
21	A book's signature in a library is used... (*"to contact the author", "to find the book in the library", "to find the book online", "I don't know"*) 1pt	0.619	0.842	<0.001
22	Which books are placed side by side in a library? (*"Books by the same publisher", "Books with similar content", "Books of the same size", "Books published in the same year", "I don't know"*) 1pt	0.890	0.958	0.001
23	How can you tell whether a Wikipedia article is high quality? (*"I check whether the article has bibliographical references", "I check the comments on the article's discussion pages", "I check whether the article has a lot of pictures", "I check how long the article is", "I don't know"*) 2pt	1.251	1.448	<0.001
24	If you want to use a database, which is the best way to find out what journals it contains? (*"To perform a search and look at the results", "You don't need to know this, because all databases cover all journals", "To look on the 'help' page or in the user manual", "I don't know"*) 1pt	0.567	0.612	0.190
25	You are looking for information about the effects of air pollution on human health. Which of the listed sources is likely to be the most objective? (*"Automobile manufacturers", "Medical research institute", "Environment organization", "Energy supplier", "I don't know"*) 2pt	1.498	1.787	<0.001
26	A summary of a scientific article is found: (*"In the abstract", "In the bibliography", "In the introduction", "I don't know"*) 1pt	0.835	0.839	0.893
27	Which tags (keywords) would you use for the following image of the Brooklyn Bridge if you wanted to upload it to a photo sharing service for other users to find? (*"Bridge", "Brooklyn", "Water", "Brooklyn Bridge", "My city", "East River", "House", "New York", "Photo", "Suspension bridge", "Day", "World"*) 3pt	1.978	1.715	<0.001
28	When quoting a short sentence by another author in a homework paper, how should you label this sentence? (*"Via quotation marks "", "Via square brackets []", "Via round brackets ()", "The sentence doesn't have to be labelled", "I don't know"*) 1pt	0.921	0.960	0.028
29	When must you identify another author's text in your own work? (*"When using an entire sentence word by word", "When using an entire paragraph word by word", "When reproducing a paragraph in your own words", "When translating a sentence from another language", "I don't know"*) 4pt	3.021	3.158	0.101
30	Why is there a need for citations? (*"To prove your own statements", "To help you out when you can't think of anything", "To not pass off other people's ideas as your own", "I don't know"*) 2pt	1.237	1.629	<0.001

(*continued*)

Table 1. *(continued)*

#	Question	Ø CAN	Ø GER	p
31	Which facts must you include when using a quote from a book? *("Author's last name", "Author's year of birth", "Author's place of birth"*, "Date of publication", "ISBN", "Title", "Total number of pages", "Illustrator's last name", "Name of publisher", "Publisher's location", "I don't know")* 5pt	3.244	4.258	<0.001
32	The following is what type of publication? Knautz, K. (2012). Emotions felt and depicted. Consequences for multimedia retrieval. In D. R. Neal (Ed.), Indexing and Retrieval of Non-Text Information (pp. 343-375). Berlin, Boston, MA: De Gruyter Saur. *("Chapter in a collection", "Monograph", "Chapter in a specialized journal", "Chapter in conference proceeding", "I don't know")* 1pt	0.247	0.611	<0.001
33	Take a look at the following bibliographical reference and then answer questions a-c. Stock, W.G. (2011). Informationelle Städte im 21. Jahrhundert. Information - Wissenschaft und Praxis, 62(2), 71-94.			
33 a	What is the title of the journal? *("Stock, W.G.", "Informationelle Städte im 21. Jahrhundert", "Information – Wissenschaft und Praxis", "I don't know")* 1pt	0.536	0.639	0.004
33 b	How many pages is the article? *("60 pages", "62 pages", "24 pages", "11 pages", "2 pages", "I don't know")* 1pt	0.643	0.755	0.001
33 c	What is the volume of the above-mentioned journal? *("2", "62", "2011", "71–94", "I don't know")* 1pt	0.478	0.463	0.672
34	How do you sort your search results when looking for articles that have attracted the most attention in the scientific community? *("By citation frequency", "By author", "By date of publication", "By the length of the articles", "I don't know")* 1pt	0.770	0.822	0.075
35	What does it mean when an article has passed peer review? *("The article has been checked and corrected by friends and colleagues of the author", "The article has been checked by experts and changes have been suggested", "The article has been edited by the publisher", "I don't know")* 1pt	0.749	0.469	<0.001
36	Which of these terms describes a knowledge organization system? *("Open Access", "World Wide Web", "Classification", "Bibliography", "I don't know")* 1pt	0.436	0.517	0.023
37	Which of these programs are reference management systems? *("Citavi", "Mendeley", "Facebook", "Wikipedia", "Bibsonomy", "Twitter", "Microsoft PowerPoint", "Endnote", "I don't know")* 2pt	0.366	0.730	<0.001
38	What is meant by online netiquette? *("A set of rules for communicating with people online", "This way I allow the site's owner to use my private information", "A seal of quality for secure web pages", "I don't know")* 1pt	0.674	0.647	0.439

(continued)

Table 1. (*continued*)

#	Question	Ø CAN	Ø GER	p
39	What does it mean when a piece of information (e.g. an image) is labelled "Public Domain"? (*"The author is unknown"*, *"It is forbidden to copy it"*, *"You're allowed to copy it as often as you like"*, *"You can only copy it for private usage"*, *"I don't know"*) 1pt	0.753	0.724	0.357
40	What does it mean when the following symbol is attached to an image on the Internet? (*"The image may be used without any restrictions"*, *"The image may not be used for commercial purposes"*, *"The image may not be edited"*, *"The image may not be passed on"*, *"If the image is used, the original author's name must be stated"*, *"The image must be passed on under the same conditions"*, *"I don't know"*) 3pt	0.828	0.945	0.074
41	Do you think that web pages often appear to be adjusted to your own individual profile (e.g. ads that precisely fit your interests)? (*"Yes, I think so"*, *"No, I don't think so"*, *"I don't know"*) 1pt	0.821	0.943	<0.001

References

1. Stock, W.G., Stock, M.: Handbook of Information Science. De Gruyer, Berlin (2015)
2. Stock, W.G.: Informational cities: analysis and construction of cities in the knowledge society. J. Am. Soc. Inf. Sci. **62**(5), 963–986 (2011)
3. Dornstädter, R., Finkelmeyer, S., Shanmuganathan, N.: Job-Polarisierung in informationellen Städten. Inf. Wiss. Prax. **62**(2–3), 95–102 (2011)
4. Gust von Loh, S., Stock, W.G.: Informationskompetenz als Schulfach? In: Informationskompetenz in der Schule, pp. 1–20, De Gruyter Saur (2013)
5. Gross, M., Latham, D.: Attaining information literacy: an investigation of the relationship between skill level, self-estimates of skill, and library anxiety. Libr. Inf. Sci. Res. **29**(3), 332–353 (2007)
6. Julien, H., Barker, S.: How high-school students find and evaluate scientific information: a basis for information literacy skills development. Libr. Inf. Sci. Res. **31**(1), 12–17 (2009)
7. Cameron, L., Wise, S.L., Lottridge, S.M.: The development and validation of the information literacy test. Coll. Res. Libr. **68**(3), 229–237 (2007)
8. American Library Association: Information literacy competency standards for higher education. http://www.ala.org/acrl/sites/ala.org.acrl/files/content/standards/standards.pdf. Accessed 17 Sept 2017
9. Smith, J.K.: Information literacy proficiency: assessing the gap in high school students' readiness for undergraduate academic work. Libr. Inf. Sci. Res. **35**(2), 88–96 (2013)
10. Kent State University: Project SAILS Skill Sets. https://www.projectsails.org/SkillSets
11. Beutelspacher, L.: Erfassung von Informationskompetenz mithilfe von Multiple-Choice-Fragebogen. Inf. Wiss. Prax. **65**(6), 341–352 (2014)
12. Mainka, A.: Public libraries in the knowledge society: core services of libraries in informational world cities. Libri **63**(4), 295–319 (2013)

13. Hargittai, E.: Whose space? Differences among users and non-users of social network sites. J. Comput.-Mediat. Commun. **13**(1), 276–297 (2007)
14. Selwyn, N.: Faceworking: exploring students' education-related use of Facebook. Learn. Media Technol. **34**(2), 157–174 (2009)
15. Gray, K., Annabell, L., Kennedy, G.: Medical students' use of Facebook to support learning: insights from four case studies. Med. Teach. **32**(12), 971–976 (2010)
16. Bogen, K.: The effect of questionnaire length on response rates: a review of the literature. In: Proceedings of the Section on Survey Research Methods, Alexandria, VA, pp. 1020–1025. American Statistical Association (1996)
17. Cronbach, L.J.: Coefficient alpha and the internal structure of tests. Psychometrika **16**(3), 297–334 (1951)
18. Gliem, J.A., Gliem, R.R.: Calculating, interpreting, and reporting Cronbach's alpha reliability coefficient for Likert-type scales. In: Midwest Research to Practice Conference in Adult, Continuing, and Community Education, Columbus, OH, pp. 82–88. The Ohio State University (2003)
19. Beutelspacher, L., Dreisiebner, S., Henkel, M.: Informationskompetenz – Forschung in Graz und Düsseldorf. Inf. Wiss. Prax. (in press)
20. PISA (2012). http://www.compareyourcountry.org/pisa-digital?cr=oecd&lg=en&page=1&visited=1. Accessed 17 Sept 2017
21. Henkel, M.: Educators of the information society: information literacy instruction in public and academic libraries of Canada. In: Proceedings of the 78th ASIS&T Annual Meeting, St. Louis, Missouri (2015)
22. Bortz, J., Döring, N.: Forschungsmethoden und Evaluation: Für Human- und Sozialwissenschaftler. Springer, Heidelberg (2006). https://doi.org/10.1007/978-3-540-33306-7
23. American Library Association: Framework for Information Literacy for Higher Education (2015). http://www.ala.org/acrl/standards/ilframework. Accessed 17 Sept 2017
24. Beutelspacher, L., Henkel, M., Schlögl, C.: Evaluating an information literacy assessment instrument. The case of a bachelor course in business administration. In: Proceedings of the 14th International Symposium on Information Science, pp. 482–491. Verlag Werner Hülsbusch, Glückstadt (2015)
25. International Computer and Information Literacy Study. https://icils.acer.org/. Accessed 17 Sept 2017

Information Encountering on Social Q&A Sites: A Diary Study of the Process

Tingting Jiang[1,2(✉)] , Chaojian Zhang[1] , Zhezhe Li[1] ,
Chang Fan[1] , and Jiaqi Yang[1]

[1] School of Information Management, Wuhan University, Wuhan, Hubei, China
tij@whu.edu.cn
[2] Center for Studies of Information Resources, Wuhan University, Wuhan,
Hubei, China

Abstract. Social Q&A sites, which enable information seeking through the direct interaction between human askers and answerers, demonstrate the environmental characteristics that conduce to information encountering (IE). The purpose of this study is to reveal how IE occurs in this specific context. A diary study based on the critical incident technique (CIT) was conducted, and 108 IE incidents were collected from 83 users of Zhihu, a representative social Q&A site. The diary questionnaire was developed according to three existing general IE process models. The content analysis of these incidents engendered a context-specific model in which the micro-process of IE consists of noticing a stimulus, (stopping), examining the content, and capturing information, and is extended by including both the foreground and follow-up activities. This study not only enriches the understanding of human information behavior, but also provides useful implications for the design of social Q&A sites. The successful attempt to introduce CIT-based diary study to IE research also shows methodological significance.

Keywords: Information encountering · Social Q&A sites · Diary study
Process model

1 Introduction

It has been widely recognized that when people are looking for information relating to one topic, they may accidentally discover useful or interesting information relating to another topic. That is, low or no involvement and low or no expectation can also result in the acquisition of information [1]. Such phenomenon is known as information encountering (IE). Nowadays, the overload of information and the abundance of ways to access information make IE unavoidable and ubiquitous [2]. Despite decades of research efforts to conceptualize, model, and interpret IE, there still lack context-specific studies which are able to engender more practical implications for developing IE friendly environments.

Social question and answer (Q&A) sites, such as Quora and Zhihu, essentially support a questioning-based information seeking process in which users pose their information needs as questions in natural language to a community and receive targeted

© Springer International Publishing AG, part of Springer Nature 2018
G. Chowdhury et al. (Eds.): iConference 2018, LNCS 10766, pp. 476–486, 2018.
https://doi.org/10.1007/978-3-319-78105-1_52

answers from peer users who are willing to share their knowledge [3]. Often, social Q&A sites categorize questions into topics and allow commenting on answers to ensure objectivity and quality [4]. As typical social media, they provide a vigorous environment where pivotal navigation is enabled among various elements, including questions, answers, users, topics, and comments, etc. [5].

It's interesting to notice that social Q&A sites demonstrate the environmental characteristics that may facilitate the occurring of IE, such as enabling exploration, trigger-rich, highlighting triggers, enabling connections, and leading to the unexpected [6]. However, the phenomenon of IE has been basically ignored in the existing literature on social Q&A. To fill the gap of research, this study aims to reveal how people encounter information in this particular context. Real users' IE experiences on social Q&A sites were collected through a diary study combined with the critical incident technique (CIT), and a context-specific IE process model was established based on both qualitative and quantitative analysis of the incidents.

2 Literature Review

2.1 IE Process Models

A number of models have been created to describe the process of serendipity or IE. McCay-Peet and Toms's [7] model of serendipity process embodies the following components: search for solution to Task A, precipitating conditions, a bisociation between previously unconnected pieces of information, a trigger that activates the bisociation, unexpected solutions to both Tasks A and B. Recently, they consolidated several previous models into a new one that consists of trigger, connection, follow-up, valuable outcome, unexpected thread, and perception of serendipity. In particular, the trigger is "a verbal, textual, or visual cue that initiates or sparks an individual's experience of serendipity" [8].

Existing IE process models place an emphasis on users' behavioral characteristics that are observable. Erdelez [9] indicated that IE is embedded within a high-level process of information seeking. A typical IE episode contains five steps, i.e. noticing, stopping, examining, capturing, and returning. A further development is the integrated model of online IE which provides a global view of the three phases respectively accommodating the pre-, mid-, and post-activities of IE. Specifically, IE may happen during online browsing, searching, or social interaction; the acquisition of interesting/useful information is preceded by noticing an information stimulus and examining the content; and the encountered information may be explored further, used immediately, saved, and/or shared. The stimulus, which can be identified and consumed within an instant, is a navigational representation of the content [10].

The above models have laid a solid theoretical foundation for IE research. Nevertheless, the environment has an important impact on what users will do by defining what they can do. As IE research evolves, context-specific models are needed to reflect more accurately the subdivisions of the field.

2.2   IE on Social Media

Thanks to the broad coverage of topics, natural style of human-to-human querying, and enriched means of participation and interaction, social Q&A sites are gaining popularity among information seekers [4]. Previous related studies can be categorized into two major streams: content-centered and user-centered [11].

Despite the ignorance of the IE phenomenon on social Q&A, IE researchers have considered the more general context of social media. In Dantonio et al. [12], interviewees reported that they had come across content serendipitously when undertaking unfocused browsing on academic social media. Panahi et al. [13] found through the interview of physicians that social media supports IE in six ways including publicizing, dissemination, personalization, keeping up to date, documentation, and retrieving.

Users might share their everyday life serendipity experiences on blogging or microblogging services. For examples, Rubin et al. [14] retrieved naturally occurring accounts of chance encounters from GoogleBlog, Bogers and Björneborn [15] crawled a large quantity of tweets containing the word "serendipity" on Twitter, and Tsai [16] used selected tweets to stimulate IE on Twitter in the laboratory setting. In addition, microblogging provides context for the discussion of serendipitous learning which occurs in browsing through the stream of social updates [17].

Millions of questions and answers have been accumulated on mature social Q&A sites and they are usually searchable with internal search tools and browsable by topical classifications. User ratings and comments are aggregated to rank and recommend popular questions, best answers, and active users. The high visibility and accessibility of available content increases greatly the chance of IE. This study is interested in how IE occur on social Q&A sites.

3   Methods

3.1   Research Setting

This study chose Zhihu (http://www.zhihu.com/), the most influential Chinese-language social Q&A site, as the research setting. It has attracted 65 million registered users, including 18.5 million daily active users. In 2016, there were more than 6 million questions posted to the site and engendering 23.33 million answers. Zhihu was chosen not only for its prevalence, but also for its representativeness as an IE-prone environment that provides various triggers.

Zhihu consists of three basic page categories, i.e. Q&A pages, topic pages, and user pages. Q&A pages display questions and their affiliated answers and comments with the users who ask, answer, or comment. Comments may be made on questions and/or answers. One can also find system-recommended related questions and user-created collections of questions on Q&A pages. Topic pages exist mainly for navigational purposes, allowing users to browse for questions within a loosely structured multi-level hierarchy. Topics are actually the system-supplied tags (e.g. "art" and "health") that askers select to describe the questions upon submission. Finally, user pages show users' profiles and their activities on the site, such as asking, answering, sharing, following, collecting, and so on. It should be mentioned that Zhihu has especially introduced a column where users can contribute thematic articles.

3.2 Data Collection

The CIT has been widely employed to capture people's experiences and perceptions in IE research. It "outlines procedures for collecting observed incidents having special significance and meeting systematically defined criteria" [18]. It is common that the CIT was applied in interviews, but the integrity and accuracy of the descriptions provided by the interviewees may be affected by their abilities to retrieve the incidents from memory. Also importantly, the quantity of the IE incidents collected through time-consuming and cost-intensive interviews may be very limited, varying from 20 to 30 incidents per study.

This study instead combined the CIT with diaries for data collection. Diary studies ask participants to record the event of interest as soon as it happens, especially suitable for capturing easily changeable and indiscernible information. Diaries are also superior to interviews in terms of both sample representativeness and size due to the absence of geographic restrictions [19]. Participants were recruited via multiple channels with small incentives. They needed to complete an online questionnaire (https://sojump. com/jq/13713854.aspx) as soon as they encountered information on Zhihu.

The questionnaire divides into three parts. The first part (Q1) begins with a brief description of IE according to Erdelez's [1] definition of the concept. Also provided are a couple of real-world examples of IE incidents, and the participants are invited to give an account of their own IE incidents on Zhihu similarly. Such free-style narration may include unexpected interesting facts about their IE experiences, but it may also be lack of desirable details. So the second part (Q2–Q17) asks a series of questions that help the participants recall and think their experiences in terms of smaller components. These questions were created and arranged based mainly on the models by Erdelez [1], Jiang et al. [10], and McCay-Peet and Toms [8] as mentioned above. This part will be described in more details in the next section. The last part (Q18–Q22) of the questionnaire collects the participants' background information.

3.3 Data Analysis

The CIT-based diary study was conducted between July 28th and August 14th, 2016. A total of 163 IE incidents were collected, but 55 eliminated for containing contradicting and/or inaccurate information. The remaining 108 incidents were contributed by 83 participants as one might submit multiple responses over the time. The top participant contributed 7 incidents while the majority only one. The narrative descriptions of the IE incidents were analyzed in combination with the answers provided for the questions in the second part that can be divided into 6 major sections:

- Q2 to Q4 were created based on the pre-activities phase in Jiang et al.'s [10] model, including the type of the foreground activity, its urgency, and the participant's emotional state;

- The inclusion of Q5 to Q8 reflects the importance of a trigger [8] or a stimulus [10] that diverts people's attention from the foreground activity. Q5 and Q7 ask respectively about the noticing and stopping steps in Erdelez's [9] model, with Q6 and Q8 eliciting the reasons behind the actions;
- The examining of the content associated with the trigger or stimulus considered in all three models is explored through Q9 to Q12, including the specific content examined as well as its relevance to the foreground activity and value type and level;
- Q13 focuses on the capturing step in Erdelez's [9] model or the post-activities phase in Jiang et al.'s [10] model, i.e. how one deals with the encountered information;
- Q14 focuses on the returning step in Erdelez's [9] model, i.e. what one does after IE;
- Q15 and Q16 collect one's overall IE frequency and attitude.

Such division enabled a natural framework for the content analysis of the 108 valid IE incidents collected in this study. The qualitative data analysis tool NVivo 10 was employed to perform the analysis. The written texts exported from each response were unitized according to the above sections, and concepts were extracted and categorized section by section. In addition, the statistical analysis software package SPSS was employed to perform independent-samples T tests and correlation analysis.

4 Results

In general, the 83 participants of the diary study were well-educated young people (pursuing bachelor's or master's degree, N = 74, 89.16%) aged between 19 and 25 (N = 68, 81.93%), with female (N = 47, 56.63%) slightly more than male (N = 36, 43.37%). 81.93% (N = 68) of them were familiar with Zhihu (4 points and above). Their information seeking on this social Q&A site featured keyword searching (N = 77, 92.77%), monitoring followed sources (N = 68, 81.93%), and browsing popular (N = 55, 66.27%) and personalized recommendations (N = 52, 62.65%), while direct question asking (N = 28, 33.73%) and topic classification browsing (N = 17, 20.48%) not so frequently seen. Based on their frequencies of IE on Zhihu, "encounterers" (4–5 points) dominated (N = 46, 55.42%), followed by "occasional encounterers" (1–3 points, N = 28, 33.73%) and "super encounterers" (6–7 points, N = 9, 10.84%). The majority (N = 75, 90.36%) had a positive attitude toward IE (4 points and above).

4.1 Foreground Activities

Foreground activities are the activities that people intentionally or consciously get themselves involved in (Q2). All of the above mentioned information seeking activities were found to have provided context for IE to occur on Zhihu, and they basically divide into:

- **Purposeless scanning** (N = 46, 42.59%) usually involves no specific need or goal. When visiting Zhihu as a daily habit or pastime during their spare time, the participants tended to browse popular or personalized recommendations provided on the homepage.
- **Purposeful searching/browsing** (N = 43, 39.81%) is a goal-driven activity that may in turn belongs to a higher-level task. Some participants would distinguish "searching" from "browsing", while others used the general term "looking for".
- **Monitoring** (N = 19, 17.59%) refers to following a topic, a question, or a user of interest to obtain updates. Most related incidents explicitly indicated a source that had been identified at an earlier time and checking for updates from the source regularly.

When engaged in the foreground activities, the participants in general were in a relatively positive emotional state (Q3, M = 4.72) and felt the activities not so urgent (Q4, M = 2.88). Independent-samples T tests were performed to find significant differences between searching/browsing and scanning for both emotional state (t = 2.088, p = .04) and urgency level (t = 2.771, p = .007). And the participants' emotional state in monitoring is significantly more positive than that in scanning (t = 3.228, p = .002).

4.2 Noticing and Stopping

Embedded in the above foreground activities are various information stimuli from the basic elements of Zhihu. If the stimuli are not components of the foreground activities or closely related, users need to stop the foreground activities, probably temporarily, so as to deal with the stimuli, which initiates the process of IE [9]. The information stimuli involved in the IE incidents (Q5) present themselves in different formats:

- **Texts** (N = 95, 87.96%) are words, phrases, and short sentences that convey linguistic meanings. Such stimuli might appear in question titles and descriptions (N = 40), answers (N = 34), topic tags and descriptions (N = 11), column articles (N = 7), user profiles (N = 2), and comments (N = 1).
- **Images** (N = 22, 20.37%) as stimuli took two primary forms: affiliated pictures (N = 15) which were inserted into answers, question descriptions, or column articles to support surrounding texts, and avatars or icons (N = 7) used to recognize specific users or topics.
- **Numbers** (N = 15, 13.89%) refer to the frequencies the questions, answers, topics, users, and articles being liked, followed, and/or commented. Zhihu keeps track of the liking, following, and commenting activities and generates total counts to imply popularity. High popularity tended to attract special attention.

Nevertheless, in some uncommon situations an information stimulus is not a necessity. For examples, participants P51, P54, and P57 reported that they clicked on some random links by mistake but opened pages that happened to contain desirable information. These situations should be deemed pure chance.

The participants were attracted by the stimuli for two major reasons (Q6). First, the stimuli were perceived to be interesting (N = 71, 65.74%): they might evoke curiosity through novelty or engender resonation through commonness. Second, the stimuli were perceived to be useful (N = 37, 34.26%): they might be connected to existing problems in one's life or work or one's current feelings that needed adjustment.

Stopping the foreground activities is a reaction to the stimuli. The stopping act may last for a very short time before the next tangible act, i.e. clicking. According to the responses to Q7, the participants clicked on the stimuli immediately in most incidents (N = 83, 76.85%), while clicking on the stimuli after a moment is much less frequent (N = 25, 23.15%).

Q8 elicits the reasons for the difference in stopping durations. Immediate clicking was explained in multiple ways: Zhihu was highly trusted for its secure environment and high-quality information; the value of the stimuli was easy to recognize; and the stimuli helped escape from the fatigue of prolonged purposeful searching/browsing or the boredom of prolonged purposeless scanning. In contrast, deferred clicking allowed time for the participants to think so that they could search in their memory for existing problems to which the stimuli were relevant. It is also possible that they hesitated to click for fear of hindering the foreground activities or just because the value of the stimuli was doubtful.

4.3 Examining

Upon accessing the information content that a stimulus represents and is usually hyperlinked to, one may examine it through various mental actions in order to determine the relevance, quality, and value of the content. This study found by analyzing the responses to Q9 that all basic elements of Zhihu had been examined as content encountered:

- **Answers** (N = 91, 84.26%). The commonest stimulus-content pair is question-answer (N = 40). The participants tended to be attracted by question titles or descriptions and then examined the affiliated answers. Also frequently seen is the answer-answer pair (N = 35).
- **Questions** (N = 31, 28.70%). The top pairs in this category include answer-question (N = 13), topic-question (N = 8), and question-question (N = 5). The descriptions of questions would be examined in more detail in response to the stimuli from their answers, topics, or related questions.
- **Users** (N = 30, 27.78%). Once a question or an answer caught one's attention, it was naturally desirable to know more about its contributor, thus resulting in examining his or her profile and activities.
- **Topics** (N = 26, 24.07%). As questions and answers are typical semantic objects, another inclination after noticing a question or an answer was to examine the descriptions of the topics to which it had been assigned to.
- **Other** (N = 12, 11.11%). This mainly refers to examining the content of a column article as preceded by noticing the title or the number of likes of the article.
- **Comments** (N = 10, 9.26%). The examination of comments usually resulted from the noticing of questions or answers.

The participants thought the above information content not so relevant to their foreground activities (Q10, M = 3.86), suggesting that the incidents provided basically met the unexpectedness criterion of IE. Significant difference was found between searching/browsing and scanning in terms of relevance (t = 2.277, p = .025). This is understandable because the relevance was evaluated against purpose and the weaker the purpose, the lower the relevance.

The value of the content (Q11) consists either in its usefulness in helping solve a problem or in its interestingness to satisfy curiosity, each explaining half of the incidents (N = 54, 50.00%). The value of the content was evaluated to be high (Q12, M = 5.30), with the value scored 4 points and above in the vast majority of the incidents (N = 103, 95.37%). And the interesting content demonstrated significant higher value than the useful content (t = 2.072, p = .008). Furthermore, content value is positively related to the relevance to foreground activities, but only moderately (r = .317, p = .001).

4.4 Capturing

Zhihu is a well-established social Q&A site, and it enables users to capture encountered information in the following modes by providing corresponding functionalities (Q13):

- **Collecting** (N = 71, 65.74%) is the most popular way of capturing. Most participants (N = 65) collected encountered answers or column articles to their Zhihu Favorites, while a few (N = 6) bookmarked the pages as the medium carrying any encountered content in Web browsers.
- **Exploring** (N = 47, 43.52%) can be considered as extended efforts to enhance the examination of the content. The participants proceeded to exploration in order to understand the content more deeply.
- **Sharing** (N = 41, 37.96%) encountered answers, question, topic and column articles to the social networking service WeChat or the microblogging service Sina Weibo as supported directly by Zhihu (N = 15). Other content was shared by sending the page URLs via Web browser functions (N = 13). However, the channels and/or targets of sharing were not specified in the remaining incidents.
- **Using** (N = 29, 26.85%) is applying immediately the encountered information to satisfy existing needs or personal interests.
- **Saving** (N = 12, 11.11%) the desirable content as texts or screenshots to the local disks on computers (N = 1) and cell phones (N = 1), online cloud storage (N = 1), or other unspecified places (N = 9).
- **Following** (N = 7, 6.48%) refers to monitoring a source for updates.

As the total frequency of the above modes of capturing exceeds 108, some participants actually adopted multiple modes in the same incident. Combining two modes is the commonest (N = 62, 57.41%), and the most frequent combinations are "collecting + exploring" (N = 13, 12.04%) and "collecting + sharing" (N = 11, 10.19%). Since no significant difference was found among different modes or mode combinations for the value type (useful/interesting) or level (from low to high) of the encountered information, the adoption of capturing modes should be attributed basically to user habits or preferences.

4.5   Follow-Up Activities

Erdelez [20] deemed it natural that people would return to the "initial information seeking task", i.e. the foreground activity, after IE. This study, however, identified more possibilities for the follow-up activities (Q14):

- **Terminating** (N = 63, 58.33%) refers to ending IE and also abandoning the original foreground activity.
- **Returning** (N = 27, 25.00%) is reconnecting with the foreground activity.
- **Probing** (N = 18, 16.67%) is a follow-up activity that deserves special attention in spite of its lower frequency. Following the cues that appeared in the IE process, one might initiate information seeking in new directions, with the original foreground activity continuing to stay in the background.

Again, there exists no significant difference in value type or level among the three follow-up activities.

5   Discussion and Conclusions

5.1   Research Methods in IE Research

This study developed a CIT-based diary questionnaire to add structure to users' recording of their IE experience. Obviously, the quantity of incidents collected in this study far exceeded those in other IE studies employing interviews. The increased sample size resulted in the abundance of data, which made it easier to detect trends. More importantly, the combination of free-style narration of IE incidents and targeted questions addressing each basic incident components did conduce to data complete-ness, allowing complementation and verification between user-concerned and researcher-concerned details. Grounded on the common steps or phases in established models, the questions in the second section of the questionnaire are mostly directly applicable to the research of IE in other contexts. However, a special observation is that when one participant contributed four or more incidents, these incidents tended to be similar. Hence the distribution of the questionnaire should be as wide as possible to avoid such bias. Also, since the questionnaire requires text input that is time-consuming, appropriate incentives are necessary to encourage participation.

5.2   Design Implications for Social Q&A Sites

An IE process model (Fig. 1) emerged from the above phased analysis. This context-specific model suggests that social Q&A sites have reshaped the IE process. The facilitation of IE is reflected in the greater variety of foreground activities and capturing modes, and the differences in follow-up activities reveal the multifold roles of IE to users.

This study differentiated purposeless scanning and purposeful browsing as fore-ground activities of IE. The latter often involves a need or goal and relies on systematic

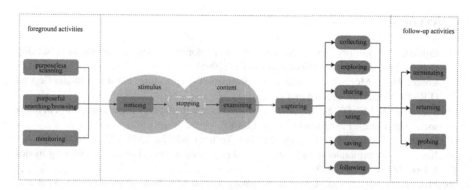

Fig. 1. A model of the IE process on social Q&A sites

strategies of relevance recognition. In addition, monitoring was for the first time identified as a type of foreground activity as popularized by the convenience of following various elements (i.e. topics, questions, and users) on social Q&A sites. One actually specifies a direction of information seeking when establishing a source of monitoring since the topic or question followed is associated with a theme and the user an interest. Although it is difficult to control the occurrence of IE in purposeless scanning that is near random, stimuli can be intentionally embedded into or reduced from other information seeking activities to induce (e.g. providing associative query suggestions in searching) or prevent (e.g. simplifying source presentation in monitoring) IE as needed.

"Capturing" in the IE process originally refers to "the extraction and saving of the encountered information for future use" [20]. As found in this study, even more modes were enabled and adopted which realized personal information management and collaboration. Given the prevalence of collecting for future use, however, social Q&A sites need consider how to revitalize the encountered information in storage and help users utilize it at a later time. Or more powerful support should be provided to encourage the immediate using of encountered information that can be easily forgotten.

Previous studies mostly neglected the activities that happen after the encountered information is captured. On social Q&A sites, the original information seeking could be totally overwhelmed by the occurrence of IE. The actual reasons behind different follow-up activities are worth further exploration. It is important to realize that the value of IE should not be achieved at the cost of jeopardizing the main information seeking task. As returning is not natural, the system should consider providing reminders and/or shortcuts that help users return to what they originally come for.

Acknowledgement. This research has been made possible through the financial support of the National Natural Science Foundation of China under Grants No. 71774125 and No. 71420107026.

References

1. Erdelez, S.: Information encountering: an exploration beyond information seeking. Dissertations, School of Information Studies (1995)
2. Rosenfeld, L., Morville, P., Arango, J.: Information Architecture: For the Web and Beyond. O'Reilly Media Inc., Sebastopol (2015)
3. Shah, C., Oh, J.S., Oh, S.: Exploring characteristics and effects of user participation in online social Q&A sites. First Monday 13(9) (2008)
4. Gazan, R.: Social Q&A. J. Assoc. Inf. Sci. Technol. 62(12), 2301–2312 (2011)
5. Jiang, T.: An exploratory study on social library system users' information seeking modes. J. Doc. 69(1), 6–26 (2013)
6. McCay-Peet, L., Toms, E.G.: Investigating serendipity: how it unfolds and what may influence it. J. Assoc. Inf. Sci. Technol. 66(7), 1463–1476 (2015)
7. McCay-Peet, L., Toms, E.G.: The process of serendipity in knowledge work. In: Proceedings of the Third Symposium on Information Interaction in Context, pp. 377–382. ACM, New York (2010)
8. Mccay-Peet, L., Toms, E.G., Kelloway, E.K.: Examination of relationships among serendipity, the environment, and individual differences. Inf. Process. Manag. Int. J. 51(4), 391–412 (2015)
9. Erdelez, S.: Towards understanding information encountering on the web. In: Proceedings of the ASIS Annual Meeting, vol. 37, pp. 363–371. Knowledge Industry Publications for the American Society for Information Science, New York (2000)
10. Jiang, T., Liu, F., Chi, Y.: Online information encountering: modeling the process and influencing factors. J. Doc. 71(6), 1135–1157 (2015)
11. Shah, C., Oh, S., Oh, J.S.: Research agenda for social Q&A. Libr. Inf. Sci. Res. 31(4), 205–209 (2009)
12. Dantonio, L., Makri, S., Blandford, A.: Coming across academic social media content serendipitously. Proc. Am. Soc. Inf. Sci. Technol. 49(1), 1–10 (2012)
13. Panahi, S., Watson, J., Partridge, H.: Information encountering on social media and tacit knowledge sharing. J. Inf. Sci. 42(4), 539–550 (2016)
14. Rubin, V.L., Burkell, J., Quan-Haase, A.: Facets of serendipity in everyday chance encounters: a grounded theory approach to blog analysis. Inf. Res. 16(3) (2011)
15. Bogers, T., Björneborn, L.: Micro-serendipity: meaningful coincidences in everyday life shared on Twitter. In: iConference 2013, pp. 196–208 (2013)
16. Tsai, C.H.: Serendipity and search a study of browsing behaviour on social network stream. M.A. thesis. University of Nottingham, Nottingham (2013)
17. Buchem, I.: Serendipitous learning: recognizing and fostering the potential of microblogging. Form@ re-Open J. per la formazione in rete 11(74), 7–16 (2011)
18. Flanagan, J.C.: The critical incident technique. Psychol. Bull. 51(4), 327 (1954)
19. Alaszewski, A.: Using Diaries for Social Research. SAGE Publications, New York (2006)
20. Erdelez, S.: Investigation of information encountering in the controlled research environment. Inf. Process. Manage. 40(6), 1013–1025 (2004)

From Accessibility to Assess-Ability:
An Evaluation Heuristic Based on Cognitive
Engagement in Search

Frances Johnson(✉)

Department of Languages, Information & Communications,
Manchester Metropolitan University, Manchester, UK
F.Johnson@mmu.ac.uk

Abstract. This investigation into information searching behaviour focuses on the users' critical assessment of information when found in response to an information need, and on the cognitive aspects of search involving in the user in the assimilation of the information found. The meta analysis of a questionnaire based survey seeks to identify the constructs of the users' assessment of information. Factor analysis of the participants' responses identifies the assessment of the 'cognitive relevance' as vital in distinguishing the searcher who appears to be intent on finding information as opposed to one engaged in the relatively simple task of looking up information. The value in the development of the questionnaire designed to identify the users' cognitive engagement in search is considered for testing the interface designed to optimize the user's involvement in search. Turning to the question of the design of the interface itself, the heuristic of assess-ability (of the information retrieved) is proposed for use in the expert review of the search interface, and to support the user in their critical assessment and verification of the information relevancy, quality and credibility.

Keywords: Search behaviour · Information credibility · Usability

1 Introduction

As Wilson et al. [1] stated in the introduction to their monograph 'From keyword search to exploration: designing future search interfaces for the web", the techniques for retrieving and visualising search results has been well researched and "[are] usually remarkably effective". However they continue to suggest that "recent work has shown that there is substantial room for improving the support provided to users who are exhibiting more exploratory forms of search, including when users may need to learn, discover, and understand novel or complex topics". Current interfaces designed to help the user query, formulate complex search expressions, navigate taxonomies and drill down using facets are indeed remarkably effective and the developments that may define potential future user search interfaces, using technologies from gesture to voice to mind control, chatbots and augmented reality look set to be transformative in the way we interact with search systems to find, learn and discover.

© Springer International Publishing AG, part of Springer Nature 2018
G. Chowdhury et al. (Eds.): iConference 2018, LNCS 10766, pp. 487–497, 2018.
https://doi.org/10.1007/978-3-319-78105-1_53

In research and development, design and evaluation go hand in hand and with developments in design we need metrics to indicate success. One approach is to set up an information retrieval experiment and measure the performance of search technology in terms of the recall and precision of the search results. However as developments focus on the user, interface and interactivity, approaches to evaluation have developed to take into consideration the complexity of the search processes and to base measures of success in terms of what a successful search might mean to the user. The aim being to design for usability and for the quality of the experience, that is user centered design.

In this investigation into information searching behavior, specifically the users' critical evaluation of information in response to an information need, we aim to identify and characterize the users' involvement in the cognitive aspects of search as they learn about the information sought and assimilate the information found. The searchers' involvement in some critical evaluation of information retrieved is crucial [2] as it is assumed to have a vital role in the assimilation of the information found and in the learning that occurs in the process of searching for information. With regards to an 'anomalous state of knowledge' [3] it is thought that this helps shift the searcher from an uncertain exploratory state to one where the information need is (ideally) clearly defined. The aim of this investigation is to work towards developing a framework for the heuristic based evaluation of the interface designed to optimize users' core activities in search and discovery. This seeks to complement the use of existing and well known heuristics in interface design and metrics to gauge user satisfaction and engagement. The framework proposed is based on key questions the user might ask when searching – such as 'has the retrieval engine worked?', 'is the information retrieved relevant?', 'is the information credible?', 'has my query worked?', 'what have I learnt'? 'what else do I need to know?', and overall, to evaluate the assess-ability of the information retrieved and presented at the interface. This critical approach which leads the user to actively search for information, *with intention*, assessing both the information retrieved and the interface supporting this activity is arguably a vital literacy necessary for instances of search where the user (with the information need) is bought back into decision making, and for a better experience of searching with current search technologies.

The study on which the new evaluation heuristic is proposed is outlined following a brief background review into past research into users' search behaviour. This is a large body of literature and, as such, is a highly selective look at the cognitive aspects to search, posing the questions: how do we evaluate information found online, what role does this assessment have in the search for information and what are the key influencing factors of the judgments formed? The study itself is questionnaire based and required the participants to respond to a bank of statements relating to their assessment of the information found for given tasks. This involved users making an assessment of the information usefulness that, when made in the dependency state of the searcher and their quest for information, may result in learning and cognitive shifts with respect to searchers' knowledge state. Through factor analysis of the participants' responses, the constructs in a possible model of the user's evaluation of information identifies the assessment of the 'cognitive relevance', the judgment of the information in relation to the individual's knowledge and goals, as critical for the development of the proposed interface evaluation of assess-ability.

2 Interactive Search Behaviour

The traditional framework for the study of search behaviour depicts the process of search as a series of steps with a goal driven information task. An assessment of relevance would be made to end the search, or to provide feedback in tasks requiring interactivity. The more innovative conceptual frameworks (such as foraging [4]) suggest an unravelling of this process with the view of a planned outcome dismissed in favor of an evolving and adaptive process. Here the path is not a straight trajectory but a process of learning and thus an evolving search. The searcher gathers and interacts with the information creating a personal perspective and learning as the search progresses. This shift in the view of search is conceptualized in models that recognize a user's anomalous state of knowledge and interactions with the information encountered. Toms [5] explains search has become more an 'immersion in a body of information'.

The shift in the concept of search can also be suggested in the development of the search interface. The relationship of the user, information and search as discussed in [6] and with regards to early interface designs, reviewed in [7] focus on the searcher in learning how to search or, more precisely, learning how to query on the index. Experimental visual interfaces for example, that show the impact of formulating the query with Boolean operations, or the visualization of the frequency of the query terms in the retrieved results, arguably invite the searcher to think about and learn how best to formulate the query to match against the system's index. Furthermore user studies of the searcher, in formulating the query and controlling the search as an effective series of moves (e.g., in [8]), are by and large based on an assumption that the searcher has a good idea of the target information sought and is learning how to best ask for the information. In comparison, the modern search interface, with for example visuals of clusters of extracted terms, appear better suited to the conceptualisation of search as exploration as the searcher evaluates the information retrieved and assimilates this information with respect to their current knowledge state. Supporting the users' exploration the interface design ultimately is for the searcher to experience 'flow' [7] again suggesting a subtle shift in the concept of search in the interface design supporting the searcher in learning how to search, for example how to submit the query, to inviting the searcher to learn from the information retrieved so as to continue the query. In this view of search as learning, the users' critical evaluation of information has a vital role.

An effective retrieval system is one which performs, both in terms of providing and facilitating access. The interest in the user and their interactions shifts the evaluation from that of system performance to questions on and around how well the interface supports the user in this task-directed goal of finding information. That is, to ask the questions, how usable and how useful are the interface features and their design? According to the definition of usability provided by the ISO standard (9241, 1994) we should be designing the system with respect to "the effectiveness, efficiency, and satisfaction with which specified users achieve specified goals" and further assess usability as a "measure of the quality of a user's experience when interacting with a service or resource" [9]. To obtain a user evaluation we can measure 'task success on finding items on a subject, along with other measures such as the user's perception of satisfaction. Usability heuristics may also be deployed both in the design and in the evaluation of the interface optimized to assist users in accomplishing the task. Thus evaluation metrics have an important role in user centered design. For example, [10] found significant effect of visually appealing interfaces on performance including completion time, and that there is positive correlation between the interface design and interest levels when searching for complex search tasks or self-chosen tasks [11]. Central to Human Computer Interaction is the maxim that the interface itself should disappear from the user's focus so that they concentrate only on the task in hand. For this, arguably design needs to go beyond usability assessment and evaluate the enabling of the search process taking into consideration the complexity of the users' interactions, both behavioural and cognitive. That is, the evaluation of the user experience demands an understanding of the search processes. One in which the user endeavors to- *find the query terms, - formulate search expressions, - refine the search based on feedback, - spot relevant items, - decide what to do next - compare information retrieved* and, - *attempt to ensure that relevant information is not overlooked.* Once we begin to think about what a successful search might mean to the user we can identify the design (and the evaluation) to support user-information interaction in search.

2.1   Research Questions

This study investigates users' interactions with information when involved in its critical evaluation conducted in a dependency context between user and the information. Broadly speaking the questions posed are, what do we think when engaged in the critical evaluation of the information found online, on what criteria do we assess the information and what might be the factors influencing the judgments formed? Thus, following Toms [5], the intention is to focus on the cognitive activity of search. The core criteria in evaluating information retrieved in a search context is relevance, an assessment of the topic match between the query and the information retrieved. Previous researchers have distinguished 'topical' relevance from 'situational' relevance that relates to the perceived utility of the document to the users' real situation or task in hand [12] and that may have a prerequisite judgment of 'cognitive' relevance, that the document is understandable and informative given the users' current state of knowledge. It is therefore assumed that formation of cognitive relevance judgments are critical activities in conducting an effective and dynamic search. The study, asks how searchers, in evaluating the information, form a personal perspective on the information and the factors that can influence this judgment. This insight is sought to inform interface design perceived to be supportive of the users' cognitive behaviour in carrying out the search.

3   Factoring the Constructs of Relevance Judgments

The aim of the study was to obtain a characterisation of participants' interactions with the retrieved results from two assigned search tasks. The participants were 102 students from Information related courses at a UK university. The task to find information was set as an exercise to be completed for the following week's class and participants were asked to complete the questionnaire following completion of each search. Using

Google, participants were asked a 'general' task to find information on Alan Turing and his contribution to the development of Computing. The expectation being that one or two encyclopaedic type of articles would satisfy this information quest. Whilst the query put to Google Scholar was more open ended to find backgrounder information on the topic of young people's use of Short Message Services (SMS) and its effect on their written language. The expectation being that the participants would have to learn a bit about this topic and find several sources to satisfy the information quest.

A questionnaire was designed to collect data on the assessments made with regards to the relevance of the information found and the assessment of the search engine used. The questions (items) were drawn from previous research which identifies and describes the judgements people make when assessing information retrieved as relevant (as detailed in [13]). The (meta) analysis here is to highlight the differences in the assessments made (of the retrieved information) and in the perceptions formed (of the search engines) when the participants' task was a straightforward 'look up' task and one where there was some simulation of a gap in knowledge and the need to look up and learn about the topic. The comparison thus described was between the 'look up' task using Google and on the 'research task' on Google Scholar (GS) and aimed to provide a characterisation of the cognitive processes when involved in search.

The Likert-style statements (items) aimed to reflect the constructs of information evaluation in the search context. Previous research identifies three types of relevance judgements, topical, cognitive and situational and these were drawn upon to suggest their assessment of the information retrieved. From these a series of statements were drawn up to include in the questionnaire and to avoid asking the participants to respond directly about their assessment of the relevance of the retrieved results. As follows:

- Topical relevance, a judgment of information 'aboutness' and the relation to the query topic is fundamental to search and participants were asked to give their level of agreement to statements such as, *the information is related to the topic of interest.*
- Cognitive relevance refers to some judgment of the informativeness with respect to the user's state of knowledge and, in this personal perspective there is some assimilation of the information. Participants were asked to consider the information retrieved and respond to statements such as, *the information has helped me to learn about the subject* as a possible indirect measure of cognitive relevance.
- The assumption is that these judgments are formed as a prerequisite for the application of the information to resolve the problem. The two stages of information interaction is clear in Blandford and Attfield's [2] definition where first the information is acquired and then applied to the situation. In this study the participants were required to find information only therefore only a measure of confidence that the information would be useful was sought in responding to items, such as *if I knew someone was looking for this information, I would tell them about this.*

To investigate the influence of the factors that may be used in making relevance judgments, including document style, recentness, novelty and scope, the questionnaire included 4–5 items relating to these and which as such may further distinguish the users' assessment of the information retrieved, such as *the information is accurate, I can believe the content, the information appears authoritative, the information is well written.*

With respect to the interactive context, and the user assessment of the interface two further constructs were considered as having key importance. Firstly, information interaction may be viewed as a dialogue between the user and the information retrieved with the interface facilitating the cognitive processing involved. It is possible then, if not likely, that the perceived ease with which the user can form the relevance judgments will affect and influence the judgment itself. Thus, a small number of items were included to measure this construct, such as, *it was easy to identify what the information was about* and *I felt that my query had been understood.* A further group of items, such as *the system is good at finding information that matches my query* were included to measure the perceived system effectiveness – that is, 'does it work?' The questionnaire was thus developed to manifest the participants' cognitive processing in search through their responses to this bank of items based on the constructs of topic relevance, cognitive relevance, situational relevance/confident use, information content, style and scope, and on the perceived support and effectiveness of the interface and system. The questionnaire was developed as a psychometric tool to investigate the core factors in users' assessment of the information and of the system in the interactive search.

3.1   Exploratory Factors

The statistical procedure of factor analysis was used to extract intended constructs when measured with the multiple statements. If the items for a construct are well designed, they should converge and form a major factor [14]. The Kaiser-Meyer-Olkin (KMO) values were greater than the recommended value 0.6 indicating sampling adequacy of the data prior to conducting factor analysis. Cronbach's alpha coefficient confirmed the reliability of the data in terms of internal consistency. These ranged from 0.706 to 0.926, which is higher than the minimum cut-off of 0.7. Table 1 reports the principal component analysis results with varimax rotation using SPSS. Two separate analyses were conducted on each of the datasets (the Google task and the Google Scholar (GS) task) in turn. An alignment across the factors for the Google and GS tasks was sought with a slight difference in the labelling of the factors, and the actual differences in the composition of these comparable factors are as follows. When asked to think about using the information retrieved using Google (query: Alan Turing), all of the items in the factor [1G] 'Content Credible' also appeared in the factor [1GS] 'Content Credible and Relevant' formed when thinking about the information retrieved using Google Scholar (for the query topic: use of Short Message Services). These were *I can believe the content, [...] is accurate* and *appears to be authoritative.* The factor [1GS] additionally included the statements, *the content is totally related to the topic of interest, is very easy for me to understand, is well written* and *tells me most of what I need to know.* These additional items might indicate that the participants were assessing the relevance of the information retrieved, as well as the credibility of the information retrieved. The sense that the participants were assessing the relevance of the information retrieved when searching for the task on Google Scholar is further borne out in the different items distinguishing the factor [2G] and factor [2GS], labelled as

'Expected Relevant' and 'Cognitive Relevant' respectively. These factors had in common the items *The information found seems to be the right amount for me, is a sufficient to complete the assignment,* and *I expect to feel well informed on this topic.* Factor [2GS] additionally included the items, *I expect this information to be very easy to read, easy to understand, I would use this information* and [it] *has helped me to learn about the subject.* Factor [2G] on the other hand additionally included only the item *I expect to know more about the topic once I have read this information.* Further indication that the participants were involved in assessing the information retrieved when using Google Scholar is in the items forming the factors [3GS] labelled 'Confident Useful' when compared to the factor [3G] in the Google task. In common were the statements, *If asked, I think that other people would value this information,* and *If I knew someone was looking for this information, I would tell them about this.* Whereas factor [3GS] contained the items, *this information would help me to complete the assignment,* and *I expect to know more about the topic once I have read this information* whilst factor [3G] included the items *I expect this info to be very easy to read* and *I would use this information to work on the task in hand.* The factors formed represent the users' assessment of the information as credible, relevant and useful with

Table 1. Factors in the evaluation of the information retrieved

Google Scholar factors			Google factors		
Item (abbreviated)			Item (abbreviated)		
1GS	... content is accurate	.831	1G	... believe the content	.850
	... *related to topic of interest*	.765		... appears authoritative	.847
	... *easy for me to understand*	.753		... *of good quality*	.815
	... believe the content	.747		... content is accurate	.717
	... appears authoritative	.658			
	... *is well written*	.652			
	... *tells me most of what I need*	.613			
2GS	... the right amount for me	.855	2G	... is sufficient	.834
	... is sufficient	.757		... *I expect to know more once read*	.769
	... *will be easy to read*	.756		feel well informed	.734
	... *will find easy to understand*	.731		... helps me complete the assignment	.631
	... *I will use this information*	.666		... the right amount for me	.550
	... *has helped me to learn*	.656			
	... feel well informed	.637			
3GS	... other people would value this	.854	3G	... *will find easy to understand*	.810
		.834		... if looking I would tell someone about this	.794
	... if looking I would tell someone about this	.675			.743
		.606		... *will be easy to read*	.734
	... helps me complete the assignment			... *I will use this information*	.665
	... *I expect to know once read*			... other people would value this	

common items found in both data sets. The major differences, however, relate to the assessment of relevance in the GS task. Of particular note is the inclusion in Factor [2GS] of the item which mentions learning, *'this information has helped me to learn about the subject'* in assessing relevance. It is further noted that the highest loading item in Factor [3GS] labelled 'Confident Useful' refers to the *value of the information* whereas in [3G] instead the highest item refers to *ease of understanding*. This may suggest that 'ease of reading/use' influences the user's judgment of usefulness in the 'look up' context, whereas in the 'research task' the assessment of information usefulness is made with greater respect to the task context or situation.

The questionnaire also asked the participants to respond to a set of items relating to the assessment of the system. These either related to the perception that the system worked (Factor 5), *the system works well in suggesting information, is good at finding information for my query* and *I can use to get the best results* or with respect to the support the participants felt they experienced (Factor 6), *my query had been understood, it was easy to identify what the information was about* and *easy to see why retrieved*. There was little variation found in these factors when assessing Google and when assessing Google Scholar. However running multiple regressions on this data does show these factors account for about half of the variance (45%) in factor [2GS] Cognitive Relevant; but, only 29% of the variance, in [2G] Expected Relevant judgment on Google. Factor 5 relating to user perception of system effectiveness also held a moderate association at $p < .001$ ($\beta = .457$) with factor [2GS] and again a weaker association with factor [2G] at $p = .007$ ($\beta = .331$).

4 Discussion: Assess-Ability as a New Evaluation Heuristic

With regards to the premise that search involves learning in the context of a gap in knowledge, this study explores the user's critical assessment of the information found. In the analysis of the questionnaire relating to the users' assessment, this study provides some evidence that the participants formed slightly different judgments according to the task. Assessment of relevance appeared to be more embedded in the evaluation of the GS task with the user engaged in assessing 'cognitive relevance' assimilating the information found. In the 'look up' task on Google assessment of the information appears to be less critical based on an expectation of topic relevancy. That is, the evidence presented here tentatively points to a difference in behaviour, especially cognitive, when searching with intention to find information (when compared to looking up information). The limitations of the study are, however, acknowledged and further investigation is recommended with the deployment of the psychometric questionnaire to further research the user's critical assessment of information found in search contexts. Further insight could be usefully gathered in user studies which involve the participants searching for different types of tasks for example with 'real' information needs, and in differing professional contexts. Further validation of this data collection instrument may be sought in correlating the searchers' critical assessment of information with some further measure of satisfaction or engagement. A searcher who appears to be involved in assessing cognitive relevance and assesses the search engine as supportive may report feeling more engaged in exploring new or complex topics.

Developments in the design of the interface to enhance the user experience may also be gauged using the questionnaire to collect data on their interaction with the information found.

Furthermore, identifying the core activity of assessing cognitive relevance may allow design to focus in the property of the 'assess-ability' of the interface to support the user in their critical assessment of the information retrieved. Nielsen's usability heuristics are de facto in user experience design comprising the ten usability principles which if adhered to can help ensure that the interface uses the users' language, helps user recognize rather than recall, gives consistent feedback on the system status and generally instil a confidence in using the interface. The development of the principle of assess-ability, as a heuristic, would question the support given to assist the user in assessing the information retrieved and help design to support this vital component of search behaviour. The types of questions that may be posed in developing the assess-ability heuristics may be drawn from recent studies that reveal the features that people claim to use when assessing information. The C3 (Content Credibility Corpus) [15] containing 15,750 evaluations of 5543 Webpages by 2041 participants, for example includes over 7071 annotated textual justifications of credibility evaluations of over 1361 Webpages. Analysis of these comments involved labelling the factors mentioned as influencing credibility assessment and were grouped into six categories. Each of these represent questions that someone might ask when assessing credibility, as: What kind of Web page is it? • Is the content of commercial character? • Who is the author or publisher? • How is the Web page designed? • Is the textual content of high quality? • Is the information on the Web page verifiable? The extent to which the presentation of the information retrieved enables the user to ask and answer some or all of these questions could form the basis of the assess-ability heuristics. For example, to ask: Is the user able to assess who is the author or publisher? Can the user determine what kind of web page/the type of article? Can the user assess the quality of the information, for example in assessing the metadata of date and the article references? The presentation of this information may make use of devices to separate out types of content, for example adverts on the page, or thumbnail to signal the type of page, and novel visuals such as 'Wikitrust' [16] designed to show editorial control and help the user to see which parts of the article are credible. The premise being that the more the user is able to assess the information retrieved, the more they will engage with the information, as is vital to searching for information. It is less obvious, however, how to provide support in asking the questions that rely more on the semantic features of the source, i.e., its relevance, completeness, scope and neutrality [17]. Asking the question – 'Can the user verify the information?' requires the user to interact with the infor-mation on a deeper level and to check accuracy and completeness and, in search contexts, to relate the information found to one's prior knowledge. In identifying the factors influencing the users' verification of information Brand-Gruwel [18] found that the strategies used involved the user in checking consistency with other sources, making connections to previous knowledge and interestingly, a verification strategy of 'trying to discern author's motive'. The design to assist the user in making this assessment is challenging but may be partly achieved by enabling the searcher to look up the author (if known) and to assess credibility markers of the author's transparency related to their motive in providing the information. Links may be followed enabling the searcher to verify content and, critically design tactics (such as the highlighting query terms in retrieved results) may be used to encourage assessment with regards to the users' information need. Here the assess-ability of the information refers to a less tangible property with its relevancy drawing on user's personal knowledge and information requirements. The value of the assess-ability heuristic is therefore not to determine design but rather to draw attention to the impact of design and features that the user perceives as supporting their interaction when assessing the credibility, relevance and usefulness of retrieved information.

5 Conclusion

A novel approach to investigating the users' cognitive activity in the critical assessment of information is presented here, and analysis suggests the constructs of the users' judgment. Interestingly, a distinct evaluation could be discerned in which the users appear to form a personal perspective on the information, critically evaluating the information in respect to their goal to find information. As a core and vital aspect of search activity, the study on assessing information provides a framework for thinking about how the information may be presented at the interface and designed for assess-ability. The framework of the heuristic based evaluation of assess-ability, supporting assessment of credibility and relevance, whilst in an early stage of development, provides an approach for interface design to support and evaluate the user's cognitive engagement in search.

References

1. Wilson, M.L., Kules, B., Schraefel, M.C., Shneiderman, B.: From keyword search to exploration. In: Wilson, M.L., et al. (eds.) Foundations and Trends in Web Science, pp. 1–97 (2010)
2. Blandford, A., Attfield, S.: Interaction with Information. Morgan & Claypool, San Rafael (2010)
3. Belkin, N.J., Cool, C., Stein, A., Theil, U.: Cases, scripts and information seeking strategies: on the design of interactive information retrieval systems. Expert Syst. Appl. 9, 379–395 (1995)
4. Pirolli, P., Card, S.K.: Information foraging in information access environments. In: Proceedings of Conference on Human Factors in Computing Systems, pp. 51–58. ACM, New York (1995)
5. Toms, E.: Information interaction providing a framework for information architecture. J. Am. Soc. Inf. Sci. 53(10), 855–862 (2002)
6. Johnson, F.C.: Shifting contexts: relating the user, search and system in teaching IR. In: Efthimiadis, E.N., Fernández-Luna, J., Huete, J., MacFarlane, A. (eds.) Teaching and Learning in Information Retrieval. Springer, Heidelberg (2011). https://doi.org/10.1007/978-3-642-22511-6_6
7. Hearst, M.A.: Search User Interfaces. Cambridge University Press, Cambridge (2009)
8. Wilson, M.L., Schraefel, M.C., White, R.W.: Evaluating advanced search interfaces using established information-seeking models. JASIST 60(7), 1407–1422 (2009)

9. Nielsen, J.: Usability 101: introduction to usability (2017). https://www.nngroup.com/articles/usability-101-introduction-to-usability/. Accessed 17 Sept 2017
10. Moshagen, M., Thielsch, M.T.: Facets of visual aesthetics. Int. J. Hum. Comput. Stud. **68** (10), 689–709 (2010)
11. Arapakis, I., Jose, J.M., Gray, P.D.: Affective feedback: an investigation into the role of emotions in the information seeking process. ACM SIGIR, pp. 395–402 (2008)
12. Saracevic, T.: Relevance reconsidered. In: Proceedings of Conceptions of Library and Information Science (CoLIS 2), pp. 201–218. ACM Press, New York (1996)
13. Johnson, F., Rowley, J., Sbaffi, L.: Information interactions in the context of Google. J. Assoc. Inf. Sci. Technol. **67**(4), 824–840 (2016)
14. Hair, J.F., Tatham, R.L., Anderson, R.E., Black, W.: Multivariate Data Analysis, 5th edn. Prentice Hall, Uppper Saddle River (1998)
15. Kakol, M., Nielek, R., Wierzbicki, A.: Understanding web content credibility using the Content Credibility Corpus. Inf. Process. Manag. **53**, 1043–1061 (2017)
16. Wiki-Watch: evaluate the quality of Wikipedia's articles. http://blog.wiki-watch.de/?p=497
17. Lucassen, T., Schraagen, J.M.: The influence of source cues and topic familiarity on credibility evaluation. Comput. Hum. Behav. **29**(4), 1387–1392 (2013)
18. Brand-Gruwel, S., Kammerer, Y., van Meeuwen, L.: Source evaluation of domain experts and novices during web search. J. Comput. Assist. Learn. **33**(3), 234–251 (2017)

The Role of Self-efficacy in Cancer Information Avoidance

Yuting Liao[✉][iD], Gagan Jindal, and Beth St. Jean[iD]

University of Maryland College of Information Studies, College Park, MD, USA
{yliao598, gjindal, bstjean}@umd.edu

Abstract. Our study highlights the roles of health- and information-related self-efficacy in individuals' tendency to avoid cancer information. Drawing on a large ($n = 3,677$), nationally representative survey data, we explored differences between information avoiders vs. non-avoiders and identified the contributing factors to individuals' health and information efficacy. We then developed a path model of information avoidance to investigate two main issues. First, we ascertained that the relationship between people's health efficacy and their preference for information avoidance is mediated by their healthcare use and perceived quality of care. Second, we discovered that individual's trust toward health information sources is a key component in understanding their information efficacy and their preference for information avoidance. Trust is positively associated with information efficacy and mediates the relationship between information efficacy and information avoidance. Understanding who prefers to avoid health information and in which situations and why is critical to improving the state of health justice in this country.

Keywords: Information avoidance · Health information behavior
Self-efficacy · Trust

1 Introduction

While many people seek information to cope with an illness [1–5], some prefer to avoid information on the topic [6, 7]. Information avoidance can involve avoiding discussing a particular topic, avoiding situations where one may encounter unwanted information, and purposefully selecting which information to pay attention to and which to not [6]. In short, information avoidance includes the active or passive prevention of potentially unwanted information exposure, even when the information is readily available [8]. Information avoidance is not an uncommon phenomenon – as Case et al. wrote, "It has long been noted that people may avoid information if paying attention to it will cause mental discomfort or dissonance... [Maslow] recognized that sometimes we would rather not know that we are at high risk for a disease or disaster" [7, p. 354]. Unfortunately, however, information avoidance has been linked with negative health outcomes, such as disease progression and disease spread [9]. It eventually leads to significant costs, including increased morbidity and mortality and increased healthcare expenditures [10]. These losses, however, are frequently not borne equally across various segments of society, as evidenced by the large disparities in life expectancy

© Springer International Publishing AG, part of Springer Nature 2018
G. Chowdhury et al. (Eds.): iConference 2018, LNCS 10766, pp. 498–508, 2018.
https://doi.org/10.1007/978-3-319-78105-1_54

based on household income [11] and educational attainment and race [12]. Health justice, an ideal state in which everyone has equitable capabilities to live a long and healthy life [13], remains unattainable for large swathes of the U.S. population.

Self-efficacy is defined as people's beliefs and perceptions of their capabilities to influence events that affect their lives [14]. People with high assurance in their capabilities approach difficult tasks as challenges to be mastered rather than as threats to be avoided [14, 15]. While previous scholars have investigated the psychological predictors and socio-economic factors of information avoidance, there is less empirical work that examines the role of self-efficacy. One notable exception, however, is Wilson, whose 1996 Model of Information Behaviour invokes Folkman's stress and coping theory and Bandura's Social Learning Theory (particularly, the central concept of self-efficacy) to explain why people may not seek information despite having a need for it [16]. To better inform health and information professionals in creating future interventions, we seek to address this gap in understanding to what extent information avoidance is linked with health efficacy (one's degree of confidence in their ability to take care of their health) and information efficacy (one's degree of confidence that they can get advice or information about cancer if they need it). More specifically, we address the following research questions:

RQ1: What differences—if any—exist between individuals who would rather not know their chance of getting cancer ("information avoiders") and those who would rather know ("non-avoiders") this information?

RQ2: To what extent are people's health and information efficacy levels related to their individual characteristics and their socioeconomic status?

Finally, a major goal of this paper is to consider public health and educational initiatives focused on mitigating information avoidance behaviors regarding serious diseases such as cancer. We also seek to better equip people to make decisions about finding rather than avoiding health information. To do this, we must understand the interrelationships between the various factors that influence a person's preference for information avoidance, as well as their health and information efficacy. We used path analysis and mediation analysis to explore a third research question:

RQ3: How is information avoidance associated with health and information efficacy, as well as other individual characteristics?

2 Related Work

Many studies [2–5, 17] have found that among people with a life-threatening illness, there is a sizeable subpopulation that prefers to avoid information about their health condition. Prior research illustrates that social determinants can play a major role in information avoidance behaviors. Survey data from a major cancer hospital revealed that cancer survivors with lower incomes and greater debt were more likely to avoid information [18]. Relatedly, the same survey respondents in the lowest income bracket also reported lower levels of self-reported health [19]. Other studies have similarly found participants with lower educational levels to be more likely to avoid health information [20, 21].

Another line of research examines the psychological predictors of information avoidance. Often, these individuals are motivated by a desire to control their anxiety [22] and/or to retain hope [6, 23]. Information behavior theorists, including Wilson [16] and Johnson, have recognized a link between lower levels of self-efficacy and information avoidance behaviors [7]. Relatedly, Miles et al. found that individuals with greater levels of cancer fear and cancer fatalism (believing that death is unavoidable after one has been diagnosed with cancer) are also more likely to avoid information, which can limit their exposure to critical cancer prevention and control information [24]. These findings are concerning when considered in parallel with recent data indicating that individuals from lower socioeconomic status groups are also more likely to report cancer fatalism. The same respondents were both less positive about early detection and more afraid to ask for help with a suspicious symptom [25]. McCutchan et al. also found that individuals from lower socioeconomic groups were more likely to have cancer fear and cancer fatalism beliefs, which were associated with their lower overall cancer symptom knowledge [26].

Counteracting the effect of demographic variables on patient's information-seeking behaviors can be a difficult prospect. However, some studies have shown the possibility of mediating the effects of these types of social determinants. Hovick et al. explained how social and cognitive factors, such as social participation and health literacy, among other factors, could potentially mediate the effect of socioeconomic status, race, and ethnicity on individuals' information seeking behaviors [27]. Reducing cancer fatalism among individuals from lower income groups may also be an effective strategy for preventing information avoidance. Miller (1995) found data that seems to indicate that lower levels of cancer fatalism can mediate the association between lower socioeconomic status and lower uptake of cancer screenings [28]. These findings emphasize the importance of improving health literacy and social support and reducing cancer fatalism through new interventions targeted specifically for individuals from disadvantaged backgrounds.

More recent studies have begun to explore the relationships between self-efficacy and information avoidance. St. Jean et al. found that lower self-efficacy among less well-educated individuals can pose a problem: Respondents with lower health- and information-related self-efficacy were more likely to avoid information [29]. This study extends prior work through a comprehensive examination of the roles of health and information efficacy in information avoidance.

3 Method

The National Cancer Institute conducts the Health Information National Trends Survey (HINTS) every few years to learn about U.S. adults' cancer-related perceptions and knowledge, their health behaviors, and their information access, needs, seeking, and use. This paper is based on the publicly available HINTS 4 Cycle 4 SPSS data set [30]. Data were collected from August through November 2014 via a paper questionnaire mailed to an equal-probability sample of U.S. households. A total of 3,677 questionnaires were returned, resulting in a 34.4% response rate. To analyze the data, we ran various descriptive and inferential statistical tests, including Chi-square tests and independent sample t-tests, regressions, and path analysis. We first explored characteristics that differed between information avoiders vs. non-avoiders (RQ1). We then used linear regression to assess predictors of health and information efficacy (RQ2). For RQ3, we employed path analysis, as simple multiple regression could not have accounted for the interplay between demographic factors, disease-specific beliefs, and healthcare-specific and health information related variables. Below we introduce the variable used in our analyses.

3.1 Measurements

Information avoidance. Information avoidance was gauged using respondents' degree of agreement/disagreement with the statement, "I'd rather not know my chance of getting cancer." This was deemed to be a valid measure of the construct of information avoidance, as people's desire not to know that they are at high risk for a disease has been mentioned in the literature as a specific example of information avoidance [7]. We used this as dependent variable (DV) in our statistical analyses. In RQ1, we recoded this variable to binary by combining those who selected "Strongly agree" and "Somewhat agree" as information avoider ($N = 1,109$; 31%), and the rest as non-avoiders ($N = 2,432$; 69%). In RQ3 path analysis, we treated this variable as a Likert scale (1 = strongly disagree; 4 = strongly agree), with higher values indicating greater tendency to avoid information [$M(SD) = 2.30(1.46)$].

Self-efficacy. In the context of cancer-related information avoidance, our study conceptualizes self-efficacy in two aspects: information-related self-efficacy and health-related self-efficacy.

- **Information efficacy.** Information efficacy was measured by respondents' indication of how confident they felt in their ability to get advice or information about cancer if they needed it (1 = not confident at all; 5 = completely confident). Higher values indicate greater information efficacy [$M(SD) = 2.77(1.03)$].
- **Health efficacy.** Health efficacy was measured by respondents' assessment of their confidence in their ability to take good care of their health (1 = not confident at all; 5 = completely confident). Higher scores indicate that participants have greater health efficacy [$M(SD) = 2.79(.86)$].

Perceived quality of healthcare. Perceived quality of healthcare was measured by 7-item questions (Cronbach's alpha = .94) that assess the respondents' satisfaction with their healthcare over the past year. These questions ask how often (1 = Never; 4 = Always) their healthcare providers gave them a chance to ask all of their questions, gave sufficient attention to their feelings, involved them in decisions related to their health care, etc. Scores were added to form one scale, with a higher score indicating greater satisfaction with healthcare providers [$M(SD) = 16.54(4.79)$, Range: 7–28].

Trust toward health information sources. Trust toward health information sources was measured by 9-item questions (Cronbach's alpha = .82) that assess to what extent (1 = Not at all; 2 = A little; 3 = Some; 4 = A lot) respondents trust information about cancer from various sources, including doctors, family or friends, newspapers, etc.

Scores were added to form one scale, with a higher score indicating greater trust in these sources [(*M*(SD) = 14.34(4.66); Range: 0–27].

Perceived control of health. Perceived control of one's health was measured by 5-item questions (Cronbach's alpha = .90) that assess to what extent (1 = Not at all; 2 = A little; 3 = Some; 4 = A lot) respondents believe that health behaviors determine whether or not a person will develop major diseases. Scores were added to form one scale, with a higher score indicating greater perceived control over whether or not they will develop the health condition [*M*(SD) = 12.63(3.16); Range: 0–15].

Perceived barriers to health information seeking. Among the 1,612 (54%) respondents who have sought cancer-related information, perceived barriers to health information seeking was measured by 4-item questions (Cronbach's alpha = .85). These questions focused on cancer-related information seeking and sense-making, asking respondents to what extent they concur (1 = strongly disagree; 4 = strongly agree) with the statements such as "It took a lot of effort to get the information you needed". Scores were added to form one scale, with a higher score indicating that participants encounter more barriers when they search for and try to make sense of health information [*M*(SD) = 4.53(3.17); Range: 0–12].

3.2   Control Variables

Demographic, cancer history and health insurance: Demographic variables include gender (60% F; 40% M), age [*M*(SD) = 51.9(21.17)], education (1 = less than 8 years; 4 = vocational or technical training; 7 = Postgraduate) [*M*(SD) = 4.83(1.64)], household income (1 = less than $20,000; 3 = $35,000 to < $50,000; 5 = more than $75,000) [*M*(SD) = 3.14(1.56)]. Additionally, cancer history and health insurance were treated as binary variables.

Social support. Social support [*M(SD) = 1.76(0.57)*] was measured (Cronbach's alpha = .75) by adding two binary variables from the following survey questions: (1) "Is there anyone you can count on to provide you with emotional support when you need it?" and (2) "Do you have friends or family members that you talk to about your health?" Most respondents indicated that they do have social support (78%).

Disease anxiety: Respondents were asked how worried they are about getting cancer (1 = not at all worried; 5 = extremely worried). Higher scores indicate greater disease anxiety [*M*(SD) = 2.58(1.22)].

Pessimistic mentality: Pessimistic mentality is measured by 4-item questions (Cronbach's alpha = .89). Respondents were asked to indicate over the past 2 weeks, how often they have been bothered by negative emotions, feeling down, depressed or hopeless (1 = not at all; 2 = Several days; 3 = more than half the days; 4 = nearly daily). Higher scores indicate a higher level of pessimistic mentality [*M*(SD) = 2.00(2.89)].

Fatalism: Fatalism is measured by a participant's agreement with the statements, "There's not much you can do to lower your chances of getting cancer", "It seems like everything causes cancer" and "In adults, cancer is more common than heart disease". Higher scores indicate a higher degree of fatalism [*M*(SD) = 8.06(1.05); Range: 3–12].

4 Findings

4.1 RQ1: Characteristics of Information Avoiders Vs. Non-avoiders

Patterns between these two groups based on their preferences regarding information avoidance and their demographic, psychological, and disease-related characteristics are examined below. To extend previous work [24], healthcare and health information specific factors were also included in our analysis.

Socio-economic and psychological characteristics. Information avoiders tend to be older [$M(SD)$ = 55.82(16.16)] than non-avoiders [$M(SD)$ = 54.58(16.49)] (t (2056) = 2.05, $p < .05$). They also tend to have less education [$M(SD)$ = 4.53(1.71)] than non-avoiders [$M(SD)$ = 4.98(1.6)] (t(1957) = , −7.40, $p < .001$), and lower household incomes [$M(SD)$ = 4.81(1.55)] than non-avoiders [$M(SD)$ = 5.3(2.26)] (t (1890) = −5.20, $p < .001$). Information avoiders tend to live in less urban places (t (1983) = −2.61, $p < .01$). Disabled respondents are significantly more likely to be information avoiders (X^2 (1) = 12.96, p < .01, Φ = .11). In terms of psychological differences, information avoiders scored higher on pessimistic mentality (t (1851) = 2.35, p < .05).

Health efficacy, perceived control, and fatalism beliefs. Information avoiders have a significantly lower level of health efficacy (t(1,952) = −1.81, $p < .5$) and lower perceived control regarding their health (t(1693) = −6.58, $p < .001$. They also tend to feel more fatalistic regarding their health (t(1889) = 11.74, $p < .001$), as they were more likely to agree with views such as "Everything causes cancer" and "There's not much you can do to lower your chances of getting cancer".

Healthcare access, utilization and quality. Information avoiders are less likely to have health insurance (X^2(1) = 9.90, $p < .01$, Φ = .05). They also have a statistically significant lower frequency of doctor visits (t(2067) = −3.65, $p < .002$), are less likely to have a regular doctor (X^2(1) = 18.46, $p < .01$, Φ = .07), and tend to have a lower perceived quality of health care (t(1502) = −1.7, $p < .05$).

Health information access, trust, and information efficacy. Overall, information avoiders have a lower level of information efficacy (t(1952) = −1.81, $p < .05$), and are less likely to use the Internet (X^2 (1) = 33.46, $p < .001$, Φ = .09) and to seek health information (X^2 (1) = 38.96, $p < .001$, Φ = .15). Even when they do engage in health information seeking, they perceive significantly greater barriers in finding and making sense of the information (t(633) = 1.9, $p < .05$).

4.2 RQ2: How Are People's Health and Information Efficacy Related to Their Individual Characteristics?

Various factors (see Table 1) emerged as significant predictors of respondents' health and information efficacy. Although health efficacy is largely affected by an individual's self-rated general health (β = .52, $p < .001$), perceived healthcare quality is also positively associated with health efficacy (β = .12, $p < .001$). So among people with poor health, those who have better perceived healthcare quality tend to have greater health

Table 1. Summary of regression analysis for predicting information avoidance

Variable	Health efficacy			Information efficacy		
	B	SEB	β	B	SEB	β
Age	−0.01	0.00	−0.09***	0.00	0.00	−0.08*
Education	0.01	0.02	0.03	0.02	0.02	0.04
Household income	0.03	0.01	0.09**	0.00	0.01	−0.01
Urbanization	0.01	0.01	0.02	−0.04	0.01	0.06*
Pessimistic mentality	−0.05	0.01	−0.08**	−0.01	0.01	−0.02
Social support	0.05	0.05	0.03	−0.06	0.05	−0.03
General health	0.45	0.02	0.52***	−0.01	0.03	−0.01
Cancer history (Yes)	0.00	0.06	0.00	0.16	0.06	0.07*
Cancer anxiety	−0.06	0.02	−0.09*	−0.01	0.02	−0.02
Perceived control	0.02	0.01	0.06	0.01	0.01	0.02
Fatalism	−0.06	0.02	−0.06**	−0.02	0.02	−0.04
Health insurance (Yes)	−0.11	0.09	−0.03	0.02	0.10	0.00
Healthcare utilization	−0.02	0.01	−0.04	0.01	0.01	0.02
Healthcare quality	0.03	0.01	0.12***	0.01	0.01	0.07**
Perceived barriers	0.01	0.01	0.02	−0.12	0.01	0.42***
Trust toward sources	0.00	0.01	0.00	0.04	0.01	0.16***
Information efficacy	0.13	0.03	0.11***	–	–	–
Health efficacy	–	–	–	0.14	0.03	0.12***
R^2	0.40			0.33		
$F(18,1070)=$	39.48***			28.65***		

*$p < .05.$ ** $p < .01.$ *** $p < .001$

efficacy, as they are more confident in their ability to take good care of their health. Also, annual household income positively correlated with health efficacy ($β = .09$, $p < .01$), while age was negatively associated ($β = −.12$, $p < .001$). Health efficacy was negatively associated with a pessimistic mentality ($β = −.18$, p $< .001$) and fatalism ($β = −.10$, p $< .001$). So respondents who are more pessimistic (i.e., agree that "There's not much you can do to lower your chances of getting cancer") have lower health efficacy than those who are more optimistic.

With regard to information efficacy, perceived barriers to health information seeking play a major role ($β = .42, p < .001$); however, an individual's degree of trust toward sources of cancer information is also a significant contributing factor ($β = .16$, $p < .001$); that is, people with greater trust in sources of cancer information tend to have greater information efficacy. Respondents' perceived health status ($β = .07$, $p < .01$) is also positively associated with their information efficacy – people who perceive their health to be poor are more likely to have lower information efficacy, indicating they find it harder to get advice or information about cancer. Additionally, age ($β = −.07$, $p < .01$) is negatively associated with information efficacy, while urbanization ($β = .06, p < .01$) of one's residence is positively correlated. Thus, older people and residents in more rural areas tend to have lower information efficacy.

To summarize our analysis related to RQ2, we found different factors that contribute to differences in individuals' health and information efficacy. The variation across these two dependent variables motivated our decision to build a multi-factor model in evaluating the phenomenon of information avoidance, which we present below.

4.3 RQ3: How is Information Avoidance Associated with Health- and Information-Related Efficacy and Other Individual Characteristics?

Our final RQ builds on prior analyses to consider the interrelationships between health and information efficacy, demographic factors, psychological predictors, and disease factors in explaining information avoidance. We used the preference to avoid information as the primary dependent variable to build the path model (Fig. 1).

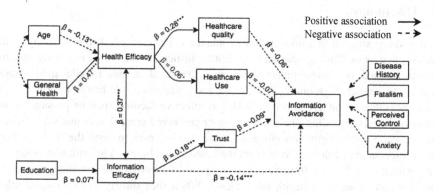

Fig. 1. Path model with β weights and direct and indirect pathways

The final model provided a strong fit to the data, $(X^2(25,1,957) = 31.281, p = .275;$ CFI = .92, RMSEA = .04). All paths shown were significant. We found negative correlations between information avoidance and several other variables, including information efficacy $(\beta = -.14, p < .001)$, perceived healthcare quality $(\beta = -.06, p < .05)$, healthcare use $(\beta = -.07, p < .05)$, and trust in cancer information sources $(\beta = -.09, p < .05)$. In line with prior research looking at the effect of disease-related beliefs on information avoidance, we found that perceived control over one's health $(\beta = -.10, p < .01)$ and disease anxiety $(\beta = -.17, p < .05)$ were negatively correlated with information avoidance, and fatalism was positively correlated $(\beta = .09, p < .05)$ with information avoidance.

Further, we examined the mediation pathways between health and information efficacy and information avoidance. We found that some of the associations between health efficacy and information avoidance were via perceived healthcare quality and healthcare utilization. Also, the relationship between information avoidance and information efficacy is mediated through people's trust in cancer information sources.

Health efficacy is negatively associated with information avoidance. This relationship remained after controlling for demographic variables and respondents' personal cancer history ($\beta = -.05$; $P < .001$). The two mediators considered were perceived healthcare quality and healthcare utilization. Based on Sobel test, both variables resulted in a significant reduction in the association between health efficacy and information avoidance (perceived healthcare quality: $z(2946) = -2.9$, $p = .003$; healthcare utilization: $z = 2.49$; $p = .013$) when entered individually. The significant relationship between health efficacy and information avoidance disappeared when either was included in the regression model. Therefore, both of these variables are mediators of the relationship between health efficacy and information avoidance.

Overall, information efficacy, perceived healthcare quality, healthcare use, and disease-related beliefs explain 13% of the variance in a person's information avoidance preferences.

5   Discussion

Our findings suggest that information avoidance is intricately linked with many of the factors that contribute to the lack of health justice in the U.S., including income disparities and the concomitant differential levels of access to education; health insurance; regular, high-quality healthcare; and comprehensible health information. In addition, information avoidance is linked to affective factors, such as pessimism and fatalistic beliefs regarding one's health, lower perceived control over one's health, and lower health and information efficacy. These results seem to echo the findings from other information behavior theorists on the connections between information avoidance and self-efficacy [7, 16]. Information avoiders in this study were less likely to use the Internet and to seek out health information. When they did try to find cancer information, they were much more likely to encounter barriers in finding and understanding information. Information avoidance was predicted by lower information efficacy, lower perceived healthcare quality, less healthcare use, and pessimistic and fatalistic beliefs regarding one's health. Further, we establish that the strong relationship between information avoidance and health efficacy is explained by healthcare use and perceived healthcare quality. Similarly, the strong relationship between information avoidance and information efficacy is explained by respondent trust in cancer information sources. Taken together, these findings underscore the fundamental contribution of health literacy to the lack of health justice in this country. Understanding the many factors that are linked with information avoidance can inform interventions aiming to help people prevent the potential negative consequences of information avoidance. Although some related factors, such as household income, are difficult to alter, others are potentially malleable. For example, health and information professionals can work with people to improve their health literacy and their health information seeking skills, and relatedly, their health and information efficacy. Increased health and information efficacy, in turn, can help people to feel less pessimistic and fatalistic and more in control of their health. Such interventions can ultimately help to decrease information avoidance and motivate and enable people to achieve more optimal health outcomes.

Our study aims to understand who avoids health information under what circumstances and why. The major limitation of this study is its reliance on self-reported, cross-sectional data, meaning our analyses can only identify correlations between variables and not causation. That said, our study serves as a foundation for future work in prediction modeling, such as machine-learning initiatives that aim for early detection of individuals' preference for information avoidance.

6 Conclusion

In this study, we moved beyond the socio-economic and psychological factors, and instead focus on the roles of both health and information efficacy in explaining why people may avoid health information. We also identified several mediators, including trust toward information sources, healthcare use, and healthcare quality. We recommend that information and healthcare professionals should improve people's health and information efficacy and help them to find and understand trustworthy health information. Health policymakers can also help to intervene in the progression from low health and information efficacy to information avoidance to negative health outcomes by ensuring that everyone has access to affordable, high quality healthcare. Through such interventions aimed to benefit everyone, including particularly those who are socioeconomically disadvantaged, we can help to ensure that every individual has equitable opportunities to live a long and healthy life.

References

1. Ankem, K.: Use of information sources by cancer patients: results of a systematic review of the research literature. Inf. Res. 11(3), paper 254 (2006)
2. Clark, J.: Constructing expertise: inequality and the consequences of information-seeking by breast cancer patients. Illn. Crisis Loss 13(2), 169–185 (2005)
3. Hack, T.F., Degner, L.F., Dyck, D.G.: Relationship between preferences for decisional control and illness information among women with breast cancer: a quantitative and qualitative analysis. Soc. Sci. Med. 39(2), 279–289 (1994)
4. Mills, M.A., Davidson, R.: Cancer patients' sources of information: use and quality issues. Psycho-Oncology 11(5), 371–378 (2002)
5. Wong, F., et al.: Men with prostate cancer: influence of psychological factors on informational needs and decision making. J. Psychosom. Res. 49, 13–19 (2000)
6. Brashers, D.E., et al.: Communication in the management of uncertainty: the case of persons living with HIV or AIDS. Commun. Monogr. 67(1), 63–84 (2000)
7. Case, D.O., et al.: Avoiding versus seeking: the relationship of information seeking to avoidance, blunting, coping, dissonance, and related concepts. J. Med. Libr. Assoc. 93(3), 353–362 (2005)
8. Sweeny, K., Melnyk, D., Miller, W., Shepperd, J.: Information avoidance: who, what, when, and why. Rev. Gen. Psychol. 14(4), 340–353 (2010)
9. Vargas, C.A.: Coping with HIV/AIDS in Durban's commercial sex industry. AIDS Care 13, 351–365 (2001)
10. Byrne, S.K.: Healthcare avoidance: a critical review. Holist. Nurs. Pract. 22, 280–292 (2008)

11. Chetty, R., et al.: The association between income and life expectancy in the United States, 2001-2014. J. Am. Med. Assoc. **315**(16), 1750–1766 (2016)
12. Olshansky, S.J., et al.: Differences in life expectancy due to race and educational differences are widening and may not catch up. Health Aff. **31**(8), 1803–1813 (2012)
13. Venkatapuram, S.: Health Justice: An Argument from the Capabilities Approach. Polity Press, Malden (2007)
14. Bandura, A.: Self-Efficacy: The Exercise of Control. Macmillan, Basingstoke (1997)
15. Schwarzer, R. (ed.): Self-Efficacy: Thought Control of Action. Taylor & Francis, New York (2014)
16. Wilson, T.D.: Models in information behaviour research. J. Doc. **55**(3), 249–270 (1999)
17. Baker, L.M.: Sense making in multiple sclerosis: the information needs of people during an acute exacerbation. Qual. Health Res. **8**(1), 106–120 (1998)
18. McCloud, R.F., Jung, M., Gray, S.W., Viswanath, K.: Class, race and ethnicity and information avoidance among cancer survivors. Br. J. Cancer **108**(10), 1949–1956 (2013)
19. Jung, M., et al.: Effect of information seeking and avoidance behavior on self-rated health status among cancer survivors. Patient Educ. Couns. **92**(1), 100–106 (2013)
20. Czaja, R., Manfredi, C., Price, J.: The determinants and consequences of information seeking among cancer patients. J. Health Commun. **8**(6), 529–562 (2003)
21. Eheman, C., et al.: Information-seeking styles among cancer patients before and after treatment by demographics and use of information sources. J. Health Commun. **14**, 487–502 (2009)
22. Pifalo, V., et al.: The impact of consumer health information provided by libraries: the Delaware experience. Bull. Med. Libr. Assoc. **85**(1), 16–22 (1997)
23. Brashers, D.E., Goldsmith, D.J., Hsieh, E.: Information seeking and avoiding in health contexts. Hum. Commun. Res. **28**(2), 258–271 (2002)
24. Miles, A., et al.: Psychologic predictors of cancer information avoidance among older adults: the role of cancer fear and fatalism. Cancer Epidemiol. Biomarkers Prev. **17**(8), 1872–1879 (2008)
25. Beeken, R., et al.: Cancer fatalism: Deterring early presentation and increasing social inequalities? Cancer Epidemiol. Biomark. Prev. **20**(10), 2127–2131 (2011)
26. McCutchan, G.M., et al.: Influences of cancer symptom knowledge, beliefs and barriers on cancer symptom presentation in relation to socioeconomic deprivation: a systematic review. BMC Cancer **15**, 1000 (2015)
27. Hovick, S.R., Liang, M.C., Kahlor, L.: Predicting cancer risk knowledge and information seeking: the role of social and cognitive factors. Health Commun. **29**(7), 656–668 (2014)
28. Miller, S.M.: Monitoring versus blunting styles of coping with cancer influence the information patients want and need about their disease. Cancer **76**(2), 167–177 (1995)
29. St. Jean, B., Jindal, G., Liao, Y.: Is ignorance really bliss?: exploring the interrelationships among information avoidance, health literacy, and health justice. In: ASIS&T 2017 Annual Conference (2017)
30. NCI analytics recommendations for HINTS 4 cycle 4 data, https://hints.cancer.gov/dataset/HINTS_4_Cycle_4_SPSS.zip. Accessed 9 Mar 2017 (2015a)

Conceptualizing the Role of Reading
and Literacy in Health Information Practices

Miraida Morales$^{(\boxtimes)}$ and Nina Wacholder

Rutgers University, New Brunswick, NJ 08901, USA
miraidam@scarletmail.rutgers.edu, ninwac@rutgers.edu

Abstract. This paper proposes that a focus on reading and literacy can deepen our understanding of information seeking and everyday life information practices. It conceptualizes the role of reading, readability, and literacy in health information practices as a sociotechnical system, and forms the basis for an ongoing mixed-methods study on the role of readability in the health information practices of adult emerging readers. This approach puts into question best practice guidelines for creating health information and asks what makes a useful health information document for adult emerging readers. The results of this research based on this conceptual framework will help to improve access to quality health information for members of communities that face greater health disparities.

Keywords: Readability · Health information practices · Health literacy
Adult emerging readers

1 Introduction

Exactly twenty years ago, an important paper delivered at ALISE's annual meeting warned that LIS' emphasis on "information" was obfuscating the role of reading in people's information seeking practices [31]. Though Wiegand's appeal to incorporate reading research into the LIS research agenda focused mostly on information practices associated with reading popular fiction, this also applies to other instances in which reading is deeply embedded in everyday life information practices. A constructionist approach to information literacy, for instance, defines reading as a complex social practice situated in specific communities, and conceptualizes literacy as the specific way in which a given community or group practices reading including its unique ways of interpreting, evaluating, and communicating [28]. To arrive at a deeper understanding of the intersection between reading and information practices, this paper considers reading and literacy practices in the context of health information practices.

A key aspect of health information seeking is the practice of evaluating health information. This forms part of broader everyday health literacy practices that include reading and making judgments about the usability of health information. At the same time, creating health information documents that are easy to read is part of a broader set of professional practices for health literacy professionals. Seen through a sociotechnical lens, health information documents encode the values, practices and assumptions of health literacy professionals [21]. An important part of the professional practice of

G. Chowdhury et al. (Eds.): iConference 2018, LNCS 10766, pp. 509–514, 2018.
https://doi.org/10.1007/978-3-319-78105-1_55

creating this type of health information is the use and manipulation of sociotechnical tools such as readability formulas and writing guidelines.

This type of health information is then embedded in the health information and literacy practices of another group—the intended audience. The health literacy movement focuses much of its attention on individuals with low educational attainment, low health literacy assessment scores, and on adults who read at low grade levels [3, 15]. Due to this focus, health literacy best practice guidelines often make recommendations on how to make health information easier to read for these readers. It is not clear, however, whether such recommendations are indeed effective in creating health information that supports the health information needs and practices of adult emerging readers. This paper constructs a framework based on several theoretical threads to conceptualize the situated nature of these interconnected health practices. It is the basis for a larger ongoing study that examines how adult emerging readers evaluate consumer health information documents.

2 The Practice of Evaluating Health Information

Research in library and information science has traditionally studied information evaluation almost exclusively as a cognitive process [7, 13]. One way to explain the variability these cognitive studies have found in the way people evaluate information quality and credibility is to recognize the role of social influences on this phenomenon [17]. Since people's values are constructed, sanctioned and negotiated through the social structures that organize their daily lives, it follows that how people evaluate health information is, at least in part, the result of social processes located in the observable practices of everyday life [25].

Individuals define credibility and quality in different ways, and how they define these affects the way they evaluate information [1, 22, 28]. Aspects of the information source itself also affect how participants evaluate them. These qualities include—but are surely not limited to—document readability, writing quality, the appropriateness of tone, and the use of technical vs. plain language [7, 13]. When they read information in order to evaluate its quality, credibility, relevance, or usefulness, people pay attention to cues present in the text and use these cues in their evaluation. Studying how these cues affect the way people evaluate information presents an opportunity for current and future research efforts in LIS.

3 Health Literacy as Sociotechnical Practice

An example of the way in which language use might affect the way people evaluate information is found in health literacy practices, a goal of which is to improve the health literacy of at-risk communities by creating and making accessible health information that is easy to read [20]. When seen as a social and professional practice, health literacy can be understood as the interaction between health professionals, librarians, and members of different communities as they use or manipulate different technologies in order to manage and make decisions about their own or their community's health and wellbeing. More specifically, we can study the development and implementation of standards for creating easy-to-read health information, the endorsement of certain linguistic features as gold standards, and the use of technology to measure the readability of consumer health information as part of this sociotechnical system of health literacy. It is not clear that the specific professional health literacy practices concerned with creating easy-to-read health information are in fact accomplishing their goal or even providing greater access to health information. An important question is whether and to what extent, from the point of view of adult emerging readers, consumer health information developed according to these standard health literacy professional practices is in fact useful, usable, and easy to read.

3.1 Health Literacy Reproduces Power Relations

As useful and well intentioned as the guidelines and recommendations for writing easy-to-read health materials are, they are mostly derived from empirical research based only on how adults read websites [12]. Derived this way, the guidelines do not reflect the diversity of reading practices among adults, individual differences among adult readers, or the variety of their experiences reading different kinds of texts. Applying a critical lens to this practice reveals the way in which health literacy practices are embedded within a system that reproduces inequities through practices and technologies that make assumptions about the characteristics of adults who experience greater health inequities.

3.2 The Concept of Readability and the Practice of Using Readability Formulas

Several agencies and institutions are involved in defining health literacy as a public health issue. Health literacy is defined as the ability to find, process and understand health information needed to make decisions related to one's health [18]. To help professionals create health information that supports these health literacy criteria, the U.S. National Library of Medicine and the federal government have codified what it means for a consumer health information document to be "easy to read." Practices to avoid include the use of technical jargon and writing long sentences, while practices endorsed include the use of bulleted lists whenever possible [8, 14]. Often, these guidelines recommend that information have a certain reading grade level to ensure it is "easy to read." The National Library of Medicine, for instance, recommends a reading level of 7th or 8th grade [14]. Once it has been determined that a document meets these guidelines, agencies may submit it to the "Easy to Read" collection of MedlinePlus where librarians and public health professionals can access them for distribution to members of communities they serve.

To be sure that health information is written at a specific grade level, guidelines recommend the use of readability formulas [14]. Readability is a quality that determines how easy to read texts are for a particular individual [6]. Based on this definition, a number of important findings have had a lasting impact on current understandings of reading, literacy, and readability: (1) easy-to-read texts benefit individuals who have low topic knowledge and/or low motivation; (2) improved readability increases the likelihood that someone will continue reading; and (3) texts that are easy to read increase reading speed and retention [6]. Despite these findings, defining just what makes something "easy to read" remains a complicated research problem.

Using readability formulas such as the Flesch-Kincaid Grade Level [10], the SMOG formula [23], and the New Dale-Chall readability formula [4], recommended by health literacy guidelines to assess consumer health information documents is quite problematic. Their use in this context can lead to inflated reading grade levels because the formulas are biased against long words which tend to be common in health information. They also do not adequately take into account certain linguistic features that often characterize these types of documents, such as phrases, lists, or tables. Ultimately, they are unable to account for factors that affect the way people read such as reading ability, topic knowledge, motivation, context, and genre [26]. Another limitation of these formulas is that they were developed using training corpora (also known as criterion passages) that were very short and not representative of a wide variety of texts [19, 24]. This limits the applicability of these formulas to longer passages and to texts from different domains, such as health information. Importantly, they are not adequate tools for assessing the readability of text written for adults [9]. Because of these limitations, it is easy to see why, despite great efforts, 'easy-to-read' health information remains difficult to read [2, 5, 30].

4   Empirical Study

The conceptual framework of health literacy discussed above guides an ongoing mixed methods study that investigates how adult emerging readers evaluate health information that have been identified as "Easy to Read." The study, which is the basis of dissertation work carried out by the first author, critically examines the sociotechnical tools and resulting artifacts involved in creating health information documents to improve access to health information for these adults. This study includes a quantitative linguistic analysis of a corpus of 500 health information documents to identify linguistic features that might affect how easy to read these documents are for adult emerging readers. Using features that indicate how ideas in the text are related, the simplicity of the structure of the text, as well as the level of abstraction in the text, the documents in the corpus were clustered into groups and prototypical documents were identified. These prototypical documents were then used in a series of usability studies with adult emerging readers who engaged in the task of evaluating their readability. The results from both phases of this study will be integrated into a more comprehensive set of findings about the role of reading and readability in the health information practices of adult emerging readers.

5   Conclusion

Reframing health literacy practices and related technologies as a mutually shaping system challenges two dominant conceptualizations of health literacy: (1) the behavioral model of health literacy, which defines health literacy as a set of competencies that individuals either have or lack [27]; and (2) the social movement model of health literacy, which conceptualizes health literacy as an individual good, encompassing a person's right to make decisions about one's own body and health [16]. Instead, a sociotechnical approach looks at the social context in which health literacy practices occurs, taking into consideration the people, practices, technologies, and artifacts involved in providing access to easy-to-read health information, as well as the characteristics of the system that make health literacy an important social agenda. Health literacy comprises a set of socially embedded practices involving not just the intended users of consumer health information resources, but also library professionals, health practitioners, health literacy proponents, and content creators. This approach facilitates the study of the interdependencies between the professional practices involved in providing access to easy to read health information, the technologies implicated in these practices—such as the use of guidelines and readability formulas—and the ultimate users of these materials. In doing so, we can investigate and better understand the specific challenges experienced by particular constituencies when engaged in everyday life information practices such as those related to health.

References

1. Arazy, O., Kopak, R.: On the measurability of information quality. J. Am. Soc. Inf. Sci. Technol. **62**(1), 89–99 (2011)
2. Baker, D.W., Gazmararian, J.A., Williams, M.V., Scott, T., Parker, R.M., Green, D., Ren, J., Peel, J.: Functional health literacy and the risk of hospital admission among medicare managed care enrollees. Am. J. Public Health **92**(8), 1278–1283 (2002)
3. Berkman, N.D., Sheridan, S.L., Donahue, K.E., Halpern, D.J., Crotty, K.: Low health literacy and health outcomes: an updated systematic review. Ann. Intern. Med. **155**(2), 97–107 (2011)
4. Chall, J.S., Dale, E.: Readability Revisited: The New Dale-Chall Readability Formula. Brookline Books, Brookline (1995)
5. Dollahite, J., Thompson, C., McNew, R.: Readability of printed sources of diet and health information. Patient Educ. Couns. **27**(2), 123–134 (1996)
6. DuBay, W.H.: The Principles of Readability. Impact Information, Costa Mesa (2004)
7. Eysenbach, G., Kohler, C.: How do consumers search for and appraise health information on the world wide web? Qualitative study using focus groups, usability tests, and in-depth interviews. Br. Med. J. **324**(7337), 573–577 (2002)
8. Federal Plain Language Guidelines. www.plainlanguage.gov/howto/guidelines/bigdoc/fullbigdoc.pdf. Accessed 18 Sept 2017
9. Feng, L., Elhadad, N., Huenerfauth, M.: Cognitively motivated features for readability assessment. In: Proceedings of the 12th Conference of the European Chapter of the Association for Computational Linguistics, pp. 229–237. Association for Computational Linguistics, Athens (2009)
10. Flesch, R.: A new readability yardstick. J. Appl. Psychol. **32**(3), 221 (1948)
11. Giddens, A.: The Constitution of Society: Outline of the Theory of Structuration. University of California Press, Berkeley (1984)
12. Health Literacy Online: A Guide for Simplifying the User Experience. https://health.gov/healthliteracyonline/. Accessed 18 Sept 2017

13. Hilligoss, B., Rieh, S.Y.: Developing a unifying framework of credibility assessment: construct, heuristics, and interaction in context. Inf. Process. Manag. **44**(4), 1467–1484 (2008)
14. How to write Easy-to-Read Health Materials. https://medlineplus.gov/etr.html#assess. Accessed 18 Sept 2017
15. Howard, D.H., Gazmararian, J., Parker, R.M.: The impact of low health literacy on the medical costs of medicare managed care enrollees. Am. J. Med. **118**(4), 371–377 (2005)
16. Huber, J.T., Shapiro, R.M., Gillaspy, M.L.: Top down versus bottom up: the social construction of the health literacy movement. Libr. Q. **82**(4), 429–451 (2012)
17. Kim, W., Kreps, G.L., Shin, C.N.: The role of social support and social networks in health information–seeking behavior among Korean Americans: a qualitative study. Int. J. Equity Health **14**(1), 40 (2015)
18. Kindig, D.A., Panzer, A.M., Nielsen-Bohlman, L. (eds.): Health Literacy: A Prescription to End Confusion. National Academies Press, Washington, DC (2004)
19. Klare, G.R.: Readability. Handb. Read. Res. **1**, 681–744 (1984)
20. Koh, H.K., Berwick, D.M., Clancy, C.M., Baur, C., Brach, C., Harris, L.M., Zerhusen, E.G.: New federal policy initiatives to boost health literacy can help the nation move beyond the cycle of costly 'crisis care'. Health Aff. (2012). https://doi.org/10.1377/hlthaff.2011.1169
21. Leonardi, P.M.: Theoretical foundations for the study of sociomateriality. Inf. Organ. **23**(2), 59–76 (2013)
22. Marshall, L.A., Williams, D.: Health information: does quality count for the consumer? How consumers evaluate the quality of health information materials across a variety of media. J. Librariansh. Inf. Sci. **38**(3), 141–156 (2006)
23. McLaughlin, G.H.: SMOG grading-a new readability formula. J. Read. **12**(8), 639–646 (1969)
24. Redish, J.: Readability formulas have even more limitations than Klare discusses. ACM J. Comput. Doc. (JCD) **24**(3), 132–137 (2000)
25. Savolainen, R.: Everyday life information seeking: approaching information seeking in the context of "way of life". Libr. Inf. Sci. Res. **17**(3), 259–294 (1995)
26. Schriver, K.A.: Readability formulas in the new millennium: what's the use? ACM J. Comput. Doc. **24**(3), 138–140 (2000)
27. Sørensen, K., Van den Broucke, S., Fullam, J., Doyle, G., Pelikan, J., Slonska, Z., Brand, H.: Health literacy and public health: a systematic review and integration of definitions and models. BMC Public Health **12**(1), 1 (2012)
28. Stvilia, B., Gasser, L., Twidale, M.B., Smith, L.C.: A framework for information quality assessment. J. Assoc. Inf. Sci. Technol. **58**(12), 1720–1733 (2007)
29. Tuominen, K., Savolainen, R., Talja, S.: Information literacy as a sociotechnical practice. Libr. Q. **75**(3), 329–345 (2005)
30. Walsh, T.M., Volsko, T.A.: Readability assessment of internet-based consumer health information. Respir. Care **53**(10), 1310–1315 (2008)
31. Wiegand, W.A.: Out of sight out of mind: why don't we have any schools of library and reading studies? J. Educ. Libr. Inf. Sci. **38**(4), 314–326 (1997)

Building Understanding Between Users
and Designers Through Participatory Design:
The Bonded Design Approach

Valerie Nesset[(⊠)] and J. Brice Bible

University at Buffalo (SUNY), Buffalo, NY, USA
{vmnesset, bible}@buffalo.edu

Abstract. Universities face great pressure to adopt and integrate new technologies to enhance learning. Yet, often a gap exists between IT personnel who provide support based on their knowledge of how the technologies are designed to work and the faculty users who have differing ideas about how they need them to work. To address this gap, a large research-intensive university in New York State has embarked on an initiative using the Bonded Design participatory design methodology. Working together in design teams, IT staff and faculty will learn from each other to enable creation of technology solutions that could not be done by each group alone.

Keywords: Participatory design · Bonded design · Design techniques
Innovative learning · User experience · UX

1 Introduction

Research-intensive universities are charged with the mandate to attract faculty members who are experts and leaders in cutting-edge research in their respective disciplines. In turn, students come to learn from these best and brightest. Furthermore, rapidly advancing instructional technologies have allowed for wider audiences and varied forms of interaction between educator and student yet faculty of all ranks who have been hired primarily for their subject expertise may struggle to keep up with these rapid changes. Potentially compounding the problem is the fact that IT staff are often so involved with managing the technology they do not even come into contact with faculty members unless there is a specific problem with hardware or software.

This paper will discuss the initiation of a new project at a large research-intensive university in New York State that is designed to address this disconnect. The purpose of the program is to improve user experience by facilitating meaningful interaction between IT personnel and faculty members through the use of participatory design, specifically, an adaptation of the Bonded Design (BD) methodology created to design technology in intergenerational teams [1–3]. Working together in participatory design teams using the BD method faculty and IT personnel will share expertise and learn from each other – the faculty sharing what they need the technology to do and IT personnel sharing how the technology is designed to work. By engaging in such an environment both groups begin to "speak the same language" and will be better able to

G. Chowdhury et al. (Eds.): iConference 2018, LNCS 10766, pp. 515–520, 2018.
https://doi.org/10.1007/978-3-319-78105-1_56

discuss technology issues with each other in ways they can both understand and act upon. The project consists of three stages: a university-wide technology needs assessment, participatory design sessions involving two teams each consisting of faculty and IT staff volunteers, and assessment; it is currently at the beginning of the second stage.

2 Conceptual Framework – Participatory Design

Highly comparable to the present user experience (UX) movement, the concept of participatory design (PD) originated in Scandinavia to address the increasing evidence that workers are in the best position to decide how to improve their workplace. PD involves highly iterative and inclusive methods that look to compromise rather than consensus to unite designers and users of technology in the design of information technologies that better meet the users' needs. Using two main techniques, metaphor and modeling to implement its two main principles, "mutual reciprocal learning" and "design by doing" PD involves users and designers teaching each other about work practices and technological possibilities using design-by-doing techniques such as interactive experimentation and hands-on design to develop low-tech prototypes [4, 5]. The literature is replete with references to participatory design studies conducted to facilitate interaction between users and designers of technology. Approaches such as Bonded Design [1–3], Contextual Design [6], Cooperative Inquiry [7], Informant Design [8], and Learner-Centered Design [9, 10] are but a few examples of methods developed to address the unique technology needs of specific user groups.

When deciding on an approach to use with faculty and IT personnel for the university-wide project, the most important criterion was the ability to unite two very disparate groups within a limited time frame. Bonded Design was chosen due to its potential for more flexible scheduling and number of sessions, comprehensive adoption and adaptation of elements from other participatory design models (particularly learner-centered design), and its intergenerational focus, where the designers and children were both considered "experts" in the design-team process, the children experts in being children and the researchers experts in technology design, similar to the faculty and IT staff context where the faculty members are experts in what they *need* the technology to do and the IT staff experts in what the technology is *designed* to do – not always necessarily the same thing.

3 Methodology

Using the BD methodology as a framework, the project is planned in three phases: needs assessment, participatory design sessions, and assessment, with each subsequent phase building upon the former. This section describes the elements of the three stages and provides the rationales for their implementation.

3.1   Phase 1: Needs Assessment

Any participatory design process should start with a needs assessment to determine the wants and needs of the larger user group to help inform and focus the design planning process. The needs assessment for this project took the form of the first-ever university-wide survey of the faculty in spring 2017 to determine their use of computer hardware (e.g., a PC or Mac laptop and/or desktop), the age and model of the most-used and preferred hardware, smartphone carriers and use, and instructional technology use. The survey was designed by a steering committee comprised of the university's Chief Information Officer (CIO), the information science researcher (who had recently received the title, 'IT Faculty Fellow' in recognition of her initiatives to engage faculty and IT staff and administrators in meaningful interactions) and representatives from IT and instructional facilities staff. In the spirit of BD, it was considered important for the survey to be reviewed by faculty members. To that end, before the questionnaire was administered, the questions were examined by members of the university's faculty senate IT subcommittee.

3.2   Phase 2: The Design Sessions

Adapting the Bonded Design Methodology. The key elements of BD (Fig. 1), namely collaboration between designers and users as members of a design team, the design techniques, and the creation of a low-tech prototype can quite easily be modified to facilitate interaction between university IT staff and faculty. The proposed modifications will be identified and explained in the following section.

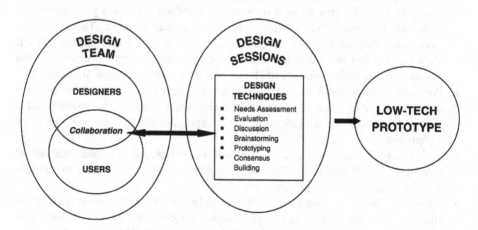

Fig. 1. The bonded design model [1–3]

Recruiting Participants – The Faculty IT Liaison Program. Omitted from the BD methodology are details regarding recruitment of participants for the design teams from a very large pool of users. In the university project, for purposes of diversity and equity, it was decided that it was important for each team to be comprised of faculty members from different academic units who are "typical" users, that is, somewhat comfortable with technology but not experts, and in recognition of faculty's busy schedules, the design sessions had to consist of enough sessions to get the job done while not overburdening the participants. To address these issues, the project designers came up with the idea of "faculty liaisons". As faculty liaisons, the faculty participants are not only actively involved in the project through the design sessions, but also at the end of the sessions along with an IT member of their team, they will go back to their academic units to serve as trainers for the technologies they have investigated. To provide control on the numbers of participants, an application form was developed explaining the purpose of the design sessions, outlining basic requirements of participation and a broad timeline, along with questions regarding the familiarity with technology, what technologies the faculty member uses and for what purposes, and an open-ended question asking why the faculty member is interested in participating. The application also made it clear that faculty members who are not IT experts were preferred for the sessions. Of 68 applicants, 13 faculty met the criteria and were asked to participate as members of two design teams each of which includes two IT staff volunteers and the researcher.

Data Collection Instruments. To better investigate the efficacy of the design team process, several data collection instruments/methods will be used:

- *Participant observation.* In this method, the researcher becomes a data collection instrument through direct interaction with the participants, actively engaging with them in meaningful ways. As Lincoln and Guba [11] assert, "it is the quality of interaction that provides the human instrument with the possibility of fully exploiting its own natural advantages". This is achieved by documenting one's perceptions and insights through such means as reflective memoing. As Miles and Huberman [12] state, "Memos are primarily conceptual in intent. They don't just report data: they tie together different pieces of data into a recognizable cluster, often to show that those data are instances of a general concept...[memoing] often provides sharp, sunlit moments of clarity or insight—little conceptual epiphanies."
- *Pre- and post-questionnaires.* For comparison, team members will be asked to complete a pre-questionnaire regarding their expectations of the process and a post-questionnaire investigating their perceptions of the process after its completion.
- *Videotapes of sessions.* Each session will be videotaped for later analysis to investigate actual behaviors. The results will then be compared with the participants' perceptions of the process.
- *Interviews.* One-on-one interviews will be conducted with willing participants in an effort to allow the researchers to gain further insights into the participants' perspectives than could be attained through the questionnaire [13].

Design Techniques. As the needs assessment is already finished, the design sessions will use the second to sixth design techniques in the BD methodology where the first task is evaluation of technology, the choice of which is directly informed by results of the needs assessment. For the present project, the technologies identified for investigation include various aspects of the course management system (e.g., student grading center, course tools), interactive instructional software, email, and cloud storage solutions. One of the first activities within the design sessions is for all team members to draw a mental model of a specific technology or create a concept map of what they think are its most important elements. Using these artifacts as a launching point for discussion, the teams will discuss the different interpretations and applications of the technology. A brainstorming session follows, where all ideas, no matter how unrealistic, are treated as equal and duly recorded. As discovered in the BD studies with the young students, it is during these brainstorming sessions where there is no judgment and where all user participants are free to voice their thoughts that innovative and often surprising potential uses of a technology are discovered [1–3]. Indeed, it is expected in the current study that the faculty users will introduce various "technology hacks" they use to get the technology to work as they need it to.

Typically, in BD, once brainstorming is finished and the ideas discussed (discussion may cover the advantages, disadvantages, and feasibility of each idea) and recorded, team members start to create low-tech prototypes in a hands-on iterative process that involves strong collaboration between team members and the frequent revisiting and revising of draft prototypes. In this project, prototyping will involve making modifications to the technology based on the faculty members' needs, along with drafting procedures and protocols that use more user-centered language. In this way, the collaborations within the design teams can benefit the much wider university community.

It is important to note that while BD has a structured protocol for each design session, flexibility is essential. As described above, participatory design is highly iterative so there must be allowances made for revisiting different design techniques throughout; however, the process must keep on track if it is to be productive within the limited time frame.

3.3   Phase 3: Assessment

Given the university environment and the higher level of education and expertise of the faculty participants, it was decided to supplement the low-tech prototypes created in the design sessions with assessment. Assessment will consist of evaluating and refining the protocols and technology hacks created by the design teams in consultation with IT, instructional design, and different faculty members so that they can be used in the wider university context. In this way, the research takes on a direct-action component.

Assessment of the project as a whole will take place after the design sessions are completed and will be conducted by the members of the research team. Evaluation will be done on each of the following aspects of the first two phases of the project:

- *Faculty IT needs assessment.* Areas covered, question structure, frequency of administration;
- *Faculty recruitment.* Efficacy of liaison program, equity of academic unit representation, cost-benefit analysis, scalability;
- *Technologies explored.* Appropriateness for design teams, scalability;
- *Design techniques.* Number of sessions, appropriateness for environment, efficacy, scalability;
- *Deliverables.* Appropriateness, efficacy, scalability.

4 Conclusion

The authors wish to make it clear that Bonded Design is only one of several partici-patory design methods that could be used in this context and it is not necessarily better than other methodologies to accomplish this task. The authors do believe, however, that BD is a feasible methodology in a context where time is a critical factor and where two disparate groups of people with different expertise need to interact with one another. Furthermore, this project seeks to explore the premise suggested by developers of the BD methodology, namely that it could be used to unite people with different expertise in a shared experience and that by bringing them together ideas and innovations that might not occur to those with similar expertise and experiences are made possible.

References

1. Large, A., Nesset, V.: Bonded design. In: Khosrow, M. (ed.) Encyclopedia of Information Science and Technology, 2nd edn, pp. 383–388. Hershey, Information Science Reference (2009)
2. Large, A., Nesset, V., Beheshti, J., Bowler, L.: "Bonded Design": a novel approach to intergenerational information technology design. Libr. Inf. Sci. Res. **28**, 64–82 (2006)
3. Large, A., Nesset, V., Beheshti, J., Bowler, L.: Bonded design: a methodology for designing with children. In: Zaphiris, P., Kurniawan, S. (eds.) Advances in Universal Web Design and Evaluation: Research, Trends and Opportunities, pp. 73–96. Idea Group, Hershey (2007)
4. Carmel, E., Whitaker, R., George, J.: PD and joint application design: a transatlantic comparison. Commun. ACM **36**(4), 40–48 (1993)
5. Muller, M., Kuhn, S.: PD. Commun. ACM **36**(6), 24–28 (1993)
6. Beyer, H., Holtzblatt, K.: Contextual design. ACM Interact. **6**, 32–42 (1999)
7. Druin, A.: Cooperative inquiry: developing new technologies for children with children. In: Proceedings of the SIGCHI Conference on Human Factors in Computing Systems, pp. 592–599. ACM Press, New York (1999)
8. Scaife, M., Rogers, Y.: Kids as informants: telling us what we didn't know or confirming what we knew already. In: Druin, A. (ed.) The Design of Children's Technology, pp. 27–50. Morgan Kaufmann Publishers, San Francisco (1999)
9. Soloway, E., Guzdial, M., Hay, K.: Learner-centered design: the challenge for HCI in the 21st century. Interactions **1**(2), 36–48 (1994)
10. Guzdial, M.: Learner-Centered Design of Computing Education: Research on Computing for Everyone. Morgan & Claypool Publishers, San Rafael (2016)
11. Lincoln, Y.S., Guba, E.G.: Naturalistic Inquiry. Sage Publications, Newbury Park (1985)
12. Miles, M.B., Huberman, A.M.: Qualitative Data Analysis: An Expanded Sourcebook. Sage, Thousand Oaks (1994)
13. Patton, M.Q.: Qualitative Research and Evaluation Methods. Sage, Thousand Oaks (2002)

Information Behavior and Filipino Values:
An Exploratory Study

Kathleen Lourdes B. Obille(✉)

School of Library and Information Studies,
University of the Philippines, Diliman, Quezon City, Philippines
kate@slis.upd.edu.ph

Abstract. This sought to determine whether Filipino values play a role in how the respondents sought, used, created and disseminated information. It gathered data on how they used information in the context of social media – whether they are active information seekers or passive information browsers; along with how identified Filipino values or characteristics are reflected. Findings show that the respondents appreciate various information sources – both online and offline, have various social media accounts and find use for each depending on the need and context, they are online most of the time and are informationally dependent. The values of *hiya, gaya-gaya* and *pagkakaibigan* reflect on their SNS use, what information to share and how they relate with their online and offline friends and relations.

Keywords: Information behavior · Information use · Social media
Filipino values

1 Introduction

The internet and social media somehow brought about different perspectives on information seeking and information use. Social media has democratized information where information creation is no longer among the select few but from anyone who has Internet connection, a mobile device and a social media account. As such, it has brought about a new way of creating, storing and accessing information. Crowd sourcing, feedback or review mechanisms (i.e. reactions or comments in blogs), reaction mechanisms (i.e. likes and reactions in Facebook, Instagram or Twitter) have paved other ways of providing and gathering information. Instead of the specific information seeking and information use, the goal of the study is to determine the overall behavior of UP SLIS students toward information and whether there are cultural factors that relate to this. Wilson [1] and Marchionini [2] have both acknowledged that the individuals and their demographics or situations have a role to play in their information behavior (for Wilson) and information seeking and use (for Marchionini).

Social media has taken a center stage in the information scene and several researches have been done to determine how factors [3] such as age, sex, motives, perceptions of social media use. Personality traits and other variables were considered [4, 5] to determine their relations to social networking support. Uses of social media permeates all aspects of life from educational, financial, social, health, leisure and more.

© Springer International Publishing AG, part of Springer Nature 2018
G. Chowdhury et al. (Eds.): iConference 2018, LNCS 10766, pp. 521–526, 2018.
https://doi.org/10.1007/978-3-319-78105-1_57

The Philippines is among the countries with the highest Internet and social media usage [6]. The recent national elections showcased how Filipinos have creatively made use of social media in the various aspects of election: from gathering information about the candidates, providing or expressing support, argue for or against, advance propaganda, or just follow and get updates on the campaign.

Filipinos are known for being hospitable, amiable, and resilient. However, there are other values or characteristics which are highly identified with Filipinos such as *utang na loob* (indebtedness or being grateful), *hiya* (to feel shame or shyness), *delicadeza* (to be cautious), *pagtitiis* (to endure), *pakikisama* (to get along with). These values have been identified as values or traits of Filipinos that have to do with smooth interpersonal relations [7]. Such values may affect or are reflected in their information behavior, as social media is an extension of social relations. The main objective of the study determined whether these values are reflected in their information behavior especially in the context of social media. The choice of the context was mainly to limit the parameter of information behavior. It also determined whether the respondents are more of active information seekers or passive information browsers in the context of social media. As this is exploratory, this was conducted in a small group of LIS students from the University of the Philippines School of Library and Information Studies (UP SLIS).

1.1 Information Behavior

Wilson [1] has defined *information behavior* as the totality of human behavior in relation to sources and channels of information, including both active and passive information seeking, and information use (p. 49). Under the umbrella of information behavior area *information seeking behavior, information searching behavior* and *information use behavior*. Several researches on information behavior have been conducted and Khoo [8] has reviewed these and some of the results of these researches include the following: younger users are more likely to use SNS; women tend to use SNS more than men; factors affecting SNS include: technology characteristics, perceived benefits, social factors, psychological factors and perceived risks; social media sites are considered as sources of information; Information behaviors include: sharing, gaining attention, social support, collaboration, hostile and/or biased information behavior; various information shared in social media: jokes; medical, educational, political, etc. information; photos; everyday life and/or special events.

Bates [9] on the other hand, has distinguished two dimensions of information seeking to include directed vs undirected information seeking and active vs passive information seeking. Thus the four modes of information seeking: searching, browsing, monitoring, and awareness.

1.2 Filipino Values

Some of the identified Filipino values that permeate most relationships, systems and beliefs include: *hiya* (feeling of shame or shyness), *utang na loob* (indebtedness or feeling grateful), *paggaya* (imitation), *pagkampi* (taking sides), *pakikisama* (to get along with) and *pagkakaibigan* (friendship) [7]. The translations however do not completely cover the meaning of the values, they will suffice to present the idea for now. There are other Filipino values or traits but these were the ones that came about in the discussion with the respondents. The use of Filipino values in explaining information behavior is covered by both Marchionini and Wilson in that personal dimensions affect information behavior. However, it is the objective of this study to determine how specific values affect information behavior specific to social media use.

2 Methodology

The study is qualitative in nature and is exploratory. This is to determine initially the information behavior of Filipinos and whether there are specific values or cultural specificities to this effect. This is a preliminary study done using a few subjects/respondents and it is hoped that this can be done quantitatively in a larger scale.

2.1 Respondents

The respondents are LIS Students of the University of the Philippines, School of Library and Information Studies (UP SLIS). There were two groups, the undergraduate and the graduate students. The undergraduate students are mostly shiftees[1] thus they have spent at least two years in their previous undergraduate programs. The graduate students are mostly studying part time since they are employed full time. They are also a mix of professional librarians[2] and non-librarians[3] working toward their licenses but are working in libraries as praprofessionals[4]. There were 11 undergraduate students (6 males and 5 females) and 11 graduate students (4 males and 7 females) who participated in the study thus a total of 22 participants. The UP SLIS students were selected as respondents for the study for the fact that they are known for their heavy usage of SNS both in their personal and academic lives. As they are heavy users, a variety of SNS use was expected. The participants were asked to keep a diary of their information use for about a week (from August 13–19, 2017). The focus group discussion was done a week later with two groups – graduate students and undergraduate students.

2.2 Data Collection

Diary. The respondents were asked to keep a diary to document how they used information. This was done for one week in free-form writing. Themes and sub-themes were determined and categorized accordingly.

---

[1] Undergraduate students coming from a previous college in the university (within Diliman) or university system (from other UP Campuses).

[2] In the Philippines, a law (RA 9246) mandates that librarians should pass the Librarian Licensure Examination (LLE) to be able to practice librarianship.

[3] At the UP SLIS, the MLIS accommodates non-graduates of BLIS and a plan is so designed for them to be able to take the LLE.

[4] Paraprofessionals are those working in the library without license to practice librarianship (i.e. clerks, technicians etc.).

Focus Group Discussion. The participants were grouped as to graduate and under-graduate groups. The focused group discussion enabled the participants to explain their social media use/activities and several realizations were made as well. This mainly expanded and articulated entries in their diary and were substantiated with specific situations and events.

3   Results

3.1   Diary

The participants were as to keep a diary to log all activities where they sought information. This was in free form as well as free in use of language (may be in English and/or Filipino). Based on their entries in their diary, the following themes were realized: Personal (sub-themes: hygiene, health/illness, homework, news, leisure, help out others, shopping); Work (sub-themes: feedback/comments from supervisor, suggestions/feedback from customers, reference work, furniture, information delivery); Food (sub-themes: recipes, places to eat); Weather (Sub-themes: forecast, flood advisory, rainfall advisory); Hobby (sub-themes: movies, DIY, music); Travel (sub-themes: traffic advisory, travel time, directions, visa).

The entries were varied, some short and straight to the point while some very lengthy and detailed. Information use also vary along with information sources. Information sources come in both personal (friends, co-workers etc.) and technical/professional (from books, journals etc.) as well as online sources (i.e. SNS, email, web). As half of the respondents are working in libraries, there are quite a number of entries pertaining to reference queries and the information sources they sought which were as expected to be sources in their own libraries. There were several entries on how the students sought information about their hobbies or about something that interested them. One entry detailed how he considered the price and sodium content of two brands of crackers but decided to try the other for curiosity. Song lyrics and information on movie characters were also sought. YouTube was also noted as a favorite source for anything and everything instructional. Google maps and Waze were also consulted for travel directions, places to eat, and traffic congestion information.

The various entries show that the respondents recognize various sources of information – from personal sources, document sources, internet and social media. The respondents also indicated their reliance on mobile phone applications such as Waze, Google Maps, Facebook, Twitter, Accuweather, Facebook Messenger, Reddit and Instagram. Their entries also indicated that they are online most of the time.

3.2   Group Discussion

The discussion started with the respondents listing the mobile applications that they have and use in their mobile devices and the top 5 applications are as follows: Chrome, Twitter, Facebook, YouTube, and Waze. Other applications include Uber, Facebook Messenger, Viber, Google Maps, Accuweather, Goodreads and notepad. It was also shared by the respondents that there are pre-installed applications in their mobile devices that they do not use. It can be noted that they do not use health applications like calorie counters, or exercise apps.

In terms of their online or onlife as Floridi [10] calls it, the undergraduate students (the younger ones) are still logging off their mobile devices. The undergraduate students have also indicated that they are screening notifications from the SNS that they have. The graduate students on the other hand were unanimous in saying that they are online all the time. It was also noted that for Twitter, they can easily log off or close the app but have difficulty doing so in Facebook and Instagram. In these two apps, they have noted that they are of the browsing type than the searching type.

As for SNS, they do not have any preference but they have considered the usefulness of the sites. For news, they would consult Twitter. For information about families and friends (and friends of friends) they would go for Facebook and Instagram. The undergraduate students have branched on to discuss their observation on the evolution of the SNS in terms of their main or original goal. Facebook for example was mainly used to connect to friends and family (like the defunct Friendster). However, this seemed to evolve to a news sharing site, advocacy site, marketing and selling site etc. The UPSLIS for one, uses Facebook and created an online community for SLIS faculty and staff, students, and alumni for announcements, invitations, news and update etc. They have also observed that both young and old are already in Facebook. This is where they have realized that the value/culture of imitating or *gaya-gaya* is reflected. They felt that once a friend posts something interesting (travel photos, black and white photo challenge, unboxing, selfies, OOTD, memes) it easily catches on especially when this friend is popular in the circle. One has detailed further that it is easy for fads to proliferate via Facebook and described how her aunt actively told the niece to take a certain photo and post it on Facebook because the neighbor just did.

In Facebook, Twitter and Instagram where likes and reactions are available, are observed varying degrees of friendships. There are those just online friends and those that are friends-friends. They have also observed that just online friends are active in reacting to posts but do not necessarily approach them. They realized that this may be due to *hiya* – that these just online friends are shy in approaching them or the fact that there are online personas that do not necessarily translate to offlife. While they interact more offlife with their friends-friends. Another manifestation of *hiya* as realized by the participants is when they self-edit their posts just because it may be offensive to some or that they don't look good in their selfie. Expressing likes in Facebook and Instagram for them is also a form of *pakikisama* to reciprocate those who have liked their posts. This can also show *pagkampi* expressing like over another post.

Crowdsourcing is one of the uses of social media for both graduate and undergraduate respondents – whether for their work, personal, technical, etc. One instance is for advice on technical specs of a computer peripheral. They do crowdsourcing either to have a layman's term/description of what they are looking for or getting confirmation or validation of their initial decision. They have also noted that making decisions is sometimes easy when doing crowdsourcing, when people bash a certain feedback or comment, then that is already off the list. They also look into crowdsourcing because people of authority or those who have experience with certain products may provide feedback and theirs is valuable. Some have indicated Reddit as a venue for such feedback or information gathering as "real people" provide answers to questions. On the other hand, they also participate in crowdsourcing mainly to reciprocate others as such a reflection of *pakikisama*.

3.3 Findings

The results show that the respondents are information dependent in most aspects of their lives whether personal, academic or professional and their information use is varied. The graduate students are online most of the time and that they tend to gather information online mostly via SNS. *Hiya, gaya-gaya, pakikisama, pagkakaibigan* and *pagkampi* are values that are reflected in their information behavior in the way they post, express their likes, post comments etc. Further study is needed to validate such findings and also to determine whether these are specific to Filipinos or not. Arguably, *gaya-gaya* and *hiya* are also experienced by others (self-editing of posts, selecting photos to post).

References

1. Wilson, T.D.: Human information behavior. Inf. Sci. **3**(2), 49–55 (2000). http://inform.nu/Articles/Vol3/v3n2p49-56.pdf
2. Marchionini, G.: Information Seeking in Electronic Environments. Cambridge University Press, Cambridge (1995)
3. Cha, J.: Factors affecting the frequency and amount of social networking site use: motivations, perceptions and privacy concerns. First Monday. **15**(12), December 2010. http://firstmonday.org/ojs/index.php/fm/article/view/2889/2685
4. Pornsakulvanich, P.: Personality, attitudes, social influences and social networking site usage predicting online social support. Comput. Hum. Behav. **76**, 255–262 (2017)
5. Maqbel, M.: Unveiling the dark side of social networking sites: personal and work-related consequences of social networking site addiction. Inf. Manag. **55**, 109–119 (2018). https://doi.org/10.1016/j.im.2017.05.001
6. Camus, M.R.: PH World's No. 1 in terms of time spent on social media. Inquirer (2017). http://technology.inquirer.net/58090/ph-worlds-no-1-terms-time-spent-social-media
7. Church, A.T.: Filipino Personality: A Review of Research and Writings. De La Salle University Press, Manila (1986)
8. Khoo, C.S.G.: Issues in information behavior. Libres **24**(2), 75–96 (2014)
9. Bates, M.: Toward an integrated model of information seeking and searching. New Rev. Inf. Behav. Res. **3**, 1–15 (2002)
10. Floridi, L.: The Fourth Revolution: How the Infosphere is Reshaping Human Reality. Oxford University Press, Oxford (2014)

Assessing Digital Skills of Refugee Migrants During Job Orientation in Germany

Juliane Stiller$^{(\boxtimes)}$ and Violeta Trkulja

Berlin School of Library and Information Science, Humboldt-Universität zu Berlin,
Unter den Linden 6, 10099 Berlin, Germany
{juliane.stiller,violeta.trkulja}@ibi.hu-berlin.de

Abstract. This paper examines the digital skill level of refugee migrants in Germany while pursuing a job, a training position, or following an educational path on the Internet. For that, we conducted a lab experiment designing tasks with varying difficulty to position the digital competencies of refugee migrants on the digital skill scale. Problems with operational and formal skills were observed whereas fact-based information seeking was often successfully completed. The most complex tasks could not be completed by any participant. The study contributes to a better understanding of the varying degrees of digital skills of refugee migrants. Results can be used to design targeted courses and curricula that address digital deficits. Further training in this area will enable refugee migrants to benefit from the many opportunities that arise through the Internet and its services, improving their chances for labor market integration.

Keywords: Digital skills · Internet skills · Information-seeking
Refugee migrants

1 Introduction

In the year 2015, over one million people sought asylum in Germany fleeing from Syria and Afghanistan and other countries where war prevails. Processing the asylum requests and integrating refugee migrants[1] into the German society is the ultimate challenge public authorities still struggle with up to now. Although the integration activities in Germany are designed to equip refugees with language skills, training in fundamental values as well as democratic participation, the activities fail to impart people with the digital skills and competences they need to help themselves online. This is particularly severe as German job-seeking activities are increasingly moving online.[2] For example, in 2013, 60% of

---

[1] As our research affects the area of forced migration we will refer to the term "refugee migrants" [1] to make clear that we apply to this group of migrants.
[2] In 2015, the top 1,000 companies in Germany published 90% of their vacancies on their company website, 7 out of 10 vacancies are offered on online job portals [2].

© Springer International Publishing AG, part of Springer Nature 2018
G. Chowdhury et al. (Eds.): iConference 2018, LNCS 10766, pp. 527–536, 2018.
https://doi.org/10.1007/978-3-319-78105-1_58

unemployed adults in Germany used the Internet to search and apply for a job [3, p. 25], whereas 10% of the refugee migrants use the Internet or newspapers to search for a job [4]. In our experience, refugee migrants with sufficient language skills (B1 and higher)[3] and all other prerequisites (such as qualifications and degrees recognized in Germany) to find a job or a training position are unable to do so as the lack of digital skills or competencies emerges to be the primary barrier to success in this area.

By assessing the digital skill level of refugee migrants, we will gain understanding in how deficits in finding, processing and analyzing information on the Internet can be tackled. This is an important aspect of forced migration research, which could be used to design targeted courses that contribute to the development of digital skills. Further training in this area will enable refugee migrants to benefit from the many opportunities that arise through the Internet and its services, improving their chances for labor market integration.

In this paper, we examined the digital skills of seven refugee migrants while pursuing a job, a training position or following an educational path on the Internet. We positioned competencies of the participants on the digital skill scale developed by van Deursen and van Dijk [6,7] and analyzed how they approach information-seeking tasks with different difficulty levels on the Internet.

The following Sect. 2 introduces relevant literature. Section 3 presents the study design and the scale that was used to assess the refugees digital skills. Section 4 describes the results of the study. The last section of the paper discusses the findings and assesses limitations to the study as well as future work.

2   Relevant Literature

Digital skills are seen as vital for living, working, studying, and entertaining oneself in the information society and defined as a crucial phase in the appropriation of digital technology [7]. Recent studies have shown that the demand for Information and Communications Technology (ICT) generic skills has increased in the majority of countries and that workers across an increasing range of occupations need generic and/or advanced ICT skills to use digital technologies effectively [8]. But digital skills are not only a prerequisite for high-quality jobs in general, they are also necessary to enable refugee migrants to obtain information about the labor market of their host country and seek employment online.[4]

So far, there is little knowledge about the digital skills and competencies of refugee migrants. It appears that this particular group of people is slowly gaining attention in information science research. Trailblazing research in information

---

[3] In the Integration courses, refugee migrants learn German language skills up to the B1-level based on the Common European Framework of Reference for Languages. On this level, learners should be able to have conversations in various contexts and cope with everyday problems [5, p. 34].

[4] A survey among German companies revealed that 59% of them advertise job offers on their homepage and use Internet job portals (42%) to find appropriate candidates for their open positions [9].

behavior of refugees was contributed by Karen Fisher. Her research is characterized by extensive field studies she conducted in refugee camps, e.g. [10,11]. Alam and Imran [12] examined the factors which influence refugee migrants' adoption of digital technology and its relevance to social inclusion in Australia. They found that there is a "digital divide among refugee migrant groups which is based on inequalities in physical access to and use of digital technology, the skills necessary to use the different technologies effectively and the ability to pay for the services" [12, p. 344].

Other studies targeted ICT usage of immigrants - not necessarily to be equated with refugee migrants - and their information behavior related to information needs, sources and grounds [13], the affection of migrants to the Internet [14], and information practices in the context of leisure and settlement [15]. Several other ethnographic studies examined Internet usage of migrant groups to maintain relationships in home countries and explored the use of different media, e.g. [16,17]. Overall, these studies suggest that Internet familiarity is high among migrants but it remains unknown how frequently the Internet is used for seeking employment. In their extensive review of research of information practices of immigrants, Caidi et al. [18] identified several research gaps. Among them is a lack of studies that focus on specific information needs: However, no studies within the information literature specifically address how immigrants find employment or make use of employment information to secure work [18, p. 520]. A better understanding of refugee migrants' digital skills is a research gap also identified by Litt [19].

With regard to information seeking strategies on the Internet or interactions with information systems, research targeting refugee migrants is very rare. A group that received more attention with regard to their information practices are international students. Although these studies focus on information literacy and challenges international students face in using ICT for academic purposes, e.g. [20,21], and everyday life [22], some of the findings might also apply to refugee migrants information seeking strategies. Participants in Mehra and Bilal's [20] study mention an inadequate level of language skills as a factor that might lead to problems in using interfaces, understanding structures and relationships between terms and formulating effective queries.

A solid base of research exists for the assessment of Internet skills[5] of various groups of people and in nationally representative surveys [19,23]. Using their developed digital skill framework, van Deursen and van Dijk [6] examined the Internet skills of the Dutch population revealing that the more complex the Internet tasks become, the less people can complete them. Similar results were obtained with Dutch secondary students [24], where only 64% of the students could complete the assignments successfully. This is intriguing as young people are considered to be especially savvy due to their frequent use of ICT. Also refugee migrants heavily use the Internet for communication and staying in touch with their home countries. Eynon and Geniets [25] studied a group of digitally

---

[5] We use the term "digital skills" which refers to the use of the Internet and can be used synonymously to the term "internet skills".

marginalized young people and found that digital skills are developed through an interplay of various factors such as access, network of support and motivation but that is very unlikely that the development of digital skills just happens due to frequent use. Whether these findings can also be applied to refugee migrants is still an open research question.

3   Methodology and Study Design

The study was conducted in August 2017 with seven refugee migrants coming from Syria and Iraq. Participation was voluntarily and the purpose was explained to all participants prior to obtain their consent to participate. The participants were recruited through the personal network of the authors and contacts to various refugee organizations. There was no compensation for participating in the study but food and drinks were provided during the duration of the study of 2,5 h. All participants were over 18 with a legal status in Germany and a proficiency level in German of at least B1. A lab-based experiment was conducted to identify the digital skill level of individuals with several tasks. Before the task-based experiment, the participants filled a short survey answering some questions about their Internet usage experience and job-seeking practices. Additionally, the survey asked for the participants' perceived digital skills regarding certain activities. For the task-based experiment, nine assignments were created based on the operational framework for digital skills from van Deursen and van Dijk [6,7], reflecting operational, formal, information and strategic skills - ranging from basic to more complex skills (Table 1). All tasks were completed online either on a laptop or a desktop computer.

Table 1. Operational framework of digital skills based on [6,7].

Operational skills	Recognize and operate the Internet services toolbars, buttons, and menus, manage different file formats saved from Internet services
Formal skills	Navigate the Internet by using hyperlinks embedded in different formats such as texts, images, menus and so on, maintain a sense of location while navigating
Information skills	Locate required information by defining information problem, choosing a Website or a search system to seek information, defining search options or queries, selecting information, evaluating information sources
Strategic skills	Developing an orientation toward a particular goal, taking the correct actions to reach this goal, making the right decisions to reach this goal; and eventually, gaining the benefits that result from the goal

Each task had to be completed within a given timeframe before it was locked and no answer was taken by the system. The participants' screens were recorded during the assignment execution for later analysis of the applied information seeking strategies. Participants were able to use all sources in the Internet to complete the tasks. They were also encouraged to use online dictionaries if they had trouble understanding the assignment. The use of mobile phones was prohibited to ensure that all relevant information seeking activities were performed on the screen that was recorded. The whole study was conducted anonymously. Participants were given tokens that allowed matching answers of the survey with the answers given for each assignment.

The assignments were tested beforehand in two pre-tests. The first pre-test aimed at evaluating the clarity of the tasks and was conducted with a German high-school student. The second pre-test was conducted with a refugee migrant to test whether tasks written in German can be understood by non-German speakers with a language proficiency level of B1. The results of both pre-tests were not included in the analysis presented in this paper.

4 Results

4.1 Internet Activities and Job-Seeking Experience

Participants were between 18–33 years old and either graduated from high school or held a university degree from their home country. Compared to the population of refugee migrants in Germany, the group was highly educated [4]. All participants came to Germany less than 4 years ago. The results of the survey, that was supposed to be filled before completing the assignment, give some insights into the refugee migrants' Internet usage and online activities. All participants have a mobile phone and a laptop to access the Internet. Figure 1 shows the activities participants do online. Overall, among the participants there is a high level of Internet affinity and familiarity.

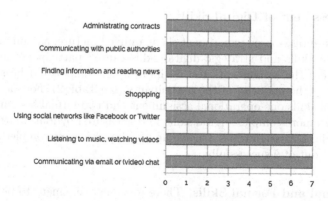

Fig. 1. Number of participants answering the question: Which activities do you use the Internet for? (n = 7).

One part of the survey asked participants to rate their skills regarding certain online and digital activities. Figure 2 shows the results. Only for the activities of creating content and programming software, the majority of participants rated their skills to be below average skills. The participants assessed their skills regarding the use of web browser, Internet search engines and social networks to be above average skills.

Another part of the survey also asked for their experience with job-seeking activities. All participants stated that they did already apply for a job. Six participants wrote the application not alone but with the help of friends, family or voluntary workers showing how a strong personal network is also important during the job-seeking process. Answers to the question about the familiarity with online career networks such as LinkedIn[6] or Xing[7] showed that four participants have a profile.

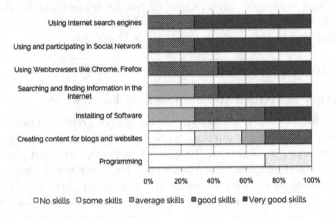

Fig. 2. Self-evaluation of participants regarding certain Internet activities.

4.2   Assessment of Digital Skills

Results of the task-based experiment show a mixed picture: assignments testing basic digital skills and strategic digital skills caused participants major problems, whereas the assignments testing information skills could be successfully completed by the majority of the participants (see Table 2). For measuring the basic digital skills one operational assignment and two formal assignments were created. The more complex digital skills were measured by four information and two strategic skill assignments. On average, each participant completed 4,2 tasks (median: 4) out of 9 successfully.

Operational and Formal Skills. There was one assignment to be completed for the operational skill. Using predefined specifications, participants had to locate and download a specific brochure from a company website and save it on the desktop of their PC or laptop. We found that only four participants were able to locate the desired file and download it to the specified location, whereby

---

[6] https://www.linkedin.com/.
[7] https://www.xing.com/.

Table 2. Descriptions of tasks and number of completions per task.

Skill level	Task	Description	Number of completions
Operational	1	Download and save a file	4
Formal	2	Use specified site search and remove filter	1
	3	Find address of jobcenter with specified query	7
Information	4	Find information on a specified website	6
	5	Determine standard size of an application photo	4
	6	Determine the minimum wage per hour	5
	7	Determine minimum vacation days	6
Strategic	8	Find three jobs with highest salary during training and career	0
	9	Match perks for employees to three given companies	0

one participant saved the file but not at the correct place. One explanation for the performance might be the adaption to smartphone use, where downloading files and saving them to specific folders is not a very common task.

For the formal skills, there were two assignments to be completed. One assignment asked for the address of a jobcenter in one of the Berlin districts. This task was easy to solve for all participants as it required them to use a search engine with a given query. In contrary, the other assignment was only solved by one participant. Here, the participants were asked to go to a company website's site search, remove a given filter, and copy the second link of the search result page. Two participants gave the link of the address of the search engine, the others failed to correctly remove the set filter. Familiarity with search engines other than web search engines seems to be rare. Also the concept of reducing results sets based on facets seems to be not known and might explain the number of completions.

Information and Strategic Skills. For the information skills, there were four assignments to be completed. In the first assignment participants were asked to find the address of a professional school for the apprenticeship of a bookseller at the website of the Chamber of Commerce and Industry of Berlin. The second assignment asked to determine the size of a photo for application documents in Germany and the third for the minimum wage per hour in Germany. In the fourth assignment participants had to find the minimum number of vacation days given for a five-day work week. Four to six participants out of seven demonstrated their information skills in the assignments, designed as open search tasks. All information tasks required the participants to formulate an information need and express it in a query. However, the observed information seeking strategies were limited to simple query formulations, because search queries were often copied from the text of the assignment. Search engines and in particular Google (used by all participants) are very good in providing the right results for verbose and fact-based queries that are linguistically very similar to a formulated question. More complex strategies such as the berry-picking technique [26] were not observed and do not seem to occur in the participant's tool box. The reasons for this result can be manifold and specifying them requires further research.

The two hardest assignments were testing strategic skills and none of the participants was able to fulfil them. In the first assignment participants were asked to select three apprenticeships and work places in which someone would earn a high salary. In order to reach this goal, participants had to find and use different web pages which offer information on high salaries for both, apprenticeships and for working places. As there are numerous web pages offering information regarding this question, participants had to conduct appropriate steps and formulate search queries which build on one another. A helpful step would have been not to find only one website which offers information specifically aimed at salaries for apprenticeships but to combine the information from different websites and verify the suggested salaries with information from other websites. In the second assignment, participants were expected to match three given criteria, i.e. perks for employees, to three given companies. All information could be found on the company websites, and company names and addresses were given to the participants. In both assignments, the lack of strategy was evident.

Strategic digital skills strongly relate to education and intellectual capacities [24]. The educational attainment of all participants was high, therefore we can not conclude that answers to the strategic skill tasks depends on the educational level. Follow-up studies will identify if the level of strategic skills depends on the educational level or other factors.

The main findings of this study can be summarized as follows:

- Only basic search strategies were observed which were often not target-oriented.
- The information seeking process is often very inefficient, advanced search functionalities are not known.
- Participants had a hard time orienting themselves on websites and lacked an understanding of the structure of websites.
- A lack of operational digital skills was observed.
- Fact-based information seeking was often successful, whereas strategic searching where information from various sources needed to be gathered was unsuccessful.
- The perceived skills of participants was better than the skills they demonstrated in the tasks.

5   Conclusion and Future Work

There is "very little known about the ways refugee migrants access and use digital technology and about their attitudes towards awareness of and skills in using the technology" [12, p. 346]. With this first study assessing digital skill and information-seeking behavior of refugee migrants in Germany, we contribute necessary and important research in the area of forced migration and information science. Insufficient digital skills can affect refugee migrants' learning, professional work and career development [12]. A better understanding of the digital skills level of this particular group can be used to design targeted courses and curricula enabling refugee migrants to enhance their Internet experience in order to obtain relevant information for e.g. education and employment [12, p. 345f]. Obtaining relevant information in the Internet and using its opportunities greatly improves chances for labor market integration.

We are aware that performance tests have their limitations as they are often limited in the definitions used, the small sample sizes and the methods for data collection (through surveys that measure skills indirectly or self evaluations) [24,27]. We are aware of the limitations of our study. First, the assessed group was very small. Secondly, the group was very homogeneous in their high educational level and their high German language proficiency. The population of the refugee migrants in Germany might have a very different personnel (there is also not much reliable data about that out there.) Nevertheless, our study provides an initial empirical data basis in this area and the thorough research design can be used for further studies in this area. For future research, we will qualitatively analyze the screen recordings to assess the information seeking strategies, queries used and approaches taken to solve the tasks.

In a follow-up study, we would like to gather more participants, which will allow us to make more generalizable assumptions about the digital skill level of refugee migrants. Additionally, we would like to further identify hindering factors that keep participants from completing assignments. For that, we are planning to complement lab-based experiments with the think-aloud method and interviews.

References

1. Lloyd, A.: Reflection on: "on becoming citizens: examining social inclusion from an information perspective". Aust. Acad. Res. Libr. **47**(4), 316–319 (2016)
2. Weitzel, T., Eckhardt, A., Laumer, S., Maier, C., von Stetten, A., Weinert, C., Wirth, J.: Recruiting Trends 2015 - Eine empirische Untersuchung mit den Top-1.000-Unternehmen aus Deutschland sowie den Top-300-Unternehmen aus den Branchen Finanzdienstleistung, Health Care und IT. [recruiting trends 2015. an empirical study of the top 1,000 companies from germany and the top 300 companies in the financial services, healthcare and IT sectors] (2015)
3. OECD: Adults, Computers and Problem Solving. OECD Skills Studies. OECD Publishing (2015). https://doi.org/10.1787/9789264236844-en
4. Brücker, H., Rother, N., Schupp, J. (eds.): IAB-BAMF-SOEP-Befragung von Geflüchteten: Überblick und erste Ergebnisse: [IAB-BAMF-SOEP-survey of refugees: overview and first results]. Number 29 in Forschungsbericht, Nürnberg (2016)
5. Council of Europe: The common European framework of reference for languages: learning, teaching, assessment (2001)
6. van Deursen, A.J.A.M., van Dijk, J.A.G.M.: Improving digital skills for the use of online public information and services. Gov. Inf. Q. **26**(2), 333–340 (2009)

7. van Deursen, A.J.A.M., van Dijk, J.A.G.M.: Digital Skills - Unlocking the Information Society. Digital Education and Learning. Palgrave Macmillan, US (2014)
8. OECD: Skills for a Digital World. OECD Digital Economy Papers. OECD Publishing (2016) https://doi.org/10.1787/5jlwz83z3wnw-en
9. Bossler, M., Kubis, A., Moczall, A.: Neueinstellungen im Jahr 2016: Große Betriebe haben im Wettbewerb um Fachkräfte oft die Nase vorn. IAB-Kurzbericht (18) (2017)
10. Maitland, C., Tomaszewski, B., Belding, E., Fisher, K.E., Xu, Y., Iland, D., Schmitt, P., Majid, A.: Youth mobile phone and internet use january 2015. zaatari camp, mafraq, jordan (2015)
11. Fisher, K.E., Talhouk, R., Yefimova, K., Al-Shahrabi, D., Yafi, E., Ewald, S., Comber, R.: Za'atari refugee cookbook: relevance, challenges and design considerations. In: Proceedings of the 2017 CHI Conference Extended Abstracts on Human Factors in Computing Systems, CHI EA 2017, pp. 2576–2583. ACM (2017)
12. Alam, K., Imran, S.: The digital divide and social inclusion among refugee migrants: a case in regional Australia. Inf. Technol. People 28(2), 344–365 (2015)
13. Khoir, S., Du, J.T., Koronios, A.: Study of Asian immigrants' information behaviour in South Australia: Preliminary results. In: Proceedings of the 2014 iConference, pp. 682–689 (2014)
14. Komito, L., Bates, J.: Migrants' information practices and use of social media in Ireland: networks and community. In: Proceedings of the 2011 iConference, iConference 2011, pp. 289–295. ACM (2011)
15. Quirke, L.C.: A study of the information practices of Afghan newcomer youth in the contexts of leisure and settlement (2014)
16. Burrell, J., Anderson, K.: 'I have great desires to look beyond my world': trajectories of information and communication technology use among Ghanaians living abroad. New Media Soc. 10(2), 203–224 (2008)
17. Yoon, K.: Korean migrants use of the internet in Canada. J. Int. Migr. Integr. 18(2), 547–562 (2017)
18. Caidi, N., Allard, D., Quirke, L.: Information practices of immigrants. Ann. Rev. Inf. Sci. Technol. 44(1), 491–531 (2010)
19. Litt, E.: Measuring users internet skills: a review of past assessments and a look toward the future. New Media Soc. 15(4), 612–630 (2013)
20. Mehra, B., Bilal, D.: International students perceptions of their information seeking strategies. In: Proceedings of the Annual Conference of CAIS/Actes du congrs annuel de l'ACSI (2007)
21. Badke, W.: International students: information literacy or academic literacy. Acad. Exch. 6(4), 60–65 (2002)
22. Alzougool, B., Chang, S., Gomes, C., Berry, M.: Finding their way around: international students use of information sources. J. Adv. Manag. Sci. 1(1), 43–49 (2013)
23. van Deursen, A.J.A.M., Helsper, E.J., Eynon, R.: Development and validation of the internet skills scale (ISS). Inf. Commun. Soc. 19(6), 804–823 (2015)
24. van Deursen, A.J.A.M., van Diepen, S.: Information and strategic internet skills of secondary students: a performance test. Comput. Educ. 63, 218–226 (2012)
25. Eynon, R., Geniets, A.: The digital skills paradox: how do digitally excluded youth develop skills to use the internet? Learn. Media Technol. 41(3), 463–479 (2016)
26. Bates, M.J.: The design of browsing and berrypicking techniques for the online search interface. Online Rev. 13(5), 407–424 (1989)
27. van Deursen, A.J.A.M., van Dijk, J.A.G.M.: Using the internet: skill related problems in users online behavior. Interact. Comput. 21, 393–402 (2009)

How Do Pre-service Teachers Work "Together" on Curriculum Development Projects: A Study on Tools and Tasks in Collaborative Information Behavior

Tien-I Tsai[1]([⊠]) and Wan-Lin Yang[2]

[1] National Taiwan University, Taipei 10617, Taiwan
titsai@ntu.edu.tw
[2] National Cheng Kung University, Tainan 70101, Taiwan

Abstract. Course preparation for teachers usually requires looking for a great amount of information. For pre-service teachers who are novice in teaching, information exchange regarding course preparation with their peers is very crucial to their professional development. Drawing upon Twidale and Nichols [1] and Shah [2–4], this study investigates pre-service teachers' collaborative information behavior when designing curriculum with their peers. Specifically, the current study examines pre-service teachers' time-space collaboration profiles and the tools being used in their collaborative information-seeking processes. 183 responses were collected via a web survey and analyzed to address aforementioned research inquiries. The results show that while nearly half of the pre-service teachers worked at different time and space, the other half either worked at the same time in the same place or worked remotely at the same time. Social media and cloud drives have become the most popular collaborative platforms for pre-service teachers to share information with their peers, and most participants used multiple online tools for various purposes during their curriculum-development group work.

Keywords: Collaborative information behavior · Curriculum development
Pre-service teachers

1 Introduction

Course preparation requires seeking a great amount of information. For pre-service teachers who are novice in teaching, exchanging information for instructional preparation with their peers is crucial to their learning and career development. Many courses in teacher education programs that aim at nurturing pre-service teachers' pedagogical competence and curriculum-development competence require pre-service teachers to develop curriculum in small groups. This curriculum-development project is typically a major learning task of those courses.

Existing literature regarding pre-service teachers' use of information has focused on their attitudes toward technology integration or assessing their levels of technological pedagogical and content knowledge (e.g., Teo and Tan [5]). Few research addressed

© Springer International Publishing AG, part of Springer Nature 2018
G. Chowdhury et al. (Eds.): iConference 2018, LNCS 10766, pp. 537–543, 2018.
https://doi.org/10.1007/978-3-319-78105-1_59

pre-service teachers' information behavior, let alone their collaborative information seeking (CIS) behavior where individuals seek information to collaboratively complete a task or achieve a learning goal. In addition, CIS research has been mostly done in experimental environment and typically focusing on the performance of collaborative search of a system or focusing more on qualitative aspects (e.g., Capra et al. [6]; Goggins and Lewis [7]; Reddy and Jensen [8]; Shah [9]; Shahvar and Tang [10]). The current study focuses on CIS in real-life settings that Hyldegård et al. [11] emphasized, and examines the perceptions of pre-service teachers on their CIS through a web survey.

Communication, including exchanging information, is one of the essential elements in CIS; co-search and co-browsing are also important features in CIS as identified in Shah [2]. Twidale and Nichols [1] proposed a model for examining users' collaborative library activities with time-space coordinates, and Shah [2–4] further elaborated it in CIS contexts. While previous studies mostly examine specific activities with this time-space framework and investigate co-search and co-browse on a specific information system, the current study views curriculum-development group project as an integrated task and depicts students' overall time-space collaboration profiles. Moreover, the current study views co-search/co-browsing in a broader sense with this time-space perspective—individuals search/browse information with their peers for the specific task at the same time in the same place.

By using a web survey, this study attempts to investigate pre-service teachers' information behavior when designing curriculum with their peers collaboratively. Specifically, the current study explores how pre-service teachers work "together" regarding time-space conditions and how they use different online tools (e.g., cloud drive, cloud documents, social bookmark tools) for information exchange with their peers while completing the learning task. Research questions of this study include:

1. What are students' perceived time-space collaboration profiles and CIS profiles when developing curriculum? How likely would they work at the same time in the same space? How frequently do they co-search, co-browse, co-locate, and co-synthesize information?
2. What online tools do students use when exchanging information for their curriculum-development group projects? Which tools were used for which tasks?

The research findings may provide insights into how teacher educators can assist pre-service teachers in conducting collaborative information seeking activities in order to achieve the ultimate goal of collaborative learning.

2   Method

2.1   Data Collection

A web survey was conducted to collect data for the current study. The questionnaire was developed mainly based on existing literature regarding collaborative information seeking and was revised according to two rounds of pilot testing. Students in teacher education programs across different universities in Taiwan were asked to address how much time they spent working "together" at the same time and in the same space for the most recent curriculum-development group project. They were also asked what types of online tools and platforms they used for different tasks while collaboratively developing curriculum for their projects. The questions in the survey included both closed and open-ended questions. Demographic questions (such as gender, field of study, teaching experience) were also asked to understand the background of our survey participants.

The sampling frame of the current study was pre-service teachers in secondary teacher education programs in Taiwan who have taken or have been taking a course that required to work on a curriculum-development group project. Data was collected through a web survey. Since survey responses rely on participants' recall and perceptions, the data collection process lasted for one month starting towards the end of semester when students may have fresh memory regarding their group projects. The researchers contacted the staff members at the center of teacher education at 30 universities that offer secondary teacher education programs in Taiwan, and asked the staff members to help distribute the web survey to the students. However, given some institutional restrictions, only seven institutions confirmed that they have passed along the web survey to their students. Additionally, since we were not able to learn whether or not the students have taken courses that required a curriculum-development group project, it was not possible to calculate the response rate.

2.2   Participants

The voluntary participants of the current study came from 183 students who were pre-service teachers in secondary teacher education programs and have taken at least one course that requires them to work on a curriculum-development group project. Most participants (70.9%) were female, and only 29.1% were male. Most of the participants (64.8%) were 21-25 years old; 21.4% were 18-20 years old; 13.7% were above 25 years old. While 17.6% were underclassmen and 47.8% were upperclassmen, 34.6% were graduate students. Participants were from various fields of study, including arts and humanities (40.1%), social sciences and education (23.6%), as well as engineering and natural sciences (36.3%). Their license fields of teaching include: language, arts, and humanities (39.8%), mathematics and sciences (31.5%), social sciences (17.4%), and others (11.2%). Nearly half of the participants were in their first year of teacher education program (41.1%) and slightly over one-third (35%) were in their second year.

3   Preliminary Findings

3.1   Students' Collaboration Profiles

Time-Space Collaboration Profiles. When students worked on their curriculum-development group project, nearly half of them (45.3%) said they mostly worked at a different time and different space, less than one-third (29.5%) mostly worked at the same time and the same space, and one-fifth (19.7%) mostly worked at the same time but different space (e.g., working through Google documents or OneDrive). Only 5.5% of the students said they mostly worked at the same space but at a different time (e.g., work in the same student office or lab at a different time).

Students were also asked to recall approximately how much time they spent working together in the same space and at the same time, and to identify a point on each spectrum (from 0 to 100, as shown in Fig. 1). Figure 1 depicts the results for all participants as well as for each group of the students with different time-space collaboration profiles. Students tended to work either at a different time and space (group 1) or at the same time (groups 2 and 3).

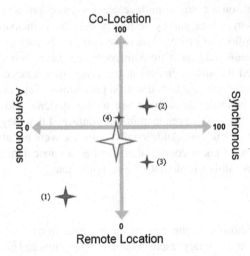

Fig. 1. Students' time-space collaboration profiles.

Note. While the center of the hallow star shows the overall average (49, 39), the center of solid stars show the averages of the following groups of students: (1) those who mostly worked at a different time and different space (34, 28) [$n = 83$], (2) mostly worked at the same time and the same space (62, 59) [$n = 54$], (3) mostly worked at the same time but different space (62, 34) [$n = 36$], and (4) mostly worked at the same space but at a different time (51, 55) [$n = 10$]. The size of stars proportionally represents the number of participants in each group.

Collaborative Information Seeking Profiles. Students were also asked how frequently they co-searched, co-browsed, co-located, and co-synthesized information with their peers while developing curriculum. A two-step cluster analysis was used to identify homogeneous subgroups within the sample. Based on students' collaborative information seeking characteristics—i.e., frequencies of co-search, co-browse, co-locate, and co-synthesize information, two subgroups of collaborative information seeking clusters were identified. Cluster one includes high CIS students, and cluster two includes low CIS students. That is, students in cluster one performed the above four CIS tasks much more frequently than students in cluster two. And this phenomenon can partially explain their time-space collaboration profiles where about one-third of the students typically worked at the same time and space, and nearly half worked asynchronous and remotely.

3.2   Collaborative Tasks and Tools Used

Students were then asked about what tools they used for exchanging information when developing curriculum with their group members (Table 1). Almost all students used social networking sites (e.g., Facebook) (95%) and cloud drives (e.g., Google Drive, Dropbox) (90.9%). Most students also used cloud documents (e.g., Google Documents) (70.7%) or instant messaging tools such as Line (58.7%). About half of the students (49.6%) used multimedia sites such as YouTube. Only 10.9% used social bookmark sites (e.g., Pinterest, Diigo). We found that most students used multiple online tools for various purposes during their curriculum-development group work.

Table 1. Tools used in collaborative curriculum development ($N = 183$).

Online tools	Percentage used in collaborative curriculum development
Social networking sites (e.g., Facebook, Google+)	95.0%
Cloud drives (e.g., Google Drive, Dropbox)	90.9%
Cloud documents (e.g., Google Docs)	70.7%
Instant messaging tools (e.g., Line, Skype)	58.7%
Multimedia sharing sites (e.g., Flickr, Instagram, YouTube)	49.6%
Social bookmarking sites (e.g., Pinterest, Delicious, Diigo)	10.9%

Table 2. Top tasks of each online tools used for collaborative curriculum development ($N = 183$).

Online tools	Top 1 task	Top 2 task	Top 3 task
Social networking sites ($n = 178$)	Content discussion (82.53%)	Task coordination (75.11%)	Information sharing (59.83%)
Cloud drive ($n = 170$)	Information sharing (80.91%)	File backup (75.91%)	N/A
Cloud documents ($n = 135$)	Information sharing (60.23%)	File backup (47.95%)	Content discussion (47.37%)
Instant messaging Tools ($n = 115$)	Content discussion (80.85%)	Task coordination (64.54%)	Task social (48.23%)
Multimedia sharing sites ($n = 97$)	Information sharing (68.07%)	N/A	N/A
Social bookmarking sites ($n = 20$)	Information sharing (48.78%)	N/A	N/A

Note 1. Task options included: task coordination, content discussion, task social, information sharing, file backup, and other (students can then fill in specific tasks). The first three options were adopted from Shah (2014) [3].

Note 2. % in each cell shows the percentage of participants who used each online tool for the specific task. N/A cells mean that the next highest tasks were with percentages less than 30%, and did not stand out from other tasks.

Specifically, while social networking sites and instant messaging tools were typically used for content discussion and task coordination, cloud drive, cloud documents, multimedia sharing sites, and social bookmarking sites were typically used for information sharing (Table 2). It is interesting that in addition to online tools that are designed for collaborative projects (e.g., cloud documents), students also use various social media to facilitate information exchange within their group.

4   Conclusion

Overall, the current study reveals that most students in teacher education programs used multiple online tools for various purposes during their curriculum-development group work, and a significant number of them typically worked at different time in different space for their group projects. It is important for teacher educators to consider how to further facilitate effective and appropriate use of various online tools to help future teachers develop a better collaborative model that helps students form curriculum plans more smoothly and effectively. Future research can further analyze the data to identify whether or not students with different collaborative information seeking profiles utilize online tools differently, and develop better strategies that help pre-service teachers collaborate with their peers in the process of curriculum development.

References

1. Twidale, M.B., Nichols, D.M.: Collaborative browsing and visualization of the search process. In: Aslib Proceedings, vol. 48, pp. 177–182 (1996)
2. Shah, C.: Collaborative information seeking. JASIS&T 65(2), 215–236 (2014)
3. Shah, C.: Evaluating collaborative information seeking: synthesis, suggestions, and structure. J. Inf. Sci. 40(4), 460–475 (2014)
4. Shah, C.: Social Information Seeking. Springer, Switzerland (2017). https://doi.org/10.1007/978-3-319-56756-3
5. Teo, T., Tan, L.: The theory of planned behavior (TPB) and pre-service teachers' technology acceptance: a validation study using structural equation modeling. J. Technol. Teach. Educ. 20(1), 89–104 (2012)
6. Capra, R., Chen, A.T., McArthur, E., Davis, N.: Searcher actions and strategies in asynchronous collaborative search. In: Proceedings of the ASIS&T, Montreal, Canada (2013)
7. Goggins, S.P., Lewis, U.A.: Collaborative information behavior: the case of an interdisciplinary Charrette. In: Proceedings of the ASIS&T, Pittsburgh, PA, vol. 47 (2010)
8. Reddy, M.C., Jansen, B.J.: A model for understanding collaborative information behavior in context: a study of two healthcare teams. Inf. Process. Manag. 44(1), 256–273 (2008)
9. Shah, C.: Toward collaborative information seeking (CIS). In: Proceedings of JCDL 2008 Workshop on Collaborative Exploratory Search, Pittsburgh, PA (2008)

10. Shahvar, S.S., Tang, R.: Collaborative information seeking (CIS) behavior of LIS students and undergraduate students: an exploratory case study. In: Proceedings of the ASIS&T, Baltimore, MD, vol. 51 (2014)

11. Hyldegård, J., Hertzum, M., Hansen, P.: Studying collaborative information seeking. In: Hansen, P., Shah, C., Klas, C.P. (eds.) Collaborative Information Seeking: Best Practices, New Domains and New Thoughts. Springer, Switzerland (2015). https://doi.org/10.1007/978-3-319-18988-8_2

Work that Enables Care: Understanding Tasks, Automation, and the National Health Service

Matt Willis[✉] and Eric T. Meyer

University of Oxford, Oxford, UK
{matthew.willis, eric.meyer}@oii.ox.ac.uk

Abstract. Automation of jobs is discussed as a threat to many job occupations, but in the UK healthcare sector many view technology and automation as a way to save a threatened system. However, existing quantitative models that rely on occupation-level measures of the likelihood of automation suggest that few healthcare occupations are susceptible to automation. In order to improve these quantitative models, we focus on the potential impacts of *task-level* automation on health work, using qualitative ethnographic research to understand the mundane information work in general practices. By understanding the detailed tasks and variations of information work, we are building a more complete and accurate understanding of how healthcare staff work and interact with technology and with each other, often mediated by technology.

Keywords: Automation · Primary care · Ethnography · Sociotechnical

1 Introduction

What do we mean when we talk about the automation of jobs? If we are to believe the most hyperbolic of public commentators, we face a near future where 'robots are coming for our jobs' and human labor is made largely redundant except in support of a large, automated, robotic workforce [1, 2]. Of course, this concern about being replaced by robots is nothing new: Time Magazine carried a cover in 1980 predicting "The Robot Revolution" [3], and similar examples have occurred periodically in media outlets going back as far as 200 years [4]. However, the rhetoric has exceeded the reality: Bessen (2016) argues only one occupation has been completely eliminated by automation over the last 60 years (namely, elevator operators) [5].

Realistically, these visions (or fears, depending on your point of view) of an automated workforce will be much more nuanced in practice in the future just as they have been in the past. Some jobs will almost certainly become fully or nearly fully automated, while others will see human labor increasingly augmented either by computers (and algorithms) or by robotic machines. Recent advances in the areas of machine learning, machine vision, computational statistics, data mining, various artificial intelligence methodologies, and mobile robotics, were made possible from large investments in both the public and private sector. Some of these technical advances are starting to see practical applications.

© Springer International Publishing AG, part of Springer Nature 2018
G. Chowdhury et al. (Eds.): iConference 2018, LNCS 10766, pp. 544–549, 2018.
https://doi.org/10.1007/978-3-319-78105-1_60

Thus, we need to ask ourselves not 'will there be widespread automation in the coming years' but instead we need to examine the ways that analogue and manual modes of work are transformed when individuals and organizations shift to digital and (partially) automated ways of working. This paper reports on work-in-progress to better understand these more nuanced shifts to digital work and automation of tasks in a single setting: the UK health sector.

2 Background: Automation and the State of NHS Primary Care in England

In a widely publicised 2013 working paper (since published in 2017) Frey and Osborne analyzed a dataset from the U.S. Department of Labor called O*NET [6]. The O*NET data captures various measures about the nature of work and the skills needed for occupational work activities. The goal of their analysis was to understand how susceptable jobs are to automation technologies given advances in machine learning and related artificial intelligence and robotic technologies. The conclusion Frey and Osborne draw from analyzing 702 detailed occupations is that about 47% of U.S. employment is susceptable to different levels of automation [7, 8]. The Frey and Osborne study is but one in many that show technologies substituting for human labor and creating widespread unemployment [9–13].

One particular pattern in the Frey and Osborne analysis is that most healthcare occupations featured a remarkably low probability for computerisation. This is, in part, due to the fact that most healthcare occupations contain features that are considered current bottlenecks to computerisation, including social intelligence, social perceptiveness, negotiation, persuasion, caring for others, originality, and creativity. The other part of the low computerisation probability for healthcare professions is because the empirical data available was at an aggregated level. Fine-grained data on the detailed work practices and skills needed to complete individual tasks and sub-tasks do not exist at any large scale, thus, we have a poor understanding of how future automation and artificial intelligence research may impact complex work arrangements that involve many heterogenous and non-repetitive tasks, as in the healthcare sector.

While automation may threaten vulnerable workers in many economic sectors, healthcare is different in that it is one of the few sectors where automation is seen by leaders, experts, policy makers, and workers as an opportunity to deal with a potential crisis. The potential crisis is particularly acute the NHS in England, where the primary care system faces staff shortages, increased workloads, increased service demand, reduced budget, skill shortages and decreased time for patient consultations in general practice services [14–16]. The reasons for the current state of NHS primary care are complex and multi factorial, the way out of this is seen to require innovation in areas such as service delivery, use of technology, staff training and patient education. One path toward relieving pressure on NHS primary care staff is the use of automation as a force multiplier, making it possible to get more done with less effort. This presents a challenge to understand where and to what extent automation can be developed, deployed and implemented into the work practices in the primary care setting. Furthermore, many technologies are developed and implemented in NHS that become cumbersome burdens to healthcare work, emphasizing the need to understand the social environment and work practices before technological interventions begin.

3 Empirical Setting and Analytical Methods

The work presented in this paper is research in development from the initial phase of the project. As we begin to collect and analyze data, we find ourselves in the position of having to classify the work practices and ways people work with technology to accomplish tasks. This granular analysis has led to thinking about how complex tasks are completed, and what information about that task a computer would need to know.

The project team includes a field researcher, who visits primary care practices and shadows every occupational role at each site to understand the work tasks that are performed by each occupation. In addition to this shadowing, we conduct interviews, gather documents, and capture photos and videos to understand how tasks flow through the primary care clinic. These far more detailed qualitative data are then linked to other data about the sector and modeled using methods developed in the original Frey and Osborne work to create a more detailed and nuanced understanding of automation in the primary health care sector in England.

At the time of this writing we have recruited four primary care general practice centers, and plan to work with 6–7 more sites in the coming year. The field researcher spends an average of a week in the field with each site observing each occupational role performing their duties. The goal is to develop an understanding for how each occupation works, what tasks they are responsible for, how they accomplish those tasks, the kinds of technologies needed to accomplish each task, and what aspects of their work rely on other people and how multiple people touch on different aspects of the same task. After gathering these detailed data the field researcher begins to synthesize the tasks across every primary care practice with a sensitization for identifying features of each task that can help to understand properties of task computerization. Qualitative coding methods including grounded theory and constant comparison approaches [7, 8], are used in analysis. The process for grounding quantitative models of task automation probabilities starts with observations of primary care work as previously described. Then, the field researcher analyzes field notes and collected documents using a constant comparative method, creating a matrix of occupations and tasks performed by each task. Once all tasks have been extracted from the data a grounded theory approach is used for qualitatively coding the tasks to develop features or classifications of each task. These features and classifications of work tasks are coded for different properties including the use of technologies, social aspects of tasks, types of interruptions, partially automated parts of the task, and other task classifications that emerge from the data.

4 Findings

Our preliminary analysis reveals the size and scope of tasks performed in primary care, indicators of partial automation, and preferences for certain practices. The heavy use of desktop computers is an important indicator for automation because it is likely that software based automation will be some of the first tasks automated through technologies like robotic process automation. We show how the configuration of the same technology in different ways presents a challenge to automation, along with the structure of certain work in primary care.

From our data, we have identified ten unique occupational roles in primary care, and some of those roles can be further divided into sub categories. For example we catalogue GPs as just one role: general practitioner. This role also includes different "ranks" or seniority of GPs such as partner GP, salaried GP, locum GP, duty GP, various levels of training (ST 1, ST3) and so on. For the purposes of this research the tasks they perform are largely the same and the titles indicate acquired knowledge and status. These ten occupations are what make primary care run and comprise a total of 135 regular tasks that we have identified. Every occupation has around 15–20 tasks that they regularly perform. For practice staff (non-clinical occupations) there are around three to eight tasks that require the collaboration of another person in the office to complete the task. This includes tasks like signing off on a prescription or letter, reviewing a document, gathering signatures, or entering in their portion of data into a system that someone else will use. Every task performed relied on a desktop computer unless it was a purely paper based task, a face to face meeting, or a phone call.

Each primary care center is home to a long list of medical technologies: needles, otoscope, stethoscope, dermascope, reflex hammer, thermometer, blood pressure meter, scale, electrocardiogram machine, and so on. However, the technology at the centre of every primary care clinic is the desktop computer. These desktop computers necessitate an ever longer list of software that enables the primary care clinic to run. Furthermore, the software that runs on every desktop computer is often configured very differently from practice to practice. The electronic medical record (EMR) that runs on every desktop computer is what all staff in primary care spend the majority of their time interacting with. Every EMR has the ability to keep and share tasks. The task EMR functionality is an analogy for a "to do" list: users create a task, add some information about the task, and it shows on their task list in the medical record. The use of this one feature varied across the three initial field sites. One site chose not to use tasks at all due to the demand of senior GPs in favor of a paper based system where receptionists would stamp (rubber stamp with ink) meta data that amounted to different tasks directly on paper documents. These paper documents then moved around the clinic in a specific order. Another clinic, on the other hand, used tasks for everything, even going so far as to communicate through task comments between GPs and practice staff. The third field site used a mix of both systems observed in the previous two sites: mostly digital tasks with specific tasks and workflows having a requirement to be paper based. Both sites that saw the use of tasks also developed a very specific strategy for tasks. The intended use of tasks is to send them to other people, similar to an email, and have them appear on a "to do" list for the recipient. In both cases GPs would also create tasks for themselves and then send them to their self. This data from EMR task use is important because it is a prime example of the configuration of technologies and software that the primary care practice to achieve certain goals using the experience and knowledge they have. It also shows that one simple technology, tasks, can be configured in at least three different ways from its intended purpose. This reconfiguration is a form of social shaping of technology, as the technology can either be shaped by use or (in the case of a preference for paper) by non-use, avoidance, or circumvention.

Our last finding to emerge from a preliminary analysis are three directions of transactional communication that occur at each primary care practice. They are communication within the practice, communication outside the practice, and communication directly to the patient. Communication within the practice includes tasks like the aforementioned tasks functionality in the EMR, as well as inter-office email, staff meetings, memos, and inter-office phone calls. Communication outside of the practice is almost exclusively letters in all three cases. Letter writing is the majority of work for secretaries as well as receptionists and some GPs. Any time that a primary care practice needs to communication information to another practice, secondary care, or another part of NHS it is done through a letter. In some instances this is also accomplished through a phone call depending on urgency of the matter and the recipient of the call. Also, in increasingly rare situations certain hospitals require a fax sent by facsimile machine. The third direction of communication is to the patient. This is done through phone calls, in some cases text messages, face-to-face while the patient is in clinic, and again through letters sent to the patient's home. These three transactional communication directions have proven to be a helpful shorthand in our analysis to show what other social actors are involved in the work of primary care, the tasks performed to communicate in and out of primary care, and lastly they show the challenges of automating certain work that happens to be a large bulk of the work in primary care.

5   Conclusion

How work will change in a future where automation and artificial intelligence are widespread is a timely and important conversation. It is a conversation that garners attention from academics, politicians, policy makers, and industry. The authors see the information field movement as an important community to bring nuance to the development, understanding, and use of automation and artificial intelligence in society, which arguably represent some of the highest-level interactions between humans and information to date. The early work presented in this paper attempts to contribute to this conversation through building a method and perspective of informing algorithms and technical development through a work practice perspective. It is our thesis that as tasks are automated, work sectors and occupations will undergo reconfiguration. In healthcare, these reconfigurations will not result in jobs disappearing wholesale, but the responsibilities, duties, and tasks performed by healthcare occupations will change (and indeed, arguably must change if the system is to survive the current socioeconomic pressures). We hope to anticipate some of this change through continued observation and analysis of the tasks that people perform and understanding, on a task based level, what can or cannot be automated.

Acknowledgements. We would like to thank all of the participants for their time and expertise. We also thank The Health Foundation for their support of this work, award # 7559.

References

1. Schmeiser, L.: Automation invasion: robots are coming for your job (2017). http://observer. com/2017/03/automation-robots-american-jobs/
2. Hammersley, B.: Think your job is safe from the robo-uprising? Think again (2016). https:// www.wired.co.uk/article/ai-robots-employment-jobs
3. The robot revolution (1980). http://content.time.com/time/covers/0,16641,19801208,00.html
4. Anslow, L.: Robots have been about to take all the jobs for more than 200 years (2016). https://timeline.com/robots-have-been-about-to-take-all-the-jobs-for-more-than-200-years-5c9c08a2f41d
5. Bessen, J.E.: How computer automation affects occupations: technology, jobs, and skills. SSRN Electron. J. (2015)
6. Frey, C.B., Osborne, M.A.: The future of employment: how susceptible are jobs to computerisation? Technol. Forecast. Soc. Change **114**, 254–280 (2017)
7. Corbin, J., Strauss, A.: Basics of Qualitative Research. Sage, Thousand Oaks (2008)
8. Glaser, B.G., Strauss, A.L.: The Discovery of Grounded Theory. Aldine, Chicago (1967)
9. Bresnahan, T.F.: Computerisation and wage dispersion: an analytical reinterpretation. Econ. J. **109**, 390–415 (1999)
10. Brynjolfsson, E., McAfee, A.: The Second Machine Age: Work, Progress, and Prosperity in a Time of Brilliant Technologies. W. W. Norton & Company, New York (2014)
11. Manyika, J., Chui, M., Miremadi, M., Bughin, J., George, K., Willmott, P., Dewhurst, M.: Harnessing automation for a future that works (2017)
12. Ford, M.: The Rise of the Robots: Technology and the Threat of a Jobless Future. Oneworld Publications, London (2016)
13. Susskind, R.E., Susskind, D.: The Future of the Professions: How Technology Will Transform the Work of Human Experts. OUP Oxford, Oxford (2017)
14. Baird, B., Charles, A., Honeyman, M., Maguire, D., Das, P.: Understanding Pressures in General Practice. The King's Fund, London (2016)
15. Hopson, C.: The sate of the NHS provider sector (2016)
16. Martin, S., Davies, E., Gershlick, B.: Under pressure: what the Commonwealth Fund's 2015 international survey of general practitioners means for the UK (2016)

Reckoning With: Information Use and Engaging with Strategic Decisions in High Tech Work

Christine T. Wolf[1,2(✉)]

[1] Department of Informatics, School of Information and Computer Sciences,
University of California, Irvine, Irvine, CA, USA
ctwolf@us.ibm.com
[2] Almaden Research Center, IBM Research, San Jose, CA, USA

Abstract. We know that *information use* features prominently in strategic decision-making, yet know little about its role in practices of assessing, evaluating, or otherwise engaging with decisions made by others. To investigate this, I draw on an ethnographic study of a high tech firm and examine a strategic direction within the organization: the development and launch of a new software product. I articulate a conceptual process I label *reckoning with*, which involves two processes of information use – *claiming a mandate* and *renewing debate* – each incorporating different types of information and producing different types of engagements with the strategic direction (*affirming* and *re-directing*). I discuss these findings and their relation to processes of organizational identity.

Keywords: Information use · Organizational identity
Strategic decision-making · Information systems implementation

1 Introduction

We know that information behavior features prominently in decision-making – both in everyday life decisions (like buying a house [24]) and in strategic decisions made in organizations [11, 18, 22]. But we know little about the role of information in practices of evaluating decisions made by others. This can be particularly complicated in the workplace, where employees must often make sense of strategic decisions made in different parts of the organization and figure out not only their import for daily work practice, but also what they mean for the organization's identity (e.g., shared concept of "who we are" and "what we do") and organizational image (e.g., shared concept of "how we think others view us") [13].

Scholars have pointed to the central role everyday talk and discourse play in shaping our social and professional worlds. The work of information professionals, in particular, often takes place within organizations at the nexus of cutting edge technologies and services and established cultural norms and values. Uncertainty can arise over the repercussions of novel tools and activities on, for example, the perception of certain occupations like librarians [23], the appropriateness of resource allocation in the public sector [35], issues of access and privilege [3] or whether organizations are

© Springer International Publishing AG, part of Springer Nature 2018
G. Chowdhury et al. (Eds.): iConference 2018, LNCS 10766, pp. 550–559, 2018.
https://doi.org/10.1007/978-3-319-78105-1_61

intentionally obscuring their motives around emergent technologies [32]. This can place workers in unique and perhaps tense positions – where they must grapple with the impacts of strategic direction and novel technical innovations on an organization's identity and image [13]. I approach this topic from the vantage of information behavior and in particular focus on *information use*, which remains an understudied component of information behavior research [6]. I am particularly interested in understanding the nexus between information use and social processes like the construction of identity and image, building on prior work [37]. In applying the insights of this work to the organizational context, in this paper I ask: *in what ways can information use figure into employees' everyday talk about their organization's strategic decisions? How do such configurations relate to organizational identity and image?*

2 Related Work

Information behavior research in organizations often examines the practices of managers, looking at, for example how their information-seeking behavior has evolved with the widespread use of ICTs [2] or the impact of their prior work experience and relationship to the firm on their information behavior [28]. Although information use remains an understudied facet of information behavior [6], a body of work has examined the question of information use in the organizational context, which frequently focuses on the context of strategic decision-making. The key function of information use is often conceptualized as the reduction of uncertainty [11, 22] with information use impacted by market factors, such as industry or business sector [26]. Häckner [18] notes that different types of information are used in different types of decision-making (with "hard" or accounting information used in defensive strategic decisions, while "soft" or ideas and vision used in expansive strategic decisions) and Citrin [10] also notes the role of information use in product development and innovation outcomes. While this work tends to conceptualize decision-making as a discrete and bounded process undertaken by managers, Choo [8] argues for a more relational view of information use in organizations, conceptualizing processes of sense-making, knowledge creation, and decision-making as inter-related and complementary. I follow such an integrated approach in my investigation of the role of information use; I am interested in the social uses of information by everyday employees in evaluating, assessing, defending (or critiquing) and otherwise "engaging with" strategic directions undertaken within an organization.

This interest is motivated by two insights into the social dimension of information behavior: that the flow of information within organizations is a social process [4, 12] and that information can be mobilized discursively to accomplish social processes [36, 37]. Borgatti and Cross [4] note that people are central sources of information within organization and that information-seeking therefore is shaped by social factors like knowing (and valuing) what other people in the organization know and the social capital needed to (and the perceived social cost of) gaining access to that information. Additionally, work looking at information behavior in teams has also pointed to social dimensions (such as team diversity) in shaping information flows [12]. Although not looking at the organizational context specifically, prior information behavior research has pointed to information use as a discursive process. Tuominen and Savolainen [36], for example, have taken a discursive approach to understanding how information use constructs authority in everyday talk. Wolf and Veinot [37] further examined how information use plays a role in social identity processes (in their case of chronic health patients, supporting the emergence of a "valued self" for those struggling with stigma by constructing the patient as an expert of their health condition).

Questions of identity construction are similarly salient in the organizational context. Distinct from a marketing-based notion of *corporate identity or brand* [33], the notion of *organizational identity* is grounded in the sociology of identity, where concepts of self and other are fluid, dynamic, and interactional [20]. Organizational identity is a collective sense of "who we are and what we do," an interactively constructed concept that is shaped by its relationship to *organizational image*, a perceived idea of "how we think others view us" [13, 17, 34]. Organizational identity and image are consequential in that they both enable and constrain actions and relationships – notions of "who we are, what we do, and what others think of us" can influence strategic decision-making [27], knowledge practices [30], and the degree to which individuals identify with their organization [1, 21]. Identity and image also influence the way organizations orient towards and interact with their stakeholders [5], blurring clear boundaries between "internal" and "external" dimensions of an organization [19]. Thus, organizations are environments rich with concerns of identity and affiliation; given this, an attention to information use in organizational identity and image processes offers a site to build on prior information research into the social uses of information [36, 37].

3   Case and Methods

This paper draws on a fifteen-month ethnographic study of a large, global technology and consulting corporation headquartered in North America (referred to throughout this paper as "the company" or "VeryNu Corp.," which, like all proper nouns in the paper, is a pseudonym). The study focus was broadly on understanding the sense- and value-making practices around emergent enterprise software that features data analytics, looking at enterprise software research and development (R&D) alongside the deployment and adoption of such programs within the organization (the organization follows an industry practice called "dogfooding" which means the corporation uses internally the technologies they sell externally). The author conducted fieldwork from June 2015 to September 2016, which included 77 semi-structured interviews, that lasted an average of 60 min and aimed to broadly understand individuals' everyday work practices (one cluster focused on R&D and included researchers, strategic product managers, technical developers, and delivery team members; the second cluster focused on "users" and included employees in a number of similar roles but working on other products and services offered by the company) and over 200 h of participant observations (including meetings and presentations on various product teams). Data analyzed included interview transcripts; detailed observation notes; as well as artifacts such as slide decks, intranet forum posts, and other organizational materials. In addition to this field site-specific data, the author also gathered market and trade news on relevant topics (e.g., mobile work; apps; future of work; data analytics; automation; and artificial intelligence, etc.) during the study period.

3.1   The Strategic Direction in Question: A New Software Product

Given this paper's interest in understanding information use in the context of evaluating and assessing strategic decisions, this paper focuses on a specific case from the larger ethnographic study. This case involves the development and implementation of a new software product, a "smart" email client. Deployed shortly before the study period, the new email program – which I call "Beta" (and the legacy email program it was meant to replace "Alpha") – is called "smart" because it features data analytics and other semi-automated features with the aim of offering a "next generation" email experience for enterprise users. I followed Beta's implementation closely, interviewing a number of "early adopters" (e.g., employees who volunteered to use the product early on in its implementation) as well as those on the Beta R&D staff and ordinary users (that began use after the "early adopter" phase). In total, 47 semi-structured interviews focused specifically on Beta with a breakdown that included 37 individuals across the following groups: Beta development team (9); Beta early adopters (14 + 10 follow up interviews 6 months later); Beta general users (14). Interviews were semi-structured and focused broadly on understanding participants' daily work practices; participants were not specifically asked to evaluate Beta's strategy. The focus in this paper was inductive and emerged through analytic approaches informed by the grounded theory method [7].

4   Findings: "Reckoning With" a Strategic Direction

This section examines two complementary sets of information practices: *claiming a mandate*; and *renewing debate*. In each, different types of information are featured, including market research; technology designs; and everyday experiences and routines within corporate life. I examine these below and elaborate on how each produce different types of engagements with the strategic direction (*affirming* and *re-directing*) and how they implicate notions of organizational identity and image.

4.1   *Claiming a Mandate*: Using "The Market" as a Warrant for Change

"The market" was a source of information commonly evoked in discussions among employees, often *affirming* the organization's strategic direction and working to construct a sense that the decision had a market-driven mandate. For example, Justin, a technical architect on the Beta team, called on "market research" to explain the strategic decision: "*What we're trying to do is we're trying to take aspects from various technology, various pieces of research, and feedback that we're getting from the market to build a very solid enterprise level piece of software...*" This account aligns with a traditional view that information behavior in strategic decision-making processes within organizations centers around surveying market conditions, often called "environmental scanning" [9], to ensure the competitiveness of a decision.

But turning to "the market" as a source of information, though, also meant acknowledging that there are already several competing software products in that market – email in particular is a rather "old" and storied enterprise topic. Given this well-trodden and saturated market, how is the company's decision to create a new email software program to be made sense of? Rather than casting the company's strategic direction as "late to market," pointing to the market's saturation can actually work to further affirm the company's position. As Sid, a project manager (PM) on the Beta team, said during a conference call: *"Focusing on mail and calendaring, it reinforces our comfort and maybe even addiction to email in the workplace. But part of the excitement of building on mail and calendaring,"* he continued *"is the richness there. Even if we start imagining a space that is much different than what we are used to, there is a big space for impact."* Though both Justin and Sid point to "the market," Sid points to it as a relational point of contrast – one against which the company's decisions are given meaning as a direction that is strategically advantageous. In Sid's account, VeryNu's strategic direction is constructed as offering something *"much different,"* with the products of other companies framed as *status quo* in comparison. In both these accounts "the market" figures into how the strategic direction is made sense of. For Justin, it serves as seemingly straightforward and rational data sources that justify and bolster the company's direction, styling it as responsive to market needs, as if to say: our product is something "the market" calls for. For Sid, "the market" takes on a different role – serving as a focal point against which to contrast the company's strategic direction as *"much different,"* his arrangement affirms the software product's novelty and ingenuity. While "the market" renders differently in each instance, we are able to see how it, as a source of information, figures in both as a resource providing a relational beacon – against which the organization's strategic direction is understood as in response (in Justin's use) or in contrast to (in Sid's use).

Information about "the market" also came from technologies themselves, with different platforms and apps pointed to as sources revealing the cutting edge of the field. Tiffany, a user experience (UX) designer on the software team, talked of turning to popular platforms like Facebook (and users' reviews of such platforms) as a register against which to measure the company's products. Are our products on par and competitive with the cutting edge? *"I know myself I've looked at reviews of other apps,"* she said. *"What do people not like about certain things? Just so we have a kind of a full picture of what is working for them and what's not working for them."* Despite the fact that Facebook is *"obviously very different than [our company's] products,"* she felt it provided *"good feedback"* because so many people use the social-networking platform. *"That's kind of what they're coming to us with knowing, that this [(meaning Facebook)] is how apps work,"* she explained. *"If we did something radically different and it wasn't better, we would really hear bad things about it."* Reflecting on how platforms like Facebook provided insight into users' expectations, she concluded: *"I feel like I'm always looking at different types of apps so we have kind of a constant knowledge of what's going on and what our users are experiencing other places."*

In these examples, information use about "the market" is relational and dynamic – it is relational in that it plays an integral role in bringing the strategic direction to life, as employees make sense of it as responsive to the broader technological market in which their company operates. This process is also situated and contingent, with information about "the market" configured dynamically by employees: the organization is not seen as simply *responding* to the market. Instead, there is a sense that the organization's mission is also to *intervene* in the market – transforming it by, in the words of Sid, *"imagining a space that is much different."* We see a similar dynamism in Tiffany's account – where she uses information about popular platforms like Facebook to make sure the company's designs are on par and competitive (i.e., *responsive* to the market). But she also allows space for the company to offer something *"radically different,"* if it is *"better."* In these ways, "the market" is a flexible source of information, whose use legitimizes the strategic direction by pivoting to bolster both the organization's identity as a rational economic actor (i.e., responding to "the market"), but also an innovative leader on the cutting edge (i.e., shaping "the market").

4.2 *Renewing Debate*: Configuring Continuity as an Alternative Rubric

Engaging with the strategic direction the software program represented did not only involve affirming it; this section also makes note of more frictive engagements. *Renewing debate* was a tactic of information use that attempted to re-direct organizational attention by offering alternative rubrics against which to measure the strategic direction. *Pointing to routines* was a type of information use that involved employees talking of their personal experiences with software products both inside and outside the organization. To illustrate this, this section examines practices of hybrid software adoption – and in particular, how employees explained their choices to only partially adopt Beta. They did so by calling out different features of software programs and the everyday work practices each did or did not support. These encompassed both comparing the company's products to each other (Beta with Alpha) as well as with features of their competitors' products (VeryNu Corp. technologies with the "best in the market"). When used in these ways, software features and their attendant work practices act as sources of information that can be mobilized to re-direct attention and scrutinize strategic choices, as if to ask: did you consider this too? In conceptualizing software features as sources of information (and in particular, in seeing employees' talk about software features as a form of engaging with the organization's strategic decision) I draw on the work of Feinberg [14–16] which points to information systems as rhetorical artifacts, whose design choices act as curatorial mechanisms. Furthermore, I find inspiration in Latham's [25] notion of "experiencing documents" (i.e., the *lived experience* of reading) and similarly see software as artifacts that are actively "read," experienced, and lived-through by our participants.

First, let us situate the deployment strategy around Beta. The software program was meant to represent a "next generation" email client, one that featured a variety of cutting-edge data analytics capabilities, as well as a web-based interface. This was in direct contrast to the company's existing email product, Alpha, which was a traditional desktop-based software program. When compared against the company's legacy email client, the new software program was undeniably a more modern product, and had many things to offer that improved the experience over Alpha. For example, Mary, who worked on one of the company's product delivery teams, described Beta's cleaner interface design as *"refreshing"* and Oskar, a technical developer and another early adopter, extolled its advanced search features as *"a huge improvement."* Only a few early adopters, though, (three of the fourteen I talked to in summer 2015, several months after Beta's launch) had "fully" transitioned to using Beta. Partial or hybrid adoption was a much more common narrative, with many workers pointing to how particular features supported in Alpha were lost in Beta. Some of these losses were confusing to workers, who audibly wondered in interviews over the strategy behind this or that feature, questioning: what's the team thinking there?

Technologies are often introduced into the workplace as a catalyst for organizational change [29]. Pointing to personal routines, then, as a rubric for new software (and asking whether it enables or hampers existing routines) can seem to run counter to the strategic role of technology as a mechanism of workplace change. Indeed, technologies are framed differently by people across an organization [31]. But the information practices here reveal the multiple vantage points around a strategic direction – and that employees mobilize different types of information as they grapple with that direction. The use of personal experiences and routines tells us that strategic decisions are actively "read" and lived-through by employees, with alternative rubrics constructed that bring high-level strategy to reside closely with their everyday work experiences.

These lived-through registers did not draw only on corporate life; employees also pointed to their experiences with consumer technologies in assessing Beta's strategic direction. Thom, a technical consultant at the company, was a Beta early adopter who felt focusing too heavily on "inside" comparators (like Alpha) was misplaced: *"I've seen some comments [on the intranet] where people from [Beta] management were saying, 'Well, you weren't able to do this before [in Alpha], so why would you need it?',"* he said. *"And I think one of the things [VeryNu Corp.] needs to readjust... You can't keep comparing it to other stuff we've done in the past... You have to compare it to the best in the business you're going into."* He then went on to list several competing products and what he thought was "the best" in different categories, (e.g., web-based versus mobile email), drawing on his personal experience with different platforms and products. This type of feature-to-feature comparison came up in many of the Beta user interviews and was also the subject of much discussion on the intranet, as Thom alludes to here. A blow-by-blow comparison is the kind of meticulous nit-picking we come to expect of product reviews – but, through accounts like Thom's, we are able to examine how personal experience is a type of information used to engage with organizational life. More than just complaints, accounts like Thom reveal an effort to renew debate within the organization, signaling the desire of employees to see their organization be strategically successful. Offering alternative rubrics against which to measure Beta's strategic narrative can be a way of vetting company products for success – with personal experiences offered up as resources to help "readjust" and refine the strategic direction (like Thom's thorough list of the "best" features in a number of technological categories).

By drawing on their personal experiences and routines with various technologies, employees offered an alternative rubric against which to measure the strategic direction: one of continuity. Whereas in the previous section we saw a mandate for change and transformation cultivated in the information use of employees – here, we see one that favors continuity and care in bringing about change. But rather than alienating, these types of debate can be integral to affiliation and belonging within organizational life.

When we approach these information practices with notions of organization identity and image in mind, we reveal their creative and affective dimensions. As employees configure information, offering personal sources of information like their experiences and routines, they animate and renew ideas of "who we are, what we do, and what others think of us," bringing grand narratives of organizational strategy to reside close to everyday life.

5 Discussion and Conclusions

This paper investigated the question of information use and strategic decisions. Rather than a focus on decision-making, as is typical, I focused on the information practices of employees as they engage with the strategic decisions made by their organization. Toward that goal, I drew on ethnographic field data from a high tech firm and took the implementation of a new software program as a strategic case. Through their ongoing processes of information configuration, employees *reckon with* the strategic direction – affirming the direction as both responsive to "the market," at the same time it is also seen as intervening in and shaping it. What's more, employees offer individual information like routines and experiences to scrutinize and refine organizational directions, re-directing the narrative to temper change mandates with the need for lived-through continuity and coherence. This builds on prior work on the social dimensions of information use [36, 37]. Extending their insights about information as a resource in social identity processes, this paper drew attention to organizational identity and image and its relation to employees' information practices. Information use plays an integral role in shaping workers' notions of organizational identity and affiliation and the continual effort to make and re-make one's organization in everyday practice. Revealing the creative and affective aspects of information use in organizations, this paper has shown how flexibilities and agencies can emerge in and through everyday work life. Organizations are not only places where grand strategic decisions are made and then carried out – they are also arenas where senses of self and identity are reckoned with in the unfolding dynamism of everyday life.

Acknowledgements. Thank you to study participants for their time and insight and to Paul Dourish, Gillian Hayes, and Jeanette Blomberg for guidance on this project. This work was supported by funds from: Achievement Rewards for College Scientists (ARCS) Fellowship; IBM PhD Fellowship; and U.S. Dept. of Education Graduate Assistance in Areas of National Need (GAANN) Fellowship. All opinions are my own and do not reflect any institutional endorsement.

References

1. Albert, S., Ashforth, B.E., Dutton, J.E.: Organizational identity and identification: charting new waters and building new bridges. Acad. Manag. Rev. **25**(1), 13–17 (2000). https://doi.org/10.5465/AMR.2000.2791600
2. de Alwis, G., Majid, S., Chaudhry, A.S.: Transformation in managers' information seeking behaviour: a review of the literature. J. Inf. Sci. **32**(4), 362–377 (2006). https://doi.org/10.1177/0165551506065812

3. Barniskis, S.C.: Metaphors of privilege: public library makerspace rhetoric. In: Proceedings of iConference (2015)
4. Borgatti, S.P., Cross, R.: A relational view of information seeking and learning in social networks. Manag. Sci. **49**(4), 432–445 (2003). https://doi.org/10.1287/mnsc.49.4.432.14428
5. Brickson, S.L.: Organizational identity orientation: the genesis of the role of the firm and distinct forms of social value. Acad. Manag. Rev. **32**(3), 864–888 (2007). https://doi.org/10.5465/AMR.2007.25275679
6. Case, D.O., O'Connor, L.G.: What's the use? Measuring the frequency of studies of information outcomes. J. Assoc. Inf. Sci. Technol. **67**(3), 649–661 (2016). https://doi.org/10.1002/asi.23411
7. Charmaz, K.: Constructing Grounded Theory. SAGE Publications Ltd, Thousand Oaks (2014)
8. Choo, C.W.: The knowing organization: how organizations use information to construct meaning, create knowledge and make decisions. Int. J. Inf. Manag. **16**(5), 329–340 (1996). https://doi.org/10.1016/0268-4012(96)00020-5
9. Choo, C.W., Auster, E.: Environmental scanning: acquisition and use of information by managers. Ann. Rev. Inf. Sci. Technol. (ARIST) **28**, 279–314 (1993)
10. Citrin, A.V., Lee, R.P., McCullough, J.: Information use and new product outcomes: the contingent role of strategy type. J. Prod. Innov. Manag. **24**(3), 259–273 (2007). https://doi.org/10.1111/j.1540-5885.2007.00249.x
11. Citroen, C.L.: The role of information in strategic decision-making. Int. J. Inf. Manag. **31**(6), 493–501 (2011). https://doi.org/10.1016/j.ijinfomgt.2011.02.005
12. Dahlin, K.B., Weingart, L.R., Hinds, P.J.: Team diversity and information use. Acad. Manag. J. **48**(6), 1107–1123 (2005)
13. Dutton, J.E., Dukerich, J.M.: Keeping an eye on the mirror: image and identity in organizational adaptation. Acad. Manag. J. **34**(3), 517–554 (1991)
14. Feinberg, M.: Ethos and the construction of a believable character for information systems. In: Proceedings of iConference (2009)
15. Feinberg, M.: Two kinds of evidence: how information systems form rhetorical arguments. J. Doc. **66**(4), 491–512 (2010). https://doi.org/10.1108/00220411011052920
16. Feinberg, M.: How information systems communicate as documents: the concept of authorial voice. J. Doc. **67**(6), 1015–1037 (2011)
17. Gioia, D.A., Schultz, M., Corley, K.G.: Organizational identity, image, and adaptive instability. Acad. Manag. Rev. **25**(1), 63–81 (2000)
18. Häckner, E.: Strategic development and information use. Scand. J. Manag. **4**(1), 45–61 (1988). https://doi.org/10.1016/0956-5221(88)90015-2
19. Hatch, M.J., Schultz, M.: Relations between organizational culture, identity and image. Eur. J. Mark. **31**(5/6), 356–365 (1997). https://doi.org/10.1108/eb060636
20. Hatch, M.J., Schultz, M.: The dynamics of organizational identity. Hum. Relat. **55**(8), 989–1018 (2002). https://doi.org/10.1177/0018726702055008181
21. Humphreys, M., Brown, A.D.: Narratives of organizational identity and identification: a case study of hegemony and resistance. Org. Stud. **23**(3), 421–447 (2002)
22. Frishammar, J.: Information use in strategic decision making. Manag. Decis. **41**(4), 318–326 (2003). https://doi.org/10.1108/00251740310468090
23. Kalsi, A.: Pervasive myth or pop culture relic? College students' experience of the librarian stereotype. In: Proceedings of iConference (2014)
24. Landry, C.F.: The home buying experience: the impacts of time pressure and emotion on high stakes deciders information behavior. In: Proceedings of iConference (2016)
25. Latham, K.: Experiencing documents. J. Doc. **70**(4), 544–561 (2014). https://doi.org/10.1108/JD-01-2013-0013

26. Lin, Y., Cole, C., Dalkir, K.: The relationship between perceived value and information source use during KM strategic decision-making: a study of 17 Chinese business managers. Inf. Process. Manag. **50**(1), 156–174 (2014)
27. Livengood, R.S., Reger, R.K.: That's our Turf! Identity domains and competitive dynamics. Acad. Manag. Rev. **35**(1), 48–66 (2010)
28. Lybaert, N.: The information use in a SME: its importance and some elements of influence. Small Bus. Econ. **10**(2), 171–191 (1998). https://doi.org/10.1023/A:1007967721235
29. Markus, M.L.: Technochange management: using IT to drive organizational change. J. Inf. Technol. **19**(1), 4–20 (2004). https://doi.org/10.1057/palgrave.jit.2000002
30. Nag, R., Corley, K.G., Gioia, D.A.: The intersection of organizational identity, knowledge, and practice: attempting strategic change via knowledge grafting. Acad. Manag. J. **50**(4), 821–847 (2007). https://doi.org/10.5465/AMJ.2007.26279173
31. Orlikowski, W., Gash, D.: Technological frames: making sense of information technology in organizations. ACM Trans. Inf. Syst. **12**(2), 174–207 (1994)
32. Proferes, N.: What happens to tweets? Descriptions of temporality in Twitter's organizational rhetoric. In: Proceedings of iConference (2014)
33. van Riel, C.B.M., Balmer, J.M.T.: Corporate identity: the concept, its measurement and management. Eur. J. Mark. **31**(5/6), 340–355 (1997). https://doi.org/10.1108/eb060635
34. Scott, S.G., Lane, V.R.: A stakeholder approach to organizational identity. Acad. Manag. Rev. **25**(1), 43–62 (2000). https://doi.org/10.5465/AMR.2000.2791602
35. Spears, L.I.: Using social networks for library funding advocacy: a discourse analysis of the Save the Miami-Dade Public Libraries Facebook campaign. In: Proceedings of iConference (2015)
36. Tuominen, K., Savolainen, R.: A social constructionist approach to the study of information use as discursive action. In: Proceedings of an International Conference on Information Seeking in Context (ISIC 1996), pp. 81–96 (1997)
37. Wolf, C.T., Veinot, T.C.: Struggling for space and finding my place: an interactionist perspective on everyday use of biomedical information. J. Assoc. Inf. Sci. Technol. **66**(2), 282–296 (2015)

Predicting Search Performance from Mobile Touch Interactions on Cross-device Search Engine Result Pages

Dan Wu[1,2](✉) and Lei Cheng[1]

[1] School of Information Management, Wuhan University, Wuhan, China
woodan@whu.edu.cn
[2] Institute for Digital Library, Wuhan University, Wuhan, China

Abstract. Search performance is one of essential indicators for search engines. Most researches predicting search performance are based on single device behavior features. However, user behaviors are more complicated in cross-device search. And little is known about how mobile touch interactions affect search performance in cross-device search engine result pages. In this paper, we conducted a user experiment based on our cross-device web search system to define and characterize mobile touch interactions on cross-device search engine result pages, and we predicted the search performance from these interactions. Besides, we divided each search result into 5 areas, including title, snippet, date, URL and recording information, and we analyzed important areas that users interacted with search engine result pages by mobile touch interactions. Moreover, we developed four models for predicting search performance on cross-device search engine result pages using features of actions, areas and inactive time collected from system logs. Our results showed that combining action features and area features can attain strong prediction accuracy, which can contribute to recommend relevant results and improve the search efficiency.

Keywords: Cross-device search · Mobile touch interaction
Search performance · Search engine result page
Information retrieval prediction

1 Introduction

People have various ways of accessing the web due to the development of mobile devices, such as mobile phones, tablets. Dearman and Pierce found that users use as many as 5 devices to access information on average [1]. Users interact with different devices in the same task, rather than just use different devices for different tasks. Especially on the weekends, the device usage sees a much greater fluctuation [2]. For example, people tend to search information in desktop at home when they are planning a vacation, however, they will access the web in mobile devices in the outside. Cross-device search is increasingly common owing to the diversity of search device. Comparing to single device search, user behaviors are more complex in cross-device search. As a result, cross-device search is becoming an important research domain [3].

© Springer International Publishing AG, part of Springer Nature 2018
G. Chowdhury et al. (Eds.): iConference 2018, LNCS 10766, pp. 560–570, 2018.
https://doi.org/10.1007/978-3-319-78105-1_62

Search performance is a core indicator of information retrieval [4]. Accurately predicting search performance has been extensively studied in desktop search and mobile search by analyzing information seeking behavior on search engine result pages (SERPs), which are referred to the relevant result list displayed by search engines with the title, snippet, URL, date in response to a query [5, 6]. In desktop search, query logs, click-through statistics, eye-fixation and mouse cursor movements are used as features to predict search performance while mobile touch interactions (MTIs) can reflect search performance in mobile search. Previous works have made great use of MTIs features to predict search performance in single device search, such as action types, touch pressure, X and Y coordinates of the touch points [7, 8]. However, researches about predicting search performance by analyzing MTIs in cross-device search are still lacking in adequate understanding. In this paper, we focused on predicting search performance from MTIs on cross-device SERPs. Not only can it improve the user interface of cross-device search, it also can help search engines recommend relevant results to users and achieve better performance.

2   Related Work

2.1   Mobile Touch Interactions

Users access information by interacting with search interface. MTIs, as unique features of mobile search, are widely used in understanding information seeking behavior. Most researches about MTIs are based on single online device, and focus on reading pattern and predicting. For example, Tran et al. compared pinch and spread performance on both phone and tablet devices in terms of performance time, actions and so on [9].

In addition, MTIs are used to understand the user's search behavior on SERPs to improve the search ranking quality. Kim et al. found that long snippets on mobile devices exhibit longer search times by analyzing MTIs [10]. Hotchkiss et al. investigated the first click decision and found that user pay more attention to ranks one and two [11].

MTIs are widely used to predict search performance as well. Action type, touch pressure, touch size, drag speed and distance [12, 13] are employed to predict search performance and achieve great prediction accuracy.

2.2   Features of Predicting Search Performance

Predicting search performance can contribute to improving the experience of search engines. Dwell time and query features are commonly used to prediction [4, 5]. Kim et al. developed a model to predict search performance by mining query associations [14].

On the other hand, mouse cursor movement and click are regarded as implicit indicators of search performance [5]. Some explicit interactions such as highlight and annotation are considered as features [15]. With the availability of eye-tracking, scanning path, viewpoint time and so on also play an important role in predicting search performance. Li et al. focused on building a prediction model that can infer user's interest ratings from attention metrics [16].

2.3 Prediction in Cross-device Search

Accurately predicting search performance in cross-device search is beneficial to improve the efficiency of information retrieval. Device transitions and whether the users will return to current task in the future are the main aspects of prediction. Wang et al. predicted task resumption using behavioral, topical, geospatial and temporal features [17]. Kotov et al. predicted whether the user will return to current task in the future according to queries, search sessions and historical features [18]. Montañez et al. proposed models to predict aspects of cross-device search transitions and the next device used for search using device information, query length and so on [3].

At the same time, predicting search performance is an important field in information retrieval, especially in cross-device search. Han et al. depended on the MTIs obtained from SERPs and subdocument to predict document quality [13].

In summary, most studies focus on predicting search performance by various features in single device search. However, little is known about how MTIs on SERPs affect search performance in cross-device search. Differing from existing studies, we aimed at predicting search performance in cross-device search. Moreover, we only concerned about the mobile touch interactions on cross-device SERPs.

3   Research Design

3.1   Research Questions

MTIs are implicit indicators of search performance [19]. In general, swiping and zooming are common actions in mobile search, and most studies pay attention to these actions to understand user reading pattern in SERPs, behavior characteristics and search performance [20, 21]. Previous studies have found that documents at the rank #1 and #2 receive most of the user's attention [22]. In this paper, we further divided each search result into 5 areas (see Fig. 1) to study which area is the most important one that users interacted with. In addition, we developed models to predict search performance using MTIs on cross-device SERPs. In conclusion, this study dealt with the following research questions (RQs):

RQ1: What are important areas interacted with users by mobile touch interactions on cross-device SERPs?

RQ2: How to predict search performance according to MTIs on cross-device SERPs?

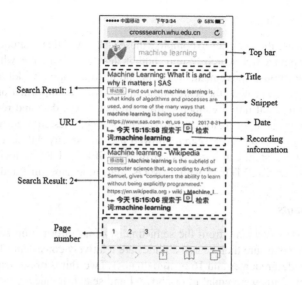

Fig. 1. SERPs of cross-device search system on mobile

3.2   Tasks and Experiment Procedure

Previous study found that entertainment information is what users search the most in mobile search, including movies, TV series, music and languages [23]. We designed four search tasks according to these topics. Each task was presented by a descriptive paragraph and contained four search points. During the experiment, the orders of the task combinations were rotated based on the Latin Square.

Our cross-device experiment included desktop search, mobile web search and mobile APP search. Firstly, we introduced our experiment to participants and conducted a survey on background and cross-device experience. Next was the search stage, each participant worked on all four tasks by 4 transition ways of desktop-mobile web browser, mobile web browser-desktop, desktop-mobile APP and mobile APP-desktop, and each task was divided into two sessions with twenty minutes. Users completed all the first devices (session 1) of 4 tasks at first and then all the second devices (session 2), so there was interruption of about 1 h between the first and second session for each task. Finally, the participants were asked to fill out three questionnaires: click questionnaire, session 1 questionnaire and session 2 questionnaire. The click questionnaire was used to obtain explicit feedback on the relevance of search results. Session 1 and session 2 questionnaires were used to collect the difficulty and the overall satisfaction about the task. Meanwhile, an interview was conducted to obtain detail information. After the experiment, we paid every participant 100–150 RMB to thank for their involvement.

3.3 Data Collection

Participants can use their devices to complete these tasks. And they searched information by login "cross-device web search system" both in desktop and mobile, which can record the search time, mouse movement, MTIs including drag up/down/left/right, tap and press. Besides, it can provide the search timestamp and query information (see Fig. 1). We divided each result into 5 elements: title, snippet, URL, date and recording information. The recording information can provide the search timestamp, current device and query information. Mobile APP search allowed user to use any APP except for search engine APP. Our system can log the load time of SERPs, URL (which contains the queries), current device, MTIs as well as MTIs' start time, stop time and areas.

3.4 Participants

We recruited 34 participants from the semi-finalist of an information search competition in order to make sure their search abilities are relatively consistent (22 females and 12 males; 18 undergraduates and 16 postgraduates). Two-thirds of participants reported that their search skills were equal to or above 4 and search frequency were equal to or above 3 on a scale of 1 to 5 (1 is the least skilled and 5 is the most skilled). The participants also reported their experiences of cross-device web search in the background questionnaire, and 97% users exhaustively reported their cross-device search experiences. The difference of participants' search abilities was not considered in our work.

4 Results

4.1 Mobile Touch Interactions and Areas of SERPs

Based on our dataset, a total of 90,737 MTIs was recorded. We counted the MTIs and their touched areas. The results were shown in Table 1.

Table 1. Mobile touch interactions and their touched areas

MTIs	Percentage	Frequent interaction area (top 6)	Percentage
Drag up	61.54%	result2 snippet	8.09%
Drag down	22.02%	result3 snippet	7.05%
Drag right	6.87%	result4 snippet	4.57%
Drag left	2.96%	search result: 3	4.47%
Tap	0.81%	search result: 2	4.44%
Press	0.02%	search result: 4	3.52%

From the perspective of MTIs, drag up was the most frequent interaction, accounting for 61.54%, followed by drag down. The interactions of drag up and drag down were closely related to the small screen of mobile device. Users needed to

Table 2. The most important areas corresponding to each interaction

MTIs	Area	Frequency	Percentage
Drag up	result2 snippet	4618	8.27%
Drag down	result2 snippet	1565	7.83%
Drag right	result3 snippet	619	9.93%
Drag left	result2 snippet	278	10.34%
Tap	result1 title	78	10.66%
Press	result3 title	2	9.09%

continue to drag up and drag down in order that they can access more information. From the perspective of areas, result2 snippet was the most frequent part of the user's interaction, accounting for 8.09%, followed by result3 snippet. To conclude, the most frequent areas users interacted with were ranks two, three and four.

Furthermore, we counted the areas of each MTIs (see Table 2). From the perspective of each MTIs, most drag up, drag down and drag left took place on result2 snippet. However, compared to drag left, drag right often interacted with result3 snippet. Tap, the most MTIs, took place at result1 title, accounting for 10.66%.

In general, user's first interaction was drag up when interacted with SERPs, accounting for 67.65%. This indicated that users tend to drag up to gain more information rather than tap on the search results. Most user's first tap decision was result1 title, followed by result2 title and result1 snippet with these datum that tap on blank area being removed (see Table 3). According to our dataset, users paid more attention to the first and second results, which was similar to Hotchkiss [11].

Table 3. First tap decision

First tap decision	Percentage	First tap decision	Percentage
result1 title	16.86%	result9 title	1.18%
result2 title	12.55%	search result: 2	1.18%
result1 snippet	10.98%	result4 snippet	0.78%
result3 title	6.27%	result5 snippet	0.78%
search result: 1	2.75%	result6 snippet	0.78%
result2 snippet	2.35%	search result: 3	0.78%
result4 title	1.97%	result2 date	0.39%
result5 title	1.57%	result3 snippet	0.39%
result6 title	1.18%	result7 title	0.39%
result7 snippet	1.18%	search result: 5	0.39%
result8 title	1.18%	blank area	34.12%

4.2 Predicting Search Performance

A set of 54 features was used for building prediction models. These included features of the MTIs types, areas that users interacted with, and inactive time in SERPs. Table 4 listed the features used in our models, a count of "x5" or "x6" denoted five or six features of that type.

Table 4. Features used in prediction models

Group		Feature	Description
Area	Title/snippet/date/URL/recording information	areacnt (x5)	Times of interact with area
		areapct (x5)	Percentage of interact with area
		areamax (x5)	Maximum of interact with area
		areanum (x5)	Result ranking that users most frequently interacted with
Action	Drag up/drag down/drag right/drag left/tap/press	actioncnt (x6)	Times of action
		actionpct (x6)	Percentage of action
		actiontime (x6)	Duration of action
		actiontimepct (x6)	Percentage of duration
		actionmaxtime (x6)	Maximum duration of single action
Inactive time		dwell time	Dwell time in SERPs
		inactive time	Time without interaction
		inactivepct	Percentage of inactive time
		inactivemax	Maximum duration of inactive

Area group refers to the 5 areas: title, snippet, date, URL and recording information. For each area, we counted the times, percentage, maximum of interactions as well as the result ranking that users most frequently interacted with. *Action* group included drag up, drag down, drag right, drag left, tap and press. For each action, we counted the times, duration and percentage and so on. This group not only indicated user's action type, but it can reflect the direction of each action. *Inactive time* group included the dwell time in SERPs, percentage and maximum of inactive time. A period of inactivity on a touch-enabled mobile device seems to be a good indicator of "reading" behavior [12]. In this group, inactive time meant the span without any interactions. All these features were counted according to our system logs.

Prediction Model. We considered three groups features for predicting search performance. To better understanding which group can attain great prediction accuracy, we developed four models based on MTIs.

Model A: This model used the action group features to predict search performance, which has been widely used in previous research [12].

Model B: This model was a variant of the model A that adapted the action group features and added the newly proposed area group features. In other words, the features of action and area are used.

Model C: This model was a variant of the model A that adapted the action group features and added the newly proposed inactive time group features. In other words, the features of action and inactive time are used.

Model D: This model was a variant of the model A that incorporated all features. In other words, the features of action, area and inactive time are used.

We treated the search performance prediction as a regression problem, and we applied a simple linear regression model to prediction with SPSS Modeler 18.0. We evaluated the search performance by calculating the standard information retrieval measure of NDCG@n (Normalized Discounted Cumulative Gain) [21] using the participants' 3-level relevance judgement on the clicked search results from the click questionnaire. We assigned the options of user's relevance feedback in click questionnaire to the corresponding values, that is, irrelevance was 1, and normal relevance was 3, and very relevance was 7. However, some errors resulted from user's wrong operation would affect the results, such as users forgot to fill up click questionnaire or they used other search engines. Finally, a total of 234 questionnaires could be used to build models.

A set of 234 results were used as training and testing. We randomly selected 75% of them were used to train the model and the rest 25% were used as the testing set. We varied the cutoff positions (named n) from 1 to 20, increasing 1 at each step and compared the prediction accuracy across all n values. The results showed that the NDCG@5 performed better than others. Table 5 showed the model parameters of predicting NDCG@5.

From Table 5 we can see that model D achieved great prediction accuracy, followed by model B and model C. This indicated that compared to the features of inactive time in SERPs, area group features were more important in predicting search performance. Moreover, we evaluated the features importance of each model. Drag up duration was the most important feature in model A and model C. However, in model B and model D, maximum duration of single drag up was the most important feature, followed by the percentage of tap. These features related to drag up play a significant role in all models, which indicated that search performance was closely related to the quantity and quality of access information.

Table 5. Model parameters of predicting NDCG@5

Model parameters	R	R-squared
Model A	0.634	0.402
Model B	0.735	0.540
Model C	0.650	0.422
Model D	0.753	0.566

Models Compared and Validated. We compared and validated the four models by evaluating RMSE (Root Mean Square Error) using the testing set. RMSE can reflect the precision of models with smaller values indicating better precision.

As shown in Table 6, surprisingly, the performance of model B was the best according to testing set, followed by model D. our results showed that the combination of MTIs and their touched areas can attain the best performance accuracy. Otherwise, the inactive time in cross-device SERPs had no significant difference by comparing model B with model C. Constrained by the screen sizes of mobile devices, users tended to keep sliding to get more information so that the inactive time performed worse in predicting mobile search performance.

Table 6. Performance of four models

Models	RMSE
Model A	0.684964
Model B	0.538975
Model C	0.723875
Model D	0.556899

5   Discussion and Conclusion

We have discussed the performance of MTIs in cross-device SERPs and our results demonstrated that MTIs in cross-device SERPs are high-quality relevance feedback that can predict search performance in cross-device SERPs.

We have two research questions in this paper. For RQ1, similar with single device search studies [21], ranks one and two were the first tap decision. Furthermore, the second and third results were the most important positions that users interacted with. This because second and third results were in the middle of screen. We also found that users started their first tap when they stayed at SERPs about 24 s in cross-device search. And the first interaction was drag up for most users. In other words, users tend to drag up to get more information when access SERPs at first, because users can access information depend on the titles or snippets of results. And this also can save most search time. Besides, user tended to tap on the result title although snippet contains more information, so the snippet sizes should appropriate for mobile devices [10]. This can help search engines to design a suitable interface of cross-device and improve the efficiency of information search.

For RQ2, we developed four models to predict search performance, differing from previous studies, we only focused on MTIs in cross-device SERPs. Previous studies found that inactive time has significant positive correlations with document relevance [13], but we found that the features of inactive time were not found to be a good indicator of predicting search performance in cross-device SERPs. One of the reason is that the screen sizes of mobile devices lead a higher chance of interacting with SERPs, according to Zhan et al. [24]; another is that users have seen these search results in the pre-switch device and there is no need to read these results again.

There are some limitations that we should acknowledge. Our dataset was based on a user experiment rather than the real cross-device search data. In the future, we will extend this research and take the types of search tasks and different screen sizes of devices into consideration. And we will use a more diverse group of participants to get the interaction data of more genuine search behavior. What is more, the machine learning methods will be used to predict search performance.

Acknowledgment. This work was supported by National Natural Science Foundation of China (71673204).

References

1. Dearman, D., Pierce, S.: It's on my other computer!: computing with multiple devices. In: SIGCHI Conference on Human Factors in Computing Systems, pp. 767–776. ACM, New York (2008)
2. Vetro Analytics. http://www.vertoanalytics.com/verto-reports/. Accessed 11 Sept 2017
3. Montañez, D., White, W., Huang X.: Cross-device search. In: 23rd ACM International Conference on Information and Knowledge Management, pp. 1669–1678. ACM, New York (2014)
4. Guo, Q., Jin, H., Lagun, D., et al.: Towards estimating web search result relevance from touch interactions on mobile devices. In: CHI 2013 Extended Abstracts on Human Factors in Computing Systems, pp. 1821–1826. ACM. New York (2013)
5. Fox, S., Karnawat, K., Mydland, M., et al.: Evaluating implicit measures to improve web search. ACM Trans. Inf. Syst. 23(2), 147–168 (2005)
6. Huang, J., White, W., Dumais, S.: No clicks, no problem: using cursor movements to understand and improve search. In: SIGCHI Conference on Human Factors in Computing Systems, pp. 1225–1234. ACM, New York (2011)
7. Han, S., Hsiao, I.-H., Parra, D.: A study of mobile information exploration with multi-touch interactions. In: Kennedy, W.G., Agarwal, N., Yang, S.J. (eds.) SBP 2014. LNCS, vol. 8393, pp. 269–276. Springer, Cham (2014). https://doi.org/10.1007/978-3-319-05579-4_33
8. Biedert, R., Dengel, A., Buscher, G., et al.: Reading and estimating gaze on smart phones. In: Proceedings of Symposium on Eye Tracking Research and Applications, pp. 385–388. ACM, New York (2012)
9. Tran, J., Trewin, S., Swart, C., et al.: Exploring pinch and spread gestures on mobile devices. In: 15th International Conference on Human-Computer Interaction with Mobile Devices and Services, pp. 151–160. ACM, New York (2013)
10. Kim, J., Thomas, P., Sankaranarayana, R., et al.: What snippet size is needed in mobile web search? In: 2017 Conference on Conference Human Information Interaction and Retrieval, pp. 97–106. ACM, New York (2017)
11. Hotchkiss, G., Alston, S., Edwards, G.: Eye tracking study. Research White paper, Enquiro Search Solutions, Kelowna, Canada (2005)
12. Guo, Q., Jin, H., Lagun, D., et al.: Mining touch interaction data on mobile devices to predict web search result relevance. In: 36th International ACM SIGIR Conference on Research and Development in Information Retrieval, pp. 153–162. ACM, New York (2013)
13. Han, S., Yue, Z., He, D.: Understanding and supporting cross-device web search for exploratory tasks with mobile touch interactions. ACM Trans. Inf. Syst. 33(4), 1–34 (2015)

14. Kim, Y., Hassan, A., White, W., et al.: Playing by the rules: mining query associations to predict search performance. In: 6th ACM International Conference on Web Search and Data Mining, pp. 133–142. ACM, New York (2013)
15. Ahn, W., Brusilovsky, P., He, D., et al.: Personalized web exploration with task models. In: 17th International Conference on World Wide Web, pp. 1–10. ACM, New York (2008)
16. Li, Y., Xu, P., Lagun, D., et al.: Towards measuring and inferring user interest from gaze. In: 26th International Conference on World Wide Web Companion, pp. 525–533. ACM, New York (2017)
17. Wang, Y., Huang, X., White, W.: Characterizing and supporting cross-device search tasks. In: 6th ACM International Conference on Web Search and Data Mining, pp. 707–716. ACM, New York (2013)
18. Kotov, A., Bennett, N., White, W., et al.: Modeling and analysis of cross-session search tasks. In: 34th International ACM SIGIR Conference on Research and Development in Information Retrieval, pp. 5–14. ACM, New York (2011)
19. Kelly, D., Belkin, N.J.: Reading time, scrolling and interaction: exploring implicit sources of user preferences for relevance feedback. In: 24th Annual International ACM SIGIR Conference on Research and Development in Information Retrieval, pp. 408–409. ACM, New York (2001)
20. Kim, J., Thomas, P., Sankaranarayana, R., et al.: Pagination versus scrolling in mobile web search. In: 25th ACM International on Conference on Information and Knowledge Management, pp. 751–760. ACM, New York (2016)
21. Guo, Q., Yuan, S., Agichtein, E.: Detecting success in mobile search from interaction. In: 34th International ACM SIGIR Conference on Research and Development in Information Retrieval, pp. 1220–1230. ACM, New York (2011)
22. Avery, J., Choi, M., Vogel, D., et al.: Pinch-to-zoom-plus: an enhanced pinch-to-zoom that reduces clutching and panning. In: 27th Annual ACM Symposium on User Interface Software and Technology, pp. 595–604. ACM, New York (2014)
23. Wu, D., Yao, X., Dong, J., et al.: Designing mobile search tasks: a context-based approach. Geomat. Inf. Sci. Wuhan Univ. **41**, 34–39 (2017)
24. Zhan, K., Zukerman, I., Moshtaghi, M., et al.: Eliciting users' attitudes toward smart devices. In: 2016 Conference on User Modeling Adaptation and Personalization, pp. 175–184. ACM, New York (2016)

Emotions Change in Pedestrian Navigation: A Perspective of User's Focuses

Dan Wu[1,2]([✉]) [iD] and Liuxing Lu[1] [iD]

[1] School of Information Management, Wuhan University, Wuhan, Hubei, China
woodan@whu.edu.cn
[2] Institute for Digital Library, Wuhan University, Wuhan, Hubei, China

Abstract. Map APPs have become daily travel helpers for people. People's emotions will influence their behaviors when they are using map APPs. This paper studies user's emotional changes in pedestrian navigation that is one of the widely used functions provided by map APPs. Two dimensions of emotional changes are analyzed. One is the changes of emotional polarities, and the other is the changes of six classifications on emotions. Factors that affect user's emotions from a perspective of user's focuses are also studied. The results show that: (1) "negative → negative" and "neutral → negative" are the most frequently emotional change patterns in pedestrian navigation. (2) Emotions on *Disgust* and *Happiness* are common in pedestrian navigation. (3) User's attention to external information and map system affects their emotions in varying degrees. We study user's emotions with the hope for giving insights for map APPs to promote their emotional learning in Artificial Intelligence.

Keywords: Pedestrian navigation · Emotional change · User's focuses
Think-aloud

1 Introduction

Emotion was the future direction of Artificial Intelligence, expressed by Fei-Fei Li, the Director of the *Stanford Artificial Intelligence Lab*, at the *Future Forum 2017 Annual Meeting*. Artificial Intelligence (AI) is the developing trend of map applications (APPs), therefore, for map APPs, it is important to learn user's emotions so that they can know their users better. This prompted us to do the research of user's emotions in map APPs. Since pedestrian navigation is one of the widely used functions provided by map APPs, we started our research from the user's emotions in pedestrian navigation.

Emotion is a basic motivation that impacts user's perceptions, cognition, social judgments and their behaviors [1]. User's emotions have been valued by many researchers. They studied user's self-reported emotional responses in mobile APPs [2], asking users to report emotional responses via questionnaires or interviews [3]. Capturing user's emotional actions could assess the effectiveness of location-based APPs at evoking particular emotions [4]. It provided inspiration for emotional learning in AI. Moreover, emotions can be divided into three polarities (positive, negative and neutral) [5] or six classifications (*happiness, fear, anger, sadness, disgust and surprise*) [6], however, previous studies mainly focused on "What are the user's emotions", but did

© Springer International Publishing AG, part of Springer Nature 2018
G. Chowdhury et al. (Eds.): iConference 2018, LNCS 10766, pp. 571–576, 2018.
https://doi.org/10.1007/978-3-319-78105-1_63

not study that "How the user's emotions change". Therefore, we put forward two research questions to study the changes of user's emotions in pedestrian navigation. That is:

RQ1: How the user's emotional polarities change in pedestrian navigation?
RQ2: How emotions on the six classifications change in pedestrian navigation?

Moreover, to study the factors that affect user's emotions, we analyzed user's focuses during pedestrian navigation. We defined user's focuses in our study as the things that users pay attention to. Previous research [7] showed that map users focused on spatial information and used it for decision-making. It revealed that there were some relationships between user's focuses and their behaviors. Therefore, it is reasonable to study factors that affect user's emotions from the perspective of user's focuses.

2   Method and Data

2.1   The Experimental Tasks and Participants

Two controlled outdoor tasks, which represented the tasks in pedestrian navigation, were designed to study user's emotions in pedestrian navigation, as be addressed below.

Task 1: Taking SHOPPINGMALL as a starting point. Searching for a nearby Hubei restaurant with the highest score and walk there.
Task II: Taking FACEMALL as a starting point. Searching for the TAIYANGSHEN HEALTH CENTER and walk there.

In Task I, participants were required to use *Explore the Surroundings* provided by Baidu Map. In Task II, they were asked to search the destination in the search box. We designed two tasks because we wanted to explore whether user's emotions would change differently when they were applying different functions in map APPs. The reason why we used Baidu Map was that 55% of participants (ranked NO.1) expressed in our pre-questionnaire that they preferred to use it.

30 university students (13 males and 17 females) who were unfamiliar with the experimental sites were recruited. Each participant had a unique user ID (number from 1 to 30). They had more than two-year experience in using map APPs (mean = 2.6 years, S.D. = 0.61). After completing the tasks, each participant, based on their performance during experiment, could obtain 100 to 150 Yuan.

2.2   Data Collection and Analysis Method

Data collection via think-aloud, an approach to study cognitive process of people [8]. It allowed us to collect data outdoors without using additional equipment. During experiment, participants were asked to speak out loudly about their thoughts and feelings. *SCREEN MASTER* (a screen-recording APP) was utilized to record user's audio speech.

Data analysis through text preprocessing and affective computing. Text preprocessing included three steps: (1) Converting audio speech into texts via a voice recognition tool[1]. (2) Segmenting sentences into meaningful words through *ICTCLAS*[2], a Chinese lexical analysis system. (3) Extracting emotional words based on *The Chinese Affective Lexicon Ontology* [11], which was an ontology giving details of intensity and polarity on emotional words. Totally, 749 sentences and 509 emotional words were obtained. In affective computing, the formulas raising by Zhang et al. [9], which were suitable for dealing with emotional words in Chinese sentences, were utilized to compute the value of emotional intensity. Meanwhile, the changes of emotions based on the six classifications raising by Ekman et al. [6] were also included.

Moreover, user's focuses were analyzed and encoded through a grounded analysis approach. It was essentially an inductive method [10] with three levels of coding. Each level was based on the previous level, just like the hierarchical encoding provided by Grounded Theory (but we do not generate theories). We directly borrowed the three levels of coding in Grounded Theory: open coding, axial coding and selective coding.

3 Results and Discussion

3.1 Change in Intensities on Emotional Polarities

Time of pedestrian navigation each participant spent was divided averagely into three periods to analyze the general change of emotional polarities (see Fig. 1).

Figure 1 reveals that the intensities on negative emotion in both tasks are greater than that of positive emotion, but the intensity difference between negative emotion and

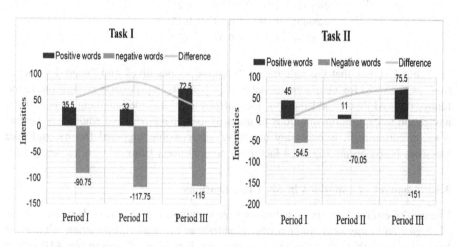

Fig. 1. Changes in intensities on emotional polarities in Task I and Task II.

---

[1] http://www.iflyrec.com/.
[2] http://ictclas.nlpir.org/.

positive emotion is decreasing, or the growth rate of the difference slows down. It is because the uncertainty about the road makes users be negative. Users will encounter different situations on the road, such as traffic jams, road construction, and inaccuracy of positioning. All the situations will influence users' uncertainties about the road. In the future, besides to promote positioning accuracy of map APPs, map APPs can offer detailed services to decrease user's incertitude of the road, such as giving details of the traffic jam, road construction, to users of pedestrian navigation. This can make users be mentally prepared, so that to reduce their uncertainties and to decrease their negative emotion.

3.2   The Change Patterns of Emotional Polarity

People's emotions may change during pedestrian navigation. For example, in our experiment, participant No.23 said, *"There is no overpass blocks my mobile positioning, so the positioning is accurate, and...what? The positioning turns to be inaccurate right now!"* According to *The Chinese Affective Lexicon Ontology*, *"accurate"*, expressed by participant No.23, is a positive emotional word, while *"inaccurate"* is a negative one. Therefore, emotion of participant No.23 changes from positive to negative at this time. We marked any change as "→". Totally, 117 pairs of changes were obtained. "Pre-", in Table 1, is pre-polarity. It is the original polarity of emotion. "Later-" means later-polarity. It represents the emotional polarity after changing.

Table 1. The probability of polarity changes.

Pre-	Later-		
	Positive	Neutral	Negative
Negative	0.06	0.18	0.2
Neutral	0.09	0.13	0.15
Positive	0.1	0.07	0.02

Table 1 shows that the patterns of "negative → negative" and "neutral → negative" are the most frequently emotional change patterns in pedestrian navigation. In the future, map APPs can add the functions of physiological measurement in pedestrian navigation to capture the emotions of users. If users have negative emotion or neutral emotion currently, it is necessary to analyze its possible triggered factors, and take measures based on the triggered factors to prevent users from being negative again.

3.3   Changes of Emotions in Six Classifications

Changes of emotions in six classifications are shown in Fig. 2. It reveals that emotions of *disgust* and *happiness* are common in pedestrian navigation. Pedestrian felt *disgust* because of something they met made them under displeasure. For example, 44% of our participants expressed that when they were facing an inaccurate positioning, they felt *disgust*. However, there are triggered factors that make users have kinds of emotions. To better understand the triggered factors, we analyzed user's focuses (see Table 2) in pedestrian navigation.

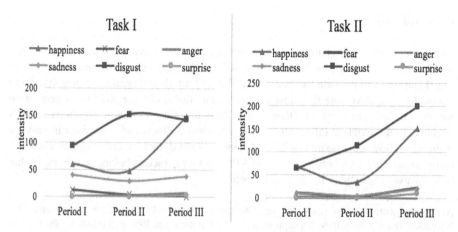

Fig. 2. Changes of emotions in six classifications in Task I and Task II.

Table 2. Codes of user's focuses.

Selective coding	Axial coding	Open coding	Percentage (%)
External information	Temperature	Outdoor temperature	12.6
		Indoor temperature	1
	Location	Current location	3.5
	Time	Time in use	3.8
	Road condition	Traffic jam	1.8
		Road construction	5.6
	Situation of destination	Position of destination	4.9
		Surroundings	1
Map system	Display of search result	Display of required time	3.8
		Display of distance	4.9
		Display of landmarks	29.5
	System prompting	Prompts of map system	12.5
	System positioning	Locating point	5.1
		Positioning accuracy	10

In pedestrian navigation, users are paying attention to external information and map system. Focusing on external information or map system affects user's emotions in varying degrees. In pedestrian navigation, as indicated by Table 2, landmarks displayed by map system are concerned by users at various times. However, a wrong positioning will mislead users to find the landmarks, which will make them be negative. Moreover, 37% of participants noticed and mentioned that the road condition affected their mood. Generally, unsatisfied situation, such as traffic jam, road construction and high temperature, makes users' emotions be negative, while satisfactory information, such as precise positioning and nice weather will make user's emotions be positive.

4 Conclusion

This paper studies the changes of emotion in pedestrian navigation that is one of the widely used functions provided by map APPs. Through our study, insights of emotional learning can provide for map APPs. We find out that "negative → negative" and "neutral → negative" are the most frequently emotional change patterns in pedestrian navigation, and emotions of *Disgust* and *Happiness* are common emotions. User's attention to the external information and map system affects their emotions in varying degrees. Follow-up research will study the triggered factors on negative emotion, recognizing what factors belong to map APPs and what factors belong to others, so that to learn user's emotions in map APPs better.

Acknowledgement. This work was an outcome of "Human-Computer Interaction and Collaboration Team" (Whu2016020) supported by "the Fundamental Research Funds for the Central Universities".

References

1. Reece, J.: Understanding Motivation and Emotion. Wiley, Hoboken (2005)
2. Mody, R.N., Willis, K.S., Kerstein, R.: WiMo: location-based emotion tagging. In: Proceedings of the 8th International Conference on Mobile and Ubiquitous Multimedia, pp. 1–4. ACM, New York (2009)
3. Huang, H., Klettner, S., Schmidt, M., Gartner, G., Leitinger, S., Wagner, A.: AffectRoute – considering people's affective responses to environments for enhancing route-planning services. Int. J. Geog. Inf. Sci. **28**(12), 2456–2473 (2014)
4. Baillie, L., Morton, L., Moffat, D.C., Uzor, S.: Capturing the response of players to a location-based game. Pers. Ubiquit. Comput. **15**(1), 13–24 (2011)
5. Xu, L.H., Lin, H.F., Pan, Y., Ren, H., Chen, J.M.: The construction of sentimental lexicon ontology. J. China Soc. Sci. Tech. Inf. **27**(2), 180–185 (2008)
6. Ekman, P., Friesen, W., Ellsworth, P.: Emotion in the Human Face: Guidelines for Research and an Integration of Findings. Pergamon Press, New York (1972)
7. Wang, J., Chen, Y.: Theoretical Cartography. Chinese People's Liberation Army Publishing House, Beijing, China (2000)
8. Nielsen, J., Clemmensen, T., Yssing, C.: Getting access to what goes on in people's heads?: reflections on the think-aloud technique. In: Proceedings of the Second Nordic Conference on Human-Computer Interaction, pp. 101–110. ACM, New York (2002)
9. Zhang, C., Liu, P., Zhu, Z., Fang, M.: A emotion analysis method based on polar dictionary. J. Shandong Univ. (Sci. Ed.) **47**(3), 50–53 (2012)
10. Thomas, D.R.: A general inductive approach for qualitative data analysis. Am. J. Eval. **27**(2), 237–246 (2006)
11. Xu, L., Lin, P., Pan, Y., et al.: The construction of emotion word ontology. J. China Soc. Sci. Tech. Inf. **27**(2), 180–185 (2008)

Why Should I Pay for the Knowledge in Social Q&A Platforms?

Yuxiang Zhao[1(✉)] ⓘ, Zhouying Liu[1] ⓘ, and Shijie Song[2]

[1] Nanjing University of Science and Technology, Nanjing 210094, China
yxzhao@vip.163.com
[2] Nanjing University, Nanjing 210046, China

Abstract. The development of online payment service enables the charging options for knowledge sharing, and morphs the social Q&A platforms into the knowledge exchange market. In the emerging trilateral payment-based social Q&A platforms, the asker needs to offer a certain amount of consulting fees to the answerer, and may also get monetary reward by the listeners' accumulated micro-payments. Thus, the asker's pay intention is one of the distinctive characteristics compared with the traditional Q&A model. This preliminary paper aims at exploring the influence factors that trigger askers' pay intention, by integrating the social exchange theory and social capital theory into examining the emerging style of trilateral payment-based social Q&A platforms.

Keywords: Payment-based social Q&A · Pay intention · Perceived value

1 Introduction

In recent years, the wave of sharing economy has stimulated the changes and innovation in business models [1]. Influenced by the proliferation of the sharing economy, the Q&A platforms unfold some new features, particularly highlighting the reward systems of knowledge transaction and monetary incentives.

Although the traditional community-based Q&A services (such as, Baidu Knows, Sogou Ask, etc.) are filled with a wealth of massive high-quality information, it also has a large amount of redundant and distorted information. For seeking the reliable information in a faster way, some askers are willing to pay for knowledge in many cases. From the answerer's perspective, as the gradual fading of the enthusiasm and freshness on the Internet, people began to pay further attention to the trade-off between their input and benefit. Hence, the payment-based Q&A services have taken the opportunity to come onto the market.

To the best of our knowledge, prior research has paid little attention to explore the askers' motivations. It is worth noting that, in the emerging style of trilateral payment-based social Q&A platforms, askers may have intricate motivations to raise their questions. Thus, the study aims at addressing the research gap by offering a theoretical perspective to explain why askers have the willingness to pay for the knowledge in the trilateral payment-based social Q&A platforms. Our potential findings may yield some implication to the managers and service providers when they design and evaluate the emerging style of social Q&A platforms.

© Springer International Publishing AG, part of Springer Nature 2018
G. Chowdhury et al. (Eds.): iConference 2018, LNCS 10766, pp. 577–582, 2018.
https://doi.org/10.1007/978-3-319-78105-1_64

2   Related Work

2.1   The Unique Characteristics of the Trilateral Payment-Based Social Q&A

When probing the context of the trilateral payment-based social Q&A platforms, we believe that this context was associated with some unique characteristics that may affect askers' perceived value and in turn their pay intention. The most notable one is the involvement of listeners in the new business model. Thus, the trilateral payment-based social Q&A platforms include three types of users, namely askers, answerers and listeners (see Fig. 1). The asker first selects an answerer to raise the question and pays a certain money set by the answerer. If the answerer doesn't respond to the question before the deadline, the money would be returned to the asker. Other users called listeners need to pay a small amount of money (1 RMB, priced by the platform) to listen to the answer, which will be split evenly between the asker and the answerer. In addition, the platform charges some commission fee. Regarding the format of Q&A, the traditional community-based model only provided the text-based interaction while the emerging platforms advocate diverse presentation styles such as text, image, voice and video, which may effectively enhance the performance and persuasiveness of Q&A interaction.

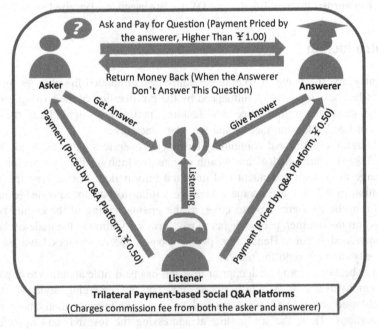

Fig. 1. Operational model of the trilateral payment-based social Q&A platforms

2.2   A Brief Review on the Askers' Motivations in Social Q&A Platforms

Most of the prior literature on users' participation motivations in social Q&A community has highlighted the issues from the answerers' perspective, yet little is known about the askers' motivations. Generally, the askers' motivations mainly include cognitive motivation, affective motivation and social motivation [2–5]. Cognitive motivation refers to the askers' needs of acquisition and further understanding of information, knowledge and skills [3, 4]. Affective motivation refers to askers' needs of receiving care, help, and support, etc., which mainly focus on psychological experiences [2–4]. Social motivation refers to the needs on building and strengthening relationships with others when asking questions [2].

To sum up, so far, there is few empirical studies on the askers' motivations in the previous research, and the asking behavior is mainly driven by the intrinsic motivations. However, in the trilateral payment-based social Q&A context, an asker may consider more about the cost and benefit. Hence, compared with the traditional model of Q&A services, the askers' pay intention is very important in the trilateral payment-based social Q&A platforms.

3   Research Model and Hypotheses

In the field of marketing, many studies have shown that perceived value has a strong prediction on consumer willingness to pay [7, 8]. The trilateral payment-based social Q&A platforms are similar to the knowledge market, involving "give" and "get" [9]. Social exchange theory can help to illuminate on people's judgement towards the exchange process from the cost and benefit perspective [10]. In addition, social capital theory posits that social capital embedded within online communities provides the contingent factors necessary for knowledge sharing and transfer [11]. Based on social exchange theory and social capital theory, we propose our hypotheses.

3.1   Perceived Value and Pay Intention

Perceived value is the personal perception after the experience on the trade-off between perceived cost and perceived benefit [6]. In our case, the trilateral payment-based social Q&A platform can be viewed as a knowledge market. On the one hand, the askers should bear some costs, such as time, money, etc. On the other hand, they can get some extrinsic and intrinsic benefits. We believe that if an asker perceives more value towards the Q&A process, she/he will form a stronger willingness to pay on the platform. Therefore, we hypothesize that:

H1: Perceived value has a positive impact on the askers' pay intention.

3.2   Antecedents of Perceived Value

Perceived cost. In this study, we will consider two types of costs, namely codification cost and financial cost. The prior research confirms that the codification cost is an important factor that influences the knowledge sharing motivation [11]. The askers inevitably spend more time and effort in designing the intriguing questions to attract more listeners. Further, the financial cost may become a significant inhibitor. In the field of marketing, Kim et al. [7], Chu and Lu [12] demonstrate that the financial cost is negatively related to perceived value. Overall, we hypothesize that:

H2: Perceived cost has a negative impact on the askers' perceived value.

Perceived extrinsic benefit. In this study, two kinds of perceived extrinsic benefits will be considered, i.e., financial benefit and social support. The askers can gain some financial benefit if the listeners pay for the answers. Prior studies have showed that the monetary reward from the organizations or platforms can stimulate the user's participate intention and attitude [11, 13, 14]. In addition, there are a lot of emotional questions in the Q&A services. If an asker perceives the support and understanding from other people, she/he will generate a strong sense of social support. Many studies have shown that social support is one of the important factors that can influence people's usage intention [15, 16]. In line with these arguments, we hypothesize that:

H3: Perceived extrinsic benefit has a positive impact on the askers' perceived value.

Perceived intrinsic benefit. In this study, we will consider two kinds of perceived intrinsic benefits, i.e., self-enhancement and entertainment. Previous literature has confirmed that information need is a driving factor to facilitate the user participation [17]. In our case, information need will enhance the learning ability, which may further lead to self-enhancement. In addition, entertainment is also an important driver of perceived value [18], and the participation intention [19]. In our case, the trilateral payment-based social Q&A platforms provide users with rich experience through gamification design. Askers in the platform can achieve the entertainment, thereby enhancing their perceived value. Overall, we hypothesize that:

H4: Perceived intrinsic benefit has a positive impact on the perceived value.

3.3 Moderating Effects

Positive reciprocity belief. In the context of the trilateral payment-based social Q&A platforms, positive reciprocal belief refers to the identification that the answer should be paid since the answerers spend their valuable time, effort, as well as their knowledge and experience in helping the askers solve their problems. Umphress et al. argue that the positive reciprocity belief can moderate the relationship between user attitude and behavior [20]. Therefore, in our case, we hypothesize that:

H5: The negative relationship between perceived cost and perceived value will be alleviated under conditions of high positive reciprocity belief.

Trust. In general, trust plays a vital role in affecting users' decision [21]. According to the different objects of trust perceived by the user, trust can be viewed as a multi-dimensional concept [22]. In this paper, we divide the trust into two dimensions, namely trust in the Q&A platforms and trust in the answerers. Compared with the traditional social Q&A communities, the new platforms in our study have more advantages on building a trustworthy ecology of online knowledge market. Some researchers have examined the moderating effect of trust on the positive impact between the adoption intention and actual participation [23]. In this study, we treat trust as a moderating construct and we hypothesize that:

H6: The positive relationship between perceived value and pay intention will be stronger under conditions of high level of trust.

4   Research Methodology

The survey methodology will be used to collect the askers' self-reported data for testing the research hypotheses. We intend to collaborate with the trilateral payment-based social Q&A platforms in China, such as Fenda, Zhihu, Weibo Q&A to conduct the empirical study. All the measures for the constructs are adapted from the items that have been used in the prior research. The perceived cost will be adapted from Kankanhalli et al. [11] and Chu and Lu [12]. The related scales for perceived extrinsic benefit will be adapted from Hau et al. [13], and Lin et al. [15]. The related scales for the perceived intrinsic benefit will be adapted from Chang et al. [18], Ifinedo [19]. The measurement items for perceived value and pay intention will be adapted from Kim et al. [7]. The construct of positive reciprocity belief will be measured by the items from Umphress et al. [20]. In terms of the trust, measurement will be adapted from Ye and Kankanhalli [14] and Zhao et al. [22]. In addition to the measurement items of these constructs, we will also set some questions to capture the askers' demographic information and their experiences about using the trilateral payment-based social Q&A platforms. Based on above data, we will use PLS to test our research model and hypotheses.

References

1. Cheng, M.: Sharing economy: a review and agenda for future research. Int. J. Hosp. Manag. **57**, 60–70 (2016)
2. Choi, E., Shah, C.: User motivations for asking questions in online Q&A services. J. Assoc. Inf. Sci. Technol. **67**(5), 1182–1197 (2016)
3. Wilson, T.D.: On user studies and information needs. J. Doc. **37**(1), 3–15 (1981)
4. Zhang, Y.: Contextualizing consumer health information searching: an analysis of questions in a social Q&A community. In: Proceedings of the 1st ACM International Health Informatics Symposium, pp. 210–219, Virginia, Arlington (2010)
5. Morris, M.R., Teevan, J., Panovich, K.: What do people ask their social networks, and why?: a survey study of status message Q&A behavior. In: Proceedings of the SIGCHI Conference on Human Factors in Computing Systems, pp. 1739–1748, Georgia, Atlanta (2010)
6. Zeithaml, V.A.: Consumer perceptions of price, quality, and value: a means-end model and synthesis of evidence. J. Mark. **52**(3), 2–22 (1988)

7. Kim, H.W., Xu, Y., Gupta, S.: Which is more important in Internet shopping, perceived price or trust? Electron. Commer. Res. Appl. **11**(3), 241–252 (2012)
8. Kwon, H.H., Trail, G., James, J.D.: The mediating role of perceived value: team identification and purchase intention of team-licensed apparel. J. Sport Manag. **21**(4), 540–554 (2007)
9. Chen, Y., Ho, T.H., Kim, Y.M.: Knowledge market design: a field experiment at Google Answers. J. Public Econ. Theory **12**(4), 641–664 (2010)
10. Homans, G.C.: Social behavior as exchange. Am. J. Sociol. **63**(6), 597–606 (1958)
11. Kankanhalli, A., Tan, B.C., Wei, K.K.: Contributing knowledge to electronic knowledge repositories: an empirical investigation. MIS Q. **29**(1), 113–143 (2005)
12. Chu, C.W., Lu, H.P.: Factors influencing online music purchase intention in Taiwan: an empirical study based on the value-intention framework. Internet Res. **17**(2), 139–155 (2007)
13. Hau, Y.S., Kim, B., Lee, H., Kim, Y.G.: The effects of individual motivations and social capital on employees' tacit and explicit knowledge sharing intentions. Int. J. Inf. Manage. **33**(2), 356–366 (2013)
14. Ye, H.J., Kankanhalli, A.: Solvers' participation in crowdsourcing platforms: examining the impacts of trust, and benefit and cost factors. J. Strateg. Inf. Syst. **26**(2), 101–117 (2017)
15. Lin, X., Zhang, D., Li, Y.: Delineating the dimensions of social support on social networking sites and their effects: a comparative model. Comput. Hum. Behav. **58**, 421–430 (2016)
16. Liang, T.P., Ho, Y.T., Li, Y.W., Turban, E.: What drives social commerce: the role of social support and relationship quality. Int. J. Electron. Commer. **16**(2), 69–90 (2011)
17. Lin, H.F.: Determinants of successful virtual communities: contributions from system characteristics and social factors. Inf. Manag. **45**(8), 522–527 (2008)
18. Chang, S.E., Shen, W.C., Liu, A.Y.: Why mobile users trust smartphone social networking services? A PLS-SEM approach. J. Bus. Res. **69**(11), 4890–4895 (2016)
19. Ifinedo, P.: Applying uses and gratifications theory and social influence processes to understand students' pervasive adoption of social networking sites: perspectives from the Americas. Int. J. Inf. Manag. **36**(2), 192–206 (2016)
20. Umphress, E.E., Bingham, J.B., Mitchell, M.S.: Unethical behavior in the name of the company: the moderating effect of organizational identification and positive reciprocity beliefs on unethical pro-organizational behavior. J. Appl. Psychol. **95**(4), 769–780 (2010)
21. Park, J.G., Lee, J.: Knowledge sharing in information systems development projects: explicating the role of dependence and trust. Int. J. Proj. Manag. **32**(1), 153–165 (2014)
22. Zhao, L., Lu, Y., Wang, B., Chau, P.Y., Zhang, L.: Cultivating the sense of belonging and motivating user participation in virtual communities: a social capital perspective. Int. J. Inf. Manag. **32**(6), 574–588 (2012)
23. Chang, H.H., Wong, K.H.: Adoption of e-procurement and participation of e-marketplace on firm performance: trust as a moderator. Inf. Manag. **47**(5), 262–270 (2010)

Digital Curation

Electronic Document and Records Management System Implementation in Malaysia: A Preliminary Study of Issues Embracing the Initiative

Azlina Ab Aziz[✉], Zawiyah Mohammad Yusof,
Umi Asma' Mokhtar, and Dian Indrayani Jambari

Faculty of Information Science and Technology,
Universiti Kebangsaan Malaysia, Bangi, Malaysia
azlinaabaziz79@gmail.com,
{zawiy,umimokhtar,dian}@ukm.edu.my

Abstract. The Electronic Document and Records Management System (EDRMS) is a software application that manages digital information, merging both document management and records management functionality which will increase the business efficacy and deliver better accountability. Literature in the area has identified that there are issues hindering organisation from implementing EDRMS. These are not ready to change, do not possess the required knowledge and skills, lack of policy and procedure in place, not receiving support from the top management and not competent over the security and privacy matter. Malaysia which is striving into a fully developed nation by the year 2020, also embarking on EDRMS to enhance its quality of service delivery. However, not all organisations particularly in the public sector succeeded in implementing EDRMS endeavour partly due to the above mentioned problems. This study seeks to identify and validate the issues which impede the materialisation of EDRMS in Malaysia public sector. Data was collected qualitatively through literature review and interview where the latter technique involved the EDRMS experts. This study could help the Malaysia public sector to discover the issues in implementing EDRMS and to develop policies, procedures, or take appropriate actions for the smooth running of EDRMS.

Keywords: Electronic Document and Records Management System (EDRMS) · EDRMS implementation challenges · Public sector

1 Introduction

EDRMS is "an automated system that supports the creation, use, and maintenance of documents and records in both paper and electronic format, with the intention of reaping an efficient organisation's workflow and processes" [1]. The implementation of EDRMS has been proven to improve effectiveness, reduce costs, keep information safe and secure, manage record versions, manage the integrity and reliability of data, improve service delivery and generally enhance business processes [2, 3]. EDRMS is

© Springer International Publishing AG, part of Springer Nature 2018
G. Chowdhury et al. (Eds.): iConference 2018, LNCS 10766, pp. 585–591, 2018.
https://doi.org/10.1007/978-3-319-78105-1_65

supposed to provide a more integrated and efficient solution for record management within the organisations. However, the public sector is suffering from a range of issues in implementing the initiative where the failure to the implementation can lead to embarrassment, reputation damage, and financial loss [1]. Previous studies have reported the failure of the system implementation was due to a variety of factors such as computer illiteracy, attitude towards technology, and poor of change management [4, 5]. Yet, few studies have actually been conducted in the context of the public sector.

1.1   System for Managing Documents and Records in Malaysia Public Sector

Malaysia is using Digital Document Management System (DDMS) for managing the documents and records of its public agencies [6]. DDMS enables significant cost savings for the agencies as it is made available through the Software as a Service (SaaS) delivery model that leverages on a multitenancy architecture. DDMS is to be extended to the entire public agencies by the year 2020 and to date, it has been implemented in 52 out of 200 agencies. From these 52 agencies, only 11,118 users (51%) are actively using the system. As the lead agency of DDMS implementation in the public sector in Malaysia, Malaysian Administrative Modernisation and Management Planning Unit (MAMPU) remarks this as unsatisfactory level of usage. Therefor this study examines issues affecting the DDMS implementation in Malaysia public sector.

2   Method

An intensive review of literature on the implementation of EDRMS initiative in the public sector was conducted alongside with semi-structured interview. For the former technique, a research question was outlined i.e. "What are the issues embraced in implementing EDRMS initiative in the public sector?". Search strings such as "EDRMS implementation", "EDRMS implementation issues" and "public sector" from various online databases were used. The latter technique has involved five experts (four experts from MAMPU and one expert from the National Archive of Malaysia (NAM)). These agencies were selected due to their role as the leading agency in the implementation of EDRMS initiative in Malaysia. The experts were selected based on their roles and experiences (as indicated in Table 1) such as involvement in the development and implementation of EDRMS, devising strategy and also policy development.

In the interview, a set of questionnaire was delivered to the selected experts comprising of questions about the implementation of EDRMS in Malaysia as follows: (1) the current scenario in managing EDRMS; (2) the issues and challenges faced by the implementing team; and (3) the impact of EDRMS to the organization. The experts were also asked to validate and rank the issues (these issues were extracted from the literature) according to their point of view using a scale of 1 to 10 (low to high priority). This ranking process is necessary to identify the issues that affect the implementation of EDRMS the most in the public sector in Malaysia. Experts were also invited to offer their opinion and insights about any issue to be added. Conversations were recorded,

Table 1. Characteristic of the expert

Expert ID	Roles in current organisation	Category	Work experience	Experience in related fields
E1	Information management expert	Top management	35 years	8 years (EDRMS, strategy and policy development)
E2	Information management expert	Senior management	12 years	7 years (EDRMS, strategy and policy development)
E3	Information management expert	Operational	11 years	7 years (EDRMS, system development)
E4	Records management expert	Operational	10 years	10 years (record management, EDRMS)
E5	ICT expert	System development	14 years	11 years (EDRMS, system development)

transcribed, and analysed. The interviews lasted between 30 to 50 min. To analyse the gathered data, the process by [7] was applied which consists of familiarisation, transcription, organisation and coding, building the description, and writing the report.

3 Findings and Analysis

The results of the preliminary study have contributed to the identification of nine issues in implementing EDRMS in the public sector as illustrated in Table 2.

Table 2. The ranking of the issues in EDRMS implementation in Malaysia

Ranking	Issues	Source		
		LR	Authors	Interview
1	Resistance to change	√	[2, 8–10]	√
2	Lack of knowledge and skills	√	[4, 11, 12]	√
3	Inadequate user training	√	[2, 9]	√
4	Lack of policies, guidelines, and procedures	√	[1, 4, 13]	√
5	Technical issues	√	[4, 12]	√
6	Security and privacy	√	[5, 14, 15]	√
7	Lack of top management support	√	[8, 12, 14]	√
8	Lack of monitoring	x	–	√
9	No enforcement	x	–	√

From the interviews, experts unanimously agreed with the identified issues from the literature but with another two additional issues such as monitoring, and no enforcement. The experts assert that these two issues need to be considered as their experience suggest in doing so. The explanation of each issue are as follows:

a. **Resistance to change** - Resistance to changes among personnel at all levels is common during the implementation of EDRMS initiative and is one of the key challenges faced by an organisation [4]. The implementation of EDRMS could cause several other changes at all levels across the organisation, especially in terms of process and work procedures. Thus, resisting to changes is unavoidable. E2 states that: *"Resistance to change is the major issue in implementing EDRMS in Malaysia public sector that is related to user adoption of the system."* E3 suggests that: *"Several approaches need to be taken to enhance the sense of responsibility and user interest in using new systems, such as by promoting the benefits of the system and rewarding the active users. The factors that influence users adoption should also be identified so that appropriate actions can be taken. Efficient change management and appropriate actions seems able to overcome these problems.*

b. **Lack of knowledge and skills** - EDRMS users should be equipped with knowledge and skills to operate the system and master the basic concepts of records management [4]. Lack of skilled personnel could resulted in EDRMS implementation failure [11]. According to E5: *"Technological skills are varied between individuals. For those employees who have limited technical skills, the thought of having to learn and use an electronic document management system for the first time can be overwhelming. We do send some of the personnel to related courses to address this issue and run the awareness program such as technology update to enhance the knowledge."*

c. **Inadequate User Training** - Sufficient trainings on information technology (IT) skills and system usage procedures play an important role in the implementation of EDRMS. The lack of training is among the main causes of EDRMS failure [8, 16]. [2] states that training should be implemented periodically to increase consumer awareness and skills in addressing EDRMS positively. According to E3: *"The implementation team has set up a schedule for training exercises and will be carried out in stages involving 35 agencies. However, the lack of staff has caused the process to take some time. Effective training should be carried out continuously and involve one-to-one or group training. Training should also be carried out according to the user's functions and responsibilities. However, there are users who do not cooperate by failing to attend these training sessions by providing various reasons."*

d. **Lack of Policies, Guidelines, and Procedures** - EDRMS in the public sector is regulated by policies, recordkeeping procedures, work processes, as well as record distribution rules and guidelines that were mostly developed independently within their respective organisations [8]. EDRMS is implemented in some organisations merely based on their instinct and initiatives, without implementing the relevant policies and procedures [13]. EDRMS needs clear and comprehensive policies [1], otherwise, its implementation is likely to fail. This is because the organisation might lack the proper directions to implement the initiative [8]. E4 states that: *"For public agencies, there are federal agencies, state agencies, and statutory bodies that have different organisational set-ups and structures. To come out with a standard EDRMS implementation policy is quite a challenge based on this variation of organisational set-ups. However, a standard policy is a must in an organisation to ensure the successful establishment of EDRMS. The implementation team are still working on it".*

e. **Security and Privacy** - Security and privacy issues are one of major concern in implementing EDRMS [5]. The users' confidence in the system will increase when organisations provide high priority and assurance related to information security. This is because the user's confidence and capabilities could also affect the implementation of EDRMS [13, 16]. Accordingly, the safety and privacy of organisational information should be taken into consideration to prevent such information from being released to the unauthorised users. According to E1: *"Security and privacy is a key criteria which should be taken into account by the management and system developer before the system is developed. The National Archive of Malaysia (NAM), Cyber Security Malaysia (CSM) and Chief Government Security Office of Malaysia (CGSO) are responsible as a security adviser for EDRMS implementation to ensure that the relevant laws and regulations are complied with."*

f. **Technical Issue** - Technical issue includes ICT infrastructure, data migration, and system integration [2, 12]. ICT infrastructure is a major requirement in EDRMS implementation comprising of the related hardware and software. Data migration that not performed according to the procedure may cause the risks of data corruption, loss, and alteration [12]. According to E3: *"ICT infrastructure for all the participated agencies were provided and coordinated by MAMPU. The different organisational set-ups and structures make these technical issues a big challenge. A complete procedures for system maintenance, data migration and system integration needs to be documented and streamlined."*

g. **Lack of Top Management Support** - The involvement and support from the most senior officers could also be the main factors contributing to the success of EDRMS. [16] states that leaders play an important role in running the organisations, especially during the first phase of EDRMS implementation. Good leadership would be able to support and control projects at all EDRMS levels, ranging from the bottom to the highest level. E1 states that: *"In terms of system usage, most of the top management depends on their secretaries and officers. However, most of the top managements provide good cooperation and support in this initiative, primarily to engage in awareness programs and training sessions. Only a handful of them have shown difficulty to cooperate due to time constraints and other important tasks."*

h. **Lack of Monitoring** - Interviews with expert stated that the strategic plan of EDRMS implementation needs to be continuously monitored to identify the problems and also to improve weaknesses and should be part of the system administrator's main tasks. Monitoring should be held periodically and be followed up with a report to identify system performance. According to E2: *"This issue has been taken into account in the ICT Strategic Plan (ISP) 2016–2020. To date, there is a monitoring plan prepared by the EDRMS implementation team in MAMPU, but no specific officer was assigned and no proper actions were taken after monitoring has been conducted. The lack of monitoring makes users indifferent to use the system. To date, monitoring is done in monthly basis through a statistical reporting of the system usage."* E1 recommended that: *"Monitoring results should be recorded and appropriate action should be taken within a prescribed time frame."*

i. **No Enforcement** - Interviews with expert also stated that enforcement is required to ensure the effectiveness of the EDRMS implementation plan. Enforcement can be executed formally or otherwise and actions can be taken if enforcement is not complied with. E2 confirms that: *"To date, no law or policy enforces the implementation of EDRMS. This means that EDRMS initiatives and programs are not compulsory, and various agencies depend on their own ICT strategic plans to execute their EDRMS practices. Enforcement needs to be considered in the future to ensure the smooth implementation of EDRMS and to enhance the sense of responsibility of users towards the system."*

4 Conclusion

The panel of experts has shown their interest and has promoted that cooperation should be given to this study as they were aware of the importance of EDRMS initiative to the public sector. The data from the preliminary study has enabled the identification of nine issues pertinent to the implementation of EDRMS initiative in the Malaysia public sector. The results of this study (the identified issues) should be able to serve as a guide for the public sector in Malaysia in developing policies, procedures, or take appropriate actions for the smooth running of EDRMS. The interviews has also suggested that monitoring and enforcement are another two additional issues to be considered as both are prevalent. Based on the top most issue listed by this study, apparently the main issue in EDRMS implementation in Malaysia is basically relate to users' attitude and behaviour. In this regard, further studies on factors affecting the EDRMS adoption (user perspective) in the public sector should be considered.

Acknowledgement. The study is financially supported by Public Service Department of Malaysia.

References

1. Yin, B.: An Analysis of the Issues and Benefits in EDRMS Implementation - A Case Study in a NZ Public Sector Organisation, Victoria University of Wellington (2014)
2. Leikums, T.: Managing human factors in implementing electronic document. Rom. Rev. Soc. Sci. **2**, 21–30 (2012)
3. Mahadi: Citizen Relationship Management Implementation in Malaysian Local Governments a Ph.D. thesis, Brunel University London (2013)
4. McLeod, J., Childs, S., Hardiman, R.: Accelerating positive change in electronic records management. J. Chem. Inf. Model. **53**(9), 1689–1699 (2013)
5. Grange, M., Scott, M.: An Investigation into the Affect of Poor End User Involvement on Electronic Document Management System (EDMS) Implementation, pp. 23–24 (2010)
6. MAMPU: Pelan Strategik ICT Sektor Awam Malaysia, vol. 2020, pp. 39–44 (2016)
7. Yin, R.K.: Qualitative Research from Start to Finish. The Guilford Press, New York (2011)
8. Nguyen, L.T., Swatman, P., Fraunholz, B., Salzman, S.: EDRMS implementation in the Australian public sector. In: Proceedings of the 20th Australasian Conference on Information Systems, ACIS 2009, pp. 915–928 (2009)
9. Mutimma Collin: Records Management in the Public Sector, University of Nairobi (2014)
10. Kalsi, N.S., Kiran, R.: A Strategic Framework for Good Governance Through e-Governance Optimization (2015)

11. Abdulkadhim, H., Mahadi, A.B., Hashim, H.: Exploring the common factors influencing electronic document management systems (EDMS) implementation in government. ARPN J. Eng. Appl. Sci. **10**, 17945–17952 (2015)
12. Mokhtar, U.A., Yusof, Z.M.: Electronic records management in the Malaysian public sector: the existence of policy. Rec. Manag. J. **19**, 231–244 (2009)
13. Dikopoulou, A., Mihiotis, A.: The contribution of records management to good governance. TQM J. **24**, 123–141 (2012)
14. Mukred, M., Yusof, Z.M., Mokhtar, U.A., Manap, N.A.: Electronic records management system adoption readiness framework for higher professional education institutions in Yemen. Int. J. Adv. Sci. Eng. Inf. Technol. **6**, 804–811 (2016)
15. Asogwa, B.E.: The readiness of universities in managing electronic records: a study of three federal Universities in Nigeria. Electron. Libr. **31**(6), 792–807 (2013)
16. Yaacob, R.A., Mapong Sabai, R.: Electronic records management in Malaysia: a case study in one government agency. Asia Pacific Conf. Libr. Inf. Educ. Pract. **2006**, 420–433 (2011)

Performative Metadata: Reliability Frameworks and Accounting Frameworks in Content Aggregation Data Models

Rhiannon Bettivia[1]([✉]) and Elizabeth Stainforth[2]

[1] University of Illinois, Urbana-Champaign, USA
rbettivi@illinois.edu
[2] University of Leeds, Leeds, UK
e.m.stainforth@leeds.ac.uk

Abstract. Metadata is not a new concept: it has existed for hundreds of years, with different forms and functions. In contemporary settings, we think about metadata serving administrative, descriptive, and technical functions. These roles are often in the service of common goals to identify information so that it can be found and used according to the discipline or industry from which it comes. But as modes of accessing and using information change, so too does the role of the data about that data, the metadata. Even if the metadata itself does not change, it comes to serve new functions, and these functions merit additional study. In this paper, we argue that in the contemporary political landscape of information, metadata schemas stemming from distinct ontological approaches take on fundamentally performative roles, and different underlying approaches mean that the performativity of the metadata is also enacted differently.

Keywords: Metadata · Semantic web · Aggregation · Performativity

1 Introduction

The word metadata literally means 'data about data', yet what it actually refers to is much fuzzier given the breadth of uses, both of the term and of metadata itself. Further, what is metadata in one context may become primary data in another. What is consistent is that metadata is used to refer to some aspect of the information object itself, at various logical levels and levels of aggregation. Metadata is bound up with identification: its role is to enable identification so that information objects can be used in the domain from which they derive. These uses are myriad, which is why the definition of metadata must be broad: metadata may be concerned with access, discoverability, rendering content machine-actionable, or enabling semantic processing and meaning-making. Any of these activities may take place in domains ranging from professional or academic spaces, to pro-am metadata spaces like Wikipedia, to quotidian personal digital activities such as tagging photos on social media.

Metadata is also an integral component of the structured data movement and the Semantic Web. While the promise of the Semantic Web remains largely unrealized, in practice this approach relies on semantically structured knowledge in the form of

G. Chowdhury et al. (Eds.): iConference 2018, LNCS 10766, pp. 592–597, 2018.
https://doi.org/10.1007/978-3-319-78105-1_66

machine-readable metadata. Structured data allows for the linking up of information from disparate sources via semantically defined associations. However, there are different approaches to structuring data, based on various factors such as domain ontologies.

We ask two research questions about structured metadata:

1. What is the motivation behind undertaking the task of converting hierarchical XML metadata into semantically structured data?
2. What roles does this metadata take on as its uses change to accommodate new forms of information consumption?

This paper presents emerging findings to these questions: we posit that metadata takes on a performative role and, within the case study domain of cultural heritage metadata, this performative role informs the non-trivial task of restructuring existing metadata into machine-readable semantic metadata. We examine how this performativity manifests itself by drawing a distinction between what we term *reliability frameworks*, unstructured or semi-structured metadata schemas with a binary view of knowledge construction, and semantically structured metadata schemas that constitute *accounting frameworks*, or schemas that enable one to account for decision-making processes.

The distinction between reliability frameworks and accounting frameworks is less focused on domain specificity than on the means of justifying defined associations. Here we undertake a comparative analysis of reliability frameworks and accounting frameworks by looking at an exemplar of each. We examine Wikipedia, a reliability framework, and CIDOC-CRM, an accounting framework. Following from this analysis, we argue that current engagements in metadata and schema-making serve a fundamentally performative role, in addition to and perhaps even superseding the roles of metadata in identification and other subsequent uses.

2   Context

The provocation for this research arose from a series of talks at the 2017 launch of the ResearchSpace semantic search and research platform, hosted by the British Museum and funded by the Mellon Foundation (https://tinyurl.com/jgewo33). An emergent theme was the evolution from relational database systems to semantic database systems and the metadata schemas designed around these systems. Wikipedia was presented as an example of the old guard, a binary model that assumes knowledge to be a set of statements that can be gathered and denoted as reliable or unreliable. Semantic data and search platforms, which do not rest on nebulous concepts like the 'notability' factor required of a Wikipedia article, support multivocality (Prescott 2017; Stead 2017). The ResearchSpace platform relies on a semantic data model to structure data for such multivocal engagements: in this case, the underlying metadata model is CIDOC-CRM and its argumentation engine extension, CRMinf. In this paper, we take up the themes introduced over the course of the Symposium. We ask what might motivate heritage institutions to take up the charge and convert legacy metadata into semantically structured data like CIDOC-CRM and CRMinf, and we extend the discussion by exploring the performativity enabled by schemas and ontologies such as these.

In the last two decades, while many projects have attempted to develop integrated heritage data systems (Oldman et al. 2014), for every expressed desire to share data there remains a reticence to do so in practice. This is partly motivated by the dislike for structured data entry (Mons and Velterop 2009): creating natively structured metadata is new to many data creators, and the task of converting legacy metadata is similarly non-trivial. Another primary implementation problem for the Semantic Web is the need to maintain control and authority over locally-created metadata, due to commercial imperatives and reasons of institutional integrity. The tension between ease of use, particularly in crowd-sourced environments, and standardization is in continual negotiation.

However, undue emphasis on data integration and interoperability can be problematic in itself - we have to consider what is lost in the process of standardization and understand how different political imperatives drive data model development (Bettivia and Stainforth 2017). More nuanced approaches to semantically structured data have gained in popularity in recent years because there is a growing recognition that making data identifiable and accessible is not sufficient for meaningful knowledge encoding. Rather, as Feinberg (2016) observes, "If we can understand and characterize the mechanisms through which ... metadata creators produce different kinds of value in aggregated datasets, we can, perhaps, develop information systems and tools that work with our theoretical commitments, rather than against them." Such value-systems are implicit in many metadata and meta-metadata schemas.

In the next section of this paper, we outline the basic operational details of the two case studies drawn from the provocation, Wikipedia and CRMinf. We explore what CRMinf tries to accomplish as a more evolved data model over binary systems like that of Wikipedia. We conclude by discussing the performativity enabled by each type of metadata model and what users of each model might perform via their creation of metadata.

3   Case Studies for Analysis

Wikipedia is a crowd-sourced web-based encyclopedia, built on the wiki concept that allows for low-cost distributed collaborative work (Stvilia et al. 2008). Established in 2001, it consists of work in 299 different languages and comprises over 40 million articles, with the English-language version being the largest at over 5 million articles (Wikipedia's article on Wikipedia, 2017). To examine its ontology, we look at two aspects of a Wikipedia page that represent forms of metadata: the citations required for an article and the optional semi-structured infobox.

Wikipedia's data model is, for the most part, domain unspecific. Content creators must establish reliability of content by linking it to published sources. Citations document the reliability of the data: if there are adequate references made, content can be considered verified. This mechanism is what we term a reliability framework because it espouses a world view that data are either based on citation and reliable or not (if not, they can be deleted via the moderated deletion model).

We also look at the metadata included in Wikipedia infoboxes. Often appearing in the top right-hand corner of an article page, these are meant to supplement articles by summarizing important information. Infoboxes are optional, but serve as a primary source for mining by Semantic Web technologies like Google Knowledge Panels and Wikidata because infobox data is semi-structured as attribute-value pairs. Content creators can select from existing templates and genre-specific attributes (https://en.wikipedia.org/wiki/Wikipedia:List_of_infoboxes) and are encouraged to maintain a consistent appearance between articles. However, it is equally possible to create new templates and attributes where an editor sees fit. Data entry into these templates does not enable the usage of citations in the way article text does, yet this is another manifestation of the reliability ontology: knowledge consists of facts that can be gathered, and their inclusion in a standardized infobox marks them as reliable.

CIDOC-CRM is a semantic ontology developed for the domain of cultural heritage. Oldman et al. (2014) describe it as "a semantically rich ontology that delivers data harmonization based on empirically analyzed contextual relationships". CIDOC-CRM differs from object-oriented metadata, instead employing an event-oriented approach that focuses on the history of the object, rather than on the object itself. This approach generates richer semantics because it takes account of relationships between past and present in the interpretation of cultural heritage objects (Amad and Bouhaï 2017). Taking an event-oriented view of objects also means that data concerning their documentation, like acquisition history, production, or conservation can be incorporated into the metadata, potentially allowing for semantically-enhanced associations between objects.

The CIDOC extension CRMinf has been developed in line with the event-oriented approach to metadata. It is a logical structure for documenting arguments using RDF triples, consisting of a subject, a predicate and an object (Bruseker et al. 2015). The argumentation structure includes 'observation', 'inference making' and 'belief adoption' (Stead 2017). In documenting arguments, CRMinf provides a tool to attribute statements to a particular entity: that is to say, it offers a tool to center the source of the information. It also allows for the emergence of multivocality (Stead 2017) within the structure of the metadata, making disagreements and contested provenance of cultural heritage objects visible within that structure. Finally, it creates a markup structure for primary data to provide evidence of argument quality without the need for citations. The formalization of the argumentation process characterizes what we have termed an accounting framework. Unlike reliability frameworks, accounting frameworks highlight the process by which the conclusion of an argument is reached. Implicitly, then, accounting frameworks challenge the citation principle upon which reliability rests.

4 Discussion

We have identified two different types of metadata framework: reliability frameworks and accounting frameworks. What defines these two types of framework are their primary goals. Reliability frameworks hinge on the legitimation of data, whereas accounting frameworks allow metadata creators to account for decisions made about the provenance of the data.

We argue that both reliability and accounting frameworks serve a performative function. In the former, users perform the cite-ability of the printed source in order to make strong statements about the data. They engage in the creation of standardized infoboxes because of the credibility gained by the consistent presentation of information that borrows its authority from references to analog markers of quality: citations and reference matter in the form of indices. In accounting frameworks, argumentation is used to perform the provenance of the data. In the case of a semantic ontology like CIDOC-CRM, metadata creators perform an account of their metadata creation process. Wikipedia authors and editors perform their authority as information producers via citations and metadata entry into infoboxes.

Academic literature about Wikipedia often focuses on two themes: quality control of aggregation, and this particular form of aggregation as a model for distributed collaborative work. The reliability framework allows authors to perform their authority and establish their reliability alongside traditional encyclopedia sources by engaging with features of analog print that connote authority. Citation and infobox metadata also allow for the performance of a type of scholarly collaboration: this takes place in the form of deletion discussions and ontological decisions about merging or deleting infobox terms among editors and administrators. CRMinf is designed to document divergent opinions, or scholarly debate, which is a form of collaborative work in that the exchange of differing ideas leads to growth in a field. The call for a reference model flexible enough to accommodate divergent data without the need for institutional application profiles speaks to an underlying desire to create a system which overcomes the collaborative barriers that often emerge in the production of highly standardized, interoperable data (Feinberg 2016).

There is an attendant concern around authority, which is imbricated in the performative role of metadata. Within Wikipedia, the emphasis is on citation to perform both authority and accuracy/quality, and the focus is arguably on the citation process more than the source itself. A similar concern with authority manifests itself differently within the accounting framework of CRMinf. First, the 'argumentation engine' provides an important means for the performance of authority by providing a documentary framework for primary sources: someone can claim authority by pointing to their original research, something not allowed within the content creation criteria in Wikipedia, which explicitly embargoes primary research. Secondly, the accounting framework encourages the performance of accounting itself, a move that also serves to establish authority by giving someone a political/moral, as well as factual, ground from which to assert their position.

CIDOC-CRM and CRMinf data are highly semantically structured and are distinct from Wikipedia's semi-structured infobox data. However, it is precisely Wikipedia's flexibility that enabled it to gain the popularity it enjoys today, similar to other highly flexible systems like Simple Dublin Core metadata. There is a constant tension between the freedom needed to encourage mass aggregation on the scale of Wikipedia and the attention to standardization needed to create highly structured and thus interoperable data. Further, semantic technologies like Wikidata strip context such as attribution and citation away from data in Wikipedia, packaging it into simple infobox statements that are machine-readable and understandable. If semantic technologies do not inherently provide the nuance necessary to move beyond the binary of reliability frameworks,

CRMinf aims to provide a means of accommodating the demand for meaningful data in this context. Yet the limits of CIDOC-CRM are that such structured metadata systems create barriers to adoption on the scale of a model like Wikipedia.

5 Conclusion

This paper has argued that semantic ontologies like CIDOC-CRM and CRMinf act as accounting frameworks, as opposed to reliability frameworks such as the model that undergirds Wikipedia: that is, the primary goal of accounting frameworks is not to provide a means to demonstrate reliability but to provide a means to account for decision-making processes in a machine-readable fashion. Usage of metadata is changing, and more study is needed into the new roles it is playing in the current information environment. Here we have presented findings suggesting the performative role of metadata in the context of semi-structured and structured data movements.

Future directions for research will examine other new roles for metadata: how it comes to stand in place of purpose-built branding efforts when Google Knowledge Panels direct traffic away from institutional websites and Wikipedia itself; or the role metadata plays in citation fetishization. Such research is all the more necessary in an era in which the very act of citation has displaced the value of the cited resource, contributing to anxieties about the reliability of public and crowd-sourced resources and about fake news and alternative facts.

References

Prescott, A.: Remediating Our Culture: Threats and Challenges. ResearchSpace Symposium, London (2017)

Bruseker, G., Guillem, A., Carboni, N.: Semantically documenting virtual reconstruction: building a path to knowledge provenance. ISPRS Ann. Photogrammetry, Remote Sens. Spatial Inf. Sci. **II-5/W3**, 33–40 (2015). Gottingen

Stead, S.: CRMinf. ResearchSpace Symposium, London (2017)

Mons, B., Velterop, J.: Nano-publication in the e-science era. In: Workshop on Semantic Web Applications in Scientific Discourse (SWASD 2009), pp. 14–15 (2009)

Bettivia, R., Stainforth, E.: All and each: a socio-technical review of the Europeana project. Digit. Humanit. Q. **11**(3) (2017)

Oldman, D., Doerr, M., de Jong, G., Norton, B., Wikman, T.: Realizing lessons of the last 20 years: a manifesto for data provisioning and aggregation services for the digital humanities (a position paper). D-Lib Mag. **20**(7/8) (2014)

Feinberg, M.: The value of discernment: making use of interpretive flexibility in metadata generation and aggregation. Inf. Res. **22**(1), 1–26 (2016)

Stvilia, B., Twidale, M., Smith, L., Gasser, L.: Information quality work organization in Wikipedia. J. Assoc. Inf. Sci. Technol. **59**(6), 983–1001 (2008)

Amad, A., Bouhaï, N.: Conservation and promotion of cultural heritage in the context of the semantic web. In: Szoniecky, S., Bouhaï, N. (eds.) Collective Intelligence and Digital Archives: Towards Knowledge Ecosystems, pp. 163–205. ISTE, Ltd., London (2017)

Earth Science Data Management: Mapping Actual Tasks to Conceptual Actions in the Curation Lifecycle Model

Bradley Wade Bishop$^{(\boxtimes)}$ ⓘ and Carolyn Hank ⓘ

School of Information Sciences, University of Tennessee, Knoxville, USA
{wade.bishop,chank}@utk.edu

Abstract. Earth science, like other data intensive sciences, requires data that are discoverable and usable by a variety of designated communities for a multitude of purposes in our transforming digital world. Data must be collected, documented, organized, managed, and curated with data sharing in mind. Actual, rather than supposed, practices of data managers provide insight into how earth science data are preserved and made available, and the requisite skills required to do so. This study's purpose is to explore the job practices of earth science data managers as they relate to the data lifecycle. Twelve earth science data managers were interviewed using a job analyses approach focused on job tasks and their frequencies. Data managers identified tasks related to preservation and curation in the data lifecycle, though the most mentioned tasks do not relate directly to sequential actions in the data lifecycle, but rather are more oriented toward full-life cycle actions. These are communication and project management activities. Data managers require domain knowledge of science and management skills beyond the data lifecycle to do their jobs. Several tasks did relate to the data lifecycle, such as data discovery, and require an understanding of the data, technology, and information infrastructures to support data use, re-use and preservation. Most respondents lacked formal education, acquiring necessary skills through informal, self-directed study or professional training, indicating opportunity for integrating information science and data management curriculum in disciplinary academic programs.

Keywords: Data curation · Job analyses · Earth science · Data management

1 Introduction

1.1 Earth Science Data

There is a high value for earth science to evaluate challenges facing the planet. The data are unique in that they are often collected at a global scale, may only be collected once in real-time, and have enduring value with a relatively long lifecycle. Many efforts exist to preserve these data in perpetuity. The longstanding data archive practices of the U.S. Geological Survey (USGS) and the U.S. National Aeronautics and Space Administration (NASA), the emergence and possible mandate of data management plans (DMPs) for others collecting earth science data, and even recent data rescue projects

© Springer International Publishing AG, part of Springer Nature 2018
G. Chowdhury et al. (Eds.): iConference 2018, LNCS 10766, pp. 598–608, 2018.
https://doi.org/10.1007/978-3-319-78105-1_67

provide some context to the importance of earth science data management. Like other data intensive sciences, earth science requires that data be discoverable, accessible, and usable, and those functions rely on data being collected, documented, organized, managed, and curated [1, 2]. These tasks require specialized human resources to manage and curate this diverse, unique, and valuable data for current, secondary and future use.

2 Background

2.1 Data Curation and the Data Lifecycle

An increased focus on scientific data curation has been growing in response to the need for improved data dissemination, preservation and openness. The space data community's need for digital archiving solutions for the massive collection of observational data led to a seven-year, international initiative resulting in publication of the *Reference Model for an Open Archival System (OAIS)* in 2002, and accepted as a recommended standard the following year, ISO 14721:2003. More recently, ISO 14721:2012 resulted from publication of the *Reference Model for an OAIS, Recommended Practice, Issue 2* [2]. While initially concerned with terrestrial and observational data, the standards are applicable to data management needs across disciplines, including earth science data.

Similar to other data, earth science data are at greatest risk for loss or not being shared when "produced by a small group or single person" [3]. Even data from larger projects may not be archived or disseminated. In a study of projects funded by the U.S. National Science Foundation (NSF) or the National Institutes of Health, participants indicated that only 12% of data produced from those awards were archived, 45% were shared informally, and 44% were never shared beyond the research team [4]. Some attribute the lack of data sharing and archiving in the recent past to a truncation of the data lifecycle, which removed the steps related to data dissemination, data deposit, data preservation, data discovery, and data repurposing [5]. The research lifecycle had typically concluded with publications that only included text. Now, to an "ever-growing extent the published report is accompanied by supplementary data" [6]. Sharing science data allows others to verify results, enables repetition of experiments, and leads to new research through data re-use [2, 6]. These approaches extend the existing producer roles of scientists from an active, research use environment to considerations for preparing their data for curation in a secondary and preservation use environment, and opens up opportunities for new or evolved roles for data curators to assist with data management.

There are several conceptual data lifecycle models that reflect the principles and recommendations of the OAIS Reference Model, including the DataOne's Data Life Cycle and Australian National Data Service's Data Curation Continuum [2]. This study uses the UK Digital Curation Centre (DCC) Curation Lifecycle model, referred to in the remainder of this paper as the DCC model, to frame the job analyses because of the clear delineation of sequential actions, acknowledgement of conceptualization as a step outside of curation activities, and the extensive use in digital curation research and application [7, 10].

The DCC model comprises four components. The first component is the center, or hub, and represents the data object, file, or dataset, as the data remains central throughout the lifecycle. The three remaining components represent actions based on frequency and intensity across the data lifecycle. These are full lifecycle, sequential, and occasional. The four full lifecycle actions are description and representation information (i.e., metadata); preservation planning; community watch and participation; and curate and preserve. These are both actionable items and mindsets, or a sort of ethos encapsulating any data curation initiative or imbued in any data management job. The sequential actions of the DCC model provide a linear framework for data, and include: (1) conceptualizing; (2) creating or receiving data; (3) appraising and selecting data; (4) ingesting; (5) preserving; (6) storing; (7) accessing, using, and reusing data; and (8) transforming data. The occasional actions, as the name implies, are not executed on a consistent basis or in a requisite, sequential fashion, but rather when needed. These occasional actions are: (1) reappraise, (2) migrate, and (3) dispose.

While a conceptual model, the specificity of the DCC model's sequential, and to a degree, full lifecycle actions provide a lens through which to illustrate applied data management tasks and responsibilities. For example, "ingesting" allows for assessment of fitness for use of data. "Preserving" actions ensure that data remains authentic, reliable, and usable, by conducting validation checks, quality assurance, and quality control. "Store" actions make sure that the data is secure to reduce the chance for data loss. The discovery actions of "access, use, and reuse" relate to the design and implementation of tools that facilitate data retrieval and use, in compliance with legal requirements, producer requirements, and end-user, or consumer, needs. "Transform" actions ensure ingested data is migrated into more usable or sustainable formats. These actions may include converting from original formats to interoperable types and formats, parsing datasets, and aggregating datasets into new data. Data that live beyond their active use environment and original purpose do so through these actions taken by data managers. Without the lifecycle actions, whether full, sequential or occasional, as presented in the DCC model, data decomposes, deteriorates, or may be deaccessioned. Data loss through producer or curator inaction, which includes lack of preparedness or lack of dedicated staff and resources, is possibly more common than purposeful or accidental deletion.

2.2   Data Curation Workforce

Data curation provides distinctive roles separate from those tasks done by scientists for science. These roles relate to portions of any data lifecycle model and both precede and follow scientific endeavors such as collection and analyses. Dedicated data management staff allows researchers to devote time and attention on the science and not these other essential tasks, which have been referred to by some as pre-science or the non-analytic parts of data science [8]. The idea that data producer and data curator roles differ in purpose is not new [9]. In consideration of the DCC model and others, effective data curation necessitates a range of skills and knowledge; expectations that producers could bear the brunt or totality of these responsibilities and know-how is unrealistic. Hence, to keep pace with funder mandates and expectations for open science, it is necessary to have dedicated, trained data curation specialists ensure data is useable and accessible into the indefinite future. The possible tenuous nature of this relationship and resulting workflows – producers creating the data that then needs to be managed into potential perpetuity by digital curation specialists most likely uninvolved in the research – is well documented in the OAIS Reference Model, and specifically addressed in a complementary standard, the Producer Archive Interface Methodology Abstract Standard (PAIMAS) [2].

Job titles and responsibilities to distinguish those working in digital curation have emerged in recent years; e.g., data manager, data curator, data librarian and data scientist [2]. However, there is a lack of workforce studies to provide an indication of the extent of professional practitioners in these areas, as reporting on the extent of data curation professionals is problematic. For example, the U.S. Bureau of Labor Statistics (BLS) does not keep data on the number of digital curation jobs. There may be disparity between job title and job responsibilities, making identification and reporting challenging. Also, many doing this type of work may not consider themselves data curators. Regardless, research infers there is a readiness gap for data curation, as demonstrated by the shortage of trained data curation professionals compared to the amount of data curation activities needed [12–14]. As stated in the U.S. National Research Council report, preparing the workforce for digital curation, an educational continuum is needed that "will include graduate-level education in digital curation for some, discrete study programs and certificates for others, perhaps supplementary courses inserted into established curricula in other fields, or exposure through online courses and conferences" [13]. Scientists, engineers, and other stakeholders all benefit from coordinated education and formal training developed and scaffolded across levels and disciplines.

3   Methods

This study adopts a qualitative, semi-structured interview method derived from the (Developing a Curriculum) DACUM approach. The approach builds on two assumptions: (1) current workers, or subject matter experts (SME), know how to do their jobs and should be the best at describing them; and (2) the best way to define a job is by describing the exact tasks conducted by a worker [11]. This study uses the first step of this job analyses approach by interviewing earth science data managers. Recruitment was conducted by snowball sampling at a national conference on earth science data with the incentive of helping create a core of expertise for earth science data management. All twelve participants managed earth science data as at least part of their position, but for most it was their entire job. The interview schedule consisted of ten questions, gathering information on: (1) current job title and work setting; (2) total years working in current job and with earth science data; (3) credentials, degrees and other applicable education or training; (4) daily, weekly and less frequent tasks associated with job; and (5) tasks not associated with the job.

Interviews were recorded, transcribed, and coded in NVivo. Emphasis was placed in identifying themes relating to the DCC model's sequential lifecycle actions that emerged in responses that detailed job tasks. Open coding was used to capture other activities mapped to the full life cycle actions, as well as activities not explicitly represented in the DCC model, the latter providing insight into non-data management knowledge, skills, and abilities needed by these job incumbents.

4   Results

4.1   Job Titles, Work Settings, Experience and Formal Education

Job titles are unique and varied. The titles are: Data Manager (2); Data Curation and Stewardship Coordinator; Branch Chief; Software Engineer; Director of a statewide Geologic Survey; Scientific Programmer; Data Scientist Level 2; Technical Project Manager and Software Engineer, Biologist; Information Architect and Principal Computer Scientist; Graduate Student; and Geographic Information Systems (GIS) Analyst. All work settings described by participants included typical office spaces. Beyond their computing equipment, participants listed other equipment related to collecting and storing earth science data, including satellites, planes, and physical samples of rock cores. The average time worked in earth science, including schooling, is 16 years. Participants' time in their respective current job ranged from a few months to 20 years, with about 7 years being the average.

All participants hold bachelor's degrees in a variety of disciplines: Computer Science (4); Biology (2); Physics (2); and several earth science related-degrees. Ten of the twelve hold master's degrees, with only one disciplinary area assumed to emphasize data curation and data management preparedness, Library & Information Science (2), and the other disciplines related to earth sciences (e.g., Geology). Three have a Ph.D. in the areas, respectively, of Geology & Geophysics, Ecology, and Atmospheric Sciences.

4.2   Professional, On-the-Job Training and Work Settings

To do data management, all participants noted the necessity for other training or referred to self-taught skills. This included: attending hands-on trainings; viewing online course modules; reading papers and workflows, and staying up-to-date on data management developments through informal, self-directed current awareness campaigns. Specific resources identified included DataOne and Globe.gov, discipline-focused, data and science programs, and Coursera and Code academy, more general instructional resources. Participants consulted these materials for "catching up" on new programming languages, software and frameworks, data carpentry, metadata standards, and information modeling (referred to collectively as "tools" in the remainder of this paper). While this study's primary focus is on mapping participants' experiences to the sequential actions of the DCC model, these activities are indicative of the DCC model's full lifecycle action for "Community Watch & Participation."

The most mentioned "tools" were Python (5) and NetCDF (5). Other tools included specific programming languages identified by participants: R (3), Java script (2), C, Fortran, Anaconda, Pearl, C+, as well as CSS, a style sheet language, and XML (2), a markup language. Specific XML editors identified are: Oxygen XML and Altova MissionKit. Frameworks for software development and big data mentioned include:

Scrum and SciSpark. Several participants identified discipline-specific tools, including ArcGIS, Quantitative Insights into Microbial Ecology (QIIME), and EmEx. DataOne's Metadata Parser, specifically, and other metadata creation tools that mint DOIs, in general, were also mentioned. The remaining tools explicitly identified by name are: PuTTY, a terminal editor; Protégé, an ontology editor; Cold Fusion, for application services; Eclipse, an integrated development environment; Hadoop, for distributed file system; Spark, a web application; and Microsoft Outlook 365 (2).

4.3 Job Tasks

The interview schedule prompted participants to describe tasks and to indicate degree of frequency, moving from daily to weekly to less frequent tasks. Rich descriptions of tasks were provided; however, information on frequency was difficult to capture due to recall, as data managers would often return to daily tasks when reflecting on weekly or less frequent tasks. Therefore, meaningful analyses of frequency of tasks by day, week or other is not possible. Instead, presented in order below are the three most frequent tasks described (communications and producer relations; management and adminis-tration; and community building), followed by data-specific tasks grounded in the DCC model's sequential actions.

4.3.1 Communicating, Managing Producer Relations, and Community Building

The most frequently described job task, communication, was characterized as vital by 11 of the 12 participants. Although communication occurs and is important in every profession, the data managers emphasized these "soft skills" over other domain knowledge or applied skills. The "collaborative nature of data management work" entails efficient and effective communication between the producer communities and these community's respective data managers. This task maps most directly to the sequential action, *Conceptualize*. As part of activity around data planning and fitness for use, data managers must adopt the role of interviewer. "You're talking to scientists and need to get information out of them." The need for a form interview was mentioned that could be similar to the existing Data Curation Profiles (DCP) interview schedule [2], but neither data lifecycle terminology nor DCPs were mentioned directly or indirectly by any participants. Through interviewing, data managers gather pieces of information needed to complete their preservation and curation tasks. One participant estimated that "50% of the time is basically working with domain experts trying to do knowledge extraction." Or, put another way, getting useful answers starts with asking the right questions in the right way. Submission agreements contain necessary infor-mation on the anticipated data to be deposited and managed such as: content infor-mation, preservation digital information, packaging information, descriptive information and the data model; as well as information on the submission's designated communities, applicable access restriction, and legal and contractual information, and the schedule for the submission.

Communications to inform successful data management, from conceptualization to other sequential, as well as full and occasional lifecycle actions, requires communi-cation with scientists working in many different places, utilizing different modes of communication, and requiring multiple contacts. With dispersed teams across an agency or several organizations, virtual meetings or weekly teleconferences are a necessity for these jobs.

Seven participants mentioned conferences as a "task" in support of their positions, serving as continuing education for the earth science data managers. While not a direct sequential action, this "task," is aligned with the full lifecycle action of *Community Watch and Participation*. Both attendance at conferences and the planning of them, were mentioned by five participants. Conference participation was highlighted as key to success in building community through an exchange of ideas and dissemination of project results. "Physically mingling with other people that are in the same domain" to keep abreast of best practices, acquire new skills, and follow trends in the science and data communities were necessary to maintain work proficiency across full, sequential, and occasional actions in this rapidly advancing field.

4.3.2 Data-Specific Tasks

Specific metadata standards and schemas were identified, including: Content Standard for Digital Geospatial Metadata (3); Dublin Core; ISO/IEC 11179, Information Technologies – Metadata Registries; and ISO 19115, Geographic Information. These standards were mentioned when participants discussed tasks related to metadata creation and assessment, essential aspects of the *Create or Receive* sequential lifecycle action, including metadata compliance (2) and dealing with incomplete or incompatible metadata (2). As reported by participants, most tasks related to "metadata discovery" simply meant talking to producers about their data to gather metadata elements. In some instances, "PI wrangling" was required as data managers were aware of data they should receive and, for a variety of reasons, scientists did not provide the data on-time for project deadlines. This task aligns with the subsequent actions, *Appraisal and Selection* and *Ingest*, as data is expected for deposit, implying that data either meets selection criteria as established by policy or, in the case of funder or other agreements, mandate.

For the next sequential stage, *Preservation Action*, participants commented on tasks related to validation checks, quality assurance, and quality control. Two participants mentioned quality assurance automation (2), writing scripts to do reviews more quickly than manual checks. Another task mentioned by one participant was testing data submission processes to ensure that once scientists submit data, that data are not transformed or otherwise damaged by the systems ingesting the data. Participants also commented on tasks relating more broadly to maintenance of the data archive's functions to protect data's authenticity, integrity, reliability, and usability.

The next action, *Store*, was not given much consideration by participants in describing tasks beyond making sure back-ups and other precautions are taken. In regard to the *Access, Use and Reuse* action, two of the participants, each with a master's degree in Library and Information Science (LIS), mentioned coursework that prepared them for the expectation and work in this area. Other participants listed tasks that fall under this action, but not with the same purposive approach to user-centered information services as the LIS-educated participants. Eight of the participants did mention answering questions about their data or the systems used to access their data as a frequent task. Some of the participants serve as technical support for tools their users have issues using. "So we built this tool, our repository, and it's not always very intuitive to people, so we're on the phone, 'okay click this button' or 'how do I write my metadata'." None interviewed mentioned collecting data on the number and types of questions asked. One participant described the complexity in enabling *Access, Use and Reuse*: "Diagraming, figuring out how these tools can work together, figuring out the ultimate workflow for somebody doing data management, and can we automate it?"

The final sequential action in the DCC model, *Transform*, related to adapting or altering the data. Nearly all participants, at some point in their extended description of job tasks, stated that they compile data to move it to other formats. The ubiquity of transformations in managing earth science may be why only a few participants detailed explicit examples that could be designated specifically to this aspect of the DCC model.

5 Discussion

5.1 Discussion

The study's purpose was to explore the job practices of earth science data managers as they relate to the DCC model. Another set of participants recruited elsewhere may have led to other tasks mentioned as well as other findings (e.g., educational background; professional training and self-directed current awareness initiatives).

The twelve participants did begin to reveal some commonalities in their job practices, even if not generalizable. Notable among these were communicating with stakeholders, including managing the data manager/producer relationship, and, to a lesser degree, providing support to data consumers for access, use and reuse. This has been an ongoing challenge in digital curation implementation. For example, in one study 91% of respondents agreed that insufficient communication and coordination between different groups of stakeholders was an impediment to effective digital curation [15]. As noted in the long list of tools used by data managers in this study, the specialization in using and building expert tools means some distinctions will always remain between producers, consumers, and curators, but some basics should help streamline communication between different teams, groups, and organizations. Communication relies on understanding between stakeholders and a shared language for data lifecycle actions should lead to more easily shared data. This job analysis found that domain knowledge is necessary to work with earth science data, but equally important are the data management skills related to communication, project management, community building and specific full- and sequential lifecycle actions, as these relate to frequent tasks performed by these workers. None of the participants, including those with LIS education, mentioned PAIMAS. PAIMAS provides explicit recommendations on what is essential to communicate, and for establishing expectations and roles for respective stakeholders in the data lifecycle (including data producers, curators and consumers). This lack of awareness is telling, as it implies that data managers and others may be resorting to improvisation and re-invention when there is a proverbial wheel, so to speak, already available to them.

As scientists are the data producers, they will always be key in any data management. One participant suggested that "it would be good for scientists of all stripes to have more experience with data, how data works, where it comes from, how it is stored, what are the problems with data." Science education must include exposure to data lifecycle models as well as the rudimentary building blocks on how to use and build the technologies that ingest, preserve, and transform data. To advance science, some shared practices and terminology to guide, evaluate, and teach those data lifecycle actions are needed. Another participant shared this view stating "I want to see domain scientists also exposed to some basic data management practices so that they understand that there might be somebody around that can help them with that instead of reinventing their own wheel." The outreach and information service activities cited by some of the data managers interviewed may help bridge the numerous data silos in earth science. Also, while graduate programs in library and information science (LIS) have been developing and delivering curriculum in digital and data curation for over a decade now [2], there is a gap in implementing domain-specific curriculum for data management in earth science and other sciences at the undergraduate and graduate level.

Although no participant directly said, "data lifecycle," participants with LIS education did explain many of their job tasks with digital curation terminology. *Preservation Action* sequential actions were discussed by most participants, but non-LIS data managers did not emphasize *Access, Use and Re-Use* actions. The following quote summarized the preservation first (or only) mindset of the non-LIS data managers: "The question I keep getting asked is, 'How are we going to search for this?' and I say, 'Don't worry about how you're going to search for it. Simply get the information into the model, and then into the archive and then you'll be able to work out a search." Obviously, some would take issue with any information organization and representation that did not consider issues of access, use, and re-use as equally important to other actions alluded to in this quote for *Store* and *Preservation Action*. If the data curation actions of tool design and question answering were considered vital tasks to these jobs and became expected data amenities by users, access, use and re-use of data would likely increase.

In many data-intensive organizations, job title and job classifications dictate career advancement. For example, the title scientist in many organization allows for higher pay and rank than the title of librarian. Therefore, in nearly all cases the titles of the data managers in this study did not directly indicate if data management was a portion of their job. The data management duties might be a significant portion of the job, but not reflected in generic job titles. Although not expressly stated, all but two of the interviewees education and background were for other roles, and they clearly gained knowledge of their data management duties through on the job experience. Without distinct data curator or data management positions, or at least mentalities, these data lifecycle tasks will continue with some elements of the data lifecycle model being undervalued or overlooked. For those participants charged with new data management duties and not provided formal training and education related to data curation, the results may not be ideal. While more experience managing data results in all workers becoming more data savvy, without exposure and adherence to data curation principles, models and practices, the resulting in-house solutions and project-specific jargon complicates stewardship of data, including emphasis on access, use and re-use. Further, where science starts and stops in the life of data management and curation needs further exploration as that demarcation of tasks will help distinguish what roles remain for the producers and the curators of earth science data.

5.2   Conclusion

Cleary, further research needs to be conducted to validate the tasks mentioned by these participants. A DACUM chart that lists the knowledge, skills, and abilities needed to work in this profession would help steer continuing education frameworks for both data producers and curators, as well as inform data literacy curriculum in degree granting science programs at iSchools and beyond. These results may also help address the need for more core science data curricula to address the workforce development issue of a shortage of data curators and data managers. Further, more research will help to distinguish the roles for data managers, data stewards, data curators, data scientists, and likely the need for them. These studies could help validate different data lifecycle models and lead to iterations for specific disciplines, with data curation profile (DCP) development as well for every type of science data. Regardless of what the job is called, those in a curator role for earth science data "need to understand the data, science, technology, and infrastructure" to make data discoverable in perpetuity. Since saving the planet benefits from saving the earth's data, there should be ample reasons to learn how to make these data as discoverable and re-usable as possible.

References

1. Strasser, C., Cook, R., Michener, W., Budden, A.: Primer on data management: what you always wanted to know. UC Office of the President: California Digital Library (2012). http://escholarship.org/uc/item/7tf5q7n3
2. Oliver, G., Harvey, R.: Digital Curation, 2nd edn. Neal-Schuman, Chicago (2016)
3. Sweetkind-Singer, J., Larsgaard, M.L., Erwin, T.: Digital preservation of geospatial data. Libr. Trends **55**(2), 304–314 (2006)
4. Pienta, A.M., Alter, G.C., Lyle, J.A.: The enduring value of social science research: the use and reuse of primary research data. In: The Organisation, Economics and Policy of Scientific Research Workshop (2010). http://hdl.handle.net/2027.42/78307
5. Jahnke, L., Asher, A.: The problem of data. Council on Library and Information Resources (CLIR), Washington, DC (2012)
6. Pryor, G.: Why manage research data? In: Pryor, G. (ed.) Managing Research Data, pp. 1–16. Facet Publishing, London (2012)
7. Higgins, S.: The lifecycle of data management. In: Pryor, G. (ed.) Managing Research Data, pp. 17–45. Facet Publishing, London (2012)
8. Kempler, S., Lynnes, C., Vollmer, B., Alcott, G., Berrick, S.: Evolution of information management at the GSFC earth sciences (GES) data and information services center (DISC): 2006–2007. IEEE Trans. Geosci. Remote Sens. **47**(1), 21–28 (2009)
9. Schellenberg, T.R.: Modern Archives: Principles and Techniques. The Union of Chicago Press, Chicago (1956)
10. Higgins, S.: The DCC curation lifecycle model. Int. J. Digit. Curation **3**(1), 134–140 (2008). http://www.ijdc.net/index.php/ijdc/article/viewFile/69/48

11. Knapp, J.E., Knapp, L.G.: Practice analysis: building the foundation for validity. In: Impara, J.C., Murphy, L.L. (eds.) Licensure Testing: Purposes, Procedures, and Practices. University of Nebraska Press, Lincoln (1995)
12. Blake, C., Stanton, J.M., Saxenian, A.: Filling the workforce gap in data science and data analytics. In: iConference 2013 Proceedings, pp. 1015–1016 (2013). https://www.ideals.illinois.edu/bitstream/handle/2142/42501/424.pdf?sequence=4
13. National Research Council: Preparing the Workforce for Digital Curation. The National Academies Press, Washington, D.C. (2015)
14. Palmer, C.L., Thompson, C.A., Baker, K.S., Senseney, M.: Meeting data workforce needs: indicators based on recent data curation placements. In: Proceedings of the iConference 2014, pp. 522–537, March 2014. http://doi.org/10.9776/1413
15. Tibbo, H.R., Hank, C., Lee, C.A.: Challenges, curricula and competencies: researcher and practitioner perspectives for informing the development of a digital curation curriculum. In: Proceedings of Archiving 2008, pp. 234–238 (2008)

Bodycam Footage as Document:
An Exploratory Analysis

Jean-François Blanchette(✉) ⓘ and Snowden Becker ⓘ

UCLA, Los Angeles, CA 90095, USA
blanchette@ucla.edu

Abstract. In the United States, bodycameras have been hailed by both civil-rights organizations and police forces as a source of superior evidence than can curtail excessive police force while protecting officers from spurious claims. Polices guiding their deployment have relied on traditional definition of body-cam footage as public record, and correspondingly focused on conditions of access to and control of the record. This paper applies the theoretical framework developed by the RTP-doc collective to analyze bodycam footage along three different dimensions—formal/material, content/semiotic, and medium/social— to provide a broader picture of the footage as document. The resulting analysis provides the groundwork for stakeholders to devise policies and ethical positions that better account for the multi-dimensional nature of the technology.

Keywords: Body cameras · Document theory · Professional ethics

1 The Rise of Bodycams

The spread of body-worn cameras (BWCs) within American police forces has been nothing less than extraordinary.[1] It is estimated that today, more than half of the 20, 00 police forces in the US have or are considering adoption of this technology. Among these, the LAPD and the NYPD have announced that they will deploy programs for, respectively, 7,000 and 22, 000 cameras. [5, 7] Indeed, in recent years, body worn cameras (BWCs) have found themselves hailed as the possible solution to one of the thorniest problems in American society: excessive use of force by police officers, particularly against African-Americans and other marginalized minorities. By providing a potentially more detailed and 'objective' account of violent encounters, bodycams could provide crucial evidence in trials that often fail to convict police offers (e.g., Rodney King), while simultaneously bringing down the costs of expensive lawsuits that police forces settle every year [4]. As such, BWC programs have been endorsed by both civil liberties organization [8] and police leaders, offering the tantalizing possibility of, as one commentator put it, a "win for all", a rare occurrence in policy making [17].

The size of the potential market has attracted the interest of many companies, new and established. In 2017, Taser, the undisputed leader in the police body camera market, simultaneously announced that it would, on the one hand, offer every police officer in the US a free body camera along with a 1-year subscription to its evidence

---

[1] Research supported by an IMLS Laura Bush 21st Century Librarian award (#RE4316005316).

G. Chowdhury et al. (Eds.): iConference 2018, LNCS 10766, pp. 609–614, 2018.
https://doi.org/10.1007/978-3-319-78105-1_68

storage service; and, on the other hand, rebrand itself as "Axon," so as to signal its reorientation from hardware manufacturer to Big Data service provider, namely the storage, management, and computational analysis of bodycam footage. As stated by CEO Rick Smith, these changes are part of a long-term strategy based on the vision that "it's time for video data to move to the center of public safety records systems, with far richer and more transparent information than historic text-only systems." [18]

Despite the complexity of such a shift, the debates that have so far accompanied the rapid spread of BWCs have focused on two main issues: (a) policies legislating *access* to footage as public record, so as to ensure that BWCs fulfill their potential for transparency; and (b) policies relative to *control* of cameras by police officers (e.g., activation and review of footage prior to filing reports), so as to ensure that BWCs fulfill their potential for providing 'objective', untainted evidence.

In this paper, we seek to broaden the scope of these discussions by proposing that BWC footage represents a particularly interesting instance of the process of "redocumentarization" described by the Pédauque collective [12–14]. We apply the collective's three-part grid (material, semiotic, social) to analyze BWC footage: (1) *as formal inscription on physical media*, and the issues the volume and authenticity of these inscriptions raises; (2) *as text* (or content) and the tension between footage as audio-visual representation vs. data aggregate; (3) *as medium* for social relations, and the development of new documentary genres (e.g., overredaction) that attempt to reconcile needs for transparency and privacy. By broadening the analytical framework driving the discussion, we seek to provide stakeholders with conceptual tools to eventually craft policy positions that better reflect their ethical standpoints.

2 Access and Control

At first sight, there seems little doubt that BWC footage meets the criteria for public records, that is, "any documentary materials, regardless of physical form or characteristics, made or received by a government entity in the conduct of public business and preserved or appropriate for preservation as evidence of the entity's organization, functions, policies, decisions, procedures, operations..." [15] Ordinary citizens, media organizations, and advocacy groups should thus all be able to use the ordinary mechanisms of public record laws to gain access in a speedy fashion to footage, and indeed, civil rights organizations have strongly argued that police forces should have clear access policies in place, guided by public records principles, in order to thwart any tendency to restrict access to footage putting officers in a bad light [8].

At the same time however, from the perspective of police forces, there are important ways in which BWC footage is *not* like other public records. BWC footage is far more readily circulated via social media channels and the press. By its very nature, it is traumatic, often portraying police use of force, injury or death and carrying enormous emotional impact for viewers and subjects, impact that may significantly shape public perception of an investigation. It is also invasive, presenting the spontaneous reaction of individuals in high-stress situations, captured with or without their consent in spaces that were not subject to such scrutiny. Finally, it differs in its scale and volume, with potentially staggering quantities of footage generated on a daily basis.

As such, various states have enacted laws that define bodycam footage as outside public records mandates. [3] North Carolina, for example, states that release is not required in cases where "disclosure would create a serious threat to the fair, impartial, and orderly administration of justice" [11], while Minnesota considers footage public only when an officer's use of force "results in substantial bodily harm." [10]

Another important focus has been the officer's control over the camera and its output, including the relationship between footage and the written reports filed by officers. For civil liberties association, again, the rules should be clear: "While some types of law enforcement interactions (e.g., when attending to victims of domestic violence) may happen off-camera, the vast majority of interactions with the public including all that involve the use of force—should be captured on video." [1] As well, civil rights organization have argued that policies should "preserve the independent evidentiary value of officer reports by prohibiting officers from viewing footage before filing their reports. ... Pre-report viewing could cause an officer to conform the report to what the video appears to show, rather than what the officer actually saw." [1]

In the next section, we broaden this focus on access and control so as to encompass additional dimensions (material, semiotic, social) of BWC footage as document.

3 BWC Footage as Document

"Roger T. Pédauque" is a collective of scholars that has theorized the current (and painful) transformation that bears the name of "paperlessness" (or, in France, "dématérialisation"). Its work provides an analytical framework that characterizes this transformation along three distinct dimensions: document as **formal inscription** on a physical media; as **text** (or sign) that conveys meaning and intentionality; and as **medium** for social relations and power.

3.1 BWC Footage as Formal Inscription on Media

The first term of Pédauque's analysis is that of the document as **trace**, that is, as a structured inscription on a physical media, governed by various rules (e.g., typography and graphic design, the manufacturing process of paper). In the case of BWC footage, the materiality of the inscription raises questions relatives to the authenticity of trace and its resulting evidential value and the sheer volume of the footage and the logistical and economic questions it entails.

Much of the rhetoric behind the rise of bodycams lies in the general perception that videos are high-grade evidence—that camera images are intrinsically transparent and truthful, as articulated by a chief of police: "the quality of information that they can capture is unsurpassed. With sound policy and guidance, their evidentiary value definitely outweighs any drawbacks or concerns." (cited in [9]) This perception extends to the court themselves: "Courts approach video cases with a strong belief that video is a singularly powerful and unambiguous source of proof, one that holds great sway with fact-finders and that may be difficult for a party to overcome. ... video is seen as a truthful, unbiased, objective, and unambiguous reproduction of reality, deserving of controlling and dispositive weight." [20]

Yet, BWC footage is routinely obtained in circumstances of high stress, chaos, and conflict. Hardware and software limitations as well as difficult operating conditions (low light, rapid movement) will often result in jerky and grainy footage. By their very design, the cameras capture a situation from a single, fixed point of view, one which does not perfectly replicate what the recording officer actually sees [2]. In addition, BWC footage is compressed, and, rather than capturing a full image for each frames, some frames are interpolated, that is, averaged from adjoining frames.

Furthermore, the big city police departments that are deploying body cameras are "likely generating more than 10,000 h of video a week." [16]. While the resulting logistical and economic issues have been a core concern of police forces, the have received scant attention from civil liberties union and archival organizations. Yet, the massive proliferation of footage and the Big Data principle of "keep everything" exerts enormous pressure on records management principles of appraisal and disposition embodied in retention schedules. For industry providers, every new video is a highly valuable input that contributes to further refinement of algorithmic functionalities, regardless of its status as public record.

3.2 BWC Footage as Text

The second RTP-Doc analytical dimension views the document as a **text** (or sign), that is, as "content" that conveys meaning, is created and consumed in a certain context, and is part of a documentary/knowledge system. In the case of BWC footage, this content is under enormous tension, as industry leaders are keen to sell not only cameras, but cloud-based storage and evidence management services. But the real money lies the computational analysis of footage through machine learning techniques. TASER/Axon, for example, recently announced its new "Axon AI platform," which offers agencies means of quickly isolating and analyzing "the most important seconds of footage from massive amounts of video data" and "making the visual contents in video searchable in real time." Clearly, vendors have no intention of treating BWC footage just as static records but rather, as vast stores of data, ripe for further mining. The low-hanging fruit here is personal identification, further on the horizon lies science-fiction candy like real-time event detection.

Video analysis is a difficult and computationally intensive tasks, one, as noted above, highly sensitive to operational conditions such as light and movement. Analysis can be greatly helped by pairing video with whatever metadata is available. Such metadata can only be obtained in two ways: manually, as officers review footage at the end of their shifts (e.g., indicating whether it is "(non-)evidential"); or automatically, by coupling footage with external data sources. These currently include the camera itself (e.g., GPS coordinates), police dispatching systems, or in the future, sensors capturing officers' biometric information, such as movement, heart rate, etc.

As such BWC footage blurs the line between records and data, a line that is already under tension because of open data initiatives, and legislation that struggles to account for the difference between data and metadata, e.g., [19] Indeed, the difference between the two has been an issue since the very birth of electronic records management. As BWC footage becomes more widely used in court cases and more diverse and complex types of metadata becomes embedded within it, the tension between its status as record and as data will be severely tested, from a technical, juridical, and epistemological standpoint.

3.3   BWC Footage as Medium

The third dimension analyses the document as **medium**, that is, as a vector of social relations, an element of identity systems and a vector of power. These dimensions are particularly visible in the case of BWCs, as various civil rights organizations have created new means for citizens to capture more easily their own footage of police incidents. The ACLU, for example, makes available a "Mobile Justice" app that allows for one-button activation of the camera and automatic transfer of the footage to ACLU servers, while Witness provides ObscuraCAm and CameraV, apps that allow for easy creation and sharing of footage. Indeed, among the proliferation of footage produced by incident bystanders, many police forces have emphasized to their officers that wearing BWCs would allow them to better show their side of the story.

At the same time, police forces are experimented with new modes of distribution and circulation of footage: some have created channels on YouTube to post footage of not only BWC footage, but also recordings of police scanners, surveillance cameras, and other kinds of records that were already considered public. In order to mitigate with the privacy invasions this might constitute [21], some police forces (notably Seattle) have experimented with new genres of document processing, such as 'over-redaction', the application of digital filters to BWC footage so as to obscure people's faces, locations (street names, house numbers), and embarrassing private information. [6] The idea is that automatically releasing such over-redacted video would allow citizens and the media to determine whether a particular piece of footage contains relevant material before filing a public records request.

4   Conclusion

Debates surrounding the spread of BWCs have made for surprising bedfellows, such as the ACLU effectively advocating for large-scale deployment of surveillance capabilities by police forces. Civil liberties and archival organizations have engaged in such debates by arguing that footage should be subjected to the same policies as traditional paper records. Yet, BWC footage represents a new kind of object whose characteristics clearly stretch the boundaries of traditional archival theory and practice, as made clear by Pédauque's three part analysis: (a) as a *physical inscription on media*, whose sheer volume requires new institutional arrangements between industry and public institutions and whose presumption of authenticity will be severely tested by the evidential requirements of the legal system; (b) as *text* which functions both as a visual representation and collection of data points to be mined through computational means, putting in tension traditional archival principles of appraisal and disposition; (c) as *medium* giving rise to new power relations between citizens and law enforcement, through new modes of creation, circulation, and processing of footage. The exploratory analysis proposed here lays the groundwork for further development of a framework that can help stakeholders articulate more comprehensive ethical and policy positions that account for the multi-faced dimensions of their objects.

References

1. ACLU, others: Civil Rights Principles on Body Worn Cameras (2015)
2. Boivin, R., et al.: The body-worn camera perspective bias. J. Exp. Criminol. **13**(1), 125–142 (2017)
3. Chokshi, N.: These are the states that want to regulate police body camera videos. Washington Post (2016)
4. Elinson, Z., Frosch, D.: Cost of Police-Misconduct Cases Soars in Big U.S. Cities. Wall Street Journal (2015)
5. Fasick, K., Gonen, Y.: NYPD launches court-ordered body camera program. New York Post (2017)
6. Harris, M.: The Body Cam Hacker Who Schooled the Police. Wired (2015)
7. Mather, K., Zahniser, D.: City Council vote resumes $57.6-million rollout of LAPD body cameras. Los Angeles Times (2016)
8. Meyer, R.: The People's Manifesto on Police Body-Cameras (2015)
9. Miller, L. et al.: Implementing a Body-Worn Camera Program. Office of Community Oriented Policing Services, Washington DC (2014)
10. Murguia, S.: More states set privacy restrictions on bodycam video, Reporters Committee for Freedom of the Press (2016)
11. North Carolina General Assembly: House Bill 972 (2015–2016 Session)
12. Pédauque, R.T.: Document et modernités (2006)
13. Pédauque, R.T.: Document : forme, signe et médium (2003)
14. Pédauque, R.T.: Le Texte en Jeu (2005)
15. SAA Committee on Public Policy: Issue Brief: Police Mobile Camera Footage as a Public Record (2017)
16. Sanburn, J.: Storing Bodycam Data is the Next Big Challenge for Police. Time (2016)
17. Stanley, J.: Police Body-Mounted Cameras: With Right Policies in Place, a Win For All, ACLU (2015)
18. TASER: TASER makes two acquisitions to create "Axon AI" (2017)
19. Toutant, C.: Justices: Data Fields Extracted Email are Public Records. New Jersey Law Journal (2017)
20. Wasserman, H.M.: Orwell's Vision: Video and the Future of Civil Rights Enforcement. Social Science Research Network, Rochester (2009)
21. Williams, T.: Downside of Police Body Cameras: Your Arrest Hits YouTube. New York Times (2015)

Using Citizen Science Projects to Develop Cases for Teaching Digital Curation

Amber L. Cushing(✉)

School of Information and Communication Studies, University College Dublin,
Dublin, Ireland
amber.cushing@ucd.ie

Abstract. Previous research suggests that citizen science project may involve many digital curation issues. In order to develop real world cases for teaching digital curation, seventeen managers of citizen science projects were interviewed. After digital curation issues were identified, findings were used to create teaching cases for digital curation education. One case related to the conceptualise phase of the DCC lifecycle is described. Utilising existing research data to develop cases could be useful for researchers who wish to teach concepts contextualised by "real world" events.

Keywords: Digital curation · Pedagogy · Case method teaching

1 Introduction

Digital curation and digital stewardship education has only developed in the past decade. Grant supported work in US graduate programmes have investigated what digital curators should know and the skills that they should develop, but there is a lack of material available about how best to teach digital curation that is based on real world examples. Previous research has found that citizen science projects involved data curation issues, suggesting it might provide context for learning about digital curation. This project aimed at exploring how existing research data can be used to create teaching cases for digital curation. Specifically, this project sought to answer the following questions: what digital curation issues exist in citizen science projects and how can these identified issues be used to create cases for the teaching of digital curation?

2 Literature Review

According to the Digital Curation Centre (DCC), digital curation "involves maintaining, preserving and adding value to digital research data throughout it's lifecycle" [3]. Digital curation activities can include conceptualising, creating, accessing and using, appraising and selecting material, disposing material, ingesting material, preserving and reappraising material, storing material, making material available for access and reuse and finally transforming material into something new.

Existing work has explored the development of digital curation education programmes by exploring what digital curators need to know and what skills they should be

© Springer International Publishing AG, part of Springer Nature 2018
G. Chowdhury et al. (Eds.): iConference 2018, LNCS 10766, pp. 615–619, 2018.
https://doi.org/10.1007/978-3-319-78105-1_69

taught [6, 8, 10]. In general, all previous work suggested that digital curation involved competencies in intrapersonal skills, information technology, the ability to work with data and execute archival functions and the ability to advocate for support and management skills. The Simmons Digital Curriculum Laboratory provided one example of how digital curation can be taught [2]. Scenarios were developed for the site by project staff and did not appear to be based on actual cases. Cases were developed to teach specific tools, rather than general concepts or selection of a tool to solve a problem.

Teaching case method has been described as "a story, describing or based on actual events and circumstances, that is told with a definite teaching purpose in mind that rewards careful study and analysis" [9]. Cases could be actual previous cases such as in medicine or law, or they could be created by the instructor [9].

The case method of teaching has been associated with active teaching models and cognitive learning theory. This pedagogical approach is based on the concept that "real world" solutions are not always found in textbooks. The case method of teaching has been associated with increasing the ability of students to relate theory to practice, developing critical thinking and analytical skills through synthesis, confronting "real world" situations and complexities, developing interpersonal skills and mastering course concepts through application [5].

Citizen science has been defined as "a form of scientific collaboration that engages non professionals in research" [11]. One concern facing citizen science projects that information scientists have explored is data quality assurance. The data life cycle explained in the Dataone guide is similar to the steps identified by the digital curation lifecycle, the most commonly applied model in digital curation practice [4, 12]. Researchers argued that many citizen science project managers did not possess the necessary data management skills, resulting in a lack of adherence to metadata standards and provenance [11]. A focus on data management has led to the start of a discussion about data curation and citizen science. Lagoze argued that the data curation practices implemented in eBird allow for improved data quality due to the fact that eBird collects metadata about it's volunteers and intended use of the eBird application [7].

3 Method

This project attempted to explore data management issues in citizen science to develop cases for teaching digital curation and digital stewardship for digital curation postgraduate and professional development programmes. In order to develop cases, the researcher first interviewed citizen science project managers at the 2015 Citizen Science conference to understand the digital curation issues that they experienced. Participants were recruited via an email sent to the citizen science listserv. Interviews were semi-structured and lasted approximately 30 min. Data was then used to create cases.

4 Findings

Seventeen interviews were conducted with citizen science project managers. Interview data was audio recorded, anonymised and transcribed. Transcripts were analysed using nVivo for Mac 10.2.2. Memoing and coding were used, via methods described by [3].

In the first round of coding, transcripts were coded according to interview protocol prompts including, but not limited to discussion of data issues, backup, data plans and the project context. In the second round of coding, transcripts coded as "data issues" were further coded into categories associated with digital curation, including, but not limited to use, collect/conceptualise, interoperability, management, archiving and organisation.

After analysis, three areas were selected to develop case studies for digital curation: the conceptualise phase, data use and organisation. Due to space constraints, only the conceptualise case will be detailed in this paper. A learning outcome in many introduction to digital curation modules/classes is to "Describe the elements of the digital curation lifecycle." The cases will be developed to meet this learning outcome. Developed cases will include elements from several interviews to protect anonymity of research participants. One case is described below, while two more will be developed.

4.1 Exploring Issues Described by Participants

According to the digital curation lifecycle, the conceptualise phase is described as a sequential action, or a "key action needed to curate data as they move through their lifecycle" [10]. Conceptualise is defined as "conceive and plan the creation of data, including capture method and storage options" [3]. In the citizen science projects, conceptualise activity was expressed as data collection issues. These issues were described as lack of trained volunteers to collect the data, lack of standard collection formats, collection techniques that did not lend to easy data entry and data that was not easily stored or could be made available to the public in the future. For example, participants 13, 2 and 9 described data collection issues as follows:

Participant 13: What I hear from a lot of people who manage projects like this is that volunteers are notoriously bad at data entry, unless you find some elderly person who used to be a p.6 secretary or something. If you find a kid, the people who we tend to find, they're really, really bad at it.

Participant 2: We have quality control issues with that project. A fair amount of the data are entered by the volunteers themselves through the online database, and then our project staff enter the rest from the paper copies, so there's always a chance for mistakes in the data entry.

Participant 9: We might lose a piece of data because we're not managing this very well. Figuring out, we don't actually have anybody double check so maybe typos, we're analyzing based on, maybe, typos.

With an understanding of how the data would be stored and used going forward, better collection techniques could be developed and volunteers could be better trained.

4.2 Developing the Case

The conceptualisation phase of the lifecycle can be difficult for students to grasp, as most students who are new to digital curation have associated it with archiving and do not understand the need to consider preservation before an item is collected or created. According to [3], the goal of a case writer "is to create a story that rewards careful study and analysis." Further, case content should include setting, the decision maker and main actors, issues, problems and interests, constraints and opportunities and decision and actions.

Considering these points, a "conceptualise" case was developed that included the following characteristics:

The setting for the case was the Clean up the beach! citizen science project, in which volunteers collected and logged beach trash to collect data on pollution. Decision maker and main actors included project manager, Mary Blake (decision maker); project director, Mark Byrne; researcher, Prof. Hazel Nolan; and volunteers, Sinead Keogh and Rory Morgan.

The case included several issues to address: Mark, the director, needs analysed data for a grant application, due in a few weeks; Hazel, the professor, needs good quality data to write an article and submit it for peer review; Sinead and Rory, the volunteers, feel that they received inadequate instructions, suffer from a lack of motivation and do not have access to appropriate data collection tools. Mary, the project manager, is being tasked with addressing all these issues in a short period of time.

Students will be required to put themselves in the role of Mary, and help her plan her priorities, address the issues and explain how the issues relate to *conceive and plan the creation of data*, or the conceptualise phase of the DCC lifecycle and how making informed decisions can ease other lifecycle issues down the line while integrating intrapersonal skills and management skills identified as competencies in previous literature.

5   Discussion

Developing the Clean up the Beach! case based on interview data grounded the issues/problems, constraints/opportunities and decisions/actions included in the description provided to students. Students often report a gap between theory and practice in learning about digital curation. Recent efforts attempt to address this, as in Simmons' development of the Digital Curriculum laboratory [1]. The current project attempts to address these concerns, by providing students a case which mirrors conceptual issues and challenges they may find in practice.

Postgraduate study of digital curation requires that students develop hands on experience using technology, including preservation programs. Much has been written about this [1, 2, 7]. Less has been written about students' abilities to practice the application of digital curation concepts. The development of cases based on collected data allows for this application.

Finally, researchers who also teach may find it useful to take examples from their own data to develop practice cases for students to understand concepts. This works particularly well for qualitative data, in which cases can be peppered directly or paraphrased from quotes. Future research could further explore the potential usefulness of such an endeavor.

6   Conclusion

Creating teaching cases based on existing research data has the potential to provide students with real word cases to improve their understanding of digital curation concepts. Further cases will be developed to teach students about organisation and archiving actions in digital curation and how the DCC lifecycle can relate to real world examples. Cases will also be integrated in Storyline Articulate software and made available via the Online Professional Certificate in Digital Information Management, launching in September 2018. Once utilised, students will be asked about their use of the case and how it impacted their learning, specifically their ability to understand the conceptualise phase of the digital curation lifecycle.

References

1. Bastian, J.A., Cloonan, M.V., Harvey, R.: From teacher to learner to user: developing a digital stewardship pedagogy. Libr. Trends **59**(4), 607–622 (2011)
2. Bastian, J., Plum, T.: Building a virtual archives and preservation curriculum laboratory at Simmons GSLIS. Proc. Assoc. Inf. Sci. Technol. **47**(1), 1–2 (2010)
3. Corbin, J., Strauss, A., Strauss, A.L.: Basics of Qualitative Research. Sage, Thousand Oaks (2014)
4. Digital Curation Centre. What is digital curation? http://www.dcc.ac.uk/digital-curation/what-digital-curation
5. Goebel, D.J., Humphreys, M.A.: The relationships among student learning styles, course delivery method, and course outcomes: a quasi-experiment investigating the case method of course delivery. Atlantic Market. J. **3**(2), 33–48 (2014)
6. Kim, J., Warga, E., Moen, W.: Competencies required for digital curation: an analysis of job advertisements. Int. J. Digit. Curation **8**(1), 66–83 (2013)
7. Lagoze, C.: eBird: curating citizen science data for use by diverse communities. Int. J. Digit. Curation **9**(1), 71–82 (2014)
8. Lee, C.A., Tibbo, H.R., Schaefer, J.C.: Defining what digital curators do and what they need to know: the DigCCurr project. In: Proceedings of the 7th ACM/IEEE-CS Joint Conference on Digital Libraries, pp. 49–50. ACM, June 2007
9. Lynn Jr., L.E.: Teaching and Learning with Cases: A Guidebook. CQ Press, Washington, D.C. (1999)
10. Madrid, M.M.: A study of digital curator competences: a survey of experts. Int. Inf. Libr. Rev. **45**(3), 149–156 (2013)
11. Sheppard, S.A., Wiggins, A., Terveen, L.: Capturing quality: retaining provenance for curated volunteer monitoring data. In: Proceedings of the 17th ACM Conference on Computer Supported Cooperative Work & Social Computing, pp. 1234–1245. ACM, February 2014
12. Wiggins, A., Bonney, R., Graham, E., Henderson, S., Kelling, S., LeBuhn, G., Litauer, R., Lots, K., Michener, W., Newman, G.: Data management guide for public participation in scientific research. DataOne Working Group, 1–41 (2013)

Semantic Mediation to Improve Reproducibility for Biomolecular NMR Analysis

Michael R. Gryk[1,2]([⊠]) [iD] and Bertram Ludäscher[1] [iD]

[1] University of Illinois, Urbana-Champaign, Champaign, IL 61820, USA
{gryk2,ludaesch}@illinois.edu
[2] UCONN Health, Farmington, CT 06030, USA

Abstract. Two barriers to computational reproducibility are the ability to record the critical metadata required for rerunning a computation, as well as translating the semantics of the metadata so that alternate approaches can easily be configured for verifying computational reproducibility. We are addressing this problem in the context of biomolecular NMR computational analysis by developing a series of linked ontologies which define the semantics of the various software tools used by researchers for data transformation and analysis. Building from a core ontology representing the primary observational data of NMR, the linked data approach allows for the translation of metadata in order to configure alternate software approaches for given computational tasks. In this paper we illustrate the utility of this with a small sample of the core ontology as well as tool-specific semantics for two third-party software tools. This approach to semantic mediation will help support an automated approach to validating the reliability of computation in which the same processing workflow is implemented with different software tools. In addition, the detailed semantics of both the data and the processing functionalities will provide a method for software tool classification.

Keywords: Ontology · Computational reproducibility · Provenance

1 Introduction

1.1 Computational Reproducibility

Researchers in the natural sciences are becoming increasingly concerned about the repeatability and reproducibility[1] of their studies [1–4]. Biomolecular NMR (bioNMR) is a well-established spectroscopic technique which uses the same principles as MRI in order to observe biomolecules at atomic resolution. It has been common practice to deposit the completed, derived bioNMR datasets with national repositories (e.g., the Protein Data Bank (www.pdb.org) or the BioMagResBank (www.bmrb.org)) while

---

[1] In this paper, we use the definitions of Vitek and Kalibera [3] that repeatability is the ability for the same researcher to get the same results with the same computational environment, while reproducibility is the ability for others to get similar results with similar computational tools.

© Springer International Publishing AG, part of Springer Nature 2018
G. Chowdhury et al. (Eds.): iConference 2018, LNCS 10766, pp. 620–625, 2018.
https://doi.org/10.1007/978-3-319-78105-1_70

embedding natural language descriptions of the computational analysis within the publications which report the findings.

This traditional approach has its limitations when considering computational reproducibility and repeatability for bioNMR. First, with the continuing increase in the complexity of the computational pipeline [5, 6], it is nearly impossible to document the process in enough detail for it to be reproduced. Second, the computation itself (in the case of bioNMR) requires dozens of specialized software tools built by academic labs. While typically free to use, these software tools are usually poorly documented, difficult to install and often minimally maintained and/or abandoned.

These issues are being addressed by the new National Center for Biomolecular NMR Data Processing and Analysis (www.nmrbox.org) – a joint NIH-funded project at UCONN Health, the University of Wisconsin and the University of Illinois. The Center has provisioned Ubuntu Virtual Machines (VMs) with more than sixty of the software tools used by bioNMR spectroscopists [7]. (Virtual machines were chosen over container technology as the various software tools are often graphical and used in concert.) These VMs (referred to as NMRbox) are hosted on a private cloud platform at UCONN Health and are available for access through the internet to spectroscopists in non-profit institutions. Since the initial release in the summer of 2016, NMRbox has over 700 registered users. Images of the VMs are also available for download and local installation. Importantly, images of the VMs will be stored indefinitely, giving future researchers the computational infrastructure with which to reproduce prior bioNMR studies, one of the recommendations of Piccolo and Frampton [8]. Of course, this long-term reproducibility requires maintenance of hypervisors capable of running the VM.

Software persistence is only one barrier to reproducibility, however. The other barrier is documenting the analysis workflow in sufficient detail that others can independently reproduce it [2, 8, 9]. This requires the capture of the various pieces of metadata regarding software configuration and data manipulation which are necessary to track the process from raw, observational data to the final, derived datasets. Referred to as *provenance* [2], this metadata would ideally be stored in a neutral format which is both human and machine-readable. Importantly, provenance metadata should be readily translatable to any of the software tools capable of performing computations on the data.

1.2 Software Ontologies

In this paper we report preliminary work in developing the infrastructure within NMRbox to gather this important metadata. An important challenge in this endeavor is the diversity of software tools itself. There exist multiple software tools capable of performing each computational step. The choice of one tool over another can be simply a matter of personal preference (as in the choice of Chrome over Firefox) or it can be due to some subtle differences in the software whereby one tool performs better for a specific set of use cases than another tool. Regardless of the rationale, it is doubtful that the bioNMR field will ever unite in support of a single software tool for all computation. Thus, bioNMR workflows more closely resemble those of analyses which combine and compare data from disparate sources, such as genomic bioinformatics [2].

The multiplicity of software tools has consequences for metadata capture and data curation. Considering that multiple tools are capable of performing the same general task, it would be expected that much of the metadata required to be recorded is conceptually similar. However, since the various tools were developed by different labs at different times, the tools do not use precisely the same vocabulary or nomenclature when referring to parameters or configuration settings. Along the same lines, the parameterization of computational steps often use different units of measure or parametric weights such that the metadata from one tool cannot be used with another without recalibration. Finally, recognizing that some tools are better at some computations than other – this suggests that there may be subtle but profound semantic differences between seemingly similar functional tasks.

Our current approach to mapping this diverse landscape of metadata is inspired by semantic mediation [9, 11, 13]. The general idea is to model the function or functionality of each software tool in order to identify the key metadata necessary to recapitulate the computation. A separate, tool-specific ontology will be created representing the metadata model for each individual software tool. These ontologies will be conceptually linked within the NMRbox VMs – providing a kind of "internal semantic web" for facilitating tool integration and mediation. This will allow for the simple cases of identifying when two different software terms refer to the same thing (the *sameAs* relation) as well as when the same term is used by two software tools to refer to different things (the *differentFrom* relation). Most importantly, it will allow complex mappings when terms from different software tools are similar but not identical. For instance, it is often the case in bioNMR that two implementations of a mathematical operation will use different sign conventions. This can easily be modeled as a *negativeOf* relation. More complex mathematical relationships can be modeled using the terminology defined by MathML and OpenMath.

2   Research Model

Our general strategy for semantic mediation is to construct separate ontologies expressing the semantics of each software tool supported within the NMRbox VM's. These ontologies are linked with each other to support semantic conversion between the various data and process elements for computation. As there is not a complete overlap between the various tools, a core ontology representing the basic data relationships inherent with bioNMR data is used as a foundation for metadata interchange. Ontologies by their nature are always "under-development"; the ontologies described here are accessible through GitHub (https://github.com/CONNJUR/Ontology_Development).

2.1   Core Ontology

The core ontology attempts to model the fundamental concepts of bioNMR experiments and their supporting data/metadata which are used by the various supported software tools. Where possible, we have attempted to use existing, established ontologies for concepts which are not bioNMR specific; for instance, the Friend of a Friend (FOAF) ontology for referring to the various data collectors and curators along the computational workflow; the Event Ontology for referring to data collection events; and the Prov-O model for referring to provenance information along the computational workflow.

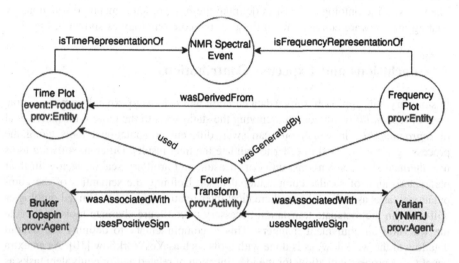

Fig. 1. Schematic showing a portion of the core ontology for bioNMR spectra (white circles) along with tool-specific elements (beige and gray circles). Where appropriate, entities are mapped to other top ontologies such as the Event and Prov-O ontologies (purple text). As illustrated above, the "Bruker" and "Varian" implementations of the Fourier Transform differ in the sign convention used for the integration (Color figure online).

As shown in Fig. 1, the core ontology deals with both time domain and frequency domain representations of bioNMR spectra, which are mathematical duals of each other. There are many mathematical methods for interconverting between time and frequency, but by far the most common is the Fourier Transform. The core ontology uses the Prov-O vocabulary for defining the provenance of the generation of a frequency spectrum from the time domain recording. The details of the implementation of the Fourier Transform are defined within the tool-specific ontologies.

2.2 Software-Based Ontologies

There are many software tools available for converting time domain bioNMR data to frequency plots [7, 12]. This is a multistep process involving several data cleaning steps in which mathematical operations are applied to the data in order to enhance the signal and suppress the noise [5]. The key operations are the Fourier Transform and concomitant phasing of the spectrum to provide so-called absorptive spectral peaks. Both the transform and the phasing operations can be done with either of two sign conventions associated with the integration along the time axis. Of the four major tools supported by Nowling *et al.* [12], two choose a default of a positive sign convention and two with a negative sign convention.

A consequence of the differing sign conventions is that if the primary data are fed naively into each of the four tools, the resulting frequency plots will be reversed and the process would appear irreproducible. However, by correcting for the sign convention during the parameterizing of the Fourier Transform, reproducible results are achieved. The tool-specific ontologies assist in defining these important semantic distinctions by relating the software conventions to those of the core ontology as shown in Fig. 1.

3 Conclusions and Expected Contributions

In summary, this approach to metadata curation will help us to expand from the simple level of *repeatability* inherent in archiving the static VMs to the more informative goal of *reproducibility*, in which one can swap different computational tools along the processing workflow [13] in order to validate the final results. Different software tools use alternate sign conventions, units of measure and arbitrary scaling factors in their parameterization of similar computational tasks. Defining the semantics of the computational tasks as well as the mathematical inter-relationships within linked ontologies will assist in the metadata translation necessary to configure alternate tools to execute the workflow in equivalent manners. This is complimentary to defining the overall dataflow of the workflow, as is done with tools such as YesWorkflow [10]. As an extra benefit, this process will allow for the identification of related and/or equivalent tasks as a method of software tool classification. It is also anticipated that by modelling the variants and variations, these linked ontologies will suggest alternative implementations of equivalent workflows (as shown by Bowers and Ludäscher [13]) – also assisting in validating that bioNMR computational results are reproducible.

The software-specific ontologies described in this paper are a similar approach to data integration and reproducibility as proposed by Rijgersbert *et al.* with the ontology of units of measure [14]. A major difference for bioNMR computation is that many of the scaling factor differences between software tools are either unit-less or tend to be arbitrary conversions to non-standard units of measure done for the ease of computation, not as a standardize method of reporting findings. Thus a more detailed level of parametric definitions is required than would be supported simply by defining units of measure.

Future work will be the continued development of this ontological framework by expanding the core ontology, adding additional software-specific ontologies, and continued inclusion of other controlled vocabularies such as MathML and OpenMath. In conjunction with the developers of NMRbox, these ontologies will be used for semantic data management within their supported VM's to help support more detailed data curation, assist with workflow management and reuse, validate workflow reproducibility, and eventually enhance data depositions to the BioMagResBank public repository. These ontologies will also be used within the CONNJUR Workflow Builder workflow management system [15] in order to provide a broader abstraction of the individual processing actors which does not rely on the underlying software tool implementation.

Acknowledgment. This work was supported in part by the National Institute of General Medical Sciences of the National Institutes of Health under Award Number GM-111135.

References

1. Munafò, M.R., Nosek, B.A., Bishop, D.V.M., Button, K.S., Chambers, C.D., Percie du Sert, N., Simonsohn, U., Wagenmakers, E.-J., Ware, J.J., Ioannidis, J.P.A.: A manifesto for reproducible science. Nat. Hum. Behav. **1**, 1–9 (2017)
2. Kanwal, S., Khan, F.Z., Lonie, A., Sinnot, R.O.: Investigating reproducibility and tracking provenance – a genomic workflow case study. BMC Bioinform. **18**, 337 (2017)
3. Vitek, J., Kalibera, T.: Repeatability, reproducibility, and rigor in systems research. In: Proceedings of the Ninth ACM International Conference on Embedded software (EMSOFT 2011), pp. 33–38 (2011)
4. Stodden, V., Miguez, S.: Best practices for computational science: software infrastructure and environments for reproducible and extensible research. J. Open Res. Softw. **2**(1), e21 (2014)
5. Verdi, K.K., Ellis, H.J., Gryk, M.R.: Conceptual-level workflow modeling of scientific experiments using NMR as a case study. BMC Bioinform. **8**, 31 (2007)
6. Ellis, H.J.C., Nowling, R.J., Vyas, J., Martyn, T.O., Gryk, M.R.: Iterative development of an application to support nuclear magnetic resonance data analysis of proteins. In: Proceedings of the International. Conference on Information Technology: New Generations, pp. 1014–1020 (2011)
7. Maciejewski, M.W., Schuyler, A.D., Gryk, M.R., Moraru, I.I., Romero, P.R., Ulrich, E.L., Eghbalnia, H.R., Livny, M., Delaglio, F., Hoch, J.C.: NMRbox: a resource for biomolecular NMR computation. Biophys. J. **112**(8), 1529–1534 (2017)
8. Piccolo, S.R., Frampton, M.B.: Tools and techniques for computational reproducibility. GigaScience **5**(1), 30 (2016)
9. Bowers, S., Ludäscher, B.: Towards a generic framework for semantic registration of scientific data. In: Semantic Web Technologies for Searching and Retrieving Scientific Data (SCISW) (2003)
10. McPhillips, T., Song, T., Kolisnik, T., Aulenbach, S., Belhajjame, K., Bocinsky, K., Cao, Y., Chirigati, F., Dey, S., Freire, J., Huntzinger, D., Jones, C., Koop, D., Missier, P., Schildhauer, M., Schwalm, C., Wei, Y., Cheney, J., Bieda, M., Ludäscher, B.: YesWorkflow: a user-oriented, language-independent tool for recovering workflow information from scripts. Int. J. Digit. Curation **10**(1), 298–313 (2015)
11. Madin, J.S., Bowers, S., Schildhauer, M., Jones, M.: Advancing ecological research with ontologies. Trends Ecol. Evol. **23**, 159–168 (2008)
12. Nowling, R.J., Vyas, J., Weatherby, G., Fenwick, M.W., Ellis, H.J.C., Gryk, M.R.: CONNJUR spectrum translator: an open source application for reformatting NMR spectral data. J. Biomol. NMR **50**(1), 83–89 (2011)
13. Bowers, S., Ludäscher, B.: Actor-oriented design of scientific workflows. In: Delcambre, L., Kop, C., Mayr, Heinrich C., Mylopoulos, J., Pastor, O. (eds.) ER 2005. LNCS, vol. 3716, pp. 369–384. Springer, Heidelberg (2005). https://doi.org/10.1007/11568322_24
14. Rijgersberg, H., van Assem, M., Top, J.: Ontology of units of measure and related concepts. Semant. Web Interoper. Usabil. Appl. **4**, 3–13 (2011)
15. Fenwick, M., Weatherby, G., Vyas, J., Sesanker, C., Martyn, T.O., Ellis, H.J.C., Gryk, M.R.: CONNJUR workflow builder: a software integration environment for spectral reconstruction. J. Biomol. NMR **62**, 313–326 (2015)

Creating Digital Collections: Museum Content and the Public

S. E. Hackney[✉] and Zoe Faye Pickard

University of Pittsburgh, Pittsburgh, PA 15260, USA
{s.hackney, zfp2}@pitt.edu

Abstract. The internet is a valuable asset for making cultural heritage accessible to a broader audience, and in recent years many museums have experimented with methods of sharing their collections online. This move towards a digital presence for museums has raised questions about the role of curators, librarians, and other information professionals in creating and maintaining digital collections. If anyone can collect images, and display them together on their personal website, what work remains for cultural heritage professionals to do?

Using data collected from webscraping using Python, we evaluate the explicit metadata associated with online collections of objects created by both the public and museum professionals. We look at museum websites which offer the public the ability to develop their own, personal collections from the museum's digitized holdings, (namely the Rijksmuseum) as well as collections utilizing similar technology on the Pinterest platform, in order to answer questions about the difference between professionally curated online collections, and ones created by the public. With the understanding that perceptions of images can be manipulated and altered by the context within which they are situated, we argue that distinguishing between professional and public collections can help information professionals better manage and anticipate patrons' expectations and the methods they use to make meaning out of digital cultural heritage objects.

Keywords: Collections · Museums · Pinterest · Human information interaction
Curation · Online communities

1 Introduction and Background

At the turn of the 21st century, professionals and scholars in the GLAM (Gallery, Library, Archive, and Museum) fields looked toward the future of their work online. The internet was seen as a valuable asset for making cultural heritage accessible to a broader audience, especially as digital infrastructure became better able to support high-quality image and other media files. As a result, GLAMs began making parts of their collections available online. The availability of collections in the digital space raises a number of questions pertaining to collections management and categorization. Public engagement with these collections has the potential to alter the process of collection development and even the formation of exhibitions. Issues such as cataloging terminology and object classification become more poignant when a greater number of individuals engage in this process. The application of tagging by the public

© Springer International Publishing AG, part of Springer Nature 2018
G. Chowdhury et al. (Eds.): iConference 2018, LNCS 10766, pp. 626–631, 2018.
https://doi.org/10.1007/978-3-319-78105-1_71

has the potential to alter the way in which a collection is viewed and how accessible it is (Bearman and Trant 2005; Marty 2011). The ability of the information professional to manage this process, or indeed if there is a need to manage it, raises questions about the ability to define any one collection in a space when everything is infinitely remixable.

Past notions of collections have depended at least partially on physical proximity of tangible objects, or a shared history of collocation, and literature around defining online collections grapples with the absence of physical provenance in digital space (Lee 2000). Likewise, GLAMs' engagement with the public through digital means is an expectation, and institutions have been grappling with ways to present their collections to a digital public in an impactful and sustainable way (Hughes 2012; McGann 2010). Although some presence on social media is all but required, the choice of platform and the way in which individual museums choose to utilize social media varies greatly and can impact the way in which the public converses with the museum (Kidd 2011). With the move towards a greater digital presence there is also a move towards digitization of collections, with an aim to secure, preserve and increase accessibility to collections (Johnson et al. 2015).

Hur-Li Lee (2000) and Currall et al. (2005) begin to address these questions in their articles, both entitled "What is a Collection?" Both papers grapple with the absence of physical provenance in digital space as a means of defining a "collection" of information objects. Lee calls for information professional to conduct further research into understanding "how users view and use collections" (p. 1112) before diving headfirst into creating digital collection platforms that simply mirror their physical counterparts. Currall, Moss, and Stuart, likewise forefront questions of realism in collection-making, both in the physical and digital worlds. In the decade and more since these papers raised their titular question, the tools and methodologies of online collection-making have expanded, and our work seeks to provide answers to them, at least in a single, specific context.

The current professional climate is heavily focused around the move towards digitalization. But beyond the act of digitizing objects from an institution's collection, there is ongoing debate about how and where digital engagement should take place, and whether priority should be placed on increased access to the collections, or on the potential revenue that digital licensing can provide (Bertacchini and Morando 2013). It has been said that "digital innovations have become companions in our daily life" Lohrmann and Osburg 2017). The expectation of a digital presence is one which GLAMs have been working towards over the past decade. The increased presence of museums on social media has been intended to facilitate engagement with visitors in a way which creates a feeling of involvement with the institution (Kidd 2011). This has begun to develop into a means by which the public can engage with museum collections rather than simply viewing pieces from the museum's collection on their website.

Some institutions have attempted to address the question of their digital presence by providing tools and platforms for visitors to their websites to "curate" their own sets of images (or other digital objects) from their larger collections. This aims to keep visitors engaged with the institution, and to maintain copyright and ownership of collection materials by allowing a space to explore and remix within the "confines" of the museum's digital domain (Cooper 2006). Conversely, social media platforms not associated with cultural heritage have become popular places for the creation of informal collections, often using digital assets from museum websites. Along with this have come questions about the role of curators, librarians, and other information professionals in creating and maintaining collections online. If anyone can collect digital images, and display them together on their website, what work then is left to do for trained professionals to do? These questions will form the foundations of our inquiry, shaping the investigation into an analysis of the possibilities of publically created collections in contrast to what is offered by those curated and managed by professionals.

2 Purpose

This project attempts to answer these questions through the evaluation of publicly-available data from social media and the Rijksmuseum website, in order to highlight the differences between online collections created by the public and those created by museum professionals. The Rijksmuseum's *Rijkstudio* tool allows visitors to their website to make their own collections out of more than 200,000 images of objects in the museum's holdings, and represents the cutting edge of museum digital engagement (Pijbes 2015). With this type of engagement in mind, we present this work as a way to develop a foundation for further research, with the aim of facilitating new directions of museum engagement with the public in the future, as well as fostering theoretical discussions of collection-making practice online.

In order to accurately assess the implications of community developed collections both those curated within the context of the museum developed service "Rijksstudio" at the Rijksmuseum in the Netherlands, and those curated within the Pinterest platform will be analyzed. Pinterest is a social media platform which provides users with the ability to "discover and save ideas". According to Pinterest "every idea is represented by a 'Pin' that includes an image, description and link back to the image's source online" (Pinterest 2017). Pinterest users are referred to as "Pinners" within the context of the platform; content is provided by individual users and businesses from any online source both within the platform itself or from outside online sources, utilizing Pinterest's own browser extensions and the "Save" button.

The assessment of both museum and more general collection tools allows for discussion on how community curated collections are likely to differ by platform due to the intention behind engagement with the platform itself. Actively seeking out museum websites and collections speaks to a targeted searching approach which is not reflected within the Pinterest platform, which supports a more serendipitous interaction with the information. It is proposed that this difference will likely be evident within the content of the produced collections, where more integration and diversity may be seen as opposed to a more focused and detailed product. We believe that this study, by articulating and highlighting differences in public and professional digital collections across platforms will be able to guide the decision-making process of GLAMs in the future to create high-impact digital spaces that showcase their collections.

3   Methods

The choice to focus on the Rijksmuseum, specifically was made as they have an active presence on Pinterest and provide a tool for the public to develop their own collections on the institutions website. This purposive approach to sampling will allow for in-depth analysis within the context of a mixed methods approach (Patton 2002; Pickard 2013). Beginning with an initial evaluation of the collections available across both platforms, curated both professionally and by the public, the 25 most recent collections were chosen in each collection category.

Using Python and the REST API protocol, we collect data from the collection-building tools associated with the Rijksmuseum (https://www.rijksmuseum. nl/en/rijksstudio). This metadata includes: username of collection creator, association of the creator (if any) with the museum, collection title and description, number of items in the collection, item titles and descriptive metadata (creator, date, etc.) associated with each item, and any "likes," "shares," or comments associated with the collection. In addition, we collect similar data from the Pinterest platform, using the Pinterest API, focusing on the official Pinterest pages of the Rijksmuseum, as well as "Boards" created by Pinterest users explicitly labeled as being about or containing objects from the collections of the Rijksmuseum. This results in 2 sites of data collection (*Rijksstudio* and Pinterest), with 4 specific categories of object-collection data (Rijks-professional, Rijks-public, Rijks-professional-pins, and Rijks-public-pins).

Using this data, we evaluate the general methods of practice among and between these groups, via the application of grounded theory methodology of iterative assessment and categorization (Mansourian 2006). Individual collections are sorted into types by their content and explicit description, such as collections centered around a particular subject matter, art form or artist, or those associated with a particular aesthetic. Once categorized in this manner, we assess the demographics of the platforms and professional level of the creators for trends in who is making what, and where. Within the context of our initial qualitative evaluation this closer assessment will allow for the development of theories primed for further research into the evolution of the digital museum and opportunities provided by open access to collections.

4   Preliminary Findings

From an initial qualitative evaluation of the Rijksmuseum's online professionally-curated collection it is apparent that there are a number of standard components which each digital exhibition contains. These include an overview of the collection including contextual information regarding the artist, theme or time period along with images of all 'objects' in the collection. This space offers more detail than the professionally curated content available on the museum's Pinterest account, where there is little to no information regarding each one of the available "Pins". The boards available on Pinterest which have been created by the museum do appear to reflect the same organizational structure which is apparent on the museum site.

In contrast, the community created collections (those pulled together by the public) seem to differ in the content and level of intellectual engagement. Those available on

Pinterest do not merely reuse the images which are available of the collection but also appear to include a number of images of the museum itself, in addition there are images of services provided by the museum. This changes the nature of the board from a representative depiction of the museum's collection to a representation of the museum experience as a whole. This is not the case with the collections which are created by the public within the museum website. The disparity here indicates a blurring of the line between "content" and the "institution" in public conceptions of the museum. These collections, although heavily laden with images of the museum's collection, do not fit the traditional museological definition of exhibition or collection, and indicate a difference in both the practices and goals of professional curators, and the public which until now, has only consumed their work. Making this distinction clear presents both a new challenge and a new opportunity for the role of the information professional within the museum sphere.

5 Conclusion

From the initial evaluation of the factors which are to be considered for this study it is evident that there are a number of variations on the concept of a 'collection' within the selected sample. By analyzing the way in which images are used within two online contexts, we aim to provide a level of guidance on the opportunities which GLAMs have to engage with visitors in the digital sphere. We believe that an increase in engagement with the public, as well as allowing for a space of personal meaning-making, can only result in a broader reach and deeper appreciation of the valuable cultural heritage and art objects held in the collections of galleries, libraries, archives, and museums worldwide.

References

Bearman, D., Trant, J.: Social terminology enhancement through vernacular engagement: exploring collaborative annotation to encourage interaction with museum collections. D-Lib Mag. 9(11) (2005)

Bertacchini, E., Morando, F.: The future of museums in the digital age: new models for access to and use of digital collections. Int. J. Arts Manag. 15(2), 60–72 (2013)

Cooper, J.: Beyond the on-line museum: participatory virtual exhibitions. In: Trant, J., Bearman, D. (eds.) Museums and the Web 2006. Archives & Museum Informatics, Toronto (2006)

Currall, J.E.P., Moss, M., Stuart, S.A.J.: What is a collection? Archivaria 58, 131–146 (2005)

Hughes, L.M.: Live and kicking: the impact and sustainability of digital collections in the humanities. In: Proceedings of the Digital Humanities Congress. University of Sheffield (2012). https://www.hrionline.ac.uk/openbook/chapter/dhc-hughes0

Johnson, L., Adams Becker, S., Estrada, V., Freeman, A.: NMC Horizon Report: 2015 Museum Edition. The New Media Consortium, Austin (2015)

Kidd, J.: Enacting engagement online: framing social media use for the museum. Inf. Technol. People 24(1), 64–77 (2011)

Lee, H.-L.: What is a collection? J. Am. Soc. Inf. Sci. 51(12), 1106–1113 (2000). http://doi.org/10.1002/1097-4571(2000)9999:9999<::AID-ASI1018>3.0.CO;2-T

Lohrmann, C., Osburg, T.: Introduction. In: Osburg, T., Lohrmann, C. (eds.) Sustainability in a Digital World: New Opportunities Through New Technologies, p. xiii. Springer, Cham (2017). https://doi.org/10.1007/978-3-319-54603-2_1

Marty, P.F.: My lost museum: user expectations and motivations of creating personal digital collections on museum websites. Libr. Inf. Sci. Res. **33**(3), 211–219 (2011)

Mansourian, Y.: Adoption of grounded theory in LIS research. New Libr. World **107** (1228/1229), 386–402 (2006)

McGann, J.: Online Humanities Scholarship: The Shape of Things to Come. OpenStax CNX (2010). http://cnx.org/contents/3d5747d3-e943-4a39-acf9-beb086047378@1.3

Patton, M.Q.: Qualitative Research and Evaluation Methods. Sage, London (2002)

Pickard, A.J.: Research Methods in Information, 2nd edn. Facet Publishing, London (2013)

Pijbes, W.: Netherlands: the battle for beauty in a virtual world: how museums can profit from the digital revolution. Uncommon Cult. **6**(2), 138–145 (2015). http://www.firstmonday.dk/ojs/index.php/UC/article/view/6212/5062

Pinterest. How Pinterest Works (2017). https://business.Pinterest.com/en/how-Pinterest-works

Toward Identifying Values and Tensions in Designing a Historically-Sensitive Data Platform: A Case-Study on Urban Renewal

Myeong Lee[✉], Shiyun Chen, Yuheng Zhang, Edel Spencer,
and Richard Marciano

College of Information Studies, University of Maryland, College Park, USA
{myeong, schen122, yzhang63, espence2, marciano}@umd.edu

Abstract. Urban renewal was a national initiative from the 1960s through the 70s aimed at improving so-called "blighted" areas, and resulted in the displacement of many vibrant communities. While the underlying mechanisms of urban renewal have been examined, there have been very few data-driven, evidence-based studies that take into account the histories and interests of former residents. The "Human Face of Big Data" project started as a digital curation effort to design and develop a web-based platform that provides insights and analytics into the mechanisms of this process. However, it was found from user feedback that designing these kinds of platforms is not trivial; rather it needed to be carefully approached as diverse values and tensions exist surrounding the design of a historically-sensitive data system. This paper aims to report on the initial system design process, and provide a preliminary design framework constructed using a top-down approach. This framework can be used to examine possible dimensions of design concerns for historically-sensitive data platforms by system designers. Also, human-computer interaction (HCI) and archival science researchers can potentially benefit from this new perspective that considers both value sensitivity and archival values.

Keywords: Digital curation · Value-sensitive design · Urban renewal

1 Background

Urban renewal was a national initiative from the 1960s through the 1970s to transform "blighted" neighborhoods into living spaces with modern amenities. Local housing authorities used a series of realty appraisals to establish property values and acquired most of the properties in the areas that were to be redeveloped. While the economic value of this initiative has been emphasized, many vibrant neighborhoods including families, businesses, and organizations, most of which were in minority communities, were displaced, forcing residents to leave their own communities. Fullilove describes this as "the traumatic stress reaction to the loss of some or all of one's emotional ecosystem" and conceptualized community displacement as "root shock" [8]. In October 2007, the Asheville City Council approved the transfer of the records of the Housing Authority of the City of Asheville (HACA) to the D.H. Ramsey Library Special Collections & University Archives at the University of North Carolina

© Springer International Publishing AG, part of Springer Nature 2018
G. Chowdhury et al. (Eds.): iConference 2018, LNCS 10766, pp. 632–637, 2018.
https://doi.org/10.1007/978-3-319-78105-1_72

Asheville [15]. In 2016, we started this research project as part of a digital curation effort to make historical documents easily searchable and navigable in favor of inter-active user interfaces and databases. The target collection is comprised of legal doc-uments for over 900 properties documenting the property acquisition process during the urban renewal period in the *Southside* neighborhood (the *East Riverside* as of 1960s). Each case file captures the entire sales history, from appraisals, to offers being made, including cases of rejection by former residents and ensuing court cases, to final deed transfers to HACA. Beyond these near-complete transactions, the stories and daily tribulations of former residents are embedded in the business records; this is why the project was named the *Human Face of Big Data*. As with other archival systems, the target data platform had to be designed in ways that support high accessibility for diverse users [17]. Due to the lengthy and unstructured nature of the collection, a systematic approach to digitally curating the collection was necessary. This led us to adopt well-known design methods, the iterative, scenario-based design approaches, along with our own methods to digitize historical materials [2, 13].

However, adopting a particular design method was found to be non-trivial in the context of urban renewal. User feedback on the first prototype of the data platform revealed that diverse values and tensions exist surrounding the curation of this data. This type of sensitive artifact could be conceptualized as a *contentious object,* since conflicts and tensions are unresolved and focused within an object or activity [11]. By limiting the scope of these objects to historical ones, in the urban renewal case, it is possible to focus on people's perceptions, identities, and backgrounds regarding historical incidents. We characterize urban renewal documents as *historically-sensitive data* where tensions exist and unresolved within a historical event. This paper reports on the initial system design process and user feedback on the first prototype system. Then, we construct a preliminary design framework that can be used to explore values and tensions surrounding *histori-cally-sensitive data systems* as a way to systematically consider their structures. As an early work for developing this design framework, we take a top-down approach that reviews and synthesizes the existing literature. This work can potentially contribute to the value-sensitive design literature by providing design implications for archival systems with controversial data. Also, digital curation and archival science researchers can benefit from a new perspective that, since it considers user values and data sensitivity, is broader than traditional archival science has focused on in designing digital platforms.

2 Digitization Process and Initial System Design

Since a property acquisition document corresponds to a parcel, we began with digi-tizing a parcel map from 1973, the original urban renewal map created for the planning purpose, to provide access points to the documents. Using Photoshop, ArcGIS, and QGIS, it was possible to adjust distorted images, geo-reference them, and geo-trace parcel polygons on the modern online map. Subsequently, interfaces were designed using the scenario-based method [2]. User personas were created based on potential users of the future system. Stakeholders included former residents, HACA, researchers, and archivists. Based on these user personas, user scenarios were generated to identify possible ways for users to utilize the data platform. User scenarios were listed for each user persona, and directly used for creating user requirements. These requirements were used to design user interfaces and databases.

While our user requirements were generated from a scenario-based, top-down approach, unlike many other user interfaces, some parts of the archival system design were also driven heavily by the contents of the original documents, or a bottom-up approach. Furthermore, human stories from the legal documents could affect the system design significantly as they can shed light on values that were overlooked in the urban renewal. This motivated us to qualitatively identify data patterns that could potentially indicate meaningful but previously unknown details. The list of these patterns was prioritized based on potential significance level and was used for interface and database designs along with the user requirements. Based on the user scenarios and data patterns, wire-frames and database schema were created. Finally, the prototype system was implemented with a part of the dataset in the database. The interface provides search functionality based on street name or person name, map-based visualization of property acquisition process by color-coding parcels, and photos and people's names associated with each parcel (more details about digitization/design processes and prototypes are available in [12]). This prototype system was presented at *The Digital Curation and the Local Community Workshop* in April 2017, which was attended by potential users and community members.

3   Challenges and Motivations

After this workshop, we were able to receive useful feedback from many different stakeholders, including a former resident, interface designers and other community members. This helped us to identify a few challenges that could improve the data platform design. The first challenge was that a former resident provided instances of tensions between stakeholders that we were not aware of previously. For instance, she mentioned that the city designer and HACA officials focused on "getting rid of the blight" in the neighborhood, whereas the residents were concerned with the effect of the process on the people of the neighborhood. Another challenge, difficulties in communicating with diverse stakeholders, also came out of the former resident's experience and perception:

> "People will shut down and shut you out when they don't want to discuss a topic as sensitive as urban renewal."

Another finding was that value tensions existed not only between different groups of stakeholders, but also within the same group. For example, former residents who had lived in the neighborhood through the period of urban renewal as adults might not have the same opinions about the process as former residents who were young and not aware of the ongoing social process at the time. Finally, an HCI researcher indicated that starting a system design with made-up user personas might be problematic in truly understanding the community:

> "I was intrigued that we, and by "we" I say the university, as a university, made up people, we made user personas to represent people who might be affected, and yet there *are* people who are affected [...] some of our methods are beautiful methods. But they don't understand in the community. There's a disconnect if we're not really clear about the "what" and the "why" [...]"

All these challenges led us to re-think the design process and to conduct this research study to better understand the value tensions and users so that we can proceed to the next step of the system implementation in a more sensitively-informed and deliberate fashion.

4 A Preliminary Framework for the Design of Historically-Sensitive Data Platforms: A Top-Down Approach

In order to consider various perspectives towards value-driven systems and archival data, we reviewed both value-sensitive design and archival systems literature. Value-sensitive design (VSD) is an approach to the design of technology, which prioritizes the inclusion of the values of users and designers [7]. Studies from the value-sensitive design explored diverse dimensions that designers could take into account in understanding user values; these include moral values and normative considerations such as fairness in representing diverse positions [1], "individual position" such as a user's stance towards a system [1], value reflection such as developer's consciousness of philosophy behind a system [16], and social boundaries of users [6, 18]. Often, considering these aspects was challenged by other system- or context-oriented values such as implicit demand for value neutrality for system developers [16] and difficulties in balancing between different stakeholders [5].

Archival systems for historical data present similar challenges as context-driven values and cultures are dominant amongst organizations that design the data platforms. Traditionally, accessibility to archived artifacts including searchability and ease of browsing has been an important goal of archival systems among other values. This qualification along with demands for archival neutrality, record authenticity, and preservation accuracy might cause archival scientists to focus less on the value-sensitivity and tensions in designing historical data platforms [3], despite concerns for archives users [17] and ongoing research on value biases of archivists [9]. Of course, there have been notable efforts to overcome this persisting challenge: an HCI study focused on tensions and values regarding ongoing archival practices and reported that authenticity can be promoted through identities established by key stakeholders [4]. Particularly, a control-openness tension was found within the same archivist group, which confirms the importance of *individual position*, i.e., one of the key VSD concepts as a dimension of design concerns [4]. Also, an archival study identified the roles of users in archiving practices and recognized the need for contextualizing archives users and curators [10].

However, it is still unclear what dimensions need to be examined in designing an archival system, since the process of identifying diverse stakeholders' values has not been established in a systematic way in the context of historically-sensitive data platforms. In order to explore this gap, a preliminary design framework was created as an initial effort to identifying possible causes of value tensions by synthesizing VSD and archival science literatures (Table 1).

Table 1. A preliminary design framework for historically-sensitive data platforms.

Conceptual dimension	Description	Sources
Accessibility control	Whether there are any concerns on increasing people's accessibility to archival data among stakeholders and designers	[4, 17]
Individual position	Whether people have different views towards the archival data and systems in a same stakeholder group (e.g., archivists team, researchers, or designers team)	[1]
Authenticity-digitization tension	Whether users are concerned with the degradation of authenticity due to digitization processes	[3, 17]
Value reflection and neutrality	Whether developers or archivists are committed to reflect their values or to guarantee neutrality	[9, 16]
Boundary	Whether different stakeholder groups have different expectations or cultural backgrounds regarding the archival data	[6, 18]
Guardianship and ownership	Whether there are tensions that come from a thought that particular stakeholders own the archival data or guard it while not owning it	[4, 7]
Collection development	Whether there are any concerns on developing the collection further after implementing a system	[14]
Transparency towards the digitization process	Whether there are needs or concerns about making the digitization process transparent	[1]

5   Discussion and Future Work

The proposed framework is not complete as it only covers part of the wide spectrum of literature, so this work should be seen as the first step to building a design framework for historically-sensitive data systems. Also, using only a top-down approach cannot be justified; we need to use both top-down and bottom-up approaches to iteratively refine the design framework. In order to do so, we are planning to conduct interview studies targeting diverse stakeholders of the urban renewal data system. Specifically, former residents, interface designers, archivists, historians, and other community members will be recruited and interviewed in a semi-structured way with protocols generated based on the proposed dimensions. The analysis results of the interview data will be used to adjust the framework along with more extensive literature reviews. We, as system designers and researchers for historically-sensitive but socially meaningful data platforms, have reported on the initial design process of the prototyping system [12]. These kinds of systems, particularly those that contain historical significance as well as people's memories and daily tribulations, have the potential to contribute to identifying data-driven, evidence-based mechanisms underlying social and historical incidents such as urban renewal. We believe that the proposed framework can be used as a preliminary examination tool for generating protocols for user studies and checking possible aspects of design concerns that can be otherwise overlooked in the context of historically-sensitive data platforms.

References

1. Borning, A., Muller, M.: Next steps for value sensitive design. In: Proceedings of CHI, pp. 1125–1134 (2012)
2. Carroll, J.M.: Making Use: Scenario-Based Design of Human-Computer Interactions. MIT press, Cambridge (2000)
3. Duranti, L.: Archives as a place. Arch. Manuscr. **24**(2), 242–255 (1996)
4. Durrant, A.C., Kirk, D.S., Reeves, S.: Human values in curating a human rights media archive. In: Proceedings of CHI (2014)
5. Flanagan, M., Howe, D.C., Nissenbaum, H.: Values at play: tradeoffs in socially-oriented game design. In: Proceedings of CHI, pp. 751–760 (2005)
6. Friedman, B., Kahn, P.H., Borning, A., Huldtgren, A.: Value sensitive design and information systems. In: Doorn, N., Schuurbiers, D., van de Poel, I., Gorman, M.E. (eds.) Early engagement and new technologies: Opening up the laboratory. PET, vol. 16, pp. 55–95. Springer, Dordrecht (2013). https://doi.org/10.1007/978-94-007-7844-3_4
7. Friedman, B., Kahn Jr., P.H.: Human values, ethics, and design. In: the human-computer interaction handbook: fundamentals, evolving technologies and emerging applications, pp. 1177–1201. Lawrence Erlbaum Associates, Inc., Mahwah (2003)
8. Fullilove, M.: Root Shock: How Tearing Up City Neighborhoods Hurts America, and What We Can Do About It. One World/Ballantine, London/New york (2009)
9. Gilliland, A.: Neutrality, social justice and the obligations of archival education and educators in the twenty-first century. Arch. Sci. **11**(3–4), 193–209 (2011)
10. Huvila, I.: Participatory archive: towards decentralised curation, radical user orientation, and broader contextualisation of records management. Arch. Sci. **8**(1), 15–36 (2008)
11. Joyce, E., Butler, B., Pike, J.: Handling flammable materials: Wikipedia biographies of living persons as contentious objects. In: iConference Proceedings, pp. 25–32 (2011)
12. Lee, M., Zhang, Y., Chen, S., Spencer, E., Dela Cruz, J., Hong, H., Marciano, R.: Heuristics for assessing computational archival science (CAS) research: the case of the human face of big data project. In: IEEE Big Data (2017)
13. Nielsen, J.: Iterative user-interface design. Computer **26**(11), 32–41 (1993)
14. Palmer, C., Weber, N. M., Renear, A., Muñoz, T.: Foundations of data curation: the pedagogy and practice of "purposeful work" with research data. In: iConference (2013)
15. Shawgo, K.: City of asheville donates urban renewal files to UNC asheville (2009). https://www.hastac.org/documents/city-asheville-donates-urban-renewal-files-unc-asheville
16. Shilton, K.: Engaging values despite neutrality: challenges and approaches to values reflection during the design of internet infrastructure. Sci. Technol. Hum. Values (2017)
17. Sinn, D., Soares, N.: Historians' use of digital archival collections: the web, historical scholarship, and archival research. J. Assoc. Inf. Sci. Technol. **65**(9), 1794–1809 (2014)
18. Voida, A., Dombrowski, L., Hayes, G.R., Mazmanian, M.: Shared values/conflicting logics. In: Proceedings of CHI (2014)

Is There a Solution to the Orphan Works Problem? Exploring the International Models

Brenda Siso-Calvo[1] , Rosario Arquero-Avilés[1(✉)] ,
Gonzalo Marco-Cuenca[2] , and Silvia Cobo-Serrano[3]

[1] Complutense University, Madrid, Spain
{msiso, carquero}@ucm.es
[2] University of Zaragoza, Zaragoza, Spain
gmarco@unizar.es
[3] PhD in Library and Information Science, Madrid, Spain
s.cobo@ucm.es

Abstract. Aspects related to copyright and orphan works become a real obstacle for cultural institutions wishing to undertake major projects for the digitisation and on-line availability of their collections. Although some countries have already established models to try to solve the problem of orphan works, others are still discussing possible options. The paper explores the current situation of the schemes in place internationally to deal with the problems associated with orphan works and how these are being applied by cultural institutions regarding the digital dissemination of their collections. The methodology consisted in a systematic review of the research results as an exploratory analytical technique for the collection of relevant information. Results highlighted that global situation is uncertain and none of the formulas studied enables full and effective digitisation and digital dissemination of the world's cultural heritage. Further advances are necessary for the creation of diligent search procedures.

Keywords: Orphan works · Digitisation · Online dissemination
Libraries · Cultural heritage · Documentary heritage · Copyright
Diligent search

1 Introduction

Digitisation of documentary heritage for its online availability is already a reality. Cultural institutions are considering the digitisation of their collections for their digital conservation and, mainly, to ensure that the public can access worldwide cultural heritage [1]. Major digitisation projects are under way or being implemented across the globe: World Digital Library, Digital Public Library of America or Europeana.

Although a digital setting offers many possibilities for making cultural material more accessible, institutions must bear in mind several key points regarding copyright. The main challenge consists in understanding the feasibility of copyright, and this is the moment at which orphan works become an obstacle for the dissemination of cultural heritage. "Works are called orphan when rights holders cannot be identified or, if they are identified, they cannot be located in order to ask the necessary permissions" [2, p. 63].

© Springer International Publishing AG, part of Springer Nature 2018
G. Chowdhury et al. (Eds.): iConference 2018, LNCS 10766, pp. 638–644, 2018.
https://doi.org/10.1007/978-3-319-78105-1_73

Although some countries have already established models to try to solve the problem of orphan works, others are still discussing possible options. "In most solutions there is a need to define a criterion on what constitutes a diligent search[1] that needs to be performed prior to the use of a work" [2, p. 63].

2 Goals and Methodology

The paper focuses on explore the current situation of the schemes in place internationally to deal with the problems associated with orphan works and how these are being applied by cultural institutions relating to the digitisation and digital dissemination of their collections. Our specific goals are to describe the current models in order then to characterize the degree of development of guidelines and standards for carrying out diligent searches prior to declaring a work as orphaned or applying for a copyright licence. Another element of significance for analysis, given the focus on Library and Information Science area, is the existence of lists of information sources and identification of databases or registers aimed at monitoring diligent search efforts at both national and entity level. Lastly, to identify some of the initiatives undertaken by different cultural institutions to solve copyright aspects.

We undertook a systematic review of the research results published by expert authors and research groups working in the field under study, as well as official reference documents and regulations from domestic and international authorities. Initial phase included the review of scientific literature and a subsequent analysis of the data and the summary of this information.

3 Results and Discussion

3.1 Statutory Exception-Based Model

Also known as the European model was adopted by the European Union through the approval of European Directive 2012/28/EU on the authorized uses of orphan works [4], which established the legal framework to facilitate the digitisation and dissemination of certain copyrighted works by cultural institutions.

Article 3 of European Directive stipulates that beneficiaries shall ensure a diligent search is made in good faith for each protected work, consulting appropriate sources for the purpose depending on the category of work. The results obtained by multiple research teams [5–7] have confirmed through relevant evidence that only the United Kingdom has set up detailed procedures or guidelines to deal with diligent searches about orphan works.

The Directive also promotes the adoption by member states of the measures necessary to ensure that information about orphan works is recorded on a central on-line

---

[1] Diligent search refers to a search procedure whose aim is to identify and locate the copyright holder(s) of a possible orphan work. This procedure is compulsory and must be carried out before an item is declared an orphan work [3].

database accessible to the public. To this end, the European Union Intellectual Property Office (EUIPO) handles the European Union Orphan Works Database, on which each competent national authority can register the information necessary to identify a work as an orphan in a country, so that it receives the same recognition throughout the European Union [3].

The total number of orphan works declared and registered on the European Union Orphan Works Database comes to 5,142 records [5], implying an increase of 3,712 records with respect to the data reflected in the EUIPO Report for 2015 [8, p. 50].

3.2   Fair Use

Fair use is a copyright principle based on the belief that the public is entitled to freely use portions of copyrighted materials for purposes such as criticism, comment, news reporting, teaching, scholarship, or research [9]. In the United States, this principle is governed by Title 17 of the Copyright Law and is being used as an effective solution for the problem posed by orphan works[2].

Cultural institutions wishing to engage in digitisation projects must rely on fair use to make their documentary heritage available on line. Library of Congress [10] believes relying on fair use may be a risky, inappropriate and costly solution, particularly if lawsuits ensue. The Copyright Office "does not believe that reliance on judicial trends, which may turn at any point, is a sufficient basis to forgo a permanent legislative solution" [11, p. 43]. On the other hand, some authors defend this model. The Library Copyright Alliance [12] maintains that libraries do not require any legislative reform to be able to make use of orphan works on the basis that fair use has ceased to be uncertain in practice, court orders are less likely and massive digitisation is more commonplace.

Cultural institutions have developed unofficial codes of best practices[3] that constitute useful documents so that institutions can apply fair use correctly. However, no comprehensive search procedures or lists of information sources have yet been developed, nor is there any official evidence that diligent search processes must be recorded on a database. It is possible to infer that those entities opting to make their collections accessible on-line probably have a record of the diligent search carried out.

There are several well-known cases of digitisation of collections in the Library of Congress. These would include the "The Hannah Arendt Papers" or "Prosperity and Thrift: The Coolidge Era and the Consumer Economy" and, in view of their historical and cultural value, they have been placed on-line partly by means of fair use formulas[4], including usage clauses in the corresponding sections of "Copyright and Other Restrictions" [10].

---

[2] The two largest digitisation projects, Google Books and HathiTrust Digital Library, have been supported by American judges in favour of fair use.

[3] Code of Best Practices in Fair Use for Academic and Research Libraries; Statement of Best Practices in Fair Use of Orphan Works for Libraries & Archives; Orphan Works: Statement of Best Practices.

[4] https://memory.loc.gov/ammem/arendthtml/res.html.

3.3   Extended Collective Licensing

ECL consists in extending a licence from a representative management entity to rights holders who are not members of that management entity. "The government authorizes a collective organization to deal licences for a class of works or a class of uses" [13, p. 36]. Within ECL regimes, searches may be carried out by the Collective Management Organizations (CMOs) (not the end user), and the search can be deferred until a later moment (after the orphan work has been used), when the CMO must distribute the royalties to the rights holders it represents [14].

In the United States, the Copyright Office proposes the implementation of this regulatory framework to solve the problem of orphan works, in such a way that licences can be used to authorize projects on the terms established by the parties under governmental supervision. In this Copyright Office proposal, no provisions are made regarding diligent search procedures or lists of information resources for the identification and location of copyright holders.

3.4   Non-exclusive Licensing

This model enables users to use certain kinds of orphan works following a case by case analysis. If applicants can prove that they made a reasonable effort to locate the rights holders, but these could not be located, then the competent authority will approve the application and issue non-exclusive conditional licence [11].

Canada opted for this model even though it is not in favour of large-scale digitisation. The *Orphan Works Report* identified some difficulties in the Canadian system and claims that several studies have highlighted that it is rarely used [15].

According to the on-line guide published by the Copyright Board of Canada, one of the requirements for the granting of licences is to demonstrate the efforts made to locate the rights holders and the results achieved. Nonetheless, only general recommendations[5] are given, so it is not possible to view exhaustive procedures and information sources for conducting diligent searches. For example, no mention is made of the Copyrights database, which enables the on-line search for copyright information recorded or eliminated since October 1991.

The Copyright Board of Canada keeps an online register of licences issued[6]. To date, 296 licences have been awarded, of which 36 belong to 16 cultural institutions. Nonetheless, the licences respond to requests to use few documents. The National Film Board of Canada is the entity with the most licences granted, 16, almost half the total.

We can infer that institutions with repeated requests for licences have records and case files for the search process to identify rights owners that are more complete than the recommendations mentioned, which are not accessible.

---

[5] http://www.cb-cda.gc.ca/unlocatable-introuvables/brochure2-e.html.

[6] http://www.cb-cda.gc.ca/unlocatable-introuvables/licences-e.html.

3.5   Fair Dealing Exceptions

Under this scheme, a series of exceptions are set out in statute as not constituting an infringement of the copyright in the work.

Australia contemplates in Division 3 of the Copyright Act [16] a series of exceptions covering fair dealing for several purposes. With respect to cultural institutions, the Australian law includes provision 200AB[7], which determines certain uses by libraries and archives that would not be considered as an infringement, but no specific exception is set out for the use of orphan works.

In view of this situation of "legislative vacuum", the Australian Law Reform Commission[8] [17] recommends the introduction of legislation on fair use exception and the limitation of legal remedies where a diligent search has been conducted; this would include cultural institutions and the use of orphan works.

Nonetheless, on this occasion we have also been unable to find any official documents detailing the diligent search process. Some general recommendations can be found in the guidelines drawn up by the National and State Libraries of Australasia [18]. Nor is there any mention in the law of the existence of a register or database listing the works considered, a priori, to be orphans.

Under provision 200AB of the 1968 Copyright Act, Australian libraries provide on-line access to different collections of orphan works after declaring that a diligent search has been carried out. This would be the case of the National Gallery of Victoria which explains, in its section on "Copyrights and Reproductions"[9], that the works whose rights holders have been impossible to locate are published on-line with the argument that this is the also the best way to discover the owners of the rights. In the same line, the State Library of South Australia publishes certain items under the premise of good faith[10].

4   In Search of Solutions: Summary and Projection

The search for solutions to overcome the obstacles imposed by orphan works for the digitisation and digital dissemination of collections continues to be a topic of interest and a pending issue in the international arena.

Within the European Union, the option adopted has been to implement a model driven by the interest to make all necessary efforts prior to having the works declared as orphans so that they can be used by all member states. In view of the results, the European model is gradually gaining ground thanks to the advances made by member states relating to detailed diligent search procedures and databases enabling this process to be documented.

---

[7] "Use of works and other subject matter for certain purposes".

[8] Federal agency in charge of investigating, conducting consultancy activities and drawing up recommendations for the government.

[9] https://www.ngv.vic.gov.au/about/reports-and-documents/copyright-and-reproductions/.

[10] http://www.samemory.sa.gov.au/site/page.cfm?u=70&c=540.

In the United States, the lack of a consensus on orphan works legislation has meant other alternatives have to be explored. Although the Fair Use model causes uncertainty, the LCA [19] argues that other models also fail to provide an effective solution for mass digitisation.

In this quest for solutions, we can see that Australia tends towards a model based on Fair Use, like that currently in place among North-American cultural institutions.

The Non-Exclusive Licensing model used by Canada also seems not to be effective in view of the results, especially for large digitisation projects.

As for the initiatives to resolve the problems associated with protected works, in Europe, the declaration of such works as orphans and their registration on the European database enable the material to be digitalised by cultural institutions. In the United States and Australia have opted to include notices of their procedure in the Copyright clauses, as well as serving as a means for legitimate holders to claim their rights.

In short, we have seen that the global situation is uncertain and that none of the formulas studied enables full and effective digital dissemination of the world's cultural heritage. It is evident that the path for finding solutions and responses to the challenges posed undoubtedly passes through the need to achieve advances in the formulation of diligent search procedures and mechanisms enabling the results and best practices to be shared among institutions.

Acknowledgments. This paper is the result of research carried out as part of the RDI project Digitalización del Patrimonio Documental en España. Prospección y propuesta metodológica para facilitar el acceso y uso de obras huérfanas. Reference: CSO2015-64292 (MINECO/FEDER, UE).

It has also been possible thanks to the assistance of the Ministry of Education, Culture and Sport which supports training for young researchers via its university teacher training programme (FPU).

References

1. Lucas-Schloetter, A.: Digital libraries and copyright issues: digitization of contents and the economics rights of the autor. In: Iglezakis, I., Synodinou, T.E., Kapidakis, S. (eds.) E-publishing and Digital Libraries, pp. 159–179. IGI Global, New York (2011)
2. Koskinen-Olsson, T., Lowe, N.: Educational material on collective management of copyright and related rights. WIPO (2012). http://www.wipo.int/edocs/pubdocs/en/wipo_pub_emat_2014_4.pdf. Accessed 17 Sept 2017
3. Arquero-Avilés, R., Marco-Cuenca, G.: Análisis del estado de la declaración de obras huérfanas en Europa. Revista General de Información y Documentación **26**(2), 365–385 (2016). https://doi.org/10.5209/RGID.54707
4. European Parliament: Directive 2012/28/EU of the European parliament and of the council of 25 October 2012 on certain permitted uses of orphan works (2012). https://goo.gl/WSPsdQ. Accessed 17 Sept 2017
5. Arquero-Avilés, R. (coord.).: Estudio comparativo y análisis de la situación actual de las obras huérfanas en Europa, Observatorio de Obras Huérfanas y Búsqueda Diligente, Madrid (2017). ISBN 978-84-697-4066-8. https://www.researchgate.net/publication/318085151. Accessed 17 Sept 2017

6. Bertoni, A., Guerrieri, F., Lillà, M.: Requirements for diligent search in 20 European countries (2017). http://diligentsearch.eu/wp-content/uploads/2017/06/REPORT-2.pdf. Accessed 17 Sept 2017

7. Favalle, M., Schoroff, S., Bertoni, A.: Requirements for diligent search in the United Kingdom, the Netherlands and Italy (2016). https://goo.gl/zBQiKS. Accessed 17 Sept 2017

8. EUIPO: Annual report: European Union Intellectual Property (2016). https://goo.gl/eKmNmU. Accessed 17 September 2017

9. Stim, R.: Getting Permission: Using & Licensing Copyright-Protected Materials Online & Off. NOLO, Berkeley (2016)

10. Library of Congress: Comments of the library of congress in response to the copyright office notice of inquiry (2013). https://goo.gl/voAYMa. Accessed 17 Sept 2017

11. United States Copyright Office: Orphan works and mass digitization (2015). https://www.copyright.gov/orphan/reports/orphan-works2015.pdf. Accessed 17 Sept 2017

12. Library Copyright Alliance: Comments of the library copyright alliance in response to the copyright office's notice of inquiry (2013). https://goo.gl/419yvA. Accessed 17 Sept 2017

13. United States Copyright Office: Legal issues in mass digitization: a preliminary analysis and discussion document (2011). https://goo.gl/GC5a3y. Accessed 17 Sept 2017

14. Hansen, D.R., Hinze, G., Urban, J.: Orphan works and the search for rights holders: who participates in a 'diligent search' under present and proposed regimes (Berkeley digital library copyright project, White Paper No. 4) (2013). http://ssrn.com/abstract=2208163

15. United States Copyright Office: Report on orphan works (2006). https://www.copyright.gov/orphan/orphan-report.pdf. Accessed 17 Sept 2017

16. Copyright act 1968 (consolidated as of 27 June 2015). http://wipo.int/wipolex/en/details.jsp?id=15724. Accessed 17 Sept 2017

17. Australian Law Reform Commission: Copyright and the digital economy, final report (ALRC Report 122) (2014). https://www.alrc.gov.au/publications/13-orphan-works. Accessed 17 Sept 2017

18. National and State Libraries Australasia: Procedural guidelines for reasonable search for orphan works (2010). https://goo.gl/hexYtw. Accessed 17 Sept 2017

19. Library Copyright Alliance: Additional comments of the library copyright alliance in response to the copyright office's notice of inquiry concerning orphan works and mass digitization (2014). https://goo.gl/TToucd. Accessed 17 Sept 2017

Uncovering Hidden Insights for Information Management: Examination and Modeling of Change in Digital Collection Metadata

Oksana L. Zavalina[(⊠)], Shadi Shakeri, Priya Kizhakkethil,
and Mark E. Phillips

Department of Information Science, University of North Texas,
1155 Union Circle 311068, Denton, TX 76203-5017, USA
oksana.zavalina@unt.edu

Abstract. This paper reports the study which measured and categorized metadata change in the digital collection of patents. The descriptive metadata in this collection is based on the local version of Dublin Core. The moist frequently occurring categories and subcategories of change are identified, as well as metadata fields that are edited the most often. Comparative analysis between multiple editing events is conducted. Results and future/concurrent research are discussed.

Keywords: Metadata change · Metadata evaluation · Metadata management

1 Introduction and Related Literature

Challenges in handling the large volume of documents highlight the need for improved quality of metadata and higher level of automation in the processes of ingestion, validation, transformation, enrichment and storage, as well as adherence to standards, and continuous assessment of workflow to maintain metadata quality (e.g., [7, 19]). Data cleaning – a strategic process performed manually or automatically for enhancing the quality of data, including metadata – deals with detecting and removing inconsistencies and significant errors in the dataset [17]. Automated data cleaning typically utilizes data mapping tools and algorithms [5] and necessitates a profound understanding of the structure of data sources and the use of schemas [6]. Completeness, consistency and accuracy criteria are used for evaluating data quality [1, 10, 17]. A family of commercial products, referred to as Extract-Transform-Load (ETL) tools, is commonly adopted for optimization of aggregated data. The ETL tools extract data from a data repository, transform data into a usable format, and then load the data into a target system. In addition to removing inconsistencies (e.g., data normalization) and errors (i.e., fixing accuracy errors, supplying missing data, and removing duplications), this process typically involves filtering, sorting, categorizing data, and so forth. The ETL framework employs semantic technologies (e.g., URl, OWL, SPARQL, RDF, etc.) for extracting data via queries for transformation [2].

© Springer International Publishing AG, part of Springer Nature 2018
G. Chowdhury et al. (Eds.): iConference 2018, LNCS 10766, pp. 645–651, 2018.
https://doi.org/10.1007/978-3-319-78105-1_74

A number of automated methods have been suggested for calculating metadata quality metrics based on the measurements of aggregations of metadata records [9, 12, 14]. Measuring metadata quality is often done to either compare the metadata against metrics of other collections, or to generate a baseline for the set of records being evaluated. Once a baseline or target is identified, the next step is often to identify an aspect of the metadata that is of interest to modify with the goal of increasing quality (e.g., increasing the number of subject headings in a record, addition of a more descriptive abstract, fixing typographical errors or normalizing name forms). Once improvements to metadata have been made the quality is measured again; the process is repeated until the desired effect has been reached. Metadata quality has traditionally been most often identified through completeness, consistency, and accuracy criteria (e.g., [3, 4, 16]). A recently proposed metadata quality assessment framework for open data portals [13] lays out 5 criteria: existence (related to completeness), conformance, retrievability, accuracy, and open data. The studies of metadata quality often focus on the completeness (e.g., [8, 15] etc.).

Existing metadata quality frameworks and assessment certifications could potentially benefit from taking into account metadata change and its impact on quality, as shown by research. For example, a recent study that automatically assessed quality metadata in terms of accuracy, completeness, and consistency [11] found that the metadata that underwent modification had higher quality compared to their original creation versions. However, versioning is not common for metadata management systems which makes it challenging to obtain change data as whenever a record is updated in most systems, the latest version overwrites the previous version (e.g., [18]). Even with these difficulties, there has been some investigation into metadata change at an aggregation level, including development and testing of a metadata change framework (e.g., [19, 20]). The study reported in this submission attempts to further develop understanding of metadata change and to contribute to updating the metadata change framework, using the data from the specialized collection of historical patents.

Although historical patents are available and full-text searchable through Google Patents, the accessibility is limited due to lack of descriptive metadata. The State digital repository that hosts and maintains the N State Patents historical collection provides descriptive metadata to facilitate worldwide access for all interested audiences. The N State Patents collection contains almost 14,000 official patents issued by the U.S. Patent Office between 1840 and 1920s. The state digital repository uses an XYZ local metadata application profile based on the qualified version of Dublin Core. The XYZ metadata scheme includes 21 metadata elements, with 20 descriptive elements which represent the information object and 1 administrative metadata element which describes the record itself. Unlike many other digital repositories, the State Repository employs the metadata versioning. While the end users can only see the latest version of a metadata record, each version of a metadata record is stored and available for analysis. Each addition of a new version of a metadata record indicates a metadata change event. The study of metadata change some results of which are presented below focused on a specialized collection. The analysis of metadata change in the N State Patents collection undertaken by our team is intended to support the metadata quality assurance, as well as to contribute to developing understanding of metadata change in digital collections and the effective ways to analyze it.

2 Methods

Our study combined automatic and manual content analysis to identify the level of metadata change in the N State Patents collection and explore the ways in which the records change. At the time of data collection there were 13,732 patent records in the collection: 11,807 visible to the public with completed metadata and 1,925 that are hidden to the public (usually the initial versions that have not been completed yet and consist of several pre-populated fields that share the same data values across the collection: e.g., *format*, *collection*, etc.). All of the 11,807 visible records have been edited at least once; the largest group of visible records (5,204 or 44%) had 3 versions, i.e., were edited twice: from version 0 to version 1, and from version 1 to version 2.

The data sample for analysis was constructed by selecting 400 records (that are visible to the public which had a total of three versions (8% of the 5,204 population). The built-in functionality of the full-text Solr search system operated by state repository – to return records in a random order – was used to generate a list of 400 records for further analysis. Records were collected in XML format and then pre-processed for normalization purposes. The summaries of metadata change from version 0 to version 1 and from version 1 to version 2 were generated automatically (with the help of a Python script) for each record. The metadata change in each of the 400 records was then categorized by three coders, using the coding manual which included 3 broad categories of change (addition, deletion, and modification), multiple subcategories for each category and codes to represent these subcategories (e.g., addition of a second instance of existing field coded as AEFI; modification in the form of replacement of data value in a field instance coded as MRD, etc.). The coding manual included guidelines for coding each subcategory of change and examples. Some results are reported and discussed below.

3 Findings and Discussion

Examination of change in metadata between version 0 to version 1 revealed that very few metadata fields bore little or no change. For example, the Relation and Primary Source fields only changed in 2% (n = 8) and 1.75% (n = 7) of records. Also, no change was observed in the Source, Collection, Institution, Resource Type, and Format fields. On the other side of the spectrum, Title and Creator fields were changed in almost all (99.75%) records in the sample. These fields also often (i.e., 117 and 360 records respectively) underwent more than one category of change. The most occurring category of change in Title field was MRD, which happened due to the replacement of the placeholder "[]" with the actual data value. The MRD category of change was followed by the AEFI, which occurred in 117 records, through the addition of alternate titles. An example of these two change categories in the same instance of a Title field is replacing the "usp019/00578525" (a placeholder) with the official title, "Tire-Tightener," and the addition of the alternative title, "Tire Tightener."

One interesting observation (Table 1) was that Contributor underwent a much higher number of categories of change than any other field (10 categories including ANS, AEFI, AQ, DF, DEFI, DQ, MRD, MAMD, MTIF, and MRQV. The MRD (n = 397), ANS (n = 260), AEFI (n = 105), DEFI (n = 90), and MTIF (n = 50) changes occurred the most often. An example of the ANS change is the addition of an Info subfield, which allows for the provision of further information about the contributor (e.g., specifying the contribution as illustration witness). Similarly, an MRD change in the Contributor field of most records occurred due to the replacement of a placeholder with a data value.

The AEFI category was observed in 9 fields, with the maximum number of instances occurring in the Subject field (n = 383). Analyses demonstrate that all records in version 0 had two assigned subject headings from two different controlled vocabularies. In version 1, additional instances of the subject field were added from the both vocabularies, as well as natural language keyword terms. The second most noted change category was MRD, occurring in 7 fields, with maximum occurrences in Title and Creator (n = 399) in the 1st editing event (from version 0 to 1).

Date field changed in 99.5% of the records on the 1st editing event. Most often, it underwent two kinds of change: MRD and AEFI. In 398 records, a placeholder was replaced by a data value; in 338 records, a new instance of the field was added. In contrast, in the 1nd editing event (from version 1 to version 2), only 2% of the records had changes in this field's data values. Similarly, the Coverage field was changed in 97.25% (n = 389) of the records in version 1. The most common categories of change in this field were MRD (n = 235) and MAMD (n = 133). An example of an MRD change is where the data value, "United States," was extended to "United States - Texas - Galveston County – Galveston." On the contrary, we observed the change in the Coverage field, in only 2.75% of the records (n = 11) between version 1 and version 2. Likewise, the Identifier and Note fields were both changed in 65% of the records (n = 260) in the sample between version 0 and version 1. The highly occurring categories of change in the Identifier field were MRD (n = 204), MRQV (n = 141), and AEFI(n = 79). The AF and AEFI changes occurred in the Note field of 69 and 191 records respectively.

The overall volume of change made in the 2nd editing event (from version 1 to version 2) was much lower than in the 1st editing event. In 57.5% of records (n = 230), the Publisher was the most changed field in version 2, followed by the Contributor with changes observed in 27.25% (n = 109). The MAMD was the most observed category of change in the Publisher, mostly due to punctuation corrections (observed in 230 records), followed by AEFI and MRD in the Subject and Contributor fields, found in 19 and 11 records respectively. The average number of changed fields per record in the 1st editing event was 8.25 with the standard deviation of 1.16, whereas in the 2nd editing event (from version 1 to version 2), the average number of changed fields per record was 1.21 with the similar standard deviation level of 1.04. Among all the change categories, MRD and AEFI were the most highly occurring categories of change observed on average 5.57 and 3.17 times per record in the 1st editing event. The MAMD and AEFI change were observed 1.02 and 0.11 times on average in 1st and 2nd record editing events.

Table 1. 14 metadata change categories observed at least once.

Category: code	Category: name	% of records in 1st editing event	% of records in 2nd editing event	Top field with category: 1st editing event	Top field with category: 2nd editing event
AF	Add a field	20.75%	3.50%	Note	Relation
AEFI	Add a 2nd+ instance of existing field	99.5%	8.25%	Subject	Subject
ANS	Add new subfield to a field	96.5%	1.50%	Creator	Creator
AESI	Add a 2nd+ instance of existing subfield	–	0.75%	–	Contributor
AQ	Add a qualifier to existing field	0.25%	0.25%	Contributor	Contributor
DF	Delete a field completely	4.25%	0.25%	Contributor	Note
DEFI	Delete a 2nd+ instance of existing field	22.5%	1.50%	Contributor	Contributor
DESI	Delete a 2nd+ instance of existing subfield	1.50%	0.50%	Coverage	Contributor
DQ	Delete a field qualifier	0.25%	–	Contributor	–
MRD	Modify: replace existing data value with new	99.75%	4.75%	Title, creator	Contributor
MAMD	Modify: amend existing data value	99.50%	87.50%	Description	Publisher
MTIF	Modify: transpose multiple instances of a field	12.75%	–	Contributor	–
MRQV	Modify: replace a value for field qualifier	37.00%	–	Identifier	–

4 Conclusions

The data collected and analyzed in this metadata change study demonstrates high level and variability of change in the N State Patents collection metadata. While the vast majority of change occurs in the first editing event, subsequent editing events also include substantial amount of change to some of the fields. The metadata fields that provide access by subject (e.g., Subject, Description) and by names of agents (e.g.,

Creator, Contributor, Publisher) were found to be edited the most throughout the lifecycle of metadata records. Modification is the most common among the three major types of metadata change, with amendment of data value occurring at the highest levels in both the early and the later stages in the life of a metadata record. Although this sample represented the most common category of records, expansion of the sample to include records with more than 3 versions would allow to make more generalizable conclusions to entire populations of rerecords in this collection.

Concurrent research compares the level and distribution of categories of metadata change in multiple digital and physical collections using different metadata schemes: Dublin-Core-based applications, MODS, and MARC. It also looks into commonalities and differences in bibliographic metadata and authority records. The results of these mutually complementary studies will allow to develop an integrated framework of metadata change applicable in various contexts.

References

1. Arenas, M., Bertossi, L.E., Chomicki, J.: Consistent query answers in inconsistent databases. In: Proceedings of the Eighteenth ACM SIGMOD-SIGACT-SIGART Symposium on Principles of Database Systems (PODS 1999), pp. 68–79 (1999)
2. Bansal, S.K., Kagemann, S.: Integrating big data: a semantic extract-transform-load framework. IEEE Computer Society (2015)
3. Barton, J., Currier, S., Hey, J.M.N.: Building quality assurance into metadata creation: an analysis based on the learning objects and e-Prints communities of practice. In: DCMI International Conference on Dublin Core and Metadata Applications (2003)
4. Bruce, T.R., Hillmann, D.I.: The continuum of metadata quality: defining, expressing, exploiting. In: Hillman, D., Westbrook, L. (eds.) Metadata in Practice, pp. 238–256. American Library Association, Chicago (2004)
5. Cong, G., Fan, W., Geerts, F., Jia, X., Ma, S.: Improving data quality: consistency and accuracy. In: Proceedings of the 33rd International Conference on Very Large Databases (VLDB), pp. 315–326 (2007)
6. Dasu, T., Johnson, T., Muthukrishnan, S., Shkapenyuk, V.: Mining database structure; or, how to build a data quality browser, pp. 240–251. Association for Computing Machinery. ACM (2002). 1-58113-497-5/02/06
7. Degerstedt, S., Philipson, J.: Lessons learned from the first year of E-legal deposit in Sweden: ensuring metadata quality in an ever-changing environment. Cataloging Classif. Q. **54**(7), 468–482 (2016). https://doi.org/10.1080/01639374.2016.1197170
8. García, P.A.G., García, A.F., Alonso, S.S.: Exploring the relevance of Europeana digital resources: preliminary ideas on Europeana metadata quality. Revista Interamericana De Bibliotecología **40**(1), 59–69 (2017)
9. Király, P.: A Metadata Quality Assurance Framework, September 2015
10. Kruse, S., Papenbrock, T., Harmouch, H., Naumann, F.: Data anamnesis: admitting raw data into an organization. In: Lomet, D.B., Jermaine, C., Kemme, B., Maier, D., Zhou, X. (eds.) Bulletin of the Technical Committee on Data Engineering, Special Issue on Data Quality, vol. 39, no. 2, pp. 8–20. IEEE Computer Society (2016)
11. Marc, D.T., Beattie, J., Herasevich, V, Gatewood, L., Zhang, R.: Assessing metadata quality of a federally sponsored health data repository. In: AMIA Annual Symposium Proceedings, vol. 2016, p. 864. American Medical Informatics Association (2016)

12. Margaritopoulos, M., Margaritopoulos, T., Mavridis, I., Manitsaris, A.: Quantifying and measuring metadata completeness. J. Assoc. Inf. Sci. Technol. **63**(4), 724–737 (2012)
13. Neumaier, S., Umbrich, J., Polleres, A.: Automated quality assessment of metadata across open data portals. ACM J. Data Inf. Qual. **8**(1) (2016)
14. Ochoa, X., Duval, E.: Automatic evaluation of metadata quality in digital repositories. Int. J. Digit. Libr. **10**(2–3), 67–91 (2009)
15. Palavitsinis, N., Manouselis, N., Sanchez-Alonso, S.: Metadata quality in learning object repositories: a case study. Electron. Libr. **32**(1), 62–82 (2014)
16. Park, J., Tosaka, Y.: Metadata quality control in digital repositories and collections: criteria, semantics, and mechanisms. Cataloging Classif. Q. **48**(8), 696–715 (2010)
17. Rahm, E., Do, H.H.: Data cleaning: problems and current approaches. In: Lomet, D.B., Gravano, L., Levy, A., Sarawagi, S., Weikum, G. (eds.) Bulletin of the Technical Committee on Data Engineering, Special Issue on Data Cleaning, vol. 25, pp. 1–48. IEEE Computer Society (2000)
18. Stvilia, B.: Measuring Information Quality (Dissertation). University of Illinois at Urbana-Champaign (2006)
19. Van Kleeck, D., Langford, G., Lundgren, J., Nakano, H., O'Dell, A.J., Shelton, T.: Managing bibliographic data quality in a consortial academic library: a case study. Cataloging Classif. Q. **54**(7), 452–467 (2016)

Information Education and Libraries

Diversifying the Next Generation of Information Scientists: Six Years of Implementation and Outcomes for a Year-Long REU Program

Kayla M. Booth[1]([⊠]), Bryan Dosono[2], Elissa M. Redmiles[3], Miraida Morales[4],
Michael Depew[1], Rosta Farzan[1], Everett Herman[1], Keith Trahan[1],
and Cindy Tananis[1]

[1] University of Pittsburgh, Pittsburgh, USA
{kbooth,mdepew,rfarzan,everttherman,kwt2,tananis}@pitt.edu
[2] Syracuse University, Syracuse, USA
bdosono@syr.edu
[3] University of Maryland, College Park, USA
eredmiles@cs.umd.edu
[4] Rutgers University, New Brunswick, USA
miraida.morales@rutgers.edu

Abstract. The iSchool Inclusion Institute (i3) is a Research Experience for Undergraduates (REU) program in the US designed to address underrepresentation in the information sciences. i3 is a year-long, cohort-based program that prepares undergraduate students for graduate school in information science and is rooted in a research and leadership development curriculum. Using data from six years of i3 cohorts, we present in this paper a qualitative and quantitative evaluation of the program in terms of student learning, research production, and graduate school enrollment. We find that students who participate in i3 report significant learning gains in information-science- and graduate-school-related areas and that 52% of i3 participants enroll in graduate school, over 2× the national average. Based on these and additional results, we distill recommendations for future implementations of similar programs to address underrepresentation in information science.

1 Background

Within the United States, the computer, library, and information sciences are broadly recognized as lacking racial diversity, particularly at the graduate and faculty levels [2,5,17]. This lack of diversity can stifle innovation, reduce self-efficacy and access to role models, and create social inequity. Only 5% of full professorships in science and engineering are held by underrepresented minorities; doctorates earned by minorities, though having risen slightly since 1991, remain well below 10% [9]. A non-diverse faculty and graduate student body is

© Springer International Publishing AG, part of Springer Nature 2018
G. Chowdhury et al. (Eds.): iConference 2018, LNCS 10766, pp. 655–664, 2018.
https://doi.org/10.1007/978-3-319-78105-1_75

hardly representative of the larger population—and thus, research in the information sciences is less likely to address the most critical challenges facing minority and marginalized groups [12].

Lack of connection to a mentor has been particularly associated with lower likelihood to pursue a graduate degree in STEM or information science (IS) [1,15]. Research experiences for undergraduate programs (REUs) can help develop these connections and improve student retention, especially for minority students in computing [6,17]. A significant body of prior work has shown that REUs can increase students' interest in graduate programs and academic research careers [10,17]. Yet, minority students tend to participate in REUs at much lower rates than their White counterparts [13]—an even greater loss since prior work shows that participation in REUs more positively affects outcomes for minority students than White students [13,14].

The iSchool Inclusion Institute (i3) is an REU that specifically focuses on preparing underrepresented populations for graduate study and careers in IS and related fields. For the purposes of the program, underrepresentation refers to race, ethnicity, gender, socioeconomic status, and intersections of other identity characteristics that are not often present in the information sciences. The goal of i3 is to build a pipeline of underrepresented students to enter the professoriate and larger workforce in IS-related fields. To this end, students accepted into the program engage in hands-on, team-based IS research projects, participate in professional development seminars and instructional modules, and receive direct mentorship from faculty and graduate research advisors. Cohorts range in size from 20 to 25 students. Students from STEM and non-STEM majors are encouraged to apply to ensure greater diversity in participation from scholars interested in a broad range of academic disciplines. Our findings show that i3 has been effective: 52% of i3 students enter graduate programs, 2× the national average for all graduate programs [8], let alone IS-focused programs. As such, we distill recommendations for the deployment of similar programs at other institutions and outline suggestions for future evaluations.

2   Curriculum

The i3 curriculum is separated into three phases. In the first phase, students come to the University of Pittsburgh campus for the month-long summer Introductory Institute to learn about the information sciences, research design, programming, research topics, and graduate school. In the second phase, they participate from their home institutions in a year-long group research project in IS, conducted under the supervision of a senior doctoral student or a faculty member. Finally, a year after the Introductory Institute, students return for the third part of i3: a two-week, on-campus, Concluding Institute, during which they present their research projects and network with the incoming i3 cohort.

2.1   Introductory Institute

During the month-long Introductory Institute, students are introduced to potential research mentors, attend research talks given by CS and IS scholars, and participate in professional development workshops. Minority scholars from universities across the country are invited to present their research, which provides a holistic overview of the topical areas within IS.

Additionally, students participate in two 10-day teaching modules focused on research design and computing methods. These modules are taught by four PhD candidates, who are selected each year as Teaching Fellows. The Fellows co-teach the modules in weeks two and three of the Introductory Institute and live alongside the students to encourage the development of mentoring relationships. Each 75–90 min module session engages students in learning activities that provide collaborative and practical instruction. Active learning is particularly emphasized, as underrepresented students who engage in active learning opportunities such as group projects have been found to be more likely to stay in school and have better grades [13,14]. Additionally, the curriculum of the two modules is synchronized as much as possible, such that the lessons on research concepts and computational methods are complementary and enhance knowledge acquisition.

Research Design Module. This module focuses on the empirical philosophies of experimental, quasi-experimental, and non-experimental designs as a way to present the objective of research as ultimately a problem-solving endeavor [17]. Students learn how epistemology affects methodology, how to turn research problems into research questions, what makes a good research question, how to choose a research method to help answer your research question, and how to analyze data. Important topics also include how to conduct ethical research, how to develop a conceptual framework, and how to present and publish their research.

Programming Module. The programming module provides students with a toolkit of computing and quantitative analysis methods that they can draw upon during their year-long research project. Throughout the two weeks, students are exposed to and experiment with languages and tools such as Python, Tableau, and R to scrape, analyze, visualize, and present data. The programming module sessions typically involve an introductory lecture, a working session in which the students divide into two groups based on prior experience and learning pace, and a full group recap during which challenges and key points from the day are summarized.

2.2   Year-Long Research Projects

During the Introductory Institute, i3 Scholars self-select into research project teams of four to six students. Over the year, teams collaborate remotely to conduct a full IS research project with the goal of producing a conference-quality research poster or paper and an hour-long final presentation. Teams conduct a comprehensive literature review, design their study, and collect and analyze their data under the guidance of a research advisor.

2.3   Concluding Institute

After a year of working remotely, students return to i3 for the Concluding Institute, which overlaps with the last two weeks of the Introductory Institute for new students. Teams finalize and present their research papers and posters. During the Concluding Institute, the returning cohort also lives with and mentors the new cohort of students, who are preparing to embark on their year-long research projects. Finally, students also learn about the publication process and how to submit their project to research conferences in their field, such as iConference, ACM CSCW, and IEEE SeGAH.

3   Evaluation Methods

We evaluate the i3 Program using several metrics. We evaluate learning outcomes across three domains: (1) the information sciences, (2) the research process, and (3) how to navigate graduate program applications and selection.[1] Our evaluation follows a pre-post design, surveying students before and after the Introductory Institute, to enable a comparison of student understandings of IS and the research process, as well as academic plans related to IS before and after the Introductory Institute.

In addition to evaluating learning outcomes from the Introductory Institute, we evaluate the overall i3 program via two metrics: (1) the number of teams who successfully published their research projects at the end of the program, and (2) the number of program alumni currently enrolled in or graduated from graduate programs. Below we detail the data we used in our evaluation, our analysis method, and the limitations of our work.

3.1   Data and Analysis

Survey Instruments. Prior to attending the Introductory Institute, students completed the pre-institute baseline survey questionnaire which asked questions about their knowledge about IS, their interest in graduate school, and knowledge about the graduate school application process on a 5-point Likert-type scale (see Tables 1 and 2 for the questions). At the end of the Introductory Institute, students completed a post-survey questionnaire which contained the same questions, as well as open-ended questions asking them to assess the curriculum. Participants completed all survey questionnaires online via Qualtrics.

Based on the recommendations of research advisors and program alumni, the Programming and Research Design modules were added to the Introductory Institute in 2014 (year 4). Accordingly, we added open-ended questions to the post-institute survey asking Cohorts 2014–2016 for feedback on the modules. Open-ended questions allowed respondents to reflect on which aspects of the

---

[1] We did not collect any identifying respondent information as part of our surveys, and thus our institution's ethics review board determined that this was not human subjects research.

modules were particularly meaningful and/or helpful to them. We identified patterns and themes across responses from all three years of the research design module to complement our survey data with a rich qualitative evaluation of the students' perspective.

To analyze pre- and post-institute survey results, we use paired t-tests – a standard statistical method for comparing pre- and post-treatment sample means [11] – to evaluate whether pre- and post-responses differed significantly. This was complemented by our content analysis of the open-ended responses. Finally, i3 maintains contact with alumni through an annual survey questionnaire, reunions and local meetups, providing letters of recommendation for applications and scholarships, and mentoring. We use data collected through alumni correspondence and via the alumni survey to calculate the number of research publications and graduate program enrollments/completions for each cohort.

3.2 Limitations

As is true of many evaluation studies, not all participants in the program chose to respond to the survey questionnaires. Thus, our data may not fully represent all student experiences. However, given that our mean response rate is 95%, we feel that our data provide a reasonable basis for evaluation. Additionally, it is possible that data validity may have suffered due to desirability bias. To mitigate desirability bias, we collected no identifying information from participants and assured them that all data would be aggregated for analysis.

4 Results

4.1 Knowledge Gains in the Information Sciences and Research

Overall, we find that participation in i3 significantly increases students' perceived knowledge about IS (see Table 1). We find a significant, nearly two out of five-point increase in perceived knowledge of subject areas in IS ($\overline{\Delta} = 1.91$) and a significant, one-point increase in perceived understanding of the impacts of technology ($\overline{\Delta} = 1.02$) following the Introductory Institute.

In addition to learning about IS fundamentals, participants reported learning about the research process. Students reported feeling that they were effectively and "thoroughly" introduced to the basic steps of conducting research, expressing sentiments such as *"I thought [the Research Design module] did a great job putting each step of the research project into perspective."*

For some students, research was new or uncomfortable territory. Participants explained how they felt after the institute, stating *"[The Teaching Fellows] aided me to understand in such small amount of time how the research process works,"* and *"I most definitely know how to plan an analysis, make a literary review, and not look stupid during a research presentation ever again."* For other participants who had prior research experience, many indicated that the program helped clarify or deepen their knowledge, explaining *"What I found helpful was the*

Table 1. Mean Likert ratings (from 1–5) on knowledge of each topic. P-value statistics are calculated based on paired t-test comparison of the baseline and post survey scores; significant p-values (<0.05) are marked with *.

Question	Cohort	Baseline	Post	p-value
The diversity and breadth of subject areas within the information sciences	2011	2.38	4.65	<0.0001*
	2012	2.24	4.74	<0.0001*
	2013	2.40	4.47	<0.0001*
	2014	2.96	4.59	<0.0001*
	2015	2.73	3.96	<0.0001*
	2016	2.81	4.55	<0.0001*
The social, political, legal and ethical impacts of technology	2011	3.29	4.50	<0.0001*
	2012	3.41	4.16	0.0201*
	2013	3.30	4.32	0.0016*
	2014	3.54	4.32	0.0008*
	2015	3.35	4.33	0.0004*
	2016	3.31	4.68	<0.0001*

clarification...[I gained] a deeper appreciation for research design. I can now clearly and confidently speak and identify various types of research design in different studies."

When commenting on the Research Design module, participants particularly highlighted two effective elements: (1) the use of concrete examples: *"clear examples and ke[pt] it simple. It made it very easy to understand the concepts and topics each day."* and (2) the direct application of concepts, *"The best takeaway from the Research Design Modules was the hands-on approach of applying the information within each session. By breaking up into groups and creating research questions, as well as mock proposals for grant money I had a better understanding of the material as well as the realization on how it gets applied."*

4.2   Interest in Pursuing Graduate Programs

In addition to assessing increases in perceived knowledge and what they valued about the new research module, we also examined students' interest in pursuing graduate programs in IS and the application process. Table 2 presents the mean across cohorts of students' perceived likelihood of pursuing a graduate degree in IS and their perceived learning about the application process.

Our results suggest that i3 students are already interested in graduate school upon their arrival to the Introductory Institute, and thus while we see an increase in interest in graduate school across all cohorts, this increase is significant for only two of six cohorts. However, we do observe a significant, nearly two-point increase in students perceived understanding of how to apply to graduate school and select which programs to which to apply ($\overline{\Delta} = 1.86$). This is especially important, as prior work has found that self-efficacy and confidence in ability are essential elements of success within IT, CS, and other STEM fields [16].

Table 2. Mean Likert ratings (from 1–5) on knowledge of each topic. See Table 1 for detailed caption.

Question	Cohort	Baseline	Post	p-value
Knowledge of processes and requirements for applying to graduate school and selecting an academic program	2011	2.62	4.75	<0.0001*
	2012	3.00	4.58	<0.0001*
	2013	2.45	4.72	<0.0001*
	2014	2.75	4.57	<0.0001*
	2015	2.88	4.42	<0.0001*
	2016	2.77	4.57	<0.0001*
Likelihood of pursuing a graduate degree in IS	2011	3.90	4.40	0.0538
	2012	3.31	4.29	0.0235*
	2013	3.65	3.72	0.8222
	2014	3.67	4.13	0.0866
	2015	3.65	3.88	0.4132
	2016	3.65	4.29	0.0141*

4.3   Research Publications and Graduate School Enrollment

To evaluate i3 in general, we analyze two non-self-reported metrics — research productivity and graduate school enrollment — which are believed to be key indicators of REU program success [3]. At the time of this paper's submission, 23 of 28 research teams have successfully published and presented their projects at an academic conference, resulting in a total of 24 peer-reviewed publications (one team published twice). This level of productivity is at least comparable to and generally higher than similar REU programs in other fields [4,7]. Twenty-one of these publications were papers or posters at iConference, one was a poster at ACM Computer-Supported Cooperative Work and Social Computing (CSCW), one was a poster at IEEE Serious Games and Applications for Health (IEEE SeGAH), and one was a paper at the Serious Play Conference.

Of the 135 students who were accepted to and enrolled in Cohorts 2011–2016, 117 completed i3; 32 of these alumni are still enrolled in undergraduate programs. Of the 85 alumni who have completed an undergraduate degree, 44 (52%) are currently enrolled in or have completed graduate programs, 2× the national attendance for underrepresented minorities [8]. Of those 44 graduate students, 35 (80%) are enrolled in or have completed programs in or related to IS.

5   Discussion and Recommendations

Our analysis highlights three key findings. First, i3 scholars indicate increases in their understanding of the information sciences and self-efficacy regarding conducting research. Second, students who largely arrived with an interest in graduate school learned about programs specific to IS, and gained self-efficacy and knowledge about how to apply to and select IS graduate programs. Finally, the i3 program results in high rates of research productivity, with 23 out of 28 teams publishing a poster or paper at an academic conference, and results in high rates of graduate school enrollment: 52% of i3 students enroll in graduate programs and 80% of those graduate programs are in IS. Thus, we conclude that i3 is an effective approach to developing a pipeline for underrepresented students to enter the information sciences field.

Upon completing the program, students reported an increased awareness of the information sciences as a multi-disciplinary field. Several factors may contribute to this increase in awareness. First, students across a variety of undergraduate majors were recruited to i3. This resulted in research teams comprised of students with diverse approaches, experiences, and interests collaborating with one another to conduct research, underscoring the interdisciplinary nature of the IS field. Additionally, i3's curriculum is built on workshops delivered by numerous iSchool faculty and PhD students from different departments and schools across the country whose areas of research represent the full range of the IS field. This exposes i3 scholars to the vast topical breadth of the field and to the various methods employed. Our analysis shows this curriculum design may encourage a holistic understanding of the field in ways that a single instructor may not. The variation in research topics and methodologies helped students explore the intersections between people, information, and technology across different contexts. Participants expressed feeling they could apply what they were passionate about in their own disciplines to opportunities and areas within IS. This holistic curriculum design encourages students to see the ways in which different topics within IS and their current majors intersect.

Respondents also indicated that their skills and confidence conducting IS research increased. This perception of increased skill and ability is noteworthy in that much of the extant literature suggests that self-efficacy and confidence in their abilities is a key component of retention for underrepresented students in STEM [6]. Additionally, the majority of the research projects were accepted to conferences, which may demonstrate to students that their contributions are valuable to the field, and may enhance to their sense of belonging to a research community outside of i3. Additionally, the year-long project gave students an opportunity to work with a research advisor, which provides students with another mentor (in addition to i3 faculty and staff). This perception of skill building, successful completion of their year-long projects, connections to mentors, and subsequent publications may all contribute to increased self-efficacy, a hypothesis worthy of further investigation.

Participation in i3 also increased participants understanding of how to apply to and select graduate programs in IS. Additionally, i3 scholars come from a myriad of academic disciplines, yet the majority of scholars who are enrolled in or have completed graduate school have done so in IS. This indicates the potential of REUs to play a meaningful role in the recruitment of underrepresented students into IS.

This evaluation and analysis of the i3 program serves two functions: (1) it details a pipeline initiative that positively addresses underrepresentation within IS, providing a curriculum outline and outcome metrics that we hope will encourage other iSchools to adopt a similar approach; and (2) it provides a basis for deeper investigation into the role of REUs and associated curriculum in IS. As these results draw from North American contexts, we encourage researchers to analyze learning outcomes of REUs in IS across the globe to extrapolate broader implementation strategies among the international iSchool community. In the next section we outline recommendations for future evaluation work.

6 Future Work

This evaluation and analysis shows that participants feel they are learning research skills and are successfully publishing their projects at peer-reviewed IS-related conferences while working with peers and mentors. i3 Scholars learn how to select and apply to graduate programs and 44 i3 alumni are enrolled in or have completed graduate school (the majority of which were IS-related programs). Though these findings suggest that the i3 program is successful in building a pipeline for underrepresented students into the information sciences, these indicators of success are only a preliminary step to fully understanding the implications of such a program.

The next step is to conduct a deeper qualitative analysis of the subjective experiences i3 Scholars attribute to helping them succeed in the program, as well as how they relate their time in the program to their post-graduate paths. Through this work, we can better understand how, why, and in what ways the different components of the program are meaningful to emerging scholars and their professional trajectories.

7 Conclusion

The results of our analysis suggest that i3 is a successful intervention for contributing to the creation of a pipeline of underrepresented students heading to IS graduate programs. It suggests that an immersive, team-based, and research-focused approach to IS is an effective way to introduce students to the breadth of the field. Our evaluation is one of the first, to our knowledge, to explore an intervention specifically designed to address underrepresentation in the information sciences and the iSchool community. Our results align with extant literature that demonstrates the potential for undergraduate research to build confidence and self-efficacy important for recruitment and retention in STEM fields. Additionally, these results provide a foundation for deeper research into how participants experience different program components, and what aspects of the program they most value and why. Further exploration of i3 offers a unique opportunity to iteratively design and evaluate a curriculum that addresses one of IS deepest challenges: inclusion and diverse representation. More broadly, future work for the iSchool community as a whole may involve the creation and evaluation of additional, similar programs at iSchools around the world as we work to "transform digital worlds" and create a more diverse community of information scientists.

References

1. Ashcraft, C., Eger, E., Friend, M.: Girls in IT: The Facts. National Center for Women & IT, Boulder (2012)
2. Aspray, W., Bernat, A.: Recruitment and retention of underrepresented minority graduate students in computer science. In: Report on a Workshop by the Coalition to Diversity Computing (2000)
3. Beninson, L.A., Koski, J., Villa, E., Faram, R., OConnor, S.E.: Evaluation of the research experiences for undergraduates (REU) sites program. The emerging role of exosomes in stress physiology (2013)
4. Brey, E.M., Campanile, M.F., Lederman, N.G.: Evaluation of a nine year summer undergraduate research program in biomedical engineering. In: ASEE Annual Conference and Exposition (2015)
5. Cuny, J., Aspray, W.: Recruitment and retention of women graduate students in computer science and engineering: results of a workshop organized by the computing research association. SIGCSE Bull. **34**(2), 168–174 (2002)
6. Dahlberg, T., Barnes, T., Rorrer, A., Powell, E., Cairco, L.: Improving retention and graduate recruitment through immersive research experiences for undergraduates. SIGCSE Bull. **40**(1), 466–470 (2008)
7. Follmer, D.J., Zappe, S.E., Gomez, E.W., Kumar, M.: Preliminary evaluation of a research experience for undergraduates (REU) program: a methodology for examining student outcomes. In: ASEE Annual Conference and Exposition (2015)
8. National Center for Education Statistics: Status and trends in the education of racial and ethnic minorities
9. National Center for Science and Engineering Statistics: Women, minorities, and persons with disabilities in science and engineering. Technical report (2013)
10. Hernandez, P.R., Schultz, P., Estrada, M., Woodcock, A., Chance, R.C.: Sustaining optimal motivation: a longitudinal analysis of interventions to broaden participation of underrepresented students in STEM. J. Educ. Psychol. **105**, 89–107 (2013)
11. Hsu, H., Lachenbruch, P.A.: Paired t test. In: Wiley Encyclopedia of Clinical Trials (2008)
12. Jaeger, P.T., Franklin, R.E.: The virtuous circle: increasing diversity in LIS faculties to create more inclusive library services and outreach. Educ. Libr. **30**(1), 20–26 (2007)
13. Kinzie, J., Gonyea, R., Shoup, R., Kuh, G.D.: Promoting persistence and success of underrepresented students: lessons for teaching and learning. Technical report 115 (2008)
14. Kuh, G.D., Kinzie, J., Cruce, T., Shoup, R., Gonyea, R.M.: Connecting the dots: multi-faceted analyses of the relationships between student engagement results from the NSSE, and the institutional practices and conditions that foster student success. Technical report 547556 (2006)
15. May, G.S., Chubin, D.E.: A retrospective on undergraduate engineering success for underrepresented minority students. J. Eng. Educ. **92**(1), 27–39 (2003)
16. Trauth, E.M., Cain, C.C., Joshi, K.D., Kvasny, L., Booth, K.M.: The influence of gender-ethnic intersectionality on gender stereotypes about IT skills and knowledge. SIGMIS Database **47**(3), 9–39 (2016)
17. Weinman, J., Jensen, D., Lopatto, D.: Teaching computing as science in a research experience. In: SIGCSE. ACM (2015)

Where Are iSchools Heading?

Vikas Yadav[✉], Farig Sadeque, Bryan Heidorn, and Hong Cui

School of Information, University of Arizona, 1103 E 2nd St., Tucson, AZ 85721, USA
{vikasy,farig,heidron,hongcui}@email.arizona.edu

Abstract. iSchools are highly interdisciplinary in nature - hence the direction and vision of iSchools have attracted researchers from various disciplines in recent times. In this paper, we analyzed the contents of the courses offered by 22 iSchools from different parts of the world. Our system extracts information from the course descriptions offered by different iSchools and visualizes the current trend of offering more courses with substantially more emphasis on computation than other paradigms. The architecture of our system is simple yet powerful - which may encourage others to implement similar techniques in different iSchool-related research.

1 Introduction

iSchools are emerging as one of the most exciting fields in academia all over the world. Being interdisciplinary and heterogeneous in nature, iSchools never focuses on one single field of study. Many researchers, faculties, students with completely different expertise and interests are working together in iSchools to innovate with technologies. Most of these iSchools have originated from conventional Library and Information Sciences departments [2], whereas only a handful originated from other related departments. Our study has suggested that it is difficult to explore the entire spectrum of research visions of an iSchool from the introductory page of that school, which could confuse prospective students and researchers trying to identify their respective research interest on iSchool websites. For example, many iSchools promote library science research in their websites, while the faculty continuously try to broaden the horizon using informatics, information technology, data science, machine learning etc. The contents of the offered courses, on the other hand, more truthfully reflect research/instructional domains of an iSchool and those are the primary source this study targets.

In this paper, we propose a novel information extraction and visualization technique that studies the course contents offered by 22 iSchools and reflects the shift in research and teaching focus towards a more computationally intensive paradigm. Our goal is to help researchers and students understand the vision, research focus and, most importantly, future directions of the iSchools. This paper also attempts to encourage other iSchool researchers by providing the idea of a simple web tool that can be used for similar analysis on iSchools' data.

© Springer International Publishing AG, part of Springer Nature 2018
G. Chowdhury et al. (Eds.): iConference 2018, LNCS 10766, pp. 665–670, 2018.
https://doi.org/10.1007/978-3-319-78105-1_76

2   Previous Works

Andrew Dillon focused on various attributes of iSchools like intellectual coverage, interdisciplinarity and research commitment in his 2012 paper [4]. He also talked about the growth of iSchools in last 2 decades and about different universities who started this revolution of transforming conventional LIS schools to iSchools. Wiggins and Sawyer [13] analyzed faculty hiring trends among those involved in the iSchool community to better understand the intellectual heritage and major influences shaping the development of the individual and collective identities in iSchools. They presented a classification of the intellectual domains of iSchool faculty and visualized the development of iSchools in terms of interdisciplinary research, computational courses and inclusion of many social studies fields which were absent in the LIS schools. Bertot [2] wrote a report on engagement events and speaker series on re-envisioning process of LIS. The report depicts an excellent view of how LIS has changed, and now under the name of iSchool, covers broader scope of Information Sciences of community and people. Nathan et al. [10] explored how an iSchool's prospective has been different from that of an LIS school and observed that iSchools are uniquely centered for designing proactive and adaptive policies for social and online media. Mulder and van Weert [9] published a report about effective course curriculum in informatics field, which are quite similar to our findings of courses in iSchools. Hildreth [6] presented a report on merging of LIS schools with neighboring informatics and computing school for overall development of LIS schools. Marchionini et al's report on careers, educational pathways, potentials and scopes of information specialists and graduates by 2050 covered aspects and reason of the recent transformations in iSchools [8]. Rathbun-Grubb [11] presented a poster tracking careers of information graduates from iSchools where she stated that career tracking of graduates can provide iSchools with useful data for strategic planning of programs and engagement activities.

3   Proposed Work and Findings

As we have already mentioned, information science is vastly interdisciplinary - it concerns itself with the collection, analysis, classification, manipulation, storage, retrieval, use, etc. of information [12]. iSchools are the institutions that enable researchers to focus on these tasks. The main reason of iSchools covering this many number of disciplines is the immense demand of information scientists in various domains. There has been a boom of information science jobs in recent years and this trend is expected to grow exponentially in the coming years [3,5]. With this trend, demand for information scientists has also increased exponentially. Information security, cyber security, Information policy, digital archiving, information extraction, Human Computer Interaction (HCI), Machine Learning etc. are the new core fields where the demand of information scientists are at its all-time high. Online social networking platforms, online education societies, data science, health informatics are some important areas where Information scientists are required. There is a similar trend of shifting towards computational research in other fields also like chemistry and biology [1].

Here we propose a simple information extraction and visualization system which extracts course names and descriptions from iSchools course webpages and visualizes the extracted information in 2 classes - courses in LIS and courses in computing. This system is still in the early process of development which will later turn into an online iSchool webpage monitoring system and we aim to monitor multiple informations.

Our current visualization system has the following steps:

- Takes input of the list of course webpages links of iSchools.
- Extracts text (course names and course description) from HTML pages.
- Preprocesses the extracted text - applies stemming and also lowercases the words. We have used Porter Stemmer stemming technique [7] for stemming the words.
- Develop the count of courses-related terminologies in each domain by dictionary lookup from pre-built domain specific dictionaries.
- Plots the histogram of collected counts.

We have run our system on webpages of 22 iSchools which are mostly from iCaucus and related organizations. We have considered only those iSchools which have provided course descriptions along with the course names. This was done to avoid ambiguity from the names of the courses. For example - course named "Information Science" can be both in Computing domain and LIS domain. After selecting iSchools from iCaucus lists, we selected few more iSchools from different countries which provided the course descriptions. The downloaded course webpages of selected iSchools can be found on Github[1]. We have built a small dictionary for words in computing domain and words in LIS domain. We first selected the most frequent words from the HTML pages after removing stop words and then we manually selected a set of words similar to course names and created dictionaries containing unigrams - which are shown in Table 1.

Table 1. Dictionaries of unigrams for LIS and computing domains

	Unigrams
Computing	Health, computational, human, computer, interaction, informatics, cyber, security, game, design, web, development, search, machine, learning, technology, digital, graphic, game, language, software, coding, programming, cryptography, data, science, mining, computing, artificial, intelligence, database
LIS	Library, archive, privacy, information, privacy, policy, security, digital, curation, collections, cataloging, society, media, management, art, law, records, public, librarianship, resources, digitization, preservation, knowledge, librarians, services, administration, communities

---

[1] https://github.com/vikas95/I-Conference-2018/tree/master/HTML_pages.

To ensure that we are not missing derived variations of words, we used stemming. Stemming is the process of reducing derived words to their root or base form. For example, the word "archive", along with its multiple variations like "archival" or "archiving" is reduced to "archiv" after applying Porter Stemmer stemming algorithm. Because of stemming, we can compute the count of each word in each dictionary more efficiently. The code for this project can be found on Github[2].

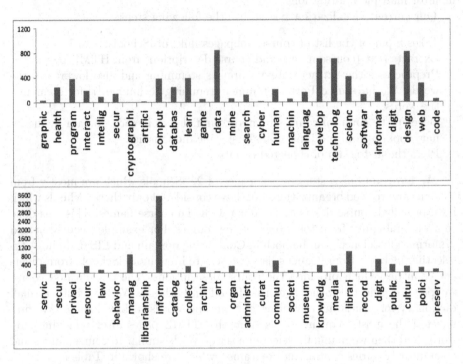

Fig. 1. Histogram of unigram counts from dictionary, top: computing, bottom: LIS.

We are representing 2 categories: "computing" and "LIS" in this paper to show iSchools' focus in LIS and computing domains. We have not included course webpages of Ischool programs which completely focus on Computing domain. For example - we have not included course web pages from programs like MS in data science and MS in Information management (similar to MIS degree) as these can heavily bias our analysis towards computing domain. We also ignored analysis on bigrams because of huge variability in the bigrams of course names in LIS domain across different universities. For example, courses like "Information theory" is named as "Fundamental theory of information" and "Information science and theory" in different schools.

---

2 https://github.com/vikas95/I-Conference-2018.

Table 2. Words distribution of course webpages of 22 iSchools

Domains	% of domain words
Unigrams belonging to conventional LIS	59.36
Unigrams belonging to computation	40.64

The distribution of computing and LIS words from course webpages of iSchools are shown in Table 2. Figure 1 has the histogram plots of occurrences of unigrams in respective categories. Few unigrams like "inform*" are skewing the final results since inform* (after stemming of "information") kind of fits for both computing and library domain.

As mentioned before, we have analyzed only information science course webpages and we got 40.64% of unigrams belonging to computing domain. This number indicates that iSchools are focusing a lot more on computational paradigm albeit being historically dominated by library science, archival science, data curation etc. As there are many more job and research opportunities in computing domain as compared to conventional LIS [3], this approach makes sense too-focusing more on computational studies can help broaden the horizon of iSchool graduates and researchers.

4   Future Work

As we have seen in Sect. 2, there have been works where researchers analyzed a school's research interest by surveying faculty hirings and looking into the jobs of the recent graduates. Incorporating these techniques in our task will certainly improve the quality of the analysis. Increasing the number of schools in the analysis dataset will give us a broader scope, and adding schools from different parts of the world will hopefully add a global perspective to this research. Improving upon the dictionaries based on their relevance with a certain research field will improve the quality of the analysis, and adding more tokens like word n-grams can also help.

Temporal aspect of this research can also be an exciting opportunity. We have analyzed the current status of the schools, but attempts can be made to analyze this from a temporal perspective. We can gather old course information from archived websites of the iSchools and try to establish the fact that indeed iSchools are moving towards a more computation-oriented research. This research can be done annually to establish a timeline of research interests of iSchools, and can help future students and researchers tremendously.

5   Conclusion

Our paper analyzes course contents provided by select iSchool websites and from the analysis we can observe that information science schools are using significant computing-related course contents. This analysis has hinted that iSchools are moving towards a more computationally relevant course and research structure, and a future temporal study will be able to confirm this. This apparently high focus on computational courses may translate into a better future research and job opportunity for iSchool graduates with more computational experience. Our analysis also suggests that it can be beneficial to observe the evolution of course contents over time, and a web monitoring system can come in extremely handy for this purpose.

References

1. Amos, M., Dittrich, P., McCaskill, J., Rasmussen, S.: Biological and chemical information technologies. Procedia Comput. Sci. **7**(Suppl. C), 56–60 (2011). http://www.sciencedirect.com/science/article/pii/S1877050911006843. Proceedings of the 2nd European Future Technologies Conference and Exhibition 2011 (FET 2011)
2. Bertot, J.C., Sarin, L.C., Percell, J.: Re-envisioning the MLS: findings, issues, and considerations. University of Maryland College Park, College of Information Studies, College Park (2015). Accessed 15 Aug 2015
3. Boumarafi, B.: Linking library profession and the market place: finding connections for the library in the digital environment, March 2015
4. Dillon, A.: What it means to be an iSchool. J. Educ. Libr. Inf. Sci. **53**, 267–273 (2012)
5. Frey, C.B., Osborne, M.A.: The future of employment: how susceptible are jobs to computerisation? Technol. Forecast. Soc. Chang. **114**, 254–280 (2017)
6. Hildreth, C.R., Koenig, M.: Organizational realignment of LIS programs in academia: from independent standalone units to incorporated programs. J. Educ. Libr. Inf. Sci. **43**, 126–133 (2002)
7. Loper, E., Bird, S.: NLTK: the natural language toolkit. In: Proceedings of the ACL 2002 Workshop on Effective Tools and Methodologies for Teaching Natural Language Processing and Computational Linguistics, ETMTNLP 2002, vol. 1, pp. 63–70. Association for Computational Linguistics, Stroudsburg (2002). https://doi.org/10.3115/1118108.1118117
8. Moran, B.B., Marchionini, G.: Information professionals 2050: educating the next generation of information professionals. Inf. Serv. Use **32**(3–4), 95–100 (2012)
9. Mulder, F., van Weert, T.: IFIP/UNESCO's informatics curriculum framework 2000 for higher education. SIGCSE Bull. **33**(4), 75–83 (2001). https://doi.org/10.1145/572139.572177
10. Nathan, L.P., MacGougan, A., Shaffer, E.: If not us, who? social media policy and the iSchool classroom. J. Educ. Libr. Inf. Sci. **55**(2), 112–132 (2014)
11. Rathbun-Grubb, S.: What happens to iSchool graduates? using career data to support iSchool engagement initiatives (2011). http://wilis.unc.edu/files/2011/09/Rathbun-Grubb-iSchools-poster-FNL.pdf
12. Stock, W.G., Stock, M.: Handbook of Information Science. De Gruyter Saur, Berlin (2013)
13. Wiggins, A., Sawyer, S.: Intellectual diversity and the faculty composition of iSchools. J. Am. Soc. Inform. Sci. Technol. **63**(1), 8–21 (2012)

Drawing the "Big Picture" Concerning Digital 3D Technologies for Humanities Research and Education

Sander Münster[(✉)] [iD]

Media Center, Technische Universität Dresden, 01062 Dresden, Germany
sander.muenster@tu-dresden.de

Abstract. Digital 3D modelling and visualization technologies have been widely applied to support research in the humanities since the 1980s. Since an academic discourse on these methods is still highly application-oriented, this article reports about both completed and planned investigations that are part of an ongoing post doc thesis work intending to drawing a "big picture" of digital 3D technologies for humanities research and education on EU level. Incorporated studies investigate scholarly communities, usage practices, methodologies as well as the development of technologies and generate design implications as well as educational strategies.

Keywords: Digital 3D technologies · Digital humanities
Practice-based education · Design implications

1 Introduction

For more than 30 years, digital 3D modelling and visualization technologies have been widely used to support research and education in the humanities, especially but not exclusively on historical architecture. In focus of 3D workflows are spatial, temporal, and semantic virtual models (c.f. Fig. 1) of material and immaterial (e.g. rites or dances) objects. Another essential differentiation affecting digital modelling is between those objects which are no longer existent or which have never been realized (e.g. the current status of plans which were not implemented) and objects which still exist [1], which closely relates to different workflows for modelling [2]. While technological backgrounds, project opportunities, and methodological considerations for the application of digital 3D technologies are widely discussed in literature [e.g. 3–5], my interest is to drawing a currently missing "big picture" and to deriving implications for further organizational and methical development by investigating the following research questions:

- What marks a scholarly culture concerning 3D modelling and visualization in the humanities?
- What are conceptual, technical and designal implications and workflows?
- How can digital 3D technologies be learned and taught?

© Springer International Publishing AG, part of Springer Nature 2018
G. Chowdhury et al. (Eds.): iConference 2018, LNCS 10766, pp. 671–676, 2018.
https://doi.org/10.1007/978-3-319-78105-1_77

   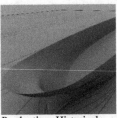

| Visualization: Non-realized baroque garden architecture | Schemes: Column order and vault arrangement of a medieval crypt | Simulation: Visibility analysis of main structures of Santiago de Compostela | Production: Historical ship hull modelled from original blueprint for rapid prototyping |

Fig. 1. Exemplified application scenarios for 3D modelling technologies in the humanities

As many other novel academic fields the community dealing with 3D technologies in the humanities incorporates various disciplinary perspectives. From the perspective of the digital humanities, the application of computing to support humanities research is in focus [c.f. 6]. Since cultural heritage is object of 3D modelling and visualization, another community focuses on the use of computing to preserve, educate and research cultural heritage [c.f. 7]. Furthermore, there are also specific communities in the involved humanities disciplines as for instance digital art and architectural history [8] and digital archaeology [9], which uses 3D technologies to cope with the "material evidence" of past culture. Even if these communities attract different people, it would be questionable and is part of my research if approaches, technologies and methodologies are similar.

2 Research Design

The research presented is part of an ongoing post doc thesis work. Against this background, my own and my department's activities include to investigate (1) the scholarly communities, (2) usage practices occurring within single projects and to gain implications for (3) further methodical development. We develop (4) technologies and workflows to enhance both, the creation of 3D models and of user-centered interfaces, and investigate how 3D models are (5) perceived and how 3D modelling techniques can be used in (6) education (c.f. Table 1). Research methods and guiding theories derive from many fields such as information studies, environmental and cognition psychology, sociology (as e.g. for the constitution of *diciplines*), education but also from economy studies (as e.g. for project management principles), computing (e.g. visualization, data architecture and usability engineering), historic disciplines and philosophy. Research has been carried out since 2010 in 12 projects on local, national and EU level so far.

Table 1. Investigational parts

Area	Research interest	Investigation
Scholarly community	Who are main authors? What are academic structures?	[A] Social network and bibliometric analysis of publications from major conferences in the field of digital cultural heritage 1990–2015 (n = 3917). Results: [7]
	What are topics?	[B] Automated topic mining of 3917 articles, manual classification of 452 articles plus 26 project reports via qualitative content analysis. Results: [10]
	Who funds projects?	[C] Qualitative content analysis of 518 projects in the field of digital cultural heritage. Results: [7]
	What marks a disciplinary culture?	[D] Three stage investigation including a questionnaire-based survey during three workshops with 44 participants to gain a general overview; 15 guideline based interviews with researchers to investigate research culture in depth; online survey with 988 participant to quantify findings. Results: [11]
Usage practices	What are phenomena and strategies for cooperation?	[E] 4 case studies: Data collection via expert interviews and observation. Data analysis via heuristic frameworks and grounded theory. For results see [2, 12]
	How to support cooperation in 3D modelling projects?	[F] Employment and evaluation of SCRUM as agile project management approach in an educational project seminar with 3 student teams [13]
Methodological development	What are current challenges?	[G] Three group discussions during workshops at national/international conferences (~60 participants); online survey with 700 participants. See [14, 15]
	How to systematize?	[H] Classification scheme developed and applied for 8 projects yet. For results see [16]
Technologies	How to create 3D models?	[I] Development of workflows and toolsets to automatically create 3D models from historic photos and semi-automatic creation from GIS data. See [17]
	How to improve user interaction with 3D models?	[J] Development and testing of 4D geo browsers; browser-based augmented and virtual reality interfaces for mobile devices. For results see [18]
Perception	What factors are influencing perception of 3D models?	[K] 2 expert workshops and literature survey yet to identify influencing factors
	How are virtually represented structures perceived?	[L] Two studies to investigate how virtually represented architecture is perceived, involving 21 persons and using usability testing. Results: [19]
Education	How to teach 3D modelling techniques?	[M] 3 student seminars to develop and test team project-based learning approaches via formative & summative assessment. See e.g. [20]

3 Results

What are the results at a glance? Considering a scholarly community on digital 3D technologies in the humanities, discourses on major conferences during the last 25 years were mainly led by institutions from European Mediterranean countries, covering primarily technological topics and being mainly driven by technological trends. Especially statues and buildings in Mediterranean countries dating from all periods Anno Domini deliver rich content for such reconstruction. Concerning the relevance of individual topics, especially data management was most frequently named, ranging from GIS and BIM to metadata schemes and data architecture. It was followed by data acquisition by photogrammetry, laserscanning and other surveying technologies. Due to the high complexity and team-based workflows, aspects and usage practices for communication, cooperation, and quality management are of high relevance within projects for 3D modelling and visualization of no more extant architecture. Especially if people with different disciplinary backgrounds are involved, visual media are intensively used to foster communication and quality negotiations, for example by comparing source images and renderings of the created virtual reconstruction. Furthermore, several projects successfully adopted highly standardized conventions from architectural drawings for interdisciplinary exchange. To support a methodological development we ran five workshops to identify prospects and demands for further development, involving around 60 researchers, and an online survey with 700 participants to verify findings from these workshops. Money and missing awareness were named as currently most pressuring issues. Demands are the development of human resources. Further requests included sustainable and practicable approaches to access wider scientific communities, widely interoperable documentation and classification strategies, an overarching cataloguing of projects and objects as well as strategies and technologies for an exchange between different technological domains [c.f. 14, 15]. With regards to technologies, a big hurdle for employing augmented and virtual reality is the current need to download and install additional software as well as use specialized hardware. Since current browser generations allow the visualization of 3D content natively, our focus is on user-friendly interaction concepts to access both visualizations and underlaying informations [c.f. 18]. Regarding the perception of virtual 3D models, relatively little visual information is needed to allow observers to distinguish buildings from each other or to identify single buildings and to gain information about its spatial relation and shape [19]. Moreover, we adopted and evaluated team project-based learning approaches to support student education in digital 3D reconstruction. As observed in two courses so far, strategies for cooperation within student project teams for creating virtual representations evolves slowly, and mostly as reaction of upcoming problems and demands. Related competencies are highly based on implicit knowledge and experience. As consequence, a teaching of best practices prior to a project work is less effective than coaching during the project work [c.f. 20].

4   Outlook

Since it is my vision to establish digital 3D technologies as a scholarly accepted and widely used method for humanities research and education, it seems to be crucial to add a critically reflected methodological basis and anchor it in academic culture. What are next steps? Since 3D models in the humanities are primarily accessed via visualizations, a toolset for assessing visualization and interactivity of 3D models and presentations is currently missing and will be in focus of a next research stage. Many of the already completed investigations are of qualitative nature or focus on particular aspects.

Consequently, a further validation for adjacent aspects as well as a verification of findings are alltime tasks. To proceed, further investigations on the scholarly use of 3D technologies and historical photographs or the design of interfaces for virtual museums are under development. Since the research is intended to enhance the validation and dissemination of 3D modelling and visualization technologies in the humanities, both education and organizational development are key issues. Beside the further development and establishment of teaching concepts and university courses, especially strategies for self-driven and scalable learning as MOOCs or open educational resources seems promising. Finally, beneficial and methodologically grounded best practice examples, an institutionalization of chairs and institutes as well as an increased awareness seem to be crucial for a further organizational establishment.

References

1. De Francesco, G., D'Andrea, A.: Standards and guidelines for quality digital cultural three-dimensional content creation. In: VSMM (2008)
2. Münster, S.: Workflows and the role of images for a virtual 3D reconstruction of no longer extant historic objects. In: ISPRS Annals of the Photogrammetry, Remote Sensing and Spatial Information Sciences (XXIV International CIPA Symposium), vol. II-5/W1, pp. 197–202 (2013)
3. Arnold, D., Geser, G.: EPOCH research agenda – final report, Brighton (2008)
4. Frischer, B.: Beyond Illustration: 2D and 3D Digital Technologies as Tools for Discovery in Archaeology. BAR International Series, vol. 1805. Tempus Reparatum, Oxford (2008)
5. Bentkowska-Kafel, A., Denard, H., Baker, D.: Paradata and Transparency in Virtual Heritage. Ashgate, Burlington (2012)
6. Schreibman, S., Siemens, R., Unsworth, J.: A Companion to Digital Humanities. Blackwell, Oxford (2004)
7. Münster, S, Ioannides, M.: The scientific community of digital heritage in time and space. In: Guidi, G., Scopigno, R., Torres, J.C., Graf, H. (eds.) 2nd International Congress on Digital Heritage 2015, Granada (2015). ISBN 978-1-5090-0048-7/15
8. Burdick, A., Drucker, J., Lunenfeld, P., Presner, T., Schnapp, J.: Digital_Humanities. The MIT Press, Cambridge (2012)
9. Evans, T.L., Daly, P.T.: Digital Archaeology: Bridging Method and Theory. Routledge, London (2006)
10. Münster, S.: Employing bibliometric methods to identify a community, topics and protagonists of digital 3D reconstruction in the humanities. In: Sterzer, W. (ed.) iConference 2017 Proceedings, iSchools, pp. 40–55 (2017). https://doi.org/10.9776/17100
11. Münster, S.: A survey on topics, researchers and cultures in the field of digital heritage. In: ISPRS Annals of the Photogrammetry, Remote Sensing and Spatial Information Sciences, vol. IV-2/W2, pp. 157–162 (2017)
12. Münster, S.: Interdisziplinäre Kooperation bei der Erstellung geschichtswissenschaftlicher 3D-Rekonstruktionen. Springer, Wiesbaden (2016)
13. Herrmann, I., Münster, S., Tietz, V., Uhlemann, R.: Teaching media design by using scrum. A qualitative study within a media informatics' elective course. In: Sampson, D.G., Spector, J.M., Ifenthaler, D., Isaías, P. (eds.) Proceedings of the 14th International Conference on Cognition and Exploratory Learning in the Digital Age, pp. 227–232. IADIS Press (2017)

14. Münster, S., Kuroczyński, P., Pfarr-Harfst, M., Grellert, M., Lengyel, D.: Future research challenges for a computer-based interpretative 3D reconstruction of cultural heritage – a German community's view. In: ISPRS Annals of the Photogrammetry, Remote Sensing and Spatial Information Sciences (XXV International CIPA Symposium), vol. II-5-W3, pp. 207–213 (2015)

15. Münster, S., Ioannides, M., Davies, R.: International stakeholder survey on demands in the field of digital cultural heritage (2017)

16. Münster, S., Hegel, W., Kröber, C.: A model classification for digital 3D reconstruction in the context of humanities research. In: Münster, S., Pfarr-Harfst, M., Kuroczyński, P., Ioannides, M. (eds.) 3D Research Challenges II. LNCS, vol. 10025, pp. 3–31. Springer, Cham (2016). https://doi.org/10.1007/978-3-319-47647-6_1

17. Maiwald, F., Vietze, T., Schneider, D., Henze, F., Münster, S., Niebling, F.: Photogrammetric analysis of historical image repositories for virtual reconstruction in the field of digital humanities. In: ISPRS International Archives of Photogrammetry, Remote Sensing and Spatial Information Sciences WG V/5, 3D-Arch 2017 – 3D Virtual Reconstruction and Visualization of Complex Architectures, vol. XL-5/W5, pp. 447–452 (2017)

18. Bruschke, J., Niebling, F., Maiwald, F., Friedrichs, K., Wacker, M., Latoschik, M.E.: Towards browsing repositories of spatially oriented historic photographic images in 3D web environments. Paper presented at the Web3D 2017, Brisbane, Australia (2017)

19. Münster, S., Kröber, C., Weller, H., Prechtel, N.: Researching knowledge concerns in virtual historical architecture. In: Ioannides, M., Fink, E., Moropoulou, A., Hagedorn-Saupe, M., Fresa, A., Liestøl, G., Rajcic, V., Grussenmeyer, P. (eds.) EuroMed 2016. LNCS, vol. 10058, pp. 362–374. Springer, Cham (2016). https://doi.org/10.1007/978-3-319-48496-9_29

20. Kröber, C., Münster, S.: Educational App creation for the Cathedral in Freiberg. In: Spector, J.M., Ifenthaler, D., Sampson, D.G., Isaías, P. (eds.) Competencies in Teaching, Learning and Educational Leadership in the Digital Age, pp. 303–318. Springer, Cham (2016). https://doi.org/10.1007/978-3-319-30295-9_19

An Exploration of Design Cues
for Heuristic-Based Decision-Making About
Information Sharing

Joslenne Peña[1]([⊠]), Mary Beth Rosson[1], Jun Ge[1], Eunsun Jeong[1],
S. Shyam Sundar[2], Jinyoung Kim[2], and Andrew Gambino[2]

[1] Center for Human Computer Interaction,
College of Information Sciences and Technology, Penn State University,
University Park, PA, USA
{jop5190,mrosson,jug264,ezj5050}@psu.edu
[2] Media Effects Research Laboratory, College of Communications,
Penn State University, University Park, PA, USA
{sss12,juk315,aug268}@psu.edu

Abstract. We report an exploratory study of web application interface cues that were designed to trigger cognitive heuristics thought to influence personal information disclosure. Building from prior work focused on identifying the presence and nature of such heuristics, we designed prototypes of simple web information applications that request personal information and inserted specific visual elements intended to evoke a heuristic . Using a combination of application walkthroughs (with think aloud comments) and retrospective interviews about what users' experiences and reactions were, we investigated the possible impact of the interface cues and corresponding heuristics. Although we found little direct impact of the interface cues, users did share a variety of concerns and strategies related to their decision making. We discuss implications for the heuristics used in this study, as well as for the design of privacy-preserving interfaces.

Keywords: Privacy by design · Decision-making · Design
Cognitive heuristics · Information disclosure

1 Introduction

Privacy researchers have shown that user interface designs can affect users' decisions about information disclosure [6]. For example, Acquisti and Grossklags [1] argue that decisions are influenced by the completeness of information provided within a user interface, presumably because this affects the calculation of risk and benefit. Research on social cognition has shown that humans often act as "cognitive misers" [10], making decisions that are quick but perhaps not accurate. In these cases, people may be relying on cues that activate cognitive heuristics, or mental shortcuts, thereby lessening the need for deep thinking and rational analysis.

Our research team is exploring decision-making that takes place in this more holistic fashion, that is a decision process that is guided by cognitive heuristics or rules

© Springer International Publishing AG, part of Springer Nature 2018
G. Chowdhury et al. (Eds.): iConference 2018, LNCS 10766, pp. 677–683, 2018.
https://doi.org/10.1007/978-3-319-78105-1_78

of thumb that serve as "short-cuts" in decision making [10]. As an example, a "bandwagon heuristic" may lead a user to disclose information if he or she believes that most people have already agreed.

We conducted an exploratory study that investigated two simple **research questions**: How can a privacy heuristic be "designed into" a software application? And, if we create such designs, will users recognize and respond to it the cues in deciding whether to disclose their personal information? In what follows, we describe how we designed simple web apps to convey cognitive heuristics that might influence information disclosure. We summarize what the users told us and discuss implications for designing systems that depend on disclosure of personal information.

2 Research Methods

Our design exploration was grounded in the findings of a focus group that explored users' privacy and security-related beliefs and behavior [5]. That study introduced familiar activities such as social networking and e-commerce, inviting participants to share experiences and thoughts about information disclosure in different contexts. Participants shared that they often do make decisions using rules of thumb, rather than going through a systematic analysis of the pros and cons of sharing. They offered many examples of this, such as trusting Google when surfing online and never questioning the intentions of Snapchat. We used these findings to identify decision heuristics that were mentioned frequently, but that are also distinct from one another. We selected the four heuristics: *Bandwagon, Community Building, Gatekeeping, and Fuzzy Boundary.* For the sake of page space, these are further described in the results section.

We followed several general rules in designing the web prototypes (we used Axure RP): we tried to isolate the target heuristic, so that no competing heuristics would interfere. We created designs with a user interface that had a reasonable degree of face validity. Finally, we illustrated usage scenarios that supported everyday activities, so that the users would not be distracted by unusual hypothetical tasks. In the end, we created four different web app contexts illustrating the four heuristics (two of the heuristics appeared in two different applications):

1. A professional networking app that attempts to evoke the Bandwagon heuristic by showing the user how many members are sharing personal details.
2. A local activities calendar that attempts to evoke the Community Building heuristic by showing competing university logos as part of a blood donation campaign; it also introduces the Fuzzy Boundary heuristic by presenting event recommendations that it says are drawn from your Google history.
3. A fitness discussion forum that attempts to evoke the Community Building heuristic by inviting you to submit fitness information to expand the community.
4. A secure payment app that attempts to evoke the Gatekeeping heuristic by adding two extra layers of dialog before confirming the transaction; it implements the Fuzzy Boundaries heuristic by reusing your account information from a site you were just browsing.

We recruited 11 participants (aged 18–23; 47) using advertisements in college classes and word of mouth, offering a $25 gift card as compensation for participating in individual sessions that lasted from 60–75 min.

Participants were given an overview of the task, explaining that they would be working with semi-functional web applications and thinking aloud about their goals, actions and reactions as they worked. They were given a printed list of tasks to work through step by step, including fictitious personal information[1] to use when information disclosure was invited. As the participants completed the tasks, a researcher observed and took notes, and both audio and screen recordings were captured. After using the prototypes, the experimenter conducted retrospective interviews, during which the screen recordings were reviewed and participants were asked whether they had noted the heuristic design cues and to reflect on their decisions about what to disclose.

We analyzed the audio and screen recordings with an open coding procedure to uncover emergent themes, as well as a more directed coding to identify comments related to the four heuristics. Not many comments were made during the tasks, even though we requested and reminded participants to do so. In hindsight, participants were attending closely to the task scripts and made-up information; we recognize that this may have led to a cognitive demand that made concurrent verbalization difficult or impossible [7]. However, we did collect many comments in the retrospective interviews. All comments were categorized using a cross-tabulation approach [9], first with a single theme, and secondly a heuristic as relevant. Coding issues were resolved by discussion.

3 Findings

Broadly speaking, participants reported that they had behaved in ways that were familiar to them, and that they believed they had made sharing decisions that were both safe and efficient. None reported feelings of privacy intrusion; it may be that our test tasks did not request information that was sensitive enough to activate information sharing concerns or the use of fictitious information reduced feelings of risk. Disappointingly, participants also reported that they were rarely aware of the user interface details intended to evoke heuristics. They were able to understand the cues during the retrospective interviews but in most cases only after we pointed to them. Thus to answer our first research question: yes, we were able to design cues evoking several cognitive heuristics with privacy implications but with varying levels. However, users' perceptions and reactions to these cues were not as strong or consistent as we had hoped.

In fact, no one explicitly mentioned a heuristic during the tasks, in any way that could be mapped to our design goals. This suggests that any impacts of the visual design cues were not strong enough to bring a heuristic into conscious awareness. During the post-task interviews, participants did start to speculate that their decisions

---

[1] We recognize that the use of fake information detracts from the study's ecological validity, but as an exploratory study we saw this as a reasonable tradeoff for ensuring actual privacy.

may have been based on rationale that does not fully match their beliefs about privacy and information sharing; this is consistent with other studies that have reported a mismatch between what people think they know and feel about privacy and how they behave [6]. For example, when pushed to explain their behavior in the presence of a user interface cue designed to evoke a heuristic, participants often did a sort of "second-guessing," trying to rationalize their behavior with respect to how they think about personal privacy. At times, even after we pointed out a cue, participants were not able to infer its privacy implications. Table 1 lists which heuristics were most strongly experienced as a result of the visual cues we designed. For instance, 10/11 users were able to describe an impact of the **gatekeeping** cue, but only 3 out of 11 (about 27%) explained how the **community building** heuristic might have influenced their privacy decisions.

Table 1. Heuristic evocation summary

Heuristic	# of Ns[a]	Evoked (Yes/No)
Bandwagon	5/11 ($\sim$45%)	N
Community Building	3/11 ($\sim$27%)	N
Gatekeeping	10/11 ($\sim$90%)	Y
Fuzzy Boundary	3/11 ($\sim$27%)	N

[a]Here we refer to Ns' as number of participants.

The **bandwagon** heuristic refers to the greater likelihood of disclosing personal information if one believes that many others are already doing so. Participants barely noticed the cue, only a few acknowledged this; instead many were surprised and said, "Oh I did not notice that!" In this scenario setting, they felt that the application had been designed to encourage sharing of the requested information and they did not feel threatened by doing so. In fact, they cited other factors that increased their comfort, such as past experiences with similar websites (e.g., LinkedIn), and their own expectations about what sorts of applications would be secure or private.

The **gatekeeping** heuristic refers to the increased comfort a user may experience if the system collects sensitive information in a multi-step way, even though this may mean it takes more work to convey. When we asked participants about the extra steps included in submitting financial information as part of the secure payment app, the majority (10) had a positive reaction. They felt that the extra steps made the entry of financial information more secure, helping them to them feel more at ease. At the same time, some participants noted the tradeoff: extra steps needed to complete a task or process is bothersome. *"The payment scenario, very secure, more secure than anything I can remember because you just hit pay and then it prompts you to re-enter the information, password, and security code from your phone"* – P8.

The **community building** heuristic implies that sharing personal information can contribute to feelings of community amongst participating users. Participants indicated that the information requested was plausible and they had no issues sharing such information to this type of community. Many compared this scenario to wearable devices such as the FitBit, which collects your health data and uses it to make rec-ommendations on fitness, training, and health improvement. However, most of them failed to grasp that by contributing information in this way they might be helping to build a health community. *"For what you are putting in information-wise from any-thing else, like myself, fitness data is not the biggest deal with me. Other types of information are not as big. Like other information I don't really mind if it is not as secure"* – P2.

According to the **fuzzy boundary** heuristic, users may feel uneasy if personal information might be shared with third parties. For the case of the community forum, there seemed to be little attention to the preferences brought in from Google; it could be that participants are so accustomed to marketing and advertising tactics that they simply ignore them, or it might be that the personal information shared through community activities does not raise privacy concerns. With respect to the secure payment scenario, participants also did not notice the cue implying that other entities will be using the financial information entered. In the retrospective interviews, most participants understood the risk such sharing would raise. One participant says that she generally feels anxious and hesitant about sharing financial information online. However, she is perfectly happy to give this information to Amazon. *"I feel like for example Amazon is an online only store, they do not have any physical stores and with online shopping I hate putting my credit card information online but they are an exception."* – P2.

4   Discussion, Limitations and Future Work

We saw little direct reaction to the design cues we hoped would activate specific cognitive heuristics relating to information sharing decisions. However, our subsequent discussions with the users were more promising, with many recognizing and in many cases validating the intended meaning of the visual cues. The gatekeeping heuristic was particularly welcome and effective in these discussions as 10 out of 11 participants were able to recognize this heuristic and its impacts. In other words, participants attested to understanding what this heuristic is, how it was implemented within the interface prototypes, and how it relates to the behaviors they exhibited. This may be due to its natural applicability to truly sensitive information (e.g., financial disclosure), as it appeared as part of the secure payment scenario. Gatekeeping can be illustrated into a two-step authentication design principle which seems more common to users in privacy practice. This could explain why this was an easier connection and interpre-tation to make.

Our findings are consistent with Egelman's [3] work that shows how users exploit privacy indicators in usage contexts but fail to recognize (and then ignore) the same indicators later in a task process. Fiesler et al. [4] explore the predictors of social media content sharing and privacy settings on FaceBook. They report that users stick to default settings rather than tinkering unnecessarily with them. Less action in exercising granular control over privacy settings and only prompted if required such as an update, a bad experience, or obtained knowledge. While this research focused on FaceBook, it is very likely to be generalizable among other interfaces like our prototypes.

Participants did not question appearances that seemed odd and out of place, and they did not test alternative options. There was considerable variation among users' ability to interpret or perceive a value in the different cognitive heuristics conveyed through design. However, we argue that having a design can be important to capture accurate accounts of users' perception that may create a bridge between heuristic, design principle, and their decision-making. Marmion et al. [8] describe an interview study that discovers heuristics of disclosure decisions through recall. While we view this work as important, it does not translate decision-making practices into user interfaces which is needed to guide designers, researchers, and privacy policy makers. Despite the relatively modesst results, our design-based approach exemplifies an important type of work that is needed in this space.

The preliminary study has several limitations. Our sample size could have been larger to reach saturation and consistency with the themes in our findings. Our participants were mostly college student-aged users who may follow different privacy standards than older users. Consequently, these results may not be completely generalizable. We also worry that the use of simulated personal information had an impact on results. It was impossible to wholly persuade participants to use this personal information as if it was their own. P3 said "*If I should put my real information I feel hesitation, but for this data, I didn't feel any caution because I knew it was fake information*". An interesting approach might ask users to work with familiar platforms (native to them) to increase their sense and likelihood of disclosure. Finally, the semi-functional prototypes were incomplete; this has advantages in terms of feedback for design [2] but arguably can be a detriment as several elements on the interfaces were not implemented. We hope to address these limitations in our next study with a more robust experimental design, larger sample size, and improved interface designs to build on this work.

Acknowledgements. This research was partially supported by the U. S. National Science Foundation via Standard Grant No. CNS1450500.

References

1. Acquisti, A., Grossklags, J.: An online survey experiment on ambiguity and privacy. Commun. Strat. **88**, 19–39 (2012)
2. Carroll, J.M.: Five reasons for scenario-based design. Interact. Comput. **13**(1), 43–60 (2000)
3. Egelman, S., Tsai, J., Cranor, L.F, Acquisti, A.: Timing is everything?: the effects of timing and placement of online privacy indicators. In: Proceedings of the 27th SIGCHI Conference on Human Factors in Computing Systems, Boston, MA, pp. 319–328. ACM, April 2009
4. Fiesler, C., Dye, M., Feuston, J.L., Hiruncharoenvate, C., Hutto, C.J., Morrison, S., Khanipour Roshan, P., Pavalanathan, U., Bruckman, A.S., De Choudhury, M., Gilbert, E.: What (or Who) is public? Privacy settings and social media content sharing. In: Proceedings of the 2017 ACM Conference on Computer Supported Cooperative Work and Social Computing. ACM, February 2017
5. Gambino, A., Kim, J., Sundar, S.S., Ge, J., Rosson, M.B.: User disbelief in privacy paradox: heuristics that determine disclosure. In: Proceedings of the 2016 CHI Conference Extended Abstracts on Human Factors in Computing Systems, pp. 2837–2843. ACM, May 2016

6. Kokolakis, S.: Privacy attitudes and privacy behaviour: a review of current research on the privacy paradox phenomenon. Comput. Secur. (2015)
7. Kuusela, H., Pallab, P.: A comparison of concurrent and retrospective verbal protocol analysis. Am. J. Psychol. **113**(3), 387 (2000)
8. Marmion, V., Bishop, F., Millard, D.E., Stevenage, S.V.: The cognitive heuristics behind disclosure decisions. In: Ciampaglia, G.L., Mashhadi, A., Yasseri, T. (eds.) SocInfo 2017. LNCS, vol. 10539, pp. 591–607. Springer, Cham (2017). https://doi.org/10.1007/978-3-319-67217-5_35
9. Merriam, S.B., Tisdell, E.J.: Qualitative Research: A Guide to Design and Implementation. Wiley, Hoboken (2015)
10. Sundar, S.S., Kang, H., Wu, M., Go, E., Zhang, B.: Unlocking the privacy paradox: do cognitive heuristics hold the key? In: CHI 2013 Extended Abstracts on Human Factors in Computing Systems, pp. 811–816. ACM (2013)

Transformative Spaces: The Library as Panopticon

Gary Paul Radford[1]([⊠]) ⓘ, Marie Louise Radford[2] ⓘ,
and Jessa Lingel[3] ⓘ

[1] Fairleigh Dickinson University, Madison, NJ, USA
gradford@fdu.edu
[2] Rutgers University, New Brunswick, NJ, USA
[3] University of Pennsylvania, Philadelphia, USA

Abstract. This paper seeks to describe and understand the nature of library experiences that both conjure immersion in different worlds, and yet relate to the physical spaces in which they occur. What does the library space make possible and what does it prohibit? Using Foucault's account of panopticism to unpack layers of surveillance, docility and agency within library sites, this paper seeks to gain a richer understanding of panopticism and the library as a social institution. A discussion of Foucault's panopticism is followed by the identification of areas where application of his concept might be useful to scholars and practitioners seeking to understand the experience of library users in their interaction and encounters with information interfaces, both interpersonal and technological.

Keywords: Michel Foucault · Panopticon · Panopticonism · Libraries

1 Introduction

There is something about library spaces that conjure experiences of different worlds. Moran [1] writes that, "A library in the middle of a community is a cross between an emergency exit, a life raft, and a festival. They are cathedrals of the mind; hospitals of the soul; theme parks of the imagination" (p. 92). However, a darker side to the library experience is evoked by novelist King's [2] recollections as a young boy: "I had loved the library as a kid – why not? It was the only place a relatively poor kid like me could get all the books he wanted – but as I continued to write, I became reacquainted with a deeper truth: I had also feared it. I feared becoming lost in the dark stacks. I feared being forgotten in a dark corner of the reading room and ending up locked in for the night" (pp. 386–387).

One can find countless examples of reflections which both celebrate [3] and offer dark warnings about [4] the experiences made possible by library spaces. This paper seeks to describe and understand the nature of these experiences and their relationship to the physical spaces in which they occur through a consideration of Foucault's [5] account of panopticism. Areas are identified where his concept might be useful to scholars and practitioners seeking to understand library users' experiences in interaction and encounters with interpersonal and technological information interfaces. It is

© Springer International Publishing AG, part of Springer Nature 2018
G. Chowdhury et al. (Eds.): iConference 2018, LNCS 10766, pp. 684–692, 2018.
https://doi.org/10.1007/978-3-319-78105-1_79

proposed that by unpacking the layers of surveillance, docility and agency within library sites, a richer understanding of panopticism and the library as a social institution can be gained.

2 From Heterotopia to Panopticon

Radford, Radford, and Lingel [3] conducted an examination of the library experience using Foucault's [6] concept of heterotopia. A defining feature of a heterotopic space is its capacity to give rise to "a sort of mixed, joint experience" (p. 24) where one is neither in one place or another, but has the potential to experience multiple places at once within the same physical space. The library as heterotopia is much more than a room or building that contains a collection of objects. It is also a place which makes possible the experience virtual spaces opened up by experiences when reading books and other texts. For example, Anand [7] writes that the library is a place where "you could lose your mother and then lose yourself in a book of Greek myths, or somebody's struggle to find love in class 5C or the life cycles of a ladybird" (pp. 5–6).

However, there is more to library experiences than the joys found in creativity and imagination. There are also profound feelings of fear [8–10]. In her much-cited article on library anxiety, Mellon [8] sought to articulate and understand the experiences and feelings of 6,000 undergraduate students as they encountered the space of an academic library for the first time. She asked them questions such as, "What were your experiences using the library?" and "How did you feel about the library and your ability to use it?" Mellon reported that the overwhelming number of responses were framed in terms of fear: "75 to 85% of students… described their initial response to the library in terms of fear or anxiety" and "terms like *scary, overpowering, lost, helpless,* and *fear of the unknown* appeared over and over again" (p. 162). Mellon also reported that these expressions of fear were not reflective of the students' perception of the actual assignments they were required to do in the library. She writes that it was these "feelings of fear that kept them [the students] from beginning to search or that got in the way of their staying in the library long enough to master search processes" (p. 163). The students' fear ran to a "deeper truth" about the library itself as expressed by Stephen King earlier. Indeed, Radford and Radford have argued that the library experience is inextricably linked to and informed by an underlying "discourse of fear" [4].

Such negative experiences may be due, in part, to an awareness that library space is dominated by surveillance and order. This is the hypothesis put forward by panopticism based in the work of Englisher utilitarianist philosopher Jeremy Bentham (1748–1832) and French postmodern philosopher Michel Foucault (1926–1984) and is the subject of the following section.

3 Panopticism

Foucault's problematization of space bear relevance on two fronts, first in heterotopic experience, discussed earlier. A second aspect of the experience of the library space is eloquently captured in Foucault's [5] concept of "panopticism," which Brunon-Ernst

[11] characterizes as "the theorization of surveillance society, derived from Bentham's project of a prison, with an all-seeing inspector" (p. 2). Bentham [12] proposed a panopticon prison in letters written from 1786–1787, in which he describes a circular building, called an "Inspection House." Prisoners are incarcerated in individual cells located on the perimeter of the structure and are supervised by an inspector housed in a central tower. The Inspection House's defining feature is that the inspector can see prison inhabitants, but the prisoners cannot see the inspector. In an ideal situation, the inspector would be able to surveille all of the inhabitants at all times. However, the architecture of the panopticon makes it possible for actual continuous surveillance to be replaced with the *illusion* of continuous surveillance. The illusion would be equally effective because prisoners have no way of knowing whether an inspector is actually present in the central tower. As Bentham notes, since total surveillance as a practical matter is impossible, "the next thing to be wished for is, that, at every instant, seeing reason to believe as much, and not being able to satisfy himself to the contrary, [the prisoner] should conceive himself to be so" [12, p. 34].

Foucault was drawn to Bentham's panopticon through a prior study of the gaze in medical institutions where "the whole problem of the visibility of bodies, individuals and things, under a system of centralized observation" is enacted [13, p. 146]. In hospitals, one needed to avoid any undue contact, physical proximity and over-crowding to reduce disease contagion and, also, to ensure proper air circulation. So, one needed to: (a) divide space, (b) keep space open, and (c) create a global and individualizing surveillance. In response to such conditions "the sovereignty of the gaze gradually establishes itself – the eye that knows and decides, the eye that governs," and, thus, "the clinic was probably the first attempt to order a science on the exercise and decisions of the gaze" [14, p. 89].

In writing *The Birth of the Clinic*, Foucault initially had thought that such concerns were specific to 18th century medicine, but he also found them in the reorganization of penal systems in early 19th century. He notes, "There was scarcely a text or a proposal about the prisons which didn't mention Bentham's 'device' – the 'panopticon'" [13, p. 147]. He realized that the panopticon was not just an architectural design intended to solve a specific problem concerning the incarceration of prisoners. According to Foucault, Bentham "invented a technology of power designed to solve the problems of surveillance" [13, p. 148].

> There is no need for arms, physical violence, mental constraints. Just a gaze. An inspecting gaze, a gaze which each individual under its weight will end by interiorizing to the point that he is his own overseer, each individual this exercising this surveillance over, and against, himself. A superb formula: a power exercised continuously and for what turns out to be minimal cost [13, p. 155].

Foucault takes Bentham's self-surveillance as a central feature of his broader notion of panopticism, where the principles of a panoptic architecture can be applied to a wider range of institutions, including the library. He asserts that one objective of panopticism is to produce "docile bodies" that may be "subjected, used, transformed, and improved" [5, p. 136]. Foucault uses the term "disciplines" to identify those methods used to achieve this docility. The panopticon's architecture is offered as a model of how space becomes a focal point for the administration of power through discipline. Foucault [5] writes: "He who is subjected to a field of visibility, and who knows it, assumes responsibility for the constraints of power; he makes them play spontaneously upon himself; he inscribes in himself the power relation in which he simultaneously plays both roles; he becomes the principle of his own subjection" (pp. 202–205).

The genius of Bentham's panopticon is that it does not matter if an inspector is present in the inspection tower. All that matters is that the cell's inhabitants believe this to be case. Power does not come from the person doing the surveillance, but from the building's architecture, which becomes a "cruel, ingenious cage" that "automatizes and disindividualizes power" [5, p. 202]. As Foucault explains, "Power has its principle not so much in a person as in a certain concerted distribution of bodies, surfaces, lights, gazes; in an arrangement whose internal mechanisms produce the relation in which individuals are caught up" [5, p. 202]. It is worth considering the extent to which libraries as institutions have always been sites of authority and control, not only of books, but of bodies. What is revealed when the space of the library is considered in terms of panopticism? How are bodies, surfaces, lights, and gazes distributed in the library space to produce effects of power and self-surveillance?

4 The Experience of Panopticism in the Library

The premise of Bentham's panopticon building is that the architecture itself would be enough to induce a particular kind of feeling that, in turn, would lead to particular kind of desired behavior. He writes: "The greater chance there is, of a given person's being at a given time actually under inspection, the more strong will be the persuasion – the more *intense*, if I may say so, the *feeling*, he has of being so" [12, p. 44]. There are clear elements in the library space that communicate either actual or perceived surveillance and have the power to structure the way one feels and acts. For example, actual or perceived surveillance is communicated is by overt displays of rules and regulations. At first, these displays of rules derived from a setting in which books were quite expensive and rare. For example, the following are taken from library rules at Harris-Manchester College, Oxford, from 1817 [15]:

> The Librarian is empowered to lend the key of the Library-room to any student who has passed through the first two years of his course, & who may be desirous of consulting any book or books in the Library, but no books shall be taken out, unless the Librarian be present under the penalty of two shillings & sixpence. The Librarian, upon delivering a book from the Library, shall enter, in a book provided for that purpose, the number of the book delivered, the name of the student who receives it, and the date of its deliver: and when the book is returned he shall mark the date of its return, signing the whole entry with the initials of his name. For every neglect to do so he shall forfeit sixpence.

Remnants of these regulations, including overdue fines, remain in most libraries today. Physical or online displays of rules are a constant reminder to the library user that her use of books is constantly subject to surveillance and sanction by the librarian/inspector.

Another expression of surveillance is represented in stereotypes of the perpetually "shushing librarian" [16]. Although many libraries have long embraced noise and activity as positive signs of institutional use, the presumed need for silence endures, especially in academic and special libraries where scholars expect to be able to read, think, and write in quiet.

Another anxiety-inducing mechanism is the sheer magnitude of the order that surrounds one in library spaces. The user, in withdrawing texts from the shelves presents a threat of disorder (in Douglas' [17] terms, introducing dirt into the purity of library organization). Such threats are constantly acknowledged by library notices which inform the user not to return the books to the shelves, a task entrusted to qualified staff. The stereotype of the librarian firmly date-stamping the book with a loud thud and displaying the damning stare of scrutiny emphasizes the dichotomous arrangements of power between librarians as in control and library users as being at their disciplinary mercy. The use of the library book is temporary, it can only leave the collection for so long, and the consequences of the user not complying (and thus having overdue books) are conveyed by the implied violence of the stamp striking the book, a theme so starkly brought to life in King's [2] novella, *The Library Policeman*.

Panopticism as a principle of internalizing self-surveillance can also shape our experiences interacting with an electronic interface, such as the home screen of the Google search engine. The home screen consists of a mostly white and bare background with a search box in the middle, almost like a letter box in the door to a large and ornate house. When we type our inquiries into the search box, we are, in a sense, peering through the letter box. We know that what we see, as revealed by the search results that the system gives to us, is always an incomplete reflection of what is actually there. But there is another gaze that is signified by the Google screen. The box in the middle of the screen can works two ways. We know, if only implicitly, that each search not only asks the system for information, it also becomes information for the system. However, where that information goes, how it is stored, and how it used, is unknown to us. It remains hidden behind the blank white screen of the Google page, just as the omnipotent inspector remains permanently hidden from the prisoners by the very architecture of the building.

5 Heterotopia in the Panopticon

In an interview, Foucault was asked, "Are there revolts against the gaze?" [13, p. 162]. Foucault replied, "Oh yes, provided that isn't the final purpose of the operation. Do you think it would be much better to have the prisoners operating the panoptic apparatus and sitting in the central tower, instead of the guards?" (pp. 164–165). Clearly, just shifting the actors in the panopticon is like rearranging the deck chairs on a sinking Titanic. The inhabitants may be in different places, but the building and its effects remain the same. But what would be the "final purpose" that goes beyond controlling the building? The inspector is as much a docile body produced by the panopticon as the prisoners.

The lesson from Foucault's observation is that there is no escape from panopticism. It is embodied in the very spaces that we occupy, including the library, and the effects are clearly seen in the accounts of library users such as those recorded by Mellon and others [8–10]. However, the library is a paradoxical place because, on the one hand, it demands that the library user be docile and adhere to the many regulations it imposes. These demands in large part evoke the feelings of fear so often reported by library users. On the other hand, the library communicates that it is a place which encourages people *not* to be docile, but rather to be creative, to explore, discover, and express themselves in ways that are more akin to Foucault's account of heterotopia [3, 6]. Unlike the home screen of the Google search engine, one does not need to peer through the letter box to see what is in the library. One can open the door and see the library as it is. One may feel confused or overwhelmed by the perceived size and complexity of the library space (this was a main source of fear reported by Mellon [8]), but it is nevertheless not hidden from us. Unlike the home screen of the Google search engine where the relationship between your search query and results retrieved are unknown to you, the library space allows you to physically experience the direct correlation between the library catalog and the organization of the empirical books on an empirical shelf. You actually walk to a physical object in a physical location guided by the numbers on the catalog card. But you are not bound by the catalog number on the card. You can reach for and look at any book on the shelf, or any shelf. In the context of panopticism, such messages are practically subversive! And yet the same systematic, rule-driven, panopticism of the empirical library space creates the conditions for heterotopia. As well as the fear-riddled and docile bodies reported by Mellon, the architecture of the library also has the potential to create the wonder and joy of the library user. Semiotician Eco [18] expresses his experience in the library space as follows:

> I can decide to pass a whole day there in bliss: I read the papers, take the books down to the bar, then I go and look for some more. I make my discoveries. Having gone in to work on, say, British Empiricism, I start to follow commentaries on Aristotle instead. On getting the floor wrong, I find myself in an area I hadn't thought to enter, on medicine, but then I suddenly find works on Galen, and hence complete with philosophical references. In this sense the library becomes an adventure (p. 11).

Hill [19] recounts a similar experience browsing the book stacks of the London Library: "There is something extraordinarily liberating and exciting about being let loose in such a place, allowed to wander, pick out this and that, read a bit here, a page there, take out the book, then wander to another bay in search of something related to it" (p. 111). The physical movement from book to book, shelf to shelf, and floor to floor are all made possible by the physical space of the library, forming the basis of Eco's "adventure" and Hill's "liberation." What Eco describes as an adventure, Foucault [11] will describe as a "fantasia of the library" [20], or what more recent scholars refer to as serendipity [21]. The order that is embodied in the physical space of the library (in its shelves, its floors, its sections, and so on) makes possible the disorder and the creativity of the imagination. Crucially, the message here is not about celebration replacing fear. Rather it is to acknowledge fear and to celebrate anyway. Spaces that privilege serendipity can highlight rather than obscure the arbitrary nature of organization, when these rationales of control are loosened, this facilitates possibilities of dissent.

6 Libraries in Prisons

This paper concludes by briefly considering a space that combines the two sites of panopticism discussed here: the library and the prison. According to the World Prison Brief (http://www.prisonstudies.org/country/united-states-america) there are over two million people in the U.S. prison population in 2017, the largest prison population in the world. Educational programming and media access have been shown to have significant efficacy in reducing recidivism [22] and libraries facilitate both functions. Yet, libraries for the incarcerated are micro-spaces of constraint within macro-spaces of constraint, a layered arrangement of organization, control and surveillance. Book censorship in prison libraries is pervasive, with wardens and guards making decisions about appropriate and inappropriate content [23]. Books can be censored for a number of reasons, including violent or explicitly sexual content, as well as racially charged or politically controversial works. Some institutions only allow books that are soft-cover, others only allow books to be donated to the library if they are brand new, rather than previously owned. Content, format, provenance: there are many modes of restricting library books (not to mention capricious decisions to exclude books for arbitrary reasons), measures of surveillance that emerge before the books are even on the shelf. When books are finally allowed into prison and jail libraries, users' reading choices can be monitored by prison staff, to the point of affecting parole outcomes [24]. Although experiences of jail and prison libraries involve heightened feelings of regulation, they also entail precious access to choice, entertainment and intellectual play. Even with all the mechanisms for censoring and controlling books within prison libraries, once there, they are powerful instruments of fantasy, education, distraction and play. It is this contradiction that perhaps explains the reoccurring presence of the library in fictional portrayals of prison including *The Wire, A Clockwork Orange, Orange Is the New Black,* and *The Shawshank Redemption.*

Yet, while books can be transformative, they can also be tools of control. Narratives of working in a prison library suggest that rather than acting as a site of resistance, libraries foster a demeanor of docility [25]. Docility is not concerned with the imposition of power through punishment or force, a principle inherent in Bentham's design of the panopticon. The panopticon will "be kind: it will prevent transgressing; it will save punishing" [12, p. 105], at least from the point of view of the inspector. Foucault [5] writes that docility will be ensured by "The meticulousness of the regulations, the fussiness of inspections, the supervision of the smallest fragment of life and of the body" (p. 141). These rules and regulations are strictly enforced by librarians and library staff, who hesitate to bend the rules to make exceptions (such as allowing overdue books or extended time in the library), often because they fear reprisals from their supervisors. In the context of jails and prisons, the library is no escape from regulation, it is rather the normalization of discipline in a familiar setting. Lingel [26] has argued that libraries can offer a sense making function of institutional legibility in contexts that are otherwise chaotic or incoherent, such as massive protests or, (as asserted here) jails and prisons. In contexts of incarceration, libraries provide a form of panopticism that hails from outside prison walls. Moreover, the surveillance and docility of the library is more palatable than those of the prison itself, where the veneer of choice over what to read can help mask forms of control. Considering the prison library in particular draws attention to the obvious, although often overlooked, modes of control and constraints around choice in collection development policy, service provision, and management of space. Prison libraries demonstrate the contradiction of managed access to information and intellectual freedom: while books and media are available for use and meaning-making, people and texts are continually surveilled and controlled according to rules that can vary from the arcane and arbitrary to the cruel and ingenious.

7 Conclusion

The goals of this paper have been to consider the library through a frame of panopticism, a reframing meant to counterbalance to fetishizing libraries as sites of endless imagination and play without recognizing the ways that these sites are also institutions of surveillance and control. The paradoxical phenomenology of the library allows for pleasure and trepidation, curiosity and strictly-imposed access constraints of access, intellectual freedom and surveilled bodies. That libraries organize books is all but tautological – that they also organize, monitor and constrain bodies is a crucial recognition for a nuanced understanding of the social and political realities of library space. By considering the above convergences and divergences in how different library spaces and contexts institute surveillance and produce docile bodies, scholars are better placed to theorize practices of resistance and subversion within libraries, especially regarding marginalized populations, such as the incarcerated, or formerly incarcerated.

References

1. Moran, C.: Alma mater. In: Gray, R. (ed.) The Library Book, pp. 91–94. Profile Books, London (2012)
2. King, S.: The library policeman. In: King, S. (ed.) Four Past Midnight. Signet, New York (1990)
3. Radford, G.P., Radford, M.L., Lingel, J.: The library as heterotopia: Michel Foucault and the experience of library space. J. Doc. 71(6), 1265–1288 (2015)
4. Radford, G.P., Radford, M.L.: Libraries, librarians, and the discourse of fear. Libr. Q. 71(3), 299–329 (2001)
5. Foucault, M.: Discipline and Punish: The Birth of the Prison. Vintage Books, New York (1979)
6. Foucault, M.: Of other spaces. Diacritics 16(1), 22–27 (1986)
7. Anand, A.: Character building. In: Gray, R. (ed.) The Library Book, pp. 5–8. Profile Books, London (2012)
8. Mellon, C.A.: Library anxiety: a grounded theory and its development. Coll. Res. Libr. 47(2), 160–165 (1986)
9. Onwuegbuzie, A.J., Jiao, Q.G., Bostick, S.L.: Library Anxiety: Theory, Research, and Applications. Scarecrow Press, Lanham (2004)
10. Carlile, H.: The implications of library anxiety for academic reference services: a review of the literature. Aust. Acad. Res. Libr. 38(2), 129–147 (2007)

11. Brunon-Ernst, A.: Beyond Foucault: New Perspectives on Bentham's Panopticon. Ashgate, Burlington (2012)
12. Bentham, J.: The Panopticon Writings. Verso, New York (1995)
13. Foucault, M.: The eye of power (Trans. by, C. Gordon). In: Gordon, C. (ed.) Power/Knowledge: Selected Interviews and Other Writings 1972–1977, pp. 146–165. Pantheon Books, New York (1980)
14. Foucault, M.: The Birth of the Clinic: An Archaeology of Medical Perception (Trans. by, A. M. Sheridan Smith). Vintage Books, New York (1975)
15. Sheekey, N.: Librarian at the Harris-Manchester College of the University of Oxford, 17 March 2016
16. Radford, M.L., Radford, G.P.: Power, knowledge, and fear: Feminism, Foucault, and the stereotype of the female librarian. Libr. Q. 67(3), 250–266 (1997)
17. Douglas, M.: Purity and Danger: An Analysis of Concepts of Pollution and Taboo. Routledge, New York (2003)
18. Eco, U.: De bibliotheca (Trans. by, A. McEwan). In: Hofer, C. (ed.) Libraries, pp. 7–14. Schirmer/Mosel, Munich (2005)
19. Hill, S.: A corner of St. James. In: Grey, R. (ed.) The Library Book, pp. 109–113. Profile Books, London (2012)
20. Foucault, M.: The Fantasia of the library. In: Bouchard, D.F., Simon, S. (eds.) Michel Foucault: Language, Counter-Memory, Practice, pp. 87–109. Cornell University Press, Ithaca (1977)
21. Makri, S., Blandford, A.: Coming across information serendipitously – Part 1: a process model. J. Doc. 68(5), 684–705 (2012)
22. Tynan, D.: Online behind bars: if internet access is a human right, should inmates have it. The Guardian (2016). https://www.theguardian.com/us-news/2016/oct/03/prison-internet-access-tablets-edovo-jpay
23. Miller, S.: The banning of books in prisons: "It's like living in the dark ages". The Guardian (2016). https://www.theguardian.com/us-news/2016/oct/03/prison-internet-access-tablets-edovo-jpay
24. Green, A.: Interview with a prison librarian. Ask a manager. http://www.askamanager.org/2015/10/interview-with-a-prison-librarian.htmlk
25. Conrad, S.: Collection development and circulation policies in prison libraries: an exploratory survey of librarians in US correctional institutions. Libr. Q.: Inf. Commun. Policy 82(4), 407–427 (2012)
26. Lingel, J.: Occupy wall street and the myth of technological death of the library. First Monday 17(8) (2012)

Librarians as Information Intermediaries: Navigating Tensions Between Being Helpful and Being Liable

Jessica Vitak(✉), Yuting Liao, Priya Kumar,
and Mega Subramaniam

College of Information Studies, University of Maryland, College Park, MD, USA
{jvitak, yliao598, pkumar12, mmsubram}@umd.edu

Abstract. Librarians face numerous challenges when helping patrons—particularly those with low socioeconomic status (SES)—meet information needs. They are often expected to have knowledge about many different technologies, web services, and online forms. They must also navigate how to best help patrons while ensuring that personally identifying information (PII) is kept private and that their help will not hold them or their library system liable. In this paper, we explore data collected in eleven focus groups with 36 public librarians from across the U.S. to understand the information challenges librarians encounter when working with patrons who have low digital literacy skills but must increasingly use the internet to request government assistance, apply for jobs, and pay their bills. Findings highlight the thin line librarians must walk to balance issues around privacy, trust, and liability. We conclude the paper with recommendations for libraries to provide additional training to librarians and patrons on privacy and information technology, and we suggest ways for librarians to fulfill their roles as information intermediaries while minimizing legal, ethical, and privacy concerns.

Keywords: Libraries · Technology · Digital literacy · Privacy
Trust · Liability

1 Introduction

Librarians are at the forefront of responding to the changing landscape of technological innovations that affect how we conduct daily activities, from paying bills to filling out job applications. Librarians are no longer limited to helping patrons locate physical resources at the library; they also regularly help patrons navigate websites and use digital tools to accomplish tasks that previously were conducted offline. Many of these tasks involve patrons disclosing personally identifying information (PII)—ranging from passwords to social security numbers to financial information—through online portals. Research has highlighted the implicit sense of trust patrons feel toward librarians [7, 10, 11], which may explain why patrons freely share this information with librarians. In addition, for many patrons with low digital literacy skills, librarians may represent the only source of knowledge to help them evaluate information credibility, avoid online scams, and accomplish practical tasks, such as creating accounts, downloading documents, and submitting forms online.

© Springer International Publishing AG, part of Springer Nature 2018
G. Chowdhury et al. (Eds.): iConference 2018, LNCS 10766, pp. 693–702, 2018.
https://doi.org/10.1007/978-3-319-78105-1_80

Yet, librarians are not trained to be legal, medical, or financial experts, nor are they trained to assist patrons with specific tools like government forms for Medicaid or other types of support. While librarians want to help patrons resolve their information needs and can facilitate digital literacy through one-on-one or group-based technology training, they must also ensure their assistance does not lead to undesired outcomes—especially those that could create financial or legal problems to their library system.

In this paper, we explore how public librarians in the U.S. navigate tensions between reducing the liability associated with helping patrons resolve their sensitive information needs and still serving their community. The following two research questions guide our evaluation of libraries, PII, and liability concerns:

RQ1: What are librarians' primary liability concerns when assisting patrons with low levels of digital literacy?
RQ2: What guidelines or policies do libraries use to reduce liability concerns when dealing with patrons' sensitive information?

In the following sections, we provide an overview of literature on the unique, trust-based relationship between librarians and patrons, the challenges information technologies raise for librarians, and the legal constraints librarians face when helping patrons resolve information needs. We then present findings from an analysis of 11 focus groups with U.S.-based public librarians to unpack the liabilities they face as they assist their patrons. We also explore the guidelines and policies librarians use to balance issues around privacy, trust, and liability. We conclude with recommendations for policies and other resources to help librarians address these challenges.

2 Related Work

2.1 Challenges Faced by Those Without Sufficient Digital Literacy Skills

Technological proficiency is increasingly essential, not only to obtain a high-paying job, but also to access government resources, apply for non-technical jobs (which often require Web-based application submission), and comply with financial and legal requirements. Individuals with low socioeconomic status (SES) face compounding problems: they must use the Web or other communication technologies to access important resources, but they often lack both direct access to these technologies and the requisite knowledge and skills to successfully navigate them [4, 19, 23, 24].

Americans making less than $30,000 per year have lagged far behind other income groups in broadband internet adoption, only crossing the 50% adoption rate at the start of 2017 [18]. Because of this, low-SES individuals are much more likely to rely on public computers—such as those in public libraries—than those with greater financial means [9]. This too, raises a tension for low-SES patrons; at least one study has highlighted that people may be reluctant to use library computers for financial matters due to privacy and security concerns [3]. When they do use public devices, these patrons may unknowingly share sensitive information with others through simple errors like not logging out of an account, saving a file to the desktop, or submitting information to an insecure website.

2.2 Interpersonal and Institutional Trust

Trust is a central component of human interactions; to trust a person or institution requires one to make themselves vulnerable by disclosing PII and relying on another's goodwill to not misuse that information [2, 21]. Therefore, trust can be viewed as a decision-making process whereby an individual uses available information to determine another person's or institution's reliability to hold to a contract or agreement [6]. Individuals rely on a number of cues when deciding whether to trust an *unknown* other, such as asking a stranger for help or sharing sensitive information with a business. In cases where risks and/or uncertainties are high—for example, when prompted to enter one's social security number into a web form—one may consciously or subconsciously assess the trustworthiness of that source and base a decision to disclose information on how trustworthy they *perceive* that source to be [7, 20].

2.3 Patron Trust in Librarians

As information intermediaries, librarians help patrons exchange and disseminate PII, translate technical information, and make information easier to use [23, 26]. Around the world, libraries are viewed as having high credibility, which plays an important role in developing trust [7]. Libraries also have some of the highest institutional reputations, especially in regards to providing access to education and information [22].

Several researchers have approached the question of trust in librarians through a social capital framework, focusing on the resources exchanged between librarians and their patrons. The highly interpersonal nature of librarians' interactions with patrons, including one-on-one assistance and providing both informational and social support, helps foster a deep trust in librarians [11]. For marginalized groups, including immigrants and low-SES individuals, libraries may be one of the only trusted resources in their local community, and libraries often cater services to local demographics, such as offering free English classes in communities with a large proportion of non-English-speaking patrons [25].

2.4 PII Privacy Challenges, and Liability Concerns

In the digital age, librarians' jobs are no longer limited to finding information; rather, librarians are increasingly approached to solve information needs or technological challenges that patrons face. Because of this, librarians work with patrons on a variety of internet-based tasks that involve PII, ranging from setting up email or social media accounts to submitting tax documents, job applications, and health forms. Patrons are often quick to trust librarians, a unique characteristic of this relationship. This may stem in part from the fact that patrons expect their library records—including the questions they ask librarians, the books they read and check out, and the information they enter on library computers—to be confidential [5].

However, library-related laws and regulations do not sufficiently address patrons' privacy [17]. Kang [12] revealed that, while most librarians recognize the importance of protecting patrons' PII, few libraries have regulations or policies for doing so. Additionally, librarians are not formally trained in dealing with private and sensitive information [7, 16]. High trust in librarians does not mitigate libraries' concerns about their liability related to protecting patrons' sensitive information. Healey [8] argues that if librarians adhere to the scope of their duties and the standards of their fields, they can be exempt from personal liability. Yet librarian liability may still emerge due to the lack of clear guidelines regarding patron privacy [11, 12, 17]. To minimize liability concerns, libraries may seek to limit services for patrons [8]. However, Healey [8] notes that "erring excessively on the side of avoiding liability can cause services to be limited, information to be withheld, and users to go unserved."

In the following sections, we probe librarians' dilemma between being helpful and being liable by asking them about the challenges they face when helping patrons to complete tasks that involve private and sensitive information.

3 Method

Between January and September 2017, the research team held 11 focus groups with 36 public librarians at local and national library conferences, as well as virtually using the WebEx conference call tool. Two of the planned focus groups became interviews when additional participants did not attend; the other nine focus groups ranged in size from 2–11 people and lasted between 60–90 min each. Moderators took detailed notes during each focus group, and the sessions were audio recorded and transcribed.

In total, 36 librarians throughout the U.S. participated (34 female, two male). Of those, 25 completed an online short form providing demographic and branch-specific data. Many had worked in libraries for several years ($M = 10$ years, median = 7.5, range: 1–30). They varied in location, with 40% working at libraries in rural areas, 40% in suburban areas, and 20% in urban libraries. Half of participants identified as reference librarians, 30% as branch managers or directors, and 20% as technical services librarians or staff.

For all focus groups (in person and virtual), participants reviewed and signed a consent form (approved by our university's Institutional Review Board). After introducing the study, the moderator posed a series of questions to the group to understand the information challenges librarians faced and especially how they handled information requests that involved sensitive information. The session ended with a discussion of the types of resources and training participants wanted to enhance their and their library's ability to handle the information requests they regularly received.

We uploaded transcripts of the focus groups to the qualitative analysis program Dedoose to enable an iterative coding process across multiple authors. One author created a draft codebook, and each author used it to independently code one of the transcripts. The full team then iteratively revised the codebook. The same transcript was then recoded with the updated codebook to ensure the list captured all desired themes. Next, each transcript in the corpus went through two rounds of coding. In the first round, an author applied codes using the codebook. In the second round, a different author reviewed the coding to ensure reliability. Finally, codes relevant to our research questions were exported from Dedoose and used to generate meta-matrices [14] to explore patterns in themes across sessions and to synthesize individuals' experiences regarding our research questions.

4 Findings

4.1 What are Librarians' Primary Liability Concerns When Assisting Patrons?

When evaluating our first research question, we identified three emergent themes related to how liability concerns manifest as librarians serve patrons in their role as information intermediaries. We discuss each theme in detail below.

Speed and immediate needs matter more than learning. In our focus groups, librarians described regularly providing support for patrons who have little to no knowledge of how to use the internet to complete important life tasks—such as applying for subsidized housing and health insurance or completing tax forms—that require submitting PII online. Librarians mentioned being bombarded with requests from patrons, including filling out tax forms, setting up bank and email accounts, and logging into existing accounts. Librarians consistently shared scenarios where patrons asked librarians to complete online transactions for them, rather than asking the librarians to *teach* them to complete these transactions on their own.

Librarians highlighted how patrons are driven by immediate needs rather than developing long-term skills that librarians could teach them. For example, a branch manager from a rural North Carolina library said, "*There are the people who just try to give you all of their information and they're handing you their credit card and they don't even stop to think that there might be an issue with that.*" A librarian from a rural Maryland library shared her experience helping a patron who "*was trying to sell property online, and he's sitting there telling me his whole password naming scheme.*" Likewise, a librarian from an urban North Carolina library, said, "*...you can't help but see people's private information, either because you're helping or because they're simply careless. It happens all the time. They leave their social security card on the copy machine, they're shoving their tax forms in your face.*"

These anecdotes highlight how patrons who lack skills to complete internet-related tasks on their own place significant trust in librarians to help complete tasks, often without stopping to consider how their PII is protected or expressing concerns about the vulnerability of that information. Some librarians framed these scenarios in terms of patrons' *desperation* to get things done, and they worried about who patrons would turn to if librarians could not (or would not) help them complete these forms. In these cases, librarians were likely seen as a trustworthy party that had the technical skills to help when the individual (and likely their family members) lacked those digital skills.

It's the librarian's fault. Due to patrons' lack of digital skills—which was evident in librarians' descriptions of patrons' inability to complete basic tasks such as clicking on pull-down menus or positioning their mouse on the screen—librarians said they often had to sit next to patrons and guide them through each step of an online transaction. To librarians' frustration, library-offered classes that teach basic digital literacy skills often have poor to no attendance. Many librarians also expressed concern about being accused of making errors while helping a patron complete online transactions that involve PII. As the technical services supervisor from a suburban Illinois library described, "*...I had a patron call who claims that one of my staff members signed her*

up for online social security and now she's not getting her paper checks anymore...
She feels that her benefits were taken away because of her working with a librarian.
I think that that's where the liability issues come in." A librarian from a suburban New
York library shared a similar example of a patron who blamed her for not getting a job
and implying she should have assisted more with preparing the patron's résumé.

These interactions place librarians in a precarious position where they may be
faulted for simply fulfilling their role as an information intermediary. If librarians
choose not to help a patron because a task deals with PII, they may be labeled as not
being helpful and/or not doing their job (which creates additional challenges).

In librarians we trust. As seen in prior research [7, 10, 11], patrons appear to
inherently trust librarians when it comes to handling PII. Librarians in our focus groups
described how patrons saw them as neutral entities and shared everything from family
stories to financial information with them. One librarian from a rural Maryland library
described how she thinks patrons view her: "*This is actually really personal infor-*
mation but, it's my librarian, I know her. I see her all the time.' Sometimes I think that
filter disappears..." Likewise, a branch manager from an urban North Carolina library
described the level of trust her patrons have in her, saying:

> *I have not had the experience of [patrons] ever pausing to consider the privacy issues or later*
> *coming up and asking, concerned about their privacy. It does seem often like it never crosses*
> *their minds, which I'm not sure how much of that is not being educated enough with tech-*
> *nological problems that can happen. Or whether it's a case of because we're in a trusted*
> *position.*

To summarize, librarians in our focus groups felt uncomfortable viewing PII but
said they feel obligated to help patrons complete tasks that involved sensitive information, even in cases when it raised liability concerns.

4.2   What Guidelines or Policies Do Libraries Use to Reduce Liability Concerns?

In addressing our second research question, participants described a range of library
policies for handling sensitive patron information. Some libraries have detailed policies
that try to capture all possible patron scenarios; however, most lack any policy, and
librarians handle each patron on a case-by-case basis. For example, the branch manager
from an urban North Carolina library said her library has very detailed policies and
procedures that explain what staff can and cannot do for patrons. Her library has posted
signs near computer labs to tell patrons what librarians cannot do. Librarians at this
library cannot handle patrons' passwords and credit card information or complete
online transactions that require submitting PII.

Some library policies are designed to address liability concerns by preventing
librarians from handling devices or entering information for patrons. For example, a
librarian from an urban New York library shared that her librarians tell patrons "*...we*
can help you as much as we can, but we can't do it for you, and we can't touch your
devices." A librarian from a suburban Maryland library described a similar policy at her
library, where librarians will not enter information on the computer or another device,
but they will tell the patron exactly how to do it. On the other hand, some librarians

said they are willing to bend the rules to help a patron in need. For example, a technical services librarian in rural Tennessee said he's willing to loosely interpret his library's policy when needed: *"You may have to fudge the rules a little bit, just so they can get unemployment [benefits]. You don't want people to starve or anything like that."* Likewise, a librarian from a urban California library said that many children come to her library without their parents, and librarians will maintain login credentials for regular patrons so they can get onto the sites they access at the library.

The majority of librarians in our focus groups affirmed that their branches do not have explicit policies in place regarding how to handle sensitive information when helping patrons complete online transactions. While some felt that implementing such policies could reduce liability concerns or would be helpful in conveying their stance to patrons, not all librarians felt the need for policies. For example, a branch manager in rural New York said, *"It would be awkward to have a policy. If we had a policy, we'd probably end up turning people away and saying, 'I'm sorry, we can't help you because this is outside what were allowed to do,' and that would be a shame."* This sentiment reflects the challenges librarians may face in crafting a policy that enables them to accomplish their mission.

Overall, these situations highlight the tensions librarians face between helping patrons, who rely heavily on them to complete important tasks, and protecting themselves and their libraries from potential legal issues. In many cases, librarians were willing to put themselves at risk rather than turn away a patron in need.

5 Discussion

In this study, we talked with 36 public librarians from around the U.S. to understand the challenges they experience when serving their patrons in their role as information intermediaries. Librarians' jobs are becoming increasingly technical as patrons turn to them for assistance with requests that involve different devices, tools, and services. Furthermore, patrons who may not own personal computers or have reliable internet access at home increasingly come to libraries to submit sensitive information ranging from job applications to forms for government assistance. And when patrons lack basic digital literacy skills to complete these tasks, librarians are often the trusted source to whom patrons turn for assistance.

Findings from our analysis highlight an important tension that librarians struggle with when assisting patrons with these requests. On one hand, librarians recognize and embrace their trusted position and know they may be the only people who can help patrons. On the other hand, librarians have valid concerns about how their help could turn into a liability for their library and themselves. These concerns were reflected in some of our participants' anecdotes of patrons "blaming" them for not getting a job or things not working out how they wanted.

Drawing on these findings, we offer the following four recommendations to help public libraries reduce liability concerns without placing too many limitations on the information assistance librarians provide. First, we recommend that librarian preparation programs and in-service professional development for practicing librarians increase their focus on facilitation strategies for working with patrons on public computers. Many librarians described being pressured to break the rules and not knowing how to respond (e.g., *"How do we tell them we can't do this for them politely, without the patron becoming frustrated or angry at us?"*). Training sessions that involve walking through a range of scenarios can help prepare librarians to facilitate the range of information technology requests they receive.

Second, we believe librarians need clearly articulated guidelines that describe what they can and cannot do when assisting patrons with information requests that include PII. While policies exist in some libraries, most participants in this study described having little to no guidelines to deal with such situations, which potentially increases libraries' liability. We believe the safest guidelines would state that librarians should never enter PII into a form for patrons. Clearer policies would also help librarians respond to patrons who express frustration or anger when librarians refuse a request.

Third, we recommend that local, state, and federal agencies make a more coherent effort to provide libraries with assistance to serve patrons who lack digital literacy. Our participants repeatedly said that government agencies direct patrons to the local library to get help with the online transactions; however, librarians rarely received any training to help patrons with those transactions. Some agencies, such as U.S. Citizenship and Immigration Services,[1] have started programs whereby libraries and other organizations can become "authorized providers" of information services; however, this is far from standard practice. If librarians received training on navigating popular services, they could better serve their patrons without increasing liability concerns.

Finally, our focus groups revealed that while there are serious privacy concerns to be addressed, the majority of patrons who use public computers need basic digital skills. Lacking those, patrons often feel completely helpless, and just completing their transaction supersedes concerns about who sees their PII. Many libraries already offer classes and other training resources to patrons on the basics of using computers and the internet. As highlighted in some participants' comments, however, the biggest challenge is getting patrons to *attend* these classes. To increase attendance, libraries can partner with community organizations as well as agencies that require people to complete transactions online (government agencies, financial institutions) to hold joint digital literacy programs. These programs can also be held in places where people already gather (e.g., community centers, churches). In addition, libraries should consider ways to partner with these patrons' children—who are often more literate digitally or keen toward developing digital literacy—and provide them with training opportunities that children could then pass along to other family members [13, 15].

6 Future Research, Limitations, and Conclusion

While the American Library Association (ALA) continues to fight to protect patrons' privacy through various initiatives and key communications to government and private agencies [1], librarians themselves often walk a tightrope that pits refusing to help a patron with information requests against providing services that could expose libraries

---

[1] See https://www.uscis.gov/avoid-scams/become-authorized-provider for more information.

to liability. This paper is one of the first attempts to systematically tackle this tension by talking to librarians from around the U.S. about these challenges and how libraries address them. We found that while librarians recognize the concerns that stem from handling patrons' PII, they feel an obligation to help patrons complete online transactions. This tension is further exacerbated by patrons' resistance to *learning* the digital skills that could help them complete these tasks on their own; rather, they often come to librarians on a deadline and seeking a quick solution. Furthermore, many of the librarians we talked to said their branches have no formal policies regarding how to respond to the many potential scenarios they encounter involving PII.

The study is somewhat limited by its recruitment strategy, which focused on using mainstream library organizations like ALA to advertise sessions and relied on librarians to volunteer to participate; furthermore, we did not attempt to obscure the focus of this research, so our participants may be more privacy conscious than the average librarian. Future research should examine these questions with more diverse populations, as well as in non-U.S. contexts to shed light on whether this tension exists in communities with different library and legal cultures.

We believe that academics, libraries, and community organizations need to work together to identify the best ways to help low-SES patrons obtain the necessary digital literacy skills to navigate the internet and to complete online tasks. In addition, these stakeholders should provide needed resources to librarians to help them better assist patrons with information needs while minimizing liability to the library.

References

1. American Library Association: Privacy, surveillance, and cybersecurity fact sheet (2017). http://www.ala.org/advocacy/advleg/federallegislation/privacy
2. Baier, A.: Trust and antitrust. Ethics **96**, 231–260 (1986). https://doi.org/10.1086/292745
3. Becker, S., et al.: Opportunity for all: how the American public benefits from internet access at U.S. libraries (IMLS-2010-RES-01). Institute of Museum and Library Services, Washington, DC (2010)
4. Blank, R.M., Strickling, L.E.: Exploring the digital nation: home broadband internet adoption in the United States. US Department of Commerce, Washington, DC (2010)
5. Bowers, S.L.: Privacy and library records. J Acad. Librariansh. **32**, 377–383 (2006). https://doi.org/10.1016/j.acalib.2006.03.005
6. Ermisch, J., et al.: Measuring people's trust. J. Roy. Stat. Soc.: Ser. A **172**, 749–769 (2009). https://doi.org/10.1111/j.1467-985X.2009.00591.x
7. Gomez, R., Gould, E.: The "cool factor" of public access to ICT: users' perceptions of trust in libraries, telecentres and cybercafés in developing countries. Inf. Technol. People **23**, 247–264 (2010). https://doi.org/10.1108/09593841011069158
8. Healey, P.D.: Professional Liability Issues for Librarians and Information Professionals. Neal-Schuman, New York (2008)
9. Horrigan, J.: Libraries 2016. Pew Internet Project, Washington, DC (2016). http://www.pewinternet.org/2016/09/09/libraries-2016/
10. Jaeger, P.T., Fleischmann, K.R.: Public libraries, values, trust, and e-government. Inf. Technol. Libr. **26**, 34 (2007). https://doi.org/10.6017/ital.v26i4.3268

11. Johnson, C.A.: How do public libraries create social capital? An analysis of interactions between library staff and patrons. Libr. Inf. Sci. Res. **34**, 52–62 (2012). https://doi.org/10. 1016/j.lisr.2011.07.009

12. Kang, S.: A study on ethic of librarians and information services job. Libr. People **4**, 20–59 (2003)

13. Katz, V.S.: How children of immigrants use media to connect their families to the community: the case of Latinos in South Los Angeles. J. Child. Med. **4**, 298–315 (2010). https://doi.org/10.1080/17482798.2010.486136

14. Miles, M.B., Huberman, A.M.: Qualitative Data Analysis: An Expanded Sourcebook, 2nd edn. SAGE, Thousand Oaks (1994)

15. Mills, J.E., Romeijn-Stout, E., Campbell, C., Koester, A.: Results from the young children, new media, and libraries survey. Child. Libr. **13**, 26–35 (2015)

16. Noh, Y.: Digital library user privacy: changing librarian viewpoints through education. Libr. Hi Tech **32**, 300–317 (2014). https://doi.org/10.1108/LHT-08-2013-0103

17. Noh, Y.: A critical literature analysis of library and user privacy. Int. J. Knowl. Content Dev. Technol. **7**, 53–83 (2017). https://doi.org/10.5865/IJKCT.2017.7.2.053

18. Pew Research Center: Internet/Broadband Fact Sheet (2017). http://www.pewinternet.org/fact-sheet/internet-broadband/

19. Powell, A., Bryne, A., Dailey, D.: The essential internet: digital exclusion in low-income American communities. Policy Internet **2**, 161–192 (2010). https://doi.org/10.2202/1944-2866.1058

20. Roberts, J.: From know-how to show-how? Questioning the role of information and communication technologies in knowledge transfer. Technol. Anal. Strateg. Manag. **12**, 429–443 (2000). https://doi.org/10.1080/713698499

21. Rooney, T.: Trusting children: how do surveillance technologies alter a child's experience of trust, risk and responsibility? Surveill. & Soc. **7**, 344–355 (2010)

22. Rozengardt, A., Finquelievich, S.: Public access to information & ICTs final report. University of Washington Center for Information & Society, Seattle, WA (2008)

23. Thompson, K.M., et al.: Digital Literacy and Digital Inclusion: Information Policy And the Public Library. Rowman & Littlefield, Lanham (2014)

24. Tripp, L.M.: 'The computer is not for you to be looking around, it is for schoolwork': challenges for digital inclusion as Latino immigrant families negotiate children's access to the internet. New Media Soc. **13**, 552–567 (2011). https://doi.org/10.1177/1461444810375293

25. Vårheim, A.: Gracious space: library programming strategies towards immigrants as tools in the creation of social capital. Libr. Inf. Sci. Res. **33**, 12–18 (2011). https://doi.org/10.1016/j.lisr.2010.04.005

26. Warren, M.: The digital vicious cycle: links between social disadvantage and digital exclusion in rural areas. Telecommun. Policy **31**, 374–388 (2007). https://doi.org/10.1016/j.telpol.2007.04.001

Boundaries, Third Spaces and Public Libraries

Rachel D. Williams(⌐)

Simmons College, Boston, USA
rachel.williams@simmons.edu

Abstract. This study relies on semi-structured interviews with twenty-four public library staff to understand how they navigate professional boundaries when providing information services to people experiencing homelessness. Analysis of the interviews indicated that public library staff perform work related to managing their professional roles and responsibilities, particularly in the context of the public library as a third, or transitional space. This boundary work refers to situations or activities in which actors construct, manage, and challenge professional boundaries, as originally described by Gieryn [13]. The results of the interviews show that public library staff perform boundary work as it relates to the public library as a third space, or transitional space, used by any number of community members and as I argue, particularly by those experiencing homelessness. In the case of public librarians' provision of information services to people experiencing homelessness, the library acts a day shelter or transitional space, which has several implications for the public library and for the staff.

Keywords: Public libraries · Boundary theory · Homelessness · Third spaces

1 Introduction

Public library workers facilitate access to a variety of information to the public, and to special populations, such as immigrants, children and families, the elderly, and others (see for example, [7]). Additionally, they provide information to homeless individuals, who are at times characterized as 'problem patrons' [12]. Comparing the stigmatization of homelessness to other forms of poverty, Phelan et al. [25] explain that because they live in public spaces, homeless individuals may be even more stigmatized because their homelessness is more visible and disruptive, and they may be more aesthetically unappealing. Assumptions between homelessness and mental health issues or addiction are also prevalent [30]. Thus, supplying information to individuals experiencing homelessness is a complex and often challenging process.

Public library staff are increasingly required to serve the needs of people experiencing homelessness [5]. At times, these needs involve answering a variety of information questions or referring individuals to agencies that can answer health questions [18]. Research has not extensively considered what public library workers' experiences are in this area of service provision to people experiencing homelessness.

Examining the information interactions between public library staff and library users experiencing homelessness, I explore how public librarians create, navigate, and

© Springer International Publishing AG, part of Springer Nature 2018
G. Chowdhury et al. (Eds.): iConference 2018, LNCS 10766, pp. 703–712, 2018.
https://doi.org/10.1007/978-3-319-78105-1_81

question their professional boundaries. This paper applies 'boundary work' theory [3, 4, 13] to interviews with twenty-four public librarians to explore their experiences providing information services to individuals experiencing homelessness. It applies concepts related to 'boundary work' by considering how public library staff construct and negotiate professional boundaries when interacting with library users experiencing homelessness. This investigation examines public library workers' experiences providing information services to individuals experiencing homelessness as well as the challenges that arise in providing those services. It also considers how the public library acts as a third space for people experiencing homelessness, which results in particular kinds of boundary work. In this paper, I argue that public library staff perform boundary work when providing information services to library users experiencing homelessness, and outline some of the ways in which these boundary making activities occur within the context of public libraries as third spaces.

1.1   Studies of Boundary Work

Previous works have utilized the theoretical concept of boundary work to analyze the professions. Boundary work is a social construct that has to do with constituting, negotiating, and breaking boundaries between abstract fields of knowledge. Gieryn [13] came up with the term 'boundary work' when demarcating what constitutes science and non-science. Gieryn [13] describes what science is, and what science is not. He uses descriptions of 'science' and 'science as not-x or y' to demonstrate the ways in which boundaries are created to delineate what a domain of knowledge is and is not. Gieryn [13] further argues that threats to the professions are struggles over boundaries, which are often rooted in conflicting or evolving ideological issues.

As Abbott [3] describes, there are two ways of understanding what a profession entails. One understanding of professions relies on hands-on techniques, often referred to as crafts, and the other relies on practical skills designed to maintain control over a domain of abstract knowledge. Public librarianship falls under the second understanding of professions, since the abstract knowledge of librarianship is born out in very practical ways.

Librarianship as a profession is perpetually in flux. According to Abbott [4], the future of librarianship as a profession is influenced by larger cultural and social forces, competing professions, and competing organizations. Public librarians are constantly negotiating their own professionalism in the context of these competing areas. Additionally, as public libraries expand positions to include those that do not require master's degrees, the understanding of the profession has begun to include not just degreed professionals, but a variety of roles, including for example, those of para-professionals, social workers, and technology specialists. Boundary work research generates theoretical insight into broader social processes by explaining how symbolic resources help create, maintain, transgress, or 'dissolve institutionalized social differences' [20]. Recent work also considers boundary work as a method for creating connections rather than distinctions, particularly in collaborative contexts [26].

Research exploring boundary work and the profession of librarianship is extremely limited [29]. For example, one recent study examined boundary work in the context of public libraries and makerspaces [31]. Exploring the boundary work of public librarianship facilitates a novel approach to considering the profession of public librarianship, as well as the challenges public librarians experience when providing information services to library users experiencing homelessness.

1.2 Homelessness and Public Libraries

Although recent scholarly literature concerning public libraries has referred to issues related to individuals experiencing homelessness, no articles have examined public librarianship in the context of boundary work. Some scholarship describes the challenges public librarians face when facilitating access to services for homeless library users, including, for example, rights issues and the ethics of policies that affect people experiencing homelessness [12]. Other literature explores issues related to ethics and information access, or how reductionist perceptions of homeless individuals can result in policies (e.g. no sleeping) that differentially impact them [6]. Hersberger [16–18] explores the everyday-life information needs of homeless people and how information is transferred via social networks for those experiencing homelessness.

Beyond focusing on the specific challenges of individuals experiencing homelessness, limited literature on homelessness and public libraries has examined how public libraries can better serve the needs of the homeless by enhancing library collections and services and creating partnerships with local government organizations and agencies [9, 23]. Other research examines how library services can be better structured to serve the needs of homeless children, teens, and families [28].

Few studies of public libraries and homelessness explore issues related to social inclusion for homeless individuals in public libraries. Similarly, research is limited regarding the connections between social workers and public librarians. In an article exploring the potential for blurring the boundaries between social work and professional librarianship, Cathcart [10] examines e-government and community information referral in the public library. Kelleher [19] surveyed homeless community members to learn why they do or not use the public library.

1.3 Third Spaces and Public Libraries

Many recent studies have discussed the role of public library as place and particularly as a 'third space' [1, 21, 22]. Mehta and Bosson [24] define a third space as a "place of refuge other than the home or workplace where people can regularly visit and commune with friends, neighbors, coworkers, and even strangers" (p. 779). Some recent articles have described ways in which public libraries can market themselves as third spaces and as places that sup- port social inclusion [15]. Recent research on the role of the library as space, and specifically as a 'third space' will be used in this study to contextualize the way public librarians perform boundary work when providing information services to library users experiencing homelessness [1, 21, 22].

Mehta and Bosson [24] describe several characteristics that support social interaction in third spaces. These include shelter (the environment itself), personalization (ability to modify the physical environment), seating (how seating impacts whether a person can relax and enjoy the space), and permeability (ability to discern what is happening inside buildings from the exterior, or the street). As Snow and Mulcahy [27] argue, people experiencing homelessness most often seek out marginal or transitional spaces for engagement and to acquire resources and services. These authors distinguish between primary spaces, or those used by a community for recreational, residential or commercial reasons, and marginal space, which is of little to no value to most residents. Marginal spaces may be unused land, abandoned buildings, alleys, or vacant lots [Snow, Mulcahy]. Snow and Mulcahy introduce the third space as a transitional one for which its "use and functions are blurred and ambiguous" and that is used by a variety of individuals, including citizens, residents, entrepreneurs, and marginalized individuals such as those who are homeless (p. 157). A public library can thus be considered a transitional space, or a nexus, for people with a variety of backgrounds and experiences to come together into this third space for any number of reasons.

While people experiencing homelessness lack housing in a conventional sense, and may or may not have established workplaces, I contend in this study that the public library does indeed function as a third space in this context. Arguably, people experiencing homelessness do not reside in what one may consider to be a home. People experiencing homelessness are individuals without permanent residences. They may reside in shelters, couch surf among friends and family members, live on the street, or reside in any kind of unstable and/or temporary living situation. With that in mind, how is it possible for the public library to act as a third space for people experiencing homelessness? As Wasserman and Clair [30] note, while people who are homeless may work sporadically, they do overwhelmingly work very hard. These authors explain that oftentimes people experiencing homelessness accept any kind of work they can find, even if they are underpaid, paid late, or not paid at all. Similarly, perceptions of what it means to have a home and to be housed are variable among people experiencing homelessness. As Hill (1991) argues, possessions often function symbolically as either reminders of a recent stable living situation or of future and hopefully better living circumstances. For others, the notion of home is associated with negative life experiences, while life in a shelter or in a car is associated more with home as an escape from abusive environments. For people experiencing homelessness, then, the concept of 'home' is a complex combination of identity, value assigned to possessions, and emotional attachment to spaces. While understandings of home and work blurry how people experiencing homelessness may perceive the public library as a third space, it is apparent that they use the library as such. People experiencing homelessness use the library for entertainment, as a place to spend time, and engage with their communities, and in this way, the public library serves as a third space for them.

The major goal of this paper is to explore the experiences and challenges public librarians express when assisting people experiencing homelessness using a boundary theory approach. How public librarians understand their boundaries and navigate them may also help explain some of the underlying dynamics of information interactions with those experiencing homelessness in public libraries, which often act as third spaces for people in general as well as those facing the challenge of experiencing homelessness.

2   Methods

This study explores how, in the context of the public library as a third space, public library staff perform boundary work as they provide information services to people experiencing homelessness. To answer this question, public library staff were interviewed regarding their experiences and challenges in providing information services to library users experiencing homelessness.

Semi-structured, in-person interviews at three library systems in three different states in the United States were used for the study. Following the pattern of recent studies of boundary work [11], a naturalistic inquiry was implemented to gather rich, in-depth data concerning how public library workers navigate their professional boundaries. The interviews explored the kinds of health and other information resources and services provided by public library workers and the boundaries they construct, maintain, and break when interacting with homeless library users. Individuals were considered eligible to participate if they were currently employed at a library system and spent the greater part of their day providing information directly to the public.

The three library systems participating in the study were situated in three Midwestern cities that serve 4-year university populations of similar sizes, between 45,000–50,000 students. All three of the included cities provide many services designed to assist the large number of community members experiencing homelessness. In one location, over 3,500 people experience homelessness in a given year. In the other city, approximately 2,500 individuals experience homelessness. A total of twenty-four library staff, from three library systems, agreed to participate in the study. All participants were either library assistants whose work focused on reference, librarians, or library managers. The majority of participants were librarians with master's degrees in library and information science. Two participants were library assistants. Interviewees had a wide range of experience in their respective libraries, from less than a year to over 10 years.

Interviews were audio recorded, transcribed, and checked by two individuals to ensure accuracy. Two coders conducted a thematic analysis of the interview transcripts based on respondents' experiences and distill the primary issues described in the interviews. The coders began by going through transcripts and identifying emergent themes. Each coder read through all the interview transcripts and identified areas in which the codes were represented and identified any additional themes not established in the initial codebook construction.

Several major themes related to providing information services to library users experiencing homelessness emerged through the analysis of the twenty-four interviews. These include: descriptions of the library as a day shelter, issues related to patron privacy/confidentiality, descriptions related to the stigma of homelessness, comparisons between professional roles as librarians and social workers or healthcare professionals, descriptions of professional limits, and librarians' stories of crisis triage. These themes relate to previous concepts identified in studies of boundary work, the professions, and library users. Beyond the major themes identified, public library workers also answered questions related to providing health information to the public and their health information seeking strategy. The analysis which follows focuses on boundary work as it relates to the library operating as a day shelter, or third space.

3 Analysis: Boundary Work and Managing the Third Space of the Library as a Day Shelter

Public library staff often performed boundary work as they navigated the distinction between considering the library in its traditional role and as a day shelter or third space. This in turn caused tension for library staff as they worked to navigate professional boundaries. Public library workers' experiences providing information to those experiencing homelessness indicated that they saw the space of the library as creating both physical and interactional boundaries between public library staff and library users experiencing homelessness. Recent research on the role of the library as place, and specifically as a 'third space' helps contextualize the way public library staff perform boundary work when providing information services to library users experiencing homelessness [1, 21, 22]. Mehta and Bosson [24] describe third places as a "place of refuge other than the home or workplace where people can regularly visit and commune with friends, neighbors, coworkers, and even strangers" (p. 779).

Mehta and Bosson [24] further describe the characteristics that support social interaction in third spaces. These include shelter (the environment itself), personalization (ability to modify the physical environment), seating (how seating impacts whether a person can relax and enjoy the space), and permeability (ability to discern what is happening inside buildings from the exterior, or the street). From the perspective of public library workers, the library operates as a third space for people experiencing homelessness, and their boundary work involves managing that space and the social interactions within it. The public library and the boundary work performed by library staff exemplify the criteria for third spaces that encourage social behavior. For example, one participant noted that the library staff removed seating to ensure that less individuals experiencing homelessness would 'hang around' the library. Other participants explained enforcing no bathing or no sleeping policies, and encouraging some areas of the library to be used more than others.

Many library staff expressed the tension between the role of a library as such and its surrogate role as a day shelter for homeless community members. The library's function as a third space brings large numbers of people experiencing homelessness into proximity with public library workers. As a result, library staff are often required to construct and enforce both physical boundaries (e.g. seating, opening the library early on cold days) and interactional boundaries (e.g. determining whether answering a question is appropriate, or how much assistance one can provide).

As Seth pointed out, "Not 100% of the homeless people go to the shelters but 100% of the homeless people use the library." Touching on the social interaction of those using the library as a third space, Seth described the library as a 'community center' that provides both virtual and in-person social networking access. The public library is 'the place to be' during the daytime for several reasons, including access to computers, restrooms, and because the library is a good place to be when the weather is bad or when it's hot outside (Alice, Janine, Dylan). Another librarian, Patrick, surmised that many people experiencing homeless come into the library to use the computers, the restrooms, or to have a safe and dry place to be. Determining whether to give a homeless person bus fare, or a ride home, or finding the best options for shelter, healthcare, and food were often described as very difficult and emotional experiences for public library workers.

One librarian was conflicted about the comparison between the public library and a day shelter. At one point he said, "As a public building open to all for extended hours, we're an obvious place to go if you don't have a home." However, later in the interview, Tim explained the limitations of the library as compared to a day shelter:

You know our services are limited, we're not a day shelter, we're not gonna allow you to keep your personal belongings here. We're not gonna allow you to bathe your entire body in our restroom... So people might be disappointed in those types of services but I honestly don't know where we stand or even if there is a consensus among the homeless about the library.

Tim's comments allude to the tension between the role of the public library and its operation as a third space. Public library staff perform boundary work physically and spatially as they work to negotiate how those experiencing homelessness personalize the space of the public library. Restrictions on sleeping, bathing, seating, and access to certain areas of the library help with controlling and monitoring social interactions. Signs restricting behavior, behavior policies, and the use of security are ways by which the public library regulates itself as a third space. As Erin explained, the public library is a third space for all sorts of people. As a result, public librarians struggle with the best way to regulate how social interaction occurs in the public library. They commented often on the conflict between the desire to provide more services to users experiencing homelessness and their inability to help because of all the other groups that use the library. This conflict catalyzed the boundary work performed by public librarians, who sought to regulate space in a way to serve the mission of the public library and used their interactions with library users experiencing homelessness to support their understanding of how the public library as a third space should operate.

Issues of space, and the tension between the public library as a primary space and a third space was an issue discussed by participants at all three library systems. As Snow and Mulcahy [27] assert, this kind of space negotiation is a familiar form of social control exerted on people experiencing homelessness, particularly in urban settings, but also in transitional or third spaces such as the public library. Maintaining control of the space of the library has become an important part of the work of library staff. At one library system that involves managing different populations of people experiencing homelessness, along with their established turfs within the library. At another library system, it involved redesigning public space outside the library to strategically redefine the kinds of interactions that take place between people experiencing homelessness and the general public. While people experiencing homelessness may often find the library a welcoming third space for engagement with the community and as a source of entertainment and comfort, other members of the community may feel differently. For example, many public library staff also expressed uncertainty and frustration regarding community perceptions related to allowing people experiencing homelessness in the library. They experienced pressure from some parts of the community to limit services to or exclude people experiencing homelessness, whether in the form of direct comments from patrons or community media coverage of the public library. Library staff often described handling these situations as uncomfortable and at times problematic, resulting in their pondering whether this kind of management was within their perceived work boundaries.

As argued by Cameron [8], continuously negotiated and contested professional boundaries are points of conflict. Understanding the professional boundaries of public librarianship as points of conflict may result in challenges reconciling the historical and emerging roles of public librarians. Abbott [2–4] describes a similar phenomenon related to changes in public librarianship in the initial growth of the computing occupations. Librarians were required to shift their perspective and their professional boundaries to include control over a particular aspect of computing: the information domain. With this shift came an alteration of professional boundaries and the role of the public library as a place that not only keeps print materials but provides information to the public. Cameron [8] explains that questioning professional boundaries and challenging them is an initial part of accepting a new role. It may be the case that public librarianship is in the midst of a similar shift regarding providing community services to vulnerable populations. They question their own professional boundaries as they relate to meeting the needs of people experiencing homelessness while maintaining the public library as a third space welcome to all within the community.

Although not addressed specifically as a boundary, the stigma of homelessness may contribute to the establishment or maintenance of distance in the relationship between public library workers and people experiencing homelessness. Snow and Mulcahy point to strategies of space management common in urban communities that may help explain how public library staff control behavior and interaction within public libraries. These strategies enacted within urban spaces include limiting the visibility of people experiencing homelessness, discouraging particular kinds of behavior (and removing individuals who exhibit that behavior), and actively excluding people experiencing homelessness in some cases. Perhaps, with greater clarity on these boundary issues, recommendations can be created as to concepts of boundary making and breaking that can help inform the ways in which public librarians assist homeless library users.

4   Conclusion

Overall, this study examined the boundary work performed by public library staff as they interact with people experiencing homelessness in the context of the library as a third or transitional space, as a nexus for social interaction. It also explored the tension experienced by public library workers as they manage the space of the public library as a day shelter. Finally, this paper took a boundary work approach to exploring what underlying professional roles and limitations are perceived by public librarians. Subsequent work will focus on more in-depth analysis related to the professional boundaries constructed by public librarians as they provide information to homeless library users, what the implications of those boundaries are in practice, and how these boundaries are situated in broader institutional dynamics.

References

1. Aabø, S., Audunson, R.: Use of library space and the library as place. Libr. Inf. Sci. Res. **34** (2), 138–149 (2012)
2. Abbott, A.: The System of Professions: An Essay on the Division of Expert Labor. University of Chicago Press, Chicago (1988)
3. Abbott, A.: Things of boundaries. Soc. Res. **62**, 857–882 (1995)
4. Abbott, A.: Professionalism and the future of librarianship. Libr. Trends **46**(3), 430–443 (1998)
5. Ayers, S.: The poor and homeless: an opportunity for libraries to serve. Southeast. Libr. **54** (1), 13 (2006)
6. Bardoff, C.: Homelessness and the ethics of information access. Ser. Libr. **69**(3-4), 347–360 (2015)
7. Burke, S.K.: Use of public libraries by immigrants. Ref. User Serv. Q. **48**, 164–174 (2008)
8. Cameron, A.: Impermeable boundaries? Developments in professional and inter-professional practice. J. Interprof. Care **25**(1), 53–58 (2011)
9. Cart, M.: America's front porch–the public library. Publ. Libr. Q. **21**(1), 3–21 (2002)
10. Cathcart, R.: Librarian or social worker: time to look at the blurring line? (2008)
11. Deverell, K., Sharma, U.: Professionalism in everyday practice. In: Professionalism, Boundaries and the Workplace, pp. 25–46. Routledge, London (2000)
12. Ferrell, S.: Who says there's a problem? A new way to approach the issue of "problem patrons". Ref. User Serv. Q. **50**, 141–151 (2010)
13. Gieryn, T.F.: Boundary-work and the demarcation of science from non-science: strains and interests in professional ideologies of scientists. Am. Sociol. Rev. **48**, 781–795 (1983)
14. Gieryn, T.F.: Cultural Boundaries of Science: Credibility on the Line. University of Chicago Press, Chicago (1999)
15. Harris, C.: Libraries with lattes: the new third place. Australas. Publ. Libr. Inf. Serv. **20**(4), 145 (2007)
16. Hersberger, J.: Everyday information needs and information sources of homeless parents. New Rev. Inf. Behav. Res. **2**, 119–134 (2001)
17. Hersberger, J.: A qualitative approach to examining information transfer via social networks among homeless populations. New Rev. Inf. Behav. Res. **4**(1), 95–108 (2003)
18. Hersberger, J.: The homeless and information needs and services. Ref. User Serv. Q. **44**(3), 199–202 (2005)
19. Kelleher, A.: Not just a place to sleep: homeless perspectives on libraries in central Michigan. Libr. Rev. **62**(1/2), 19–33 (2013)
20. Lamont, M., Molnár, V.: The study of boundaries in the social sciences. Ann. Rev. Sociol. **28**(1), 167–195 (2002)
21. Leckie, G.J., Hopkins, J.: The public place of central libraries: findings from Toronto and Vancouver. Libr. Q. **72**(3), 326–372 (2002)
22. Lin, H., Pang, N., Luyt, B.: Is the library a third place for young people? J. Librariansh. Inf. Sci. **47**(2), 145–155 (2015)
23. Mars, A.: Library service to the homeless. Publ. Libr. Mag. **51**(2), 32–35 (2012)
24. Mehta, V., Bosson, J.K.: Third places and the social life of streets. Environ. Behav. **42**(6), 779–805 (2010)
25. Phelan, J., Link, B.G., Moore, R.E., Stueve, A.: The stigma of homelessness: the impact of the label "homeless" on attitudes toward poor persons. Soc. Psychol. Q. **60**, 323–337 (1997)
26. Quick, K.S., Feldman, M.S.: Boundaries as junctures: collaborative boundary work for building efficient resilience. J. Publ. Adm. Res. Theory **24**(3), 673–695 (2014)

27. Snow, D.A., Mulcahy, M.: Space, politics, and the survival strategies of the homeless. Am. Behav. Sci. **45**(1), 149–169 (2001)
28. Terrile, V.C.: Library services to children, teens and families experiencing homelessness. Urban Libr. J. **15**(2), 2 (2009)
29. Trosow, S.E.: Jurisdictional disputes and the unauthorized practice of law: new challenges for law librarianship. Legal Ref. Serv. Q. **20**(4), 1–18 (2001)
30. Wasserman, J.A., Clair, J.M.: At Home on the Street: People, Poverty, and a Hidden Culture of Homelessness. Lynne Rienner Publishers, Boulder (2010)
31. Williams, R.D., Willett, R.: Makerspaces and boundary work: the role of librarians as educators in public library makerspaces. J. Librariansh. Inf. Sci. (2017)

Developing Library Services for International Students in China's Universities: What Does the Literature Tell Us?

Lihong Zhou[1,2(✉)], Yingying Han[1], Ping Li[1], and Jie Xu[1]

[1] School of Information Management, Wuhan University,
Wuhan 430072, China
L.zhou@whu.edu.cn
[2] Institute for Digital Library, Wuhan University, Wuhan 430072, China

Abstract. Despite the rapid growth of international students in China's universities, university libraries are not fully prepared. The new requirements of this rapidly emerging community have not been fully understood nor well addressed. This paper reports on a research study that aims at developing library services for international students, on the basis of identifying and understanding of their requirements. This study adopted an inductive literature analysis approach for the analysis of 52 articles retrieved from international and Chinese academic databases. Fourteen library service requirements emerged from the analysis in four main categories: academic support requirements, physical environment requirements, resource and collection development requirements, and librarian outreach support requirements. Further conceptualisation of the research findings revealed three core library service requirements: academic development requirements, leisure/recreational requirements, and language and cultural learning requirements. This study focuses on China's university libraries; however, the research findings provide useful implications and insights that can be shared across international borders.

Keywords: Chinese universities · International students · Literature review
Library services · Requirements

1 Introduction

The recent achievement and development of China's economy has encouraged its universities to build and enhance their international presence and reputation. This internationalisation strategy has been heavily weighted by the Chinese central government [1]. In 2010, the China's Ministry of Education launched a "Study in China" program, which ambitiously aimed at attracting at least 5,000,000 international students to study in China's universities [2]. In the 2015/2016 academic year, 442,773 international students studied in China, and the number is expected to be significantly higher in 2016/2017 [3]. To support this program, the central government provided a total of 20 billion CNY (approximately 3 billion USD) in for setting up scholarship packages, and upgrading university teaching, research and social facilities, including university libraries and library services [4].

© Springer International Publishing AG, part of Springer Nature 2018
G. Chowdhury et al. (Eds.): iConference 2018, LNCS 10766, pp. 713–718, 2018.
https://doi.org/10.1007/978-3-319-78105-1_82

International students have different information needs from those of the native students [5–7]. Zhao and Mawhinney [8] claim that non-native and native language speakers demonstrate evident differences in the searching, evaluating, writing and citing processes. Therefore, Dimartino and Zoe [9] point out that university libraries should provide well-tailored academic instructional services to international students, which are critical to their academic success in the new environment. Saw et al. [10] claim that university libraries have a vital role in helping international students adapt to their new environment, reducing cultural and language barriers, and obtaining information about the social and university environments.

Some Chinese researchers assert that Chinese university libraries should become the support platform for this new and fast-growing community [11, 12]. Nevertheless, China's university libraries are simply unprepared to provide the services international students need [11, 13]. Some researchers [14, 15] claim that no comprehensive services have been provided, nor has any attention or systematic effort been made to investigate and resolve this problem.

Thus, in China's universities, international students are not sufficiently included in the current provision of library services. This paper reports on one of the very early research studies, which aims to articulate specific and pragmatic strategies for the development of library services in China's universities through identifying and understanding the requirements of international students. This paper focuses on the literature review stage of this research project and its findings.

2 Review Methods and Processes

The literature review was carried out in two stages. The first stage aimed to perform a general review and to provide a theoretical and contextual basis for more systemitised literature retrieval and analysis in the second stage. Specifically, the review has two main aims: (1) to identify what library services have been provided to international students on a global scale; (2) to gain a general understanding of the present international student services provided in China's university libraries.

Stage two systematically retrieved and analysed academic works both in English and Chinese. Two sets of databases were systematically searched. The first set included three international databases: Web of Science, ScienceDirect and Emerald. As the second set, three Chinese academic databases were searched: CNKI, Wanfang and CQVIP. In general, the search returned 532 articles, including 63 articles in English and 469 articles in Chinese. After careful screening, 57 articles were included for the analysis: 40 in English and 17 in Chinese.

An inductive analysis approach was adopted. Specifically, a grounded theory (GT) analysis approach was adopted, as proposed by Strauss and Corbin [16], which is widely recognised as particularly useful for generating a theory closely related to the context of the phenomena being studied [17, 18]. Specifically, the data analysis adopted two GT analytical techniques, coding (open, axial and selective) and constant comparative analysis. Open coding was used to anticipate and label new library service requirements as indicated in data. When a new requirement emerged and was open-coded, it was compared with the existing list of open-codes to check and verify if it was completely new, if it already existed or if it could be merged with the existing codes to formulate new requirements. Axial coding was used to develop vertical relationships between different codes, which connected the individual requirements that emerged and formulated subcategories around the axis of a category. Finally, selective coding focused on identifying horizontal relationships among the emerging categories and on checking and verifying the research findings [16]. Theoretical saturation was achieved in the literature analysis-until no new open codes emerged from the data analysis.

3 Literature Review Findings

The analysis pointed to fourteen library service requirements in four categories: academic support requirements, physical environment requirements, resource and collection development requirements, and librarian outreach support requirements. These categories and individual requirements are shown in Table 1:

Table 1. Categories and requirements emerged from the analysis

Categories	Requirements	Requirements	Categories
Academic support requirements	1. Understanding academic principles and rules 2. Orientation courses 3. Information literacy education 4. Academic writing training	5. Comfortable and convenient space for study 6. Flexible space for seminar/discussion 7. Onsite technological facility 8. Bilingual environment	Physical environment requirements
Resource and collection development requirements	9. Academic resources 10. Leisure resources 11. Language learning resources	12. Multicultural librarians with good communication skills 13. Special liaison librarians 14. Convenient online/offline accesses to librarians' support	Librarian outreach support requirements

Effective academic support services are essential to international students [19]. International students often study with a limited understanding of the academic rules of the new educational institution. This results in major challenges, including problems with attitudes toward intellectual property [19] and understanding the academic rules for using information properly to avoid plagiarism [20]. As suggested by Gunnarsson et al. [20], university libraries should provide an introduction to the academic principles and rules. In this case, as emerged in the analysis, three types of library services are extremely useful: library orientation courses, information literacy education and academic writing education [8].

Library facilities are frequently used by international students. For them, university libraries are often seen as quiet and relaxing places [21]. However, Song [22] identified that international students used the library primarily as a place to study, while domestic students viewed it as a place that provided resources for their research. Also, a bilingual library environment is highly valued for adjusting into the academic community, quickly locating library resources and services [15].

Moreover, the literature review showed that electronic resources are strongly preferred over print resources. However, a large proportion of international students do not know very much about the extensive databases and e-journals available to them [21]. Apart from using information for academic purposes, Datig [21] states that it would be "a nice perk" if university libraries could offer leisure reading in both English and student's own language.

Also, through analysis, three specific librarian outreach support requirements have emerged from the literature analysis. The literature analysis shows that international students from different cultural backgrounds may have very different expectations of the librarians' help. Curry and Copeman reveal that in Asian collectivist cultures, people tend to avoid disturbing others. Therefore, librarians need to show cultural sensitivity in their delivery of library services [19]. Additionally, Shao and Scherlen [23] assert that international students expect librarians to avoid the use of slang, jargon or long complex sentences, which may result in miscommunication between students and librarians.

4   Discussion

The findings were further conceptualised to understand the relationships between the requirements. Thus, a conceptual model is developed, as shown in Fig. 1. According to this diagram, four response strategies can be articulated.

- Librarian involvement: librarians are closely related to almost all requirements of international students. Librarians need to be culturally sensitive and bi-/ multi-lingual and should always be reachable and ready to help when needed.
- Resource and collection development: international students require academic resources, leisure resources and language learning resources.
- Online/offline support: if on-site assistance is only available during library opening hours, international students should be able to receive 24/7 online supports through library web services.
- Space allocation: university libraries should provide easy and convenient access to technological devices, as well as flexible, moveable spaces for group work.

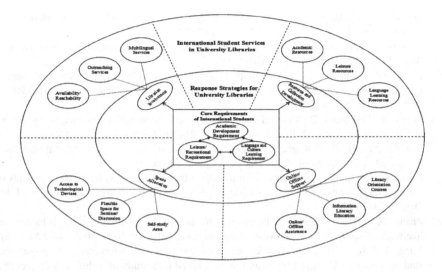

Fig. 1. Core requirements from international student and response strategies and services

5 Conclusion

This paper reports on one of the early research efforts, which aims to articulate strategies for the development of international student services in China's university libraries. The literature analysis revealed three core library service requirements: academic development requirements, leisure/recreational requirements, and language and cultural learning requirements. Furthermore, four response strategies were formulated: librarian involvement, resource and collection development, online/offline support and space allocation. Among these strategies, librarian involvement has emerged as the central strategy and thus should be prioritised.

References

1. Ministry of Education of the People's Republic of China - National Outline for Medium and Long-Term Plan for Educational Reform and Development (2010–2020). http://www.moe.edu.cn/srcsite/A01/s7048/201007/t20100729_171904.html. Accessed 15 Sept 2017
2. The Central People's Government of the People's of China - Plan of Studying in China. http://www.gov.cn/zwgk/2010-09/28/content_1711971.htm. Accessed 15 Sept 2017
3. Ministry of Education of the People's Republic of China - Statistics of International Students in China in 2016. http://www.moe.gov.cn/jyb_xwfb/xw_fbh/moe_2069/xwfbh_2017n/xwfb_170301/170301_sjtj/201703/t20170301_297677.html. Accessed 15 Sept 2017
4. Ministry of Education of the People's Republic of China - Department Budget of Chinese Ministry of Education in China in 2017. http://www.moe.edu.cn/srcsite/A05/s7499/201704/t20170407_302152.html. Accessed 15 Sept 2017
5. Yi, Z.: International student perceptions of information needs and use. J. Acad. Librariansh. **33**(6), 666–673 (2007)

6. Shaffer, C., Vardaman, L., Miller, D.: Library usage trends and needs of international students. Behav. Soc. Sci. Libr. **29**(2), 109–117 (2010)

7. Hughes, H.: International students' experiences of university libraries and librarians. Austral. Acad. Res. Libr. **41**(2), 77–89 (2010)

8. Zhao, J.C., Mawhinney, T.: Comparison of native Chinese-speaking and native English-speaking engineering students' information literacy challenges. J. Acad. Librariansh. **41**(6), 712–724 (2015)

9. Zoe, L.R., Dimartino, D.: Cultural diversity and end-user searching: an analysis by gender and language background. Res. Strateg. **17**(4), 291–305 (2000)

10. Saw, G., Abbott, W., Donaghey, J., McDonald, C.: Social media for international students – it's not all about Facebook. Libr. Manag. **34**(3), 1–19 (2013)

11. Chen, Y.: Exploration and practice of information literacy education of overseas students in research universities—taking Harbin Engineering University library as an example. Libr. Dev. **9**, 73–76 (2011)

12. Zhang, X., Liu, H.: Study on the model of attributions on library using behaviors of international students and decision-making guidance. Libr. Inf. Serv. **60**(8), 44–52 (2016)

13. Yang, B., Liu, L., Tong, W.: A study on the current situation and problems of international student service in Chinese University libraries: based on a study of websites of project 985 university libraries. Res. Libr. Sci. **19**, 48–52 (2015)

14. Liu, J.: A study on the evaluation of the importance of international student service in university library and the innovation strategy of service. Libr. Work Study **1**(6), 100–103 (2013)

15. Wang, Q., Chen, H.: Probe into the information service of university students in university library. Libr. Work Study **6**, 105–107 (2012)

16. Strauss, A., Corbin, J.: Basics of Qualitative Research: Techniques and Procedures for Developing Grounded Theory. Sage Publications, London (1998)

17. Creswell, J.: Qualitative Inquiry and Research Design: Choosing Among Five Traditions. Sage Publications, London (1998)

18. Zhou, L., Nunes, M.: Identifying knowledge sharing barriers in the collaboration of traditional and western medicine professionals in Chinese hospitals: a case-study. J. Librariansh. Inf. Sci. **44**(4), 238–248 (2012)

19. Curry, A., Copeman, D.: Reference service to international students: a field stimulation research study. J. Acad. Librariansh. **31**(5), 409–420 (2005)

20. Gunnarsson, J., Kulesza, W.J., Pettersson, A.: Teaching international students how to avoid plagiarism: librarians and faculty in collaboration. J. Acad. Librariansh. **40**(3–4), 413–417 (2014)

21. Datig, I.: What is library?: international college students' perceptions of libraries. J. Acad. Librariansh. **40**(3–4), 350–356 (2014)

22. Song, Y.: A comparative study on information-seeking behaviors of domestic and international business students. Res. Strateg. **20**(1), 23–34 (2004)

23. Shao, X., Scherlen, A.: Chinese academic libraries serving international students and scholars: an assessment of three case studies. Int. Inf. Libr. Rev. **43**(1), 53–61 (2011)

Author Index

Printed in the United States
By Bookmasters